Landscape, Tradition and Power in Medieval Iceland

The Northern World

NORTH EUROPE AND THE BALTIC C. 400–1700 AD.
PEOPLES, ECONOMIES AND CULTURES

Editors

Jón Viðar Sigurðsson (*Oslo*)
Piotr Gorecki (*University of California at Riverside*)
Steve Murdoch (*St. Andrews*)
Cordelia Heß (*Greifswald*)
Anne Pedersen (*National Museum of Denmark*)

VOLUME 80

The titles published in this series are listed at *brill.com/nw*

Landscape, Tradition and Power in Medieval Iceland

Dalir and the Eyjafjörður Region c.870–c.1265

by

Chris Callow

BRILL

LEIDEN | BOSTON

Cover illustration: Litli-Hóll, known formerly as Espihóll inn syðri, seen from south-west. ©Photograph by Chris Callow.

Library of Congress Cataloging-in-Publication Data

Names: Callow, Chris, 1971- author.
Title: Landscape, tradition and power in medieval Iceland : Dalir and the Eyjafjörður region c.870-c.1265 / by Chris Callow.
Other titles: Dalir and the Eyjafjörður region c.870-c.1265
Description: Leiden ; Boston : Brill, [2020] | Series: The northern world: North Europe and the Baltic c. 400-1700 ad. peoples, economies and cultures, 1569-1462 ; volume 80 | Includes bibliographical references and index. | Summary: "Chris Callow's Landscape, Tradition and Power critically examines the evidence for socio-political developments in medieval Iceland during the so-called Commonwealth period. The book compares regions in the west and north-east of Iceland because these regions had differing human and physical geographies, and contrasting levels of surviving written evidence. Callow sets out the likely economies and institutional frameworks in which political action took place. He then examines different forms of evidence - the Contemporary sagas, Landnámabók (The Book of Settlements), and Sagas of Icelanders - considering how each describes different periods of the Commonwealth present political power. Among its conclusions the book emphasises stasis over change and the need to appreciate the nuances and purposes of Iceland's historicising sagas"-- Provided by publisher.
Identifiers: LCCN 2020007362 (print) | LCCN 2020007363 (ebook) | ISBN 9789004278875 (hardback) | ISBN 9789004331600 (e-book)
Subjects: LCSH: Iceland--History--To 1262--Sources. | Iceland--History--To 1262. | Human geography--Political aspects--Iceland. | Human settlements--Iceland. | Power (Social sciences)--Iceland. | Sagas--History and criticism.
Classification: LCC DL352 .C35 2020 (print) | LCC DL352 (ebook) | DDC 949.12/01--dc23
LC record available at https://lccn.loc.gov/2020007362
LC ebook record available at https://lccn.loc.gov/2020007363

Typeface for the Latin, Greek, and Cyrillic scripts: "Brill". See and download: brill.com/brill-typeface.

ISSN 1569-1462
ISBN 978-90-04-27887-5 (hardback)
ISBN 978-90-04-33160-0 (e-book)

Copyright 2020 by Koninklijke Brill NV, Leiden, The Netherlands.
Koninklijke Brill NV incorporates the imprints Brill, Brill Hes & De Graaf, Brill Nijhoff, Brill Rodopi, Brill Sense, Hotei Publishing, mentis Verlag, Verlag Ferdinand Schöningh and Wilhelm Fink Verlag.
All rights reserved. No part of this publication may be reproduced, translated, stored in a retrieval system, or transmitted in any form or by any means, electronic, mechanical, photocopying, recording or otherwise, without prior written permission from the publisher.
Authorization to photocopy items for internal or personal use is granted by Koninklijke Brill NV provided that the appropriate fees are paid directly to The Copyright Clearance Center, 222 Rosewood Drive, Suite 910, Danvers, MA 01923, USA. Fees are subject to change.

This book is printed on acid-free paper and produced in a sustainable manner.

Contents

Acknowledgements VII
Note on Spelling and Pronunciation IX
List of Illustrations X

1 Introduction 1
  1 Debates and Frameworks 1
  2 Landscapes and Seascapes 26

2 Frameworks of Power: *Goðorð* and Elite Marriage Networks c.1100 to c.1265 44
  1 The Twelfth Century 45
  2 From c.1200 to c.1265 47
  3 *Goðorð* c.1100–c.1265 56
  4 *Goðorð* in Dalir 57
  5 *Goðorð* in Eyjafjörður and the North-East c.1150–c.1265 62
  6 Conclusion 68
  7 Elite Marriage Networks 68
  8 Marriages in Dalir and Northern Snæfellsnes 70
  9 Elite Marriages in Eyjafjörður and the North-East 77

3 Patterns of Power c.1100–c.1265 85
  1 The Early Twelfth Century in Dalir: Local Leaders and Political Networks in *Þorgils saga ok Hafliða* 85
  2 *Goðar* and *þingmenn* in *Sturlu saga* 92
  3 Dalir c.1185–c.1215 98
  4 Sturla Sighvatsson and Þórðr Sturluson in Dalir 102
  5 Dalir and Þórðr *kakali* Sighvatsson, c.1242–c.1250 112
  6 Dalir c.1250–c.1265 117
  7 Political Power in Dalir from c.1185-c.1265: Some Conclusions 124
  8 The Eyjafjörður Region 126
  9 *Prestssaga Guðmundr góða* and *Guðmundar saga dýra* 126
  10 After Guðmundr *dýri*, c.1200-c.1265 134
  11 Conclusion 145

4 Settlers and Settlement Mythologies in *Landnámabók* 147
  1 Genealogical Charters and the Origins of *Landnámabók* and *Íslendingasögur* 147
  2 *Landnámabók* 154

    3 *Sturlubók*   158
    4 Dalir and Northern Snæfellsnes   164
    5 Eyjafjörður and the North-East   187
    6 Conclusions   201

5 The Worlds of Snorri *goði* and Guðmundr *ríki*   205
    1 The Dalir *Íslendingasögur*   213
    2 Eyjafjörður and the North-East in the *Íslendingasögur*   270
    3 Conclusions   307

6 Conclusion   308

    Appendix: *Sturlunga Saga*   319
    Bibliography   327
    Index   362

Acknowledgements

This book has taken a long while to write. The longer it has taken to write the more debts I have accrued, and the more time there has been for me to forget to whom I owe thanks, regardless of how significant their help has been. I have benefited from so many people's knowledge, advice and practical support over the years. All errors of fact and interpretation remain my own.

I would like to acknowledge the financial support of the AHRC for matching study leave in 2006-7, and for periods of institutional leave from the University of Birmingham which also funded the PhD whence this book originates.

I have benefited enormously from conversations with Icelandic scholars, especially Helgi Þorláksson, Sverrir Jakobsson and Ármann Jakobsson, but above all from Orri Vésteinsson whose friendship and sharp thinking has been invaluable since we first met in a UCL refectory in 1996. Since I was accepted to take part in the first Hofstaðir archaeological fieldschool in 1997 Orri and his colleagues in Fornleifastofnun Íslands, have done their best to keep me up-to-speed with Icelandic archaeology and have always been ready to answer questions and provide reports: Birna Lárusdóttir, Howell Roberts, Mjöll Snæsdóttir, Hildur Gestsdóttir, Adolf Friðriksson, as well as Tom McGovern and Ian Simpson and fellow Hostaðir '97 students. Ragnheiður Traustadóttir and colleagues kindly supported my participation in the Hólar Rannsóknin conference in 2006. I wish there was more to show for all of this friendship, support and expertise in this very unarchaeological book.

I was fortunate to be awarded Stofnun Árna Magnússonar's Snorri Sturluson fellowship in 2013. My three months at Árna Stofnun were productive, both for this project and my next one. Conversations with Emily Lethbridge, Erika Sigurdson, Úlfar Bragason, Gísli Sigurðsson, Rósa Þorsteinsdóttir, Giovanni Verri, Greg Cattaneo and Elizabeth Walgenbech and others have all helped shape this book.

Staff at the university libraries of Birmingham, UCL and Cambridge, as well as Jökull Sævarsson and Chris Astridge then at Landsbókasafn Íslands, helped with greater and smaller requests for unusual publications and/or maps. I am very grateful to Rick Beck for the use of his photograph of Grenjaðarstaður.

At the University of Birmingham numerous colleagues have been supportive and shaped my thinking, often by encouraging me to read new things. These include Niall McKeown, Mary Harlow, Gareth Sears, Simon Yarrow, William Purkis, Christina Pössel, Andy Howard, Amanda Forster, Chris Dyer, Steve Bassett, Philippa Semper, David Griffith, Roger White, Will Mack, Andrew Bayliss, Kate Sykes, Kate Smith, Megan Cavell, Vicky Flood, and Chris Markiewicz.

Students at Birmingham, especially those doing my Special Subject, have kept me on my toes and made me revisit my assumptions on several occasions.

Other academic colleagues and collaborators over the years who have more or less directly influenced my thoughts include Matthew Innes, Judith Jesch, Christina Lee, Jayne Carroll, Alison Finlay, Dale Kedwards and Wendy Davies; Wendy enabled me to benefit from the 'People and Space' project.

Marcella Mulder at Brill has been incredibly supportive and patient throughout the long gestation of the book, while Anita Opdam has carefully managed the production process. Jón Viðar Sigurðsson and two anonymous readers offered valuable comments on the draft.

I would also like to thank Bethan Strange for excellent copy- and senseediting, Ryder Patzuk Russell for reading and suggesting changes to the introduction, Rebecca Merkelbach for discussing *Svarfdæla saga* and correcting an error, and Poppy Forshaw-Perring for drawing the original maps.

I owe an enormous debt of thanks to Chris Wickham, an inspirational tutor, PhD supervisor and colleague for longer than either he or I would care to remember. He has given up far more time than I could have expected in reading drafts of this book at many stages of its evolution, and made it better.

I owe special thanks to friends in Iceland: Guðmundur Jósepsson and family for putting up with me and putting me up since 1994; Phil Roughton and Kristin Birna Kristjánsdóttir for similarly unstinting hospitality and introducing me to Palli Lárusson Rist (1921–2016) and Stína at Litli-Hóll who in turn hosted me and gave me a valuable guided tour of Eyjafjörður in October 2010.

It also feels fitting that I should thank friends in Kings Heath Running Club, especially the Beer and Intervals WhatsApp group, for keeping me physically and mentally fit since 2014.

My mum and dad, Pat and Wendy, have been supportive throughout my strange choice of career and the saga of this book's writing. Growing up somewhere rural and working on a farm in my late teens means that storytelling and how people think about the past have long been an interest. My mum's parents, Ralph and Betty Dale, provided much of my interest in history although they might have been surprised to know it. James (1972–2004) and Jimmy Jermy have been supportive friends for years. I'm sorry neither James nor my grandparents lived to see this book completed.

My wife Helen Fisher will be gladder even than I am to see this book completed; she kindly proofread and edited an earlier draft. Above all else her love, support, intelligence and good humour have made writing this book possible.

Note on Spelling and Pronunciation

Following modern Icelandic convention, ö has been used as the standard symbol for hooked 'o' (ǫ) and ø. Thorn (Þ, þ, usually seen in its upper case form) and eth (usually in its lower case form, ð) are used throughout. They are pronounced like the variations of 'th' in English, respectively like *th*ink, *th*en.

For the names of farms I have tried to be consistent in using the most commonly used standardised spellings but for valleys I have used modern Icelandic spellings, such as Laxárdalur rather than Laxárdalr and Eyjafjörður rather than Eyjafjörðr. For modern Icelandic scholars' names I have used first names and patronymics in all references.

Figures, Maps and Tables

Figures

1. Photograph of Hvammur (Hvammr) in Hvammssveit   XXIII
2. Photograph of farmstead excavations in Ólafsdalur in August 2018   XXIII
3. Photograph of Helgafell on Þórsnes   XXIV
4. Photograph of Narfeyri on Skógarströnd   XXIV
5. Photograph of Sauðafell in Miðdalir   XXV
6. Photograph of Staðarfell on Fellsströnd   XXV
7. Photograph of Staðarhóll in Saurbær   XXVI
8. Photograph of Skarð on Skarðsströnd   XXVI
9. Photograph of Kársstaðir in Álptafjörður   XXVII
10. Photograph of Bakki in Öxnadalur   XXVII
11. Photograph of Hörgárdalur looking inland from near Möðruvellir   XXVIII
12. Photograph of the modern church at Grund in Eyjafjörður   XXVIII
13. Photograph of Munkaþverá and neighbouring farms   XXIX
14. Photograph of Jórunnarstaðir in Eyjafjarðardalur   XXIX
15. Photograph of Fnjóskadalur and Ljósavatnsskarð seen from Vaðlaheiði   XXX
16. Photograph of Ólafsfjörður   XXX
17. Photograph of Grenjaðarstaður (Grenjaðarstaðir)   XXXI
18. Simplified genealogy of the Sturlungar   71
19. Genealogy of Þuríðr Þórðardóttir, wife of Hafliði Másson   87
20. Genealogy in S109   168
21. Genealogy in S104   170
22. Genealogy in S106   171
23. Genealogy in S103   173
24. Genealogy in S98   174
25. Genealogy in S85   178
26. Genealogy of the descendants of Bolli Bollason in chapter 78 of *Laxdæla saga*   215

Maps

1. Iceland   XII
2. Dalir and north Snæfellsnes   XIII
3. Eyjafjörður and the north-east   XIV
4. Western Snæfellsnes   XV

5. Skarðsströnd, Fellsströnd and Skógarströnd XVI
6. Saurbær XVII
7. Hvammssveit, Laxárdalur and Miðdalir XVIII
8. Outer Eyjafjörður XIX
9. Inner Eyjafjörður XX
10. Reykjadalur, Bárðardalur and Mývatnssveit XXI
11. North-east Þingeyjarsýsla XXII
12. The *landnám* in Dalir and northern Snæfellsnes according to *Sturlubók* 166
13. The *landnám* in Eyjafjörður and the north-east according to *Sturlubók* 188

Tables

1. Summary table of *Sturlubók*'s chapters covering northern Snæfellsnes 175
2. Table showing Helgi *inn magri*'s dependent colonists in Eyjafjörður and their *landnám* 190

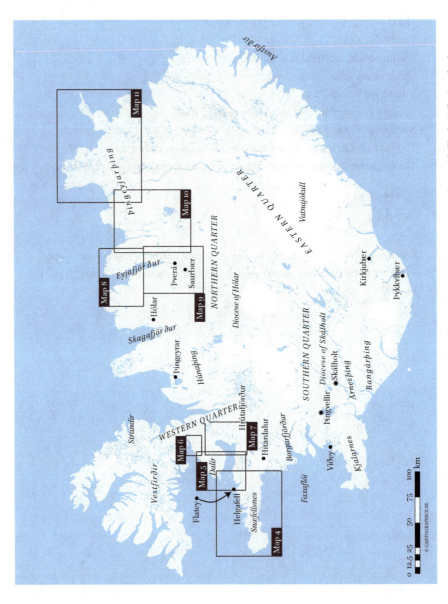

MAP 1   Iceland. The map shows the sites of the Alþing (Þingvellir), two episcopal sees (Skálholt, Hólar) and religious houses.

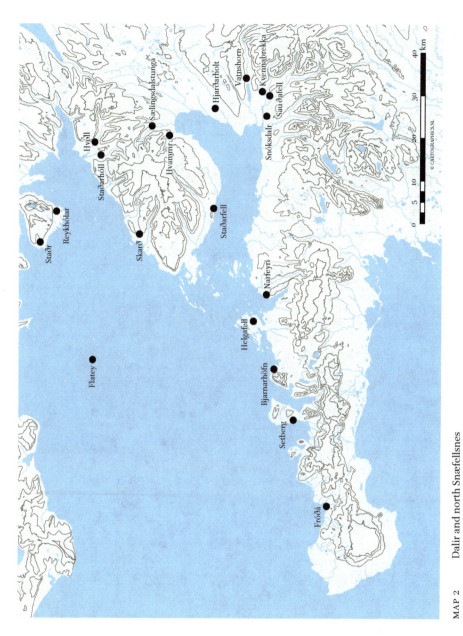

MAP 2   Dalir and north Snæfellsnes

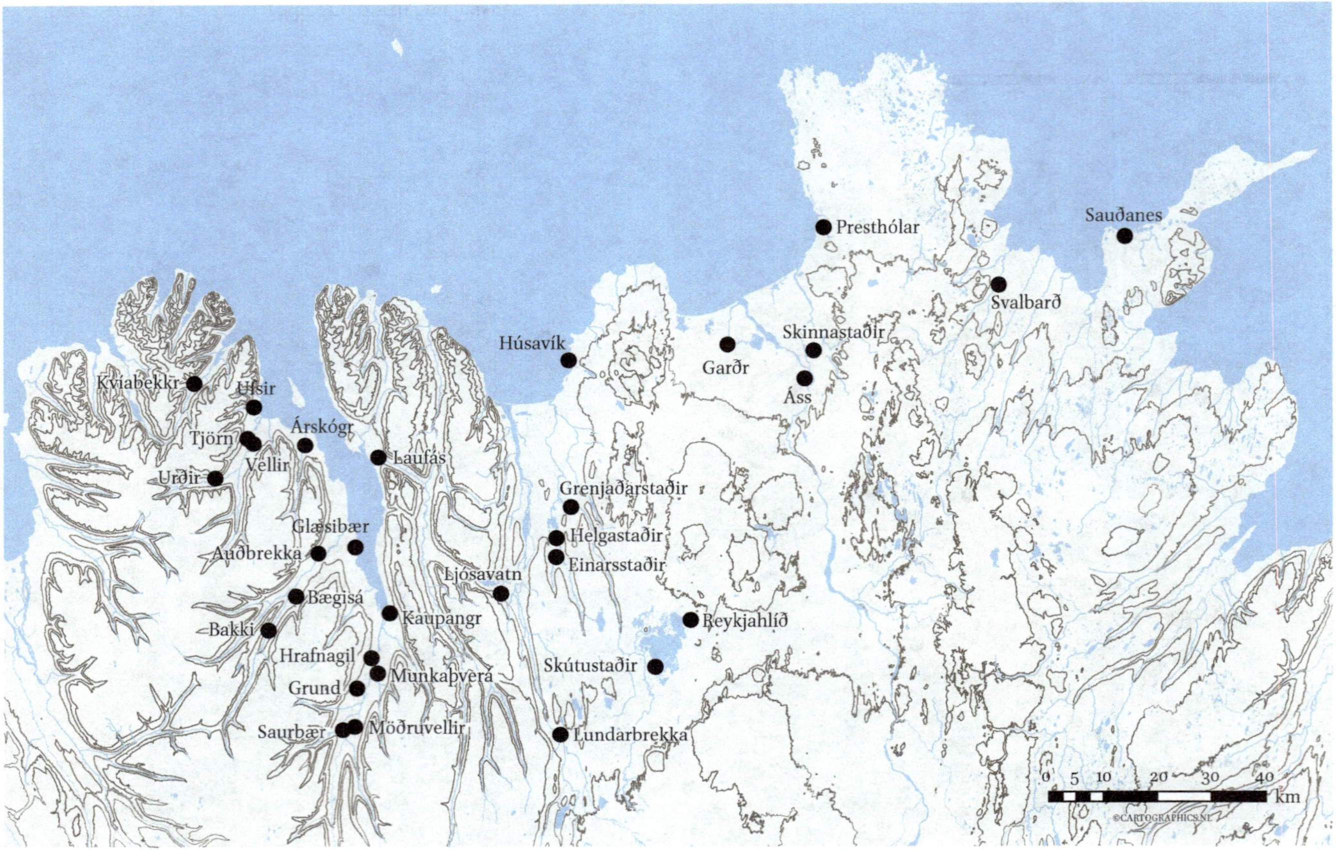

MAP 3   Eyjafjörður and the north-east

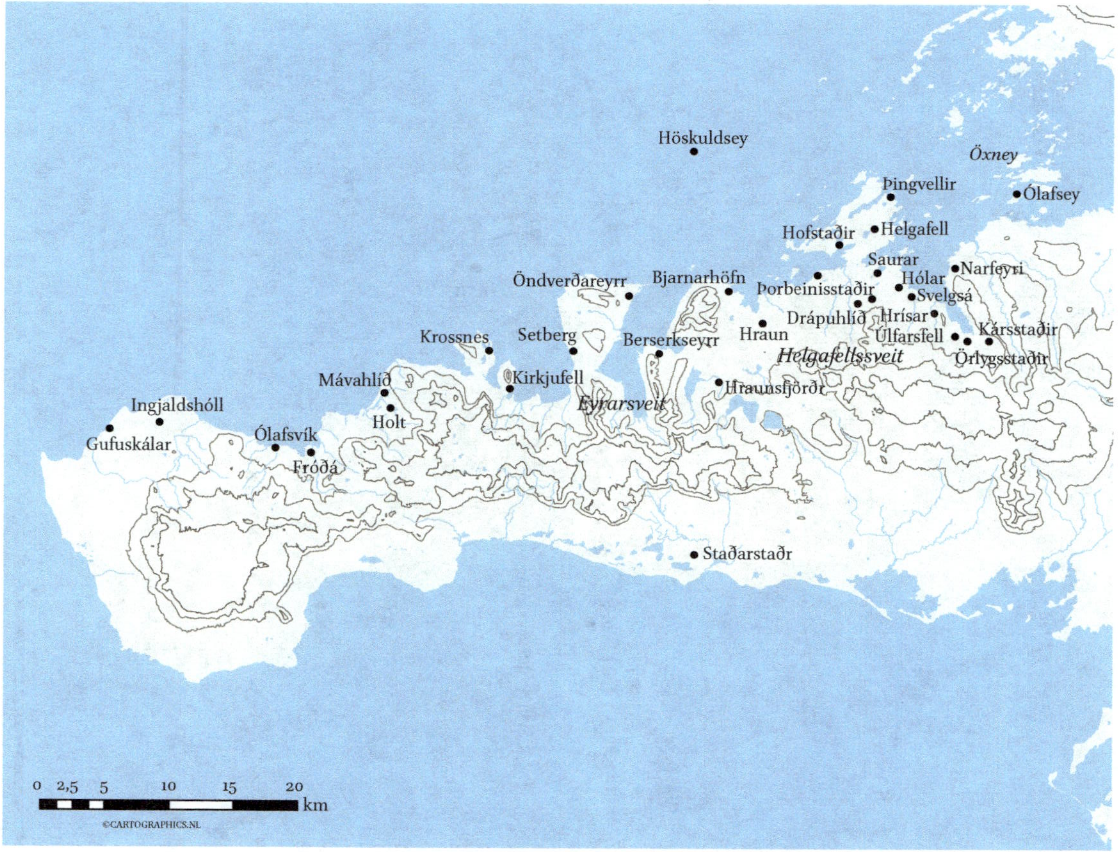

MAP 4   Western Snæfellsnes

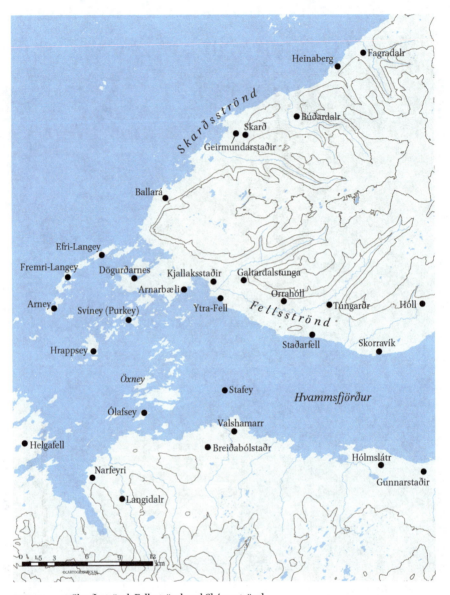

MAP 5   Skarðsströnd, Fellsströnd and Skógarströnd

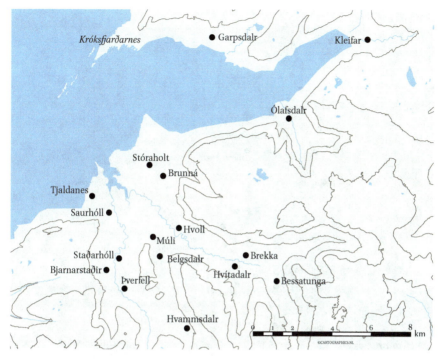

MAP 6   Saurbær

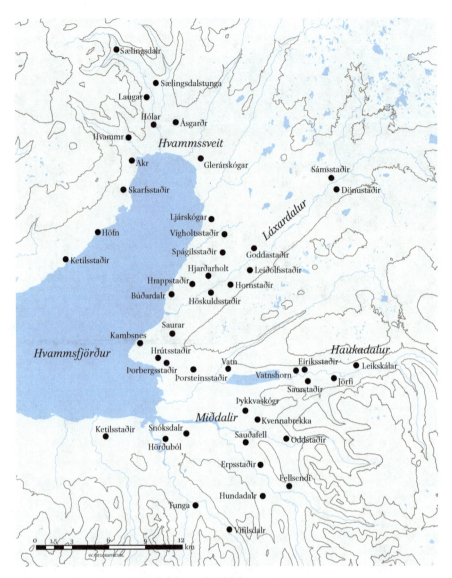

MAP 7   Hvammssveit, Laxárdalur and Miðdalir

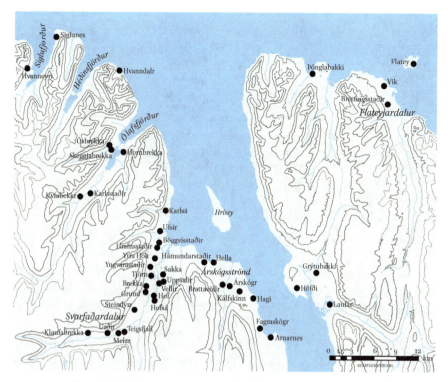

MAP 8   Outer Eyjafjörður

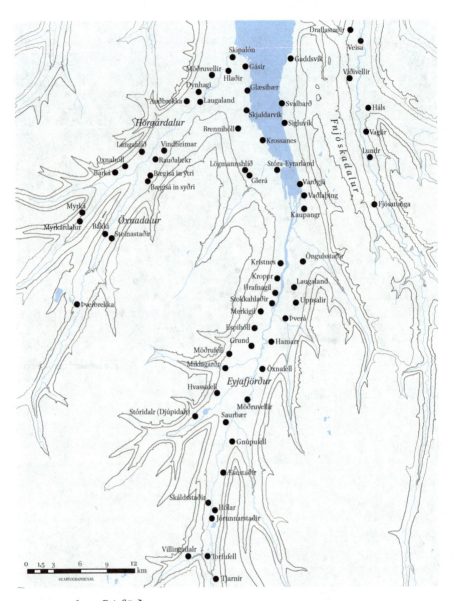

MAP 9 Inner Eyjafjörður

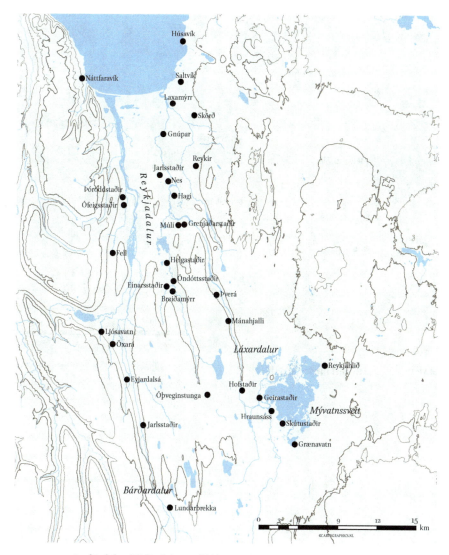

MAP 10   Reykjadalur, Bárðardalur and Mývatnssveit

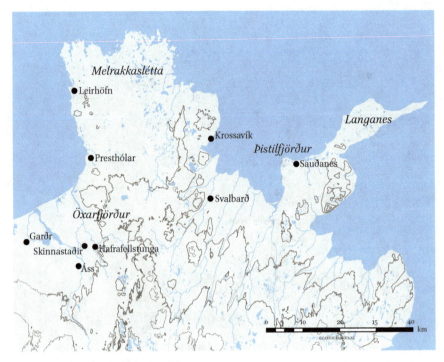

MAP 11   North-east Þingeyjarsýsla

FIGURE 1 Photograph of Hvammur (Hvammr) in Hvammssveit

FIGURE 2 Photograph of farmstead excavations in Ólafsdalur in August 2018.

FIGURE 3   Photograph of Helgafell on Þórsnes

FIGURE 4   Photograph of Narfeyri on Skógarströnd

FIGURE 5   Photograph of Sauðafell in Miðdalir

FIGURE 6   Photograph of Staðarfell on Fellsströnd

FIGURE 7   Photograph of Staðarhóll in Saurbær

FIGURE 8   Photograph of Skarð on Skarðsströnd

FIGURE 9   Photograph of Kársstaðir in Álptafjörður

FIGURE 10   Photograph of Bakki in Öxnadalur

FIGURE 11   Photograph of Hörgárdalur looking inland from near Möðruvellir

FIGURE 12   Photograph of the modern church at Grund in Eyjafjörður

FIGURE 13   Photograph of Munkaþverá (left) and neighbouring farms

FIGURE 14   Photograph of Jórunnarstaðir in Eyjafjarðardalur

FIGURE 15   Photograph of Fnjóskadalur and Ljósavatnsskarð seen from Vaðlaheiði

FIGURE 16   Photograph of Ólafsfjörður

FIGURE 17 Photograph of Grenjaðarstaður (Grenjaðarstaðir) Image © Rick Beck.

CHAPTER 1

Introduction

1 Debates and Frameworks

Histories of the regions of early medieval western Europe have long been considered an important form of historical writing.[1] As part of the development of the *Annales* school French historians in the post-war era wrote sizeable studies of French regions of the central middle ages, the most iconic being Georges Duby's *La société aux xie et xiie siècles dans la region mâconnaise* (1953). The region, variously defined, has remained a productive unit of analysis ever since. For medieval Iceland, four Icelandic-language regional studies have appeared; two published in the late 1980s on the south, and now recently one on Breiðafjörður in the west and a fourth on the middle-sized northern valley of Svarfaðardalur.[2] This book is therefore a methodological exercise, an attempt to see what regional histories for medieval Iceland might look like, particularly as in recent decades historians have become ever more reflective on how they interpret medieval texts.

Using two regional case studies, one from the central-west of Iceland, the other from its north-east (Maps 1–3), the objective of this study is to assess the extent and causes of changes to socio-political structures in Iceland, from the start of its colonisation in the century through to the formal concession of overlordship by the country's elite to the Norwegian king in the 1260s.[3] Throughout this period Iceland appears unusual when considered in the context of western European society, being materially poorer than almost anywhere else in the Scandinavian mainland, let alone regions further south in Europe. There was no king and rarely a single power or overlord in Iceland itself. There was no

---

1   E.g. Bisson 2002 for an overview of French studies. Examples in English by British scholars include Davies 1988, Wickham 1988, Innes 2000, and Balzaretti 2013.
2   Jón Thor Haraldsson 1988; Helgi Þorláksson 1989a; Sverrir Jakobsson 2015; Árni Daníel Júlíusson 2016. Sverrir Jakobsson's study of Breiðafjörður covers the period from the *landnám* to c.1500. See also Sverrir Jakobsson 2002 on Breiðafjörður and contributions on the west by Helgi Þorláksson, first on the farm of Sauðafell and now Breiðafjörður over the *longue durée* (Helgi Þorláksson 1991a, Helgi Þorláksson 2013).
3   Patricia Boulhosa (2005) has convincingly argued that one document supposedly recording the agreement between the Icelanders and King Hákon Hákonarson is essentially an early fifteenth-century forgery but this does not call into question the basic submission of Iceland's elite recorded elsewhere.

administration, no standing armies, and Iceland's Christian institutions were slow to establish themselves. There is no surviving written evidence from before 1100, which fits with the absence of a literate administrative structure. Iceland was always entirely rural, sparsely populated, had an economy based on sedentary-pastoralism – mainly of cattle and sheep – and on fishing and, of course, it was far from other landmasses. In its documentary record it is only after the 1260s that Iceland looks more like other parts of the Norwegian kingdom, which itself was coming to look more like other polities in western Europe.

While the form and scope of this study have something in common with studies of other medieval regions, the evidence it uses is unique to Iceland in many respects. Our sources are almost entirely literary, in the form of various kinds of saga, and most of these are written by anonymous authors. They are unlike the conventional range of sources used by medieval historians such as charters, annals, saints' lives or, to an extent, the kinds of histories which cover other western European regions.[4] That is not to say that documentary evidence does not exist for Iceland. The period being examined here, however, might be described as 'spattered' with such sources, as Wendy Davies has aptly described a similar situation for pre-tenth-century Spain.[5] Documents are so few that, even in combination with the compilations of legal provisions which survive, they provide only a vague idea of how Icelandic society functioned before 1300. The challenge of trying to understand social change in medieval Icelandic society up to the 1260s is in making sense of this particular balance of sources. That said, this challenge is still a lesser one than that facing anyone trying to write the history of late thirteenth- or fourteenth-century Iceland, for which we have almost no narrative sources.[6]

The structure of this book is a statement about the way one might 'do' the history of medieval Iceland, using these narrative sources but focussing on two regions. The book's shape recognises the importance of literary texts as whole entities and how their construction affects what we can say about social action. The regional framework allows texts to be investigated, not just to mine them for detail, but often to allow space to see what is particular to those texts as representations of the past. Discussion of the representation of the period *after* 1100 is dealt with first and is split into two complementary chapters.

---

4   A reasonably good parallel might be Lindy Brady's study, *Writing the Welsh borderlands in Anglo-Saxon England* (Manchester, 2016) which deals with literary texts complemented by slightly stronger non-literary material.
5   Davies 2007: 1.
6   Sigurdson 2016 is a rare study of this period.

Chapter 2 is a discussion of *goðar* (sing. *goði*), the legal postholders who are sometimes referred to in English as chieftains, and of the marriage alliances created by members of Iceland's elite from which *goðar* were usually drawn. Chapter 3 uses the so-called *samtíðarsögur* (contemporary sagas) to consider geopolitical relationships, mostly framed by the narratives of the collection of texts known as a whole as *Sturlunga saga*, named after the family that played a leading role in politics and in writing these texts (see Figure 18 on p. 71). The sub-divisions within this chapter recognise the fact that our view of politics and society are heavily shaped by the individual sagas concerned. Going from the better-known to the less certain, Chapter 4 is concerned with the way *Landnámabók* (*The Book of Settlements*) constructs a picture of early social organisation in each region. *Landnámabók* is an unusual text, a kind of catalogue of facts about the colonisation, which has rarely been subjected to intensive study in the context of the history of particular regions. Chapter 5 is a discussion of the well-known and much-translated genre of saga, *Íslendingasögur* (known as the *Sagas of Icelanders* or *Family Sagas*). While it has become far more common in the Anglophone world to study 'the sagas' synthetically for understanding social practices or cultural history, here they are studied for what they tell us about ideas about the operation of local politics specific to each region. This means that the specifics of local geography, mostly in terms of particular farms, are considered in detail; readers unfamiliar with Icelandic geography will find it necessary to refer to the maps.

As with any book, chapters have to be in a particular order. The order chosen here is one which is shaped by the sources more than themes. The main focus of the respective chapters are texts that cover the twelfth and thirteenth centuries themselves, then the colonisation and the tenth and eleventh centuries. The choice of this structure does not presuppose that particular literary genres actually provide the kind of empirical truth that historians and their readers sometimes want of a time and place. It would be fallacious to suppose that this were possible given the kinds of evidence we have. Related to this is the issue of the dates of composition of *Landnámabók* and the *Íslendingasögur*: it is proposed in this study that these texts do at least predate the writing of the *samtíðarsögur* and most likely reflect twelfth-century ideas which relate to the realities of twelfth-century politics. This represents something of a departure from most scholarship and will be justified in Chapters 4 and 5.

1.1.1   The Choice of Regions

The regions I have chosen are artificial ones, as are most regions to some extent, in that they were not necessarily seen as coherent, self-evident polities or administrative regions in the middle ages. The first region centres on Dalir or what is called Dalasýsla by the early modern period, the region largely formed by the coast of the bay known as Breiðafjörður (Map 2). As shorthand, this region will be referred to as Dalir in the present study. Also included within this region, however, is the north coast of the Snæfellsnes peninsula to its south. This latter area is included because so much of the literary evidence suggests that there were close interactions between people on each side of the part of Breiðafjörður known as Hvammsfjörður, after the famous farm of Hvammr (Figure 1). The end of Snæfellsnes marks something of a natural boundary between its north and south, because the tip of the peninsula is marked by the glacier Snæfellsnesjökull and, below it, uninhabitable lavafields. Post-medieval administrators may have eventually decided that Snæfellsnes was separate from Dalir, but the fact that it is possible to see from one side of Hvammsfjörður to the other, and that it was quick to row across the bay, means that people who lived in these districts had a lot to do with each other. Either end of the region is marked by administrative boundaries which are visible in early modern sources and no doubt existed earlier, i.e. the edge of Saurbæjarhreppur in the north, and of Neshreppur on Snæfellsnes. The area chosen could well have been the whole of Breiðafjörður, the subject of Sverrir Jakobsson's 2015 monograph mentioned in passing in this book's first paragraph. A justification for not looking at the whole of Breiðafjörður is that the sources mention the northern coast of Breiðafjörður less than other parts of it, even if the people who lived there will sometimes feature in what follows. Last, to give some sense of scale to the chosen region, the reader needs to know that from the south-easternmost point of Miðdalir it is about 50km north as the crow flies to the coast in the district of Saurbær. Going west it is about 100km from Miðdalir to the westernmost tip of the Snæfellsnes peninsula.

The second study region is, in effect, two neighbouring early modern administrative regions, *sýslur*, namely Eyjafjarðarsýsla and Northern Þingeyjarsýsla (Map 3). It will be referred to as the Eyjafjörður region, and has at its core the large valley system of Eyjafjörður, within which sits Akureyri, Iceland's largest town outside the Reykjavík conurbation. The region includes districts to Eyjafjörður's east, including the valleys of Fnjóskadalur, Reykjadalur and modern Aðaldalur.[7] Further to the north-east it also includes the remote and sparsely populated districts of Tjörnes, Öxarfjörður and Melrakkaslétta, as well as Mývatnssveit, the distinctive area around the 37km^2 lake Mývatn, 'midge lake' (Maps 10 and 11). The eastern boundary of this area was originally the boundary between the medieval Northern and Eastern Quarters before it was a *sýsla* boundary. From modern Akureyri it is about 40km north to the mouth of Eyjafjörður and the same distance south to the last, narrow inhabitable part of the

---

7 Following the usage of the medieval texts, Reykjadalur will often be used in what follows to refer to the more modern, adjacent districts of Reykjadalur or Reykjahverfi, and Aðaldalur.

valley system (Eyjafjarðardalur, Figure 14). West to east it is c. 100km as the crow flies from Svarfaðardalur on the western side of Eyjafjörður to Mývatn.

Why should these particular regions be studied? The main reason is to consider developments (or the lack of them in some respects) in two contrasting physical environments with roughly the same human population. The use of the word landscape in the title of this book reflects the fact that, as other Icelandic historians (and archaeologists) have suggested, it is appropriate to assume a fairly high level of geographical determinism in understanding Icelandic social relations. The differing kinds of landscape and seascape each of these two regions make for useful comparisons; Dalir and Snæfellsnes consist almost entirely of coastal districts, while the Eyjafjörður region has a mixture of coastal districts and inland districts up to c.50km away from the sea. It is almost impossible to give a good sense of the microgeography of the various districts discussed in this book but the reader is referred to the photographs to get a sense of some key farms and landscape settings alongside the maps; a full discussion of landscapes and seascapes follows in section 1.2 below.

The human geography of these regions suggests similarities and differences between them. Early modern evidence suggests that the Dalir region consisted of just over 430 farms (c.320 in Dalasýsla itself, 115 on northern Snæfellsnes) while the Eyjafjörður region had over 650, shared almost equally between Eyjafjarðarsýsla and Norður Þingeyjarsýsla. It is usually assumed that on average households had something like six to eight inhabitants in the middle ages, on the basis that this was the case in the eighteenth century when we first have detailed population data for Iceland. We might therefore estimate that the Dalir region studied here had about 3000 inhabitants and that Eyjafjörður and the north-east had about 4500. The legal status of individual households could vary, however, being either legally distinct farms (*lögbýli*), whether owned by a landlord or not, or else dependent cottages (pl. *hjáleigur*, sing. *hjáleiga*) which were owned by a landlord who lived nearby on a 'main' or 'head' farm (*aðalból* or *höfuðból*).[8] A rough count suggests approximately a quarter of farms in the two study regions were *hjáleigur* in the eighteenth century, when we first have detailed records. This compares with somewhere between a third and a half in regions in the south where many coastal households in the eighteenth century concentrated on fishing.[9] Everywhere in Iceland,

---

[8] The term manor has been used recently in English to describe larger farms which include cottages (e.g. Árni Daníel Júlíusson 2010) but Icelandic landlord-tenant relations lacked one of the core elements of the classic manor as conceived of for the medieval west, i.e. that labour services were performed by tenants on the main farm. See Magnús Már Lárusson 1970 generally for the very sketchy evidence for relations between *höfuðból* and other farms that formed part of an estate.

[9] Ólafur Lárusson 1944: 37.

medieval and post-medieval, the landscape was conceptualised as a series of districts based on its physical geography: a valley or coast might be known by words which loosely mean 'district,' namely *sveitir* (sing. *sveit*), *byggðir* (sing. *byggð*) or *hverfi* (sing. *hverfi*). Dalir had far fewer such districts than the larger Eyjafjörður region although there is nothing obviously different in their character except that more of Dalir's districts were coastal.

For all the differences in their landscapes, these regions share the fact that they are considered to have undergone a process of political centralisation, although Dalir less completely. They are regions for which we have texts which seem to show this happening in the twelfth century. Political centralisation had happened earlier in other parts of the north and south close to the seats of the bishops: in the south around Skálholt, home to Iceland's first bishop from 1056 and, in the north, in Skagafjörður, where the bishopric had been established at Hólar since 1106. Whether the time and place of the establishment of the bishops were strictly a cause or effect of political centralisation is not entirely clear. Given that there was a fifty-year gap in the establishment of the dioceses, and that Dalir and Eyjafjörður and the north-east were in different dioceses – in Skálholt's and Hólar's respectively – there is at least the potential for this to have affected their histories. A brief discussion in this chapter of what we can (and cannot) say about early, local church organisation suggests that this would be difficult to determine, however.

Last, but by no means least is the fact that these regions have what might be considered the full 'set' of written sources, notably the genre of texts known as *Íslendingasögur* and the compilation called *Sturlunga saga*, which both recount events in these regions, and which cover other regions less well. When synthetic works for Iceland discuss twelfth century political developments or political practices, they are often discussing Dalir or Eyjafjörður. Such works do not, however, pay enough attention to the different realities of regions which had their own specific histories.

1.1.2 Archaeology and Prehistory

What this study will not do is analyse what we might call the prehistory of Iceland, the period before 1100, using archaeological evidence. Most archaeological excavation is no longer carried out as if it were there to prove or disprove 'what the sagas say' for those early centuries, in the belief that the sagas are there to be proved or disproved and the archaeology likely to relate to the 'real' people mentioned in them.[10] There has been an impressive amount of research-driven archaeology in Iceland in the last few decades which itself has

---

10   See, for example, Adolf Friðriksson & Orri Vésteinsson 2003, Birna Lárusdóttir 2007, Callow 2017b.

built on almost a century's worth of less concerted and less rigorous excavation. The nature of the archaeological record in Iceland and the interests of archaeologists means that considerable attention has been paid to the archaeology of settlements abandoned before c.1100. For all that, there is a huge imbalance between the fairly plentiful data for the Eyjafjörður region and the almost complete absence of it for Dalir; the ongoing excavation of the tenth-century farmstead in Ólafsdalur in Dalir is a rare exception (Figure 2). It is still worth briefly summarising the picture for Iceland as a whole because it does provide several indications as to the nature of early Icelandic society.[11]

More will be said about the written evidence for the colonisation, or at least ideas about it, but archaeological evidence confirms that there are some signs of human activity in the late ninth century before there was permanent settlement.[12] It has also been suggested, on the basis of archaeological evidence from Mývatnssveit in the north-east, that Iceland was settled within a few decades either side of 900, just as the written sources have suggested.[13] Much of the settlement archaeology has been dateable via two tephra layers, the so-called *landnám* (colonisation) tephra and one deposited in 1104, between which buildings were constructed and abandoned. Refinements to dating techniques, however, mean that early archaeology is being ever more carefully dated including even an adjustment to the supposed date of the *landnám* tephra from 871 ± 2 to 877 ± 1.[14]

Much of the data for this has come from the various research projects over the last 20 years, including some large international collaborative projects under the umbrella of the North Atlantic Biocultural Organisation (NABO). The picture seems to be that settlers built Norwegian-style longhouses in those lowland regions which were best suited to cattle farming, in an attempt to continue the preferred economy of Norway.[15] These lowland farms were wealthy from the beginning and latecomers or dependents were given poorer land with access to fewer natural resources: from the outset Icelandic society was more hierarchical than older, nationalist-influenced Icelandic scholarship had thought.[16] The fact that we have large numbers of farms abandoned at all before 1100 is testament to one of two possible phenomena. In some places it simply indicates that new dwellings were built within the same property and is evidence of continuity of settlement (e.g. Figure 2).[17] In

---

11   For a detailed survey of scholarship see Zori 2016.
12   E.g. Schmid et al. 2018.
13   Orri Vésteinsson & McGovern 2012.
14   Schmid et al. 2017.
15   See, for example, McGovern et al. 2014.
16   Orri Vésteinsson 1998b.
17   Bolender et al. 2011.

other places we can see upland areas being settled slightly later and often being abandoned after a century or so, although also sometimes clinging on for longer. This does not necessarily indicate that valleys were abandoned, rather that people ceased living in them, exploiting their pastures remotely.[18]

Building materials remained conservative, people relying on turf and stone construction, although the move from dwellings consisting of a longhouse with outbuildings to larger multi-room dwellings by the thirteenth century is evidence of adaptation to the Icelandic situation.[19] The only evidence so far of significant social differentiation or display by means of a dwelling does not occur in Iceland until the thirteenth century: at politician Snorri Sturluson's home at Reykholt in Borgarfjörður a structure akin to a contemporary Norwegian urban house was built with stone foundations.[20]

Iceland's burial archaeology of the period before 1100 has also received a significant boost from deliberate efforts to detect early furnished burials. These have often been popularly thought of as isolated 'pagan' or 'viking' burials with grave goods (often poorly furnished but in Iceland frequently including horses and dogs) but are increasingly being found clustered in small cemeteries. Several churches with accompanying cemeteries which pre-date 1100 have also been excavated. The standard 'pagan' burial catalogue compiled by Kristján Eldjárn in the 1950s has seen two new editions due to increasing numbers of new discoveries, one published in 2000, the other in 2016.[21] Even though numerous new sites have been published, and improved excavation techniques have vastly increased the value of cemetery excavations, the data is still insufficient to be useful in a study like the present one.[22] The most significant recent development, however, has been the suggestion that the traditional dichotomy between pagan and Christian burial should be challenged: several different rites might have been practised in the late tenth and early eleventh century.[23]

For reasons that will become clear it is the assumption of this work is that it is very difficult to write a history of these regions for the period from the

---

18   McGovern et al. 2007: 39; Orri Vésteinsson et al. 2014.
19   Hörður Ágústsson 1987: 229–46.
20   Guðrún Sveinbjarnardóttir 2012.
21   Kristján Eldjárn 1956, 2000, 2016.
22   Cf. Árni Daníel Júlíusson (2016: 41–78) who argues that *kuml*, burial mounds, are found in the richer, lowland part of Svarfaðardalur and reflect the wealth or power of that part of the valley. For excavation techniques see the detection of above-ground structures over accompanied graves by Roberts & Elín Ósk Hreiðarsdóttir (2013).
23   Orri Vésteinsson et al. 2019.

landnám to c.1100 using texts but for now a regional archaeology for this period is not possible either.[24]

1.1.3 Texts, Institutions and Scholars

The key problem in writing a history of Iceland that includes the period before 1200 is that much of our written evidence is from the thirteenth century and almost all of this is in the form of sagas. Each chapter will discuss the source-critical issues relevant to the particular genre of saga and other texts relevant to that chapter. In order, these are the contemporary sagas, i.e. the compilation of sagas known collectively as *Sturlunga saga* together with the bishops' sagas (*biskupasögur*), then, respectively, *Landnámabók* and the *Íslendingasögur*. This section will outline some institutions and scholarly debates.

The use of writing probably began in Iceland at the beginning of the twelfth century.[25] By 1106 Bishop Jón Ögmundarson had established a cathedral school at Hólar in the northern diocese on the model of a school at Iceland's other cathedral at Skálholt where he had been taught. Major farms in the south, Haukadalur and Oddi, are also known to have educated priests from about the same time.[26] Quite what was taught at these early centres of literacy is unclear but by 1117 Icelanders had turned from readers to writers when it was decided that their laws should be written down. 'Christian' laws had also been written down before 1133, as had Ari Þorgilsson's potted history of early Iceland, *Íslendingabók* (*The Book of Icelanders*). The production of each of these texts involved the bishops of Skálholt and Hólar and they were all written in the vernacular. While writing was restricted to a small group of people in this early phase, it is notable that this group readily wrote in Icelandic rather than Latin.[27] The *First Grammatical Treatise*, an attempt at explaining how one should write Icelandic down, dateable to the mid-twelfth century, illustrates that Icelandic had been written by this stage but that writers were still grappling with how to do so using the Latin alphabet.[28] That Ari Þorgilsson almost certainly wrote the first version of *Landnámabók* (*Book of Settlements*) also suggests that this group was keen to write about the Icelandic past.[29]

---

24 For one on a smaller scale looking at Skagafjörður see Carter 2015.
25 Whaley 2000 provides a succinct overview. See also de Vries 1964–7, Turville-Petre 1953, Byock 1988, Miller 1990.
26 Jónas Kristjánsson 1988: 116–17.
27 The role of Latin in Iceland has often been played down but the novelty of Iceland's production of vernacular texts is still striking. See, for example, Clunies Ross 2009 and Patzuk Russell 2017.
28 Haugen 1972: 1–6.
29 See below pp. 154–56.

While historians have often treated *Íslendingasögur* with caution, Ari Þorgilsson's early history of Iceland, *Íslendingabók*, has often been supposed to give a faithful account of early constitutional development probably because it is terse and there is no other 'historical' text with which to contradict it.[30] Until recently nothing has been made of the potential for Ari to have had a poor memory, or poor sources, or for the existence of collective memory which had forgotten or simplified the past.[31] Yet his account of the development of political institutions is extremely simple and schematic. He says that the first settler arrived in Iceland in around 870 and that Iceland was completely settled within 60 years.[32] The constitution of the Commonwealth (*Þjóðveldið*) was established relatively soon after the settlement period with the Alþing established at Þingvellir presided over by an official, the lawspeaker (*lögsögumaðr*).[33] In these early decades it also came about that Iceland was divided into Quarters (North, South, East and West) and each had a fixed number of local assemblies (*þing*, sing. and pl.) established in them.[34]

Grágás, the collection of medieval Icelandic law dating to the twelfth and thirteenth centuries, provides numbers of *goðar* which have been interpreted in conjunction with Ari's dates.[35] Thus it has often been accepted that Iceland had its four administrative Quarters from 930, each of which contained nine *goðar* and three *vorþing* (spring assemblies).[36] In about 965 the Northern Quarter, including Eyjafjörður, is said to have been given another *þing* with three more *goðar*. There is some archaeological evidence in the north for other assemblies having existed outside the strictures of this pattern.[37] The establishment of this new *þing* appears, at least in the minds of the compilers of *Grágás*, to have led to three new *goðar* being created in each of the other Quarters. All, 'old' and 'new' *goðar*, seem to have had the ability to appoint men to the *lögrétta*, the legislative council held at the Alþing. These bare statements are questionable and could be reconstructions designed to explain a later political situation. Even Konrad Maurer, the classic early analyst of Icelandic law,

---

30 E.g. Helgi Þorláksson 2011: 207 on Jón Johannesson's faith in Ari.
31 See now, though, the work of Pernille Hermann, e.g. Hermann 2007.
32 ÍF I: 4, 9. Archaeological evidence would seem to more or less confirm this at present (Orri Vésteinsson & McGovern 2012, Orri Vésteinsson et al. 2014).
33 ÍF I: 8, 19.
34 ÍF I: 12.
35 *Goðorðsmaðr* (plural, *goðorðsmenn*), a term synonymous with *goði*, is also often used in sagas.
36 *Grágás* Ia 38; ÍF I: 12. Three autumn assemblies, *leið*, were also supposed to take place in each Quarter but these did not have judicial functions like *vorþing* (*Grágás* Ia 111–12).
37 Orri Vésteinsson et al. 2004; Orri Vésteinsson 2006a: 317.

admitted that he could not say how many *goðorð* (the legal position owned by a *goði*; sing. and pl., *goðorð*) and *þing* there were before 965 but we should be sceptical about the significance of this date.[38] If we trust some elements of Ari's account it is possible to see particular assembly sites in the Southern Quarter as having served larger areas than *Grágás* would suggest, as might the Þórsnessþing in Breiðafjörður, and possibly predating any attempt to regulate the number of *þing*. Those *þing* in the Northern Quarter fit a pattern whereby one *þing* served each major population centre (Húnaþing, Skagafjörður, Eyjafjörður, Þingeyjarsýsla).[39] However we read the sagas, it is debateable whether we can ever see a pattern of 36, 39 or 48 *goðorð* at any given time, or indeed, because of the serendipity of the sagas, whether we should ever expect to see this pattern.[40] It seems as likely that political patterns varied from region to region or even from valley to valley. Settlement patterns and densities, the decisions and will of small communities, and personal relationships, must all have dictated how power structures developed.

The possibility that a neat pattern of institutions and institutional evolution might not have been a reality in the earliest centuries has been commented on before, particularly for *goðorð*.[41] Jón Viðar Sigurðsson sums up his 1989 work on twelfth- and thirteenth-century political developments by stating that the analysis of political development portrayed in the *Íslendingasögur* had still to be done.[42] More recently he set out the evidence from *Íslendingasögur* which identify a large number of *goðar* and *goðorð*: 27 references to *goðorð*-owning groups in the Western Quarter, for instance, rather than the nine prescribed by *Grágás*.[43] The problem is unpicking these references, and trying to work out the logic of the texts when they make them, something which has not been attempted. Texts cannot necessarily be 'cherry picked' to identify institutional facts when the status of individuals described as *goðar* is linked to the role they play within a given narrative.

What we can say, though, is that *goðorð* were alienable possessions which could be sold or given away and, if not, inherited by the *goði*'s kinsmen, something evidenced in both *Grágás* and sagas. A single, finite *goðorð* could also be run by two or more men at once, provided only one of them undertook legal duties at court in a given year.[44] One major benefit of being a *goði* was that one

---

38   Maurer 1852: 52.
39   Orri Vésteinsson 2009: 303–06, 309–10.
40   For a full discussion of the issues see Gunnar Karlsson 2004: 63–77.
41   Sigurður Nordal 1942: 105–6; Jón Jóhannesson 1956–8 I: 177, 269–73; Orri Vésteinsson 2009.
42   Jón Viðar Sigurðsson 1989: 137.
43   Jón Viðar Sigurðsson 1999: 47–54.
44   Miller 1990: 23–24.

could appoint judges to the Quarter's court. This court was held every summer at the Alþing, the summer assembly (at which all Quarter courts were held and the court of appeal, the *Fimmtadómr* or Fifth Court). At the same time, the *goði*'s position was underpinned by the stipulation that farmers (pl. *bændr*, sing. *bóndi*) of a prescribed minimum wealth had to declare themselves to be the supporter of a *goði* of their choice. These men, *þingmenn* (sing. *þingmaðr*), were obliged to pay a fee (*þingfararkaup*) to ensure that their *goði* could afford to go to the Alþing. *Goðar* and *þingmenn* were expected to aid one another; *goðar* were expected in particular to represent their *þingmenn* in court. Such a relationship might have worked for the *þingmaðr* because *þingmenn* were theoretically allowed to break off the formal allegiance to a *goði* and chose another one.[45] *Goðar* are also often said to have *mannaforráð*, best translated as 'leadership', with the strong implication that this has the assent of *þingmenn* or another way of saying someone owned a *goðorð*. In practice the *goði-þingmaðr* relationship most often worked as between a patron and client.[46]

The *goði-þingmaðr* relationship is widely accepted as having operated widely in the period before the thirteenth century. It is visible occasionally in both *Íslendingasögur*, set in the tenth and eleventh centuries, and those *samtíðarsögur* covering the twelfth. There is debate, however, over how idealised this representation might have been and whether or not such a system, if it really operated, broke down over time as the power of the elite grew. Associated with this possible change are ideas about the potential for increasing territoriality. It has been assumed that *goðar* probably got richer, and fewer and fewer men held *goðorð* or else that some *goðorð* disappeared altogether.

Indeed there has been much concern to explain the apparent disappearance of the supposed 39 *goðorð* and the rate of growth of territorial lordships (*ríki*, sing. and pl.) Fundamental is an article by Gunnar Karlsson, 'Goðar og bændur,' 'Goðar and farmers,' published in 1972.[47] His view then was that individual leaders were first able before 1150 to take up more than one of the recognised *goðorð* in Hegranessþing (Skagafjörður) and Árnesþing (southwest Iceland), in other words the regions surrounding the episcopal seats, first around Hólar and then Skálholt. Rangárvellir, another region in the south, and the Eastern Quarter witnessed this phenomenon next. Jón Viðar Sigurðsson and others have since suggested earlier or later dates of power concentration in different regions but the same question continues to be asked.[48] *Ríki* run by a single leader are generally agreed to have existed almost everywhere by 1200

---

45 *Grágás* Ia 136–37; Jón Jóhannesson 1956–8 I: 79; Jón Viðar Sigurðsson 1999: 120.
46 Orri Vésteinsson 2007; Callow 2018.
47 Gunnar Karlsson 1972, 1977.
48 Jón Viðar Sigurðsson 1989, 1999; Helgi Þorláksson 1989a; Gunnar Karlsson 2004, 2007.

at the latest, in place of the multitude of local leaders who we can still see at this point.⁴⁹

Gunnar's article was more significant, however, for the debate it sparked with Helgi Þorláksson across various publications from 1979 to 1983. They discussed the causes of increased political centralisation and the relationship between wealth and social power, mostly concerning themselves with political developments in Eyjafjörður and Skagafjörður; they gradually agreed to disagree less. Gunnar contended that wealth played a large part in the political power of individual leaders, and that the elite had got richer. He argued that *stórbændr* (literally 'big farmers,' rich farmers who were not *goðar*) only emerged as a distinct class in the 1250s as a result of their financial exploitation of *staðir* (church-farms; sing. *staðr*); Helgi was suspicious of the idea that there had even been a significant increase in church-held land or donations to churches in the first half of the thirteenth century to enable this.⁵⁰ Helgi tried to demonstrate that wealth and power were not directly connected, stressing continuity for the role of *stórbændr*, a group he saw as wealthy and influential throughout the Commonwealth period although their power did not correlate with their wealth.⁵¹ That is to say, they had more combined wealth than *höfðingjar* (sing. *höfðingi*, in the thirteenth century, an increasingly common synonym for *goðar*) but that this was irrelevant to politics. It is hard to say whose views have had the greater influence although both scholars have continued to argue aspects of their respective cases about what underpinned elite power.⁵²

Such discussions helped pave the way for more social historical or anthropologically-derived analysis of *Íslendingasögur* and *samtíðarsögur* which has often been the specialism of non-Icelandic historians, whose work was especially prominent in the 1980s.⁵³ The early work of William I. Miller, Jesse Byock and Paul Durrenberger sought to rehabilitate *Íslendingasögur* as a source.⁵⁴ Their work, particularly Miller's, has concentrated on explaining social processes

---

49   E.g. Orri Vésteinsson 2007: 121.
50   Gunnar Karlsson 1980a: 6, 24, 30; 1983; Helgi Þorláksson 1982b: 87–88.
51   Helgi Þorláksson 1982b: 91, 105–6.
52   E.g. Gunnar Karlsson 2004; Helgi Þorláksson 2001. Jón Viðar Sigurðsson (1999: 209–12) followed Gunnar in emphasising the significance of wealth over honour or reputation. Gunnar Karlsson (2004:316–33) restated his case, reasserting the main point about the vast growth in wealth from the twelfth to thirteenth century among the very wealthiest, and also questioned some of the detail of Jón Viðar's calculations of the wealth of *höfðingjar*. Viðar Pálsson 2003 sides with Helgi in an extended exploration of Snorri Sturluson's fortunes.
53   Although see, for example, Viðar Pálsson (2017) on feasting.
54   Miller 1983a, 1983b, 1986, 1988a, 1988b, 1990; Byock 1982, 1984a, 1988, 1989; Durrenberger 1992. Miller went on to publish books on broader themes but has returned to his earlier focus on Iceland (Miller 1993, 1997, 2003, 2006, 2008, 2014).

rather than examining diachronic change, looking at issues such as the creation of social networks, kinship, the use of violence and vengeance, the operation of peace-making processes,[55] and relations between *þingmenn* and *goðar*.[56] Guðrún Nordal's impressive *Ethics and Action in Thirteenth-Century Iceland* provided a more detailed social and cultural analysis of the contemporary sagas.[57] Although this sort of approach to sagas has been widely accepted as valid for Iceland, just as it has now for Norway, there have been occasional criticisms.[58] The present work takes it for granted that there were common patterns in the way Icelandic disputes worked. Scholars' focus on social practice is often coupled with agnosticism over the dating of texts and, especially for Miller, a scepticism that within *Íslendingasögur* the 'descriptions of various social arrangements and mechanisms of social control' cannot be assumed to pertain to the period before the twelfth century.[59] A parallel development, however, has been literary scholars' success in demonstrating the literariness of the texts in the *Sturlunga* compilation. This has further blurred the division which used to be assumed between the 'unhistorical' *Íslendingasögur* and the 'historically accurate' *Sturlunga saga*.[60]

The partly artificial division between *Íslendingasögur* and *samtíðarsögur* can be illustrated by briefly considering *Þorgils saga ok Hafliða* and *Sturlu saga*, two sagas which form part of the *Sturlunga saga* collection. *Þorgils saga ok Hafliða* records the dispute between two *goðar* in western Iceland over the period 1117 to 1121 while *Sturlu saga* records the rise to power of Sturla Þórðarson from about 1150 to 1180. Both cover events much later than those recorded in *Íslendingasögur* but earlier than those in the rest of the *Sturlunga saga* compilation. Both texts as we have them now can be dated to some time in the thirteenth century but no earlier.[61] They are therefore not particularly 'contemporary' but they do include a great deal of detail about the people in them. Like most *Íslendingasögur* they cover events within a fairly restricted geographical range, unlike the longer sagas in the *Sturlunga saga* compilation which cover thirteenth-century events. In fact, all of these narratives were written at some

---

55   Miller 1990: 13–22.
56   See especially Byock 1988: 71–6, 114–18; Byock 2001: 63–65, 128–32, 341–43.
57   Guðrún Nordal 1998.
58   E.g. Bagge 1991b, Orning 2008 for elite social practice in Norway; see Helle 2011 for various concerns about the incautious use of sagas in recent decades.
59   Miller 1990: 51.
60   Úlfar Bragason 1981: 161–70.
61   For further detail see the Appendix.

chronological distance from the events they describe, and probably by people from the same general background. As a conventional category *samtíðarsögur* include the sagas about bishops but this subgroup do not warrant particular attention. Some of them have the same fundamental interests in Icelandic politics and involve the same kinds of people as do the *Íslendingasögur* and *Sturlunga saga*, and they sometimes discuss events in the two case study regions in the twelfth and thirteenth centuries.[62]

As the main source used by Icelandic historians for examining the period c.1100 to c.1265, much space could be devoted to a critique of the origins and purpose of *Sturlunga saga* and its component parts; such comment is relegated to the Appendix. While attempts have been made to show that the different extant forms of some of these sagas have their own separate perspectives on events,[63] it is rarely the case that two distinct accounts of the same thirteenth-century events exist. The exception to this is *Hákonar saga Hákonarson* which provides a kind of alternative view to some events in Iceland. This text was commissioned by the Norwegian king Magnús *lagabœtir* Hákonarson who asked Sturla Þórðarson (d.1284) to write an account of his father's life. Sturla wrote the saga in 1264–5 but then wrote the longest text in the *Sturlunga saga* compilation, *Íslendinga saga*, in the 1270s. Where the two sagas cover the same events there can be differences of emphasis. These can be explained by Sturla's own changing knowledge or perspective on events not necessarily because the earlier saga was written for a Norwegian patron and the one without a patron.[64]

---

62 Bishops' sagas cover the lives of three bishops of Skálholt: Þorlákr Þórhallsson (bishop from 1178 to 1193), Páll Jónsson (1195–1211) and Árni Þorláksson (1269–98); and three bishops of Hólar, Jón Ögmundarson (1106–21), Guðmundr Arason (d.1237) and Lárentíus Kálfsson (1324–31). Preceding all of these is a chronicle of the bishops of Skálholt, *Hungrvaka* (Hunger-waker), which covers the earliest Haukdælir bishops to 1176. These texts are diverse. They includes the lives of Iceland's saints, Þorlákr (*Þorláks saga helga*) and Jón (*Jóns saga helga*), which are akin to hagiography because of their partial focus on the miracles associated with the bishops. These two texts also both survive in three different versions (Jónas Kristjánsson 1988: 181–84). The canonization of Bishop Jón, in the northern diocese, seems to have been carried out in direct response to that of Þorlákr, in the south. The sagas of the two later bishops, *Árna saga* and *Laurentius saga*, differ from the earlier sagas about bishops in that they are clearly based on other (surviving) written sources (Magnús Már Lárusson 1965b). This marks them out from most other sagas about Iceland in this period. *Páls saga* stands out as having been written very soon after the death of its focal character while *Laurentius saga* is almost entirely about the ecclesiastical world. *Guðmundar saga biskups*, of which *Prestssaga* is a version, has the most complicated textual history, for which see Björn Sigfússon 1960b. Haki Antonsson (2017) analyses *Árna saga*.
63 Úlfar Bragason 1986; Jakob Benediktsson 1972a: 355.
64 Ármann Jakobsson 2015.

This book will not discuss *Hákonar saga* because it does not add much to our understanding of events in Iceland. [65]

The majority of the sagas in *Sturlunga saga* were probably put together in the collection we have now sometime in the fourteenth century.[66] Two similar manuscripts survive of the same basic compilation of sagas, *Króksfjarðarbók* and *Reykjarfjarðarbók*, neither of which survives complete.[67] *Reykjarfjarðarbók* contains two sagas, *Sturlu þáttr* and *Þorgils saga skarða*, which are not in *Króksfjarðarbók*. In the case of what has been identified as *Þorgils saga skarða*, the saga exists only as dismembered chunks within *Reykjarfjarðarbók*'s version of *Íslendinga saga* rather than as an independent work; the inclusion of this text for the period 1242–50, possibly in place of other narrative material, looks like the deliberate act of a compiler.[68] It is clear that the sagas in the compilation have been changed to suit the purposes of writers and compilers as they have been transmitted so that their original form and message may sometimes have been lost. Many of the earliest of these sagas were probably written within a few decades of the events they describe. They often do, in fact, give a high level of description which may reflect the involvement of the saga writers or someone they knew. But this is not the same as assuming, as some have, that we can rely on what has been supposed to be their 'restraint and objectivity';[69] the writers' closeness to events may well have provided a very one-sided view of events. Modern scholars who sit either side of the literary/historical divide still take different approaches to them. As historian Jón Viðar Sigurðsson puts it in his otherwise sympathetic review of Úlfar Bragason's 2012 book *Ætt og saga*, 'It is unlikely that literary scholars will ever come to a unanimous conclusion about the narratology of *Sturlunga saga*, and I do not have the luxury of waiting for that event to occur.'[70] There are some obvious signs of the literary shaping of some of these sagas, and their original authors and the compiler must be guilty of deliberate and accidental omissions or misremembering, and just plain ignorance. It is sometimes obvious where the sympathies of particular authors lie, including those of Sturla Þórðarson, because they almost make them explicit, but their selectivity and other genuine attempts to

---

65 Scholars of Iceland rarely refer to it. E.g. Gunnar Karlsson (2004: 361–63) only discusses *Hákonar saga* in relation to royal control of Iceland in 1258–62.
66 Úlfar Bragason 1992, 2010.
67 SS II: xiv.
68 MS fragments of an independent *Þorgils saga skarða* survive (SS II: xlvii; Úlfar Bragason 1981: 161).
69 Hallberg 1993: 617; see also, for example, Meulengracht Sørensen 1993: 144.
70 Jón Viðar Sigurðsson 2013: 864.

mislead will always be hard to detect.[71] It is hoped that the readings of them in this book show an awareness of the problem at least, even if Chapters 2 and 3 only work on the basis that we often have to suspend our caution.

Other problems of dating and interpretation are discussed in the Appendix. Here it will suffice to note the individual sagas in the *Sturlunga* compilation, most of which the reader will see referred to. These are: *Geirmundar þáttr heljarskinns, Þorgils saga ok Hafliða, Ættartölur (genealogies), Haukdæla þáttr, Sturlu saga, Formáli (Prologue), Prestssaga Guðmundar Arasonar, Hrafns saga Sveinbjarnarsonar, Guðmundar saga dýra, Íslendinga saga, Þórðar saga kakala,* and *Svínfellinga saga*. *Reykjafjarðarbók* also included *Þorgils saga skarða, Sturlu þáttr, Jarteinasaga Guðmundar biskups* (a miracle collection), and *Árna saga*, the saga of Bishop Árni of Skálholt (1269–98). In addition to these, a biographical text, *Arons saga Hjörleifssonar*, records events surrounding the life of Aron Hjörleifsson (d.1255), the foster-brother but then enemy of Sturla Sighvatsson.[72]

Returning to historical scholarship, the intervention of Miller and other scholars has had some impact on medieval history in Iceland but arguably not enough, despite the diverse topics covered by historians of medieval Iceland in recent years.[73] Scholars have considered how the political system evolved and operated, however, often positing a more organic or varied pattern than the laws would suggest.[74] Jón Viðar Sigurðsson attempts to look at the means by which 'chieftains' maintained their social position, drawing on Byock and Miller, but his distinctive contribution has been to raise again the issue of what the *Íslendingasögur* might tell us about the number of *goðar* in Iceland before 1100.[75] Based on the sagas' collective recording of more than the 39 or 48 proposed by the normative evidence, he suggests that there was no clear sense of how many *goðar* people in the twelfth and thirteenth century really thought there ought to be. Although his counting up all the individuals who might be considered chieftains suggests an overly empirical approach to the sagas, his conclusion is more measured: that there would have been '50 to 60 chieftaincies at any one time during this [early] period.' Helgi Skúli Kjartansson came up with a similar suggestion in a published lecture given in 1988

---

71 Cf. Helgi Þorláksson 2017.
72 Aron was the older brother of Óláfr who was abbot of Helgafell (1258–1302). *Arons saga* is included in the 1946 edition of *Sturlunga saga* (SS II: 237–78; Úlfar Bragason 2013).
73 Published papers from Iceland's main, regular history conference reveal a wide range of topics since its inception in 1997 but more recent overviews largely eschew the issues discussed by Miller.
74 E.g. Orri Vésteinsson 2009.
75 Jón Viðar Sigurðsson 1999.

using worked case studies from *Laxdæla saga*, *Eyrbyggja saga* and *Ljósvetninga saga* (three of the texts discussed in this book). In effect he suggests that the number of *goðorð* might have been fixed but that there might have been any number of *höfðingjar* who were trying to acquire them because of the influence *goðar* could have on court cases.[76] He sees being a *goði* as being a local legal representative who attends the Alþing, and no more, thus playing down the role of *goðorð*-ownership as a basis for political influence. Orri Vésteinsson has, more recently still, argued against Byock over the relationship between *goðar* and their *þingmenn*, proposing a weaker legal role for *goðar*, and noting that not all powerful figures were necessarily *goðar* and vice versa.[77] These suggestions warrant closer attention; the evidence for leadership and *goðorð* ownership needs to be given more careful consideration in the context of individual texts. The late Gunnar Karlsson's (1939–2019) monumental 2004 book, *Goðamenning*, is the most significant, recent contribution to this debate but is structured around traditional political-historical themes. It is symptomatic, perhaps, that on this specific issue Gunnar favoured the view of the laws on the number of *goðorð*, *contra* Jón Viðar's suggestion, and that, as he said explicitly, he did not think he should discuss dispute processes.[78]

Stronger arguments have been put forward for greater levels of territorialisation too, which this study will support. Orri Vésteinsson posits small blocks of fairly exclusively controlled territory around each chieftain's residence, surrounded by more politically divided districts inhabited by men tied to various chieftains. This makes Iceland appear less exceptional than it has often been portrayed, and contributes to the broader argument that Orri makes about the significant inequalities of wealth in Iceland that underpin his model of territorial control for the twelfth century.[79] Jón Viðar Sigurðsson has made a similar case but especially emphasised the importance of the *hreppr* (pl. *hreppar*) or commune. *Grágás* identifies the *hreppr* as an association of a minimum of 20 neighbouring farms, led by a small committee, who have rights of mutual obligation, including the feeding of the poor of the *hreppr* and the collecting of tithe. Jón Viðar suggests that in effect *höfðingjar* must have controlled *hreppar* in some way and thereby exerted territorial control.[80] Although *hreppar* seem to have existed by the late eleventh century, their virtual absence

---

76 Helgi Skúli Kjartansson 1989.
77 Jón Viðar Sigurðsson 1989 shared this view but, in his more recent work (1999), also proposed a model of earlier territorialisation.
78 Gunnar Karlsson 2004: 70–77, 147.
79 Orri Vésteinsson 2007, esp. 124–25.
80 Gunnar Karlsson 2004: 154–57.

from sagas or documents makes it uncertain whether they operated at all or else were just so mundane as to not warrant discussion.[81]

1.1.4 Local Ecclesiastical Structures

One last issue remains to be considered by way of introduction: the establishment of local ecclesiastical administration. As a general cause of political change, the introduction of the tithe in 1097, and its potential for increasing the elite's incomes, has had a long historiographical life. Björn Sigfússon credited Árni Pálsson (1878–1952) with first suggesting that the influence of the church led to a concentration of power around the two episcopal seats, Skálholt and Hólar.[82] Through their exploitation of the tithe the bishops are supposed to have upped the political stakes, forcing *goðar* to compete more fiercely, with the result that some of them lost or gave up their *goðorð* to others.[83]

The power of the tithe to transform social relations has been put forward most recently and convincingly by Orri Vésteinsson.[84] Tithe is seen as having been an additional income for church owners, who tended to be the wealthiest people in the first place. Farms with wealthy churches on them, *staðir*, usually a church owning half of the farm plus property elsewhere, in effect did not have to pay tithe because one quarter of the tithe went to the church owner (with a quarter going to each of the bishop, the priest and the poor).[85] The major difficulty in such arguments, however, is that we know next to nothing about the rate of the development of churches or specifically *staðir* – although many were clearly being established by members of the elite in the twelfth century – or the actual rate at which the tithe was imposed, or whether it was always collected. Even in theory, by comparison with tithe payments elsewhere in Europe, Iceland's tithe was very small, effectively a one percent property tax, and so its effect may have been weak.[86] The organisation of the Icelandic church at a local, pastoral level was hierarchical, featuring 'full' churches with resident priests and annex churches (most often a *hálfkirkja*, a 'half-church')

---

81 Eventually, by the early modern period if not before, *hreppar* had fixed boundaries and did function as administrative districts, potentially making them a vehicle for localised influence.
82 Björn Sigfússon 1960a: 56; Jón Viðar Sigurðsson 1999: 11–12.
83 Björn Sigfússon 1960a: 57; Byock 1988: 94–95. Guðmundr *inn ríki* who appears in *Íslendingasögur* and Hafliði Másson are the two *goðar* associated with more than one *goðorð* (both in the north of Iceland) before c.1120 (see e.g. Jón Viðar Sigurðsson 1999: 56; Gunnar Karlsson 2004: 248–55, 261).
84 Orri Vésteinsson 2000: esp. 67–92, 238–46; Orri Vésteinsson 2017.
85 Orri Vésteinsson 2000: 295; Magnús Stefánsson 2000: 22–36; 2005: 117–21; Benedikt Eyþórsson 2005: 37–39.
86 *Grágás* Ib 205; II 46.

which the main church provided with, say, half the number of services.[87] It seems churches typically had the right to collect tithe from six to ten farms, but some churches had this right for over 20 farms. All the same, however low the tithe was, the creation of the need for farmers to pay tithe to a church, and then for a priest to serve a church or churches, created a small-scale territorial institution which provided another social tie between those on richer farms and their poorer neighbours. In the so-called Tithe Law (*Tíundalög*) of 1097 the assessment of the tithe payable by a farmer and the handing out of tithe to the poor or needy (*ómagar*) is not set out as the responsibility of the church but of the delegated members of the secular *hreppr*.[88] This has been noted as showing the lack of institutional coherence or reach of the church in about 1100.[89]

For all their apparently slow growth, Christian institutions probably did strengthen the influence of the secular elite. It is certainly notable that the church in Iceland failed to develop or assert its independence. Churches and their property remained private until as late as 1297, serving their owners more than the bishops, despite moves in Norway from the mid-twelfth century to establish ecclesiastical independence.[90] Christian institutions also provided the elite with new channels of communication which allowed access to material, cultural and spiritual capital from outside Iceland and some new bodies which could be controlled by secular powers, i.e. churches and the small number of monasteries. Many people we might think of as *höfðingjar* seem to have been ordained as priests in the central decades of the twelfth century which seems to coincide with the period in which many churches were first given property and, in some cases, the tithe.[91] In 1190 Archbishop Eiríkr of Niðarós banned Icelanders from being ordained if they held a *goðorð* and, whether or not this was the cause of it, very few of the major secular leaders in the thirteenth century were priests.[92] Men in leading families continued to be

---

87 Helgi Skúli Kjartansson 2005: 98; Orri Vésteinsson 2000 esp. 80–81, 85–92, 240–45, for what follows.
88 *Grágás* Ib: 206.
89 Cf. Gunnar Karlsson 2004: 282 on the general lack of references to the territorial basis of power in the narrative sources.
90 Orri Vésteinsson 2000: 112–32 for the so-called *staðamál*, the battle for control of the property individual churches owned (see also p. 48, footnote 14 below). Orri argues convincingly against the possibility that Bishop (and saint) Þorlákr Þórhallsson of Skálholt (1178–93) made progress in asserting church control.
91 Orri Vésteinsson 2000: 182–94; Orri Vesteinsson 2017: 57–59.
92 DI I: 189–91; Orri Vésteinsson 2000: 170.

ordained, just not those who were *goðar*, while there were more priests among those wealthy families who were no longer competing in secular politics.[93]

It is worth momentarily digging into the detail of some of this for the two regions under investigation because they will not form a significant part of the book later on. This is not least because the origins and impact of the church in each region are hard to decipher directly from the narrative sources and, indeed, the impact of the church within the case study regions is hard to determine at all. The general picture would seem to be that the establishment of local church institutions – the building of churches and the development of ministries or tithe areas – mirrored and amplified secular political patterns. There is some reason to believe that the boundaries of ministries might have overlapped in part with secular administrative boundaries but is harder to say more about the social and political importance of ministries. The patchy evidence we have is from the twelfth century at its earliest and we often have to look at fourteenth-century charters and try to make inferences about the earlier history of individual churches, i.e. their properties and rights, the numbers of farms which paid tithe to them, and the numbers of priests or deacons who were supposed to live at them. Most of these pieces of information are not much use in understanding political power but some inferences can be made nonetheless. It should be noted that for the two study regions most of the *máldagar* (foundation charters) for churches are later than 1265. If the dates of the charters are correct – and this is far from certain[94] – then before 1265 we have only scattered *máldagar*, all from Dalir and north Snæfellsnes, a few more in the later thirteenth and early fourteenth century and then, for the northern diocese the first, comprehensive compilations are dateable to 1318 and 1394. Our view of the church at a local level is therefore shaped by a mostly late and patchy documentary record.

If we are considering how the church evolved as an institution the first thing we can say is that the early narrative evidence mentions very few churches before 1200, the date at which we have a fairly comprehensive list of churches for the diocese of Skálholt.[95] Thus for the southern diocese, 57 churches can more or less certainly be seen to have existed before 1200, of which just twelve are in our western study region. For the diocese of Hólar, 32 churches are referred to directly or indirectly in the same period, of which 21 are in the Eyjafjörður region. These figures reflect the size of the study areas relative to the diocese rather than there having been a larger

---

93 Orri Vésteinsson 2000; Sverrir Jakobsson 2009: 162.
94 Orri Vésteinsson 1996: 37–41.
95 Compiled by Bishop Páll Jónsson (DI XII: 3–15).

number of north-eastern churches or better recording of them. So far as we can infer anything from these numbers, it would seem that locally the church was equally well-established in our two study regions and that these regions were fairly typical of the rest of Iceland by 1200. There is also a general similarity between the regions in that each had a single, significant monastery by the late twelfth century, Helgafell in the west (Figure 3), and Munkaþverá in Eyjafjörður itself (Figure 13), although their role in politics will be covered in the course of the rest of this book rather than here.

Our records for the the economic basis of individual church foundations is also patchy. Those *máldagar* we do have give the impression that, whatever might have happened before our surviving documentation appears, there were no significant new donations of property to churches before the mid-thirteenth century. For Dalir the initial establishment of the monastic community at Helgafell is remarkable for how little property seems to have been donated to it, just rights to a piece of woodland and a meadow, each on different farms.[96] By 1250, however, we can see that Helgafell comprised a large chunk of the Þórsnes peninsula although whether it had further properties is unclear.[97] In 1274, however, it owned seven neighbouring properties along with several local islands and *reki* (coastal driftage rights) in locations further north.[98] Elsewhere in Dalir the church at Skarð owned half of the farm itself by 1259 (Figure 8) plus neighbouring Geirmundarstaðir, and all or part of ten nearby islands or island groups and a farm on Strandir.[99] Smaller churches seem to have had next to no property given to them. The early *máldagar* for Geirröðareyrr (also known as Narfeyri, Figure 3) in Álptafjörður and Tjaldanes in Saurbær, both dated to 1224, and the 1270s and 1280s *máldagar* for Setberg, Bjarnarhöfn, Hvoll and Garpsdalr, show them having little or no land under their control.[100] Snóksdalr's church owned three farms and *reki* east in Hrútafjörður and Steingrímsfjörður.[101] For the remaining churches later *máldagar* also give the impression that they had limited land.[102] Thus the issue of how church land was managed

---

96   DI I: 282.
97   DI I: 576–78.
98   DI II: 116. See below on *reki*, pp. 34, 36, 40.
99   DI I: 597. See below for the strong association of Skarð with Geirmundarstaðir and its eponymous founder, pp. 181, 319.
100 DI I: 465, 466; DI II: 82, 118, 257.
101 DI II: 258.
102 Sælingsdalstunga, DI II: 633; Staðarfell, DI II: 637; Búðardalr, DI II: 650–51; Staðarhóll, DI III: 79–80; Fróðá DI III: 109; Mávahlíð DI III: 110. Orri Vésteinsson (2017: 62–63) has pointed out the peculiarity of the establishment of the small tithe area of Búðardalur *within* that of Skarð sometime between 1238 and 1268.

was most likely not an issue for any but the larger farms where the church owned sizeable amounts of property; we can surmise that secular owners or heads of household still had a large say in how these estates' resources were deployed.

In the Eyjafjörður region the fraction or value of the main farm (*heimaland*) each church owned is mentioned most of the time and conforms usually to one of three patterns: churches tended to own all, half or one-third of the home farm.[103] In Eyjafjörður and its tributary valleys, for example, the churches of Árskógr, Saurbær, Glæsibær, Laufás and Höfði owned all the estate on which they sat in 1318. Hrafnagil's church owned half of its *heimaland* while two others owned one-third (Möðruvellir, Gnúpufell). It is noticeable that Grund (Figure 12), Lögmannshlíð and Laugaland are the only churches within the region which, rather than owning any part of the main farm itself, owned a smaller neighbouring farm, probably one which might be thought of as dependent on the main one in some way.[104] This suggests similar approaches to the establishment of the church by their owners. It is interesting that Grund, before 1265, and Lögmannshlíð, sometime after 1265, were home to the major political leader or official in Eyjafjörður.[105] It looks like the owners of these two farms somehow managed to avoid giving their land away to churches, potentially avoiding any ambiguity about how the farm was managed.

For other churches in the Eyjafjörður region *máldagar* suggest there might have been a particular phase of church establishments because some of them follow a similar format. Five *máldagar* share certain key features, something not visible anywhere else in the two study areas' *máldagar*. The churches at Lundarbrekka, Eyjardalsá (both in Bárðardalur), Ljósavatn and Draflastaðir (Fnjóskadalur) and Miklagarðr (Eyjafjörður) are all said to have possession of 30 hundreds of their respective farm's *heimaland*. This shared stipulation is unique across the two regions in specifying a value in hundreds (*hundruð*, sing. *hundrað*), the standard unit of value, as well as the actual number itself.[106] This

---

103   Landownership is either not mentioned, or else there is a *lacuna* in the manuscript, for these churches: Svalbarð on Svalbarðsströnd, Kaupangr, Hólar, Djúpadalr, Árskógr.
104   DI II: 452–54; DI III: 521. In the early eighteenth century the farms owned by the churches were dependent properties were of slightly different statuses but all of reasonable size and roughly in proportion to the church-farm. In *Jarðabók* (see below, p. 28), Finnastaðir (associated with Grund) was valued at 40 hundreds and independent. Hesjuvellir/Esjuvellir was rated at 20 hundreds or one-fifth of Lögmannshlíð. Laugaland's Grjótgarðr was occupied and dependent of that farm and had no value accorded to it but was probably notionally no more than 20 hundreds (*Jarðabók* x: 174–5; 198, 227).
105   See below pp. 135–40, 195–201.
106   A *hundrað* was equivalent to 120 ells of homespun cloth (*vaðmál*) or one cow or six ewes with lambs (Magnús Már Lárusson 1962b).

allocation might have occurred by chance but it looks far more likely that these farms – all among the smaller ones to have ministeries – had something in common. Perhaps these churches were founded at roughly the same time and/or one foundation formed the model for the others.[107]

Given that it is not clear that either large-scale landownership or significant differences in access to military technology existed in medieval Iceland, it has been suggested that local ecclesiastical structures enabled some people to increasingly outdo others. In other words, owning a church and controlling its finances, along with controlling others' access to religion, gave those who built and controlled churches a degree of influence over their neighbours. Orri Vésteinsson has also proposed that churches' differing ministry sizes, as measurable by the numbers of farms that paid tithes to particular churches, say something about political structures. Small ministeries in the south of Iceland close to Skálholt can be explained as the product of a political structure whereby the bishop – or the Haukdælir family who established the see at Skálholt and became its first bishops – were exceptionally powerful while, at the same time, there were also many lesser farmers each of whom could only establish small ministeries. By contrast, a single, more even tier of church founders, perhaps establishing churches later in time as well, would create few churches each with a correspondingly large ministry. Nuancing his model, Orri Vésteinsson has proposed that competition for local influence along routeways, whether to aid travellers spiritually or to benefit from the additional social ties created by providing lodgings for travellers, meant that ministeries along routeways were smaller. The principle here is that more people founded churches along routeways meaning that, again, churches here had smaller ministeries.

Orri chose Dalir as a regional case study in his synthetic work on the Icelandic church because it has the best early documentary record of churches. Even here, however, the documentation is largely no earlier than the early fourteenth century and so we cannot be sure if ministry sizes had remained the same; we can certainly see at least one instance where ministry sizes changed early in the fourteenth century.[108] Orri's ideas work for Dalir, in that Dalir (and the Western Quarter as a whole) has a higher average size of ministry than all other regions of Iceland at just over 14 farms per ministry. Most of Dalir's

---

[107] 30 hundreds might have equated notionally to half of each farm's property but might have been less for the probably larger Miklagarðr and more for the smaller Lundarbrekka (*Jarðabók* X: 231; XI 71, 133, 147).

[108] Hvammr's ministry was enlarged in 1308, Orri Vésteinsson 2000: 245. Changes in ministry size occurred occasionally elsewhere, e.g. in the north-east for Nes in Reykjadalur between 1318 and 1394 when its ministry shrank from 13 farms down to eight (DI II: 435, DI III: 558).

churches with small ministeries lay along the north-south land route from Saurbær to Miðdalir with some of the otherwise notable farms which feature in our narratives (Staðarhóll, Hvammr, Sælingsdalstunga, Sauðafell) having churches but small ministeries. This might be an argument for not overemphasising the significance of tithes as a source of income – some significant church-farms did not extract tithes from many farms – but noting the importance of location for these no doubt already well-off farms.

Returning to the larger scale, Orri calculates that the Southern Quarter and Eastern Quarter had an average of between eight and nine farms for every full church, and the North Quarter had eleven. Following this reasoning, this would suggest that the social hierarchy in the north was generally flatter than that in the south and east. It should be noted, however, that the surviving data for the south and east is the least complete, based on *máldagar* for no more than half the likely churches. By my calculation Eyjafjörður and Northern Þingeyjarsýsla churches have almost exactly the same average number of farms per ministry (eleven) as for the remainder of the Northern Quarter. Here, among those we have figures for, the ministry sizes range from one (Miklagarðr in Eyjafjörður) up to 19 (Grenjaðarstaðir) and by far the largest, 30 of Vellir in Svarfaðardalur, actually the largest across the Northern Quarter.[109] There would appear to be some smaller ministeries in valleys which acted as routes for longer distance travel, such as in Öxnadalur or Hörgárdalur (Figures 10 and 11). This could explain the small ministeries of Miklagarðr and Djúpadalr in Eyjafjörður which might be considered to be on routes from upper Eyjafjörður to Skagafjörður. And, while some larger ministeries (of 15 or more farms) seem to be off the beaten track and associated with the only major farm in a district (Prestshólar, Húsavík, Grýtubakki, Barð), Grenjaðarstaðir (Reykjadalur) and Hrafnagil (Eyjafjörður) were not. If these latter two had large ministeries in earlier centuries then this must represent the pre-eminence of those church-farms in some way. Orri also suggests that the demand for priests might influence the size of ministeries, i.e. that there was high demand initially in the south and in Skagafjörður near the bishops' seats, and less so elsewhere. If this was the case then perhaps Grenjaðarstaðir, Hrafnagil and Vellir were early foundations and their owners were able to prevent new churches being built nearby. As we shall see, the occupants of these farms were often prominent figures in local politics but no more so than, say, the occupants of Grund in Eyjafjörður, or many other farms with churches, and regardless of the size of their ministeries, and whether or not their farm was wholly or partly under church ownership.

---

109   Árni Daníel Júlíusson 2016: 236.

This framing of the scholarship on socio-political change and the excursus into the detail of church establishment show the variety of regional patterns of all kinds in medieval Iceland. The limited nature of the evidence for the evolution of the church, particularly for Eyjafjörður and the north-east in this case, reminds us of the potential value of revisiting the narrative material for understanding local political patterns.

As a whole, this introductory section has aimed to demonstrate the development of the relevant literary and historical fields and to give a basic sense of the nature of the material to be used in this study. What is clear is that the historiography of medieval Iceland has changed significantly over the last thirty or forty years but that there is still a need to integrate some of the approaches taken by different kinds of scholar in order to consider how and why Icelandic society changed, or did not change, during the period from the *landnám* up to the 1260s. Significant space will still be devoted below (Chapters 4 and 5) to contextualising the writing down of *Landnámabók* and *Íslendingasögur* because, despite their contingent nature, and the doubts of some scholars as to the value and necessity of even trying to pin these texts down in time and space, this study aims to demonstrate that the texts still provide an under-utilised source for Iceland's history.

As alluded to above, finding a way of interpreting medieval narrative material is an important part of this study and there needs to be more debate about these how these texts' contents relate to the world in which they were composed. It will be argued here, crucially, that *Íslendingasögur* do amount to an interpretation of the past shaped by local socio-political patterns, rather than as some kind of fiction, and that we ought to try to interpret the saga texts as attempts at writing history rather than simply entertainment. It will be argued that just as is more obvious in the case of *Landnámabók*, genealogy and geography form a key element in other texts' construction of the past, particularly for *Íslendingasögur*. Before we look at different texts' views of the past, however, we need to understand fully the different landscapes and economy of the regions under consideration because in a relatively poor society like that of medieval Iceland their impact was significant.

2 Landscapes and Seascapes

The regions examined in this book include a variety of environments which have always had an impact on their economies at a local and wider level.

Colonists arrived in Iceland with what might be termed a productive 'imported domestic mammal package' of sheep, goat, cattle, pigs, and horses but this could soon be deployed differently and was supplemented by natural resources.[110] All had a measurable value and helped distinguish one farm from another. Medieval Icelanders had few choices but to exploit their environment in certain obvious ways. Basic economic patterns also most likely remained the same throughout the period from the *landnám* into the early modern period. Using later written sources, reasonably sound inferences can be made about patterns of both farming and the availability of natural resources in the period before 1300.[111] Historians are aware of the varied natural resources across Iceland but not enough has been made of this for the medieval period beyond a generalised consideration of the potential for landownership to be an underpinning of leaders' power.[112]

Clearly by the time our first texts were written, Icelandic farms showed great variety in their size and value; this inequality seems to have been created in the *landnám* period itself, to judge by the way farm boundaries ensure that some farms owned a variety of lowland resources while others were denied access to them.[113] The most valuable farms – they will often be described below simply as 'large farms' – were usually close to larger rivers and had not only good pastures for cattle but access to a wide array of other resources such as salmon-fishing, peat, and birch woodland. In terms of their value, we can see in later sources that such farms were typically worth 60 hundreds or more, sometimes over 100 hundreds, way beyond the 'modal' size of farm of 16 to 24 hundreds. An average or typical farm, of which there were many, might have poorer or less varied pasture, and fewer other resources. The smallest independent farms, i.e *lögbýli* as opposed to the dependent *hjáleigur*, might occasionally be as small as 12 hundreds or less. As we shall see, the most influential people in all our texts lived at those wealthier farms with varied resources while it is noticeable in particular for *Sturlunga saga* that hardly any people from the very smallest farms appear at all.[114]

---

110 McGovern, Harrison & Smiarowski 2014: 154.
111 Changes to regional economies in later centuries can also often be filtered out. A good example of a regional specialism is the exploitation of sulphur in north-east Iceland which was exported from the later middle ages onwards, see e.g. Mehler 2015.
112 E.g. Jón Viðar Sigurðsson 1999: 101–19; Gunnar Karlsson 2004: 316–33. See, though, Helgi Þorláksson 2003 for the interests of *höfðingjar* in fishing in the West Fjords.
113 Orri Vésteinsson 1998b gave the classic argument for this, using Borgarfjörður as his case study.
114 Orri Vésteinsson 2007.

While it is important to be aware of the varied access to resources at the level of the individual farm, we need also to consider how intra-district or intra-regional ties might be created by broader differences in resource distribution for our two regions. Breiðafjörður, especially the southern part of the bay with its hundreds of tiny islands, represents a very specific kind of natural environment. It has its own marine resources and specific climatic characteristics which distinguish it from other regions.[115] In the north-east, Eyjafjörður and its tributary valleys provide larger lowland areas suitable for pastoral farming. The inland landscape east of Eyjafjörður is less characterised by mountain ranges and supported pastoral farming in some places, while marine resources were exploited by the relatively smaller numbers of coastal farms.

As to our sources, sagas and pre-1400 charters offer sporadic evidence on landscape and resources but our most detailed source is the early eighteenth-century tax survey known as *Jarðabók Árna Magnússonar og Páls Vídalíns*.[116] *Jarðabók* is a farm-by-farm description of the natural resources and livestock holdings of Iceland. Unlike previous, seventeenth-century registers which only recorded rent payments, this one recorded both quantitative and qualitative data.[117] Livestock numbers and subjective commentaries on pasture and other natural resources were included. Despite the fact that this register is centuries later than the period studied here, *Jarðabók* gives a good general sense of natural resources, whether because they were still abundant or, sometimes, because the exhaustion of those resources is recorded.[118] We can see that there had been a great conservatism over the centuries in the notional values of individual farms as measured in hundreds. *Jarðabók* is undoubtedly testament to one big economic change in Iceland: the growth of

---

115 Cf. Sverrir Jakobsson 2015: 155–62.

116 For saga references to past vegetation conditions, for example, see Sigurður Þórarinsson 1944. Inferences can also be made about the likely extent of church possessions in earlier centuries. It is not within the scope of this study, however, to piece together patterns of landownership in the medieval period. The evidence is highly fragmentary even for the late medieval material. Various other digitised modern resources for individual farms are now readily available via http://jardavefur.skjalasafn.is/ including descriptions of modern farm boundaries (http://jardavefur.skjalasafn.is/landamerkjabaekur/#pg-1) but they have not been consulted.

117 Björn Lárusson 1982: 14–24.

118 These accounts require contextualised reading because they were compiled over the period 1702–14 and the methods of recording vary from year to year, from district to district. The survey was interrupted by a significant outbreak of smallpox in 1707–9 whose impacts are visible in the registers compiled afterwards. In the west, for example for Eyrarsveit (October 1702) and Neshreppur (June 1711), most of the north-east was surveyed in 1712 but some districts in Eyjafjörður had been surveyed in late 1706.

commercial fishing, as shown by the large numbers of fishing booths in different regions, including Snæfellsnes, the West Fjords, and, in the north, the island of Grímsey. Even in this instance, however, archaeological evidence is starting to suggest that texts have misled us into exaggerating change. Fishing may have taken place on a larger scale at an earlier date.[119] Climatic change and some environmental degradation must also have effected slow changes in the pastoral economy. Underlying all this, however, is a basic continuity of settlement pattern and farming techniques. The regional and local variations in *relative* abundance of vegetation and the land's ability to support livestock probably did not alter significantly between the time the sagas were written down and the time the Danish authorities commissioned *Jarðabók*.

The fundamental point to make about what these sources show is perhaps obvious but needs stating nonetheless. Access to natural resources in Iceland, just as anywhere else, was uneven. Some farms or districts had access to particular natural resources that others had in smaller quantities or not at all. People's needs or desires for resources they did not have encouraged interaction, either at the level of the farm or else regionally. As will also be discussed below, secular landowners and religious institutions can be seen to have been in possession of more land and of particular, remote, finite resources as early in time as our sources enable us to see.

Before considering the variations in natural resources, it is worth noting that Dalir and the Eyjafjörður region had slightly different climates, such that Dalir might have produced better hay growth and therefore supported more livestock. By most standards, the climate of modern Iceland is harsh: it has relatively low average temperatures, is notoriously windy and some areas are snow-covered for up to six months of the year. Modern temperature statistics for Iceland show that the coasts of Breiðafjörður are relatively mild but wetter than the north-east, as shaped by the Gulf Stream and proximity to the coast. Stykkishólmur, close to Helgafell in northern Snæfellsnes, has average monthly temperatures ranging from − 1.3 Celsius in February to 10.1 Celsius in July.[120] Akureyri shows almost no difference in average annual temperate, being only 0.2C colder yet with greater variability. Stykkishólmur has far greater annual precipitation than Akureyri, however, c.700mm compared to c.500mm.[121] On a day-to-day basis such differences are/were barely noticeable but they are significant for pastoral farming in that the higher temperature and rainfall in

---

119   Björn Þorsteinsson (1978: 209–16) for an older account; For some more recent developments: Mehler & Gardiner 2007; Callow 2010.
120   Hanna, Jónsson & Box 2004: 1198, Figure 5.
121   Wastl, Stötter & Caseldine 2001: 194, Figure 5.

the west are likely to facilitate greater hay growth over the year.[122] Districts further inland than Akureyri have harder winters, whether in Eyjafjörður itself, or in districts like Bárðardalur, Reykjadalur or Mývatnssveit.[123] Indeed, planned, sparser settlement in the tenth and eleventh centuries in areas far inland may have been a response to the harsh climate.[124] Here, deep, settled snow on the ground in the Eyjafjörður region will have hindered movement more often than in Dalir.[125]

The cultivated part of Iceland's medieval landscape, just as it is now, consisted mainly of hay fields surrounding the farm (*tún*), other lowland pastures (*hagi*, pl. *hagar*) and waterlogged meadows close to rivers (*engi*, pl. *engjar*). Of the three types the meadows were the most valuable because they could be grazed by cattle, the most valued form of livestock. Larger farms, usually owned or occupied by the most powerful *höfðingjar*, and/or partly or wholly owned by the church, tended to include the best meadows and therefore most cattle.[126] Although ownership or access to good pasture must have been key in the period being studied, it is hard to gauge because it is not until the early twentieth century that we have any real sense of the size of pastures associated with particular farms.[127] Almost all plants have been used in Iceland as animal fodder but those most readily available at lower altitudes with most nutritious value were of greatest importance.[128] Grazing for sheep mattered slightly less

---

122 Relatively modern studies suggest that a change in summer temperature of just one degree Celsius can affect the growth of hay by 15 percent. Bryson 1974 and his contribution in A.B. Pittock et al. 1978: 325.
123 It is possible, but hard to prove, that the north-east might have been subject to more frequent harsh winters, such as devastated the far north-east of the country in the late seventeenth century and apparently caused over two hundred deaths in Vopnafjörður, just outside the Northern Quarter (Þorvaldur Thoroddsen 1908–22: II 383).
124 Orri Vésteinsson et al. 2014: 61.
125 Despite these relatively harsh conditions, there is now evidence for the presence and likely cultivation of barley in several places across Iceland, including two locations in the north-east. It was once thought that climatic constraints had limited cereal cultivation to the south and west. The Dalir region provides one rare instance of medieval cereal cultivation (SS I: 27). Generally see Gunnar Karlsson 2009: 155–66; Riddell et al. 2018: 682.
126 Orri Vésteinsson 1998b for the argument that this situation originated early in Iceland's settlement.
127 The beautiful colour, hand-drawn maps produced by the Danish *Geodætisk Institut* in the first two decades of the twentieth century provide the best, but hardly ideal, guide on the areas likely to have been used for different forms of grazing. For an attempt at assessing pasture in early Svarfaðardalur in the north-east see Árni Daníel Júlíusson 2016: 93–108.
128 Þorvaldur Thoroddsen (1908–22: II 422) was very enthusiastic about the woolly willow on the heaths of the north-east but this kind of fodder would not necessarily have been a first choice of feed.

INTRODUCTION

because they were left to roam the mountains during the summer, making use of lower quality grass.

A further distinction can be made between our regions because of the excellent pastures provided by the islands in Breiðafjörður, a resource not available in the Eyjafjörður region. So-called *fjörubeit* is a general Icelandic term for shoreline grazing areas, usually made up of seaweeds, and often used to describe the coasts of many of Breiðafjörður's islands.[129] This additional resource was also relatively accessible because of the lack of lowland snow cover.[130] Such resources were rarely available in the Eyjafjörður region, not least because so few farms were near the coast.

The real significance of grazing in medieval Iceland was its impact on livestock herds. Here our data is not good but there are some clear patterns.[131] The general picture is one of gradual change with sheep farming becoming increasingly important, with rising herd sizes, as cattle numbers remained steadier. By 1200 these were the main livestock types with pigs and goats seemingly unimportant. There was a difference between the farming practices of larger and smaller farms, and between regions, but detecting regional difference is difficult. Certainly for the large estates owned wholly or partly by the church the cattle numbers remained a larger part of the economy. Archaeology suggests ratios of cattle to sheep could be as high as 1:3 on richer farms – the excavations at Hofstaðir in Mývatnssveit in the Eyjafjörður region had this ratio throughout the period c.940 to c.1310 – while smaller farms tend to have ratios of 1:6 or above, but rarely so high as to suggest the extensive sheep farming of later centuries.[132] Written evidence seems to indicate that households typically had anywhere between five and twenty cattle in the thirteenth century and the

---

129 Lúðvík Ingvarsson 1980–86: I 93–95. *Fjörugrös* is another term for seaweeds which were grazed by livestock, or as a famine food for humans. It occurs in many places in Iceland but with concentrations in the west. Flatey in Breiðafjörður had, at the beginning of the eighteenth century, as much as the farm needed ('Fjörugrös so mikil að nýtast kunna,' *Jarðabók* VI: 240). *Fjörubeit* seems to have been more important. Many farms in Helgafellssveit, Eyrarsveit and Neshreppur for example, had *fjörugrös* but *Jarðabók* comments that they did not always exploit it (*Jarðabók* V: 280, 283, 284, 288, 293, 322, 341, 343, 346, 355, 358; VI: 240, 312, 313, 315).

130 Significantly, livestock produced milk year-round when grazed on these pastures. See Stefán Aðalsteinsson (1991: 289–90) on ewes' milk; Þorvaldur Thoroddsen (1908–22: III 255, III: 379, IV 34–35) specifically on cows in Eyrarsveit and elsewhere enjoying beneficial dining on *fjörubeit* in milder weather. See also Lúðvík Ingvarsson 1980–86: I 113, 114; *Jarðabók* V: 288, 293.

131 For what follows see Callow 2001: 299–305.

132 McGovern, Harrison & Smiarowski 2014. These figures might partly reflect consumption patterns at a farm rather than production but either way they suggest the availability of particular species for the household.

wealthiest farms could have anything from 40 to 100 dairy cows, figures possibly including animals on *hjáleigur*.[133]

The uncultivated landscape was clearly not uniformly advantageous, either for Iceland's colonists or its later inhabitants. Woodland is a resource famously in short supply in Iceland and only available in the form of smaller tree species unsuitable for building. The lack of timber (*viðr*) for building meant it could be imported by the wealthy, or a lower grade of timber could be obtained from the coast as part of the rights to *reki* which will be discussed below.[134] Woodlands (*skógar*) were, however, large and more widespread in particular places in the medieval period than they were in later centuries. The arrival of humans had a major impact on existing tree cover. Prior to the *landnám* it is generally thought that birch woodland at the lowest altitudes and willows at higher altitudes together covered over half of Iceland's total area.[135] Settlers are thought to have cleared the woodland to create pasture for their cattle and used the wood extensively as fuel (and possibly for building or fencing material); many sagas refer to charcoal production.[136] It is thought that burning, deliberate and accidental, was common in early centuries.[137] The decline in vegetation is also blamed in part on the overgrazing of sheep and, perhaps, the pigs thought to have been relatively common before 1200.[138] Environmental modelling suggests that the land may have been able to support far more sheep than had previously been thought, suggesting that the decline in vegetation generally may have some other cause.[139] *Íslendingasögur* certainly retain the idea of a more densely wooded landscape having existed in the tenth century. *Laxdæla saga* is notable in depicting Laxárdalur and Sælingsdalur as having been thickly wooded in the past. The saga stories suggest the locations of woodland in the

---

133   Gunnar Karlsson 2009: 125.
134   Gunnar Karlsson 2009: 240. Of the three mentions of imported timber in *Sturlunga saga*, one is from our case study regions. In about 1120 Þorgils Oddason is said to obtain it from a ship in Hrútafjörður to build a new room or hall (*skáli*); Hafliði Másson then makes sure to obtain some of it as part of the fine when Þorgils is outlawed (SS I: 37–38).
135   Andrés Arnalds 1987; Þóra Ellen Þórhallsdóttir 1996; Sigurður Þórarinsson 1976.
136   Particularly noteworthy is *Ölkofra þáttr* in which the main character accidentally burns down a wood close to the Alþing (ÍF XI: 82-95). There is archaeological evidence too, e.g. Smith 1995.
137   Þorsteinn Þórarinsson 1974.
138   Stefán Aðalsteinsson 1996: 78. The existence of early place-names with the element *svín-* or *grís-*, meaning pig or piglet, are often supposed to indicate that there were pigs in medieval Iceland although there are few references to them otherwise. See, for example, the story in *Sturlubók* about the pigs said to have given Svínadalur in Hvammssveit its name (ÍF I: 158).
139   Simpson et al. 2001; Brown et al. 2012.

twelfth and thirteenth centuries and are evidence of its significance. Whatever the nature of the decline and its causes, it is certain that everywhere was more wooded than when *Jarðabók* was compiled.[140]

It is, however, inequality of access to woodland that is of most relevance. Often a district has one or more farms that derives its name from woodland but it is larger concentrations which were of more significance.[141] Each study region would appear to have districts which retained significant woodland which was used for firewood into the thirteenth century and beyond. For Dalir, both *Jarðabók* and place-name evidence indicate concentrations along the innermost districts around Hvammsfjörður, from Fellsströnd southwards round to Skógarströnd, literally 'woodland shore,' and where 16 farms still had woodland in c.1700.[142] Dalir and north Snæfellsnes was one of the few places in the country in c.1700 where some farms were charging other people a fee (*skógartollur*) to collect wood or dig charcoal pits, something not recorded at all in the north.[143] At the same time, the relatively densely-populated Saurbær district in Dalir was noticeably without either woodland or peat.[144]

In general the use of peat as a fuel was also characteristic of many farms in early modern Iceland but less so in Þingeyjarsýsla where *skógar* still existed to be used as the fuel of choice and peat-cutting was rare. In particular in the north-east, fuel-rich districts included those ones immediately east of Eyjafjörður, from Fnjóskadalur (Figure 15) and throughout Reykjadalur, whose woodland could (still) be utilised for firewood or charcoal production.[145] Within Eyjafjörður itself only Glæsibæjarhreppur, arguably the nodal point for communications within the whole valley, had notable woodland.[146] This would suggest a similar broad division to that in Dalir between those more densely

---

140 *Jarðabók* generally refers to just a few sources of fuel: wood or woodland (*skógar, hrís, rifhrís*) and peat (*móskurður*, literally peat cutting). Woodland is generally referred to as being available to burn for charcoal making and/or as firewood (*til kola og eldiviðar*). *Hrís* andr *rifhrís* are only referred to a lot for Húnavatnssýsla, the region between the two studied here. *Sturlunga saga* records a single dispute over *viðirif*, tellingly for Borgarfjörður rather than Dalir or Eyjafjörður (SS I: 232).
141 E.g. Krákunesskógr in Álptafjörður, regarded as best woodland in that small fjord by *Eyrbyggja saga* (ÍF IV: 85). More generally see Ashwell & Jackson 1970: 158–66.
142 The place name elements *skógr/-ar* and *holt* may both reflect the early presence of woodland. Many farm names including these elements can be confirmed as having been wooded areas simply because there is still some significant woodland near them.
143 *Jarðabók* V: 367, 368; VI: 35, 36, 81, 83, 85, 101, 101, 115, 116, 135, 160.
144 See discussion of population above p. 5.
145 *Jarðabók* XI *passim*.
146 See pp. 195–201 and 318 for Glæsibæjarhreppur's political importance.

settled districts with more extensive pastures, and other districts which retained, or had always had, a more diverse landscape.[147]

Some medieval Icelanders also benefited from access to the shoreline. The owners of rights to exploit the coast could be farm owners or tenants who lived on coastal farms or else inland farms – often monasteries and *staðir* in later centuries – which had bought or been given the rights.[148] These rights enabled the gathering of driftwood, beached whales, sea birds, their eggs or else eider ducks and their valuable down. The combination of varied dominant sea currents and the varied nature of the shoreline itself ensure that some coasts were sought-after resources while others were of negligible importance.

The one resource which the whole of Breiðafjörður lacked but which was common across much of northern Iceland was *reki*. For the Eyjafjörður region there were many farms on the coasts, especially on Melrakkaslétta and Tjörnes, which were able to collect *reki*, 28 of these were owned by the monastery of Þingeyrar in Húnavatnssýsla by the late thirteenth century and no doubt long before.[149] If analogies can be made between Iceland and other parts of medieval western Europe, it would seem likely that wealthy landowners had donated rights to *reki* to churches at some point before we can see those churches owning it. We can also see at least a couple of major farms in Eyjafjörður which were not *staðir* but owned *reki*: Grund had *reki* on Tjörnes in 1285 and both it and Espihóll had *reki* in multiple locations in 1391.[150] Given what else we know about the lack of practical independence of the Icelandic church, even when it had been nominally donated to the church, *reki* was probably controlled by the lay occupant of the church-farm. The significance of *reki* was not just that it provided timber and/or whale meat but that it encouraged communication from the coast to the interior for those wealthy farms and ecclesiastical institutions which owned it.

Dulse or *söl* (*rhodymenia palmata* or *palmaria palmata*) was apparently also in the hands of secular owners but its distribution varied from that of *reki*. *Söl* was a resource exploited around much of south and west of Iceland including

---

147   *Jarðabók* X: 162–73.
148   The so-called *Spákonuarfr*, the rights to the coast along Skagaströnd in Húnavatnssýsla, is an early documented example, a record of which survives from c.1200. The monastery of Þingeyrar had taken possession of some other farms' rights but presumably in the relatively recent past because this fact was recorded, DI I: 304–6, Bjarni Einarsson 1980.
149   DI II: 90–92, 306–10. Lúðvík Kristjánsson 1980–86: I 231–32; Gunnar Karlsson 2009: 203–5.
150   DI III: 3–4, 457–58, 458–59. For their roles in narratives see, for example, pp. 135–40, 278–83.

a notable concentration in Saurbær in Dalir.[151] In later centuries it was sold to people from outside Breiðafjörður as a source of food for both people and livestock, being regarded as medicinal, perhaps because of its iodine content.[152] The earliest charter evidence concerning *söl* shows several churches owning or being given rights to it in the fourteenth century. *Sturlunga saga* mentions *söl* twice, both in connection with Saurbær, with one reference suggesting it was being sold.[153] The earliest charters demonstrate the extent to which significant amounts of the Saurbær coast was owned by churches.[154] The church at Skarð is said to have owned half the shore (*fjörv halfa*) in its oldest extant *máldagi* (1259).[155] Of 17 churches that had rights to *söl*, 13 of them were from modern-day Dalasýsla while three of the other four were nearby.[156] Churches on Snæfellsnes did possess *söl* rights elsewhere, but Saurbær was clearly the most important source in western Iceland.[157] By contrast, all that can be said about *söl* for the Eyjafjörður region is that it is almost absent from *Jarðabók*, being mentioned just eight times as opposed to over 50 times for Dalir.[158]

Fishing was also vital for people in our regions in the middle ages.[159] The obvious fish that people are likely to have caught in the medieval period are the same as in later centuries: cod and haddock from the sea, salmon and trout from numerous rivers. Again, the story is one of Breiðafjörður's greater diversity of resources. All the major species of saltwater fish and *crustacea* found around

---

[151] Lúðvík Kristjánsson 1980–86: I 47, 55. Wrack was the other notable seaweed, consumed for its salt, and was used as a fertiliser in the south of Iceland but seemingly not around Breiðafjörður (Lúðvík Kristjánsson 1980–86: I 127–28, 136, 160).

[152] Bell 1981: 118 generally. Eyrarbakki on Iceland's southern coast was the only other noteworthy source from which *söl* was sold (Þorvaldur Thoroddsen 1908–22: IV 232–33). Lúðvík Kristjánsson (1980–86: I 70, 80–83) gives evidence of *söl* having been eaten around Stykkishólmur and Skógarströnd at the end of the nineteenth century.

[153] A group of men are mentioned incidentally as going *til sölvakaupa*, to buy *söl* (SS I: 22). The other reference, probably amounts to the same thing when a woman was said to be travelling to the *sölvafjara* in Saurbær (SS I: 65).

[154] For what follows see also Lúðvík Kristjánsson 1980–86: I 53–55.

[155] Identifiable as belonging to the farm Frakkanes on Skarðsströnd (DI I: 597).

[156] DI III: 166, 535. Garpsdalur, Staður on Reykjanes and Fell in Kollafjörður; the most distant (Melr in Miðfjörður) had grazing rights for the horses of its *söl* collectors.

[157] Elsewhere *söl* is recorded among the possessions of Helgafell on the land of Hraunskarð in about 1360 which was held in exchange for fishing rights (DI III: 140; Lúðvík Kristjánsson 1980–86: I 58). Further west on the Snæfellsnes coast there is a record of rights to *söl* belonging to people from Saxahvoll in about 1380 (DI III: 348). A further church (Akranes, in Iceland's south-west) had rights to *söl* on Snæfellsnes in/by the 1360s (DI III: 250).

[158] *Jarðabók* XII: 97.

[159] See generally Þorkell Bjarnason 1883.

Iceland are common in Breiðafjörður but it also has a relative abundance of *crustacea* and additional species, which are relatively rare elsewhere. By the early modern period Breiðafjörður and Snæfellsnes saw significant seasonal sea fishing. *Jarðabók* records the fishing 'booths' (*verbúðir*) on the coast where fishermen based themselves. By contrast, the Eyjafjörður region is notable for its excellent river fishing. It has certain rivers which are especially good for salmon and trout although these local supplies are not visibly significant beyond forming part of the rights which *staðir* and churches eventually had.

If we take sea fishing first, it is clear that by the early modern period Breiðafjörður was one of the places in Iceland where fishing was of greatest economic significance. This seems likely to have been the case before 1300. Even if fishing is rarely visible in written evidence, archaeology is starting to suggest that fishing was significant in the medieval period, possibly even for the export of dried fish (*skreið*).[160] For Dalir *Laxdæla saga* mentions people from Sauðey fishing at the fishing station at Bjarnareyjar,[161] presumably in a similar way to people in the eighteenth century. Nevertheless *Íslendingasögur* references to the sale of dried fish on Snæfellsnes demonstrate there was a trade in fish in Iceland's earliest centuries.[162] In the north, the owner of the farm of Grenjaðarstaðir is said to have had some kind of great 'catch' from the island of Flatey as well as having *reki* rights on Grímsey, the latter hinting at early fishing rights.[163] A *bóndi*'s setting out to get *föstumatr*, probably stockfish, from Siglunes on the outermost edge of Eyjafjörður might also indicate large scale fishing in the north before 1200.[164] Undoubtedly there were changes in the fishing industry and social practices which related to it – improved technology (the introduction of nets and harpoons) and an increased tendency for people living inland to migrate to the coast to fish when farming was difficult – but marine resources had always been key, especially in Breiðafjörður. For Breiðafjörður *Jarðabók* reveals a wealth of detail about different fishing stations and where individuals went fishing, details almost entirely absent for the

---

160   Amundsen et al. 2005; Callow 2008. None of the references to *skreið*, stockfish, in *Sturlunga saga*, for example, tell us anything about its export, merely its production and/or storage, mostly to be consumed by the people who feature in the text (SS I: 158, 312, 390, 397, 507). In the 1220s it would also seem that the English King Henry III was legislating for the import of fish from Iceland. Who was doing the fishing is unclear, however (DI I: 482).

161   ÍF V: 29; Helgi Þorláksson 1991: 442. These islands also formed part of a property deal between the Sturlungar in 1240 (SS I: 447).

162   ÍF III: 156, note 4 for references.

163   *Reykdæla saga ok Víga-Skútu* (ÍF X: 170, 171).

164   SS I: 169; Birna Lárusdóttir, Howell M. Roberts & Sigríður Þorgeirsdóttir 2011: 7–8.

north, a phenomenon which, again, could well have existed by the period this book largely covers.[165]

Over recent centuries cod has been the fish caught in greatest numbers around Iceland.[166] Fishing seasons everywhere around Iceland were defined by the weather and the availability of cod; the two study regions both had long fishing seasons but that in the west dovetailed slightly better with the rhythm of the pastoral year than that in the north.[167]

Beyond these broad patterns it is clear that Breiðafjörður has always had excellent fishing resources because it is home to species that were rare or absent elsewhere around Iceland. The most significant herring spawning ground is to the west of Iceland between Eldey and Breiðafjörður; *beinahákarl* (*selache maxima*) was often seen off Breiðafjörður in the summer, and sometimes elsewhere in the west. In the eighteenth century, at least, it was sometimes harpooned.[168] The lumpfish or *hrognkelsi* (*cyclopterus lumpus*) is strongly associated with Breiðafjörður because it prefers shallow waters and feeds off the *crustacea* which inhabit Breiðafjörður.[169] Nineteenth-century sources indicate that lumpfish was often eaten in spring in Breiðafjörður when other sources of

---

165 Bjarnareyjar were visited by many fishermen from Skarðsströnd. Along Breiðafjörður's southern shore, Hjallasandur was a focal point, while many people from this area went further south and fished off Dritvík at the end of Snæfellsnes. Place-names including the elements *búð* or *búðir* may also indicate temporary settlements which, in some cases, were probably used as fishing stations. Búðardalr in Laxárdalur may have served such a function, judging by its coastal location; Skallabúðir and Vatnabúðir in Eyrarsveit certainly did in the eighteenth century and probably earlier.

166 Fishing seasons referred to in *Jarðabók* without reference to a particular fish, i.e. spring and autumn, coincide with the cod fishing season of the last two centuries but the connection to cod is not made explicit (Ogilvie 1981: 239–40).

167 In early modern sources there is some suggestion that there were two specific cod fishing seasons in Breiðafjörður two (10th April-12th May, 29th September-23rd December). *Jarðabók* makes it clear that many farmers living along northern Snæfellsnes fished all year round. The main season for them was undoubtedly spring but fishing went on all through the year. It is often said that people went to sea whenever they could manage to. The exact phrase varies from account to account in *Jarðabók*. The north of Iceland also had fairly lengthy sea fishing seasons covering spring, summer and autumn but perhaps with greater chance of the hay harvest having to take precedence over fishing (Aðils 1926–27: 514–15; Ogilvie & Jónsdóttir 2000).

168 Þorvaldur Thoroddsen 1908–22: II 570.

169 Other areas of south-west Iceland are home to lumpfish too (Lúðvík Kristjánsson 1980–86: IV 364). Kristjánsson's map of farms recorded in *Jarðabók* with access to *hrognkelsi* ignores some farms around Hvammsfjörður which were described as having little or virtually no *hrognkelsi*. It must, however, be of some significance that these kinds of comment are only recorded at particular farms i.e. these farms did or had had *hrognkelsi*.

food were scarce.[170] Unfortunately the lack of archaeological excavations in the west makes it hard to say more about how this ecosystem was exploited in the middle ages, but it must have been.

Freshwater fish were undoubtedly a major source of food for people living in our regions but it is much harder to see this as having any significance for social action. Many farms had access to rivers that provided salmon and trout, with the former appearing in many river names (the common Laxá meaning salmon-river). There are at least five 'Laxár' in the western study region but some really significant rivers with this name in the north-east, most notably that running just west of Mývatn, past the famous excavated farm at Hofstaðir, and into Reykjadalur. *Jarðabók*'s vast catalogue of entries for trout confirms their ubiquity, too, and probably explains why rivers were never named after them.[171]

Besides Iceland's potential attraction as a fishing station in the ninth and tenth centuries, marine mammals were also an important initial and later resource. While walrus ivory may also have attracted early colonists,[172] it was ultimately seal-hunting that was far more widely practised in the medieval North Atlantic, especially in western Iceland.[173] Seals provided skins as well as food.[174] In Breiðafjörður there was an exploitable population of seals at hand

---

[170] It is noticeable that the sources for lumpfish being eaten by necessity in spring are only from Breiðafjörður; people in the south were not so desperate (Lúðvík Kristjánsson 1980–86: IV 363). Harbour seals, *hákarl* (the small shark common all around Iceland) and seabirds in turn feed on lumpfish (Þorvaldur Thoroddsen 1908–22: II 552).

[171] At a regional level, however, it is perhaps worth noting that the West Fjords, had no salmon rivers but instead most likely had excellent sea fishing. It is hard to see that this made either region dependent on the other, however (Þorvaldur Thoroddsen 1908–22: II 542).

[172] Helgi Þorláksson 2006; Ævar Petersen 1993. In the last century walrus have usually only been found off Reykjanes, in the south of Iceland. A fairly recent study suggests that even hunting in recent centuries has reduced walrus numbers such that there might have been larger numbers in Iceland in the middle ages (Erlingur Hauksson 1993b: 213). Findings of walrus bones in Iceland, however, have been most common in the north-westernmost areas of the West Fjords and at the very end of the Snæfellsnes peninsula. This seems to suggest that the walrus has generally visited the more remote, rocky parts of Iceland's western coast. Breiðafjörður's more sheltered southern and western coasts are unlikely to have seen many walrus and its population can rarely have hunted them for ivory or food.

[173] Bonner 1982: 19–34.

[174] Ogilvie et al. 2009: 66. Although *Sturlunga saga*, for instance, has an abundance of references to seals and their products, only once does it refer directly to their consumption, SS I: 84. DI generally, however, provides abundant evidence of their importance to churches. To take DI II as an example, and which covers the later thirteenth and early fourteenth centuries, its index contains references to seals (*selr*, 153, 376), seal boats (*selabátr*, 635),

throughout the year[175] while in the north-east seal-hunting was also practised along outer Eyjafjörður and along the north-eastern coast, especially Tjörnes. *Jarðabók* and the abundant seal-related place-names in Breiðafjörður suggest that it has always been the habitat for exploitable seal populations for some or all of the year.[176] Exactly how productive such seal populations were is unclear given the uncertainties of the size of even modern seal populations (of which there might have been six species).[177] With so little research done in the modern era, attempting to trace changes in Iceland's seal populations back in time is almost impossible.[178] What we can say, however, is that in the west, Skarðsströnd seems to have had best access to seals, whereas Tjörnes had the best resource in the north.[179] The sum of the evidence, including the handful of references in *Íslendingasögur*, would seem to suggest that western Iceland and the West Fjords was able to exploit seals more than other regions.[180] Rights to seal-hunting, however, do not necessarily seem to have been in the hands of

---

Grey seal hunting (*útseladráp*, 768), seal skin and seal skin book covers (*selskinn*, 235, 435, 436, 437, 443, 424), and seal hunting (*selveiðr*, 114, 376, 431, 475, 615, 620, 768, 769).

175   Ogilvie 1981: 255 notes the benefit of sea-ice in bringing seals to where people could catch them. See also Björn Guðmundsson 1944: 149.

176   Luðvík Kristjánsson 1980–86: I 309–16. Harbour seals and Grey seals, for example, have tended to spend all year round in Breiðafjörður and to not migrate (Bigg 1981: 5). Thoroddsen picked out certain islands or coasts as being especially favoured by the Grey seal in Breiðafjörður: Skarð, Fagradalur, the Akureyjar, Rúfeyjar, Rauðseyjar, the tiny island of Sviðnur as well as Hergilsey (Þorvaldur Thoroddsen 1908–22: II 474). Modern research shows that the distribution of seals around Breiðafjörður's islands has changed since the nineteenth century but not sufficiently to invalidate Thoroddsen's general account (Erlingur Hauksson 1993a: 189).

177   This point is illustrated by the lack of data for Icelandic seal populations in many of the articles collected in Ridgeway & Harrison 1981. Riddell 2015 counters the older assumption that harp seals might only have been exploited when sea-ice was present. Certain species were rare in particular places when they might have been more plentiful earlier or preferred southern Iceland (Þorvaldur Thoroddsen 1908–22: II 476–77; Ronald & Healey 1981: 61).

178   In general see Þorvaldur Thoroddsen 1908–22: II 472–73; Bigg 1981: 5.

179   One of the best farms for *selveiði*, in the north-east, though, was Harðbakur on Melrakkaslétta, further to the north-east, owned by the monastery at Munkaþverá when *Jarðabók* was compiled (Lúðvík Kristjánsson 1980–86: I 314). Among the few relevant archaeologically excavated sites, only the post-medieval midden deposits at Svalbarð in Þistilfjörður show a large dependence on seals for food. See Ogilvie et al. 2009: 65 (Fig. 4), 66 for references.

180   That would seem to be the implication of *Íslendingasaga* references based on Lúðvík Kristjánsson 1980–86: I.

the church before 1300; many donations occurred in the later middle ages.[181] Unless the surviving documentary record is misleading, it seems likely that seal-hunting rights were too precious for lay men to give away.

Whales, a potential source of food and other products, were no doubt common around Iceland's shores in the middle ages, although they were apparently not scuttled in the way that they have been in other regions of the North Atlantic. While commercial whale-hunting is a relatively modern phenomenon, beached whales provided an irregular but prized resource in medieval Iceland, forming another key part of *reki*.[182] Neither of the study areas was blessed with shores on which whales were beached, and no sagas make much mention of them or distinguish between species of whale.[183] However, as with *reki* in general, certain coastal areas were favoured for whale beaching and formed part of the standard sought-after rights which eventually ended up in ecclesiastical ownership. There is some limited evidence of the potential for whales to be beached on Skarðsströnd, but *reki* was instead most likely gathered from Strandir (Map 1); in *Laxdæla saga* the Helgafell-based *höfðingi* sought whale meat from Steingrímsfjörður.[184] In the Eyjafjörður region, Tjörnes made a credible location for a bumper year of whale beachings in *Ljósvetninga saga*, something which the saga says came to the attention of the pre-eminent Eyjafjörður-based *höfðingi*.[185] This fits the pattern we see elsewhere whereby Tjörnes' *reki* was controlled from larger farms in Eyjafjörður or Reykjadalur, whether they were wholly owned by the church or not.[186]

Coastal-dwelling birds and their eggs have always formed a potentially significant form of food around Iceland's coast, with puffins, arctic tern, gulls, and ducks being among the most commonly consumed.[187] The islands of Breiðafjörður, and to an extent the coast of the bay, provided a more

---

181   Even in later centuries churches in the mid-west generally did not possess seal breeding grounds. Well after the period studied, Öndverðareyrr or Hallbjarnareyri's church was given half of Selsker in Eyrarsveit (DI IV: 173), and the church at Búðardalr owned Helluhólmr, both of which could have provided seal hunting, *selveiðarflögum* (DI VII: 72). See Lúðvík Kristjánsson 1980–86: I 312–14 for the vagaries of the evidence for the church's holdings.
182   Byock 1982: 69, 70, 229–30.
183   Lúðvík Kristjánsson 1980–86: V 30–31 gives the *Íslendingasögur* and *Sturlunga saga* references.
184   ÍF V: 218.
185   ÍF X: 47.
186   This would seem to be the implication of the availability of (stored) whalemeat and eggs to Eyjólfr Hallsson of Grenjaðarstaðir in *Guðmundar saga dýra* recorded for 1187 (SS I: 165, 166).
187   See Ævar Petersen 2008 for modern seabird harvesting.

than average supply. In one modern study it was found that, just on Flatey and a few surrounding islands, at least 29 different species of bird had nested there over a five year period.[188] While the eggs of many different species have traditionally been eaten, duck eggs are consumed in preference to other species,' either fresh or preserved to be eaten in the winter.[189] Eider ducks are also significant as producers of eggs and down, the latter used for bedding.[190] In the north-east the obvious corollary to this is not only the most north-easterly coasts of Tjörnes and Melrakkaslétta but also the significant inland resources of Mývatn. At Mývatn numerous species of duck thrive there during the summer such that now 10,000 eggs a year can be harvested from nests; the ducks themselves are not eaten.[191]

Direct medieval evidence for the exploitation of birds in Dalir is limited. *Sturlunga saga*, for example, makes just a few short references to down (*dún*) in Breiðafjörður and *máldagar* make only a handful of explicit references to the wildfowl resources of church estates in the west.[192] For eider and their down *Jarðabók* suggests that they were quite common; presumably their ubiquity meant that larger landowners did not need to lay claim to specific properties which had them.[193] This absence of references to wildfowl contrasts with *Jarðabók*'s interest in wildfowl resources. In the early twentieth century the

---

188 Ævar Petersen 1979.
189 *Iceland* 1942: 301. *Jarðabók* records that swans' eggs were exploited on some of the more upland farms in Laxárdalur in Breiðafjörður but nowhere else in the west, suggesting that these were an alternative (*Jarðabók* VI: 69, 70, 72, 73, 74).
190 Few modern studies of the bird population in Iceland have been published but the richness of Breiðafjörður's birdlife stands out. A 1970s study of the eider population of Flatey and some islands surrounding it measured the total number of nests as exceeding 700 in each of three separate counts (carried out when down was collected). These islands make up a very small fraction of the total number of islands in Breiðafjörður which the eider occupy, suggesting that the total number of individuals amounts to several thousands. Other species heavily outnumbered the eider in the above census (Ævar Petersen 1979: 234 (Table 1), 243, 248, 253). For eider on the Flatey in the north-east see Ævar Petersen 2010: 14–16.
191 There is abundant archaeological evidence for the consumption of duck eggs from Hofstaðir, the excavated tenth- and eleventh-century site. McGovern et al. 2007: 41–42.
192 SS I: 494, SS II: 95; Lúðvík Kristjánsson 1980–86: V 146.
193 In particular it is noticeable that none of the churches in Dalir and around Hvammsfjörður are said to have had *eggver* or *dúntekja* (egg and down resources) in their late medieval *máldagar*. This contrasts first of all with the frequent assertion of rights to *söl* in the same documents. This is not easily explained except in that wildfowl were more readily available than *söl* and therefore not so valuable. It is also possible that church estates, generally larger than average farms, were better endowed with livestock and less dependent on hunting (*veiði*) than smaller farms.

island of Flatey in Breiðafjörður was a particularly large producer of down, ahead of mainland districts (Klofningur, Skarð and Reykhólar).[194] Districts of the north-east were also notable producers, mostly in the same districts already identified for coastal resources.

To anyone not from a North Atlantic community it would be easy to assume that this relatively harsh environment was almost uniform and that there were few human and physical geographical features which could lend themselves to social differentiation or even exchange. What this section has aimed to demonstrate is that while the core activity of everyone, from poorest *bóndi* to the wealthiest *höfðingi* and their respective households, was pastoral farming, but both pastoral farming and other subsistence and surplus-generating activities could vary. The value of a farm and the quality of life of its inhabitants was mostly determined by the quality and quantity of pasture one could get for one's livestock in the summer and then the quantity of hay one could cut and store to feed animals through the cold and dark winter. People knew how to make use of any other resources on their properties to produce food and surplus; all other resources contributed to the values of farms which we see being measured in hundreds.

What has also been shown is that natural resources varied from region to region and farm to farm, as we might expect. This typically resulted either in wealthier people and institutions owning property away from their residence, or else, although it is rarely recorded, for people to travel to buy or exchange goods. There are some obvious likely links between areas with different resources. In Dalir marine resources of all kinds might be exchanged within and outside the region; *söl* in particular was sought after. Even within the region, although distances were short, many farms in Laxárdalur might lack rights to marine resources and operate an almost exclusively pastoral economy. In the Eyjafjörður region there were larger distances between coast and interior and greater variations in access to resources between districts. It is likely that by 1100 much of the lowland areas of the valleys feeding into Eyjafjörður had little immediate access to woodland while Fnjóskadalur and upland areas probably had far more, and probably carefully managed. Mývatn also provided resources which were rare.

It is tempting to ask which of the two regions we might consider to be wealthier or which districts within them were the wealthiest. There is no easy answer to this. As has been implied, it depends how we measure it. In all areas there were great differences between the wealth of individual farms which

---

194   *Iceland* 1942: 300.

means that it really becomes a question of sheer population size or density. At the same time, by 1100 it seems as if people had largely adapted their farming strategies to suit the environment such that in a given region there was a correlation between available resources and population. What we might say, then, is that Eyjafjörður itself stands out as the most extensive, relatively densely-populated area across either region. At the same time, Dalir's almost uniquely varied marine and bird resources meant that it was likely to have been buffered against the worst effects of prolonged bad weather and thus famine.

CHAPTER 2

Frameworks of Power: *Goðorð* and Elite Marriage Networks c.1100 to c.1265

Before beginning to look at the regional picture it is necessary to give a basic outline political narrative of recorded events in the period c.1100-c.1265, the period for which we can create the most certain account and analysis. At times the detail of the contemporary sagas is bewildering, especially for the first time reader, but it needs to be sketched so as to frame the regional analyses.[1] It is also true that for Iceland in the twelfth century it is hard to produce a narrative for much of the country beyond the two regions being studied here. As a result, modern overviews tend not to feature accounts of the twelfth century at all; the increased coverage of events in the thirteenth century still means that this account gives the latter more space. This basic, scene-setting narrative is not an attempt to create a significantly new narrative for Icelandic political history. It should also be noted that the account below reads as if the narratives is unquestionably accurate, or was universally agreed upon. This cannot be the case but the difficulty is in being able to actually suggest an alternative view when this is all we have. The great joy and frustration of these texts, especially the lengthy *Íslendinga saga*, is that there is just so much one might question, but it would be a complex task to try to get behind their wording.

The two 'frameworks' considered in this chapter, however, *goðorð* and elite marriages, do require much more critical engagement. The stability and continuity of the *goðorð* as an institution has been argued for most forcefully by Lúðvík Ingvarsson, while some doubt has been cast on Lúðvík's conclusions in a thorough critique of them by Gunnar Karlsson.[2] However, the account below will argue that the existence of particular *goðorð* is not nearly as clear as has been suggested before. That is not to say that many did not continue to exist into the thirteenth century but merely that we have little credible information with which to be able to trace the notional 36, 39 or 48 *goðorð* which the normative texts suggest existed.

---

1 For what follows cf. Jón Jóhannesson 1956–8 I; Björn Þorsteinsson 1980: 128–60; Lúðvík Ingvarsson 1986–87; Jón Viðar Sigurðsson 1989, 1999; Orri Vésteinsson 2000; Gunnar Karlsson 2004; Sverrir Jakobsson 2016.
2 Lúðvík Ingvarsson 1986–7; Gunnar Karlsson 2004: 205–70.

Alongside this is a re-examination of what might be seen as the representation or outward signs of inter-dynastic politics, namely recorded marriages. These are rarely considered critically, perhaps because the superficial impression is that Iceland's elite simply continued to marry within itself in an almost random fashion. The aim of this section therefore is to try to identify either geo-political patterns or else the political strategies of the people, usually men, whose familial networks we can identify.

1   The Twelfth Century

It is possible to write a kind of skeletal account of politics in each region for the twelfth century stitched, together mostly from *Sturlunga saga*, the bishops' sagas and snippets of information from elsewhere. This is not the kind of history of events, however, that we will see below for the thirteenth century because there are not the obvious personalities, beyond those mentioned for each of the case study regions, who are really worthy of note other than those mentioned in the discussion of marriages set out below.

In Iceland's south, two kin groups seem to have held regional power in parts of the Southern Quarter. As early as 1100, if not before, the Haukdælir seem to have been the only kin group to hold any political power in Árnesþing (Map 1). The fact of their establishment of the bishopric of Skálholt and their subsequent role as self-appointed bishops would seem to suggest this.[3] The Oddaverjar, named after their farm Oddi, have two iconic figures within their ranks, Sæmundr *fróði* (1056–1113) and Jón Loptsson (d.1197). Many scholars have suggested that Sæmundr had complete control of Rangárþing and the power of the Oddaverjar remained great, while a 'minimalist' position would see Jón Loptsson as only getting complete control of the region in c.1190.[4] Either one or two families seem to have shared control of the whole of the Eastern Quarter.[5] In the south and the east, then, there are signs of the concentration of power at some point in the twelfth century. In the west and the north it was different. For the West Fjords we know very little in the twelfth century but there is a visible concentration of power only after 1200. In Dalir and Eyjafjörður, as we

---

3   See generally Jón Viðar Sigurðsson 54–60; Jón Viðar Sigurðsson 1999: 64; Orri Vésteinsson 2000: 20–24; Gunnar Karlsson 2004.
4   Helgi Þorláksson 1989: 14–18 has argued for the latter; Jón Viðar Sigurðsson 1999: 64–65; Gunnar Karlsson 2004: 281–82.
5   Gunnar Karlsson 2004: 279–81.

shall see, institutional and social power was also divided between different leaders in the twelfth century.

The history of the twelfth century can also be seen through the lens of the church (Map 1). While the first see at Skálholt had been established in 1056, it had taken until 1106 for the north to get its own see, at Hólar in Hjaltadalur (at the northern end of Skagafjörður), which served the Northern Quarter. The north led the way in establishing monasteries, however, the first appearing at Þingeyrar in Húnavatnssýsla, in 1133.[6] Þverá in Eyjafjörður, already an important political centre was set up in 1155 by Bishop Björn Gilsson (often known as Munkaþverá, Figure 13).[7] In the west Þorleifr *beiskaldi* founded a house at Hítardalr in the 1160s, which may not have survived long, while a house which had originally been on the island of Flatey in Breiðafjörður in 1172 moved to the major political focus of Helgafell in 1184/5. As an institution, the church was undoubtedly only gradually finding its own identity. Whereas *goðar* often seem to have had themselves ordained as priests earlier in the twelfth century, by its end it was becoming more common for priests to come from the wider population and to be seen as more akin to servants.[8]

At the end of the twelfth century the scale of politics for the leading figures in Dalir and in Eyjafjörður started to change. Between 1185 and 1202 the Sturlusynir, sons of Sturla Þórðarson from Hvammr in Dalir, built up a geopolitical platform which would allow them, and Snorri Sturluson in particular, to play leading roles in Icelandic politics. The three Sturlusynir each married into a wealthy family. Þórðr took over his father-in-law's farm at Staðarstaðr on Snæfellsnes. Sighvatr is said to have moved from farm to farm around Dalir before marrying into the north-based Ásbirningar and living at Sauðafell in Miðdalir (Figure 5).[9] In 1215 he moved out of Dalir, to Grund in Eyjafjörður (Figure 12). Snorri's marriage brought with it control of Borg in Borgarfjörður before he moved to Reykholt. Each of Hvamm-Sturla's sons was a *goði* with Sighvatr and Snorri, by virtue of their connections, taking over several *goðorð*.

At roughly the same as the Sturlusynir were apparently achieving wider influence through their marriages, Guðmundr *dýri* (the worthy) Þorvaldsson and

---

6   Orri Vésteinsson 2000: 133–4; Gunnar Karlsson 2008.
7   IA 115, 252, 322. The first abbot of Þverá, Nikulás Bergsson (d.1159) does not feature in *Sturlunga saga*. Such institutions were small and family-run; Björn's brother was abbot at Þverá (1162–81). It is possible that both Björns were descended ultimately from Eyjólfr Valgerðarson through his son Einarr (see below esp. pp. 274, 279–83, 288–90). Orri Vésteinsson 2000: 135, 149–50.
8   Orri Vésteinsson 2000: 134–35, 136, 179–94; Sverrir Jakobsson 2009.
9   SS I: 243.

Kolbeinn Tumason were building up their power in the north, based at Bakki in Öxnadalur (Figure 10, Map 9) and Víðimýrr in Skagafjörður respectively. By 1188 Guðmundr *dýri* held multiple *goðorð* which previously had belonged to separate individuals in the north.[10] Guðmundr had won his conflicts with other local leaders for dominance in Eyjafjörður. Kolbeinn Tumason held *goðorð* (of unspecified number) which covered most of the western half of the Northern Quarter.[11] By co-operating, these two leaders were remembered as extinguishing the last threat to their complete domination of the north in 1197 by burning to death Önundr Þorkelsson in his home in Hörgárdalur in the so-called *Önundarbrenna*.[12]

A settlement was arranged to atone for Önundr's killing through the Oddaverjar *höfðingi* Jón Loptsson, based in the south. Jón had brought about a settlement between Sturla Þórðarson and Páll Sölvason in 1118 and was obviously remembered as being the major power broker in Iceland right up to his death in the autumn of this same year, 1197.[13] His power seems to be regarded by all the texts as a major reason for the absence of much elite conflict in this period. This may well have been wishful thinking on the part of thirteenth-century writers, or else the product of memories willing to contrast the strife of the mid-thirteenth century with an era about which they knew comparatively little. Yet the idea that Jón Loptsson was somehow an altruistic mediator does not ring true; the whole reason for his involvement in the accounts we have was most likely that he had a very large number of supporters to ensure others' compliance.

2   From c.1200 to c.1265

The remainder of the period covered by this book can be subdivided roughly according to the presence of particular leaders in Iceland: c.1200-c.1220, c.1220-c.1242, c.1242-c.1250 and c.1250-c.1265.

The death of Jón Loptsson in 1197 probably allowed some kind of 'pressure release' whereby *goðar* with grievances took advantage of the absence of a

---

10 See below pp. 63–64.
11 SS I: 243.
12 This, like the *Flugumýrarbrenna* the burning-in of Gizurr Þorvaldsson in 1255, is one of a clutch of iconic events that get referred to as a means of dating other events. It is a key event in the annalistic literature and clearly remembered in association with Jón Loptsson's death in the same year (SS I: 234; IA 22, 62, 121, 181, 254, 324, 477).
13 SS I: 51, 104, 192–94.

pre-eminent leader. Guðmundr *dýri*'s retirement to the monastery at Þingeyrar may have had the same effect on a smaller scale in Eyjafjörður. Certainly one theme which is highlighted in the first decades of the thirteenth century is the conflict between the bishop of Hólar, Bishop Guðmundr Arason (d.1237) and *höfðingjar* based mostly in northern Iceland. Bishop Guðmundr, of quite good family himself, seems to have wanted what Kolbeinn Tumason would not allow him: full control of churches and church property, i.e. some of the wealthiest farms in the diocese. At Víðines in Skagafjörður in 1208 Kolbeinn Tumason was killed in a battle against the bishop's forces. Sighvatr and Snorri Sturluson were part of a group of several *höfðingjar* who banded together a few years later to try to prevent the bishop from rising above what they saw as his station. On this occasion the bishop was forced to leave Hólar, something which drew a written response from the Archbishop of Niðarós to the *höfðingjar* concerned. Then followed a cooling-off period in which first some of the secular leaders and then the bishop went to Norway. For a few years relations between the bishop and the *höfðingjar* were less openly hostile; the bishop seems to have accepted the continued existence of private churches and to have travelled about the north expecting *bændr* to provision his large group of supporters.[14]

Other than events surrounding Bishop Guðmundr, the period from c.1200 to c.1220 is fairly thinly covered. Of greatest significance, however, was the growing confidence of Snorri Sturluson. Snorri had been elected lawspeaker in 1215 and been to Norway to become a supporter (*lendr maðr*) of King Hákon Hákonarson. In 1224 he arranged dynastic marriages for some of his daughters which guaranteed his involvement in politics in all of the major regions in the western half of Iceland. That same year Snorri acquired significantly more property and territory when he married the widow Hallveig Ormsdóttir, after the killing of her Haukdælur husband by the Oddaverjar, his foster-brothers.[15] Snorri seems to have been the first recorded western leader to have such significant support from the south. When Snorri married his daughter to the young Ásbirningr leader Kolbeinn *ungi* Arnórsson in 1232 part of the deal was

---

14 It was not until 1253 that a more firm commitment was made at the Alþing for church property to be fully given over to ecclesiastical control according to *Árna saga biskups* (*Biskupa sögur* I 720, DI II: 1). *Árna saga* undoubtedly overstates the case for its eponymous hero's success in gaining control of churches. It took until 1297 for an agreement to be made whereby the Icelandic aristocracy gave up control of church-farms where the church already owned more than 50 percent of the estate. The less well-off farms with churches on them were never taken from private hands (DI II: 324–25; Orri Vésteinsson 2000: 131–32).

15 SS I: 278–82, 304.

that Snorri was to have half of the wealth and *goðorð* (pl.) which Kolbeinn owned in the north, i.e. the western part of Húnavatnsþing.¹⁶ By this time, if not earlier, it is clear that Snorri Sturluson had acquired something like the influence which his foster-father Jón Loptsson had had, at least in those three Quarters for which there is reasonable evidence. The east seems less important and is less well-documented. *Íslendinga saga* claims Snorri was the wealthiest person in Iceland.¹⁷

As early as 1221 we see renewed conflict in the north and west. Sighvatr Sturluson was now based in Eyjafjörður and, working with his brother-in-law Arnórr Tumason, was called upon to use military means to move Bishop Guðmundr Arason out of Þingeyjarsýsla. This they did successfully but a later battle resulted in the death of Sighvatr's son, Tumi. The bishop was forced to go to Norway in 1222.¹⁸ The move of Sighvatr's son Sturla from the north to Sauðafell in Dalir (1221) brought with it renewed conflict in Dalir because Sturla's uncles, Snorri and Þórðr Sturluson, seem to have feared that Sturla Sighvatsson would attempt to build up some kind of influence in collaboration with his father.¹⁹ The root of the problem was probably the *Snorrungagoðorð* which Þórðr Sturluson and his son Jón *murti* managed to take over. Sturla Sighvatsson responded aggressively in 1227, raiding Þórðr's home, Hvammr, and in 1228 having Snorri's ally Þorvaldr *Vatnsfirðingr* killed.²⁰ Þorvaldr *Vatnsfirðingr's* sons responded by raiding Sauðafell when Sturla was away. This only led to Sturla having them in turn killed, despite Snorri's attempts to bring peace.²¹

In the north the growing power of Kolbeinn *ungi* prompted Snorri Sturluson to make an agreement with him in 1232 that allowed Snorri to retain some control there. At about the same time Sturla Sighvatsson left Iceland. He and his father had received a critical letter from the archbishop of Niðarós about their hostility towards Bishop Guðmundr Arason; Sturla travelled to Norway to meet King Hákon and then went on to Rome.²² Sturla had had influence in the West Fjords and left a deputy in charge of his *þingmenn* there.²³ The lessened threat from the west gave Snorri and his son Órækja the opportunity to make progress. Órækja took over the *goðorð* of the Vatnsfirðingar and

---

16 Gunnar Karlsson 2004: 296–97.
17 SS I: 304.
18 SS I: 293.
19 SS I: 284 for Sturla's move.
20 SS I: 315–17, 322.
21 The *Sauðafellsför* is lamented as being especially cruel and thus as a spur to Sturla Sighvatsson's revenge (SS I: 347–58).
22 His father Sighvatr did not feel the need to respond to the criticism (SS I: 360, 361).
23 SS I: 363.

used his newly-acquired influence in the north-west to raid Dalir. Here, in encroaching on the territory of his Dalir-based kinsmen, Órækja is sometimes portrayed as his father's lieutenant, sometimes his own man.

When Sturla Sighvatsson did return to Iceland in 1235 the tensions between the four major political factions in the north-west of Iceland resurfaced, between: Snorri Sturluson and Órækja; Sighvatr Sturluson and Sturla; Þórðr Sturluson and his sons; and Kolbeinn *ungi*. Three of these factions were Sturlungar, who despite their kinship, appear to have often competed with one another for power. Kolbeinn *ungi* and Sighvatr had made a pact against Snorri and Órækja and upon Sturla's return gathered forces and went to Borgarfjörður, ostensibly with the intention of forcing Snorri to put an end to Órækja's designs on Sturla's western territories. In the event Snorri fled rather than face his opponents' sizeable army leaving Órækja to be captured and supposedly gelded, either literally or metaphorically, depending on how we read *Íslendinga saga*.[24]

Over the next two years the leading *höfðingjar* realigned themselves again. Órækja and Snorri went to Norway and in Snorri's absence Sturla Sighvatsson and his father were in the ascendant. Sturla intervened in the politics of the south, hardening the opposition to him: when Sturla forced Gizurr Þorvaldsson of the Haukdælir to swear an oath of allegiance to him Kolbeinn *ungi* readily became Gizurr's ally. The two sides' collected forces eventually fought at Örlygsstaðir in Skagafjörður in August 1238. Sighvatr and Sturla were both killed at this battle, a great set-piece event in *Íslendinga saga*.[25]

Kolbeinn *ungi* took over the *goðorð* which Sighvatr had controlled in the north while in 1239 Snorri and the recovered Órækja returned to Iceland. Snorri may have been returning to Iceland with the authority of the Norwegian king to assert the rights of the crown over Iceland but, either way, the returning father and son took an increased interest in the west.[26] Soon after his return Snorri outlawed one of the local leaders from the West Fjords who had taken part in the raid on Borgarfjörður in 1237. Snorri was also given control of Sauðafell by Solveig, Sturla Sighvatsson's widow, and placed his nephew Sturla Þórðarson in charge of it.[27] Órækja, meanwhile, bought the island of Flatey

---

24   SS I: 395. Gåde 1995 demonstrates that Sturla Þórðarson has recast the story of Órækja's alleged maiming in the form of a miracle story; Órækja is said to have had a testicle removed and then been able to ride a horse almost immediately afterwards.
25   See generally Úlfar Bragason 2012: 161–74.
26   SS I: 444.
27   *Íslendinga saga* says that the deal also included the islands Bjarneyjar and Skáleyjar and *reki* at Drangar on Strandir as well as 14 dependents: "Solveig fær í hendr Snorra búit at Sauðafelli, en hann fekk Sturlu Þórðarsyni, frænda sínum. Tók hann við búinu ok

(from Þórðr *tiggi* Þórðarson) but contested the rights of Sturla Þórðarson, thereby challenging the kinsman whom his father supported.

Snorri and Órækja, like Sighvatr and Sturla before them, enjoyed only a brief dominance before they were successfully challenged by other *höfðingjar*. A dispute over the legacy of Hallveig Ormsdóttir, Snorri's wife who died in 1241, led to Snorri's stepsons having him killed. Gizurr Þorvaldsson famously joined with Hallveig's sons to do so. Órækja, now accompanied by Sturla Þórðarson, went to Reykholt and gained a swift revenge, killing one of Hallveig's sons. By this stage Gizurr and Kolbeinn *ungi* had already made an unsuccessful raid on the mid-west in the hope of killing their Sturlungar adversaries. With the violence and speed of the power struggle escalating, attempts were made to reach another settlement. The first stage of negotiations happened at the *Hvítár-brúarfundr*, literally, meeting at the bridge over the river Hvítá, in Borgarfjörður. We are told that Gizurr tricked Órækja into leaving his own forces and crossing the Hvítá, thus having no option but to grant Gizurr his demands. A settlement was arranged by Kolbeinn *ungi* that same year by which Órækja was forced to leave Iceland and had to give Kolbeinn those *goðorð* which Snorri had owned.[28] Kolbeinn was able to get oaths of loyalty from many men from the west and West Fjords, some more willingly than others. They included Sturla Þórðarson who managed to avoid being exiled.[29]

Órækja Snorrason never returned to Iceland, dying in Norway in 1245, but his cousin Þórðr *kakali* Sighvatsson came back in 1242 and it was he who effectively maintained Sturlungar political interests. Gizurr Þorvaldsson also went to the Norwegian court, no doubt to win the support of the king, while Gizurr's cousin Hjalti, the son of Bishop Magnús of Skálholt, acted as his locum in Iceland.[30] The pattern of events repeated itself. In Gizurr's absence Þórðr *kakali* set about gathering support across Iceland from a mixture of his kinsmen, their supporters, and other leaders opposed to Kolbeinn *ungi* and Gizurr. Þórðr gained a reasonable number of supporters, sufficient to feel able to challenge Kolbeinn militarily. The two sides fought the *Flóabardagi*, a sea battle off Iceland's northern coast from which Þórðr's side seems to have come off worse.[31]

When Gizurr returned to Iceland there were renewed attempts to bring about peace. He had made peace with Jón, the son of Sturla Sighvatsson who

---

Bjarneyjum ok Skáleyjum ok Drangareka ok fjórtán ómögum." (SS I: 447). Helgi Þorláksson 2001: 114.
28 SS I: 470–71.
29 SS I: 471–72, SS II: 1–3.
30 SS II: 1.
31 SS II: 56–67. See below p. 115.

was still based in Dalir.[32] These negotiations, which had got as far as Kolbeinn and Þórðr agreeing to seek the Norwegian king's mediation, came to a halt when Kolbeinn died. Kolbeinn is alleged to have granted his *goðorð* (pl.) to a kinsman, Brandr Kolbeinsson, and to Gizurr. Gizurr apparently declined to take up Kolbeinn's offer, however, perhaps not wishing to incite Þórðr *kakali*. As it emerged, Þórðr felt he had a claim to the authority which his father had held in Eyjafjörður. After Brandr Kolbeinsson had taken all of Kolbeinn *ungi*'s territory, Þórðr was able to gain support in Eyjafjörður and took a force into Skagafjörður to attack Brandr Kolbeinsson. In another set-piece battle Brandr was killed.[33]

Gizurr reacted swiftly to Þórðr *kakali*'s success in the north. He took an army of four hundred men into Skagafjörður and was able to persuade Þórðr to agree to let the king arbitrate their dispute. When Þórðr finally got to Norway it was decided – on what basis we are not told – that he should return to Iceland and Gizurr should remain as a royal retainer in Norway. Thus in 1248 Þórðr had control of Snorri Sturluson's former *goðorð* and estates[34] as well as the whole of the Northern Quarter and maintained supremacy in the Western Quarter. Þórðr seems to have been able to levy a tribute on the 'Southerners' (*Sunnlendingar*) in Gizurr's absence.[35]

Þórðr's rapid rise to an unprecedented dominance in Iceland led to the king's questioning of his loyalty and a request for him to return to Norway.[36] In this period the dependency of the Icelandic elite on the support of the Norwegian king becomes even more visible. The Sæmundarsynir, from Oddi in the south, supposedly gave up their *goðorð* (pl.) in return for a *ríki* granted by the king that probably amounted to the same package of rights.[37] Despite their apparent importance, it is unclear who the Sæmundarsynir were, making the precise impact of their action unclear.

It would seem that the Norwegian king continued to try to establish his right to control territory in Iceland. When Gizurr Þorvaldsson and Þorgils *skarði* Böðvarsson[38] returned to Iceland, however, they were beholden to the king

---

32 SS II: 67.
33 SS II: 73–80. See below p. 80.
34 We are told that by this stage King Hákon claimed these as royal property (SS II: 72; Jón Viðar Sigurðsson 1999: 73–74).
35 SS II: 86; SS I: 474.
36 Jón Viðar Sigurðsson 1999: 73–74; Jón Jóhannesson 1956–8: 232.
37 SS I: 474; Jón Viðar Sigurðsson 1989: 55.
38 Bishop Heinrekr of Hólar and a certain Finnbjörn Helgason also returned to Iceland at the same as Þorgils and Gizurr. Finnbjörn was from a fairly minor family and was granted the estate of Grenjaðarstaðir in north eastern Iceland by the king.

and expected to act on his behalf in a way which Þórðr *kakali* Sighvatsson had not been. Þorgils *skarði* clearly also came to Iceland with a large military retinue, no doubt supplied by the king. Gizurr and Þorgils were expressly assigned territories rather than automatically returning to control the *goðorð* they had inherited. Thus Þorgils *skarði* controlled Borgarfjörður and part of the Northern Quarter (much as his kinsmen had before him), and Gizurr was given either much of the Northern or Southern Quarter depending on which of *Íslendinga saga* or *Hákonar saga* one believes.[39] Þórðr *kakali*, meanwhile, never returned to Iceland.

In Dalir Sturla Þórðarson remained in control of Staðarhóll in Saurbær (Figure 7) and a former ally of Þórðr *kakali*, Hrafn Oddsson, had by now lived at Sauðafell for several years. Sturla and Hrafn appear to have maintained a firm hold on Dalir while the more ambitious *höfðingjar* had been taking greater political risks. This is far from saying that Sturla and Hrafn were not involved in the machinations of the 1240s and 1250s: crucially, they tried to drive Gizurr out of Skagafjörður in 1253.

Other leaders also emerged after Þorgils *skarði* had returned. Eyjólfr Þorsteinsson, a son-in-law of Sturla Þórðarson, and Hrani Koðránsson – of unknown family background – acted on Þorgils' behalf in the north. It was they who maintained hostility to Gizurr Þorvaldsson after Sturla Þórðarson had come to terms with him. Sturla and Gizurr sealed their new friendship by the marriage of Sturla's daughter to Gizurr's son. Eyjólfr Þorsteinsson and Hrani Koðránsson, acting in their own interests and accompanied by other northern leaders, trapped Gizurr and his family in their home (Flugumýrr in Skagafjörður) after the wedding and burnt down the farm. Gizurr was fortunate to survive when all the rest of his immediate family perished, notoriously hiding in a barrel of whey to shield himself from the heat.[40] Gizurr had immediate revenge on some of the *brennumenn* with local leaders banished from the north: Hrani to Flatey in the west, Eyjólfr Þorsteinsson to live with Finnbjörn Helgason at Grenjaðarstaðir (who had been appointed by King Hákon to run part of northeast Iceland, from Reykjadalur east to the river Jökulsá).[41]

Having failed to bring Iceland peacefully under the king's jurisdiction, Gizurr was summoned to Norway in 1254. This time he made Oddr Þórarinsson (of the Svínfellingar) his deputy in Skagafjörður; Oddr, like Gizurr, is said to have been a popular leader with the locals. Oddr was able to get revenge for the burning-in at Flugumýrr by having Hrani Koðránsson killed.

---

39   Jón Jóhannesson 1956–8: 246–47.
40   SS I: 484–94.
41   SS I: 476.

In 1255 the enmity among the highest rank of Icelandic leaders continued unabated with the result that three of them were killed: Oddr Þórarinsson, Eyjólfr Þorsteinsson and Finnbjörn Helgason. Hrafn Oddsson and Eyjólfr Þorsteinsson killed Oddr in January of that year, swiftly creating enemies in the process. That opposition came from not only Oddr's brother Þorvarðr but also Þorgils *skarði*, Sturla Þórðarson and Finnbjörn. These four took part in the inevitable battle which followed, at Þverá in litla in Eyjafjörður. It was here that Eyjólfr and Finnbjörn, on opposing sides, lost their lives.

Tension seems to have momentarily subsided because the *bændr* of Eyjafjörður and Skagafjörður were no longer able or willing to choose successors to their dead leaders. Þorvarðr Þórarinsson and Þorgils *skarði*, however, each proceeded to try to get accepted as the leader of regions which had no reason to be loyal to them: Þorvarðr sought the support of the Eyfirðingar while Þorgils *skarði* tried to win over the Skagfirðingar. The former are famously said to have called Þorvarðr Þórarinsson arrogant to his face and dared to say they preferred to have no leader at all.[42] Both regions paid tribute direct to the Norwegian crown in 1256 rather than a local leader.[43]

That same year saw the death in Norway of Þórðr *kakali* Sighvatsson. Gizurr Þorvaldsson was presumably being detained by the king who, *Þorgils saga skarða* says, now chose Þorgils *skarði* as his representative in Eyjafjörður. Apparently Þorgils had also been able to persuade the *bændr* of Skagafjörður to accept him as their leader. This final rise in Þorgils' fortunes had the not unsurprising effect of galvanising opposition to him. Þorvarðr Þórarinsson laid claim to Eyjafjörður as his inheritance (as a kinsman of Þórðr *kakali*) and pursued his claim to the full: Þorvarðr had Þorgils *skarði* killed in Eyjafjörður in early 1258.

Following Þorgils *skarði*'s death Gizurr Þorvaldsson was allowed to return to Iceland once again. At this point in the texts the emphasis on Gizurr's role as king's agent is far greater than on the many previous occasions where a king had tried to get Icelandic leaders to work on his behalf. Gizurr was given the title *jarl* and he persuaded Sturla Þórðarson, and Sighvatr Böðvarsson (Þorgils *skarði*'s brother and Sturla's cousin) to become his men.[44] For the first time a vocabulary more fully akin to that of western European feudalism appears.[45]

---

42   SS II: 192.
43   Jón Jóhannesson 1956–8: 319.
44   SS I: 527.
45   In particular the term *handgenginn maðr* seems to be used to describe someone who had sworn fealty to the Norwegian king. *Íslendinga saga* points out that in 1235 Kolbeinn *ungi* did not become a *handgenginn maðr* (SS I: 386); for the use of the term for the 1240s see SS I: 525, 527; II: 111, 113, 115, 116, 274. Terms with similar connotations are also used for Icelanders but earlier too, and not in relation to their Icelandic landed possessions: *lendr*

At the same time Gizurr claimed jurisdiction on the king's behalf over more of Iceland than anyone had done before him: all of both the Southern and Northern Quarters and Borgarfjörður. This was probably recognition that these were the areas over which Gizurr could take direct control. By now there were apparently only weak challengers to Gizurr. While Sturla Þórðarson had had designs on Borgarfjörður he now effectively gave in to Gizurr by swearing allegiance to him. Þorvarðr Þórarinsson might also have maintained a claim on Eyjafjörður but is unlikely to have been able to gather a sufficiently threatening army from the sparsely-populated east. One short-lived challenge to Gizurr was made in 1259: Þórðr Andréassson of the Oddaverjar sought co-conspirators from Skagafjörður but when Gizurr discovered their plans and raided Rangárvellir Þórðr quickly conceded defeat. Þórðr swore allegiance to Gizurr but eventually rose against him a second time in 1264. This time Gizurr had Þórðr killed for his treachery.[46]

For the period 1260–1264 the surviving sources are relatively scarce. A rather complex pattern of conflicting loyalties and authorities probably remained, it would seem, but two notable things emerge. First, Hrafn Oddsson had managed to ingratiate himself with the king in order to be granted control of Borgarfjörður. This was in preference to either his former ally Sturla Þórðarson or Gizurr himself. In all probability this decision was designed by the king to curb Gizurr's power. The king probably wanted Gizurr to be sufficiently powerful to guarantee the payment of a large tribute from Iceland but not so powerful that he could do without the king's support. With regard to Dalir, this move clearly made Sauðafell a northern outpost of a polity centred on Borgarfjörður and gave Hrafn greater power than Sturla.

The second significant development was the formal agreement by Icelandic leaders to pay tribute to the Norwegian king. Every group of regional leaders was faced with the difficult task of maintaining some kind of independence of both Gizurr and the king without allowing themselves to be deemed actively hostile to either. Again the public swearing of oaths would seem to be the key event which determined leaders' stance. The texts give the impression that events were more critical now because of the presence in Iceland of the king's retainer, Hallvarðr *gullskór*, but Gizurr's power must have been the most significant factor behind the deal made in 1262 by which Iceland's leaders agreed

---

maðr (literally 'landed man,' SS I: 120, 278, 527), *hirðmaðr* (retainer) is used 24 times in *Sturlunga saga* (SS II: 479 for full list of references). In some of these examples men become the *lendr maðr* or *hirðmaðr* of Gizurr Þorvaldsson rather than the king (Gunnar Karlsson 1975b: 51).

46 SS I: 529–34; SS II: 235.

to pay the king a tribute. The presence of Norwegian leaders in Iceland may be underplayed in the contemporary saga by writers emphasising the independence of their forebears.

Much Icelandic historiography has not tried to get beyond the world-view of the elite writers of these narratives who were obviously disappointed to have to give up some of their own revenue to the king. The agreement of 1262[47] was clearly of significance to them and the narratives sometimes seem to have been written with the attitude that everything that went before led to this event. It seems reasonable, however, to suppose that less powerful *höfðingjar* might have welcomed the king's ability to contain the power of figures like Snorri Sturluson and Gizurr Þorvaldsson. For *bændr* there may have been a reduction in violence: if leaders were less able to call upon resources from Norway, in the form of either weapons or armed men, they were less likely to instigate large scale armed conflict.

3 *Goðorð* c.1100-c.1265

We need to turn now to examine the potential secular institutional underpinnings of power in our two regions. Tracing *goðorð* from *Landnámabók*, through *Íslendingasögur* and into the contemporary sagas poses more of a problem than is usually admitted. Little attempt has been made to understand why or under what circumstances given texts identify *goðorð* by different prefixes often expressing ownership by a kin group or individual. If, for instance, we are too keen to assume that two *goðorð* with different names are in fact the same *goðorð* then there is a risk that we are imposing a continuity in institutions which never existed and are failing to understand both the nature of *goðorð* and the narratives themselves. Thus the names given to *goðorð* below are used for the sake of convenience, and, as will be shown, in some cases evidence of the continued existence of a *goðorð* is circumstantial. The purpose in trying to track the existence of *goðorð* over time is to assess the importance of this institution.

For Dalir four possible *goðorð* are of importance, the first three being part of Þórsnesþing[48] (*Snorrungagoðorð*,[49] *Þórsnesingagoðorð*,[50] *Rauðmelingagoðorð /'Hítdælagoðorð*'[51]) and the last, *Reyknesingagoðorð*, which formed a part of

---

47 DI I: 619–25.
48 See above p. 11.
49 SS I: 64, 235, 303, 304, 315, 319, 447.
50 SS I: 235.
51 SS I: 243, 359.

Þorskfjarðarþing to the north.[52] For the Eyjafjörður region the *goðorð* associated with two local assemblies are of potential significance: Vaðlaþing (*'Esphælingagoðorð,' 'Þveræingagoðorð'* and *Fljótamannagoðorð*/*'Möðruvellingagoðorð'*) and Eyjarþing (*Ljósvetningagoðorð, 'Reykdælagoðorð'* and *'Öxfirðingagoðorð'*).[53] This list is maximal and follows the nomenclature proposed by Lúðvík Ingvarsson and critiqued by Gunnar Karlsson.

4 *Goðorð* in Dalir

Despite the doubts expressed above, there is reasonable evidence for the continued existence of *Snorrungagoðorð* in *Sturlunga saga*, even if not of its earlier existence. This is the *goðorð* which Sturla Þórðarson inherited and passed on to his sons and so its earlier history is worth an especially close look. On the one hand the Sturlungar claim to have inherited it through the male line going back to Snorri *goði*, the significant figure who features prominently in *Íslendingasögur* (Chapter 5), making it look like retrospective justification for their continued authority. On the other hand, it is impossible to put forward an alternative history for the *goðorð* given the sparse but fairly coherent account that can be created for its owners.

Sturlu saga credits Þórðr Gilsson with sole control of the *Snorrungagoðorð* and it is passed down through the male Sturlungar in the thirteenth century. Þórðr Gilsson is said to have inherited it directly from one Mána-Ljótr, who is elsewhere identified as the son of Ljótr, a son of Snorri *goði*.[54] *Sturlu saga* is our only source for the connection between Þórðr and Mána-Ljótr while it is only in the short genealogical text known as the *Ævi Snorra goða* that we learn of the ancestry of Mána-Ljótr. In the *Ævi* it is said that Mána-Ljótr was the most illustrious of Snorri's grandsons, that he lived at Sauðafell and that his (surprisingly unpraised) father was Máni.[55] The result is that a continuous familial line can be traced from Snorri *goði* to Hvamm-Sturla but no one seems to have felt the need to set this out for us in one place. The association of Mána-Ljótr with Sauðafell also seems entirely plausible on a general level because Sauðafell was a major farm in Dalir although there is no other evidence for a connection between the Sturlungar, or Snorri *goði*, with Sauðafell before Sighvatr Sturluson lived there in about 1200.[56] It is hard not to draw the

---

52 SS I: 13, 23.
53 Of these only *Fljótamannagoðorð* is identified by name in *Sturlunga saga* (SS I: 168).
54 'Þórðr Gilsson tók við goðorði Snorrunga eftir Mána-Ljót.' (SS I: 64).
55 ÍF IV: 182.
56 See above p. 46. It is also curious that while the *Ævi* places Mána-Ljótr at Sauðafell the main part of *Eyrbyggja saga* does not mention Sauðafell at all. Actually the *Ævi* or the

conclusion that this connection was one manufactured or cultivated by the Sturlungar.

To return to the later twelfth century, it appears that Hvamm-Sturla's eldest son, Þórðr, briefly took over the *goðorð* but he then acquired half of another one, *Þórsnesingagoðorð*,[57] and *Snorrungagoðorð* passed into the sole possession of Sighvatr Sturluson for over 30 years. Sighvatr gave it to his son Sturla in 1224. This arrangement, whereby the father and son both controlled *goðorð* simultaneously (Sighvatr having taken over other *goðorð* in the north) aroused the anger of Þórðr and Snorri Sturluson. Þórðr Sturluson apparently convened the Þórsnessþing in 1227, which Sturla Sighvatsson did not attend, and at which Jón Snorrason was granted two-thirds of the *goðorð* and Þórðr the remaining third.[58] This was undoubtedly designed to curb Sturla Sighvatsson's influence. Conflict between Sturla Sighvatsson and his uncles continued but nothing more is said by the contemporary sagas about the *Snorrungagoðorð* for some time. If Sturla Sighvatsson was indeed deprived of a share in the *Snorrungagoðorð* then it did not hold him back politically and we are entitled to ask what all the fuss had been about in 1226–27; his influence was bolstered by his possession of the *Dýrfirðingagoðorð* in the West Fjords.[59]

In 1240, following his brothers' deaths and his rise to power in the south, Snorri Sturluson seems to have had effective sole control of the *Snorrungagoðorð*. *Íslendinga saga* says that in that year Snorri gave Sturla Þórðarson one-third of the *goðorð* but that before this Böðvarr Þórðarson, Sturla's brother, had also given Sturla a third of it.[60] Böðvarr had presumably inherited this third of the *goðorð* when his father had died in 1237. This would seem to confirm that the *goðorð* was seen as only being divisible into thirds in 1240, just as it had been in the 1220s, perhaps because Þórðr, Sighvatr and Snorri had inherited it jointly. Thus what Sturla Sighvatsson had been deprived of in 1227 was probably only one-third of the *goðorð* and Jón Snorrason simply gained Sturla's entitlement to add to his inherited portion.[61]

After this it would seem that Sturla Þórðarson retained his two-thirds share until he swore allegiance to the Norwegian king. The other third is

---

concluding part of the saga proper almost exclusively names farms *not* mentioned in the rest of the saga, e.g. Ballára on Skarðsströnd, Laugarbrekka on the southern coast of Snæfellsnes, and Lambastaðir in Mýrar.

57 SS I: 235.
58 SS I: 315.
59 Lúðvík Ingvarsson 1987: III 159.
60 SS I: 447.
61 Lúðvík Ingvarsson 1987: III 158.

usually assumed to have belonged to Jón, the son of Sturla Sighvatsson, because he was likely to have inherited his father's or grandfather's claim to it. In 1248 Jón shared control of Þórðr *kakali* Sighvatsson's territories with Sturla Þórðarson when he left Iceland, seemingly confirming Jón's political prominence.[62]

The account of the *Snorrungagoðorð* highlights the fragile connection between the accounts of it in *Íslendingasögur* and the *Sturlunga* compilation. The same is true for *Þórsnesingagoðorð* for which even the confident account of its existence by Gunnar Karlsson has a lacuna for the period c.1110 to 1170.[63] With rather unhelpful brevity, Chapter 6 of *Íslendinga saga* says, in a sentence, that Þórðr Sturluson acquired half of the *Þórsnesingagoðorð* from Þorgils *prestr* (priest) Snorrason of Skarð (d.1201) but that Ari *inn sterki* Þorgilsson had owned the other half of it. Þórðr seems to have acquired the whole *goðorð*, getting Þorgils' half at some unspecified time, and Ari's half when Ari went abroad with Þórðr's mother in the late 1180s, never to return.[64] It is not clear how Þorgils and Ari had come to share control of the *goðorð* but the division might have reflected their different locations and enabled them to divide *þingmenn* on geographical lines: Þorgils lived at Skarð on Skarðsströnd while Ari lived at Staðarstaðr on the southern coast of Snæfellsnes.

If we look back to the earlier twelfth century it makes sense for Þorgils to have inherited some or all of the *goðorð* from his father Snorri whom *Íslendinga saga* identifies as lawspeaker, a precondition for which is likely to have been once being a *goði*.[65] Þorgils' own ordination as a priest, and then that of his sons, also suggests that he was one of those *goðar* who was intentionally getting out of secular politics, either willingly or under duress from the Sturlungar.[66] As for the other half of the *goðorð*, its owner Ari *inn sterki* was also the descendent of someone well-known: he was the grandson of Ari *inn fróði* Þorgilsson, the historian. It could be that he inherited his part of the *goðorð* through Ari *fróði*.[67]

Moving into the thirteenth century, it seems probable that Þórðr Sturluson kept the *Þórsnesingagoðorð* but it is not mentioned explicitly at all. Two of Þórðr's sons, Böðvarr and Þorgils *skarði*, could have possessed it. Perhaps both

---
62   SS II: 86; Lúðvík Ingvarsson 1987: III 163, 172; Jón Viðar Sigurðsson 1999: 74.
63   Gunnar Karlsson 2004: 240–41.
64   SS I: 229–31, 235.
65   SS I: 235.
66   Haukr Þorgilsson married a priest's daughter and moved to Hagi on Barðaströnd, SS I: 223. His uncle Narfi was also apparently without a *goðorð* (Orri Vésteinsson 2000: 192, note 18).
67   Gunnar Karlsson 2004: 240.

these sons held the *goðorð* and, ultimately, it came into the possession of Böðvarr's son Sighvatr who, like his father and grandfather, lived at Staðarstaðr on Snæfellsnes. Sighvatr Böðvarsson swore the oath to the Norwegian king in 1262 which suggests he was influential and, perhaps, a *goði*.[68]

For the third *goðorð* in the west, *Reyknesingagoðorð*, the issue of its representation is similar to the first two discussed. It is another case of 'now you see it, now you don't' in the narratives. As will become clear in Chapter 3, Þorgils Oddason passed his *goðorð* onto his son Einarr but after Einarr there is no sign of his patrilineal line wielding any political power for a long time, let alone concrete evidence of their owning *goðorð*. In the first two decades of the twelfth century Þorgils Oddason, the eponymous leader in *Þorgils saga ok Hafliða*, got the *goðorð* from Ingimundr *prestr* Einarsson when Ingimundr's father died.[69] As a priest, and as in the case of Þorgils Snorrason, Ingimundr seemingly did not wish to take a leading role in local or regional politics.[70]

But the name *Reyknesingagoðorð* is only used in *Þorgils saga ok Hafliða*. After this it is not until we hear of a man called Vigfúss Gunnsteinsson, Þorgils' great-great grandson and a major politician in the 1250s, that we can see someone who *might* have made use of that same *goðorð*. What is striking about Vigfúss is that, like Sighvatr Böðvarsson, he was one of the five men from the Western Quarter swearing an oath to the king in 1262.[71] Again it is unclear whether this confirms his being a *goðorðsmaðr* or merely that he was one of the most significant landowners in the region with the right kind of social network.

Between these dates, we can see that some men descended from Þorgils Oddason were still well-off and based at larger farms. Vigfúss' father was wealthy enough to consider buying Hvammr in the 1220s but not actually able to produce the payment. He moved to Brunná then later bought Garpsdalr (which Vigfúss inherited, Map 6).[72] Vigfúss' uncle, Páll *prestr* Hallsson, owned Staðarhóll, lived at Narfeyri and Langidalr (Map 5), and, like Vigfúss, was apparently on good terms with Sturla Þórðarson. Either of these brothers

---

68 SS II: 281–82; Lúðvík Ingvarsson 1987: 111 122.
69 SS I: 13, 23.
70 As in the case of Þórðr Sturluson's receipt of a gift of half a *goðorð* from Þorgils Snorrason, this could be exactly what happened. On the other hand it seems the transference of authority, away from a traditional seat of power or a line of patrilineal descent (in this case from Reykhólar to Staðarhóll and from cousin to cousin), is most likely to have happened under pressure from Þorgils.
71 SS II: 281–82. Vigfúss is only named in the *Króksfjarðarbók* version of *Sturlunga saga*. By stating that Vigfúss and the other named individuals were each accompanied by three *bændr* the text is implying that these men were all *goðar*.
72 SS I: 309. Gunnsteinn was still alive in 1253 (SS II: 160).

could have been a *goðorðsmaðr*; both lived in Saurbær at one point and Páll was heavily involved in local politics. The remaining generations between Vigfúss and Þorgils can be traced but the individuals' actions are not visible. For example, the death of Hallr *prestr* Gunnsteinsson, Vigfúss' grandfather, is commemorated in an annal but he is not recorded in *Sturlunga saga* at all.[73] It would seem that this line probably only managed to regain influence only once it had married into both the Skarðverjar (Vigfúss' mother was from Skarð) and the Sturlungar (when Vigfúss married Sturla Sighvatsson's daughter) having *perhaps* held onto a *goðorð* for generations.

The origins and continued existence of the last relevant western *goðorð* also suffer for the absence of evidence for the earlier period. Often known in secondary literature as *Hítdœlagoðorð* or *Rauðmelingagoðorð*, the *goðorð* of the people from Hítardalr or Rauðamelr, it is more obscure than those named above. The term *Rauðmelingagoðorð* is used just once, in the *Íslendingasaga Eyrbyggja saga*, where, in connection with the tenth century, it is said to have been in the possession of Þorsteinn from Hafsfjarðarey.[74] There is no recorded genealogical connection between this Þorsteinn and Þorleifr *beiskaldi* (d. 1200) at Hítardalr who, in the 1170s, we see owning a *goðorð* in *Sturlu saga*.[75] Þorleifr's biography is difficult to write. He is generally credited with establishing a monastery at Hítardalr although this institution might barely have outlived him. He is remembered in *Páls saga byskups* as an associate of Bishop Páll and as being present among a group of influential *höfðingjar* when the bones of Bishop Þorlákr were excavated in 1198.[76] Seen from the perspective of *Sturlu saga*, Þorleifr *beiskaldi* was indeed a *goði* but one who was relatively weak: he supported Einarr Þorgilsson when Einarr was the dominant politician in the mid-west but after Einarr's death he supported Ari *inn sterki* Þorgilsson when Ari was fined for aiding Einarr's killers.[77]

In spite of Þorleifr's passivity, he kept a *goðorð* to pass it on to his daughter's son, Þorlákr Ketilsson, rather than letting it fall under the control of the Sturlungar.[78] Þorlákr, unlike his grandfather, was on good terms with the

---

73 IA 128.
74 ÍF IV: 156. Haffjarðarey/Hafsfjarðarey is an island off the coast of modern Hnappadalssýsla, where Snæfellsnes meets the Mýrar region.
75 Gunnar Karlsson 2004: 239.
76 Lúðvík Ingvarsson 1987: III 84; ÍF XVI: 97, 308, 332.
77 SS I: 231.
78 IA 22, 62, 121, 181, 324. Þorleifr had two daughters, both of whom married the sons of Þorsteinn *ranglátr* from Grund in Eyjafjörður, which could explain why the *goðorð* skipped a generation. See below pp. 107, 134 & 135 for Þorlákr Ketilsson.

Sturlungar, not least because he fostered Sturla Sighvatsson.[79] This arrangement, and Þorlákr's rather limited presence in *Sturlunga saga*, might well suggest that he was by far the weaker partner in his alliance with Sighvatr Sturluson but it certainly helped guarantee his political survival.[80] While Þorlákr did not live at Hítardalr, both he and his son Ketill were at nearby Kolbeinsstaðir and so retained their association with that district. Ketill was a priest as well as becoming *lögsögumaðr* in 1259.[81] For both Þorlákr and Ketill the evidence for their having controlled a *goðorð* is indirect, but it seems possible they did, given that when they do appear in *Sturlunga saga*, they are involved in politics at a high level, Ketill in particular, even if he did not swear the oath to the king in 1262.[82]

The small number of references to *goðorð* in and around Dalir after 1200 is in part because who owned which *goðorð* was simply not something which needed to be stated for the purposes of the story; *goðorð* usually only impinge on the narrative when they form part of a dispute. Nevertheless it seems possible that the western *goðorð* survived as institutions, at least until 1262, when three of the four owners swore fealty to the king of Norway. Ketill Þorláksson's position is more ambiguous, but to become lawspeaker he presumably had the trust of Gizurr Þorvaldsson and, indirectly therefore, the king. Ketill probably gave up any *goðorð* he controlled in or before 1259. Second, it is important to note that the number of *goðorð* in this region corresponds quite well with the number supposed to have existed in *Grágás*. In other words, the more cautious approach to institutional stability of Gunnar Karlsson seems to be borne out by the evidence.

5 *Goðorð* in Eyjafjörður and the North-East c.1150-c.1265

Goðorð in the earlier twelfth century in this region are less tangible than those around Breiðafjörður. Lúðvík Ingvarsson's trust in the existence of the number of *goðorð* set out in the normative texts looks particularly ill-advised for

---

79   SS I: 267. Þorlákr also fostered Aron Hjörleifsson whom Sturla Sighvatsson later tried to have killed.
80   *Arons saga* calls Þorlákr and Sighvatr 'dear friends,' *kærir vinir* (SS II: 238).
81   Orri Vésteinsson 2000: 170, 192, notes 17 & 18, 223, 229.
82   Gunnar Karlsson 2004: 239. Þorlákr and Ketill were also, for example, at the head of a group of what are called their *hreppsmenn*, men/people of their *hreppr*, when they went to meet Þórðr Sturluson, SS I: 386. *Hreppsmenn* is perhaps not quite a synonym for *þingmenn* but implies leadership of men within at least one *hreppr*.

this region.[83] A useful starting point is Chapter 18 of *Íslendinga saga* which gives us a snapshot of *goðorð* in Eyjafjörður because of its interest in Sighvatr Sturluson. The last paragraph of that brief chapter is worth citing in full:

> North [i.e. north-east] of Öxnadalsheiði Ögmundr *sneis* [Þorvarðsson] and Hallr Kleppjárnsson owned *goðorð*. Þorvaldr, the son of Guðmundr *dýri*, gave Sigurðr Ormsson those *goðorð* which he had owned. Sigurðr gave those *goðorð* to Tumi Sighvatsson and thus Sighvatr came to own them afterwards.[84]

As this description comes just after the brief statement identifying Kolbeinn Tumason as owner of all the *goðorð* to the east of Öxnadalsheiði, it neatly sums up a particular point on the way to greater political centralisation in northern Iceland. The text is unambiguous about Þorvaldr having owned more than one *goðorð*, but it is less clear whether that was the case for Ögmundr *sneis* and Hallr. No names or locations are given for the *goðorð* concerned, except for the signficant physical boundary of Öxnadalsheiði, the heath dividing Skagafjörður from Öxnadalur and the political orbit of Eyjafjörður. What might have actually lain behind this description can best be got at by considering each *goðorð* in turn.

It makes no particular difference in what order we consider the twelfth-century *goðorð* for Eyjafjörður itself so what follows considers them roughly geographically, from west to east.

Guðmundar saga dýra identifies a *goðorð* on the very edge of the Eyjafjörður region in the later twelfth century. If we trust the chronology of that saga then it was in the 1180s that this, the so-called *Fljótamannagoðorð*, was given to Guðmundr *dýri* by a man from Fljót (Jón Ketilsson at Holt) in exchange for Guðmundr's support in a legal case. It has been suggested that this *goðorð* can be equated with what Barði Guðmundsson and Lúðvík Ingvarsson called the *Möðruvellingagoðorð*, and therefore that it had a continuous existence from the tenth century, despite the absence of a good reason why the *goðorð* should be so clearly associated here with Fljót, rather than Möðruvellir.[85] It is controlled by someone from that district whose only recorded supporters are from

---

83   Lúðvík Ingvarsson 1980-86: III 446–52. Gunnar Karlsson's summarising statement on the issue for Eyjafjörður, comparing Barði Guðmundsson's account with Lúðvík's, is agnostic, 2004: 266.
84   'Fyrir norðan Öxnadalsheiði áttu þeir goðorð Ögmundr sneis ok Hallr Kleppjárnsson. Þorvaldr, sonr Guðmundar ins dýra, fekk Sigurði Ormssyni þau goðorð, er hann hafði átt. Sigurðr gaf þau goðorð Tuma, syni Sighvats, ok komst Sighvatr svá at þeim síðan.' SS I: 243.
85   Barði Guðmundsson 1937: 69; Lúðvík Ingvarsson 1980-86: III 447.

Fljót. The text identifies the *goðorð* as being 'populous and well-managed' (*fjölmennt ok vel skipat*). Such a description is still hard to reconcile with this having been the same *goðorð* as one having habitually been run by anyone living as far away as central Eyjafjörður; other *goðorð* in the late twelfth century seem to have been run by *goðar* who lived closer to their *þingmenn*, presumably because some kind of regular physical presence by a *goði* ensured he could protect his clients.[86]

It is telling for our understanding of the general operation of *goðorð* that we have barely any indication of the names or origins of the *goðorð* (plural) of the most powerful figure in the Eyjafjörður region in the late twelfth-century, Guðmundr *dýri* of Bakki in Öxnadalur. Guðmundr is said to have been given the *Fljótamannagoðorð* as we have seen. It is also said that his son, Þorvaldr, gave two or more *goðorð* to Sigurðr Ormsson. This latter statement is helpful on one level because it does confirm that *goðorð* were still perceived as individual, but at the same time it is utterly opaque as to what, besides, the *Fljótamannagoðorð*, Þorvaldr and his father might have controlled. Lúðvík Ingvarsson contended that Guðmundr and Þorvaldr were controllers of what he called the *Þveræingagoðorð*, but there is too little evidence to go on. The only other thing said anywhere in *Sturlunga saga* about Guðmundr's original *goðorð* (singular or plural) is that his brother and nephew had it/them before him.[87] The brother, mentioned in *Sturlunga* just this once in relation to the *goðorð*, died in 1178, while the more visible nephew, Þorvarðr *auðgi*, died in 1186.[88] One possibility is that Guðmundr inherited a recognised *goðorð* from his half-brother Þórðr Þórarinsson who lived at Laufás: Laufás was certainly a wealthy farm, and *Njáls saga* does mention a *Laufæsingagoðorð*. Of all the *Íslendingasögur* one might expect to give an accurate picture of northern traditions (even if not past realities), the south-centred *Njáls saga* is hardly it, but it is an intriguing possibility. Barði Guðmundsson wanted to equate the *Laufæsingagoðorð* with the *goðorð* of Guðmundr *ríki* and his descendants based at Möðruvellir,[89] and although this is a difficult fit, this might be a better solution than seeing the *Fljótamannagoðorð* as identical to another *goðorð*, especially as Guðmundr *dýri* owned more than one. In geographical terms there might be 'space' for a *goðorð* in and around Laufás and in districts to the east, as we shall see. The broader point to note is that the *goðorð* of Guðmundr *dýri* were most

---

86   SS I: 167–68.
87   SS I: 163. The name *Þveræingagoðorð* is used by Barði Guðmundsson (1937: 68) but he thought that this was what Önundr Þorkelsson and Einarr Hallsson controlled (cf Gunnar Karlsson 2004: 259–60).
88   Ásgrímr *auðgi*: IA 118; Þorvarðr Ásgrímsson: IA 22, 61, 119, 180.
89   Barði Guðmundsson 1937: 67–69.

likely passed onto his son Þorvaldr who in turn gave them to Sigurðr Ormsson (in around 1203). These were passed to Tumi Sighvatsson before the latter's father, Sighvatr Sturluson, took them over in 1215.

The evidence is equally unclear for other *goðorð*. The *goðorð* associated with Hallr Kleppjárnsson in the quotation above may or may not have had a continuous existence since the tenth century. In the *Ættartölur* section of *Sturlunga saga* there is a single line of patrilineal descent from the *goði* Þórir Hámundarson of Espihóll, of *Víga-Glúms saga* fame, to some possible *goðar* of the twelfth century.[90] But, as Gunnar Karlsson has noted, this possible line of *goðar* really is no more than a list of names.[91] After the evidence of the *Íslendingasögur*, it takes until the later twelfth century to see less ambiguous evidence of this *goðorð* operating within Eyjafjörður itself. Even then the evidence is of leadership rather than explicitly control of *goðorð*. Thus in *Guðmundar saga dýra* one Óláfr Þorsteinsson (of Saurbær in Eyjafjörður), a descendant of Þórir Hámundarson, appears to have shared local leadership with Hallr's father, Kleppjárn Klængsson of Hrafnagil. Óláfr is said to have asked Kleppjárn whether he would prefer to go to the Alþing to support one of the Reykjardalur-based protagonists in a legal case or else to stay at home to protect the district (*gæta heraðs*). While these two men are being portrayed as pre-eminent in Eyjafjörður, and possibly beyond it, there is no explicit mention of *goðorð*.[92] We know nothing else about Óláfr except that he became a canon at Saurbær while Kleppjárn's death is recorded in one annal for 1194.[93] After this, the murder of Hallr Kleppjárnsson by Kálfr Guttormsson from Grund in 1212 brings to an end any identifiable *goðorð*.[94]

Guðmundar saga dýra also identifies a pair of men, Önundr Þorkelsson of Laugaland and Einarr Hallsson of Möðruvellir, who are said to share *goðorð ok*

---

90 See below pp. 191, 278–283 for Þórir and the Esphælingar.
91 Gunnar Karlsson 2004: 258. The relevant section of the *Ættartölur* in *Sturlunga saga* centres on Þorsteinn *ranglátr* who, as with other sections, was alive in the first half of the twelfth century. The line traced to him was: Hámundr-Þórir-Þorvaldr *krókr*-Ketill-Einarr-Þorsteinn *ranglátr*. Þorsteinn *ranglátr*'s children and grandchildren are then listed.
92 Gunnar Karlsson draws the opposite conclusion despite the fact that he sees none of Óláfr's paternal kin as *goðar*, 2004: 258.
93 For Kleppjárn's death: IA 121; Lúðvík Ingvarsson 1980-86: III 609. This is an unusual entry but it could make sense as one of interest to people in northern Iceland. Kleppjárn's death is listed with that of an otherwise unknown Þorvarðr Ormsson. This Þorvarðr, if from the north, could be the son of Ormr Fornason, a priest at Urðir in Svarfaðardalur whose son Víga-Haukr was connected to Loftr Markússon and Hrafn Sveinbjarnarson in the West Fjords. He left Iceland before 1208 to end up in Greenland (SS I: 196, 214–16).
94 SS I: 258; Lúðvík Ingvarsson 1980-86: III 611. See below, esp. 78, 80, 131, 134, 135, 139 for Kálfr.

frændsemi, goðorð and kinship. We know little about either of these men and this has a possible significance for understanding the importance of their *goðorð*. It is impossible to trace the ancestry of either man with certainty, and Einarr Hallsson's home is uncertain: he could have lived at either of the two important farms called Möðruvellir. When we consider the evidence for this *goðorð* alongside that for the possible *Laufæsingagoðorð* or *Möðruvellingagoðorð*, it is perhaps slightly more likely that Einarr lived at the Möðruvellir in Eyjafjörður but only because Möðruvellir in Hörgárdalur was apparently occupied by Þorvarðr Þorgeirsson at the time.[95] It has sometimes been assumed that Önundr and Einarr shared the *Reykdælagoðorð* of the much earlier Áskell *goði*, but no connections can be made between the evidence of the *Íslendingasögur* and the later twelfth century.[96] Recent commentators have said nothing about the number of *goðorð* being shared, or rather have assumed that we are talking about just one, and have made no suggestion as to the geographical scale of this shared enterprise. It has been suggested that Einarr was a kinsman by blood of the family associated closely with both Saurbær's religious house and Grenjaðarstaðir in Reykjadalur, but this clarifies nothing.[97] What we do know is that there is no clear evidence of this *goðorð* being used by anyone after them. Önundr died in 1197, but the date of Einarr's death is not recorded. As was the case with the *Fljótamannagoðorð*, it is likely that Guðmundr *dýri* somehow prevented the *goðorð* from functioning.

It still remains for us to consider the *goðorð* said to have been owned by Þorvarðr Þorgeirsson (d.1207) and his son Ögmundr *sneis* (d.1237). As with other *goðorð* discussed here, there is still an issue about how safely this can be taken towards the apparently *goðorð*-owning Ljósvetningar of the *Íslendingasögur* (Chapter 5). There is circumstantial evidence that Þorvarðr's father, Þorgeirr Hallason, was a *goði*: Þorgeirr was seen as significant on the political stage in about 1120[98] and when his daughter married Hvamm-Sturla (1148) he was described as *mikill höfðingi*, a great leader, and lived at Krossanes in Kræklingahlíð.[99] By the late 1160s, Þorgeirr was living at Hvassafell in Eyjafjörður until shortly before his death in 1169 when he took holy orders and enterred the monastery at Munkaþverá, leaving Þorvarðr to take over Hvassafell.[100] Krossanes and Hvassafell were no doubt among the top tier of farms in their

---

95   E.g. SS I: 162, 164.
96   Gunnar Karlsson 2004: 264. See below pp. 284–90.
97   SS II: 43. *ættskrá*. Here and elsewhere genealogies (*ættskrá* (sing.), *ættskrár* (pl.)) are identified by number as provided in appendices of SS II.
98   SS I: 35.
99   SS I: 66. See below pp. 70, 72, 80–81.
100 *Byskupa sögur* I: 31; IA 117; SS I: 123.

districts, but not among the very largest for the region. These men plus Ari, Þorgeirr's other son and father of the future Bishop Guðmundr, are generally seen in glowing terms in the opening chapters of *Prestssaga* but it is still perhaps not surprising that we do not have the kind of detailed narrative about them which would mention tell-tale signs of *goðorð*-ownership such as mention of *þingmenn* or *mannaforráð*.

Þorvarðr Þorgeirsson is identifiable as a *goði* in *Guðmundar saga dýra*, however, when in the late 1180s he is said to have had a *þingmaðr* 'í dalnum,' in the valleys somewhere east of Eyjafjörður.[101] In this text he is also living at Möðruvellir in Hörgárdalur, i.e. just a few kilometres north-east of Hvassafell, but at a much wealthier farm. However, Þorvarðr and his kinsmen are seen to have a longer association with Háls in Fnjóskadalur, an impression which comes mostly from *Prestssaga* but also *Guðmundar saga dýra*. Þorvarðr's sister is said to have lived at Háls with her husband (from nearby Víðivellir) and then he and his son Ögmundr also spend time there, with Ögmundr last identified as being at Háls in 1197.[102] Where Ögmundr lives and what he does in the following decades is unclear. He might have remained in or around Eyjafjörður until 1209 when he is effectively kicked out of the north by Bishop Guðmundr's opponents along with the bishop himself; then Ögmundr moved to Hofsteigr in the east, and is only mentioned again briefly in 1234.[103] Thus should Ögmundr still have held a *goðorð*, he cannot be seen to have made use of it. As noted by others, the influence of Sighvatr Sturluson when he arrived in the area in 1215 must be the reason that this *goðorð* disappears from our view.[104] As we shall see, though, this was shortly before the establishment of a *ríki* in Eyjafjörður.[105]

Thus as Gunnar Karlsson's commentary on these *goðorð* suggests, they disappeared earlier than those in Dalir. At the same time the evidence for their earlier and continued existence is even murkier than he thought. It is probably safest to conclude no more than that in the twelfth century, Eyjafjörður always had at least two *goðorð* which were each owned by one or more *goðar*, ensuring some kind of political competition among *goðar*. One or two *goðar* probably always lived in Eyjafjörður itself, with the possibility that others lived in less populous districts to its east or west. *Goðorð* do seem to

---

101   SS I: 162.
102   SS I: 117, 123, 130, 131, 151, 192.
103   SS I: 254, 371.
104   Gunnar Karlsson 2004: 263.
105   See below pp. 135–44. Sigurðr Ormsson may already have developed similar influence after his arrival in Eyjafjörður in 1203, e.g. when Hallr Kleppjárnsson and Sigurðr Ormsson drag a monk out of Munkaþverá (SS I: 244).

have been more readily concentrated in fewer hands here than in Dalir, to judge by the tradition of Guðmundr *ríki*, the multiple *goðorð* of Guðmundr *dýri*, and the appearance of a single owner of all *goðorð* in 1215.

6 Conclusion

In essence the aim of this section has been to critically consider the assumption of institutional continuity in regional political power. Jón Viðar Sigurðsson is probably correct in suggesting that in the twelfth and thirteenth century people had no clear understanding, or need to understand, the origins of *goðorð*. The patchiness of the evidence for the history of *goðorð* is probably the product of the nature of the *goðorð* as highly malleable and relatively weak. It is more likely that the differences between the regions – in Dalir there was still some, limited competition over at least one named *goðorð* in the decades after 1220 whereas in the Eyjafjörður region there was not – is a product, in Dalir, of the some competition among rival *goðar* and thus practical functioning of these institutions. The same can certainly not be said for *goðorð* in the north in the thirteenth century. The more important point, however, is that the number and continued existence of *goðorð* in the north up to that point is even more opaque than scholars tend to suggest. In both regions it seems as if 'goðorð' was not so much a legal role waiting for someone to fill it but a synonym for *mannaforráð*, a recognition of *de facto* power even if it depended on negotiation between a *goði* and *þingmenn*. This more amorphous quality of *goðorð* means that we should not expect its or their history to be easy to write.

7 Elite Marriage Networks

To include this section feels like something of a historiographical throwback but it is necessary to help build up a picture of what shaped socio-political activity in each of the two regions. Given the importance of personal relationships in Iceland, however, who married whom had the potential to matter a great deal. At the same time a glance at the genealogical tables of the 1946 standard edition of *Sturlunga saga* can lead one to conclude simply that every identifiable elite family in Iceland married into every other group and, most of the time, everyone among Iceland's elite could claim some kind of kinship with someone else. This is partly true but also rather glib. There is a balance to be struck, and if we are to understand how and why politics worked the way it did then our goal should at least be to try to work out how the people named in those genealogical tables and mentioned in narratives were actually trying to create socio-political networks. There is, however, a difficulty in simply trying to represent 'family'. It is easy to see that familial identity is fleeting and how difficult it is to decipher the size and longevity of such groups when the narratives mention them, whether they are named after individual men (e.g. the Sturlungar, Ásbirningar, Fornungar) or farms (e.g. Staðarhólsmenn, Möðruvellingar, Grundarmenn). The accounts below do not follow a common structure, rather they are led by a concern with understanding the possible political strategies of certain elite men in relation to each region at a particular time. Who is discussed in this chapter has been dictated by a combination of (a) my own reading of who seems to have been a significant grouping whose line can be traced to a reasonable degree in *Sturlunga saga* and (b) the choices of the editors of the 1946 edition of the text who seem largely to have come to the same conclusions as I have about how to group people. The fact that only a few families are identifiable says something about the closedness of the elite which largely married within itself.

It should also be said that we have very few examples where there is an account of a negotiation of a marriage. The issue of agency is obviously an important one and perhaps in what follows it has been too easy to assume agency on the part of certain elite men or, rather, to write this account as if they had agency; reality may have been different in some cases. Given that many members of the elite socialised fairly frequently, there is no reason to doubt that some marriages did come about because the future husband and wife wanted them to; it is just hard to see it. It is perhaps more likely, however, that most marriages were contracted because that is what fathers and older brothers on one or both sides wanted, depending on the specific circumstances.

There is also an issue about how genealogy functions in or behind *Sturlunga saga*'s narratives. In what follows, genealogies in the contemporary sagas are assumed largely to work in a different way from those in *Íslendingasögur*. It is assumed that the connections which are recorded in contemporary sagas describing the thirteenth century are not so strongly shaped by the processes of social memory because the accounts were most likely written soon after the events they describe. The relationships which are recorded, most importantly, are far more numerous and complicated than those recorded within the *Íslendingasögur*. The kinship connections recorded are therefore assumed to be more credible than those recorded for the more distant past. Nonetheless it might sometimes be significant that some familial connections are either not made explicit or are so poorly explicated that the sagas' authors and/or *Sturlunga saga* compiler were trying to ignore them as best they could. The material we have for marriages in the twelfth century is more scant, just as it was for *goðorð*. Partly for that reason the marriage networks in *Þorgils saga ok Haflíða*, the saga covering 1117–21, will be dealt with discretely below in the context of that saga's core dispute, and we will begin by looking at the latter half of the twelfth century.[106]

As to the specifics of our regions, for the earlier twelfth century we have already seen some elements of elite marriage networks for Dalir and for the Eyjafjörður region. With the arrival of Hvamm-Sturla, the marriages of his sons and the move of Sighvatr Sturluson to Eyjafjörður, the elite families of the two regions are also partly linked. Beyond the fact that of Sighvatr's move there is nothing striking about this particular connection, as opposed to connections between any other regions in thirteenth century Iceland. It does not negate the fact that the Sturlungar were some of the most important figures in thirteenth century Iceland. But it also means that for the purposes of this book discussing the two regions separately becomes more problematic.

8   Marriages in Dalir and Northern Snæfellsnes

For the highest social tier in the Dalir region, it is only really possible to give a sustained analysis of the marriage networks of the Sturlungar, such is their importance. Mention will be made of other relevant kinship ties in chapter 3. When we have the first hints at the position of Hvamm-Sturla's family it is seems they were connected beyond Dalir. Hvamm-Sturla's mother would appear to have been connected to the Oddaverjar, on the one hand, while his first wife, Ingibjörg, was the daughter of Þorgeirr Hallason from Krossanes in Eyjafjörður.[107] The next notable ties to examine are the marriages of Hvamm-Sturla's children by his second wife, Guðný Böðvarsdóttir. *Sturlu saga* records the marriages of few of Sturla's children, particularly not those of Guðný. This is probably because the marriages of many of his children, including those of his most politically successful sons, Þórðr, Snorri and Sighvatr, took place after his death. While it sames safe to assume Sturla's agency in arranging the marriages of his children by his first wife, Ingibjörg Þorgeirsdóttir, and of his illegitimate children, later, Guðný and her sons are likely to have had more decision-making power. At the same time the ties created by Sturla's children by Ingibjörg, and by his concubines, also helped create potentially lasting personal ties for his children by Guðný. A clear example of this was the second partnership of Þuríðr Sturludóttir, Sturla's

---

106   See below pp. 86–90.
107   SS I: 52, 64, 66, 117.

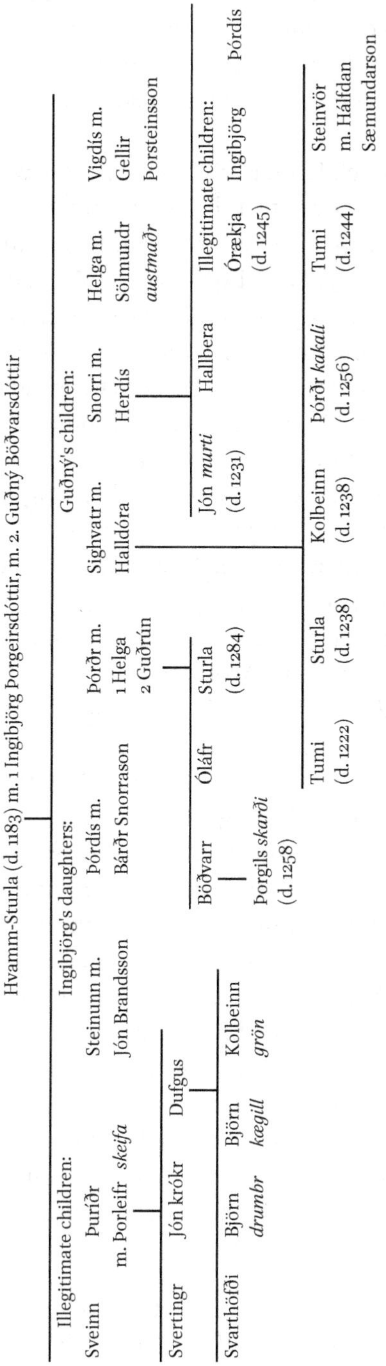

FRAMEWORKS OF POWER

Hvamm-Sturla (d. 1183) m. 1 Ingibjörg Þorgeirsdóttir, m. 2. Guðný Böðvarsdóttir

Ingibjörg's daughters:

Steinunn m.	Þórdís m.	Þórðr m.
Jón Brandsson	Bárðr Snorrason	1 Helga
		2 Guðrún

Böðvarr — Óláfr — Sturla (d. 1284)
Þorgils *skarði* (d. 1258)

Illegitimate children:
Sveinn — Þuríðr m. Þorleifr *skeifa*
Svertingr — Jón krókr — Dufgus
Svarthöfði — Björn *drumbr* — Björn *kægill* — Kolbeinn *grön*

Guðný's children:

Sighvatr m. Halldóra — Snorri m. Herdís — Helga m. Sölmundr *austmaðr* — Vigdís m. Gellir Þorsteinsson

Jón *murti* (d. 1231) — Hallbera

Tumi (d. 1222) — Sturla (d. 1238) — Kolbeinn (d. 1238) — Þórðr *kakali* (d. 1256)

Illegitimate children:
Óræka (d. 1245) — Ingibjörg — Þórdís
Tumi (d. 1244) — Steinvör m. Hálfdan Sæmundarson

FIGURE 18   Simplified genealogy of the Sturlungar

daughter by Álof, which saw her take over the farm of Hjarðarholt. Although this too was probably contracted after Sturla's death, it most likely played a part in ensuring Sighvatr Sturluson's control of Hjarðarholt: Sighvatr moved to Hjarðarholt with Þuríðr and it was Þuríðr's son Dufgus who later controlled that farm.[108]

Guðný Böðvarsdóttir's children by Sturla were those who became most influential in the course of the thirteenth century, presumably because she was alive and able to help shape their future. First, Þórðr Sturluson married the daughter of Ari *inn sterki* Þorgilsson from Staðarstaðr, on the southern coast of Snæfellsnes. This marriage was probably the result of Ari *inn sterki*'s apparently quasi-marriage with Guðný following Hvamm-Sturla's death. Ari *inn sterki*'s own death, in Norway, left Þórðr to inherit Staðarstaðr and thus greatly expand the geographical spread of his kin group's landholdings and influence. Indeed almost immediately after recounting the death of Ari, *Íslendinga saga* gives a story set in the mid-1190s of Þórðr working on behalf of a *þingmaðr* as far south as Lundarreykjadalur, the southernmost tributary of Borgarfjörður; and Þórðr had his younger brother Sighvatr actually stay in Lundarreykjadalur over the winter.[109] Þórðr's relationship with his wife seems to have ended reasonably soon, however, although he kept control of Staðarstaðr, according to *Íslendinga saga* at least, by virtue of his being Ari's heir.[110]

The account of the contracting of Þórðr's younger brothers' marriages suggests a simple and logical expansion of their collective influence. Sighvatr Sturluson appears to have married Halldóra Túmadóttir in the late 1190s. She was the daughter of a man from Áss in Skagafjörður (Tumi Kolbeinsson, d.1184) and Þuríðr Gizurardóttir of the Haukdælir (d.1247). The significant fact seems to have been that the marriage was approved by Þuríðr's son, Kolbeinn Tumason, and her second husband Sigurðr Ormsson of the Svínfellingar, based at Svínafell itself in the south-east. It was Sigurðr who is later identified as securing Sighvatr's move to Eyjafjörður. Thus, after Sighvatr spent some time working under the guidance of his older brother in Dalir, he acquired connections to key families in other regions but nevertheless moved to Hjarðarholt with his new wife, and did not (yet) live in Eyjafjörður itself.

Þórðr Sturluson himself negotiated a marriage for his brother Snorri, to the daughter of Bersi *inn auðgi* (the rich) from Borg in Mýrar. *Íslendinga saga* contrasts Snorri's new-found wealth with his earlier predicament as a poor younger

---

108 See below, pp. 101, 125. SS I: 52, 64, 234, 314, 338 for references to Álof, Þuríðr and Þuríðr's second husband/partner Þorleifr *skeifa*. Cf. Sverrir Jakobsson 2002: 173–74.

109 SS I: 232. The *þingmaðr* concerned is identified as Hámundr Gilsson from the church-farm of Lundr. If this story is true then Þórðr had a very wealthy *þingmaðr*.

110 SS I: 231. On Ari sterki's role see further Sverrir Jakobsson 2013: 166, 167, 171–72.

son, partly perhaps to praise Þórðr Sturluson's achievement in effecting such a marriage. Snorri appears to have married in 1200 but stayed at Oddi with his foster-family, only moving to Borg when Bersi *inn auðgi* died in about 1202.[111]

It is notable that Guðný's two daughters also seem to have married into wealth. Vigdís Sturludóttir married Gellir Þorsteinsson, the owner of Flatey, the largest island in Breiðafjörður and an important political and, for a while, monastic centre.[112] Helga Sturludóttir's marriage to Sölmundr *austmaðr* is only made explicit in the *Ættartölur* section of *Sturlunga saga*. Like all so-called *austmenn*, Sölmundr was most likely Norwegian, but he plays a periodic role in Icelandic politics in the 1230s, being a possible go-between in rivalries among the Sturlungar, and then outside: both he and Helga were forced to hand over the rights to Snorri Sturluson's property to Gizurr Þorvaldsson in late 1241.[113] Precisely when this couple married and under what circumstances is impossible to say, but it might well have suited Helga's brothers for them to have a Norwegian connection. Other evidence might suggest the connection with Sölmundr was made before 1220. Helga appears to have been the mother of a very long-lived son, Egill Sölmundarson, who was already an adult in 1241 when he inherited some of Snorri Sturluson's property, and lived until 1297.[114]

The allegiances forged by the Sturlusynir for their children represent yet another jump in the geographical distribution of marriage partners for this kin group. This did, however, vary from brother to brother. By the 1220s Snorri Sturluson had daughters whom he was able to marry to regional overlords like himself by the 1220s. Gizurr Þorvaldsson of the Haukdælir, Árni *óreiða* Magnússon from Kjalarnes in the south-west, and Þorvaldr *Vatnsfirðingr* from the West Fjords, all married daughters of Snorri in 1224. When Árni *óreiða* died, in 1228, his widow married Kolbeinn *ungi* Arnórsson from Skagafjörður. Órækja Snorrason married Kolbeinn *ungi's* sister to create a third tie between the Sturlungar and the Ásbirningar.[115] Sturla Sighvatsson married Solveig Sæmundardóttir of the Oddaverjar in 1223, connecting him with the family which had fostered Snorri Sturluson. With the exception of the marriage of Ingibjörg

---

111 SS I: 237, 240.
112 This was an enduring connection in as much as Vigdís' and Gellir's daughter married Gísli Markússon from Rauðasandr in northern Breiðafjörður (d.1258) who was an ally of Þórðr *kakali* Sighvatsson and other Sturlungar, e.g. SS II: 8.
113 SS I: 52, 390, 455.
114 Egill Sölmundarson, as a subdeacon, was the victim of the tightening of ecclesiastical control over property by Bishop Árni Þorláksson of Skálholt. Egill's marriage was nullified in 1275. *Árna saga biskups*: 37–38; Gunnar Karlsson 2000: 97.
115 I.e. after Sighvatr Sturluson's marriage to Halldóra Tumadóttir (pp. 71, 72 above).

Snorradóttir to Gizurr Þorvaldsson which ended in 1231, these marriages proved to be of enduring significance.[116]

Snorri's brothers appear sometimes to have been junior partners in his attempts to gain power. If we look at the status of the three Sturlusynir, even before 1224, then it is clear that Sighvatr did not have as much authority as Snorri (in terms of *goðorð*) and perhaps not the same financial means, although this is harder to measure. What is more noticeable, however, in distinguishing the political positions of the three brothers, is what we know about the marriages which they arranged for their children. Snorri's dealing has already been outlined. Of Sighvatr's children we know of only two of his children's spouses but these were both from the Oddaverjar, reinforcing the connections which had been created through Snorri's fosterage at Oddi.[117]

The recorded marriages of Þórðr and his children are worth examining because they pose questions about the relationships between the Sturlusynir and are of relevance to the control of Dalir. Þórðr himself remarried, to Guðrún Bjarnadóttir of the Flóamenn in the south, i.e. a different (or competing) elite group to the Oddaverjar in the south, with whom Sighvatr and Snorri were more strongly connected.[118] His eldest son, Böðvarr, married into the Ásbirningar, to Sigríðr Arnórsdóttir. Þórðr's daughter Halla married Tómas Þórarinsson, a member of the Seldælir, from Arnarfjörður in the West Fjords.[119] Þórðr's son Sturla married more locally, to Helga Þórðardóttir from Skarð.[120]

The first of these marriages seems qualitatively different from the latter pair. Böðvarr's marriage into the leading family from the Northern Quarter seems to have cemented an alliance of country-wide significance. Marriages with the Seldælir and Skarðverjar, meanwhile, were of more local, but not necessarily less, importance. Although the dates of these marriages are not certain it is

---

116   SS I: 346. The severance of this connection is also clearly part of the process by which Snorri and Gizurr's conflict escalated.

117   Two of his older sons, though, died at the battle of Örlygsstaðir when comparatively young. To judge by their siblings' marriages they too might have married into elite families in different regions (SS I: 436, 437, 438).

118   Sighvatr, however, married one of his illegitimate daughters, Sigríðr, into the Flóamenn (SS I: 52). This marriage was not without significance because Sigríðr and her husband, Styrmir Þórisson, were said to have inherited all of Sighvatr's wealth and property and lived at Grund in Eyjafjörður, Sighvatr's former base (SS I: 440, 472; II: 4, 5). See below pp. 136–37.

119   SS I: 52, 54; II: 10, 25. Halla's son, Þórarinn Tómasson was at Flatey with Sturla Þórðarson (SS II: 72).

120   The sources' silence on the marriage connections of the remainder of Sighvatr's and Þórðr's children but is suggestive of their lack of great political importance. This might be because, if they married, they married locally, in Dalir or Eyjafjörður, and to *bændr* rather than *höfðingjar*.

likely that Þórðr arranged them as a deliberate attempt to create allegiances within the north-west.[121] An alternative interpretation might be that some of these later marriages took place after his death and were the result of his children's weakened eligibility. Þórðr's death, and those of his brothers in 1238 and 1241, could well have affected his children's choice of partner. Interpreting Þórðr's or his family's intentions behind his second marriage is less easy. Suffice it to say that of the three brothers, Þórðr's kinsmen by marriage were the most illustrious.

The connections of the next two generations of Sturlungar, where they are recorded, show that there remained a western Icelandic elite which married within itself although about half of their marriages being to people outside the Western Quarter. Sturla Sighvatsson's daughters married: Hrafn Oddsson (from Eyrr in Arnarfjörður in the West Fjords), Vigfúss Gunnsteinsson (Garpsdalr), Sæmundr Ormsson (of the Svínfellingar from the south east) and Eyjólfr Þorsteinsson (originally from Vatnsdalur in the north).[122] Þuríðr, the illegitimate daughter of Hvamm-Sturla, had had a son who married the daughter of Þorgils Gunnsteinsson from Staðr on Reykjanes;[123] and her grandson Svarthöfði Dufgussson, married Hrafn Oddsson's sister.[124]

Böðvarr Þórðarson married his children to families associated with Hítarnes, just south of Snæfellsnes (in Kolbeinsstaðahreppur) and, possibly, Narfeyri.[125] His brother Sturla, however, married one of his daughters to the son of Gizurr Þorvaldsson and then into an East Fjords' family, and another daughter to the son of Brandr Kolbeinsson from Skagafjörður. Böðvarr's ties were far closer to home than those made by Sturla who continued to make countrywide connections, the tie with the east perhaps reflecting the scaling-up of political activity in the mid-thirteenth century.[126]

---

121 Böðvarr and Halla were both children of Þórðr Sturluson's second wife of three (he had no children with his first wife). Sturla was the son of Þórðr's concubine and born in 1214. The birthdates of Böðvarr and Halla are unknown and we do not know whether Þórðr Sturluson kept his concubine at the same time as his second wife. A *terminus ante quem* for Sturla Þórðarson's marriage is perhaps given by a reference to his marriage when he is invited by Skarð-Snorri Narfason to move to Reykhólar in 1241 (SS I: 451).
122 Only the marriages of Sturla's daughters are recorded anywhere. Þórðr *kakali* Sighvatsson's connections are not recorded here because he based himself in the north, never married, and his children by his concubine are never recorded as marrying (SS II: 19. *ættskrá*).
123 SS I: 338.
124 SS I: 447.
125 SS II: 19. *ættskrá*, 24. *ættskrá*, SS I: 54.
126 *Sturlunga saga*'s body of genealogical information relating to Dalir and the west is heavily slanted towards the history of the Sturlungar themselves. However, it is worth noting that

The marriage connections of late twelfth- and thirteenth-century Icelandic leaders set out above is not easy to analyse. The simplistic notion that kinship groups (*ætt*) are easily identifiable is clearly wrong for this material, just as has been pointed out for other societies.[127] A kin group, at least its extent outside of a nuclear family, is as large as people want it to be. People can choose what they call themselves when they are related to many other people. The terms such as Sturlungar, Ásbirningar, Oddaverjar etc. have only been used in the above account for the sake of convenience and convention. Geography and personal relationships clearly counted for as much in the practicalities of thirteenth century politics as did blood connections. That is why so much space has been devoted to identifying the choices men made for their children: by doing so they were choosing political allies, or confirming their friendship, in as strong a form as was possible. Chapter 3 will serve to illustrate this point.

For now, however, it would seem that the marriages of the Sturlusynir did mark them out from the owners or occupiers of other large farms in Dalir and, later, the north. We can see Hvamm-Sturla's sons married into the very highest echelon of Icelandic society, no doubt in part due to their father's negotiation of Snorri's fostering at Oddi. This, however, was only the first stage in their political rise. Þórðr's advantageous, but still fairly local, marriage no doubt paved the way for Sighvatr's marriage into the more established Ásbirningar and this in turn allowed Snorri to marry the daughter of one of the wealthiest men in Borgarfjörður. The fact that a leader of regional importance had three legitimate sons who were all able to marry so well, who *all* held *goðorð* and who lived so long, is certainly unusual when compared with almost any other elite family recorded in *Sturlunga saga* or the *Íslendingasögur*.[128]

The more expansive set of connections of three of Hvamm-Sturla's sons should not obscure the fact, however, that the Sturlungar remained part of a denser western Icelandic elite community. Hvamm-Sturla's other children, for the most part, married church-farm owners from the west. The Sturlungar of

---

Geirmundar þáttr heljarskinns provides a genealogy of the Skarðverjar which illustrates that other ties existed which linked some other wealthy farms in Dalir. Two of the children of Narfi Snorrason from Skarð (d.1202) married two of the children of Hallr Gunnsteinsson (whose father had taken over Staðarhóll soon after Einarr Þorgilsson's death and whose grandson was Vigfúss Gunnsteinsson) and another daughter of Narfi married the nephew of Hvamm-Sturla who controlled Staðarfell (SS II: 20. *ættskrá*). This couple's son was Guðmundr *undir Felli* who had an important part to play in politics around Hvammsfjörður. See below pp. 103, 104, 106, 109, 110–11, 112.

127 Kuper 1982.

128 Gizurr Hallsson's sons (Þorvaldr, Hallr *prestr* and Magnús biskup, who all died in the 1230s) provide the only real parallel.

any generation between c.1185 and c.1260 could claim moderately close kinship (by marriage) with almost any head of household of a church farm in the Western Quarter. There was clearly also a pattern whereby Þórðr Sturluson and his sons – the Sturlungar who most obviously based themselves in Dalir or Snæfellsnes – tried to keep themselves connected with both regionally and 'nationally' important people. Sturla Þórðarson had been married locally but married his children further afield; Böðvarr had married into the Ásbirningar but married his children more locally.

With regard to the area around Hvammsfjörður, there were, all the same, some important farms which were not obviously occupied by people married into the Sturlungar, or for that matter the Skarðverjar, the only other group for which we really have information.[129] Hvoll in Saurbær, Ásgarðr in Hvammssveit, Höskuldsstaðir in Laxárdalur, Vatnshorn in Haukadalur, Fellsendi, Snóksdalr and the Skógar farms (all in Miðdalir), the whole of Skógarströnd and Helgafell: none of these places were obviously directly controlled by members of the Sturlungar (or the Skarðverjar). To understand how these places may have fitted into local politics requires the more detailed analysis of accounts of disputes in Dalir and surrounding districts, and that will be the focus of Chapter 3.

9   Elite Marriages in Eyjafjörður and the North-East

No single family in the north-east serves as a focal point for characterizing elite marriage strategies. Þorsteinn *ranglátr* Einarsson of Grund (d.1149), however, is represented as one of the seven key genealogical figures in the *Ættartölur* section of *Sturlunga saga* and is the only one of the seven to come from Eyjafjörður or the north-east.[130] This fits well with other sources' views of Grund as an important farm, regardless of who lived there, even if that view of Grund might be deemed something the Sturlungar were especially keen on given the presence of Sighvatr and his descendants there after 1215. Þorsteinn therefore merits being the first person we consider in this section.

Þorsteinn himself is said to have married into the Reynistaðarmenn in Skagafjörður,[131] and his children's marriages give the impression of his being an important figure in countrywide politics. His sons Ketill and Björn married daughters of Þorleifr *beiskaldi* from Hítardalr in the west. Ketill moved west,

---

129   See note 126 just above.
130   SS I: 55–56; see above p. 65, footnote 91.
131   SS I: 55.

but we know nothing more about Björn bar the name of one of his daughters.[132] A third son, Óláfr, was a canon at the short-lived religious house at Saurbær in Eyjafjörður, and we know he had children and died in 1204.[133] Of Þorsteinn's daughters, one married someone associated with Keldur in Rangárvellir in the far south, a large farm where Jón Loptsson of the Oddaverjar (d.1197) built a church and monastery.[134] The other two daughters appear to have married grandsons of the iconic figure of Hafliði Másson from the Húnavatn region.[135] Taken as a whole, Þorsteinn *ranglátr*'s children's matches look like those we should expect to have been obtained by people at the very highest level of Icelandic society, and it is especially significant that there was a connection to Hafliði Másson's family or, indeed, anyone in Húnatnssýsla.

It is notable just how closely focussed on Eyjafjörður are the connections of Þorsteinn's descendants. Aside from the line from the daughter married to someone from Keldur, which leads to connections only outside the north-east, the rest of the family's known links are very geographically close to Grund. Óláfr's daughter married Eyjólfr Hallsson of Grenjaðarstaðir (Reykjadalur) who was then abbot at Saurbær from 1206 to 1212.[136] Their son, Jón, and his son (still alive in 1255), lived at Möðrufell in Eyjafjörður.[137] Jón Eyjólfsson married the sister of the Kálfr Guttormsson who lived at Grund until he sold it to Sighvatr Sturluson in 1215 and moved to Skagafjörður.[138] Thus here the marital strategy looks like a geopolitical one of sorts; unlike for many other families over the course of the period c.1100-c.1260, descendants of Þorsteinn *ranglátr* continued to stay in the same place into the mid-thirteenth century, even if they no longer lived at Grund.[139]

One of the seemingly peculiar things about the late twelfth-century north is that a leading figure like Guðmundr *dýri* Þorvaldsson could emanate from somewhere relatively remote like Bakki in Öxnadalur.[140] It seems most likely that the marriages of Guðmundr's sisters and daughters were crerated by him and his brother Ásgrímr in the 1160s and 1170s, although they were not starting from scratch. Their father is generally accepted as having been Þorvaldr *auðgi* Guðmundarson, about whom we know little more than his name and when he

---

132 SS I: 55, 56.
133 SS I: 56; IA 122.
134 Orri Vésteinsson 2000: 138.
135 SS I: 55, 56, 160.
136 Orri Vésteinsson 2000: 138.
137 Óláfr's sister and her husband had lived at Möðrufell as well (SS I: 373, 518).
138 SS I: 260. See below p. 134 for Kálfr Guttormsson's move to Grund.
139 Jón Eyjólfsson was probably still alive in 1232 when it is implied that he owned Grenjaðarstaðir (SS I: 346).
140 Helgi Þorláksson 1994. See esp. pp. 128–34 for Guðmundr *dýri*'s career.

died in 1161/2. Þorvaldr nonetheless gets given the epithet *auðgi*, rich, by the author of *Haukdœla þáttr*.[141] Guðmundr is recorded as having two sisters, whose connections contrast sharply with one another. One marriage brought a connection with the family of one Forni Söxólfsson, the Fornungar, about whom we know little except that Forni was local to Eyjafjörður.[142] In the late 1190s the couple's children lived at the farm of Myrkárdalur (in a tributary valley of Hörgárdalur) and Svarfaðardalur; their grandsons also lived in Svarfaðardalur.[143] The link was reinforced by marriage of Guðmundr's daughter into the same Skagafjörður family with which Forni was connected linked.[144]

Guðmundr's other recorded sister married Gizurr Hallsson of the Haukdælir, the lawspeaker from 1181 to 1202. Gizurr played an active role in southern politics so far as we can see, living at Skálholt and even having a say in the election of Guðmundr Arason as Bishop of Hólar in 1201.[145] Given that Gizurr is only first recorded as politically active in 1170 it would make slightly more sense to see the marriage as having been arranged by Guðmundr *dýri* or his (probably) older brother.[146] Thus it looks as though it was in the 1160s and 1170s that this family, namely Guðmundr, his brother and his father, were securing a combination of local and wider ties. just as we gave seen elite men in Dalir doing. What is notable here is that so far as we can tell they made no attempt to tie the family to other significant Eyjafjörður-region leaders.

To turn to Guðmundr's children, we know his illegitimate daughter Ingibjörg married Þorfinnr, the son of Önundr, Guðmundr's rival from Hörgárdalur. *Guðmundar saga dýra* implies that this arrangement was not Guðmundr's choice, which might be the author's way of excusing his killing of Þorfinnr in the *Önundarbrenna* of 1197. Ingibjörg then had a second husband, Hallr Kleppjárnsson of Hrafnagil, presumably chosen by Guðmundr, a relationship whose meaning ended in 1212, the year when Guðmundr died and Hallr was killed;[147] Ingibjörg did have a son and the little we know about him links him

---

141 SS I: 60, 122. Ásgrímr Þorvaldsson (d.1178) is given the same epithet in an annal but *Sturlunga saga* says nothing about him (IA 118).
142 SS I: 163, 177.
143 Söxólfr (SS I: 182, 187); Ormr *prestr* at Urðir (SS I: 196); Brandr and Klængr Eyjólfsson and other sons of Arnþrúðr Fornadóttir at Vellir and Sakka (SS I: 139, 199, 210, 272). Their sister may have been the Halldóra Eyjólfsson, abbess at Kirkjubær in the south-east, 1189–1210 (SS I: 140; IA 120, 123, 180, 182). Eyjólfr, Brandr's son, was abbot of Munkaþverá, 1254–93. See below for the Arnþrúðarsynir opposing Guðmundr *dýri*, pp. 127.
144 Söxólfr Fornason married Þórdís Daðadóttir; Signý Guðmundardóttir married Brandr Daðason (SS I: 177).
145 SS I: 139–40, 152; IA 22, 61, 118, 121 (Gizurr's death), 180, 181, 323, 324.
146 SS I: 60, 86, 94, 130, 139, 146, 152, 161,163, 229; II: 237.
147 SS I: 178, 191. See p. 135 for Hallr's killing.

to Skagafjörður.[148] What Guðmundr had planned for his son Þorvaldr is not clear because we do not know the identity of Þorvaldr's wife. Þorvaldr had two sons, however, one of whom, Geirr *auðgi*, was associated with Silfrastaðir in Skagafjörður and swore the oath to the king in 1262, confirming the sense that this family's interests had shifted to Skagafjörður.[149]

The line of Guðmundr *dýri*'s brother, Ásgrímr Þorvaldsson, is more obscure but it too eventually became based in Skagafjörður. Ásgrímr had one recorded child, Þorvarðr *auðgi* (d.1186), who, like his uncle, married into a significant family from the south (the Vallverjar). In this case the match was important enough for Þórðr Sturluson to marry Þorvarðr's widow, marriage which we are explicitly told brought Þórðr great wealth.[150] Þorvarðr's only recorded child, a daughter, however, married the aforementioned, locally-based Norwegian Kálfr Guttormsson. In this instance *Guðmundar saga dýra* is clear that Guðmundr arranged the marriage and that Kálfr was newly-arrived in Iceland, no doubt under the *aegis* of Guðmundr.[151] Kálfr and his descendants are quite soon associated only with Skagafjörður; he himself moved out of Eyjafjörður after he killed Hallr Kleppjárnsson of Hrafnagil in 1212. He and his son Guttormr were killed at home at Miklabær in Skagafjörður in 1234 by the party of Kolbeinn *ungi* and Órækja Snorrason because of Kálfr's association with Sighvatr Sturluson. Kálfr's only other recorded child is a daughter, Jórunn, who married Brandr Kolbeinsson, a blood relative of Kolbeinn *ungi* killed at the Battle of Haugsnes in 1246.[152] Her sons were the other two of the three Skagfirðingar who swore the oath to the king in 1262; one of them (Kálfr, born c.1240) married a daughter of Sturla Þórðarson, but we know almost nothing about them by now.[153] Thus in this case an elite family, such as we can see it here, retains its elite status but shifts out of Eyjafjörður entirely as a result of that killing in 1212.

Also significant is the family of Þorgeirr Hallason (d.1169) and his son the aformentioned Þorvarðr Þorgeirsson, men who held secular influence but notably supporters of the church.[154] A genealogy and potted account of Þorgeirr's

---

148　Ingibjörg had sons with Hallr one of whom, Kleppjárn, appears to have been associated with Skagafjörður and died at Haugsnes in 1246 (SS I: 257, 337, 338, 369; II: 79).

149　SS I: 497, 499, 501; II: 181, 196, 281. Geirr was still alive in the 1280s and also later at Langahlíð, and so back in Hörgárdalur like his distant forebears but not in Eyjafjörður (SS II: 385; *Biskupa sögur* I: 774). See above pp. 64, 65 on Þorvaldr and *goðorð*.

150　SS I: 232.

151　SS I: 194, 205. There are few men called Guttormr or Kálfr recorded in *Sturlunga saga* and some can be seen to have non-Icelandic connections (SS II: 394, 413). For general issues of Norwegians in Iceland see, for example, Callow 2004 and Sverrir Jakobsson 2007.

152　SS II: 68–83, esp. 81; deaths of Kálfr and Guttormr: SS I: 368–70.

153　SS I: 483, 493, 525–27; II: 279, 281.

154　See above pp. 66–67 for the *Ljósvetningagoðorð*.

children acts as the framework for *Prestssaga Guðmundar góða*.[155] His own extra-regional marriage – his wife was from Reykhólar in Breiðafjörður – confirms the impression we get from elsewhere that he was an important figure in Iceland.

Þorgeirr is also credited with ten children, five sons and five daughters. Only three of the sons have recorded partners. Two had wives: Þorvarðr married a Herdís Sighvatsdóttir (background unknown) and Ingimundr *prestr* married the daughter of Tumi Kolbeinsson of the Ásbirningar. A third son had children with a woman whose descent was also traced to the Reykhólamenn in Dalir: these two were the parents of Bishop Guðmundr Arason.[156] A fourth son, Þórðr *munkr* (monk) Þorgeirsson, seems to have been just that, dying without children at Munkaþverá. Of Þorgeirr's daughters, in order of decreasing consequence or traceability: one married locally to someone from Langahlíð (now called Skriða, Hörgárdalur) before marrying Hvamm-Sturla; another married Grímr *þingaprestr* Snorrason at Hof in Skagafjörður; the third married a man from Hólar in Eyjafjörður; the fourth someone from Fnjóskadalur (at Víðivellir then Háls); and the last to someone whose origin is unknown.[157] What this amounts to is two marriages to powerful families (to Hvamm-Sturla, to Sigríðr Tumadóttir), a third to a more middling family (Grímr of Hof), while all other connections are to spouses living at locally-important farms but not necessarily people with any influence or wealth. This really does seem to suggest a patriarch or family which had relatively small secular political ambitions, fitting well with the pattern whereby some members of the elite eschewed secular politics.[158]

The marriages of Þorgeirr Hallason's grandchildren, i.e. Þorvarðr's children, are also worthy of attention. Taken at face value it might seem that Þorvarðr's having eight daughters and just a single son would have helped him create a rather particular form of social network, enabling lots of connections with his male peers. As it turns out, it looks as if he married his oldest and legitimate children into families of most consequence while his later children, including his one son, Ögmundr *sneis*, married people who lived further away from Eyjafjörður but were of lesser social status. The geneaology at the beginning of *Prestssaga Guðmundar góða* lists his children in such a way as to suggest this.[159] Thus his legitimate daughters married: Þorgeirr (Skagafjörður, d.1186), the son

---

155   For most of what follows see SS I: 116–18.
156   SS I: 118, 120, 143.
157   Further references to the husbands: Grímr Snorrason, SS I: 134, 165, 169, 173, 184; Brandr Tjörvason, SS I: 123.
158   Orri Vésteinsson 2000: 238–40.
159   SS I: 117 also for Þorvarðr's children's marriages.

of Bishop Brandr Sæmundsson;[160] Kolbeinn Tumason (Skagafjörður, d.1208) who opposed Bishop Guðmundr Arason;[161] Klængr Kleppjárnsson (Hrafnagil, d.1219);[162] Þórðr *prestr* Önundarson (probably Möðruvellir, Hörgárdalur);[163] and a Brandr Knakansson (Fnjóskadalur).[164] His illegitimate daughters married, respectively, someone from Breiðabólstaðr (Vestrhóp), a deacon from distant Vopnafjörður in the far north-east, and the daughter he fathered in old age married an Eldjárn in Fljótsdalsherað in the east.[165] Ögmundr, listed penultimately, married a Sigríðr Eldjárnsdóttir from Espihóll (Eyjafjörður). Given that Ögmundr ultimately fled the north for the Eastern Quarter, it is possible that the two 'Eldjárns' identified here are the same person or related people from the east. Either way, Ögmundr did not marry anyone of consequence although, in the absence of other evidence, we must assume his marriage created some kind of tie to the household at Espihóll.[166] What is also noticeable here is the importance of Skagafjörður connections and the continued ties to Hörgárdalur and the western side of Eyjafjörður. Þorvarðr's children's marriages, of which the earliest ones certainly took place during his lifetime, are probably further evidence of his own lesser political importance relative to his father's. As we shall see, this fits with the fact that two of his most powerful son-in-laws (Kolbeinn and Klængr) seemingly acted against his interests.[167]

Last, but not necessarily least, we might consider the line of men associated with Grenjaðarstaðir in Reykjadalur, the only elite family to the east of Eyjafjörður we can say anything much about. Given this, it is striking that they seem so notable for Iceland as a whole.[168] Twice in *Sturlunga saga* a male line is listed (starting here with the most distant in time, rather than as in the text), each of them being lawspeakers: Gunnarr, his son Úlfheðinn and then his son,

---

160   SS I: 125. The marriage took place in 1179. Þorgeirr left Iceland with Ingimundr *prestr* and so seems to have been an active ally of Þorvarðr's, dying abroad in 1186 (SS I: 134).
161   SS I: 238.
162   SS I: 165, 166. Klængr and his father are said to have decieved Þorvarðr in selling on the farm of Helgastaðir in Reykjadalur in the *Helgastaðamál*. See below pp. 83, 133.
163   SS I: 195 where he is named; he did not take part in raiding led by his brother-in-law Þorgrímr *alikarl* in *Guðmundar saga dýra*. See below pp. 130.
164   SS I: 178, 179 is probably the same Brandr as identified at SS I: 117.
165   Of these husbands only Hjálmr Ásbjarnarson can be seen as politically active in *Sturlunga saga* (SS I: 152, 163, 211).
166   See below p. 133 for the political implications. There is an Eldjárn *prestr* Steingrímsson in Kálfr Guttormsson's party when Kálfr goes to kill Hallr Kleppjárnsson in 1212. This Eldjárn is identifiable as one of the Ásbirningar and the dates suggest no connection to Ögmundr unless he married late in life.
167   See pp. 81, 130, 131.
168   See above p. 53 on Grenjaðarstaðir as the farm intended for Finnbjörn Helgason by the king in the 1250s (Gunnar Karlsson 2004: 359).

Hrafn.[169] The next generation sees Hrafn's son and daughter linked to key positions in the church. Hallr Hrafnsson (d.1190) was at Grenjaðarstaðir but became abbot of Munkaþverá, having married into the Ásbirningar. Hallbera Hrafnsdóttir married Hreinn (from Gilsbakki in Borgarfjörður, d.1171) who became abbot of Þingeyrar and then of Hítardalr.[170] In other words this seems to be an elite family who, one might argue, as lawspeakers distanced themselves partly from secular political machinations and then aspired to continue doing so by embracing the church. Hallr's children might also be seen to have collectively been involved in the church while also largely remaining in the north east. As mentioned above (p.78), Eyjólfr *prestr* became abbot of Saurbær in Eyjafjörður. Neither Ísleifr nor Ásbjörn Hallsson are identified as clergy, but neither do they have children and, given what else we know, this could have been a reality rather than omission from *Sturlunga saga* or other sources. Other information about them is scrappy but points in the same direction: Ásbjörn Hallsson bought Helgastaðir (Reykjadalur) in 1187 and the property was certainly an ecclesiastical *staðr* later;[171] then in 1220 Ísleifr also tried to shelter Bishop Guðmundr at his home in Þverá in Laxárdalur.[172] Their sister married the nephew of Bishop Ketill Þorsteinsson of Hólar.[173] This line, then, most likely continued to try to keep out of contentious secular politics.[174]

The wider area of Eyjafjörður and the families selected here does suggest some shifts in roles. There seems to be a clear distinction between those families who chose to enter the church, such as the descendants of Þorgeirr Hallason, i.e. the family of Bishop Guðmundr and the family associated with Grenjaðarstaðir and those who retained an interest in secular politics. The latter, however, if based in or close to Eyjafjörður itself, married outside the valley. Some families with Eyjafjörður connections in the twelfth century seem to have gravitated more towards Skagafjörður later on. These included Þorgeirr's son, Þorvarðr. Guðmundr *dýri*'s family also seems to have been focussed as much on Skagafjörður as Eyjafjörður, perhaps not surprisingly for someone based at Bakki, midway between the two. This could be read as a result of the growing power of regional leaders based at Grund in Eyjafjörður. At the same

---

169 SS I: 56, 160.
170 There is the possibility that the Hallr *prestr* Gunnarsson of 'Möðruvellir' mentioned in Chapter 4 of *Guðmundar saga dýra* was the son of a Gunnarr who was son of Hrafn *lögsögumaðr* (SS II: 43. *ættskrá*).
171 DI II: 436–37.
172 SS I: 277. Ísleifr had been at Geldingaholt in Skagafjörður in 1199 (SS I: 209).
173 SS I: 55, 56.
174 In fact it is only Jón, Eyjólfr's son at Möðrufell, already mentioned, whom we might see as getting involved in secular politics in the thirteenth century and even then possibly not willingly (p. 139 below).

time there might have been an attraction in cultivating links with Skagafjörður because it was where the bishop was based. Such geographical shifts are certainly not visible in Dalir; the difference might be the result of a there being a greater concentration of power in each major valley in the north.

There were, however, a handful more powerful people in Eyjafjörður in the mid-thirteenth century who could claim to have ancestors who lived at or near the same major farm as themselves, such as the people of Hrafnagil.[175] What is noticeable, too, and it may reflect tensions within Eyjafjörður, is that we rarely see a marriage contracted between the families that controlled the major farms in lower Eyjafjörður. These farms are so close to one another, in many cases within sight of one another, as illustrated by this book's cover image. It might be argued that this pattern has somehow been shaped by the perceptions of Sturla Þórðarson or other authors of contemporary sagas, but it seems likely that this was a real pattern which came about because of the rivalry of those farms. This is a picture not dissimilar to that found in *Íslendingasögur*, something which needs to be borne in mind for what follows.

Overall this section has assessed the shifting patterns of familial networks and tried to determine whether or not these created geopolitical patterns. While the general pattern is superficially unsurprising – leading families tended to marry some of their children to other members of the elite in their Quarter, and some other children to families across the country – the detail suggests some differences at different times and places, the vagaries of numbers of children having an impact on politics too.

The most striking thing is simply that the Sturlungar were so pervasive as a kin group within Dalir itself. Their connections in this small area were to almost every large farm in almost every generation. While one might argue that this is the product of our sources, we might still expect to be able to identify other powerful families within Dalir, however 'family' is defined. This is not to suggest that other well-off people in Dalir were not producing children and marrying them off, but instead that they must have moved down a rung in the social ladder. The connections of the Sturlungar themselves suggest that they retained a strategy which saw them strike a balance between local connections and broader connections, especially in the north and south. Thinking about this in terms of the history of our two regions in the twelfth and thirteenth centuries, it would seem that the geographically smaller region, Dalir, could be increasingly controlled by a particularly astute or charismatic family. This was most likely due to both their own desire for local power but the keenness of other wealthier *bændr* to ally with them.

---

175   Guðmundr of Hrafnagil who was invited to the wedding of Gizurr Þorvaldsson in 1253 may have been a descendant of Kleppjárn Klængsson (and his son Hallr Kleppjárnsson) (SS I: 482).

CHAPTER 3

Patterns of Power c.1100–c.1265

The narrative texts cover the period c.1100-c.1265 in different ways, going from regional-focussed texts to Iceland-wide ones, but it is possible to write about intra-regional politics in Dalir and Eyjafjörður across this whole time frame. Despite the obvious signs of a far greater degree of political centralization after c.1200, and the increasing signs of the Norwegian king's influence, political power in Iceland was still weak. For this reason the narratives still show major leaders who need to operate at both a local level, as well as a region- or island-wide level, such as in the mobilization of forces in conflicts or during the settlement of disputes. Major events, such as the battle of Örlygsstaðir in 1238, had a direct impact on aspects of politics within regions, in particular Breiðafjörður and in the north-east. In 1238, for example, not only did the deaths of the father and son Sighvatr Sturluson and Sturla Sighvatsson, leaders in Eyjafjörður and Dalir respectively, affect regional politics, but even the listing of those who died serves to show the districts from which Sighvatr and Sturla drew their support. The same is indirectly the case for accounts of political action outside a given region. Contemporary sagas tell us who supported regional leaders in countrywide politics, and thus provide an image of political affiliations and geopolitics within a region. This will enable us to address how and why subtle changes in political power occurred in each region in the thirteenth century up to the point at which narrative coverage ceases. That said, the extent to which we can examine change over the longer term is shaped by the surviving narratives which is why for the period before c.1150 we can only look at western Iceland. The reader is again referred to the maps and figures to get a sense of the locations being discussed.

1 The Early Twelfth Century in Dalir: Local Leaders and Political Networks in *Þorgils saga ok Hafliða*[1]

Þorgils saga ok Hafliða is an important text in that it is the sole glimpse we have of regional politics anywhere in Iceland before c.1150. It centres on the conflict between Þorgils Oddason of Staðarhóll in Saurbær and Hafliði Másson of Breiðabólstaðr in Vestrhóp in the Northern Quarter, and covers just four years,

---

[1] See the Appendix, pp. 319–20 for the literary background to the saga.

1117–21. Hafliði Másson appears to have been a significant figure within Iceland: he is identified in Ari Þorgilsson's near-contemporary *Íslendingabók* as playing host at Breiðabólstaðr to a group of men who compiled a new set of laws for Iceland.[2] A literal reading of the saga would suggest that its main dispute represented an outbreak of unprecedented social unrest within Iceland although such a view is hard to substantiate given the lack of other accounts of the early twelfth century. In terms of wider debates about political change, *Þorgils saga ok Hafliða* suggests that some local leaders in the early twelfth century probably had influence over a considerable area, in this case either side of the border of the Western and Northern Quarters. The saga is too brief to be analysed in the same way as those covering later decades but it still presents some credible geopolitical patterns for Dalir in this period.

While we have already seen how leaders tried to construct marriage alliances, *Þorgils saga ok Hafliða* has more to tell us, partly because of its status as the only part of *Sturlunga saga* covering such an early period. The text might have undergone various reshapings to fit into the wider story that the compilers of *Sturlunga saga* wished to write but it still gives a potentially credible account of political realities. We will look at the kinship and other social networks of its two main protagonists to see what this says about the positions of those protagonists and political power before looking at the geopolitics in more detail.

The first thing to note is that there appears to have been a real significance to blood and marriage ties in shaping the conflict between Þorgils and Hafliði. The bigger picture is that during the course of their dispute, and especially in their final confrontation at the Alþing, both men drew on the support of high-profile kinsmen. Þorgils had the support of various kinsmen by marriage: Styrmir Hreinsson of Gilsbakki (Borgarfjörður), the future lawspeaker Guðmundr Þorgeirsson (geographical origin unknown), and Þorsteinn Gellisson of Fróðá (Snæfellsnes).[3] Hafliði was on good terms with Finnr Hallsson (Hofteigr in the east), his niece's husband and another future lawspeaker,[4] and he used Hallr Teitsson, an ally of the Haukdælir, for advice and support in the saga's final conflict.[5] Such widely dispersed support networks serve to confirm the importance of the dispute and of the key pair of actors.

At a regional level, Þorgils and Hafliði seem to have had or created kinship ties which had the potential to antagonise one another. There was the likely

---

2   ÍF I: 23
3   SS I: 45, 49; IA 112, 113, 320, 321, 473; Jón Viðar Sigurðsson 1989: 108. Guðmundr's geographical affiliations are unclear but he is identified as the lawspeaker for 1123–34.
4   SS I: 29. Hafliði sends an outlaw to him.
5   SS I: 38.

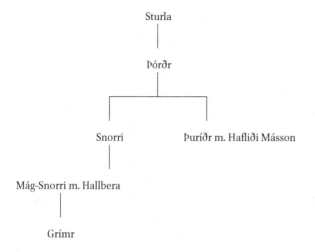

FIGURE 19   Genealogy of Þuríðr Þórðardóttir, wife of Hafliði Másson

geopolitical motive behind Þorgils' marriage to a woman from Ásgeirsá in Víðidalur (Kolfinna).[6] This tie linked Þorgils to an important farm in central Víðidalur, one of the closest larger farms to Hafliði's home in Vestrhóp. That Þorgils' father-in-law is recorded as his supporter would seem to confirm what the map suggests: Þorgils or his father are likely to have been in cahoots with Kolfinna's father in challenging Hafliði in his home district.[7] On the other side of the equation, Hafliði's familial connections suggest he had a strong interest in the Western Quarter, even if those connections are not actively drawn upon in the saga. He and two of his daughters married people from the west.[8] His wife was a granddaughter of Snorri *goði* while two of his own daughters married men in the west: Sigríðr Hafliðadóttir is said to have married into the Vatnsfirðingar (in Ísafjörður)[9] and, according to *Sturlu saga*, Jórunn Hafliðadóttir married Brandr Gellisson (Helgafell).[10]

A further piece of genealogy is recorded for Hafliði's wife, Þuríðr, in Chapter 8 of *Þorgils saga ok Hafliða* (Figure 19).[11] It serves to connect not only Hafliði's family but also that of the Sturlungar to the supposed founder of Staðarhóll,

---

6   SS I: 13, 63.
7   SS I: 49. Kolfinna's father was Hallr Styrmisson.
8   SS I: 12. *Þorgils saga ok Hafliða* only traces Hafliði back to a northern colonist, Ævarr, via a single line of male ancestors back who settled in Langidalr. This genealogy is very similar to that in *Sturlubók* (ÍF I: 224).
9   SS I: 12, 55, 103.
10 SS I: 10.
11 On genealogical charters see below pp. 147–52.

Sturla Þjóðreksson.[12] Here Þuríðr is identified as the granddaughter of Sturla Þjóðreksson, a connection which links her to Þorgils Oddason's farm.[13]

For the sake of the dispute which follows, it is also significant that Þuríðr is related to the figure of Mág-Snorri: Mág-Snorri lived at Múli in Saurbær and, after Þorgils had bought Múli, a dispute led to Mág-Snorri and son seeking Hafliði's support.[14] If this genealogy is a real one then the presence of Hafliði's kinsmen (by marriage) at Múli was another possible source of tension between Þorgils and Hafliði.

The genealogy above is, however, all that *Þorgils saga ok Hafliða* itself says about familial connections recorded within Dalir and the areas closest to it but provides a reason for the tensions between Þorgils and Hafliði by means of their each having the other's kin living close to them. One might question the veracity of these genealogies for the early twelfth century, on the grounds that they had long been shaped by social memory, but they might equally explain why the dispute between Þorgils and Hafliði was so bitter.

Beyond *Þorgils saga ok Hafliða*, *Sturlu saga* expands our picture of Þorgils Oddason's social network via the marriages he had apparently arranged for his seven daughters. Four daughters married outside Dalir, three within. The four who married outside the immediate area are said to have married: Snorri Kálfsson from Melr in Miðfjörður (only just to the east of Dalir); Örnólfr Kollason from Ísafjörður in the West Fjords; Þórhallr Finnsson from Fljótsdalsheráð (east); and Gunnsteinn Þórisson from Einarsstaðir in Reykjadalur (north-east). All four husbands were from elite families and lived at wealthy farms while three of them can be seen to actively support Þorgils' son Einarr.[15] In fact Þórhallr Finnsson's alleged housing of an outlaw sent to him by Einarr parallels his father Finnr's support of Þorgils. The point is that Þorgils can be seen to have guaranteed his sons a countrywide network of political alliances.[16]

---

12 SS I: 12, 20.
13 SS I: 52.
14 Not only are Þuríðr and Hallbera's male ancestors given the (albeit common) names of many of the thirteenth-century Sturlungar but the section in *S* where the same connection is made seems designed specifically to trace descendants of Snorri *goði*, with whom the Sturlungar wanted to be associated (Helgi Þorláksson 1992a).
15 For Gunnsteinn Þórisson, SS I: 75; Snorri Kálfsson, SS I: 74, 86; Þórhallr Finnsson, SS I: 67. Örnólfr Kollason is only referred to here which may be because his wife died relatively young, severing his connection with Einarr (SS I: 68).
16 It would seem that Snorri Kálfsson, who lived closest, is the only one of his sisters' husbands whom Einarr Þorgilsson called upon outside of the Alþing.

Þorgils' remaining three daughters married men who undoubtedly lived near Saurbær but whose homes are not properly identifiable. Two of these men were supporters of Einarr Þorgilsson and probably farmers of local significance in Saurbær.[17] The third, Böðvarr Barkarson, seems to have ended his days living at Sælingsdalstunga, having at one stage owned Hvammr.[18] Böðvarr and Einarr Þorgilsson then seemingly lived at Sælingsdalstunga simultaneously.[19]

Þorgils appears to have had only two sons, Oddi and Einarr. Oddi is said to have been fostered in the south of Iceland by the Oddaverjar, while Einarr was fostered at Brunná in Saurbær itself.[20] These arrangements mirror the pattern of local and broader connections seen in the matches of Þorgils' daughters. Þorgils' sons, however, seem to have been unsuccessful in producing children. Oddi died young and without children, something the saga regards as a tragedy.[21] While Einarr died in old age he also apparently died without children; it was his sisters who became his heirs rather than any sons.[22] As will be demonstrated below, Einarr's lack of sons, in effect, prevented his local pre-eminence from being handed on to any of his blood relations.

The marriages above confirm the impression that, like other members of Iceland's elite, Þorgils constructed a power base on two levels, one local and one countrywide. The local farms with which he can be seen to have created ties (Hvoll, Fagradalr, Hvammr or Sælingsdalstunga; see Map 2) were, as with the farms with which *þingmenn* are associated in the same texts, in the wealthiest tier of local farms. Geographically speaking, these new ties added to those districts close to Saurbær with which it can be demonstrated that he already had ties, i.e. Reykjanes and, less certainly, Skarðsströnd. Elsewhere we shall see that his kinsmen on his mother's side lived at large farms at Hjarðarholt

---

17   SS 1: 69. Halldórr Bergsson and Yngvildr Þorgilsdóttir split up and he left Iceland to go on pilgrimage never to return. Halldórr *slakkafótr* Þórarinsson, who married Guðrún Þorgilsdóttir, lived in 'Fagradalr'; their daughter married Jón Þorgilsson from Hvoll in Saurbær. It is unclear which farm in Fagradalr this was.

18   SS 1: 65, 68. Böðvarr had previously bought Hvammr, only to have to sell it to Hvamm-Sturla, no doubt under duress, when it was claimed that Böðvarr had assisted in a killing.

19   This is implied by the fact that Böðvarr moved to Sælingsdalstunga when he sold Hvammr but before Einarr moved to Staðarhóll (SS 1: 68). In all probability Böðvarr owned a share in Sælingsdalstunga. He seems to have not controlled the whole estate because both Yngvildr and Einarr Helgason are credited with shares in it at different points (SS 1: 72, 76).

20   SS 1: 63.

21   SS 1: 68.

22   SS 1: 230. *Ættartölur*, Chapter 6, does identify a daughter of Einarr as marrying Þorvaldr *Vatnsfirðingr*, but the sagas do not identify any children (SS 1: 55).

(Guðmundr Brandsson) and Fróðá (Þorsteinn Gellisson).[23] Thus we are left with the impression that Þorgils (and his son Einarr) could claim close kinship ties with many wealthy farmers in northern Dalir with the notable exception of the soon-to-emerge Sturlungar.

Overall, the various elements of Þorgils' kinship network appear credible. The connections which he can be viewed as creating, his daughters' marriages, suggest a strategy to bolster his and his daughters' status. Those connections through Þorgils' maternal line support the idea that he was part of an elite family which had extensive wealth and influence in the mid-west, although not to the same extent as we have seen that the Sturlungar were to manage in the thirteenth century.[24] There might be a territorial implication to these ties as well. Certainly the idea that Fróðá, a wealthy farm distant from the farms of later leaders Þórðr Gilsson and Hvamm-Sturla (Staðarfell and Hvammr) should have supported Þorgils makes sense. Guðmundr Brandsson at Hjarðarholt, a farm roughly midway between Saurbær and Vestrhóp, is said to have been Hafliði's friend meaning that he had ties to both parties. Nevertheless, perhaps it was the fading power of Þorgils and his son Einarr and the growing influence of the Sturlungar, that means that just a single son of Guðmundr Brandsson is recorded[25] and no descendants of Þorsteinn Gellisson at all.

The limited view we have of the operation of *goðorð* in *Þorgils saga ok Hafliða* gives a different perspective from the genealogical material. Hafliði Másson and Þorgils Oddason are visible as *goðar* with *þingmenn*[26] and as noted above, Þorgils is said to have been given the *Reyknesingagoðorð* by his kinsman Ingimundr *prestr* of Reykhólar.[27] Hafliði's *goðorð* is not identified by name but it is usually assumed that he held the *Eyvellingagoðorð* from the Northern Quarter which was later supposedly given to Snorri Sturluson.[28] The history of this *goðorð* is even more obscure than for most, however. It is not identified in connection with Hafliði in *Sturlunga saga* but it could still be the same *goðorð* given to Snorri Sturluson (by an otherwise unknown Þorsteinn Ívarsson) which, in connection with events in 1232, is called *Hafliðanautr* (Hafliði's possession or gift).[29] It is also difficult to say exactly when Snorri Sturluson was

---

23   SS I: 13, 49.
24   The genealogy of Þorgils' maternal kin, the Reyknesingar or Reykhyltingar (SS II, 21. Ættskrá), is misleading. This genealogy is a compilation of the genealogies of individuals or groups which are only recorded in certain sagas; these are never recorded together. And, while *Þorgils saga ok Hafliða* only mentions Guðmundr and Þorsteinn, there is no way of knowing if these connections are fictional.
25   SS I: 234.
26   SS I: 12, 14.
27   SS I: 13, 23. See above p. 60.
28   SS I: 243.
29   SS I: 359; Jón Viðar Sigurðarsson 1989: 51, 52, 54; 1999: 40, 61, 114.

first given the *goðorð* because this statement comes in a very brief chapter of *Íslendinga saga* (Chapter 18). One thing that is clear, however, is that the *goðorð* was considered to have had a geographically-limited sphere of influence in the early thirteenth century, at least to its east, when Kolbeinn Tumason is said to have held all the *goðorð* to the east of the *Eyvellingagoðorð*, up to Öxnadalsheiði in Skagafjörður[30] (in other words, most of the *goðorð* of the Northern Quarter). While this serves as a rough indication of the area within which Snorri had *þingmenn* it is not necessarily a good guide to any territorial divisions in the early twelfth century.

As with most other sagas, *Þorgils saga ok Hafliða* is concerned primarily with the conflict between *goðar*, and so it can also be supposed to show where the interests of *goðar* collide. In this case it would seem to be in fairly distant Strandir, the east-facing coast renowned for its good driftage (*reki*). While Hafliði had a *þingmaðr* based relatively far north on this coast, we are also told that Þorgils Oddason was used to making trips out to Strandir, hinting that Þorgils was a likely alternative advocate to Hafliði on Strandir. The text also suggests that, at one point, Þorgils was able to acquire supporters along Strandir when one of them was mistreated by Hafliði. On terms very favourable to himself, Þorgils agreed to take up the case of the wife of Hafliði's *þingmaðr* (Hneitir from Ávík) after associates of Hafliði had had this *þingmaðr* killed.[31] It is difficult to gauge the relative support of the two leaders in Strandir. Perhaps Hafliði had more influence there than Þorgils or any other leader there but did not have a monopoly of power.

Beyond the Strandir case, the only *þingmaðr* identified in the saga is one of Þorgils' who lived at Skálmarnesmúli on Barðaströnd (Map 1).[32] Together with the Strandir example it would appear that notable *þingmenn* lived at some distance from the *goðar*. Indeed the remoteness of the two *þingmenn* from their *goðar* might explain why the label *þingmaðr* was used by the writer. Barðaströnd and Strandir most likely were areas from which the saga's audience would not have expected Þorgils or Hafliði to have drawn support but, rather, were on the fringes of their spheres of influence. This begs the question of the nature of the allegiances of *bændr* closer to each respective *goði*. Was the saga author assuming that all *bændr* living closer to particular *goðar* were by default the *þingmenn* of their closest *goði*? Did it simply mean that one had a local lord, by geographical accident, or did it suppose, as *Grágás* does, a more active, symbiotic relationship between the *goði* and *þingmaðr*? The brevity of *Þorgils*

---

30   SS I: 243.
31   SS I: 19.
32   SS I: 14.

saga ok Hafliða makes this question difficult to answer for the early twelfth century but it would seem most likely that each leader's influence was strongest close to where they lived but extended into quite distant districts, the latter perhaps especially in order to control resources in remote locations. Better answers can be gleaned for Dalir from *Sturlu saga*.

2   Goðar and þingmenn in Sturlu saga[33]

Even a cursory reading of *Sturlu saga* shows that support networks are not depicted as simply based on local leaders' relationships with people identified as *þingmenn*. The text identifies nine men as *þingmenn*, very few if we assume that most of the 300 or more farms in Dalir could have each been home to one or more potential *þingmenn*, but a large number compared to many sagas, both *Íslendingasögur* or contemporary sagas. The allegiance of *bændr* at some quite large farms, such as Einarr's some-time opponents at Hvoll in Saurbær, are not made clear. But those nine whose allegiance is identified were tied to the three local *goðar*. These are: Skeggi from Skarfsstaðir (identified as *þingmaðr* of first Þórðr Gilsson and then Hvamm-Sturla), Börkr Kálfsson of Gunnarsstaðir (*þingmaðr* of Sturla), Sigurðr *kerlingarnef* from Laugar, Erlendr *prestr* Hallason from Ásgarðr, Ketill the father of Þorleifr at Ásgarðr, Þorvaldr and his son Kjartan (all *þingmenn* of Einarr Þorgilsson), Tanni from Galtardalstunga and Þórhallr Svartsson of Hólmslátr (*þingmenn* of Þorleifr *beiskaldi*). The association between most of the named *þingmenn* with the farms they lived at immediately suggests a reason for the text choosing to identify them as such. Just as in *Þorgils saga ok Hafliða*, in each case, with the possible exceptions of Skeggi, Þorvaldr and Kjartan, these men live a relatively long distance from their *goðar*.

The significance of the references to *þingmenn* in *Sturlu saga* would therefore again seem to be that they refer to areas where the reader might *not* expect a *goði* to have active support. In other words, the text might be assuming that each *goði* has almost complete adherence from the area closest to his own residence. There is an obvious argument against this in that it is easy to see how narratives of dispute in which *goðar* were called to act on certain individuals' behalf required them to be given them the tag *þingmaðr*. This provides the local leader with a motive for intervening. But at the same time, it can be

---

[33]   Cf. Gunnar Karlsson 1972, 1975a; Jón Viðar Sigurðsson 1989: 23–40; Orri Vésteinsson 2007a.

countered, these cases are being highlighted because they represent those disputes which were unusual because they involved the political status of local leaders changing, or being challenged, and take place away from their home territories. If this is the assumption of the writer of *Sturlu saga* then we can make further suggestions about the territorial control of Dalir in the late twelfth century.

The 'hypothesis of challenge' works best in relation to the disputes which bring Þorleifr *beiskaldi* into conflict with Hvamm-Sturla. Tanni's farm of Galtardalstunga most certainly lay outside the expected orbit of a leader based, as Þorleifr was, at Hítardalr. In this case Tanni is identified as a kinsman of Þorleifr.[34] No other *þingmaðr* is identified as being a kinsman of their *goði* or living so far away from him. Tanni is therefore exceptional even among this scattered group of nine *þingmen*.

The other dispute, which becomes a legal conflict between Þorleifr *beiskaldi* and Sturla, is that concerning the ownership of Gunnarsstaðir on Skógarströnd. In this case it might also be argued that the text's assertion that, of the rivals, Þórhallr (of Hólmslátr) was a *þingmaðr* of Þorleifr *beiskaldi* and Börkr (Gunnarsstaðir) a *þingmaðr* of Sturla was a narrative device created by the need to explain a conflict. This case is similar to that we have seen for Strandir in *Þorgils saga ok Hafliða*. Skógarströnd was between districts dominated respectively, to the north by Hvamm-Sturla, and to the south by Þorleifr *beiskaldi*.

In this context we must also consider the possibility of other local advocates or politicians. Support networks need not have existed only at the level of the *goðar* and we have every reason to believe that in the latter half of the twelfth century there were well-off farmers in Miðdalir and Laxárdalur who might have had more political clout than others. In *Þorgils saga ok Hafliða*, Hjarðarholt has already been mentioned as homes of someone of regional significance. Sauðafell only became the base of Sturla Sighvatsson in the thirteenth century but this farm, too, was most likely wealthy or locally significant before his father had bought it (Figure 5).[35] These three farms may have provided their late twelfth-century occupants with the resources and connections to support the likes of Börkr against someone like Þórhallr. In *Sturlu saga* Börkr does not turn to anyone more local than Hvamm-Sturla, which might indicate a significant step in Hvamm-Sturla's political ascent.

---

34   SS I: 95.
35   Cf. Helgi Þorláksson 1991a.

The other instances where the text uses *þingmaðr* can be used to shed light on the *goði-þingmaðr* relationship and the nature of political power. In the light of the argument above concerning the term's use, the identification of Skeggi from Skarfsstaðir as a *þingmaðr* of Þórðr Gilsson (and of his son Sturla) in the early part of *Sturlu saga* does not seem to make as much sense as it does elsewhere, because Staðarfell, Þórðr's farm, is relatively close to Skarfsstaðir, less than 20 kilometres away (Figure 6, Map 7). But, while this is a relatively short distance between a *goði* and a *þingmaðr* compared to those discussed so far, Skarfsstaðir is far closer to Hvammr (just five kilometres away) than to Staðarfell. Hvammr, like Sauðafell, must have been wealthy and/or strategically important for Hvamm-Sturla to want to buy it. Its owner before Sturla, Böðvarr Barkarson, was at least powerful enough to be in a position to marry Einarr Þorgilsson's sister Ingibjörg. The farm more than likely had a church by this stage too. If it is supposed that Hvammr had any kind of pre-eminence within Hvammssveit before Hvamm-Sturla moved there,[36] then it would have been more striking if Þórðr Gilsson had had a strong influence over Skarfsstaðir. That is not to say that Þórðr's influence in Hvammssveit was at the expense of another *goði* – there is no evidence to suggest that the people who lived at Hvammr before Hvamm-Sturla were *goðar* – but elsewhere the text does suggest that Hvammr's estate had recently been mismanaged, something which may have allowed Þórðr to bully its occupants.[37] If this set of suppositions is correct then Þórðr Gilsson's possession of a *þingmaðr* at Skarfsstaðir probably caused political tension, and may represent the breaking down of an earlier *de facto* local territorial division.

Indeed Sturla's move into Hvammssveit, with his purchase of Hvammr itself, must have intensified the competition between *goðar* in Dalir in the mid-twelfth century. Control of Hvammssveit is contested by Sturla and Einarr Þorgilsson for a large part of *Sturlu saga*. In the context of this dispute, reference is made to two *þingmenn* belonging to Einarr, both living in Hvammssveit, Sigurðr *kerlingarnef* (Laugar) and Erlendr *prestr* Hallason (Ásgarðr).[38] The status

---

36 I.e. under the control of its previous owners, Þorkell *prestr* and Böðvarr Barkarson. Hvammr's history is recorded briefly at the end of chapter three of *Sturlu saga*. Þorkell *prestr* owned it first before his two sons let the farm deteriorate and then sold it to Böðvarr Barkarson (SS 1: 65).

37 SS 1: 65.

38 Ketill whose son was a *húskarl* at Ásgarðr is not said to have been living at that farm himself. It would not necessarily have been the case that Ketill lived at the same farm. No comment is warranted about Ketill and son except to note that clearly Ásgarðr housed more than one active supporter of Einarr (SS 1: 82).

of these two men would appear to have been different. Sigurðr lived at a relatively small farm and was married to the daughter of a peripatetic labourer;[39] Erlendr was a priest and living at a larger farm. Sigurðr is only mentioned in one episode, when Einarr Helgason, Hvamm-Sturla's stepson, makes an unwanted visit to Laugar in order to chat to Sigurðr's wife.[40] The upshot of incident is that Einarr Helgason struck Sigurðr with his axe and *goði* Einarr Þorgilsson, who was visiting Ásgarðr, made an attempt to get Sigurðr redress. Erlendr *prestr*, however, can be seen taking a more active role in supporting Einarr Þorgilsson in Hvammssveit; Einarr stays at Ásgarðr at regular intervals. Another statement in this episode, however, suggests that Einarr Þorgilsson expected some support in Hvammssveit, which goes beyond these two dependants. This is possibly because when his father had been alive, about a decade before this, he himself had lived at Sælingsdalstunga.[41] When Einarr prepared to travel to Sælingsdalstunga he tried to gather support against Einarr Helgason.[42] The implication would seem to be that Einarr Þorgilsson, however misguidedly, expected everyone in Hvammssveit to come to his aid.

In the same chapter the saga says that Einarr was keen to stop Sturla and Einarr Helgason from intimidating his *þingmenn* but gives no hint as to where these particular *þingmenn* were living or how many there were. In fact when Einarr's call for support is heard, it would seem to have been heeded by virtually no one. He has to go to Sælingsdalstunga with just eight men, a party which could easily have been made up of his own company from Saurbær or from just Ásgarðr. The text gives the impression that Einarr had been convinced that he had support in Hvammssveit which now had simply disappeared. On balance it would seem sensible to conclude that Einarr had probably not had much active support in Hvammssveit for some time and very few supporters who, in the 1170s, would publicly declare themselves as his *þingmenn*. That one of Einarr's *þingmenn* there, Erlendr *prestr*, was wealthy should not obscure the fact that Einarr Þorgilsson's power was generally weak in Hvammssveit, no doubt as a result of the change of hands of Hvammr itself. The text does point out occasions when Einarr acts strategically in Hvammssveit but these are rare and he is only successful when he has the backing of Þorleifr *beiskaldi*.

---

39   SS I: 65.
40   SS I: 79.
41   SS I: 66.
42   SS I: 79. 'Einarr Þorgilsson sendi þá Styr Gilsson at beiða *bændr*, at þeir kæmi í Ásgarð.'

One further example serves to show how Einarr was apparently oblivious to the need to manage his group of *þingmenn*, specifically to appreciate that some *þingmenn* were more politically valuable than others. Álfr Snorrason from Fagradalur (Map 5) would appear to have been at odds with Einarr when Álfr was displeased at Einarr's bullying of the heir to Búðardalr on Skarðsströnd, whom Álfr had taken in.[43] Nevertheless Álfr Snorrason would appear still to have been Einarr's *þingmaðr* in the 1170s. Álfr now asked Einarr to support him in gaining redress against a Kjartan Þorvaldsson, who had struck Álfr's son at a horse fight in Gilsfjörður. Einarr refused, however, on the grounds that he himself was better disposed to Kjartan and Kjartan's father because they were not only his *þingmenn* but also his friends (*vinir*). Unable to get any joy from his own *goði*, Álfr went to the next nearest *goði*, Sturla, for help. Sturla was successful in getting compensation paid over and, as a result, Álfr formally agreed to become Sturla's *þingmaðr* (*Ok réðst Álfr þá at þingfesti undir Sturlu.*).[44]

The episode suggests that Einarr was making a political mistake in supporting Kjartan and his father over Álfr. Although we do not know their origins, Kjartan and father were – by virtue of the fact that their origins are not stated – probably less wealthy and locally influential than Álfr. Kjartan may have come from outside Saurbær too, if we can read anything into the location of the confrontation between him and Álfr's son. In contrast, Álfr lived at a large farm with a church very close to Staðarhóll, making him a potential problem for Einarr.[45] It may be reading too much into the fine detail of the text but it may be significant that Álfr is only said to have changed *goði after* Sturla had proved himself to be a successful advocate. Álfr may have been able to fudge the issue of his allegiance for a few months as he played off the local *goðar* one against the other.

Territorially, Álfr's switch to Sturla marks Sturla's furthest encroachment towards Einarr's home at Staðarhóll and is very signficant. Einarr Þorgilsson's sphere of influence was nowhere near that which probably pertained when his father Þorgils had lived at Staðarhóll until 1151. As mentioned above, we are told that Einarr had lived at Sælingsdalstunga, and, equally significantly, his brother Oddi had lived at Skarð, despite the line of the Skarðverjar being there before and after him. What the presence of Einarr and Oddi at these locations meant in practice can only be speculated on, but it is likely that it reflected Þorgils having *þingmenn* along Skarðsströnd and in Hvammssveit, some of whom Einarr lost to Sturla.

---

43   SS I: 83.
44   SS I: 102; Byock 1988: 121.
45   Helgi Þorláksson 1983; cf. Gunnar Karlsson 1972.

More generally, then, few *goði-þingmaðr* bonds are made explicit in *Þorgils saga ok Hafliða* or *Sturlu saga* even though both texts deal with politics at the level of the individual farmstead. Where *þingmenn* are identified it would seem, in most cases, to be due to the need of the narrative to identify an abnormal political pattern, whereby a *goði* has a *þingmaðr* some distance from his home farm. We are told of very few *þingmenn* living close to their *goðar* and the simplest conclusion to draw, therefore, is that farms closest to each *goði* were run by his own *þingmenn* or else almost powerless.[46]

One final point needs to be made about the particular farms associated with named *þingmenn* in accounts of twelfth-century Dalir and relates to both the nature of the narratives and how politics seems to have worked, both here, and, actually, in Eyjafjörður as well. It is immediately noticeable that the farms of these *þingmenn* were among the most valuable in Dalir. Tjaldanes (40 hundreds), Heinaberg (30), Fagradalr (50+), Galtardalstunga (40+),[47] Skarfsstaðir (40), Ásgarðr (100), and Hólmslátr (30) were all properties of above average value for the region (and for Iceland as a whole).[48] Laugar and Gunnarsstaðir, both valued at 16 hundreds in *Jarðabók* are the exceptions to this rule, being of roughly average size. In the case of Laugar it might easily be argued that the farm was more valuable in the twelfth and thirteenth centuries, on the grounds that it was the home of locally notable people in *Laxdæla saga* and in the contemporary sagas.[49] In most cases, then, Hvamm-Sturla and Einarr Þorgilsson were only remembered as dealing directly with the *bændr* from wealthy farms. The smaller farm of Gunnarsstaðir probably mattered in the short term because it was on the geographical boundary of the areas effectively controlled

---

46 One such farm might have been Holt (modern Stóraholt), a 40 hundred farm which largely stays out of events in *Sturlunga saga* (SS I: 321, 448). Its occupants sought help from Sturla in one dispute but Sturla did nothing much to help (SS I: 80–81).

47 *Jarðabók* VI: 149–53 gives the values of Fagradalur ytri as 50 hundreds and Fagradalur innri, where there is a *hálfkirkja*, as 40 hundreds and so 80 hundreds in total. Whether the medieval farm included one or both of these early modern farms is not clear; 50 hundreds is certainly a minimum figure for the medieval estate. Galtardalstunga also had a *hálfkirkja* in *Jarðabók* and is valued at 40 hundreds there (*Jarðabók* VI: 111).

48 See generally Orri Vésteinsson 2007.

49 There also remains the possibility that Laugar was not alone in having been broken down into smaller units in the late medieval period and that, in the twelfth century, others of these large farms were larger and included land later run as separate legally-independent farms. Clear cases in point would be Sælingsdalstunga, valued at 44 hundreds in *Jarðabók*, which had had 'Sælingsdalstunga-gierde,' valued at 16 hundreds, detached from it at some unspecified point; or Vífilsdalr neðri (24 hundreds) and Vífilsdalr fremri (16 hundreds). In both examples the values of the farms sharing a name add up to a round number, which suggests their conjoined origins. There are no clear examples of neighbouring farms which had been amalgamated, however, to judge from the evidence of farm names and values in Dalir in *Jarðabók*.

by Hvamm-Sturla and Þorleifr *beiskaldi*. The fact of these larger farms being the only ones of real significance demonstrates two things: the clear signs of greater social inequality in the twelfth century than has sometimes been suggested and, as we shall see, the continued importance of this class of larger farms.

3   Dalir c.1185-c.1215

While the deaths of major Sturlungar figures over the period 1237 to 1241 was to have a very obvious impact on politics in our study regions,[50] a smaller shift is discernible after the departure of Sighvatr Sturluson to Eyjafjörður in 1215, hence the choice of time frame for the following discussion. The sons of Hvamm-Sturla were politically preeminent in the area around Hvammsfjörður, so far as we can see, as soon as Einar Þorgilsson died in the 1180s. At the same time, however, their growing influence caused them and their sons to be rivals as much as allies.

All three of the politically prominent sons of Hvamm-Sturla retained an interest in Dalir and the west, but were enemies as well as allies. Þórðr Sturluson and his sons had the largest property interests in the Hvammsfjörður area in the first decades of the thirteenth century. They controlled Hvammr, Bjarnarhöfn and Staðr (on the south coast of Snæfellsnes) as well as many other farms. Sighvatr Sturluson spent his early adulthood in the west but his move to Eyjafjörður at least shows him passing control of his Dalir properties on to his son, Sturla, who was based at Sauðafell in Miðdalir. Snorri Sturluson, the third of the *goðorð*-controlling sons of Hvamm-Sturla, took control of Borg in Mýrar and Reykholt in Borgarfjörður, living at these farms rather than in Dalir. Snorri retained a political role in the west, however, through his kinship with the Vatnsfirðingar clan in the West Fjords and the presence of his son, Órækja, in the north-west. Thus the major political conflicts which emerged in the mid-west in the 1220s and 1230s were primarily between Þórðr Sturluson and his nephew Sturla Sighvatsson because they were the wealthiest landowners based in the region. *Íslendinga saga* portrays Sturla Sighvatsson as pursuing a rather unjust expansionist policy at the expense of his kinsmen; Órækja Snorrason is likewise seen as a belligerent nuisance to Þórðr and his sons.

While the deaths of the three Sturlusynir, Þórðr (1237), Sighvatr (1238) and Snorri (1241), and the expulsion of Órækja from Iceland (1242), ushered in a new community of political leaders in the west, it did not visibly diminish the wealth or influence of Hvamm-Sturla's descendants. Þórðr Sturluson's sons,

---

50   See above pp. 50–51.

Sturla and Böðvarr, remained in control of major farms in the west. Þórðr *kakali* Sighvatsson had authority over yet larger territories in the 1240s before Þorgils *skarði*, the son of Böðvarr Þórðarson, did so in the 1250s. It is worth it is not until this later period that the intervention of the Norwegian king is apparent when the Sturlungar vied with Gizurr Þorvaldsson of the Haukdælir for primacy over Iceland. If we begin with the late twelfth century, however, we return to a smaller scale of political activity.

The single depiction of Dalir politics after the deaths of Einarr Þorgilsson and Hvamm-Sturla is a two-paragraph anecdote in *Íslendinga saga* which would seem to have taken place in the late 1180s or early 1190s. It is said that Hvamm-Sturla's sons had an illegitimate half-brother living at Staðarhóll who had sought their assistance over a killing of another one of their half-brothers.[51] Sturla's legitimate sons are depicted travelling to Saurbær from some unspecified location.[52] This gave them the opportunity to stop at the hot springs in Sælingsdalur (*til laugar*) where apparently they intended to hang a thief. Somehow, however, a man from Höskuldsstaðir in Laxárdalur (Hallr Arason) and his sons freed the thief. While Þórðr Sturluson is said to have been physically restrained and prevented from fighting, one of his supporters killed one of Hallr's men before Þórðr called them off.[53]

This brief tale would seem to imply that Hvamm-Sturla's sons were operating in a similar political world to their father. We have also seen that Sighvatr bought half of Staðarhóll at about this time. The killing there of another son of Hvamm-Sturla would suggest local hostility towards them in Saurbær; that a second son of Hvamm-Sturla lived at Staðarhóll suggests that the Sturlungar had a significant presence there but, perhaps inevitably, that it was resented. After all, Einarr Þorgilsson's nephew is said to have taken over the *staðr* and its dependents not long before.[54] Sighvatr's inability to get on with Einarr Þorgilsson's affines in Staðarhóll and Saurbær generally may well explain why he moved out of Staðarhóll within just a few years. Resistance to the Sturlungar probably remained in Saurbær but the Sturlusynir at least aspired to power there in a way which their father could not have done even if the scuffle between the Sturlusynir and the men from Höskuldsstaðir shows they could be challenged. Clearly it would be beneficial to know exactly whom it was that the Sturlusynir considered to be have been a thief and *why* they were challenged by people from Höskuldsstaðir. Certainly, whatever the precise view that Sturla

---

51   SS I: 232.
52   The Sturlusynir are said to have stayed at Hvammr with Guðný, not to have lived there. It seems most likely that some or all of them had been at Staðr, Þórðr's main estate.
53   SS I: 234.
54   SS I: 231. Precisely when this Þorgils Gunnsteinsson moved into Staðarhóll, and whether he moved out again, is not made clear.

Þórðarson or the *Sturlunga* compiler is giving us on this story, the sons of Hvamm-Sturla look to have been operating on the same scale as their father.

After this only one other noteworthy dispute within Dalir is recorded for the entire period before Sturla Sighvatsson's arrival from the Eyjafjörður. It took place in 1217, just after Sighvatr had moved to Eyjafjörður. As part of a dispute between the Víðdælir and Miðfirðingar, elite groups from Húnaþing, one Eyjólfr Kársson had Þórarinn Grímsson, the *bóndi* at Snóksdalr, the large farm in Miðdalir close to Sauðafell (Map 7), killed.[55] Þórarinn's widow turned to Þórðr Sturluson to prosecute the case because, as *Íslendinga saga* says, Sighvatr was then in the north and his sons were too young to act on her behalf. Þórðr duly prosecuted the case against the killers.[56]

From this incident alone it might be supposed that Þórðr was either acting as Sighvatr's deputy, or, perhaps that he was treading on Sighvatr's toes by representing in court people who lived right next to Sauðafell. In fact it emerges that this dispute had more significance still. The text points out two things. First, that Sighvatr was displeased by Þórðr's intervention and, second, that Sighvatr's and Þórðr's cousin, Dufgus Þorleifsson, was Sighvatr's steward at Sauðafell and that he had been on bad terms with Þórarinn, the dead man – Eyjólfr's killing of him may have had Sighvatr's implicit support. These statements thus make most sense as an expression of rivalry between these large neighbouring farms, and as a sign of further tension between the two brothers. Unfortunately what happened to Snóksdalr in the aftermath of the killing is not clear. Arguably it was Snóksdalr's likely wealth and a potentially large household that allowed it to seek out Þórðr and incur the wrath of Sighvatr.

Þórarinn Grímsson was probably not alone in his fairly active opposition to Sighvatr when he was at Sauðafell. He was married to the daughter of Brandr Þórhallsson, the *bóndi* from Fellsendi, also in Miðdalir.[57] This marriage must have represented a significant connection between these farms. And a cool relationship may also have existed between Sighvatr and Brandr Þórhallsson, possibly of long standing. This is suggested by a second, more local dispute. In this case Brandr had been at odds with one of Sighvatr's local *þingmenn*.[58] Brandr's half-brother had been killed by Sighvatr's *þingmaðr* and Brandr had killed the *þingmaðr* in revenge. Sighvatr hurriedly brokered a settlement but how satisfactorily we are not told. This account makes up chapter eight of *Íslendinga saga* and is therefore most likely to have been remembered as taking

---

55   The deacon at Snóksdalr was also killed (SS 1: 264–65).
56   SS 1: 265.
57   SS 1: 264.
58   The *þingmaðr* Þórðr Kollason was from Dalir, a 'Dalamaðr' (SS 1: 236).

place in the late 1190s.⁵⁹ If that was the case, then the connection between Brandr from Fellsendi and Þórarinn from Snóksdalr looks like a strategic reaction to the aggression of Sighvatr and his supporters. Equally, the marriage of Þórarinn to Brandr's daughter and the likely friendship between these *bændr* may have been a source of the ill-feeling which existed between Þórarinn and Sighvatr or Dufgus by 1217. Thus Þórðr's intervention on behalf of Þórarinn's widow was most likely a hostile intervention in the micropolitics of the larger farms in Miðdalir, which could only elicit a hostile reaction from Sighvatr.

This episode usefully points out the similar tensions between the largest farms in Miðdalir in the first decades of the thirteenth century as there had been in Hvammssveit in the 1160s. These linked cases highlight the continuing expectation that *goðar* would act as managers of disputes within a district and the inherent difficulties for them in doing so. In this case the basic problem was that two local *bændr*, who controlled *staðir* which were not much poorer than Sighvatr's Sauðafell, allied against Sighvatr and his (probably poorer) supporters. There is insufficient evidence to suggest that these *bændr* actually forced him to leave the district on which he had imposed himself for over a decade, but they must have made his position difficult. What may have been more significant in Sighvatr's departure was the fact that a neighbouring *goði*, his brother Þórðr, had in effect taken a hostile stance towards him by acting in court for those wealthy *bændr*. It may have been growing tension between the two brothers which led Sighvatr to try his luck elsewhere, especially when he had, in Dufgus, a kinsman to manage Sauðafell. We cannot say, however, how Dufgus and Þórðr regarded one another, which would be especially telling because Dufgus must also have managed Hjarðarholt in this period; in so doing Dufgus was running the largest farms in two adjacent districts.

A different text gives the impression that Sighvatr was losing influence to his older brother. *Hrafns saga Sveinbjarnarsonar* records that both brothers had a role as judges or arbitrators in the conflict in the West Fjords between Þorvaldr *Vatnsfirðingr* and Hrafn Sveinbjarnarson. Sighvatr is said to have been involved sometime between 1204 and 1207, while Þórðr appears twice as a mediator, in 1211 and 1214.⁶⁰ The fact that Sighvatr had a role in this conflict early on while Þórðr had a (larger) part to play some time later would seem to mirror the decline in Sighvatr's power implied by *Íslendinga saga*. Arbitrators in these kinds of high-level disputes had to be able to make stick the settlements they brought about. Being asked to act as a go-between, or not, in other people's disputes

---

59 SS I: 236.
60 With Þorvaldr Snorrason (SS I: 215, 216, 222, 223) and with Kárr *munkr* (ironically the father of the troublesome Eyjólfr Kársson from Flatey) (SS I: 227, 228).

acted as a rough measure of a *höfðingi*'s political clout.[61] More generally, though, this dispute also implies a possible political dependence of the West Fjords, whereby either the Sturlungar or *höfðingjar* from Breiðafjörður were seen to be important for resolving disputes in the West Fjords.

4 Sturla Sighvatsson and Þórðr Sturluson in Dalir

The account of politics after Sighvatr left can be best analysed in two parts. First of all it makes sense to look at those small-scale, *Íslendingasögur*-type disputes which, still, give a sense of the loyalties of *goðar* and *bændr* at the lowest scale, and of the nature of territorial control. After this we can create a picture of the loyalties of particular *bændr* who appear throughout the disputes which embroiled the Sturlungar in wider politics. By way of introduction it makes sense to look first at the earliest dispute story, that of Sturla Sighvatsson's pursuit of Aron Hjörleifsson. It gives an idea of extent of Sturlungar control, or lack of it, on Snæfellsnes just after 1220.

Sturla Sighvatsson's desire to capture and kill Aron Hjörleifsson from Bjarnarhöf stemmed from when Aron had fought against Sturla on Grímsey when Sturla's brother Tumi had been killed.[62] Sturla and Aron had also been fostered at the same farm as children and apparently not got on.[63] This may further explain why Sturla appears to have been so intent on both getting Aron outlawed for his brother's murder[64] and then trying to kill him. After the battle on Grímsey, Aron allied himself with Eyjólfr Kársson of Flatey[65] and the sons of Hrafn Sveinbjarnarson, against Sturla. Aron's movements show that he had a strong support network across Snæfellsnes. His father Hjörleifr is said to have lived at both Bjarnarhöfn and Miklaholt. Hjörleifr also had a concubine at Berserkseyrr, a farm which sheltered Aron at one point.[66] To add to this, the Hrafnssynir already counted the abbot of Helgafell at this point, Hallr Gizurarson,

---

61   actors were also important in the choice of arbitrator but to in this case, aside from their influence, Þórðr and Sighvatr must have been equally appropriate. They had similar familial connections and lived almost equidistant from the homes of the disputants. See Miller (1990: 259–67, esp. 266). Jón Loptsson (d.1197) was the archetypal powerful third party but many *höfðingjar* were asked to mediate
62   SS I: 291–93.
63   SS I: 267.
64   SS I: 305.
65   SS I: 266.
66   SS I: 307–8.

among their kinsmen by marriage.[67] Most importantly, a farm as far east as Valshamarr, on Skógarströnd was inclined towards Aron rather than Sturla; Vigfúss from Valshamarr is described as Aron's friend (*vinr*).[68] Aron was hidden by Vigfúss at Valshamarr, an offence for which Sturla prosecuted Vigfúss and was able to award himself 20 hundreds' worth of land.[69] This dispute highlights the limitation of Sturla Sighvatsson's territorial power, all the same, because Aron survived thanks to his local supporters.[70] It is unclear whether at this point Sturla Sighvatsson could rely on any notable supporters west of Miðdalir.

Subsequent disputes show a more significant role for both Sturla and Þórðr Sturluson in Dalir itself.[71] These local cases show the ineffectualness of Dufgus Þorleifsson, a kinsmen of both men, who gets involved in disputes involving particular *bændr*, especially one from Höfn on Fellsströnd, and ultimately gets the two Sturlungar *höfðingjar* involved. There is a hint that Sturla might have been able to loosen the alliance between Þórðr Sturluson and the Fellsströnd men, of whom the most significant was the occupant of Staðarfell, Guðmundr *undir Felli*.[72] In the end, however, Þórðr and Sturla arbitrated a settlement between the Fellstrendingar and Dufgus and there were no real local geopolitical changes.[73]

Several points are worth making about this dispute, one of the fullest descriptions of a highly localised conflict in *Sturlunga saga*. At its broadest level it shows how the rivalries between the wealthier farmers could play themselves out when the opportunity arose. Sturla Sighvatsson perhaps saw this dispute, wrongly as it turned out, as a chance to break up the traditional loyalty

---

67   SS I: 305. Hallr Gizurarson was abbot of Helgafell from 1221–25 (Orri Vésteinsson 2000: 154, 156).
68   SS II: 264–65.
69   SS I: 318.
70   Ironically Aron was to be a henchman of Sturla's brother, Þórðr *kakali* Sighvatsson, after Sturla's death (SS I: 473–4, 481; II: 277).
71   SS I: 311–13.
72   'svá mundu skipta trúnaði með þeim Þórði frændum sem hann gæfist nú Þorgilsi' (SS I: 313–14). The point might also have been that Guðmundr owned Bjarneyjar; Sturla Sighvatsson's widow gave away Bjarneyjar to Snorri (who gave it to Sturla Þórðarson) after Sturla's death. *Íslendinga saga* does not make it explicit that Guðmundr had owned Bjarnareyjar but it is a suggestive coincidence that *Njáls saga* identifies the owner of Staðarfell as the owner of Bjarnareyjar (Helgi Þorláksson 2001: 114).
73   They decided that the party of Þorgils Oddsson of Höfn had to pay compensation of 40 hundreds for Dufgus' injuries and a further 20 hundreds for the killing of Bjarni Árnason, half of which Þjóstarr had to pay. Þorgils was also be outlawed from Fellsströnd for a year but he was able to ignore this stipulation, living on the island Öxney (SS I: 314). Cf. p. 267 footnote 268 below for references to Öxney in other narratives.

of the *bœndr* of Fellsströnd to Þórðr Sturluson. Guðmundr *undir Felli*, grandson of Hvamm-Sturla's brother, was a key ally, as kinsman to both Þorgils Oddsson of Höfn and Þórðr himself. Sturla, however, was in a difficult situation by having supporters on both sides of the dispute and the fact that Dufgus exited Dalir alive and not outlawed – he moved to Árnessýsla – represented a good outcome for him.[74] Sturla would appear to have worked in the arbitration on behalf of Laxdárdalr more generally, because two of his stronger local supporters most likely lived there, Torfi Guðmundarson (Hjarðarholt) and Árni Auðunarson (Hornstaðir),[75] as indeed did his future supporters, Dufgus' sons.

In Hvammssveit, the three farms involved in the disputes were among the largest (Skorravík, Höfn and Ásgarðr),[76] and it appears Þórðr Sturluson might have had associates in several households, including two *austmenn* involved in the dispute and a *bóndi* at Skorravík who had gone to Norway, also probably working for Þórðr. In other words the dispute between Dufgus and Þorgils was not one between average farmers.[77]

It is no surprise that soon after this episode in 1227, Þórðr and Snorri Sturluson managed to convene the Þórsnessþing and deprive Sturla Sighvatsson of his third of the *Snorrungagoðorð*.[78] This was undoubtedly due to the continuing threat he posed to his kinsmen, particularly to Þórðr. As if to prove the point, Sturla raided Hvammr the same year – the so-called *Hvammsför* – in a retaliatory but seemingly futile response to his loss of authority.[79] Hvammr was not damaged but men were injured on both sides, leading to a settlement at a local peace meeting in 1228 and the payment of considerable compensation

---

74 The man mentioned, Þjóstarr, an *austmaðr*, was living at Sauðafell just a few years later, and his unwillingness to harm Dufgus in 1226 may have reflected the fact that he was already an associate of Sturla as much as Þórðr Sturluson (SS I: 349). Dufgus purchased the farm of Baugsstaðir (SS I: 314).

75 SS I: 339. Árni was there in 1229 at least. He later moved to Ytra-Fell on Fellsströnd (SS I: 385).

76 Skorravík was valued at 30 hundreds; Ásgarðr at 40 in *Jarðabók* (VI: 84, 100);

77 Dufguss' original agreement to act on behalf of the alleged mother of Þorgils' child was a political move of great local significance. Unfortunately for him he handled the situation badly: he was unable to protect the advantage he had won from Þorgils by threatening him, because he did not have a large entourage and was vulnerable to a surprise attack. Fortunately for Dufgus, Sturla (and perhaps Þórðr) were well enough disposed towards him to award him a large compensation payment. Þorgils connection with Þórðr was perhaps not as strong as Dufgus,' and it could have been that Ásgarðr, Þjóstarr's home, was still not on good terms with Hvammr, let alone controlled by it.

78 See p. 58 above.

79 SS I: 315–16.

to Þórðr.[80] Sturla refused to pay some of it, giving instead the Valshamarr islands he had taken from Vigfúss.[81]

The underlying cause of these disputes would seem to be that neither Þórðr nor Sturla had the loyalty of all the farms which lay between them. Indeed, something more needs to be said about the affiliations of Dalir farms. Mention has already been made of some of Sturla's supporters in Laxárdalr but he had other local supporters, an account of which will give a sense of local geopolitics in the 1220s and 1230s.

Of Sturla's supporters of the 1220s and 1230s, Lauga-Snorri from the Laugar in Hvammssveit is the most visible and lived closest to Þórðr.[82] Lauga-Snorri first appeared with Sturla at the *Hvammsför* in 1227 and died at Örlygsstaðir in 1238. The fact that Lauga-Snorri's son is recorded defending Höskuldsstaðir in 1244 might suggest that he also chose to ally himself with Sighvatr's sons.[83]

Glerárskógar was also a farm close to Hvammr which Þórðr Sturluson had had to concede to Sighvatr Sturluson and, probably, to Sturla Sighvatsson. On their mother's death – and it is not fully explained why – Sighvatr is said to have inherited or taken the farm because it was 'nearest to him'.[84] Glerárskógar is also a source of dispute between Sighvatr and Þórðr in the aftermath of the raid on Hvammr: Sighvatr is quoted as saying that he no longer wished to argue with Þórðr over money matters (*fé*) or Glerárskógar.[85] Glerárskógar is notable for being a large farm from Hvammssveit whose occupants we are told nothing about in this period; perhaps none of the better-connected supporters of Sturla wished to live so close to Þórðr for fear of attack.

Supporters of both Sturla and Þórðr appear in a dispute which took place in 1235.[86] A man named Skíði Þorkelsson, who had been a member of Sturla's party in the *Hvammsför*, lived at Kvennahóll on Fellsströnd in 1235. His large farm, however, was divided between himself and a certain Jón Þorgeirsson, who had a concubine (*fylgjukonu*) at Kvennahóll but perhaps did not live there.

---

80 At Þorbergsstaðir, another farm on the margins of more densely populated districts (Map 7).
81 SS I: 318.
82 We can be fairly certain that "Lauga-" refers to Snorri's farm on the basis of analogy with all the other men called Snorri in *Sturlunga saga* who we know had toponymic nicknames. Eyrar-Snorri was indeed from Eyrr, Skarð-Snorri from Skarð, Garða-Snorri from Garðar, Mela-Snorri from Melar and Fell-Snorri from Staðarfell. Mág-Snorri in *Þorgils saga ok Hafliða* is the only exception.
83 In the more detailed account in the *Króksfjarðarbók* MS of *Sturlunga saga* (SS II: 287).
84 'tók til sín Glerárskóga, er honum váru næstir' (SS I: 303).
85 SS I: 318.
86 SS I: 384–86.

Skíði and his brother Ingimundr, who also took part in the *Hvammsför* in 1227, apparently took one of Jón's horses and gave him further unspecified problems. Jón turned first to Guðmundr *undir Felli* for advice, apparently because Skíði was a friend of Skarð-Snorri Narfason, with whom Guðmundr was on bad terms.[87] Guðmundr recommended that Jón should seek the help of Þórðr Sturluson, in all probability because, in turn, he knew that Þórðr was ill-disposed towards Skíði and Ingimundr: Skíði was accused of having done harm to another of Þórðr's *þingmenn*. Skíði surprisingly asked for Þórðr's aid and was turned away, although Þórðr's son Óláfr did help him.

In the end Skíði met his death after haggling with the *bóndi* from neighbouring Arnarbæli about the sale of a horse: Jón decapitated Skíði with an axe, and rode straight to Hvammr. Thereafter the pattern of events is a fairly familiar one. Jón's crime was discovered by his enemies (a man from Jörfi in Haukadalur and Kolbrandr, Skíði's son) but ultimately he escaped to southern Iceland.

This short but rich account reinforces the idea of how little full territorial control Þórðr and Sturla had, and how each had a clear, but geographically dispersed, band of supporters, a point we will come back to. It is possible that the presence of Skíði at Kvennahóll and Árni Auðunarson at Ytra-Fell represents an outward expansion of Sturla's influence, on the margins of Þórðr's main area of support; certainly Árni had not lived at Ytra-Fell a few years before. The location of Skíði's son's appearance, somewhere in or around Miðdalir, also implies that he was living at the farm of one of Sturla's supporters, if not at Sauðafell.

The personnel and geographical range of Sturla's supporters in Dalir can be traced yet further. The figure of Árni Auðunarson and his sons warrants comment first. The first evidence we have is in a situation where Sturla shows considerable loyalty to Guðmundr Árnason, who had taken part in the revenge killing of Sturla's kinsman Jón Þorleifsson.[88] Jón, living north in Gufudalur at the time of his murder, had been the brother of the Dufgus whom we have already met, and of Svertingr, who then lived at Fagrdalr.[89] Árni and Sturla enabled Guðmundr and another killer to stay at farms in Laxárdalur (Ljárskógar and Hornstaðir), despite the presence at Hjarðarholt of Jón Þorleifsson's kinsmen.[90] The killers left Dalir the same year but having enjoyed Sturla's

---

87   SS I: 384.
88   SS I: 338–39.
89   SS I: 331.
90   Although Svertingr Þorleifsson lived some distance away at Fagradalr, Dufgus had left Hjarðarholt, and his sons were possibly too young to think about taking vengeance, this still represents an insult to a group who had been and would be in the future, loyal to Sturla and his brother. The killers later accompanied Sturla on a raiding venture (aimed at

protection.[91] In 1238, nearly a decade later, Árni Auðunarson' sons assisted Sturla again. At this point the Árnasynir are said to have lived in Bitra, to the north of Dalir, but killed three 'Southerners' who themselves had killed a bull in Glerárdalur, possibly belonging to the farm of Glerárskógar, and thus to Sturla.[92]

Torfi *prestr* Guðmundarson has already been mentioned as one of Sturla Sighvatsson's most prominent henchmen. He was probably the son of Guðmundr Brandsson who had given Hjarðarholt to Hvamm-Sturla. The only time Torfi is associated with a farm, he himself lived at Hjarðarholt (in 1232). He was also a priest, like Guðmundr Brandsson, and by looking at his role in local politics it becomes clear that he was highly influential, even if not a *goðorðsmaðr* or *höfðingi*. Torfi was a lieutenant of Sturla first and foremost, but at the same time he was trusted by other *höfðingjar* to act as an intermediatory in disputes involving Sturla and other western leaders. Torfi and Skarð-Snorri negotiated a settlement (although unsuccessful) between Sturla and Þorvaldr *Vatnsfirðingr* in 1223 and he was co-negotiator with Þorlákr Ketilsson (from Kolbeinsstaðir) between the same men in 1228.[93] In the same year he was sent twice by Sturla to try to arrange a peace deal with Snorri Sturluson and the Vatnsfirðingar. As if further proof were needed of his role as Sturla's right-hand man then his appearance, alone, with Sturla in another peace meeting with Þorvaldr *Vatnsfirðingr*'s sons in 1230 provides it. Torfi's appearance living at Hjarðarholt in 1232 is also his last in *Íslendinga saga* and it may not be a coincidence that from the late 1230s the Dufgusssynir, Sturla's kinsmen from Hjarðarholt, become politically active. As Guðmundr Brandsson's son, Torfi would have been extremely elderly by now as his possible father Guðmundr had died in 1151.[94]

More evidence of Sturla's relations with local *bændr* comes from the account of his killing of the Þorvaldssynir when they attack him in Miðdalir in 1232. Torfi Guðmundarson had given Sturla advanced warning of the Þorvaldssynir's approach when they stopped at Hjarðarholt en route to Sauðafell. This gave Sturla time to gather supporters: he sent messengers 'to gather those men, such as he wanted, from Haukadalur' and also men from 'Hörðudalur and more widely about Dalir' (*til Hörðudals ok víðara um Dali ok stefndi mönnum at*

---

the sons of Þorvaldr *Vatnsfirðingr*) during which Sturla apparently maintained his distance from them by not speaking to them. Eventually Sturla accepted a truce from Svertingr Þorleifsson on their behalf, no doubt mostly due to Sturla's political superiority.

91 SS I: 340.
92 SS I: 417–18. The forces of Gizurr and Kolbeinn *ungi*, however, exacted their own revenge by cutting off the foot of a man from Laxárdalur as they left Dalir.
93 SS I: 300, 318.
94 SS I: 234.

sér).[95] From this unspecified crowd a few men are identified by name: Halldórr from Kvennabrekka, Hallr Arason from Höskuldsstaðir, a *bóndi* called Þórólfr from Hundadalr,[96] and the Hörðdælir[97] and Haukdælir (both *en masse*).[98] Lauga-Snorri also comes into the action, later, probably because he had longer to travel to Sauðafell than those others named.[99] Those named here are clearly not all the *bœndr* in Miðdalir, let alone from around the eastern end of Hvammsfjörður, but the force was clearly large enough to make short shrift of the eight-man Þorvaldssynir party they cornered in Hundadalr.

In this case we probably have a list of those of the wealthier *bœndr* in Dalir who were most loyal to Sturla in 1232, and most able to fight. (Torfi Guðmundarson was not involved in the fight, perhaps through old age.) We ought not to overestimate the support Sturla could muster from his own backyard, however. It is significant that no one was present from Fellsendi or Snóksdalr, the large farms close to Sauðafell with which Sighvatr Sturluson was on bad terms in 1217.[100] The parties of the Haukdælir and Hörðdælir represent an unknown number of men and, in the case of the former, probably do not represent men from every farm in Haukadalur. Hörðudalr proper had only five or six farms in it in 1700 and so conceivably men from each farm could have turned out for Sturla.[101] Yet Sturla also apparently had rather frosty relations with one of the more important men who appears on his side: Halldórr from Kvennabrekka, a local deacon,[102] who initially refused to be involved with the attack,[103] and whom Sturla later abuses for wanting to spare the Þorvaldssynir, saying that Halldórr would 'be quick to call them saints.'[104] Alongside his role as a deacon, a possible explanation of Halldórr's attitude is that he had been at Snóksdalr when it was raided in 1217, even though his father had lived at Kvennabrekka. In all likelihood what we are also seeing here, as in 1217, is that some church-owners were unwilling to be involved in secular politics.

Although a fairly long list has been made of Sturla Sighvatsson's supporters, very few allies can be identified for Þórðr Sturluson among local *bœndr*. Of

---

95 SS I: 348.
96 SS I: 350.
97 SS I: 351.
98 SS I: 352.
99 SS I: 352.
100 See above p. 100–1.
101 *Jarðabók* VI: 3–21.
102 SS I: 264.
103 SS I: 332.
104 'því at þú munt skjótt kalla þá helga' (SS I: 357).

these, Jón Þorgeirsson (who had to leave Fellsströnd in 1235) and Þorgils Snorrason of Skorravík have already been mentioned. The third and final one is the farm of Tjaldanes in Saurbær, easy to identify as a long term ally: Þórðr married a woman from Tjaldanes in 1224 (his third and final wife)[105] while her brother still lived at Tjaldanes and supported Þórðr in 1235.[106]

If we want to see support for Þórðr we actually have to look at three wealthier local figures. Skarðsströnd's most important politician of this period, Skarð-Snorri (d.1260), has already been mentioned as a mediator between Sturla Sighvatsson and Þorvaldr *Vatnsfirðingr* in 1223.[107] The evidence of Snorri's role seems to fit into three categories. First he acted as an advocate of people living on Skarðsströnd, as if he had been a *goði*.[108] There is just one example of this but it would seem indicative of his role as local 'big man.' In 1234 he intervened on behalf of a group of men, one from Hvarfsdalr, the other his kinsman from Búðardalr, after one of them had killed a supporter of Þórðr's son Óláfr *hvítaskáld*. Snorri persuaded Óláfr to accept a compromise solution.[109] Second, he acted as a mediator in disputes affecting Dalir which usually involved the Sturlungar. In 1234 again Skarð-Snorri was asked to act in this way, alongside Guðmundr from Staðarfell and Svertingr Þorleifsson, between Órækja Snorrason and Sighvatr Sturluson.[110] In this respect he formed a part of the second tier of locally-influential people, seemingly those below the Sturlungar and who had landed interests only in or around Dalir, who could act as fairly neutral arbiters. Thirdly, Snorri and his sons sided with the Sturlungar when it suited them. Snorri helped Þórðr Sturluson to capture and put to death a bandit whose activities had been encouraged by Óræki Snorrason.[111] Skarð-Snorri's niece had also married Sturla Þórðarson by 1241[112] and his sons fought with Sighvatr Sturluson and Sturla Sighvatsson at Örlygsstaðir in 1238.[113] Overall we are given the impression that Skarð-Snorri was quite a powerful local figure who did his best to stay out of trouble and whose prime interest was simply to

---

105   SS I: 303.
106   SS I: 384.
107   See above p. 107. The date of his death is only recorded in *Gottskálksannáll* (IA: 330).
108   It is not clear whether or not Snorri was a *goði*.
109   SS I: 376–77, 383. Orri Vésteinsson (2017: 62–63) suggests that the creation after 1238 of a small tithe area for Búðardalr's church out of Skarð's was somehow the result of this conflict.
110   SS I: 387.
111   SS I: 365–66, 383–84.
112   See above p. 74.
113   SS I: 423.

foster local political stability. His sons' presence at Örlygsstaðir can be read in the same way.

When Páll *prestr* Hallsson, the owner of Staðarhóll, is first mentioned in *Íslendinga saga* he is labelled a 'great friend' of Þórðr Sturluson.[114] Certainly Páll was not on good terms with Sturla Sighvatsson by 1226 when Sturla had abducted Páll's sister and tried to persuade her to marry one of his supporters.[115] Páll also shared with Þórðr the burden of housing Bishop Guðmundr in 1231. By this time, however, Páll had moved from Staðarhóll to Narfeyri (Figure 7, Map 6).[116] Páll is next mentioned in 1237 when he is said to have persuaded Sturla Þórðarson and a younger brother to spend Christmas with Sturla Sighvatsson at Sauðafell.[117] Páll went with the brothers and the meeting seems to have gone well, but without bringing Þórðr's sons into a closer relationship with their uncle and cousin. When Sighvatr and Sturla tried to persuade Böðvarr Þórðarson (who, significantly, was not based at Sauðafell) to let Svertingr Þorleifsson – probably on good terms with Sturla Sighvatsson – to manage Hvammr, Böðvarr refused.[118] Páll had perhaps been trying to get the Þórðarsynir to give way peacefully to their increasingly powerful kinsmen. He was certainly well-disposed towards Sturla Þórðarson when he supported Sturla's continued tenancy of Staðarhóll over Órækja in 1241.

Guðmundr *prestr* Þórðarson from Staðarfell (Guðmundr *undir Felli*) has been referred to in two local disputes, and as a kinsman of the Sturlungar and Þorgils Oddsson from Höfn.[119] Guðmundr remained politically active from the 1220s into the 1240s. He helped Þórðr Sturluson and his sons to muster forces against Órækja Snorrason in 1234. At the Alþing in 1238 he was said to have been the most senior figure in a force of men from western Iceland (*vestanmönnum*), in the absence of any of the Sturlungar.[120] In 1239 he was co-leader with Sturla Þórðarson of the Saurbæingar and Strendir (*bændr* from Fellsströnd and possibly Skarðsströnd as well)[121] who went to a peace meeting convened by Snorri Sturluson.[122] Guðmundr is last mentioned in 1245 alongside Ketill Þorláksson at the wedding of Hrafn Oddsson to Sturla Sighvatsson's daughter;[123]

---

114   'inn mesti vinr Þórðar' (SS I: 310).
115   SS I: 310.
116   SS I: 346.
117   SS I: 409.
118   SS I: 412.
119   See above pp. 103, 104, 106.
120   SS I: 416.
121   *Strendir*, 'Strandsmen,' is used four times in *Íslendinga saga* but is ambiguous. In ch. 59 it almost certainly identifies people just from Fellsströnd and not Skarðsströnd (SS I: 311, 314). In ch. 159 it most likely refers to people from Skarðsströnd (SS I: 472).
122   SS I: 446.
123   SS II: 70.

Guðmundr's brother Snorri who also lived at Staðarfell after his father is first mentioned in 1242,[124] but this perhaps hints that Guðmundr was close to retiring from the political scene in 1245.

The accounts of these local disputes suggest, then, that Þórðr Sturluson and Sturla Sighvatsson both had relatively weak local power. They could not necessarily control large farms adjacent to their own (e.g. Ásgarðr, Fellsendi). They were also clearly dependent on the support of the most prominent local *bændr* in raising forces for defensive and aggressive actions, both locally and outside Dalir. Such relatively wealthy men also acted as a kind of middle tier when it came to *bændr* seeking legal support or protection. It would seem that *bændr* were likely to turn first to the nearest church-farm owner, like Guðmundr *undir Felli* or Skarð-Snorri, and required that person to act as their sponsor in order to gain the support of a *goði*. In this respect there are clearly two tiers of *bóndi* visible in this period.

At the same time Þórðr and Sturla, although lacking control of solid territorial blocks, were able to rely on support from people quite widely dispersed across Dalir. Þórðr certainly had sympathisers in almost every *hreppr* in Dalir, excluding perhaps Miðdalir. There is less evidence for the geographical spread of Sturla Sighvatsson's supporters but he could count on some in Fellsströnd, Hvammssveit, Laxárdalur, Haukadalur, Miðdalir and Hörðudalur. Around Helgafellssveit it is unclear how political control operated in this period but Þórðr's control of Öndverðareyrr and his friend Páll Hallsson's move to Narfeyri suggest that Þórðr had real influence here (Map 4). And Hjörleifr Gilsson, who according to *Arons saga Hjörleifssonar* lived at Bjarnarhöfn,[125] was certainly no friend of Sturla Sighvatsson by the 1220s and so may have been better disposed towards Þórðr.[126]

There is therefore no evidence to suggest that there was any great change in the way politics operated on the ground in this period. *Höfðingjar* cannot be seen to have made greater demands on the local population than in *Sturlu saga*, and we will see something structurally similar in the *Íslendingasögur*. Wealthy *bændr* appear in the accounts of Dalir disputes in the 1220s and 1230s but this partly reflects the sudden depth of coverage after the thinner coverage for c.1185 to c.1220. The importance of rich *bændr* in Dalir may also reflect the

---

124 SS I: 471.
125 SS II: 237.
126 Perhaps another neutral or one-time set of allies of different members of the Sturlungar could be mentioned in this connection: the sons of Jón Brandsson, husband of Steinunn Sturludóttir, who, up to the early 1230s seem to have been based in Reykhólar and in the West Fjords, e.g, Bergþórr Jónsson (d.1232), Ingimundr Jónsson (d.1231) (SS I: 297, 315).

fact that a single leading figure was running farms in both Hvammssveit and Helgafellssveit. For *bændr* in these areas this may have represented a change in their access to legal and military help. Their nearest legal representative now lived further away than had been the case in the period covered by *Sturlu saga*. Þorgils Snorrason's gift to Þórðr Sturluson of half of the *Þórsnesingagoðorð* had had a practical effect because there was no active *goði* living in Saurbær,[127] on Skarðsströnd or Fellsströnd. If Páll Hallsson was a *goði* then his move out of Staðarhóll to the less politically important farm of Narfeyri may also show Þórðr Sturluson getting his way in Saurbær at the expense of a 'friend.' Certainly smaller farmers brought grievances to the attention of more powerful figures such as Skarð-Snorri and Guðmundr *undir Felli*, because they felt they needed an advocate before they even got to a *goði*. While this situation is one which suggests increasing social stratification, and the concentration of power into fewer and fewer hands, it is worth remembering the political situation across Saurbær and Hvammssveit before Hvamm-Sturla challenged Einarr Þorgilsson: Einarr (and probably his father) influenced both districts, i.e. things were still much the same.

5 Dalir and Þórðr *kakali* Sighvatsson, c.1242–c.1250

Whereas *Íslendinga saga* provides some quite detailed accounts of the micropolitics of Dalir in the first few decades of the thirteenth century, the accounts of later decades are sketchier. We are forced into a far patchier account of geopolitics and often have to write a more narrative kind of account.

Þórðr *kakali* Sighvatsson's return to Iceland in 1242 provided the wealthier men of the mid-west a leader behind whom they might rally against Kolbeinn *ungi* Arnórsson whose power had grown in the north of Iceland. Many of them, but not all, were forced to swear oaths of loyalty to Kolbeinn *ungi*.[128] The account of Þórðr *kakali*'s initial efforts to establish himself as a politician in 1242 suggests who his closest allies were, many of them being his kinsmen. The men who joined Þórðr during his western Icelandic recruitment drive of late 1242 (and with Dalir connections) were all kinsmen: Tumi Sighvatsson, Sturla Þórðarson, the sons of Dufgus Þorleifsson, Hrafn Oddsson (distantly related to Þórðr as brother-in-law of the Dufgusssynir) and his nephew, Teitr Styrmisson

---

[127] It is possible that either Páll Hallsson or his brother Gunnsteinn were a *goðorðsmaðr* although it is never said explicitly (see above p. 60 on Gunnsteinn's son, Vigfúss). Gunnsteinn lived at Brunná in Saurbær, the farm from which Þórðr Sturluson gained a member of his household (SS I: 307) and at which Einarr Þorgilsson had been fostered in the early twelfth century.

[128] SS II: 1.

of Flatey.[129] Aside from this group, Þórðr clearly had Norwegian leaders in his retinue (Hákon *galinn*, for instance)[130] as well as other well-off Icelanders. Events in the mid-west in the 1240s, such as we have them recorded, generally featured these men.

Þórðr's first action to affect the west was to try to build up a military presence to intimidate the regional overlords. He toured the West Fjords and Dalir to assemble a force and gathered this army, amounting to a total of about 200 ill-equipped (*lítt vapnat*) men somewhere in eastern Dalir. Such a large group of people was difficult to provision and led to the decision to travel south.[131] Þórðr took a tribute from *bændr* under Gizurr Þorvaldsson's jurisdiction before returning west. All of Þórðr's kinsmen who are named above acted as his lieutenants, leading sections of the army for particular tasks.

Kolbeinn *ungi* reacted to Þórðr *kakali*'s raid into his ally Gizurr's territory by quickly gathering his own force. On his way back from the south Þórðr took refuge first at the monastery at Helgafell but decided to retreat as far west as Flatey.[132] It is at this point that Þórðr *kakali* made an effort to persuade his cousins Böðvarr and Sturla Þórðarson to support him against Kolbeinn *ungi* and Gizurr. Böðvarr, however, refused to break his agreement not to oppose Kolbeinn, his brother-in-law. Böðvarr then tried to get Kolbeinn to agree to some kind of settlement but without success.[133] Þórðr meanwhile continued his efforts to gain martial support from the leading men in the West Fjords.[134] This may indicate that he had exhausted the possibilities of getting further support from Dalir. Teitr Styrmisson and Svarthöfði Dufgussson argued that the force should travel to southern Breiðafjörður, whence Þórðr's 'most valiant' supporters came, and because they would not find suitable troops in the West Fjords.[135]

Kolbeinn *ungi*'s eventual raid into Dalir in 1243 proved to be inconclusive. Kolbeinn had a force of nearly 600 men but failed to capture Þórðr himself or Sturla Þórðarson who, apparently, was also specifically sought.[136] Sælingsdalstunga was raided but Sturla and the rest of Þórðr's force escaped to the group of larger islands at the mouth of Hvammsfjörður. Kolbeinn's men caught up

---

129 SS II: 9–10, 13.
130 SS II: 30.
131 SS II: 13.
132 SS II: 23–24.
133 SS II: 26.
134 SS II: 27–29.
135 '...ekki mundu vera nema búkarla ok fiskimenn ok þá, er ekki mannsmót væri at...' (SS II: 29). The casual dismissal of the West Fjords as the home of only farmers and fishermen might be further evidence of the region's early economic specialisation.
136 SS II: 30.

with them there but there was a stand-off rather than a fight. Þórðr himself spent the whole time in safety on Flatey, only venturing out to (unsuccessfully) try to persuade Böðvarr Þórðarson to join him again.[137] Kolbeinn's force raided Laxárdalr as they returned north.[138]

A retaliatory raid led by Þórðr *kakali* with the support of the Dufgusssynir, Teitr Styrmisson, and brothers Hrafn and Nikulás Oddsson[139] seems to have led to a move towards reconciliation by Kolbeinn. At one point Kolbeinn *ungi* is credited with offering to give up control of his territories in Iceland (*ríki öll*) and go abroad[140] but when a deal was made by one of his deputies suggesting he might have given up his claim to Eyjafjörður, he was far from pleased.[141] A short-term truce was agreed, nonetheless.

When the truce is up, however, Kolbeinn and his supporters raided into Dalir again. By using a different route, crossing from Bitra into Gilsfjörður, the raiders attacked Tumi Sighvatsson, Þórðr's brother, now living at Reykhólar.[142] Last minute attempts to warn and assist Tumi, by Sturla Þórðarson and *bændr* from Saurbær, could not prevent his death.[143] Half of Kolbeinn's party returned by the more conventional route northwards and raided four farms in Laxárdalur, killing a man at two of them.[144] Tumi's death has no visible impact on politics within Dalir. Teitr Styrmisson ran Flatey on his own now[145] and what property Tumi had held jointly with Þórðr *kakali* in Dalir was given to Tumi's wife Þuríðr who moved to Sauðafell while Þórðr sought opportunities in the north.[146]

The culmination of events in 1244 was that Þórðr and Kolbeinn agreed to have their case arbitrated by the king in Norway. Both men spent the rest of the year trying to outflank one another militarily – particularly by trying to get more support from regions further from their respective bases – but without much success. Þórðr *kakali*, Sturla Þórðarson and Vigfúss Gunnsteinsson also led what might have been a raid into the north had they been able decide what their plan was; they returned home without even reaching Skagafjörður. But

---

137 SS II: 32.
138 SS II: 32–33.
139 SS II: 35–38.
140 SS II: 43.
141 SS II: 44–45.
142 SS II: 45–46.
143 SS II: 48.
144 SS II: 48, 287–88.
145 SS II: 72.
146 SS II: 49. Tumi had probably inherited Sauðafell from his father or brother Sturla (SS I: 447).

most well-recorded is the *Flóabardagi*, a sea battle in Húnaflói. This was equally inconclusive and nobody of any significance from Dalir died in the fight.[147] More conflict that summer, and the fact that Þórðr *kakali* had some open supporters in Eyjafjörður, and now moved there, led to the parties' willingness to negotiate, especially once Þórðr *kakali* had moved to Eyjafjörður and won a decisive military victory.[148]

Kolbeinn *ungi* died in the winter of 1244–45 and so his planned visit to Norway with Þórðr did not take place. What is recorded next, however, gives the appearance of being a natural progression of events. Gizurr Þorvaldsson's arrival in Skagafjörður with a large force precipitated negotiations between him and Þórðr which resulted in them going to Norway in 1246. Þórðr thus had to leave his territories in other people's hands. Although it is not stated, it would seem that Hrafn Oddsson – now married to Þuríðr Sturludóttir and living at Sauðafell – was able to establish himself better in the mid-west in Þórðr's absence. Þórðr entrusted his northern territory (*ríkit*) to kinsmen from the north but clearly no longer had any landed interests in the mid-west when he left Iceland.

Turning specifically to Dalir, it would seem that Þórðr *kakali*'s stint as a western-based *höfðingi* involved close co-operation with the people who controlled certain large farms around Hvammsfjörður. Þórðr's cronies are identified time and time again as his kinsmen the Dufgusssynir and Sturla Þórðarson as well as Teitr Styrmisson, Hákon *galinn* and a select number of others. There is little evidence of Þórðr's (or anybody else's) co-operation with other wealthy farmers. This is most likely in part because that is simply all *Þórðar saga kakala* tells us; the biographical focus of the saga is highly restrictive. Nevertheless it seems likely that Þórðr's concerns were not always those of the larger farmers in and around Dalir although they may have fought for him on certain occasions, most likely when he first arrived back from Norway in 1242.

As we have seen, Þórðr *kakali* tried hard to acquire support among the wealthier farmers of the West Fjords. His success here was mixed, something which demonstrates his weakness in the face of the personal ties and oaths which had already bound men in the West Fjords to Kolbeinn, or else discouraged them from political and military action. At a local level, too, we can see that Þórðr *kakali* had limited power in 1242–3 and actually operated within the same socio-political strictures as his forebears in Dalir.

---

147 SS II: 56–67. See above p. 51.
148 See above p. 52.

Chapter 12 of *Þórðar saga kakala* provides a snapshot of the geographical limitations of Þórðr's activities in winter 1242–3. He spent the winter living on Skarðsströnd, billeting his forces on two farms, Búðardalr where he himself stayed, and Ballará, where his sister Valgerðr lived with her husband (Bárðr Þorkelsson). To the south, however, Þórðr does not seem to have had much influence. Instead the centre of Dalir appears not to have been home to any major political figures at this point, with Þórðr's cousins Böðvarr and Sturla Þórðarson seemingly based at Staðr on the southern coast of Snæfellsnes. The districts in the centre of Dalir (specifically the farms of Hólmslátr and Dögurðarnes) serve simply as locations for meetings of the cousins or their representatives, as mid-points between their respective homes.[149]

Þórðr did, however, venture away from Skarðsströnd to try to deal with some raiders from Miðfjörður, just into the Northern Quarter. After his meeting with Böðvarr and Sturla he travelled around the region. Þórðr seems to have tried to catch the raiding party in Laxárdalur, chasing them up the valley, and having to give up the chase due to a lack of horses. His solution then was to leave two of his *heimamenn* in Dalir to deal with the problem, which they did in due course, killing the group's leader in Miðfjörður.[150] From this we get a mixed picture of a different kind. On the one hand people in Miðfjörður seem willing to risk raiding Dalir, perhaps because there is no nearby local leader to stop them. On the other hand, Þórðr *kakali* sees himself as the guardian of the people of Dalir, despite basing himself no closer than Skarðsströnd, and is able to secure peace for them.

As well as Þórðr *kakali*'s own activities it is important to note that his brother Tumi acted with him but he too was limited in what he could do and where within Dalir he could do it. While one gets the sense that the saga wishes to play down the role of Tumi Sighvatsson there is still a logic to the way his geopolitical power is portrayed. Thus on Þórðr and Tumi's first visit to Dalir in 1242, Tumi stopped off to stay at Hvammr where the brother's kinsman Svertingr Þorleifsson lived[151] but this is as far south in Dalir as Þórðr or Tumi stayed over the next few years.

More significant than Tumi's stay at Hvammr, is the story of his living arrangements in winter 1242–3. First he stayed on Flatey but he was only there a few months before he is said to have been dissatisfied with the place and

---

149 SS II: 25, 32.
150 The party was led by Þórarinn *balti* who was killed at Bretalækr (SS II: 27).
151 SS II: 7.

wanted to leave.[152] He went to ask Snorri *prestr* Narfason at Skarð, said to have been the wealthiest man in the West Fjords (*manna augastr í Vestfjörðum*), about taking over the running of Reykhólar. Snorri owned Reykhólar but the farm was run by his sons (Bárðr and Sigmundr). Snorri agreed to let Tumi occupy the farm but only provided Tumi could present guarantors who would swear that he would maintain it properly. Tumi moved in without providing these assurances and there was seemingly nothing which Skarð-Snorri Narfason could do to stop him. Even worse for Snorri is what happened later: Tumi's presence caused Kolbeinn *ungi* to attack Reykhólar the following year. Kolbeinn's party not only killed Tumi but also Snorri's son Bárðr, a priest, and inevitably they stole horses and other possessions as well.[153] Tumi's portrayal here may well be a brief attempt at character assassination[154] but it underscores the burden which Þórðr *kakali*'s political ambitions may well have placed on any district he lived in. By basing himself so far west Þórðr was probably trying to avoid an attack from Kolbeinn and suggests that the whole area stretching from inner Hvammsfjörður east to Miðfjörður was a kind of No Man's Land for the *höfðingjar* at this point because each saw the other as capable of mobilising sufficient force in the short term to be able to make quick attacks on the other over relatively short distances.

6 Dalir c.1250-c.1265

Þorgils saga skarða's account for the 1250s enables us to see the roles of wealthy *bændr* although not the vast majority of them. This marginally fuller account of local politics in the latter reflects the fact that so much of the conflict in the 1250s takes place between Þorgils *skarði*, his cousin Sturla Þórðarson and Hrafn Oddsson who all lived in the mid-west of Iceland. Under these circumstances it is not at all surprising that the loyalties of local people were of greater importance. Again, we have to rely on unpicking the dense narratives to try to suggest broader political practices and geopolitical patterns.

Þorgils *skarði* Böðvarsson stayed in Norway from 1244 (when he was eighteen) until 1252. His return to Iceland meant that he moved home, to Staðr on Snæfellsnes, to live with his father. *Þorgils saga* places its main character very

---

152 SS II: 33. There is an interesting parallel here with Sighvatr Sturluson's dissatisfaction with Staðarhóll (SS I: 231). Svertingr was the brother of Dufgus Þorleifsson and therefore uncle to the ubiquitous Dufgussynir.
153 SS I: 33, 40, 46–48.
154 Tumi had also taken in retainers whom Þórðr *kakali* had cast out of his own retinue (SS II: 41).

much centre stage and has very little to say about Þorgils' father Böðvarr, although he was doubtless involved in Þorgils' political plans, even if not in military activity. In 1252 Þorgils represented a threat to the established regional political scene in the mid-west. Sturla Þórðarson, Hrafn and Nikulás Oddssynir, and Þórðr *Hítnesingr* (from Hítarnes in Mýrar) seem to have formed a coherent group.[155] Þorgils' activities probably destabilised this regional block, in a way which his ageing father had probably tried to avoid.

Þorgils' need for money to meet his political ambitions put him in a similar mould to Þórðr *kakali*. Þorgils' case differs from that of his kinsman, though, in that he had brought a retinue from Norway although this is not given more than passing comment by the text. It provided him with the opportunity to attain significant political power without having to win as much support in Iceland. The problem of feeding this armed retinue, however, is what created his first visible conflict with Hrafn Oddsson, one which admittedly has a supra-regional element to it. Hrafn was still living at Sauðafell and therefore geographically Þorgils' nearest rival leader. The saga says that Þorgils went to visit a certain Halldórr Vilmundarson, the deacon at Rauðamelr (to the east of Staðr and thus marginally closer to Sauðafell), and asked him and his wife to move to Staðr to run the farm (*leitaði eftir...at þau réðist til Staðar ok væri þar fyrir búi*). When Halldórr firmly refused to do so, Þorgils stole all the cattle and sheep from Rauðamelr and drove them back to Staðr. Halldórr reacted by seeking the advice of Guðmundr *umboðsmaðr*, the overseer at Helgafell, in the hope of getting redress. Guðmundr interceded on Halldórr's behalf: he went to ask Þorgils to return the livestock. When Þorgils refused to return the animals Guðmundr suggested that Halldórr ask Hrafn Oddsson for support. Hrafn offered support of a kind: he would take up Halldórr's case on condition that Halldórr moved himself and his relatives to Sauðafell. Halldórr was clearly not satisfied with his solution and so turned to a third potential source of help. He went to Kolbeinsstaðir, where he found not only Ketill *prestr* Þorláksson but also his kinsman Narfi Snorrason (from Skarð). They, in turn, referred Halldórr to Abbot Brandr of Þykkvabær, clearly feeling that they were unable to put pressure on Þorgils (or Hrafn). When Halldórr contacted the abbot he finally got some kind of result: the abbot wrote a letter to Þorgils *skarði* requesting that he return the livestock. Halldórr is said to have delivered the letter to Staðr himself, with Ketill Þorláksson accompanying him for moral and physical support.

The sanction of the well-connected abbot (and a future bishop) from the southern diocese seemingly had much more clout than that of the *umboðsmaðr*

---

155   E.g. in summer 1252 when they all attended a feast at Geldingaholt in Skagafjörður (SS II: 119).

of Helgafell. Þorgils immediately had the livestock driven back to Rauðamelr and he and Halldórr exchanged gifts. Þorgils gave Halldórr a mass robe (*messuklæði*) while Halldórr gave three geldings and a four-year-old ox in return. The pair also brought a formal halt to their differences by redefining themselves as having *vinátta* (formal friendship).[156] Halldórr, we must assume, returned to Rauðamelr and was thereafter left in peace.

A second narrative records Þorgils making exactly the same demand – for a *bóndi* to move to Staðr and manage his farm – at a wealthy farm in another neighbouring district. This time Þorgils turned to Kolgrímr from Bjarnarhöfn and his daughter, Þuríðr. Although Kolgrímr was unwilling to comply with Þorgils' wishes, a compromise solution was eventually arranged whereby only Þuríðr Kolgrímsdóttir moved to Staðr.[157] This presumably gave Þorgils a kind of hostage, and perhaps the person with the real management skills, or even a potential concubine.

Þorgils' relationship with Kolgrímr is more ambivalent than his relationship with Halldórr but it may also have been highly exploitative on his part. When Þorgils had first arrived at Staðr, even before his request for Kolgrímr to move there, the saga says that Kolgrímr contributed five *kúgildi* (hundreds) to the establishment. The choice of the word *kúgildi*, in this instance, when *hundrað* is more commonly used as a unit of measurement, might suggest that Kolgrímr really was supplying animals. Precisely how willingly this contribution was made is difficult to ascertain. It may be, however, that Þorgils was trying to manage the burden he was placing on wealthy local *bændr*. Þorgils received the five *kúgildi* from Kolgrímr, then, instead, tried to exploit Halldórr from Rauðamelr, but when this failed returned to someone who was perhaps an easier target. In fact, Kolgrímr may have become even easier to intimidate by 1253 when Þorgils asked him to move to Staðr. By this time Þorgils' father, Böðvarr Þórðarson, had moved to Öndverðareyrr, almost the farm next door to Kolgrímr's home at Bjarnarhöfn.[158] This no doubt allowed Böðvarr and Þorgils to keep a close check on him.[159]

---

156 SS II: 150–51.
157 SS II: 152.
158 SS II: 149.
159 Bjarnarhöfn had also been occupied by Óláfr *hvítaskáld* Þórðarson, perhaps briefly, in 1234 (SS II: 377–79). It is not clear whether Hjörleifr Gilsson, father of Aron, still lived at Bjarnarhöfn (SS II: 237). His political position would be difficult to assess. It is possible that at this stage Hjörleifr favoured Hrafn Oddsson, because, firstly, his brother Sölvi had lived at Rauðamelr, secondly, Aron became a part of Þórðr *kakali*'s retinue (see note 78) and thirdly, Aron was fostered at Kolbeinsstaðir, a farm which recently had been involved in opposing Þorgils *skarði*.

These two episodes show why Þorgils *skarði*'s arrival caused tension on Snæfellsnes and suggest that he was not popular. In both instances in which Þorgils pays visits to nearby heads of major farms they were unwilling to move to his farm, most likely because to do so would mean they had to leave their farm under someone else's management and no doubt bring their own livestock to Staðr. Certainly once Halldórr or Kolgrímr had moved to Staðr they would have been in no position to prevent Þorgils from exploiting their farms. Þorgils' need for provisions is emphasised, too, by the fact that stealing livestock was his immediate concern once Halldórr refused his wish. Furthermore when Þorgils and Halldórr exchanged gifts it seems that Halldórr and Þorgils recieved the gifts which they would want: robes for Halldórr and food for Þorgils. On an earlier meeting with Abbot Brandr, when he had only just arrived back in Iceland, Þorgils had received an ox as a gift from the abbot.[160] In sum, we see a structural change in local politics. The existence of Þorgils' imported retinue were the cause of changed political relations on Snæfellsnes. Þorgils appears to have had a retinue of an unprecedented size in and around Dalir, with the result that he was forced to try to oppress wealthier *bændr* to maintain it.

The set of events presented above represent an initial phase in Þorgils *skarði*'s political life in the mid-west and, more specifically *his* relationship with wealthy landowners – possibly even a single kin group[161] – on Snæfellsnes rather than Dalir. What happened in the few years immediately afterwards shows how political relationships worked within Dalir over a longer time. In broad terms we can still see three significant *höfðingjar* – Þorgils, Sturla and Hrafn – whose relations with one another seem to be the most significant element in Dalir's politics.

The key top-level political change that we see in Dalir within the period covered by *Þorgils saga skarða* is the change of Sturla Þórðarson's loyalties from Hrafn Oddsson to Þorgils. For Sturla this was a move away from an ally of more than a decade to positively align himself with his nephew after years of ambivalent relations with his brother Böðvarr. It happened despite an initial meeting with Þorgils at Helgafell late in 1252 ending without an agreement about their respective political roles: Þorgils apparently held fast to the idea of his being King Hákon's agent in Iceland. *Þorgils saga* is also keen to stress

---

160   SS II: 149.
161   Guðmundr Óláfsson may not have been a kinsman of the Hjörleifr Gilsson and his sons Aron and Óláfr, later the Abbot of Helgafell, but he was most likely their *umboðsmaðr* rather than anyone else's. Guðmundr controlled first Helgafell and then Miklaholt, farms occupied by Óláfr and Hjörleifr respectively (SS I: 267; II: 237).

division between Sturla and Hrafn, particularly in dialogues between them over the following years.[162] Eventually, however, Sturla and Þorgils became reconciled (towards the end of 1253) although not before Sturla and Hrafn had tried to kill him.[163] Þorgils waived any compensation payment which Sturla might have paid but was less forgiving to Hrafn, from whom he did demand recompense.[164] The marriage of Sturla's daughter to Gizurr Þorvaldsson's son and the attack on Flugumýrr further served to divide Sturla and Hrafn.[165] Sturla's change of stance with regard to Hrafn and Þorgils had the major effect on local politics one would expect. After a brief period of collaboration between Þorgils and Hrafn in 1254,[166] Sturla and Þorgils always sided together against Hrafn.

The stratum of wealthy men who lived in Dalir and had regular dealings with the three *höfðingjar* in this period amounted to just a handful: Páll *prestr* Hallsson, the Dufgusssynir (Kolbeinn *grön*, Svarthöfði and Björn *drumbr*), Snorri *prestr* Narfason (Skarð-Snorri) and his sons, Snorri *prestr* Þórðarson (Fell-Snorri) and Guðmundr Óláfsson, who as *umboðsmaðr* has already been mentioned.[167] These people were all close kinsmen either to each other or to one of the *höfðingjar*.

Páll Hallsson's position would seem to have been one of the strongest among this group. Páll's daughter was briefly considered as a marriage partner by Þorgils *skarði* (although Þorgils dismissed her as too ugly).[168] While Páll is identified in *Íslendinga saga* as the owner of Staðarhóll,[169] we see him living at Narfeyri in 1252 and Langidalr in 1253, both wealthy farms on the north coast of Snæfellsnes.[170] Páll's son, Eyrar-Snorri, is remembered as living at Narfeyri in 1257 and presumably did so into the 1260s.[171] After the return of Þorgils *skarði*, Páll was very clearly a supporter of Þorgils. Not only was he on such good terms with Þorgils for the marriage tie to be contemplated but Páll was also chosen by Þorgils as a possible arbitrator in deciding compensation owed him by

---

162 SS II: 126, 140, 144.
163 SS II: 158.
164 SS II: 161.
165 See above p. 53.
166 SS II: 162.
167 Kolgrímr from Bjarnarhöfn might also be added to this list. His only appearance in *Sturlunga saga* has already been discussed.
168 SS II: 151.
169 SS I: 449.
170 SS II: 130, 151.
171 SS II: 212.

Sturla Þórðarson in 1253.[172] Sturla's refusal to allow Páll to arbitrate also suggests that Páll was regarded as very close to Þorgils.

The Dufgusssynir, who still retained control of Hjarðarholt,[173] remained loyal to Hrafn Oddsson in the same way as they had been lieutenants of Sauðafell's previous heads, the sons of Sighvatr, Sturla and Þórðr *kakali* Sighvatsson. As Hrafn was able to expand his interests in the north, so they went with him and fought for him.[174] Of the three sons of Dufgus Þorleifsson still alive in the 1250s, Svarthöfði and Kolbeinn *grön* had the most prominent political roles. Svarthöfði's marriage to Hrafn's daughter in 1240 suggests that he might have been the older or preeminent brother then.[175] Kolbeinn may have been more often a leader of military expeditions: he was at the burning of Flugumýrr (as was Björn *drumbr*), for instance, when Svarthöfði was apparently not. Svarthöfði may have only had a military role after Kolbeinn's death, such as when *Íslendinga saga* records him leading a force in Eyjafjörður in 1254.[176] Björn *drumbr* appears to have spent most time at Hjarðarholt.[177] All three of them, possibly in part due to their kinship with Þorgils *skarði* and Sturla Þórðarson, were arbitrators in the immediate aftermath of Hrafn and Sturla Þórðarson's attack on Þorgils at Stafaholt in 1252.[178] On balance the Dufgusssynir seem to have been even more important to Hrafn Oddsson than they had been to Sturla Sighvatsson and his brother Þórðr *kakali*.

After Páll and the Dufgusssynir most of the remainder of the heads of the larger Dalir farms appear as arbitrators of the settlement between Hrafn and Sturla in 1257. The increasing mutual distrust of the two *höfðingjar*, as a result of their contest for control of Borgarfjörður, led Hrafn (and Ásgrímr Þorsteinsson)[179] to attack Saurbær. Sturla managed to escape from Staðarhóll before his opponents arrived. Hrafn's party was rather restrained, only killing one man, but a settlement was still called for. The initial peace meeting failed because, we are told, Hrafn still had his mind on ridding himself of Sturla once and for all. Hrafn also raided Skarð and its environs in another fruitless search for Sturla.[180]

---

172 SS II: 158–59.
173 SS II: 195.
174 SS II: 185, 191.
175 SS I: 447.
176 SS I: 499.
177 This is the implication of a passage where Þorgils *skarði*'s party ride across Laxárdalsheiði in 1255. They expect the figure in the distance to be Björn *drumbr* rather than anyone else (SS II: 195). Björn does not appear in the raid on Stafaholt or the battle at Þverá.
178 SS II: 135.
179 Another northern Icelandic leader who had helped Hrafn against Þorgils and Sturla (SS I: 482, 484, 513; II: 177–79).
180 SS II: 208.

A second meeting brought each side together with three arbitrators named on each side. Sturla named Skarð-Snorri, Fell-Snorri and Páll *prestr* Hallsson from Langidalr while Hrafn was represented by Guðmundr Óláfsson, Þórarinn Sveinsson and a 'Þorkell *prestr*.' A geographical division exists between the two sides' arbitrators: Sturla's representatives lived closer to him than to they did to Hrafn. Guðmundr Óláfsson lived at Miklaholt on the south coast of Snæfellsnes and acted on Hrafn's behalf in spite of, or because of, his kinship with Fell-Snorri;[181] Þórarinn Sveinsson, having served Sturla Sighvatsson and his son Jón, probably still lived at Sauðafell, as might Þorkell *prestr*.[182] What is striking is that small, loose territorial blocks, indicated by the allegiances of the richest farmers to the nearest *goði*, appear now just as they did in the twelfth century.

The short *Sturlu þáttr* provides a kind of epilogue to the discernible pattern of politics around Hvammsfjörður just as it provides an epilogue to the *Sturlunga saga* compilation. Sturla Þórðarson and Hrafn Oddsson clearly continued to compete for political supremacy after Þorgils *skarði* Böðvarsson's death in 1258; unfortunately *Sturlu þáttr* only covers the short train of events (probably from 1262) which led to Hrafn Oddsson forcing Sturla Þórðarson out of Iceland in 1263 for what would be eight years. What remained at stake was wider political control than simply of Dalir, in particular of Borgarfjörður. This may explain the text's need to assert that Hrafn made Stafaholt in Borgarfjörður his home only with Sturla's permission (*en Hrafn gerði bú í Stafaholti með ráði Sturlu*).[183] Certainly such a move allowed both Sturla and Hrafn the reassurance that their rival lived further away than before, even if for Sturla this meant that Hrafn had closer control of land and men in Borgarfjörður. At the same time, however, Sturla's son, Snorri, appears on the political stage and is said to have moved to Álftanes in Mýrar. In geographical terms this again extended south the area over which Sturla had a strong interest, having already operated a farm at Hítardalr from 1255.[184] The arena of conflict for these two *höfðingjar* had moved south.

Of significant interest here is what happened to Sauðafell when Hrafn had moved out of Dalir. Vigfúss Gunnsteinsson, who had lived at Garpsdalr, was at Sauðafell in about 1261. He was living here for the same reason that Hrafn Oddsson had been able to, namely that he was Sturla Sighvatsson's son-in-law. He was thus Sturla's kinsman by marriage and joined in a pact with Snorri

---

181 It still seems feasible that Guðmundr *umboðsmaðr* was the same person as Guðmundr Óláfsson even though, when the uncle-nephew relationship of Fell-Snorri and Guðmundr is recorded, the latter is called Óláfsson (SS I: 10). Guðmundr's referral of Halldórr Vilmundarson to Hrafn (p. 118 above) also firms up the idea of their alliance.
182 SS I: 304, 436, 447.
183 SS II: 227.
184 SS II: 167–69, 195, 201–3.

Sturluson the younger and Eyrar-Snorri to protect one another. It seems unsurprising that he failed to meet up with his 'allies' to attack his brother-in-law Hrafn, although Sturla Þórðarson seems to have expected Vigfúss' co-operation in 1262.[185] Vigfúss certainly tried to stay neutral in this conflict, and perhaps he was seen as a neutral party to run Sauðafell who had been put in place with the agreement of both Sturla and Hrafn.

Other than this change, the loyalties of the Dalir-based men who appear in the few pages of *Sturlu þáttr* seem to have remained close to the way they were in the mid-1250s, although in truth we are only told of the actions of Sturla's supporters around Hvammsfjörður. Eyrar-Snorri and Snorri Sturluson the younger joined together in a raid on areas of the West Fjords loyal to Hrafn.[186] In retaliation Hrafn is said to have captured Eyrar-Snorri soon afterwards, in his final sortie into Dalir to remove Sturla. We are told that Böðvarr Þórðarson advised his son Guðmundr to support Sturla rather than Hrafn,[187] confirming that Böðvarr was still alive at this point and loyal to his brother. Finally as Hrafn closed in on Sturla he reached Bjarni, son of Skarð-Snorri, at home who was also clearly still in cahoots with Sturla: Bjarni knew where Sturla was hiding but would not go to find him unless Hrafn agreed to grant Sturla peace.[188] Bjarni, like his father, was siding with Sturla, his local *höfðingi*.

7 Political Power in Dalir from c.1185-c.1265: Some Conclusions

Eighty years is a long time, especially in politics, and particularly when those years are only described by political narratives which sometimes cover whole years in a few pages. Nevertheless some broad points can be made about the numbers of local political leaders in Dalir in this period and the nature of their power, in terms of their territorial control and support networks.

The leading political figures in Dalir as identified by the narratives are easily listed, as they have been mentioned above: Þórðr Sturluson, Sighvatr Sturluson, Snorri Sturluson, Sturla Sighvatsson, Böðvarr Þórðarson, Þórðr *kakali* Sighvatsson and, the only non-Sturlungar figure, Hrafn Oddsson. Þorgils *skarði* Böðvarsson was based on Snæfellsnes and can only be seen to have had an impact there. Of these men, only the Sturlusynir and Sturla Sighvatsson and

---

185 SS II: 228.
186 Ibid.
187 SS II: 229.
188 SS II: 230.

Böðvarr Þórðarson are clearly said to have had *goðorð* or a share in one which was based in Dalir. Þórðr *kakali* and Hrafn Oddsson, although they may have inherited or acquired *goðorð* which were dependent on support from Dalir, can only be seen to have claimed authority from the Norwegian king.

At any one time in this period it would seem that there were no more than two of the very highest level of powerful individuals living and exercising power in Dalir itself. Given what we shall see was the case in Eyjafjörður after 1200, this fragmented picture is still significant. Þórðr Sturluson was based at Hvammr while Sighvatr and then Sturla Sighvatsson lived at Sauðafell. After Þórðr Sturluson's death Hvammr ceases to appear as the base of his sons while Sauðafell is occupied by Þórðr *kakali* and then Hrafn Oddsson (and then Vigfúss Gunnsteinsson). Sturla Þórðarson was able to base himself at Staðarhóll, as he had done on and off since 1235, although sometimes living at his other estates, outside Dalir, in the 1250s (at Hítardalr and Svignaskarð) and eventually moving to Fagradalr in 1271.[189]

In territorial terms there seems to have been a division between northern and southern Dalir with Hvammssveit perhaps now being an area which acted as some kind of buffer zone. When Þórðr Sturluson was living at Hvammr there was clearly a great deal of tension with his peers at Sauðafell, particularly as Dufgus and his sons, based at Hjarðarholt, were loyal to Sauðafell. Þórðr Sturluson's support network may have been more dispersed and he may have relied on some form of support, financial or 'military,' from Saurbær and around Öndverðareyrr and Staðr on Snæfellsnes, to counter Sauðafell's power. Certainly, so far as we can see, Fellsströnd was an area which was contested by Hvammr and Sauðafell in the 1220s and 1230s; even Hvammssveit was not entirely supportive of Hvammr, assuming that Lauga-Snorri actually still had a connection there while he was affiliated to Sturla Sighvatsson. It would seem that Sturla Þórðarson's residence at Staðarhóll, regardless of whether or not he was able to live at Hvammr, would reflect the fact that it was not politically astute for him to live too close to Sauðafell.

For this region one might ask whether there really was so little solidarity among the Sturlungar; familial feeling between brothers, uncles and nephews might have been greater than is suggested by our conflict-focussed texts. Of course, at the same time, these men presumably had differing ideas as to how best to deal with *bændr* – the writer Sturla Þórðarson certainly judges his uncle Sighvatr and cousin Sturla harshly in this regard – and there was an array of other, standard factors which prohibited greater solidarity. Each of Hvamm-Sturla's sons inherited different properties and their political roles were shaped

---

189 SS II: 235.

by their marriages to women from different regions and the different kinship networks which these created. In Dalir itself the best-documented rivalry among the Sturlungar, that between Þórðr Sturluson and his nephew Sturla Sighvatsson, must also have owed something to the rough equality of their wealth and support networks, even if Þórðr Sturluson had slightly the better of it (at least according to his son who wrote about it).

As has been stressed throughout this chapter, the allegiances of those men who lived at what were wealthy farms in later centuries, and frequently the preeminent farm in each district, but who do not appear to instigate conflict, would appear to have been important to the *höfðingjar*. These men were frequently both in the company of the *höfðingjar*, seen as negotiators in their conflicts, and acted as a line of communication between local leaders and lesser farmers, those at smaller farms. Moreover, they were married into local *höfðingi* families. In many respects they appear as their equals and it would take exceptional circumstances – such as late on in the period concerned when Þorgils *skarði* returned from Norway with some kind of army – for them not to be treated as such.

8 The Eyjafjörður Region

The contemporary sagas have far less to say about twelfth- and thirteenth-century Eyjafjörður and Þingeyjarsýsla than they do about Dalir, thanks to the interests of the medieval compilers of *Sturlunga saga*. We have no equivalent of *Þorgils saga ok Hafliða* for the period before 1150, although two texts cover the last decades of the twelfth century in reasonable detail, *Guðmundar saga dýra* and *Prestssaga Guðmundar góða*. These enable us to ask the same questions about territoriality and the nature of the *goði-þingmaðr* relationship as we have done for Dalir. *Íslendinga saga* does provide occasional coverage of Eyjafjörður but for all of the valley's tens of farms, very few are mentioned. The discussion of *Íslendinga saga* and the other later texts for this region is therefore briefer and structured around the geography of the region rather than on the chronological basis which made more sense for Dalir.

9 *Prestssaga Guðmundr góða* and *Guðmundar saga dýra*

We have to begin our analysis of Eyjafjörður, then, with the two narratives which record northern politics in the late twelfth century. An outline of their contents will help explain their scope.

Prestssaga Guðmundr góða is an account of Guðmundr Arason's life until his consecration in Norway. Its coverage of northern politics in the period c.1160 to c.1203 is fairly superficial because it only really follows Guðmundr's life. The saga begins by emphasising the importance of the future Bishop Guðmundr's father and his uncle, the *goði* Þorgeirr Hallason, in the 1160s. Ari, Guðmundr's father, dies a gallant death in battle in Norway as a *lendr maðr* of Jarl Erlingr, while Þorgeirr is identified as making a notable speech at the Alþing after it had been interrupted by fighting.[190] Þorgeirr sold his farm at Hvassafell in Eyjafjörður and entered the monastery at Munkaþverá, meaning his sons were now based in Fnjóskadalur (Map 10). Guðmundr, an illegitimate child, is said to have been born at Grjótá, probably Grjótgarðr, a *hjáleiga* of Laugaland in Hörgárdalur.[191] He spent his childhood in the care of his uncle and foster-father, Ingimundr, who, after an apparently failed marriage, and took Guðmundr with him to various different prominent farms in and around Eyjafjörður. They stayed at Möðruvellir in Eyjafjörður, at Grenjaðarstaðir, at nearby Staðr in Kaldakinn, and then Guðmundr went to Saurbær to stay with Óláfr Þorsteinsson.[192] This list would seem to suggest that the secular leaders of the region were not hospitable towards Ingimundr and Guðmundr; it pre-empts events of the 1230s where Guðmundr again relied on the support of church-farms to house him.[193]

Guðmundr spends the next few years on the move, stopping off at various places including Steingrímsfjörður, Hvammr in Dalir – Hvamm-Sturla was his uncle by marriage – and the monastery at Þingeyrar in Húnavatnssýsla. Guðmundr eventually became a priest at Miklabær in Skagafjörður.[194] By 1190 he had been invited to move to Vellir in Svarfaðardalur by a kinswoman, Arnþrúðr, where he stayed until Arnþrúðr and her sons inherited a neighbouring farm (Sakka).[195] Guðmundr planned to leave but was persuaded to stay for a while, supposedly turning down a permanent benefice there. This may well have been due to the hostility of the man who ran the farm, who was only eventually removed by the Bishop of Hólar (Brandr Sæmundarson), and on the understanding that Arnþrúðr's sons would retain ownership of the property.[196] This story is retold from a different perspective in *Guðmundar saga dýra* where Guðmundr *dýri* forcibly removes the Arnþrúðarsynir from Vellir; his hostility

---

190 SS I: 117–21. See pp. 66–67, 318 for Þorgeirr and Ari.
191 SS I: 118; *Jarðabók* X: 174–75.
192 SS I: 124–25.
193 See below 142–43.
194 SS I: 136, 138, 139.
195 See below p. 132.
196 SS I: 140–41, 210–12.

might explain Guðmundr Arason's move to another farm in Svarfaðardalur (Ufsir).[197]

After this, from about 1198, Guðmundr's reputation as a healer sees him travel all over the country. It is noticeable that up to this point Guðmundr had not spent any time in Eyjafjörður proper nor the districts immediately to its east and *Prestssaga* is rather short on the detail of where he went to in Eyjafjörður in further travels dateable to 1201, north around the district around Eyjafjörður (*norðr um herað um Eyjafjörð*). Given that individual farms are often named in the text, this might be further indication that Guðmundr Arason was not that popular among the elite in Eyjafjörður.[198] In *Guðmundar saga dýra* he does appear but only in a minor way when he allows a body to be buried at Vellir; Guðmundr *dýri* may not have been his namesake's biggest fan if his treatment of the Arnþrúðarsynir is anything to go by.[199] Equally, despite Guðmundr *dýri*'s presence at the meeting to decide the next bishop and where Guðmundr Arason was chosen, he is not named as one of the new bishop's advocates.[200] It might be that Guðmundr Arason's apparent popularity was something which Guðmundr *dýri* resented and, given that Guðmundr *dýri* was able to suspend the Vaðlaþing, it is not inconceivable that he could also limit the priest's travels around Eyjafjörður. In effect, the main point to draw from *Prestssaga* is that we have a different kind of powerful figure here in the late twelfth century. This a one-off case and it is perhaps not surprising that Guðmundr Arason is based in Svarfaðardalur, roughly equidistant between Skagafjörður and Eyjafjörður, and thus reasonable distance from the homes of Guðmundr *dýri* and other local leaders of any note. As we shall see, however, Guðmundr *dýri* otherwise seems to have had a strong influence in Svarfaðardalur.

Guðmundar saga dýra, covering the period 1185–1200, is often seen as the archetypal text for demonstrating, first, the freedom of *þingmenn* to choose their *goðar* and, second, the beginnings of the amassing of multiple distinct *goðorð* by a single *goði*.[201] The boldest view of geographically-dispersed *þingmenn*, living distant from their chosen *goði* rather than cowed by one in their immediate vicinity, is in Jesse Byock's *Viking Age Iceland*. The two maps and accompanying list of *goðar* in *Guðmundar saga dýra* aimed at making this point show four definite *goðar* and two probable *goðar*.[202] There is no doubt

---

197 SS I: 141.
198 SS I: 146.
199 SS I: 173, 174, 187–88.
200 SS I: 152. The two named advocates are men from Skagafjörður and, probably, Breiðabólstaðr in Vestrhóp (SS II: 394, 403).
201 Cf. generally Helgi Þorláksson 1994.
202 Byock 2001: 128–32, 133.

that the text does record some *þingmenn* living tens of kilometres away from their *goðar* in different valleys from their *goði*. However, it is not the case that all the *goðar* on Byock's maps lived permanently where they are located, nor that *þingmenn* represented in Byock's exegesis were permanently attached to the particular *goðar* he assigns them to. Allowance also has to be made for the likely allegiances of those *bændr* not mentioned in the text. This text, just like *Sturlu saga*, can be read so as to demonstrate the presence of a certain degree of territorial power for *goðar*. It raises interesting questions about what power Guðmundr *dýri* had and what was going on in Eyjafjörður itself in this period. The fact that Guðmundr was able to prevent by force any kind of resolution of an important legal case at the Vaðlaþing in about 1187 and then to prevent it happening altogether soon afterwards shows that he enjoyed considerable support.[203]

The basic framework of the saga is formed by the political relationships between three *goðar* and their relatives and associates. Guðmundr *dýri* Þorvaldsson, whose family seem to have been powerful before him, lived at Bakki in Öxnadalur (Figure 10, Map 9), in effect, defeated two rivals.[204] His most obvious competitor was Önundr Þorkelsson, who lived first at Laugaland in Hörgárdalur before ousting the occupant of Langahlíð in the same valley.[205] After Önundr's death, his place in local politics was taken by his son-in-law Þorgrímr *alikarl* at Möðruvellir in Hörgárdalur.[206] Möðruvellir had been the home of another *goði*, Þorvarðr Þorgeirsson, when the saga began and it is unclear as to why the farm changes hands other than that Þorvarðr lost out politically to Önundr/Þorgrímr *alikarl*. This is in sharp contrast to the apparent importance of Þorvarðr's father, Þorgeirr Hallason. Þorvarðr's son, Ögmundr *sneis* Þorvarðsson, had been in Norway but returns to live at Háls in Fnjóskadalur in 1192 (Figure 15, Map 10).[207]

From across the region to the north of Hörgárdalur – Fljót, Ólafsfjörður (Map 8) and Svarfaðardalur – people still seek out either Guðmundr or Önundr as their advocate. Guðmundr *dýri* still also had the confidence of other local leaders, including Kolbeinn Tumason, and carries out the so-called *Önundarbrenna* in 1197, the arson attack on Önundr's home at Langahlíð which killed Önundr and many others. Guðmundr paid extensive compensation at the Alþing as a result of a settlement presided over by Jón Loptsson.[208] After this

---

203 SS I: 163, 170.
204 See above for his familial background, 66, 80–81, 83.
205 SS I: 178.
206 SS I: 189–92.
207 SS I: 178.
208 SS I: 192–94.

he bought off Ögmundr *sneis* by belatedly paying off the 1200 hundred fine which he had owed from their previous dispute, and which seems to result in Ögmundr's passivity thereafter.

Indeed peace seems to have broken out for a while but Þorgrímr *alikarl* and Önundr's sons made an attempt to remove Guðmundr from the political scene. As they gathered troops for a raid on Guðmundr at Bakki, they killed a known supporter of Guðmundr's who lived at Arnarnes on the west coast of Eyjafjörður.[209] They raided Bakki but Guðmundr was absent and so they removed his men's 'weapons and shields.'[210] Þorgrímr then went away to gather support from his southern-based kinsmen which allowed Guðmundr (with Kolbeinn Tumason again) to raid Laugaland and other farms in lower Hörgárdalur.[211]

A further attempt by neutrals to negotiate a long-term peace got nowhere. Þorgrímr *alikarl* led a raid on Bakki with a force of one hundred men. This raid ultimately failed and led to Þorgrímr's force being surrounded at a neighbouring farm by men led by Guðmundr, Kolbeinn Tumason (who is said to have brought 600 men) and Ögmundr *sneis*. In the settlement Guðmundr got self-judgement and thereby supposedly made Þorgrímr destitute. Þorgrímr left Hörgárdalur and is said to have moved to the farm of Geldingaholt in Skagafjörður.[212] A single sentence at the end of the saga says that Guðmundr retired to become a monk at Þingeyrar, there having been only a slight hint of Guðmundr's piety up to this point.[213]

The sketch narrative above gives a sense of the scale of the saga's action in terms of individuals' power and geographical scale. Guðmundr *dýri* seems to have been more successful than Hvamm-Sturla, for example, both to begin with and at the end of his secular career. What remains to be considered is the wider geopolitical patterns that can be discerned in the text and what they tell us about the nature of political power in and around Eyjafjörður.

The first thing to say is that it would seem that the allegiances of Hörgárdalur's *bændr* were divided on roughly geographical lines (see Map 9). Guðmundr *dýri* had more support and more land in the upper parts of the valley while Önundr/Þorgrímr *alikarl* had more support in the lower valley. Ögmundr is noticeably absent from Hörgárdalur politics in the latter half of the saga when his interests were focussed on Fnjóskadalur. Thus Guðmundr had two kinsmen living near him, Þorvaldr at Bægisá in syðri and Söxólfr Fornason at

---

209 SS I: 196.
210 SS I: 199.
211 SS I: 201–2.
212 SS I: 207–9.
213 SS I: 176, 207, 212. Otherwise Guðmundr is said to have visited his church regularly and known someone who worked as a shrine-maker in Svarfaðardalur.

Myrkárdalur (also the farm where Guðmundr had a concubine) and he owned Bakki's neighbouring farm, Steinastaðir.[214] Myrká was home to a supporter of Önundr but the saga mentions him only to show that he could be bullied by Söxólfr.[215] Thus almost the only connections in Öxnadalur and upper Hörgárdalur were to Guðmundr.[216]

Önundr and Þorgrímr *alikarl* had supporters almost exclusively in lower Hörgárdalur. They controlled Laugaland, Langahlíð and, later, Möðruvellir and had supporters at Dynhagi, Rauðalækr and Hlaðir. At the *Önundarbrenna* a man called Gálmr Grímsson from Dynhagi chose to die with Önundr, rather than escape on account of his friendship with Guðmundr and Kolbeinn Tumason, presumably died in the fire.[217] Tjörvi from Rauðalækr, a farm mid-way between Bakki and Laugaland, is also granted a truce by Guðmundr's party (but dies of his wounds). A priest at Öxnahóll was definitely allied to Önundr later in the text, once Guðmundr had had him publicly humiliated.[218] Hlaðir, close to Möðruvellir at the mouth of Hörgárdalur, was home to another figure (Illugi Jósepsson) who was initially supported by Guðmundr but ends up being supported by Þorgrímr *alikarl* (when Guðmundr aided a killer from nearby Skjaldarvík).[219] By contrast Kálfr Guttormsson at Auðbrekka is the only person in the lower half of Hörgárdalur who is not a supporter of Önundr and, even if he was associated with Guðmundr, his case is rather unusual because he had arrived in Iceland not long before 1197 and moved out of Hörgárdalur at some point too.[220] This account differs only slightly from Byock's maps but emphasises significant territorialisation within the confines of Hörgárdalur during the short period covered by the saga. Given the paucity of evidence for this valley at any other point it is difficult to see how usual this pattern was. The overall process is not that dissimilar to that seen in *Sturlu saga* when Hvamm-Sturla drives supporters of his enemy away from Hvammsveit.[221]

Of the allegiances of men outside Hörgárdalur, Svarfaðardalur (Map 8) seems to have been almost exclusively populated by supporters of Guðmundr

---

214 SS I: 171, 176, 185.
215 SS I: 187.
216 Guðmundr arguably also has connections in the opposite direction too because he buys property at Uppsalir and Hálfdanartunga, relatively close to Bakki, when he can (SS I: 171).
217 Jón Viðar Sigurðsson 1998: 111; Sverrir Jakobsson 1998: 127.
218 SS I: 186, 201, 202.
219 SS I: 176, 177, 194.
220 See p. 78.
221 See above pp. 95–96.

dýri.[222] But equally telling is the blanket statement on how Guðmundr treated the area, visiting his many *þingmenn* and close relatives there every spring and autumn. This must refer to the Fornungar but probably to others too.[223] Certainly no other *goði* seems to have had a connection to Svarfaðardalur, and Guðmundr is someone who resolves disputes between *bœndr* in Árskógsströnd as well.[224] Guðmundr appears to have been dominant in Fljót where we hear of one recorded *þingmaðr*, and then that Guðmundr was given the *Fljótamannagoðorð*.[225] While there is a man who comes from that region (Rúnólfr Nikulássson) and stayed with Önundr, he was essentially an outlaw being sheltered.[226]

In Óláfsfjörður (Map 8) it is clear that some neighbouring *bœndr* at the farms known as Brekka could have different *goðar*.[227] In one dispute a man was is explicitly the *þingmaðr* of Guðmundr while the brothers living nearby were the *þingmenn* of Önundr. A third example sees another *þingmaðr* of Önundr in this valley. Here there do appear to have been divided loyalties and what's more the three farms were probably average-sized, rather than farms of 40 hundreds or more as we have seen for Dalir, and were not even the largest within Óláfsfjörður.[228] This might perhaps be explained by the remoteness of the region to Hörgárdalur; *bœndr* from this district might have had more to gain by seeking protection from a *goði* than the *goði* would have to gain from trying to keep loyal smaller or poorer households.

Located on the coast, closer to Hörgárdalur, are two *þingmenn* with contrasting social networks. The first, the priest Helgi Halldórsson was at Árskógr, in the district of the same name, in 1191. He was the kinsman of the *goði* Þorvarðr Þorgeirsson but the *þingmaðr* of Önundr. A vignette about the love life of Helgi's mother-in-law, who lived at nearby Brattavöllr, sees Önundr and Þorvarðr work together to help Helgi. In other words one of the most important farms in this district was not an ally of Guðmundr. The second named man, however, is Guðmundr's nephew, Hákon Þórðarson at Arnarnes, the son of

---

222 Two named farms had his supporters, Tjörn, and Sakka (where Arnþrúðr's sons lived until they were exiled). We might add Vellir as a sometime home of Guðmundr's supporters, the Fornungar who were his brother-in-law's family. Arnþrúðr and her sons had lived there too, and Urðir, home of Ormr *prestr* Fornason, Guðmundr's nephew (SS I: 196). Urða-Steinn, seemingly a member of Guðmundr's household, must have been related to them somehow (SS I: 174, 176, 182, 191, 196, 197, 199, 204, 206, 234). See above for Vellir, p. 79.

223 'Guðmundr átti fjölða þingmanna út um Svarfaðardal ok náfrændr, ok fór hann þannig at heimboðum haust og vár.' (SS I: 176).

224 Guðmundr pays compensation for the killing of a man from Fagraskógr (SS I: 210).

225 See above pp. 63, 64, 66.

226 SS I: 183–86.

227 Ósbrekka and Skeggjabrekka (Map 8).

228 The Brekka farms were valued at 20h and 30h respectively. Sandr might refer to Sandkirkja, a *hjáleiga* of Hornbrekka (*Jarðabók* X: 21–24, 37–38).

Guðmundr's half-brother Þórðr Þórarinsson. Hákon was an active supporter of Guðmundr and was eventually killed by Þorgrímr *alikarl*'s men.[229] It might have made sense for Hákon to locate himself at Arnarnes because it was close to his father at Laufás, a short boat trip over Eyjafjörður, rather than because it says anything about geopolitics more widely, although it could have been useful for Guðmundr to have someone loyal to him living at Arnarnes. These two cases are of men who would have been important locally – they lived on farms of average size or larger – are probably confirmation that well-off *bændr* in this district could choose their *goði*.

A similar point can be made about the allegiances of men identified on the other side of Eyjafjörður. Mention has already been made of Þorvarðr Þorgeirsson's and his son Ögmundr *sneis*' shift to Fnjóskadalur. By the early 1190s this means that we can see these men only working within this valley. Þorvarðr's move east, out of Möðruvellir in Hörgárdalur, makes sense for other reasons. He and his father had been at Hvassafell up until the late 1160s and so Möðruvellir was the most westerly place in which he had ever lived.[230] Þorvarðr also had a *þingmaðr* who was one of the two brothers from somewhere in or around Reykjadalur (*í dalnum*) who had a claim on Helgastaðir in the late 1180s (Map 10).[231] It is also worth noting that Ögmundr's wife is supposed to have come from Espihóll. In other words Hörgárdalur was not really central to this father and son's political orbit; their presence at Möðruvellir in Hörgárdalur might have been an attempt to expand their geopolitical reach but one which ultimately failed. All of this has the effect of further tidying Byock's map into local clusters of *þingmenn*. Nevertheless the fact that the other claimant on Helgastaðir was a *þingmaðr* of Önundr still suggests that there could be a considerable distance between *goðar* and *þingmenn*. Perhaps Reykjadalur was like Ólafsfjörður in being distant from *goðar* so that the relationship was less active on both sides, and actually served the *þingmenn* more as a control on the influence of neighbours than signalling strong affiliation to a *goði*.

The sum of the alliances mentioned above is that we have changing pattern whereby Guðmundr gradually increases his influence over particular districts. He, like other leaders perhaps, could end up with influence over all the largest farms in a small valley (Svarfaðardalur) just by dint of a marriage, in this case that of his sister. He, and his rival, Önundr, also created districts around their own farms of about the same size as a *hreppr* in which most farms were probably under their sway, or else could do nothing actively against them. It is also important in the case of Guðmundr not to underestimate how much influence

---

229 SS I: 169–71, 179, 180, 186, 187, 190, 191, 196–99.
230 SS I: 168.
231 SS I: 160.

he had by c.1200 even if we do not see him with *þingmenn* in Eyjafjörður itself or further east. This also begs the question of what was going on in Eyjafjörður itself in the period 1185–1200. Önundr is said to have shared *goðorð* with an Einarr Hallsson of Möðruvellir who might have had *þingmenn* of his own. It is also curious that *Guðmundar saga dýra* has no real interest in Eyjafjörður or its apparent *goðar* at Hrafnagil and Saurbær. This might be a product of a rather selective social memory but probably reflects the fact that Guðmundr and the *goðar* in Eyjafjörður (together) regarded each other as sufficiently well-matched not to try to challenge one another. For most of the saga we are probably witness to these leading farmers, who happen to be *goðar*, avoiding conflict with Guðmundr. He, for his part, seems to have been unable to challenge the power of well-off leaders in Eyjafjörður whose interests would have been aligned with the numerous *bændr* in Eyjafjörður. It is only in the signficant conflict towards the end of the saga that we see Grund's apparent leader, Þorlákr Ketilsson, on the side of Þorgrímr *alikarl* against Guðmundr *dýri*. Guðmundr is able to get Þorlákr outlawed from Eyjafjörður and his right-hand man, Kálfr Guttormsson moves there. In geopolitical terms, Grund was the closest of the large Eyjafjörður farms to Bakki and so, at the small scale about which we are talking, it was strategically important (Maps 3 and 9). Here again the case can be made that Guðmundr was ensuring that he had a block of territory. This bolstered what was also an attempt to locate himself centrally in relation to inner and outer Eyjafjörður, and Skagafjörður.

10   After Guðmundr *dýri*, c.1200-c.1265

After the account of *Guðmundar saga dýra* come the intertwined accounts provided by *Íslendinga saga*, *Þórðar saga kakala* and *Þorgils saga skarða* which take us up to the end of the Commonwealth period in the 1260s. It arguably makes less sense to treat the thirteenth-century history of Eyjafjörður in quite the same way as Dalir has been treated. We do have particular narratives which highlight individuals' allegiances, of course, but fewer of them. Therefore this section considers geopolitics synchronically and diachronically.

10.1   *Eyjafjörður*

Íslendinga saga initially says little about the valley of Eyjafjörður itself. Guðmundr *dýri* retired to the monastery at Þingeyrar just after 1200 and so local politics almost inevitably changed. Sigurðr Ormsson, of the Svínfellingar family and from south-eastern Iceland, was invited north by the two preeminent figures in Skagafjörður, the Bishop of Hólar and Kolbeinn Tumason, to manage the diocesan estates. Sigurðr then moved to Munkaþverá, however, having been given the *goðorð* of Guðmundr *dýri* by Guðmundr's son. Sigurðr was only at Þverá a short while before moving to Möðruvellir in Hörgárdalur. While in Eyjafjörður, he also allied himself with Hallr Kleppjárnsson, at Hrafnagil, *against* the Bishop Guðmundr *góði* and the bishop's kinsman, Ögmundr *sneis* who was still at Háls in Fnjóskadalur.[232] It is also noteworthy here that Sigurðr and Hallr are portrayed as working with a leading figure from Skagafjörður, a significant connection in the short term at least and one which we will rarely, if ever, see in *Landnámabók* or *Íslendingasögur*.

Thus at this point it is Möðruvellir in Hörgárdalur, Hrafnagil, Háls and Grund which seem to be key places. Within Eyjafjörður, though, the local battle between Sigurðr at Möðruvellir and Ögmundr *sneis* ended with Ögmundr being made to leave the north of the country altogether in 1209.[233] It is only when Hallr Kleppjárnsson has been killed by Kálfr Guttormsson of Grund that Sighvatr Sturluson is invited to move to Eyjafjörður and buys Grund.[234] Like Sigurðr Ormsson, here Sighvatr had the support of the leading family in Skagafjörður, his Ásbirningar kinsmen.[235] Thus, suddenly, as Sighvatr became involved in Eyjafjörður politics, we can see Grund as the pre-eminent farm within the whole of Eyjafjörður and so it remains until the 1260s.

An argument could be made for Grund having been important earlier. Certainly Þorsteinn *ranglátr* Einarsson (d.1149) was associated with Grund and the Grundar-Ketill who is said to have died in 1173 may well have been his son.[236] His son, Þorlákr, was driven out of Eyjafjörður as part of the judgement (*sjálfdæmi*) meted out by Guðmundr *dýri* in 1199; Guðmundr and his Skagafjörður ally had surrounded the fortified enclosure (*virki*) at Grund, where Þorgrímr *alikarl* and his southern ally were holed up.[237] When we next hear of Grund, seemingly in about 1211, it is the home of Kálfr Guttormsson,[238] Guðmundr *dýri*'s Norwegian ally, which would seem to suggest that Guðmundr had been able to influence who lived there, if not perhaps even have lived there himself.

In fact Grund remained the home of the controller of what now suddenly appears to be a regional overlordship, a *ríki*, with it not seeming to matter who

---

232 E.g. SS I: 244–50
233 SS I: 254.
234 Kálfr Guttormsson kills Hallr Kleppjárnsson; Kálfr appears to be regarded as a troublemaker (SS I: 260).
235 SS I: 258.
236 SS I: 55, 124; Lúðvík Ingvarsson 1980–86: III 461.
237 SS II: 208–9.
238 SS I: 257.

ran the region, because they always live at Grund. In succession, we have a number of men who take charge of the Eyjafjörður *ríki*, including Sighvatr's sons after his death in 1238, but also others. Þorvarðr Þórarinsson was there in 1258, for example, when he had Þorgils *skarði* killed at Hrafnagil.[239] This is quite unlike what we have seen for Dalir where members of the same elite family still competed with one another and without there being any clear sense that one had primacy over the other until the 1240s with the return of Þórðr *kakali* from Norway.

Certain ways in which the history of Grund is represented merit further attention. In fact, the accounts of Þórðr *kakali* Sighvatsson's return to Iceland from Norway present differing accounts of his immediate gathering of support in Iceland. *Þórðar saga kakala* chapter 2 is significantly more verbose in describing Þórðr's arrival in Eyjafjörður and journey to the south and then west of the country, giving over two pages in the 1946 edition to events which take only sixteen lines to recount in *Íslendinga saga* (ch. 158).[240] The only purpose of the *Íslendinga saga* account seems to be to briefly remember a few minor characters who were supporters of Þórðr.[241] *Þorgils saga skarði*, however, provides a hostile account of Kolbeinn *ungi* of which two main elements are worth investigating. Kolbeinn is set up as dominating Eyjafjörður and being involved in the control of Grund. He is also supposed to have turned all the larger *bændr* in Eyjafjörður (*alla ina stærri bændr í Eyjafirði*) against Þórðr *kakali* in advance of the latter's return. He then engineered a situation whereby Sighvatr Sturluson's widow and son, Halldóra and Tumi, were deprived of Grund and forcibly moved out to Skagafjörður where Kolbeinn hoped that they (and Þórðr *kakali* when he returned) would cause him fewer problems. Sighvatr's daughter Sigríðr and her husband, Styrmir Þórisson, were apparently

---

239   SS II: 216.
240   SS I: 472; SS II: 4–7.
241   SS I: 472. *Íslendinga saga* gives a list of five men most of whom are not recorded anywhere else. Of these five, only one appears regularly in *Sturlunga saga*: Nikulás Oddsson. He appears mostly in connection with his support of Þórðr *kakali* (SS I: 472; II: 7, 34, 36, 49–51, 54, 56, 59–60, 72, 82, 84, 119, 125–27, 131, 134, 137, 140, 161, 165–66, 176, 177, 289). Two of the others (Jón Tóstason, Aron *kjúkabassi*) are only mentioned here. Öxna-Börkr/Börkr Guðmundarson is mentioned in both instances but with different names and never mentioned again (SS I: 472; II: 7) while Þorgeirr *kornasylgja* is mentioned here and in passing once more when a supporter of Þórðr in summer 1244 (SS I: 472; II: 53). Snorri Þórálfsson who accompanied Þórðr from Norway is said to have been from the north (*norðlenzkr at ætt*, SS II: 34) and had been with his father in 1235 and before that with Guðmundr Arason (SS I: 386). He was killed supporting Þórðr at the *Flóabardagi* in June 1244 (SS II: 64). He might also have been the 'Snorri *prestr*' who was gelded in 1222 in events surrounding the outlaw Aron Hjörleifsson (SS I: 292; II: 249).

moved in the opposite direction, from upper Skagafjörður to Grund. Grund is actually described as being Styrmir's *föðurleifð*, his inheritance from his father, but none of our surviving sources make it clear who Styrmir's father was. There is also mention of a rumour that Kolbeinn had bought a share in the farm, although the saga's account seems designed to discredit such a claim. Quite what we can conclude about the purpose of some of this information is unclear beyond the fact that, unsurprisingly, ownership of Grund was a contentious issue at this point. It looks as if Kolbeinn had tried hard to control the farm, if not own it, in order to control Eyjafjörður. However, the farm seems to have remained in Sighvatr's family until the rights to it were given by Steinvör Sighvatsdóttir to Þorvarðr Þórarinsson, her son-in-law, in the absence of a legitimate male heir.[242] The story of Grund and Þorvarðr end with a whimper as Þorvarðr leaves, seemingly within months, to be replaced by Steinvör's son, Loftr Hálfdanarson.[243]

Only one or two extra details need be added to this lengthy list of developments. These concern the more local-level allegiances which appear occasionally in the *Sturlunga saga* compilation that can tell us about relations between major farms and also between these larger farms and smaller ones. Such relationships are important to remember because they are, here as in Dalir, on a similar kind of scale to those in the *Íslendingasögur*. Thus we have already seen that Grund and Hrafnagil were opposed to one another at one point in the early thirteenth century. This same tension seems to have continued, to judge by a conflict set in about 1220. It is at this point that Hrafnagil is said to have been home to the killer of one of Sighvatr's other sons, a statement which becomes significant when, in the same chapter, it is related that an overseer at Hrafnagil is killed by a temporary member of the household, someone who had been at neighbouring Stokkahlaðir and was suspected of really working for Sighvatr.[244] In this early part of Sighvatr's time at Grund, there were kinsmen of the people of Hrafnagil living at Espihóll, midway between Hrafnagil and Grund, and also at Gnúpufell. By 1238, and the battle of Örlygsstaðir at which Sighvatr was killed, however, both Espihóll and Gnúpufell were remembered as being the home of members of his force.[245] Perhaps here we can see a change in the allegiance of Espihóll and Gnúpufell. And, if a throwaway line about one of the supporters of Sighvatr's sons is anything to go by – this man

---

242 SS II: 211, 216.
243 SS II: 222.
244 One of killers associated with Stokkahlaðir, between Espihóll and Hrafnagil but nearer to Hrafnagil. This killing happens before the 'full' revenge on Tumi Sighvatsson's killers, the attack known as the *Grímseyjarför* (SS I: 288–90).
245 SS I: 420.

has a girlfriend at Gnúpufell – then Gnúpufell was still identifiable as having a close relationship with Grund in 1255.[246] However, the tension between Grund and Hrafnagil seems to have been just as long-lived. In 1255, in events connected with another generation of Iceland's leaders, the opponents of Grund use Hrafnagil as a place to stay.[247] This is hardly the kind of sustained level of detail that we see for many accounts for Dalir but the high status of each farm is maintained and, significantly, it is Hrafnagil which is a rival to Grund rather than any other large farm in Eyjafjörður.

Íslendinga saga also mentions relations between Sighvatr and his associates with farms to the south of Grund, but to hardly anywhere else. In other episodes we can see that Sighvatr and his sons created some enemies here early on. Shortly after Sighvatr had moved to Grund, his sons wanted to buy a sword from two brothers, one at Möðruvellir, the other at Miklagarðr, another large farm but one which rarely gets mentioned in the *Sturlunga* compilation.[248] The brothers did not want to part with the sword but eventually the Sighvatssynir got it anyway and injured one of the brothers in doing so. Sighvatr gave the injured brother compensation but the text gives the impression that the households of Möðruvellir and Miklagarðr had been hard done by.[249] Möðruvellir is never portrayed as positively disposed towards Grund. Later on Hallr Jónsson from Möðruvellir, son of one of the abused brothers, appears to have been seen as a kind of neutral. He appears to have avoided involvement with Þórðr *kakali* Sighvatsson's politicking in the 1240s, but in one scene is keeping the peace in Borgarfjörður between Þórðr's men and those of Kolbeinn *ungi*. In 1255 he is seen, first, to be one of the key *bændr* among who refuse to accept Þorvarðr Þórarinsson as their leader, and later is sought out to mediate when the Bishop of Hólar meets *höfðingjar* at Þverá.[250]

---

246 SS I: 497. I am not suggesting here that it was unusual for people in different households to interact but that the fact that *Íslendinga saga* records this connection is more significant, given the likely distance in time from events to commitment to writing, regardless of what we hypothesise about Sturla Þórðarson's note-taking and writing activities. Rowe (forthcoming) will discuss Sturla's working practices.

247 SS I: 511–17; SS II: 218. Þorvarðr Þórarinsson goes to Grund, his opponents Sturla Þórðarson and Þorgils *skarði* to Hrafnagil.

248 Miklagarðr was a large farm but one which rarely gets mentioned in the *Sturlunga* compilation. The father and son there in 1253 are named as invitees to Gizurr Þorvaldsson's daughter's wedding (SS I: 482).

249 SS I: 260–62.

250 SS II: 21 for when Hallr prevent someone being harmed. The circumstances make it unclear whose side he is on, however. SS II: 73 for Hallr from Möðruvellir not in the north to greet Þórðr *kakali* Sighvatsson in 1246. He is among a group which includes men otherwise positively disposed towards Þórðr *kakali* who support Kolbeinn *ungi* in a raid with

Although the stories above show Grund in conflict with other (larger) farms, on the other hand, particular middle- to larger-sized farms to the south of Grund, on the western side of the main valley, seem always to support it. Hólar and Hvassafell are home to supporters of Sighvatr and his son Þórðr *kakali*.[251] Möðrufell was also home to another set of supporters, who were there from just before Sighvatr's arrival and can last be seen to be active up to 1234. The nephew of Kálfr Guttormsson – Kálfr having formerly lived at Grund himself[252] – still lived at Möðrufell in 1255 but it is not clear what this man's allegiances were at this point.[253]

The attack on Gizurr Þorvaldsson which results in the burning of the farm at Flugumýrr in 1253 provides another snapshot of the politically significant men in and around Eyjafjörður. Whether or not this constitutes a group who were regularly on good terms is less clear. Certainly most of the identifiable 'burners' gathered by Eyjólfr Þorsteinsson (Möðruvellir in Hörgárdalur) and Hrani Koðránsson (Grund) were probably from the locality, augmented with a few kinsmen and long-time associates of the Sturlungar.[254] It is only those men gathered by Eyjólfr whom we can locate and, although none of them can be connected with elite families, most came from larger farms.[255] Given that Guðmundr from Hrafnagil and Þorvarðr Þórðarson from Saurbær join this party it seems as if most of lower Eyjafjörður and Hörgárdalur provided support against

his only recorded act being to save another opponent from harm (SS II: 45, 47). SS II: 192, 198 for events in 1255.

251 Guðmundr Gíslsson of Hvassafell accompanied Abbot Árni to advise Þórðr *kakali* to leave Eyjafjörður in 1242, p. 141 below. Alongside Gnúpufell, Hólar, in the shape of Þorgils 'Hólasveinn' supported Sighvatr and his son in 1234 and when he died fighting for Þórðr *kakali* in 1244, alongside Guðmundr Gíslsson (SS I: 371, 468; SS II: 45, 79).

252 Kálfr was at Grund to invite Sighvatr Sturluson there in the second decade of the thirteenth century. He remained an ally of Sighvatr but had moved to Miklabær in the Blönduhlíð district of Skagafjörður by 1234, the year that Kolbeinn *ungi* and Órækja Snorrason had him and his son Guttormr killed at that farm (SS I: 367–70).

253 Jón Eyjólfsson at Möðrufell, brother-in-law of Kálfr Guttormsson aided him in killing Hallr Kleppjárnsson (SS I: 258). Óláfr, Jón's son, was there in 1234 and 1255 (SS I: 373, 518). There seems to be no connection from the *bóndi* at Möðrufell to the Þórólfr Sigmundarson who was there in the 1180s and whose daughter divorced Teitr Guðmundarson of Helgastaðir (SS I: 160–62). This would seem to confirm that Möðrufell was an important farm, given Helgastaðir's size.

254 The two obvious members of the extended kin group of the Sturlungar in the list are Kolbeinn *grön* Dufgussson and Ari Ingimundarson, grandson of Steinunn, the daughter of Hvamm-Sturla (SS I: 484).

255 SS I: 484–85. Jón from Bakki in Öxnadalur and his son, Ljótr; Einarr from Gaddsvík on Svalbarðsströnd on the eastern coast of Eyjafjörður; Einarr Þorgrímsson from Öxnahóll; Ófeigr Eiríksson, Andréas Brandsson, Þorgils Sveinsson of Möðruvellir in Hörgárdalur. Many of these men are either killed by Gizurr or go abroad in 1258 (SS I: 522).

Gizurr. The absence of people from further afield in this troop may reflect a combination of the fairly hasty assembling of the force and the inability of Þórðr *kakali*'s deputies to impose themselves on the districts further away from their own homes.

One last record of a few individuals' allegiances in Eyjafjörður from *Þorgils saga skarða* is also of note. Þorvarðr Þórarinsson is clearly the object of hostility from the author in the build-up to the killing of Þorgils in 1258 but it is interesting to see how this image is created in just a few sentences. We are given hints at how the local population related to each of Þorvarðr and Þorgils. It is now that Þorgils stayed at Hrafnagil because his brother-in-law lived there, while a friend of Þorgils at Öngulsstaðir – one of the largest farms on the eastern side of the river – had been maimed by Þorvarðr.[256] Þorvarðr, by contrast, had his greatest local supporter in Þorvarðr Þórðarson at Saurbær to the south of Grund.[257] In other words local allegiances which Guðmundr and Þorvarðr Þórarinsson had had as members of a wider group from Eyjafjörður whom Gizurr had invited to his wedding, and their shared role in the attack on Gizurr, seemingly counted for nothing nearer to home five years later.[258]

10.2   *East and West of Eyjafjörður*

What is striking about the smaller valleys which form part of the Eyjafjörður region is how little they feature in the accounts of the thirteenth century. This must in part be due to the myopia of the texts' writers. On the other hand it is possible to see some of these areas as having few local leaders actively interested in secular politics. We will look at what can be said for Svarfaðardalur first before looking at the districts to the east.

Svarfaðardalur's most obvious occupants were the so-called Fornungar, the family named after Forni Söxólfsson, in practice Forni's grandsons, the Arnþrúðarsynir.[259] Their role in the late twelfth century has already been touched on but they continue to play a role, albeit a different one, in later decades. Eyjólfr Valla-Brandsson is the most prominent member of this family and is someone whose identity seems only to be that of a churchman. He is the most notable figure from this valley in the thirteenth century. He goes from probably being a priest at Vellir, in 1218, when he takes in Bishop Guðmundr's

---

256   Öngulsstaðir was a 60 hundred farm in 1712 (*Jarðabók* X: 295–96).
257   SS II: 217. Guðmundr and Þorvarðr Þórarinsson had been in the same party at the *Flugumýrabrenna* (SS I: 485).
258   The only others named were Þorvarðr and his son Örnólfr from Miklagarðr (SS I: 482, 485). Others from Eyjafjörður seem to have been loyal to Gizurr, e.g. the Ásgrímr from Munkaþverá who died at Flugumýrr (SS I: 488, 492).
259   See above pp. 78, 128, 132.

displaced school master and pupils from Hólar, to being the abbot of Munkaþverá by the 1250s. He next features as part of the account of Bishop Guðmundr's death in 1237, coming from Vellir to Hólar in order to place a ring on the dead bishop's finger.[260] He then does not appear again until 1253 when he is identified as abbot and mediates following Gizurr Þorvaldsson's swift revenge against his Eyfirðingar attackers.[261] In 1255 Eyjólfr was mediator again, but this time he acted explicitly at the behest of local *bændr* rather than the competing *höfðingjar* although he had to abort his efforts and the battle at Þverá in litla was the result.[262] The same year Munkaþverá was the scene for a meeting between Bishop Heinrekr, on the one side, and Þorgils *skarði*, Þorvarðr Þórarinsson and Finnbjörn Helgason on the other. Here Eyjólfr was not so much mediator as simply host to an attempted peace meeting which ended without peace being achieved.[263] His last recorded activities, seeing to the burial of Þorgils *skarði* at Munkaþverá in 1258, and, in 1259, holding a feast in honour of the visiting Gizurr Þorvaldsson, confirm that he interacted with the secular elite but did not obviously take sides.[264] It is noticeable, too, that Eyjólfr was far more visible than his predecessor, Abbot Árni (d.1252), whose only appearance in *Sturlunga saga* is when he advises Þórðr *kakali* to leave Eyjafjörður as soon as he can to avoid the aggression of Kolbeinn *ungi*.[265] Thus Vellir, the recorded home of Valla-Ljótr of *Valla-Ljóts saga*, does not seem to be a part of the secular political game.[266] There are signs that other people living in Svarfaðardalur took part in larger conflicts, in the 1240s at least: Sökku-Guðmundr, Guðmundr from Sakka, supported Kolbeinn *ungi* and ultimately died at the so-called *Flóabardagi* in 1244.[267] But it would appear that the countrywide focus of *Sturlunga saga*, shaped by the activities of the uppermost tier of the elite, ensured that other local conflicts in and around Svarfaðardalur, which surely did happen, are not recorded.

It is also a significant question as to what the political relationship was between Eyjafjörður-based *höfðingjar* and the regions to the east such as Fnjóskadalur, Reykjadalur, Mývatnssveit and Öxarfjörður. Certainly in 1256 Þorgils *skarði* could consider the whole region as under his control but it is less clear

---

260 SS I: 400.
261 SS I: 495.
262 SS II: 184–86, 188.
263 Failed negotiations took place in Borgarfjörður in 1253 (SS II: 141–47).
264 SS I: 525; II: 218–20.
265 SS II: 5.
266 See below pp. 302–4.
267 SS I: 468; II: 53, 54, 64.

what the case was in earlier decades.²⁶⁸ Even in this situation it is not clear what kind of power a *höfðingi* or royally-appointed governor might have over this relatively remote region. Most recent commentators have inclined to the view that these districts must have been under the control of Sighvatr Sturluson and subsequent Eyjafjörður-based leaders. It is certainly hard to see any other leader in these districts at all in the period concerned and we have no accounts of anyone holding or acquiring *goðorð* there. Gunnar Karlsson points out that in 1222 Tumi Sighvatsson, eager for political independence from his father, might have been seeking *mannaforráð* north of Eyjafjörður when he was killed by Bishop Guðmundr's force.²⁶⁹ This certainly makes sense if we assume that getting support from the wealthier *bændr* in these districts was a kind of second prize, the main prize being to live in and control Eyjafjörður with its more dense population and good access to the port of Gásir.

We also see Bishop Guðmundr active in districts to the east. In an episode shortly before Tumi's death, the bishop's party travels from Svarfaðardalur to Höfði in Höfðahverfi and thence to Reykjadalur because he has no support in Eyjafjörður itself. His presence is briefly tolerated by farms or *staðir* in Reykjadalur (Einarsstaðir, Grenjaðarstaðir Múli, Staðr, Helgastaðir) but ultimately the local pre-eminent *bóndi*, together with Sighvatr Sturluson and Arnórr Tumason, is able to remove the costly guest.²⁷⁰ Guðmundr then goes, via Þverá in Laxárdalur, out to Sauðanes in the north-east (Maps 3 and 11) before coming back via Öxarfjörður (Maps 10 and 11). Perhaps what is noticeable here is that it does not appear that Sighvatr pushes Guðmundr eastwards or prevents him from going to Öxarfjörður, on his way back, for example. It is only when Guðmundr's group gets back to Reykjadalur that Sighvatr's forces push Guðmundr southwards.²⁷¹ In other words, Sighvatr is more concerned with what was going on closest to Eyjafjörður and not beyond.

Similarly we can see signs of Kolbeinn Sighvatsson having been a leader in Reykjadalur in 1232 when he and his father get control of Grenjaðarstaðir and he sets up home, and presumably until he dies at Örlygsstaðir in 1238 when he is the first-named of the Sturlungar dead from 'further north' (*lengra norðan*), i.e beyond Eyjafjörður.²⁷² None of the other nine men in this group are identifiable even though *Íslendinga saga* records patronymics for eight of them (even

---

268 SS II: 209.
269 Gunnar Karlsson 2004: 300.
270 SS I: 274–76. Oren Falk 2015, esp. pp. 131–32, points out the pre-eminence of Ívarr of Múli in this episode, a farm mentioned in *Landnámabók* (ÍF I: 274). Ívarr might be seen as the same kind of lesser *höfðingi* as Ófeigr in *Ljósvetninga saga* (see pp. 294, 297).
271 SS I: 276–77.
272 SS I: 346.

though we have some information about men from Reykjadalur from the story about Bishop Guðmundr just mentioned.) One possibility is that these men were from a diverse range of farms from around Grenjaðarstaðir in the same way as the men from Eyjafjörður came from farms close to Grund.

There are other indications that the north-east was within the political orbit of Eyjafjörður leaders but the evidence is scattered. In 1244 Kolbeinn *ungi* was able to muster a ship and its captain from as far away as Leirhöfn in Melrakkaslétta (Map 11).[273] As Gunnar Karlsson notes, later on, Þórðr *kakali* goes to Öxarfjörður in search of men willing to fight Brandr Kolbeinsson and seems to have succeeded in getting support from somewhere north-east of Eyjafjörður.[274] Later a man from Þverá in Laxárdalur (Map 10) who happened to be a kinsmen of Gizurr Þorvaldsson was maimed by Ásgrímr Þorsteinsson (1254); Eyjólfr *ofsi* Þorsteinsson had a kinsman from Öxarfjörður's major farm who fought and died at the battle at Þverá in litla; and Þorgils *skarði* also had some unspecified cause to go to Öxarfjörður (1257).[275] In 1258, while Þorvarðr Þórarinsson was based at Grund, he could apparently get Reykdœlir and Fnjóskdælir to support him at a peace meeting, even immediately after he had killed Þorgils *skarði*.[276] In fact all of the (few) places where we see northern *höfðingjar* active in the north-east are within the territory given to Finnbjörn Helgason when he was appointed, in 1252, to rule Reykjadalur and all the areas 'north' to the river Jökulsá. It is possible, although of limited consequence, that Jökulsá had been a territorial boundary for some time. It could also have been the case that communities in these areas were only too happy to be left alone by Iceland's secular leaders.

Closer to Eyjafjörður, Höfði in Höfðahverfi and nearby Laufás are likely to have been large farms in the thirteenth century but they rarely get a mention in *Sturlunga saga* either. Laufás certainly had a church as early as the 1160s and Höfði was a church property in 1318. Their absence seems to be a product of their geographical remoteness and genuine political marginality in the thirteenth century. The only mention of either farm is when Bishop Guðmundr has been driven from Hólar by Kolbeinn *ungi*. In early 1232 Guðmundr flits from one side of Eyjafjörður to the other, staying first at Laufás, where word

---

273 Hjalti Helgason of Leirhöfn provided a *ferja* and took part in the *Flóamannabardagi* (SS II: 53, 57, 58, 61, 64).
274 Gunnar Karlsson 2004: 300; SS II: 72, 76.
275 SS I: 510; Halldórr Helgason of Skinnastaðir: SS I: 519, II: 191; II: 212.
276 SS II: 222.

reaches him from the Reykdœlir that they will not support him, then at Árskógr on the opposite coast, the Eyfirðingar in the middle rejecting him. The *bóndi* at Höfði is the only person who will take Guðmundr in.[277] The fact that all three of these farms seem to play no part in secular political action in the thirteenth century may be a product of their relative geographical isolation but it is also interesting to note that all three are recorded in their later *máldagar* as being wholly in the possession of the church. It is possible that this is why we have a vignette involving these three farms supporting a bishop on the only occasion they feature in *Sturlunga saga* after 1200.[278] These are farms which were most likely not part of the secular political game and so rarely get mentioned in *Sturlunga saga*.

In summary then, the brevity of this section says a great deal about the economy with which Eyjafjörður is dealt in large parts of *Sturlunga saga*. Overall, the picture of politics of Eyjafjörður is rather changeable but it shows one significant blip in that power transfers out of the main valley in the 1180s and 1190s. After this Grund appears to function almost as a kind of official residence for the preeminent figure in the region. Despite that, the farm's occupants face periodic opposition from Hrafnagil. Grund can also draw on support from some of the larger farms to its south but it is never seen to gain support from, or else bully, any of the farms on the eastern side of the valley. Indeed very little coverage is given to the eastern side of the valley, partly perhaps because Þverá, despite being a large farm, had no active role in secular politics because it had a monastery attached to it. Möðruvellir also appears neither to be a threat to Grund nor connected to any of the larger farms in the west of the valley. The activities of the *höfðingjar* in the mid-thirteenth century, when they are actually in Eyjafjörður, seem remarkably like those of the leading men in *Íslendingasögur*.

The account above suggests remarkably little structural change to politics within Eyjafjörður, and between Eyjafjörður and the districts to its north and east, after c.1209. Svarfaðardalur and Hörgárdalur get relatively little coverage in the thirteenth century which might suggest that they have lost some importance. Like the Reykdœlir, the people of Svarfaðardalur do appear in larger scale conflicts as a group, when their presence was requested; and it was expected rather than there being the expectation that no one from Svarfaðardalur would get involved. We might suspect that Kolbeinn Sighvatsson's probable presence in Reykjadalur enabled stronger control of the region as a whole than had been seen before but the degree of control is harder to determine.

---

277   SS I: 338.
278   Orri Vésteinsson 2000: 97; DI II: 446–48, 454–55; DI III: 515–16.

11 Conclusion

In some respects the patterns of politics in these two regions could hardly be more different. In Dalir, the smaller region, we see continued competition between two or more leaders until the return to Iceland of Þórðr *kakali* in 1242 who, even though he operated at a countrywide level politically, cannot be seen to control the whole region himself. Instead he is able to galvanise his kinsmen, who are still seen as the leading figures in the region, in order to fight against Kolbeinn *ungi*, the significance of which derived from Þórðr's desire to assert his role as the leader of the *ríki* in Eyjafjörður. In Eyjafjörður and the areas to its east we see obvious signs of political centralisation at the beginning of the thirteenth century; that someone, Sighvatr, could seemingly be invited in to run Eyjafjörður, and given *goðorð*, is a sign that even at this stage there was a dominant figure in this region and less political competition than in Dalir. It is also significant that he does this only with the apparent encouragement of the bishop and leading secular figure in Skagafjörður; if this were part of the reason for Sighvatr's move to Eyjafjörður then it shows a solidarity among the elite across regions. This may be the spin put on things by the Sturlungar, as justification for their control of a region they had traditionally no connection to, but it fits with the absence of conflict recorded within Eyjafjörður in the late twelfth century. In other words, for all the detail of local power struggles centring on Guðmundr *dýri*, there was already an expectation that this region could be controlled by a single individual, regardless of who actually controlled *goðorð*. Of course, seen from outside Iceland, this level of political power was still incredibly small-scale and weak.

We have differing scales of conflict in the texts for each region as time goes on but it is important to note that most successful leaders always seem to depend on support from two sources, geographically. They seem to rely primarily on people from neighbouring farms to their own base – even in Eyjafjörður – and on leading figures in other districts, those who usually live on the larger farms. The latter most often means the largest farm in a particular cluster of farms, what might be called a *sveit* or a *byggð*, or of a whole *hreppr*. This pattern does not really change as much over the twelfth and thirteenth centuries as our sources perhaps suggest; we just tend to see a greater degree of local politicking in the late twelfth century because the sagas record where there was conflict. Most texts are only interested in the activities of *bændr* from larger farms because, in all probability, these were the only people whose support mattered consistently.

In this regard we may be seeing a difference between Dalir and Eyjafjörður in that we never hear about *stórbændr* in Dalir, only in Eyjafjörður (and

Skagafjörður for that matter) and in the thirteenth century. Such nomenclature appears to be a phenomenon of the thirteenth century and to depend on the fact that people in Eyjafjörður were conscious of a class of wealthier farmers whose allegiances still mattered. The great unknown here is simply how wealthy such *bændr* were. This brings us back to a larger problem for medieval Iceland, our inability to work out who owned land and what landownership actually signified. The *stórbændr* in the large valleys where they are referred to, Eyjafjörður and Skagafjörður, might conceivably have owned anything from a single farm of 40 or 60 hundreds, to several farms which brought in rent. At the same time we have *höfðingjar* who move home regularly without it being clear whether or not they owned the farms they lived at. In all probability both groups owned multiple farms with varied associated resources and that *höfðingjar* owned more property still, but what really set *höfðingjar* apart was their desire to exercise political control.

CHAPTER 4

Settlers and Settlement Mythologies in *Landnámabók*

The purpose of this chapter is to understand the perspectives on our regions of the key source, the *Sturlubók* (*S*) version of *Landnámabók*. This text records that most iconic of events in Iceland's history, its colonisation. We have seen that the *S* text, as with the later versions of *Landnámabók*, begins with an introductory narrative about Iceland's very first discoverers and colonists (*landnámsmenn*) but then is largely made up of short chapters, each of which include basic details about one or more colonists. It is these dense, genealogy-filled chapters which provide great interest for understanding ideas about the *landnám* even if we cannot be certain that they tell us much about what really happened in Iceland before c.1100. Mention has already been made of the limits to our current archaeological knowledge for socio-political organisation in the regions being studied.[1] *S* does not provide any definitive answers either, but it provides a different perspective on Iceland's early history. In essence this chapter will treat *S* as what scholars studying other societies have labelled a 'genealogical charter,' in this case a view of the past which it will be proposed we can date largely to before 1150. The assumption is that most of the contents of *S* predate surviving *Íslendingasögur* and therefore provides an earlier 'charter' than they do, but that they too are underpinned by genealogical charters. Two prefatory sections will make the case for the use of the term genealogical charter and how *S* is being approached respectively.

1   Genealogical Charters and the Origins of *Landnámabók* and *Íslendingasögur*

One key question which this book has yet to consider in depth but underpins both this chapter and the following one is that of how *Íslendingasögur* are structured. It is proposed that there were no novelist-like authors and that we must assume that medieval Icelanders, at least those who were interested in retelling narratives about the past, had a ready set of mental frameworks which helped them to understand and retell this past.

---
1 See pp. 6–9.

Genealogy, a large part of saga texts, would seem to offer an obvious framework for constructing chronologies and complex narratives.[2] Indeed genealogical texts have long been regarded as possible early sources for sagas, even though they have barely survived: the *Ævi Snorra goða*, a short account of Snorri *goði* Þorgrímsson's descendants is the only independent genealogy of a character named in one of the *Íslendingasögur*. Even if such texts did inform saga authors, those authors certainly would have required extensive genealogical knowledge from other sources to have created most of the *Íslendingasögur* and *Landnámabók*.

Comparative material from other societies suggests that oral genealogies can structure people's understanding of the past. Modern anthropological research and the study of modern oral literatures suggest ways of understanding how people have constructed their past in societies where history is transmitted almost entirely orally. Studies of genealogy and peoples' sense of collective identity are of particular relevance in trying to ascertain the likely function of genealogy for medieval Icelanders. These studies of later societies tell us first and foremost that genealogies get transformed over time, whether consciously or subconsciously, to explain existing political situations as people observe them. This is particularly true of the more distant parts of genealogies. In societies in which knowledge about the past is transferred almost exclusively by the spoken word, traditions change as people try to reconcile their history with their present. The classic early work on this subject is Laura Bohannan's analysis of Tiv genealogies in Nigeria.[3] The Tiv groups that Bohannan studied saw their past strictly in genealogical terms. Ancestors of a given subgroup of the Tiv were credited with genealogical relationships with the ancestors of other groups identifying themselves as Tiv. Bohannan concluded, however, that these genealogical histories were flexible:

> The way in which Tiv learn genealogies and the lack of written record allow changes to occur through time without a general realization of the

---

[2] Clunies Ross 1993, 1998: 86–96; Úlfar Bragason 1993, 2010: 51–57 for genealogy as a source which informs *samtíðarsögur* narratives. Orri Vésteinsson (1996: 31) makes a similar point: 'As people's relationships are so important to the structure of the sagas it may even be proposed that genealogical information was the medium through which events were remembered, to be, at some later time, written down in a narrative form.' Spiegel 1983 is the classic study on the use of genealogy as a structuring element in western European chronicles in this same period. West 2012 and Pohl 2016 discuss the earlier medieval west.

[3] Bohannan 1952. See also Evans-Pritchard 1940; Gluckman 1965: 271–75; Donner 1992; Mahoney 2016.

occurrence of that change; social change can exist with a doctrine of social permanence.[4]

Bohannan discovered that the same genealogical specialist in a Tiv tribe told the history of that tribe in different genealogical terms at two different recordings several years apart. In between her two recordings Bohannan noted that the political and geographical relationships of the tribes whose ancestors made up the genealogy had changed. These changes were reflected in the genealogy when, on her second visit, she asked about the history of the tribal subdivisions. Newly formed alliances were reflected in the closer genealogical ties of their ancestors; recently-broken political ties meant more distant genealogical ties for tribes' ancestors; the merging of two former subdivisions meant that the ancestor of one group disappeared from the genealogy; and the uprooting and resettling of a group to nearer or further away could mean that their ancestors moved from one branch of a genealogy to another.

A second example of the way in which oral genealogies change was described by Emrys Peters.[5] Peters' study was of the Bedouin of Cyrenaica who all claimed descent from a single female ancestor, Sa'ada. It suggests several potential patterns in the way the oral genealogies might change. Many of the features of the genealogies remembered by the Bedouin are worth listing as they are potentially relevant when looking at medieval Icelandic genealogies; these features have some striking similarities with the Icelandic ones. The Cyrenaican genealogy shows uniformity in its number of segments (i.e. divisions symbolised by a particular name) in its earliest generations and less regularity as it gets closer to 'the present.' The segments also reflect the ecology of the region in that people in the genealogy can be seen to symbolise distinctions in the landscape; all the people living within one readily identifiable part of the landscape were descended from one person. Peters also determined the degree of kinship required for an individual to take part in a vengeance killing: this, it emerged, was being determined by the Bedouin according to the current, acknowledged interpretation of people's genealogy. Several patterns emerged in naming practices. The names of living people changed according to whether or not their fathers were present; nicknames were handed down even though they were inappropriate for anyone but the original bearer; names were fused; and men were regularly named after an ancestor simply to keep that name in use in the genealogy. Stability and change in the genealogies also

---

4   Bohannan 1952: 314. For early western European medievalists drawing on Bohannan see, for example, Dumville 1977b, Thornton 2002.
5   Peters 1960: 50–53.

followed a pattern: it was at about the 'fifth ascending generation' that people differed in their interpretations of the genealogy. For the more distant past the genealogy remained very stable while for the more recent the number of divisions was more varied. A more recent study of Bedouin genealogical knowledge and storytelling, based on fieldwork in Jordan in 1989-90, has questioned the mutability of some such traditions but at the same time still recognises how the present does reshape views of the past through genealogy.[6]

For Iceland there is perhaps one individual who we might see as something like the ancestor figures remembered by other societies. This is Björn *buna*, of whom *Landnámabók* says 'from Björn are descended nearly all the powerful men in Iceland.'[7] The next few chapters in this early part of the text set out the upper part of what looks like a genealogical charter. Beyond that, if we trace genealogies to their logical ends in *Landnámabók* it emerges that a large number of the people recorded are indeed his descendants, albeit still a minority of them.

Why was Björn *buna* so important and to whom? The answer to these questions would seem to lie in the fact that he is identified as an ancestor of people from the west of Iceland, particularly those people named in surviving *landnám* texts as coming from around Hvammsfjörður. Björn *buna*'s descendants are recorded in greatest detail in the lines of descent through his son Ketill *flatnefr* (flatnose) and Ketill's children, about whom we will hear a lot later.[8] The apparent importance of Björn might reflect the interests of one of the various writers of *Landnámabók* texts from western Iceland who will be discussed below: Ari Þorgilsson, Styrmir Kárason or Sturla Þórðarson. Two possibilities as to why this might the case suggest themselves. Either this was part of the same kind of manufacturing of spurious genealogies which was common to much of north-western Europe in the twelfth century, or else we are seeing something more organic, of the kind that we see in the oral traditions discussed above. It is very hard to say for certain. Björn *buna* is only mentioned in a limited number

---

6 Shryock 1997 esp. 17–32, 111–47. I am grateful to Ben White for this making me aware of Shryock's work.
7 'frá Birni er nær allt stórmenni komit á Íslandi' (S10, H11).
8 *Sturlubók* includes a total of about 180 descendants of Ketill *flatnefr* who were associated predominantly with the mid-west of Iceland. About 120 people descended through his daughter Auðr *in djúpauðga* (Auðr the deeply-wealthy) and 60 through his son Björn *inn austræni* (Björn the easterner). The descendants of the other two sons of Björn *buna* combined number about 106. This difference in the respective numbers of descendants is more likely to represent the interests of the people recording them than the real numbers of descendants of each child, or even the claims of particular groups to be descended from a particular child. Björn also appears in *Njáls saga* (ÍF XII: 284–85).

of places and it hard to tell how and when the story about him emerged. On the one hand, it seems as though his genealogy would have taken some trouble to construct from scratch, on the other hand it is curious that he has no real back story: he is said to have been a *hersir* (lord or leader) from Sogn in Norway but he was not a colonist of Iceland himself. It is hard to know quite what purpose having someone with those attributes would have served as part of myth for Icelandic, or western Icelandic origins. Equally there is no easily-discernible pattern to those in Iceland who were and were not said to have been descended from Björn, and what political purpose being descended from him served. The meaning of Björn's seemingly unique nickname is also uncertain. One possibility is that it refers to a small river course or stream or else jet of a fluid, which might make sense for someone at the apex of a genealogy from whom others metaphorically sprang or poured. All we can safely say is that he looks *something* like a mythical ancestor and is at least evidence of how some elite Icelanders could conceive of their own genealogies.

The societies of twentieth-century Tiv and Bedouin peoples certainly cannot be seen as entirely parallel with medieval Iceland. But, significantly, these societies all shared a strong reliance on spoken communication rather than writing, and genealogical relationships formed the basis of socio-political organisation in the absence of some form of non-kin based state system.[9] In these modern case studies genealogies form a key part of people's discussions about the past and at any one time it can even be the case that different people remember them in different ways.

For this book what matters is not which genealogy was correct but to examine these differences to see if it is possible to explain how they came about. For medieval Iceland we can piece together the political affiliations suggested by the recorded genealogies and, using the evidence of the contemporary sagas, we can at least compare them to what we can reconstruct as likely contexts for their production. Where the genealogy-derived patterns do not seem to bear close relationships to the political affiliations we can see in the thirteenth-century then it is reasonable to suggest that the genealogical sources reflect memories of different, potentially earlier, political situations. Indeed arguments have been put forward for there being limits on the potential for individuals to know, or want to create, highly individualised or tendentious accounts of the

---

9 This is a different issue from that of the relationship between literary form and the political structures of the society which produces it; there does not seem to be one, at least there is no particular form of polity which correlates with the production of epic (Barber 2007: 45–58).

past.[10] This is where Iceland might differ from other places in medieval Europe because sagas less obviously provide the one-sided views of the past that are visible elsewhere. As a general analytical guide, then, Bohannan's term 'genealogical charter' will sometimes be used in what follows. Genealogical charters, it will be argued, are visible in the *Sturlubók* version of *Landnámabók* as well as in *Íslendingasögur*.

Of course looking at medieval Iceland is not merely a case of looking at the recordings of oral accounts from different points in time. By their very existence sagas of all kinds are proof of the emergent written culture in medieval Iceland. By the thirteenth century many of the elite could read, while *scriptoria* existed at Skálholt, Hólar and in monasteries. Where *Landnámabók* is concerned we have evidence of writers using pre-existing manuscripts as the basis of their text but adding their own information to them. Haukr Erlendsson, creator of *Hauksbók* in the early fourteenth century, says that he compiled his text by copying parts of two others, *S* and the lost *Styrmisbók*, but also imbued his text with his own view of the past.[11] Clearly, however, there was a first version of *Landnámabók* and sagas which their authors must have had to compose according to what they *knew* rather than what they had read. An awareness of the vitality of oral traditions and the probability that these informed many of the variations in written narratives should shape how we interpret them.[12]

One premise of this study therefore is that where there is no good evidence for textual relationships having shaped the genealogies then we can legitimately assume that they were commonly *remembered*.[13] The shape of the genealogical information which was remembered, as with any kind of narrative, was not uniform: it seems reasonable to suppose that people drew on a pool of genealogical knowledge to inform a given narrative and that different genealogies would be used to explain different stories. In what follows, therefore, the genealogy which a saga preserves is seen as being made up of a number of narrative units: these units are pieces of the genealogy which should be viewed as

---

10 E.g. Rankovic 2007.
11 Jón Jóhannesson 1941: 175.
12 Gísli Sigurðsson 1994b, 2002. It has long been recognised that many sagas have different versions which, often, seem to derive from common, sometimes lost, manuscripts. The detailed studies of Scott 2003 and Lethbridge 2007, on *Eyrbyggja saga* and *Gísla saga* respectively, show that structural variations within genealogies are rare across saga versions.
13 Fentress & Wickham 1992 is the most significant work on 'social memory' in recent decades. 'Cultural memory' as it is now often talked about in Anglophone scholarship is explored extensively for medieval Scandinavia in Glauser, Hermann & Mitchell eds. 2018.

having been remembered for specific purposes. This will often be because the cluster of names formed the basis of a story which reflected a set of political relationships across a wide area. Other people are associated with a particular place, either through the place taking their name or there being a story connecting the two. The reasons for remembering people in genealogies and sagas is complicated and so the approach in the analysis below, particularly for Dalir and North Snæfellsnes, is based on an attempt to identify particular units of genealogy which work as part of one or more narratives.

Almost all *Íslendingasögur* include short genealogies for many of their characters. By putting together all the small genealogies in a saga together a much larger genealogy can be created. This can be seen as a kind of pool of genealogical knowledge which the saga tellers deemed necessary to include in their sagas. *Íslendingasögur* are likely to be very selective in what they include despite the huge mass of names they still give in genealogies. The genealogical information included, i.e. not forgotten, by the people interested in any saga must have been preserved for some specific reason or other. The names in the saga were memorable, even if not 'accurate.' It is assumed here that people tend to remember only what seems relevant and makes sense to them; anything else gets jettisoned.[14]

Given the likely lack of historicity of the later views of tenth- and eleventh-century Iceland what the historian is left with is neither secure nor easy to interpret. We are left to analyse a series of images of the past given in narratives whose origins, precise date of composition and manuscript history are obscure. These images, however, should not be regarded as fictional. The perceptions of the Icelandic past recorded in narratives of all kinds can be supposed to mirror political situations at some point in time before about 1300. As will become clear, we have accounts of events in Dalir and in the north-east in the twelfth- or thirteenth-century. It will be argued that where twelfth- and thirteenth-century patterns do not match patterns in *Íslendingasögur* and *Sturlubók* in key respects the latter record earlier perceptions of the past rather than competing contemporary ones.

The debates about saga authors, dates of composition, and literary borrowings are extremely complex and few attempts at unravelling the problems are convincing; they will be discussed in more detail for each text in Chapter 5. Nevertheless it is still assumed that certain people wrote certain sagas or that certain sagas date from a certain absolute or relative date according to the presence or absence of literary borrowings. Some of these debates are set out

---

14   See, for example, Brooks 1989: 60–64 and Brooks 2000 for the way myth was manipulated in Anglo-Saxon England and, more generally, Vansina 1985.

below in relation to particular sagas; such literary scholarship has actually remained incredibly resilient to criticism.

Some generalisations can be made now on *Íslendingasögur* origins and ways of approaching them. However we view the exact way in which a combination of sources of information which was used to knit together the final written narrative, it is undeniable that this information was, originally, spoken by one person to another. Whether a story was 'true' or not, in essence it had to pass, for however long, from person to person without the aid of writing. The question is therefore not so much about how early a story was written down or how long a story was circulated but about how it was told and under what circumstances. We can never know how a whole saga or the shorter narratives within it were transmitted, or what kind of relation they have to actual events, but we can try to suggest a context for the stories. What follows in subsequent chapters is therefore an analysis of the origin myths contained in both *Landnámabók* and *Íslendingasögur* describing politics in Dalir and Eyjafjörður. This supposes that these myths were likely to have been known by more than one person and that they were shaped by the processes of social or collective memory. If saga-like narratives were often told by more than one person at a sitting, as suggested by Clover, then we have good reason to believe that collective attitudes had some control on anyone's views of the past. Genealogy, in combination with human and physical geography, provided the dominant frame within which people remembered the past.

2   *Landnámabók*

Various versions of this same basic text survive, each recording stories and genealogies relating to people, mostly men, alleged to have first settled in Iceland during the reign of Haraldr *hárfagri* in the late ninth century. Five versions have survived in whole or part, those from the manuscripts called *Melabók* (*M*), *Sturlubók* (*S*), *Hauksbók* (*H*), *Þórðarbók* (*Þ*) and *Skarðsárbók* (*Sk*).[15] To this list most discussions add two versions which do not survive, a supposed original text by Ari Þorgilsson and the so-called *Styrmisbók*, from which other texts are thought to have borrowed. The texts record settlers, in a geographical order, land-claim by land-claim, going clockwise around Iceland's coast. Most of the individual chapters contain genealogies which include six or seven generations forward in time from the *landnám*; this suggests that the bulk of the

---

15   All references to these texts are by the abbreviation for the text and by chapter number as given in the standard edition of *Landnámabók* in ÍF I.

information may have been recorded in around 1100.[16] The textual relationships of the various versions of *Landnámabók* have been studied in great depth.

S is the version of *Landnámabók* which will be used in this chapter because it is the earliest surviving full version of the text, even though it was probably written late in the life of Sturla Þórðarson (d.1284). Sturla most likely used a copy of a work written by Ari Þorgilsson in the early twelfth century as the basis for his text. He may also have taken information from written *Íslendingasögur* even though direct, word-for-for borrowings from extant versions of sagas are rare.[17] We can see, however, that Sturla probably made additions to a less elaborate text, but not in ways likely to have seen significant rewriting.[18] Most famously, and not insignificantly, *S* ignores the otherwise strict geographical order of chapters when it recounts Auðr *in djúpauðga*'s *landnám* in Dalir. Otherwise the source of most of *S* must be the text which Ari Þorgilsson says the Icelandic bishops asked to omit from his rewrite of *Íslendingabók*.[19] The extent of Ari's discarded writings is unclear but it seems likely that they were far greater than what remains in the very brief genealogies of four bishops in *Íslendingabók*. At the end of *Íslendingabók* Ari traces his own patrilineal line (*langfeðgatal*) for more than 30 generations although it generally only names one male per generation.[20] This does at least hint at his enthusiasm for genealogy.

---

16   Calculating the length of generations is extremely problematic. We do not know how medieval Icelanders calculated generations. See Henige 1982 for general problems relating to chronology in accounts of the past in traditional societies. For a context closer to medieval Iceland, Dumville 1977b.
17   For a brief survey of the issues see Jesch 1985b. For debates on the origins of individual *Íslendingasögur* see below pp. 213–27, 270–79.
18   Sveinbjörn Rafnsson 2001, 2017 sees Sturla as more interventionist.
19   ÍF I: 3. See also its introduction, viii–xvii, for an account of the debate up to 1968 on what people have thought Ari left out of *Íslendingabók*; the essentials of which have remained the same. *Melabók* is also thought to be a very early version. It does not borrow from other surviving *Landnámabók* but only survives itself as two pages of a fifteenth-century manuscript copy (ÍF I: li, lxxxii). Jón Jóhannesson argued that much of *Melabók* represented a direct copy of *Styrmisbók* (1941: 140–74). *Melabók*, however, also shows: i. more explicit authorial input in the form phrases making the reader aware of what has already mentioned e.g. in the form of 'X who was mentioned before' ('er fyrir var getit,' M43) or 'as has been already been said' ('sem fyrr er sagt,' M38); ii. a more clear concept of its being a record of coterminous *landnám* through the use of phrases which explicitly point out relationships between *landnám* such as, for example 'between *landnámsmaðr* X and *landnámsmaðr* Y' ('til móts við,' M36, M37); iii. most clearly an interest in the history of one single family, i.e. the history of the 'Melamenn' (because it traces many genealogies down to the parents and wife of Snorri Markússon, d.1313), when *S* and *H* have far fewer references to contemporaries of the supposed thirteenth- or fourteenth-century authors.
20   ÍF I: 26–28; Halvorsen 1965; Úlfar Bragason 1993: 27–29.

Ari was probably quite elderly when *Íslendingabók* was written in the early 1130s so he may well have been chosen to write it on the strength of earlier writings.[21] Haukr Erlendsson also identifies Ari and one Kolskeggr *hinn vitri* (the wise) as the text's writers.[22] This statement has generally been accepted as credible although it has never been agreed exactly what Ari and Kolskeggr knew or wrote on the *landnám*.[23] Ultimately, even if Ari himself was not responsible for the first *Landnámabók*, then it is very likely that one of his contemporaries in the early twelfth century was.

It has often been assumed that *Sturlubók* is also partly derived from another version which according to Haukr Erlendsson, writing in the early fourteenth century,[24] was written by Styrmir Kárssson (d. 1245).[25] Haukr says that he wrote his text based on those of Styrmir and Sturla.[26] *Styrmisbók*, however, no longer survives, which makes any comments on its detailed content speculative. Sturla might have possessed *Styrmisbók* or both he and Styrmir had access to the early twelfth-century text.[27] In the vast majority of their chapters *Sturlubók* and *Hauksbók* are identical which is why the standard, *Íslenzk fornrit* edition which uses S as its base text, rarely has to give much space to *Hauksbók*, its secondary text, to present their differences.

A central question about any of these texts about the *landnám* is simply that of their purpose. The late *Þórðarbók* version records a famous passage which suggests that the text was compiled to refute foreigners' claims that Icelanders were descended from slaves or 'bad people' (*af þrælum eða illmennum*).[28] It is generally believed that this passage originated in one of the medieval texts, either *Styrmisbók* or the earliest version, even though it does not survive in *Sturlubók*.[29] Certainly this motivation may explain why a genealogical text was

---

21 ÍF I: xvii–xviii summarises the evidence for the dating of the surviving version of *Íslendingabók*.
22 H354.
23 ÍF I: cvi–cx; Callow 2011.
24 Stefán Karlsson 1964.
25 ÍF I: lxxxii. Styrmir was lawspeaker, an associate of the Sturlungar family in the 1230s and later prior of Viðey (SS I: 323, 342, 444).
26 H354; ÍF I: xcvi–cvi.
27 Jón Jóhannesson (1941: 137–174) first put forward the argument that both *Sturlubók* and *Melabók* were derived from *Styrmisbók*. Jakob Benediktsson (e.g. 1966–9: 278) accepted this. Sveinbjörn Rafnsson (1974: 68–84) made the issue more complicated and expanded the idea of what *Styrmisbók* might have contained.
28 ÍF I: cii; Gunnar Karlsson 1996: 49.
29 Gunnar Karlsson 1996: 49–50.

written, but it does not entirely explain the format of *Landnámabók* nor how this relates to the bishops' request that Ari rewrite his first text.

Barði Guðmundsson argued for *Landnámabók*'s value as a source of information on *óðalsréttir*, rights to *óðal* property or property belonging to a distinct kin group.[30] Sveinbjörn Rafnsson suggested something similar in a monograph designed to show that the rights of owners of *aðalból* (main farms within an estate) had been recorded in the face of ecclesiastical attempts to take full control of church-farms.[31] According to this idea, tales about settlers' burial mounds (*haugar*) are included in the texts to reaffirm whose descendants held rights to any colonist's farm (a *landnámsbær*).[32] The huge volume of information in *Landnámabók*, however, does not lend itself to such a simple explanation. Many of the entries seem either to offer too much irrelevant material to have served a legal purpose in an ownership dispute, or else offer far too little.[33] More recently it has been suggested that the fundamental purpose of the text was to create a history for the whole landmass of Iceland. In other words, regardless of whether or not there were genuine traditions available, *Landnámabók*'s compilers strove to give a history to every part of the landscape. Certainly some chapters of the text conform to this idea, namely, the simplistic one-sentence accounts of sparsely populated regions with a settler whose name appears to have been invented on the basis of a place-name.[34] Beyond these, however, most chapters record meaningful boundaries between individual '*landnám*,' and the kin relationships recorded in the text might be read to infer something about political relationships when the text was compiled.[35] The boundaries can even sometimes seem to have been more significant than the genealogical material in any given chapter because it sometimes appears as if that 'data' has been set into a chapter or location where it does not fit.

As with the *Íslendingasögur*, it seems safest to assume that *Landnámabók*'s contents were derived mostly from oral traditions, perhaps, as has been argued,

---

30   Barði Guðmundsson 1938.
31   Sveinbjörn Rafnsson 1974: 151–58; Jakob Benediktsson 1974b: 211–12; Orri Vésteinsson 2000: 112–32.
32   Sveinbjörn Rafnsson 1974: 196–203.
33   Jón Jóhannesson 1941: 200; ÍF I: cxviii; Jakob Benediktsson 1969; Bruhn 1999: 175.
34   Adolf Friðriksson & Orri Vésteinsson 2003; Callow 2011.
35   Haraldur Matthíasson 1950 observed the duplication of *landnám* boundaries and those of later-recorded *hreppar* in part of the south of Iceland. He considered that boundaries recorded in *Landnámabók* influenced the later *hreppar* boundaries. Pétur Urbancic 1962, looking at part of Húnavatnssýsla, observed less overlap (Sverrir Jakobsson 2005: 294–96).

from one specifically related to the *landnám*.[36] *Landnámabók*, like many medieval texts, should be read as a whole because all aspects of its contents contain ideas about geopolitics current at the time of its compilation.

3 Sturlubók

For reasons stated above (p. 155) the *Sturlubók* version of *Landnámabók* is the one used here. Other redactions are considered only on the rare occasions where there are significant variations between them and *S*.[37] The chapters relevant for each of our regions are, for Dalir, chapters S78 to S117, roughly from Bjarnarhöfn north to Gilsfjörður; for Eyjafjörður and the north east the chapters are S214 to S261, with S262 being the last chapter for the Northern Quarter and consisting of a list of the eight finest colonists in the Quarter (*ágætistir landnámsmenn*). Far more space will be devoted here to the western region than to Eyjafjörður simply because this region presents more complex issues in relation to other texts, which give it dense coverage, and because, as we have seen, it was the home of the Sturlungar in the late twelfth and thirteenth centuries. As elsewhere in this book, but perhaps more so than in previous chapters, the reader will find it useful to refer to the maps to better understand the discussion.

The individual stories to be analysed in *S* are relatively formulaic, but rarely so clichéd as to suggest that they are not based on genuine tradition on some level. They each contain some, even if rarely all, of a list of features which are readily recognisable. They can, for instance, give the boundaries of the colonist's *landnám* or land-claim; occasionally, they retell a narrative of some kind that takes place either before the colonist's arrival in Iceland, or once they have arrived. Significantly, they also frequently give a genealogy of the settler which details the settler's kinship with other settlers as well as their own descendants. When a line of descent is traced forwards in time from a colonist it is most often five or six generations in length, i.e. down to a notional date of about 1050–1100. Sometimes, however, no geneaology is provided at all, while, for a handful of colonists, genealogies are traced far beyond six generations, in which case they usually trace a single line to a prominent individual or family in the late twelfth century, such as to a *höfðingi* like Hvamm-Sturla, the ancestor of the

---

36 Bruhn 1999: 178–79.

37 *The chapter numbers are derived from the ÍF I edition. Hauksbók's text rarely varies much from Sturlubók. Melabók, which is most clearly concerned with creating a past for a single family rather than recording genealogical charters per se, is only relevant for part of the west. Its contents include the equivalent chapters to S76–86, 99–100, 111–13 and 115–19.*

Sturlungar, or to a bishop.[38] One further, notable feature of the accounts in Dalir and Eyjafjörður respectively is the presence of the colonists Auðr *in djúpauðga* (Auðr the deeply-wealthy) and Helgi *inn magri* (Helgi the lean) who are credited with being early colonists and who take large regions before giving parts of their *landnám* to other settlers. This pair had a connection to the key figure of Björn *buna*, Auðr being his descendant and Helgi marrying one of his descendants, Auðr's sister.[39]

All of the elements of *S*'s potted *landnám* narratives are worthy of analysis. They suggest notions of geopolitical hierarchy and affiliation, in just the same way as we will see in *Íslendingasögur*. In other words, we can see how the idea of genealogical charters operate in this text. In *S* it will be supposed that hierarchy or precedence is established by a variety of features associated with a colonist: early arrival of a colonist, their legal status (free rather than freed or slave), or the importance of the colonists whose families they and their descendants marry into. Colonists can be distinguished by the general size, location and suitability for farming of the *landnám* as suggested by other evidence. We will see that individual *landnám* can range in size from not much more than a single farm to entire valleys. It is also worth noting that in almost all districts there is a demonstrable relationship between *landnám* boundaries and the boundaries of later *hreppar*, especially in more heavily populated parts of Iceland.[40] This usually sees a *landnám* mapping exactly onto a later *hreppr* or else for multiple *landnám* to fit within a *hreppr*.[41] This reinforces the idea that *S* is not simply a collection of genealogical lore but is recording a kind of meaningful set of geopolitical relationships.

Before looking at the evidence for each region in detail it seems worth making the argument for the 'innocence' of at least some of the genealogical material in *S*. This concerns one key farm whose history we might arguably expect *S* to make something of: Staðarfell on Fellsströnd in Dalir, the early home of Hvamm-Sturla and of his father before him, Þórðr Gilsson, in the mid-twelfth century (Figure 23). What is undeniable is that the important farms in the thirteenth century, all over Iceland, tend to be given impressive back stories in *S*. Hvammr, the farm which we have seen Hvamm-Sturla is said to have bought, does have a focal role in Dalir. However, Staðarfell, which he and various

---

38   There are five references to Bishop Þorlákr Þórhallsson of Skálholt, for example. One mentions his chaplain (S177), one a friend (S318), and three mention a colonist from whom he was supposedly descended (S331, S339, S360).
39   See above p. 150
40   See above p. 157, footnote 35.
41   cf. Adolf Friðriksson & Orri Vésteinsson 2003, esp. 151–54.

descendants never seem to lose control of, has a very different kind of account. For Staðarfell the relevant chapter of *S* is S111. This is actually one of the most idiosyncratic chapters in the whole of *S*, but not in the way one might expect. It records a conflict among people living on Fellsströnd which results in the death of a Kjallakr of Kjallaksstaðir but it is almost unintelligible, like an almost overly-condensed version of an *Íslendingasaga*.[42] This garbled chapter therefore does not appear to have been manipulated to fit into a thirteenth-century or Sturlungar world view, something we might expect on the basis of most interpretations of *S*: despite the widely-recognised presence of larger-scale narratives across *S* and other versions of *Landnámabók*, an absolutely key farm for the history of a major family of scholar-politicians is *not* used to create a glamorous past for them. Staðarfell is not connected in any way to Hvammr, either, nor seen as the home of anyone particularly powerful. The content of S111 implies a simpler, antiquarian interest on the part of the compiler, rather than a desire to radically rewrite the past.

It is a challenge to contextualise the localised genealogical charter which S111 preserves, but it is still instructive given what we have seen in earlier chapters of this book. More will be said about the detail of S111 below in relation to the geopolitical patterns that *S* provides for Dalir. What *S* says here must surely predate the appearance of the Sturlungar or, at best it captures local traditions which were scarcely remembered by locals at or around the time of the emergence of Hvamm-Sturla or his father. This would actually hold true for later decades too because in the early thirteenth century Staðarfell was controlled by descendants of Hvamm-Sturla's brother who were on good terms with Sturla Þórðarson.[43] Thus, as we shall see, although the 'failure' of Kjallakr's family on Fellsströnd in S111 creates space for the Sturlungar to appear as

---

42   A brief summary of S111 gives a sense of its character. The story is not unlike episodes in *Íslendingasögur* or other parts of *Landnámabók* which record stories centring on a particular large farm and it dependent properties. The story seems to be designed to explain the deaths of some of the nine sons of Kjallakr, including Þorgrímr *pöngull* of Staðarfell, at the hands of Hrafsi, the son of Ljótólfr, a blacksmith to whom Kjallakr had given the farm of Ljótólfsstaðir (probably the later-recorded Ljótsstaðir). The story serves as a kind of history of Staðarfell which helps define local social relations. Other farms or cottages are said to belong to Kjallakr's sons, but they get no real mention. Men die on both sides of the dispute but, notably, no one from Staðarfell does. The story seems to be a way of recording the demotion or elimination of certain farms on its lands: the obvious farm left at the end is Staðarfell. The chapter is also notable in not situating its characters within any wider genealogies or in relation to other local farms, except that the Kjallakr at the head of the genealogy is said to be the son of Björn *inn sterki*, a blood kinsman of Gjaflaug, the wife of Björn *inn austrœni* (see below, p. 176).

43   SS II: 17. ættskrá.

owners of Staðarfell, the chapter does not explain how the Sturlungar came to own it and control its vicinity.

For all that we are used to thinking about the purposes of particular medieval historians in writing and shaping their accounts of the past, S111 reminds us that *S* might not be shaped by the concerns of Sturla Þórðarson. Few chapters in *S* are as dense or apparently naïve as S111 but they too may retain tradition. By a similar token, although the contents of *S* bear strong similarities to particular *Íslendingasögur*, particularly *Eyrbyggja saga* and *Laxdæla saga* for Dalir and northern Snæfellsnes, *S* still preserves differences from these texts and therefore an independent voice.

3.1   *The chronology of the landnám in* Sturlubók

S sees the colonisation of Iceland in essentially two different ways, according to two different presuppositions. A major concern of the text is to record who first found and first settled Iceland. In this context stories about the very first individual discoverers and settlers, who supposedly arrived before everyone else, are set out in its initial chapters.[44] Ingólfr is identified as the first settler and *Landnámabók* begins with his *landnám* at Reykjavík.[45] After Ingólfr's settlement the text is almost always organised topographically, listing individual *landnám* in a fairly strict order travelling clockwise around the country. This much is well-known, but the effect this topographical pattern has on perceptions of the *landnám* are important. After the early chapters, *S* gives the initial impression that Iceland was settled virtually simultaneously. Sometimes, however, *S* (and *Íslendingasögur*) creates some kind of simple chronological order to the arrival of colonists, and most of the time this chimes with the idea of the genealogical charter.

For both regions being studied here there is an apparently early colonist (the sister- and brother-in-law Auðr *in djúpauðga* and Helgi *inn magri*) who takes a particularly large *landnám* as the culmination of a story in which they are associated with coastal locations on their journey into their ultimate destination, a large *landnám*, most of which they grant to others. Such accounts must be seen as additions to more localised origin stories.[46] Those more focussed stories are more significant for understanding ideas about local politics and territorial affiliation.

---

44   This concern is shared by Ari Þorgilsson's *Íslendingabók* (ÍF 1: 4–6).
45   Ingólfr's *landnám* is actually interrupted by chapters about Björn *buna* and his descendants (Sigurður Nordal 1942: 79–81).
46   Adolf Friðriksson & Orri Vésteinsson 2003: 147–49.

For Dalir there is also the addition of the sibling relationship of Auðr and Björn *inn austrœni*, which is of interest both for geopolitics and chronology. *S* makes it clear that Björn arrived and settled at Bjarnarhöfn before Auðr *in djúpauðga* came to Iceland, i.e. that the outer part of Hvammsfjörður was settled before inner Dalir. Such an account actually works on two levels. First it works as part of a narrative which sees Hvammr, and Dalir in general, as the most desirable place for Auðr to settle after its first inhabitant, Björn, had roamed the North Atlantic searching for somewhere suitable to live. Auðr homes in on Hvammr after finding her brother Helgi *bjóla's* establishment on Kjalarnes in south-west Iceland unsatisfactory, but Björn's home welcoming, if obviously already occupied. On one level the story works as part of a narrative making Auðr's settling of Hvammr seem predestined, with outer Hvammsfjörður being an acceptable stopping off point. On another level, however, it makes economic sense for Bjarnarhöfn and outer Hvammsfjörður to be remembered as a place settled first because it would have provided a wide array of coastal resources to a first wave of settlers, i.e. fish, seals, sea birds, *crustacea* etc. By the same economic logic, inner Dalir, drawing on not only coastal resources but also pastoral ones would eventually become home to the region's most prominent settler.[47]

Thinking more conventionally about absolute chronology, *S* does make explicit statements about the dates at which some colonists arrived. The most obvious statements in *S* about 'real' dates are references to colonists arriving during the reign of the Norwegian king Haraldr *hárfagri* or due to his oppression. This detail seems designed to emphasise the earliness of certain colonists' arrival and heighten their status. Thus the three major, related figures, Auðr, Björn *inn austrœni* and *Helgi magri* are connected to Haraldr's *hárfagri's* reign as part of *S*'s origin story for Iceland (S13). They form part of two significant families, Auðr and Björn as the children of Ketill *flatnefr* and grandchildren of Björn *buna*, and Helgi linked to them through his marriage to their sister and as the son of Eyvindr *austmaðr*. Here, both Ketill *flatnefr* and Eyvindr *austmaðr* function as high-status ancestors who flee Norway, settle in the British Isles, and whose children settle in Iceland.

Similar associations for a few other figures emphasise their high status in our regions. In Dalir two further colonists have an explicit association with Haraldr *hárfagri's* reign: Þórólfr *Mostraraskegg* of Helgafell (S85) and Geirmundr

---

47 The same can probably not be argued for the story of Helgi *inn magri* and his farm at Kristnes. He has little directly to do with places in the outer fjord, nor anywhere further afield with a contrasting environment to lowland central Eyjafjörður.

heljarskinn at Skarð (S112).[48] These are arguably the most prominent colonists in Dalir after Auðr *in djúpauðga* and Björn *inn austrœni*. In Eyjafjörður and the north-east it is only the brothers Ásgrímr and Ásmundr Öndóttssynir of Glerá who have the Haraldr *hárfagri* connection (S229). Given Glerá's central location in Eyjafjörður, if not its wealth, the association adds a lustre to this farm's history which matches its geographical centrality. The explicit connection with the reign of Haraldr *hárfagri* helps confirm the high status of these colonists.

The accounts of most other colonists are not framed in this way and rarely give a hint at relative or absolute dates beyond what is expressed by genealogy. We have to assume that *S* and other accounts see most settlers as arriving in the period c.870-c.930, again in the decades of King Haraldr's supposed rule, but here without *S* giving them that explicit association. The one notable exception to this is the account of Eiríkr *rauði*, supposed discoverer of Greenland, whose appearance in Dalir in the later tenth century deserves brief analysis.

Eiríkr *rauði*'s arrival in Haukadalur is said to have happened after he had settled initially with his father in the relatively inhospitable Strandir coast of the West Fjords (S89). This is the first indication that he might be a latecomer. His activities are also dated relative to the arrival of Christianity. The story goes that, following Eiríkr's expulsion from Haukadalur, and then his brief return to Dalir, he persuaded people to sail to Greenland 15 years before Christianity was accepted in Iceland, i.e. in 985 (S90). Such a date makes general sense in the context of the disputes Eiríkr was involved in, if the text's logic is that most land was settled in this region in the early tenth century. The initial settlement of Haukadalur is a special case because there is no conventional *landnám* myth associated with it: there is no colonist preceding Eiríkr, only mention of his contemporary Þorbjörn *inn haukdœlski*. Haukadalur is in effect a rare case of a fairly populous valley without a settlement story for the late ninth century. All that need concern us here, however, is that other details in *S* show Eiríkr as a latecomer: he marries the grand-daughter of a settler (S89, S122) and the protagonists in his disputes are grandchildren or great grandchildren of other Dalir colonists.[49] Eiríkr's local rival in Haukadalur, Þorbjörn,

---

48 The fact that *Eyrbyggja saga*, which focusses on the area of Björn and Þórólfr's *landnám*, says that these men were friends may explain why *S* says that they both left Norway in the reign of Haraldr *hárfagri* (ÍF IV: 6; cf. p. 220 below). For the attitude of *Landnámabók* versions towards Haraldr *hárfagri* generally see Sveinbjörn Rafnsson 1974: 203–14.

49 Eiríkr is supported by Víga-Styrr, great-grandson of Björn *inn austrœni* (S84), Eyjólfr, grandson of Kjallakr of Kjallaksstaðir (S111), the sons of Þorbrandr of Álptafjörður who were therefore great-grandsons of Finngeirr (S86) and Þorbjörn son of the settler Vífill (S100). Supporting his opponent Þorgestr were Þorgeirr *ór Hítardal*, grandson of Steinn

would seem to be the only other significant person commemorated for this valley, and he too is confirmed elsewhere as a late settler (S104).[50] In one obvious respect the dispute between Eiríkr and Þorbjörn would seem to symbolise a conflict between Haukadalur's two major farms, Vatnshorn and Vatn, with Þorbjörn/Vatn being victorious. Part of the victory would seem to be that Þorbjörn marries Eiríkr's wife, with whom he has children.[51] It is hard to be certain whether later writers thought that much about the logic of Eiríkr arriving generations after other colonists but it also makes some geographical sense that Haukadalur, with access to a narrower range of natural resources, was settled after districts adjacent to the coast, even if we cannot say how much later.

Eyjafjörður has a single example of a late arriver as well but for them there is a different story altogether, their arriving 'late in the *landnám* era' (*kom út síð landnámatíðar*, S228). This will be discussed below in connection with potentially competing views of Eyjafjörður's early history.[52]

4   Dalir and Northern Snæfellsnes

If the original political geography of Hvammsfjörður can be understood in terms of a genealogical charter, then the broadest geopolitical relationships ought to be indicated by the earliest genealogical relationships. *S* suggests that Hvammr, signified by Auðr *in djúpauðga*, was the centre of political power in Dalir, through Auðr's position at the beginning of a lengthy genealogy.[53] The position of Auðr and Björn *inn austrœni* as siblings gives some sense of unity to the combined area they settled. Other broad patterns emerge too. Þórólfr *Mostrarskegg*, who settled Helgafell and its surrounding area, is recorded as

---

        mjöksiglandi (and the son of a *landnámsmaðr* to the south of this region, S66) and the sons of Þórðr *gellir* (or great-great grandsons of Auðr *in djúpauðga*, S109).

50   Herschend (1994: 168) suggests that *S* supposes Þorbjörn to have settled before Auðr and that Þorbjörn's farm is part of Auðr's settlement, but there is no suggestion that Auðr took Haukadalur.

51   Eiríkr is associated with Eiríksstaðir, a *hjáleiga* owned by Vatnshorn at later Skriðukot, site of the modern heritage site featuring a reconstructed farm.

52   See below pp. 195–96. This formulation only occurs in five other places in *S*.

53   *Laxdæla saga* suggests the same for Auðr (Unnr *in djúpúðga* in that text), see below p. 227. There are variant spellings of Auðr's name and nickname. *Djúpauðga* was most likely understood to mean 'very wealthy'; Unnr *in djúpúðga* in *Laxdæla saga*. This chapter follows *S* in using 'Auðr'.

SETTLERS AND SETTLEMENT MYTHOLOGIES 165

having ties exclusively with descendants of Auðr (S85). Some of the districts settled by Auðr's companions are further tied to her through marriages recorded between their respective descendants. On the other hand some colonists and districts have weaker ties to Auðr: colonists along Skógarströnd are accorded connections other than just to Auðr; Sauðafell's colonist, Erpr, appears genealogically independent of Auðr despite his being her freedman (*leysingi*); Haukadalur is only linked to Hvammr indirectly through connections to Laxárdalur. We have already seen that Eiríkr *rauði* was driven out of Haukadalur by someone who later marries into the Hvammverjar. To the west there is a separate set of links. Here Björn *inn austræni*, Auðr's brother, has connections with Kjallakr who settled Fellsströnd. As we shall see, it is notable that Skarðsströnd is portrayed as a third, separate entity, united through the comradeship of the settlers here and their descendants' marriages to people in the northern half of Breiðafjörður.

While S does not give all of this region any more of a concrete identity, explicitly or implicitly, than it does any of the other narratives analysed in this book, it gives a coherence to most of it by the co-presence of the colonists Auðr and her brother Björn *inn austræni*. Auðr is one of the few women recorded as a colonist. Having arrived via the Hebrides, she is said to have taken all of the 'inner part of the fjord from Dögurðará to Skraumuhlaupsá,' in other words, the three later *hreppar* of Hvammssveit, Laxárdalur and Miðdalir, but, as we have seen, actually excluding Haukadalur. She gives out parts of her land to various named people who accompany her. Auðr's colonising activities and the *landnám* of her companions are recorded across several chapters of the text. S's coverage for this area consists of 41 chapters, S78 to S118, of which 15 concern Auðr or members of her supposed party (S95–S103, S105–S110). By contrast, Björn settled at Bjarnarhöfn, having come directly from Norway, and only one chapter describes his *landnám*, S84. S credits Auðr with multiple genealogical connections across the west of Iceland, which means that putative political relationships can be traced for them. It is worth noting, however, that while the sibling relationship of Auðr and Björn is made explicit, in other ways the text makes them distinct. Björn is neither credited with the kind of extensive and complex *landnám* which Auðr has, nor does he appear so widely in genealogies. They are distinguished by their religion too: Auðr is Christian, while Björn is buried as a pagan and in a burial mound. The significance of the geographical and genealogical division between Auðr's descendants and those of Björn will be examined below.

The finer detail of this region's *landnám* can actually be broken down into three areas: Auðr's *landnám*, northern Snæfellsnes, and the remainder of

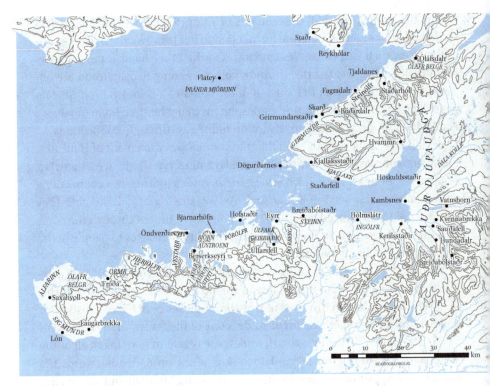

MAP 12   The *landnám* in Dalir and northern Snæfellsnes according to *Sturlubók*

modern Dalasýsla (Fellsströnd, Skarðsströnd and Saurbær). Auðr's *landnám* will be considered first because it is the largest and includes Hvammr, the farm we have seen as being so important in other contexts (Map 12). At this point it is also worth noting that the analysis for this region considers the evidence of *Laxdæla saga* and *Eyrbyggja saga* alongside S because these two texts give accounts of the *landnám* in a way in which only 17 of the 40 or so *Íslendingasögur* do,[54] but few do so so extensively or with such similarity to S.

4.1   Auðr's landnám

Auðr's story and settlement is described from S95, starting with the settlement of her followers in the south of the *landnám* and moving northwards. Unusually, however, Auðr's *landnám* is prefaced with a fairly lengthy account of her life in the British Isles before her arrival in Iceland, and the succeeding chapter gives an account of two of her companions, Kollr and Erpr. The form of Auðr's own *landnám* is, as is widely recognised, both significant and unusual. It was

---

54   Guðrún Nordal 2013: 204 note 17.

large, wealthy and relatively densely populated in later centuries, covering Hvammssveit, Laxárdalur, Miðdalir and Hörðudalur.

It is the southern half of Auðr's *landnám* which she allocates to men who sailed with her, from Hörðudalur north to Laxárdalur. Ketill was given land just to the east of Skógarströnd and lived at Ketilsstaðir (S98); Hörðr was given Hörðudalur (S99), Vífill Vífilsdalur (S100), Hundi Hundadalur (S101), Sökkólfr Sökkólfsdalur (S102), and Erpr *Sauðafellslönd* (the lands/estates of Sauðafell, S103), where he settled at Erpsstaðir. Finally, Kollr (or Dala-Kollr, Auðr's grandson-in-law) takes all of Laxárdalur (S96, S105). The narrative which describes Auðr and people connected with her (largely mirrored in *Laxdæla saga*) continues with five more chapters, four of which are almost entirely genealogy with the other one recounting Auðr's death (S106–110).

Undoubtedly Auðr's *landnám* expresses the belief that Hvammr had primacy over central Dalir, i.e. each of the named valleys or farms with which her companions are associated. That said, the varied formats of each of the S entries for these areas, and the genealogical connections which are made with other areas, suggest that there are further nuances which are worth analysis, to see how well the idea of a genealogical charter holds up. Most of Auðr's male associates seem to derive their names from farm or valley names, but the quantity and nature of other information given about each one suggests that S depends largely on some kind of earlier tradition here. Most suspicious are the single-sentence *landnám* accounts for Hundi and Sökkólfr (S101, S102) whose brevity appears to reflect the smallness of the valley each is allocated.[55] The names of most of the other dependent male settlers within Auðr's *landnám* – Vífill, Ketill, Hörðr and Erpr – also seem to derive from place-names but these figures have a genealogical importance which Hundi and Sökkólfr lack. Only one, Dala-Kollr, seems to have a less obvious connection to a particular place although his name, *kollr*, 'head' or 'mountain peak,' might make sense as part of a now-lost story in which he was a senior or early colonist. This is not out of line with his position as the dependent of Auðr's with the largest *landnám*, i.e. the whole of Laxárdalur. The idea of Dala-Kollr's primacy among Auðr's crew is reinfoced by his being the only one who marries into her line.

Although last among those chapters covering lines of descent from Auðr, S109 presents her descendents via her grandson Óláfr *feilan* and whose mother was Þuríðr, the sister of Helgi *magri* of Eyjafjörður. Óláfr *feilan* and his father lived at Hvammr. The genealogy in this fifteen-line chapter is set out in Figure 19.

---

55   Herschend 1994; Adolf Friðriksson & Orri Vésteinsson 2003: 147.

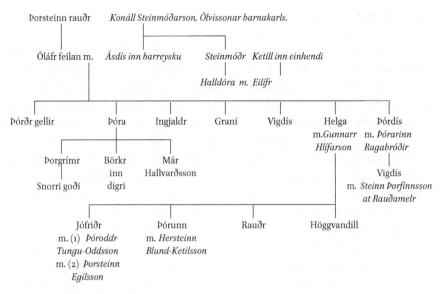

FIGURE 20   Genealogy in S109

Locally it connects Hvammr to Snorri *goði* at Helgafell,[56] but after that what is notable is that it records connections to the farm of Rauðamelr, on the southern side of Snæfellsnes, and also to two people in Borgarfjörður, all to the south of Dalir. The Borgarfjörður connection is of particular significance because this region was Snorri Sturluson's base in the thirteenth century. S109 (Figure 20) also includes obvious connections with the the well-known dispute between Þórðr *gellir* and Tungu-Oddr – outlined in *Íslendingabók* and *Hænsa-Þóris saga* – where it forms part of the myth concerning the origins of Iceland's system of assemblies.[57]

These are all extra-local ties, of course. Despite that, attempting to explain how and why this genealogy and the dispute story came about is not easy. This genealogy may not quite be emphasising Hvammr's regional hegemony over these places in the way that a narrowly-defined genealogical charter might, in terms of interregional politics the chapter makes Óláfr *feilan's* descendants look noticeably focussed to the south of Dalir. While, for instance, Óláfr *pái*, the grandson of Dala-Kollr, marries Þorgerðr Egilsdóttir from Borg

---

56   *S* had already stated Snorri *goði*'s descent from Auðr in S85.
57   S107 also traces a line of descent from Auðr to someone with Dalir connections who died fighting with Þórðr *gellir* against Tungu-Oddr.

in Borgarfjörður, his sons marry sisters from further north.[58] It contrasts with much of the material considered below in that it supposes regional-scale political relationships for Hvammr instead of predominantly local ones. At the same time the opposition between Þórðr *gellir* and Tungu-Oddr recorded in the feud story in *Hænsa-Þóris saga* and *Íslendingabók* is reflected by the segmentation of S109's genealogy.[59] The fact that these men appear at all in such close proximity in a genealogy of people associated with Dalir suggests that this is a genealogy created by Dalir people. S109 is in effect seeing events in Borgarfjörður's past as a part of that of Dalir, putting Borgarfjörður people in minor (and therefore geographically distant) segments of the genealogy. It aggrandises Hvammr and does not really fit with the more organic model and smaller scale genealogical charter we have seen so far. Potentially it may also be significant that it is one of Óláfr *feilan*'s descendants (Jófríðr) who marries men associated, respectively, with Borg and Breiðabólstaðr, next to Reykholt, both places controlled by Snorri Sturluson in the thirteenth century.[60]

For all these similarities with thirteenth-century geopolitics, the early twelfth-century *Íslendingabók* story involving Þórðr *gellir* and Tungu-Oddr, agrees with the basic story of *Hænsa-Þóris saga* and the genealogies in S (and indeed *Laxdæla saga*). The idea of connections between Dalir and Borgarfjörður is therefore probably one that we can associate with Ari Þorgilsson and his peers.[61] The implication is therefore that both Hvammr and Breiðabólstaðr might have been regionally powerful by this date.

Adjacent Laxárdalur is characterized as having a strong connection to Hvammr which is personified by the relationship of Dala-Kollr with Auðr (S105). Dala-Kollr, the coloniser of all of Laxárdalur, is said to have been a joint leader with Auðr – whether this is when they navigated to Iceland or when they got there is not clear – as well as the person whom she respected most (*hann hafði forráð með Auði ok var virðr mest af henni*, S96). Kollr also marries

---

58 Two daughters of Ásgeirr *æðikollr*'s marry two sons of Óláfr *pái* (S105, ÍF V: 137–38, 161). *Laxdæla saga* makes more of this connection (and more precisely) than S but the clear implication in both is that Óláfr *pái* had connections with the region immediately to the north and east of Laxárdalur.

59 For a summary of bookprosist views on the relationships of S, other *landnám* texts, *Laxdæla saga* and *Hænsa-Þóris saga* see ÍF III: vii–xxi. The basic similarities in all the accounts of the burning of Blund-Ketill, *Hænsa-Þóris saga*'s key event, and their associated genealogies are more striking than their differences.

60 Breiðabólstaðr was part of the Reykholt estate by the time Snorri took ownership of it in 1206 (DI I: 471; Helgi Þorláksson 2007: 214–15).

61 *Laxdæla saga* (ÍF V: 14) does not agree entirely with S over Hersteinn's father and so there can be no real question of intertextuality here (ÍF III: ix, 4, note 3).

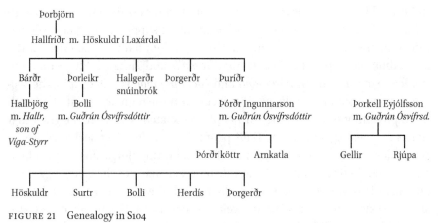

FIGURE 21 Genealogy in S104

one of Auðr's granddaughters, cementing the idea that Hvammssveit and Laxárdalur were on very good terms.[62]

To understand the more precise significance of S105, however, we need to look at S104, S106 and S107. S104, as mentioned above, records the descendants of Þorbjörn from Haukadalur and Höskuldr which creates a slight overlap between them (Figure 21).

Both S104 and S105 record the line of Höskuldr-Þorleikr-Bolli but S104 is interested primarily in two things which S105 is not. The first, the integration of

---

62   The genealogy of Kollr's descendants which is recorded in S105 works like a genealogical charter at a more local level:

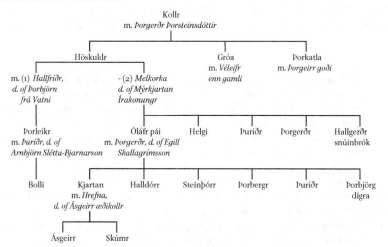

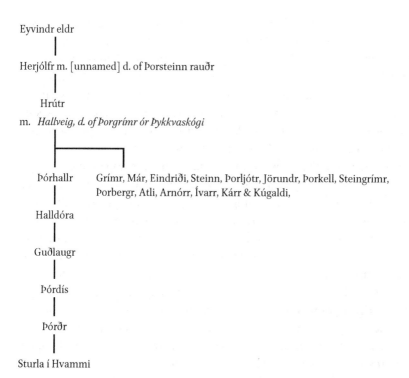

FIGURE 22   Genealogy in S106

Þorbjörn from Vatn into the genealogy of Auðr, has already been discussed.[63] The second is the genealogical relationships of Bolli and his wife Guðrún Ósvífrsdóttir, two figures at the centre of *Laxdœla saga*. That S chooses to place Bolli and Guðrún in S104 rather than in S105 serves to distance Bolli and Guðrún from the Laxdælir. S might just as easily have presented Bolli and Guðrún in connection with Kjartan Óláfsson, given the trio's close connection in *Laxdœla saga*. S is trying to diminish the couple's importance for the history of Laxárdalur by associating them with Haukadalur instead, giving precedence to Kjartan's line that was associated with Hjarðarholt.

S106 records the descendants of Hrútr Herjólfsson but in doing so reveals lower-scale political differences within the Laxárdalur area (Figure 22). Arguably it does this despite its being one of those places in S where a line is traced down to Hvamm-Sturla. The simple, explicit link down to the Sturlungar would appear to be an addition to an earlier version of *Landnámabók* or at least there is nothing here which does not chime with other parts of S that cover Miðdalir.

---

63   See above pp. 163–4.

The chapter identifies Hrútr's wife as being from Þykkvaskógr which makes some sense on the ground as Þykkvaskógr was at the northern end of the Miðdalir district, and here forms the edge of a small Laxárdalur-centred territorial unit.[64] Only in *Laxdæla saga*, however, is a more detailed set of relationships between Þykkvaskógr and Laxárdalur suggested when it records the Ármóðssynir from Þykkvaskógr helping to avenge the death of Bolli Þorleiksson. *S* and *Laxdæla saga* both see Þykkvaskógr as part of a Laxárdalur political orbit and on good terms with the major farms in Laxárdalur.[65]

Again *S*'s greater detail allows us to drill down into the apparent genealogical charter, which is clearly informed by an understanding of a story very like that preserved in *Laxdæla saga*. It might be argued that in giving such a view of the past both *S* and *Laxdæla saga* are the work of someone among the Sturlungar trying to justify their control of land in Miðdalir in the thirteenth century. It will be suggested in Chapter 5, however, that *Laxdæla saga* does not necessarily embody a partisan Sturlungar view of the past. The shape of the genealogy in S106 and the account of Hrútr's genealogy in *Laxdæla saga* both suggest that Hrútr ('ram') was viewed as a mythical *ættfaðir*. He is attributed 15 named children by one wife in S106 and 26 unnamed children by three wives in *Laxdæla saga*.[66] This most likely suggests that Hrútr's genealogical importance was relatively newly-established, because people seemed to still claim to know details about him in a way that they did not for, say, Álfr *í Dölum* or Erpr. Hrútr's large number of descendants is a typical feature of the later stages of a genealogical charter in which the number of segments are generally large and irregular.[67] This idea of a very fecund Hrútr is common to *S* and *Laxdæla* but the precise information about him in each story is significantly different and suggests their textual independence as well as a lively oral tradition about Hrútr.

While a strong affinity and almost equity characterises Dala-Kollr's relations with Auðr, Erpr and Sauðafell seem less eminent and less positively-associated with Auðr, despite or perhaps because, of Erpr's status as Auðr's freedman (*leysingi*). We have seen how significant a centre Sauðafell was in the thirteenth

---

64 Þykkvaskógr survived as a place-name only into the sixteenth century but is identical with one or other of the cluster of farms in Miðdalir with *skógur* in their name (ÍF v: 87, note 6).

65 More powerful, regional connections for Þykkvaskógr are alluded to when *Laxdæla saga* says that Gestr Oddleifsson had relatives there (ÍF v: 87)

66 ÍF v: 48–49.

67 Peters 1960: 50–52.

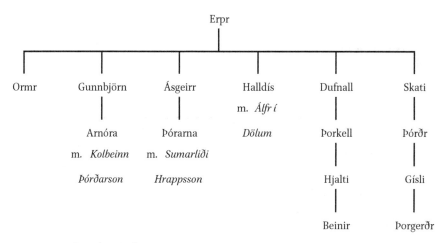

FIGURE 23   Genealogy in S103

century. By contrast *S* makes little of Sauðafell's supposed first colonist, Erpr, whose name must derive from the adjacent farm, Erpsstaðir. The neat genealogy of Erpr is not filled with well-known or important people, but it does go as far as a further four generations in two lines (Figure 23).

Within S103 the figure of Álfr *í Dölum*, a great grandson of Auðr, is, however of note.[68] Álfr (literally 'elf' or supernatural being) was someone people remembered as an ancestor of the Sauðafellsmenn and of the people of Reykjanes across the bay from Saurbær (S122).[69] It seems likely, given his name and descendants, that Álfr had been a figure of genealogical significance for locally powerful people. Perhaps here, even if Erpr is cast in the role of Auðr's dependent, the recording of Álfr is another hint at the farm's high status. Equally of note is the marriage recorded for Þórarna Ásgeirsdóttir to Sumarliði Hrappsson, which creates a tie between Sauðafell and an opponent of Hjarðarholt in Laxárdalur, a conflict made explicit in *Laxdæla saga*.[70] Thus Sauðafell's settler has important descendants locally, but the last element suggests political tension with Auðr's line. This, as we will see, is not dissimilar to the accounts for the other Miðdalir *landnámsmenn* associated with Auðr. Sauðafell certainly appears less important than we might expect given its importance in the thirteenth century.

---

68   *Laxdæla saga* has a very brief account of Erpr which agress in outline with S103 (ÍF V: 10). Álfr's descendants are set out in a later chapter, S107, which partly accords with S103.
69   Álfr *í Dölum* is mentioned once in *Sturlunga saga*, as an ancestor of Þorgils Oddason (SS I: 13).
70   Sumarliði is the son of Hrappr, inhabitant of Hrappsstaðir in Laxárdalur (ÍF V: 40).

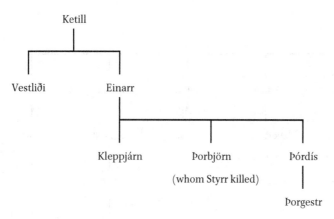

FIGURE 24   Genealogy in S98

Lastly, Ketill is given the most westerly part of Auðr's *landnám*, from Skraumuhlaupsá to Hörðudalsá. He seems to exist in *S* – he is notably absent from *Laxdæla saga*[71] – because he is on the edge of Auðr's territory and has a genealogy which flags up a conflict or contrast between Auðr's descendants and those of Björn *inn austrœni* (Figure 24). By including Ketill, *S* divides the eastern end of Skógarströnd into smaller parcels of land than does *Laxdæla saga*, and Hörðudalur effectively becomes smaller. This might imply a different political situation when the two texts were created.[72]

The main point of the S98 genealogy, however, seems to be to explain where Ketill's grandchildren fit into the story of Styrr, who killed one of them. Styrr is Víga-Styrr (Killer Styrr), a descendant of Björn *inn austrœni* whose story is recorded in *Heiðarvíga saga* and is elsewhere associated with Bjarnarhöfn.[73] In sum, although the appearance of a Ketill of Ketilsstaðir in just one version of the story of Auðr's *landnám* could lead us to believe that he was consciously manufactured, the fact that he is credited with descendants makes it more likely that he owed his existence to a genuine tradition.

4.2   Northern Snæfellsnes: Björn inn austrœni, Þórólfr Mostrarskegg *and* Skógarströnd

It is probably most useful to summarise the accounts for northern Snæfellsnes in a table (Table 1). Given the arguments of the present chapter about the early

---

71   Björn M. Ólsen 1908: 162–63; Jón Jóhannesson 1941: 215; ÍF I: 140, note 3.
72   Ketill's son Vestliði probably owes his existence to a topographical feature, Vestliðaeyrr, which lay between Skraumuhlaupsá (modern Skrauma) and the river Hörðudalsá, and is recorded in *Sturlunga saga* (SS II 194, 195, 213).
73   ÍF III: 232–33; ÍF I: 140, note 3; S98.

SETTLERS AND SETTLEMENT MYTHOLOGIES   175

TABLE 1   Summary table of *Sturlubók*'s chapters covering northern Snæfellsnes

S chapter no. and colonist's name	Farm	Area/District	Other notable features
78 (Óláfr *belgr*)	(Óláfsvík)	(Óláfsvíkurenni)	Expelled by Ormr *inn mjóvi*
79 Ormr *inn mjóvi*	Brimilsvellir then Fróðá	Gamlavík, Óláfsvík	Chapter includes partial account of dispute in *Eyrbyggja saga* that includes Þorbjörn *inn digri*, son of Ormr
80 Sigurðr *svínhöfði*	?	From Búlandshöfði to Kirkjufjörður	
81 Vestarr	Öndverðareyrr	Eyrarland & Kirkjufjörður	
82 Kolr	Kolgrafir	From Fjarðarhorn to Hraunsfjörður	
83 Auðun *stoti*	Hraunsfjörðr?	Hraunsfjörður	
84 Björn *inn austræni*	Bjarnarhöfn	From Hraunsfjörðr to the river Stafá	
85 Þórólfr *Mostrarskegg*	Helgafell?	From Stafá to Þórsá	Credited with naming Breiðafjörðr, Þórsnes peninsula and Helgafell. Established a *hof* at Hofstaðir. A *heraðsþing* was established on Þórsnes.
86 Geirrøðr, Geirríðr	Narfeyri	Þórsá to Langadalsá	Geirrøðr gives Geirríðr the farm/valley of Borgardalr
86 Úlfarr	Úlfarsfell?	Álptafjörður	Farm given by Geirrøðr
86 Finngeirr	Kársstaðir	Álptafjörður	Farm given by Geirrøðr
86 Úlfarr & Örlyggr	?	Álptafjörður?	Land given by Geirrøðr
87 Þorbergr	Stóri-Langidalr?	Stóri- and Litli-Langidalr	
88 Steinn Vígbjóðsson	Breiðabólstaðr	From Stóri-Langidalr to Laxá	
94 Ingólfr *inn sterki*	Hólmslátr	Laxá to Skraumuhlaupsá	

dates of the traditions recorded in S, it is ironic that the first and last *landnám* chapters for this entire region mention the same figure, Óláfr *belgr*, whose story looks likely to have been fabricated, either in the original *Landnámabók* or by the compiler of S. In both instances he is displaced by another colonist and his legacy is not progeny but merely place-names: the bay and/or farm of Óláfsvík on Snæfellsnes and then the valley names of Belgsdalur and Óláfsdalur adjacent to Saurbær. Beyond Óláfr, however, we have more credible colonists and genealogies.

If we return to considering the relationship between Auðr and Björn *inn austrœni*, then it is striking that the blood relationship between Auðr and Björn exists in spite of other *landnám* separating them geographically, notably all of Skógarströnd and that of Þórólfr *Mostrarskegg* at Helgafell but also, on Fellsströnd, that of Kjallakr. These other *landnám* also tell us about broad political relationships. Björn *inn austrœni* is connected to Kjallakr in S84 as Kjallakr's father,[74] implying Bjarnarhöfn's political superiority to Fellsströnd if we follow the logic of a genealogical charter. Fellsströnd is notable for not being connected to Auðr despite its proximity to Hvammssveit, which as a putative political divide is quite striking.[75]

---

74   *Eyrbyggja saga* and M both see Kjallakr as Björn *inn austrœni*'s son, and therefore dependent:

S111:
   Björn *inn sterkr*
   |_____
   Kjallakr at Kjallaksstaðir Gjaflaug m. Björn *inn austrœni*

S84:
   Kjallakr
   |_____
   Björn *inn sterkr*   Gjaflaug m. Björn *inn austrœni*
                                    |
                          Kjallakr inn gamli at Bjarnarhöfn

Eyrbyggja saga   chs.2 & 7. Key details of this genealogy are replicated in M24:

   Björn *inn austrœni* m. Gjaflaug, daughter of Jarl Kjallakr
   |_____
   Kjallakr *gamli* at Bjarnarhöfn   Óttarr m. Gróa
   m. Ástríðr
   |
   Kjalleklingar

75   ÍF IV: 12. See p. 180 for S84 and S111's contrasting views of the exact nature of the connection between Bjarnarhöfn and Fellsströnd.

Such a pattern is supported by the fact that Helgafell, Bjarnarhöfn's near neighbour, *is* associated exclusively with Auðr/Hvammr.[76] S85 records Þorsteinn *þorskabítr* of Helgafell's famous clash with Þorgrímr Kjallaksson and his brother-in-law Ásgeirr *af Eyri* regarding the sanctity of the assembly site on Þórsnes, a story also found in *Eyrbyggja saga*. This is in effect a conflict between Bjarnarhöfn and Öndverðareyrr against Helgafell. Although the dispute is not resolved, and part of the point of the story is to explain how the assembly changed location, the story depicts a political situation which emphasises division. It also seems entirely realistic that two of the major farms west of Helgafellssveit might ally with each other against Helgafell, the wealthiest farm in the district. The only genealogical information preserved in S85 serves to demonstrate connections between Helgafell and Auðr *in djúpauðga*'s descendants associated with Hvammr. Every descendant of Þórólfr *Mostrarskegg* could, according to this account, claim descent from Auðr *in djúpauðga* (Figure 25).

The further detail of *S*'s idea of Auðr/Hvammr's sphere of influence can be worked out by a combination of positive and negative evidence. The marriages of Auðr's granddaughters to men from Breiðabólstaðr and Langidalr, just east and inland from Narfeyri (S87, S88) ties Skógarströnd to Hvammr, but less directly so than for areas within her *landnám*.[77] That said, of these two colonists' farms on Skógarströnd, Breiðabólstaðr is elsewhere also tied to Helgafell and Langidalr has a recorded connection to Bjarnarhöfn.[78] The pattern of allegiances suggested by the genealogies for Skógarströnd creates the impression of some influence or ties to Hvammr but also, some connection to Helgafell.

Þórólfr *Mostrarskegg*/Helgafell's recorded relationships do, however, extend over Álptafjörður, the small valley immediately next to the east of the Þórsnes

---

[76] *Eyrbyggja saga* has a significant variation on the relationship between Björn *inn austrœni* and Þórólfr *Mostrarskegg*. It says that Björn and Þórólfr were companions but that Björn settled 'með ráði Þórólfs,' with the consent of Þórólfr (ÍF IV: 11). *Eyrbyggja saga* clearly saw Helgafell as superior to Bjarnarhöfn, both here and in the rest of the saga. See below pp. 193, 200 for instances in Eyjafjörður of the 'at ráði' formulation.

[77] Áslákr, son of Þorbergr, marries Arnleif Þórðardóttir (S87); Þorgestr, the son of Steinn *mjöksiglandi* marries Arnóra Þórðardóttir (S88). The similarity of the daughters' names strongly suggests that they formed part of the same story.

[78] The colonist located nearest to Miðdalir, Ingólfr of Hólmslátr, has no recorded connections to any others. S87 records descent from the colonist Þorbergr is traced mainly through Illugi *inn rammi*, the so-called *ættfaðir* (clan founder) of the Langdælir. Illugi has many children attributed to him and the marriages of his daughters are recorded. The key point to mention here is that none of these marriages link Illugi's descendants with Helgafell.

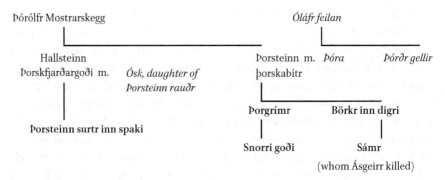

FIGURE 25 Genealogy in S85 (Normal text denotes descendants of Þórólfr *Mostrarskegg*, italicised names indicate descendants of Auðr *in djúpauðga*, and bold names indicate descendants of both.)

peninsula. S86 shows concern with Helgafell and not directly with Hvammr. It records another sketch narrative about (disputes in) Álptafjörður that includes the same basic names and features as the fuller account we will see in *Eyrbyggja saga*.[79] A key part of this is that Snorri *goði* of Helgafell, a descendant of both Þórólfr *Mostrarskegg* and Auðr, takes control of Álptafjörður. Both *Eyrbyggja saga* and *Laxdæla saga* then also identify Snorri as eventually moving to Hvammr. *S* makes no mention of this, which suggests that *S*'s author wished to play it down.[80]

S's account of the area to the west of Helgafellssveit also overlaps with the account of *Eyrbyggja saga*, although is never dependent on it. While the most obvious starting point for considering the *landnám* here is relations with Helgafell, the text shows a rather mixed picture for its five colonists, of which only three are worth discussion. Only the first, most westerly of them (S79), has a strong connection to Helgafell. This *landnám* has Fróðá as its colonist's farm, and the account consists of a potted version of *Eyrbyggja saga*'s account of its occupant, Þorbjörn *inn digri* Ormsson. Þorbjörn is linked to Helgafell through his marriage to Snorri *goði*'s half-sister. This tie means Snorri prosecutes the case against Þorbjörn's killer – Þórarinn from Mávahlíð, the farm next door – as set out both here and in chapter 22 of *Eyrbyggja saga*.[81] By contrast, it is implied by S80 that the next *landnám* to the east was remembered solely in opposition to Snorri/Helgafell: a single line of descent from the colonist Sigurðr names people associated with Mávahlíð (Þórarinn), Kjallaksstaðir and Bjarnarhöfn (Vermundr *inn mjóvi*).

---

79   ÍF I: 128, note 2; Jón Jóhannesson 1941: 95.
80   See Chapter 5 generally for the elements of Snorri's political power.
81   See below p. 252 for the occupation of Mávahlíð by people other than Snorri's family.

S81 records a fuller genealogical account for the colonist at Öndverðareyrr than does *Eyrbyggja saga* with the result that he gets a more nuanced set of ties. The *landnámsmaðr*'s son marries someone from Kjallaksstaðir, a tie clearly not with Snorri/Helgafell. However, for the next generation a marriage to Snorri's allies in Álptafjörður is recorded and then, in the following generation, a marriage to a daughter of Snorri.[82] The whole genealogy seems more grounded in the reality of familial connections between local, wealthy farms, but is shaped in such a way as to depict incremental increases in positive relations between Öndverðareyrr and Helgafell.[83] This is not what one would expect in a genealogical charter but there is a geopolitical logic to it.

If we look at all of this stretch of northern Snæfellsnes, then, we can see a diverse set of chapters, including some that tell potted versions of narratives similar to those told in *Eyrbyggja saga*, and others which are notably short. None, though, are of a single line or two such as we saw for Hundi and Sökkólfr (S101, 102). Those to the west of Helgafell would seem to be mostly a cluster of local intra-district affiliations with just Fróðá being remembered as strongly tied to any farm beyond it, namely Helgafell. Of the farms of colonists, Helgafell and, indirectly, Hvammr, is shown in clear, active opposition to Bjarnarhöfn and Öndverðareyrr, something which is reflected genealogically. Skógarströnd's colonists or their descendants are identified as having a mixture of ties with Hvammr, Helgafell and Bjarnarhöfn. There are some very clear local geopolitical patterns but for Skógarströnd the idea of a genealogical charter with clear affiliations to one part of the genealogy of Auðr and Björn does not work. The mixed ties for people in this area might instead be read as the product of this district being on the edge of the spheres of influence of the most powerful farms.

4.3   Fellsströnd, Skarðsströnd and Saurbær

This area is significant because it is not part of Auðr's *landnám*. Instead here we see two separate groups of colonists involved in the settlement and the issues of the construction of their *landnám* stories are different. As discussed above, Kjallakr, who settled most of Fellsströnd, represents the first of these 'groups' and his story has the appearance of a very simple, small-scale genealogical charter. More complex is the information we have on the colonists who

---

82   See esp. pp. 250, 251 below on Steinþórr *af Eyri* and his son Gunnlaugr.
83   The last two colonists, Kolr and Auðun *stoti* (S82, S83) are not connected explicitly with particular farms but would appear to be associated with the two small fjords, Kolgrafarfjörður and Hraunsfjörður respectively. The former has no named genealogical connections but the latter's line of descent is recorded as far as a marriage to the people of Öndverðareyrr (ÍF I: 120).

settled Skarðsströnd, Saurbær and some of the islands west of these districts. Determining whether or not these stories represent genealogical charters and, if they were, of whose construction, is less simple. A brief consideration of the complexities of the *landnám* accounts for Skarðsströnd and the relatively densely inhabited Saurbær can add to our understanding of the logic of the S account.

As noted at the beginning of this chapter, the *landnám* account for Kjallakr in S111 is one of the clearest examples of a narrative which not only sets out an origin story for a large farm and the district around it – what in later centuries was actually a *hreppr* – but also includes a kind of genealogical charter. To begin with, though, something more needs to be said about the status of Kjallakr himself. It is clear that his name derives from Kjallaksstaðir, the farm at the mouth of Galtardalsá on Fellsströnd. Genealogies in S111 and in S84 show that Kjallakr was seen as connected in some way or other to Bjarnarhöfn on the southern side of Hvammsfjörður, although they differ in arguably significant ways. As pointed out above, S84 identifies a Kjallakr *hinn gamli* (the old) in connection with Bjarnarhöfn but not explicitly with Fellsströnd.[84] S111 links the two areas, however, by stating:

> There was a man called Kjallakr, son of Björn *inn sterki*, brother of Gjaflaug who married Björn *inn austræni*; he went to Iceland and took land from Dögurðará to Klofningur and lived at Kjallaksstaðir.[85]

S111, then, supposes that Kjallakr was *not* the son of Björn *inn austræni*, i.e. not politically subordinate to him, and that he was in fact of equal standing to him, as his brother-in-law. In addition, the appearance in S111 of an extra character called Björn, Björn *inn sterki*, looks like as a pro-Fellsströnd story suggesting the district's independence. In still recording that Kjallakr and Björn *inn austræni* were related by marriage, S111 suggests the districts' political affinity. S111 effectively makes Kjallaksstaðir independent of Bjarnarhöfn, though, in contrast with S84's account, and at a more local level, it supposes the superiority of Kjallaksstaðir over nearby farms because Kjallakr grants land to others. S111 also gives Kjallakr a sphere of influence: his sons lived at Ketilsstaðir, 10km to the east, and on the island of Svíney (modern Purkey) 15km to the

---

84 See above p. 176, esp. footnote 75.
85 'Kjallakr hét maðr, son Bjarnar ens sterka, bróðir Gjaflaugar, er átti Björn enn austræni; hann fór til Íslands ok nám land frá Dögurðará til Klofninga ok bjó á Kjallaksstöðum.' (ÍF I: 147).

west, almost exactly on the boundaries of the early modern *hreppr* of Fellsströnd.[86] Equally importantly, this latter connection is consistent with a view of Svíney as being independent of Hvammr and even possibly hostile to it. S111 seems to preserve a picture of Fellsströnd that makes a sense as a 'Fellsstrendingar' view of the past while also suggesting an affinity with Bjarnarhöfn but nowhere else, not even Hvammr.

The *landnám* accounts covering Skarðsströnd and Saurbær represent an entirely separate set of stories from those for Fellsströnd. These districts are important to consider simply because they include the farms Staðarhóll and Skarð (Figures 7 and 8). What is also noteworthy is that the *S*, *M* and *H Landnámabók* texts all have slightly different accounts of the area, in particular giving different boundaries for the settlements of most colonists. While Sveinbjörn Rafnsson has interpreted *S*'s and *M*'s contrasting stories about Saurbær as the product of the dispute in 1241 between Sturla Þórðarson and Órækja Snorrason over control of Staðarhóll (the so-called *Staðarhólsmál*),[87] this is questionable given the confused accounts in the various *Landnámabók* recensions.

Geirmundr *heljarskinn*, who settled at Geirmundarstaðir on the estate of Skarð, is portrayed as the leader of a group of colonists who settled the coast of Breiðafjörður's north-western corner (S112, S113). *S* thus gives a kind of shared identity to the area. Geirmundr himself is said to have taken the coastal strip from near Dögurðarnes north to an unidentifiable 'Klofasteinar' and stayed 'in Búðardalr' initially.[88] He is said to have had another *landnám* in the West Fjords, along part of Strandir, replicating the economic link we see elsewhere for larger Dalir landowners.[89]

---

86   These claims for Kjallaksstaðir's influence are also recalled in *Íslendingasögur* covering Dalir. In S111 Svíney was supposedly occupied by an Æsa, daughter of Þorgrímr from Staðarfell. The political position of Æsa's son Eyjólfr fits with this in *Eyrbyggja saga*, *Eiríks saga rauða* and *Grænlendinga saga* where he is listed among the supporters of Eiríkr *rauði* against Þórðr *gellir* and Þorgestr from Breiðabólstaðr on Skógarströnd (ÍF IV: 59, 198, 241). In *Eyrbyggja saga* the farm Barkarstaðir, supposedly between Orrahóll and Galtardalstunga on Fellsströnd, is associated saga with Börkr *inn digri* whom Snorri *goði* tricked out of Helgafell. This is a rare example of someone from either side of this part of Hvammsfjörður appearing on both sides of it. Barkarstaðir is recorded in *Jarðabók* (VI: 111) as being abandoned and uninhabitable. Börkr is portayed negatively in *Eyrbyggja saga* and his displacement to Fellsströnd suggests conflict between the two districts.
87   Sveinbjörn Rafnsson 1985.
88   Klofasteinar have been assumed to be a landscape feature of some kind, rather than a farm, but their exact location is unclear. It seems likely that they were just north of the valley of Búðardalur (Kaalund 1877–82 I: 493; ÍF I: 153, note 9).
89   E.g. for Þorgils Oddason (p. 91) and Snorri *goði* (p. 267).

One of the problems with *S*'s account for this area is simply working out where the boundaries of *landnám* were thought to have been. Geirmundr's companion Steinólfr *inn lági*, for example, is said by *S* to take the coast immediately to the north of Geirmundr's *landnám*, from 'Klofasteinar' to 'Grjótvallarmúli' and to have lived in Fagradalur. Grjótvallarmúli has been identified as Holtahyrna, a hill at the north-western edge of Saurbær.[90] The assumption has therefore been that Steinólfr took all of Saurbær as his *landnám* although incongruously he was said to have based himself at Fagradalur, to Saurbær's south. Likewise *S* can be seen to contradict itself by claiming that both Steinólfr and Óláfr *belgr* (S118) settled at least some part of Saurbær.

Equally difficult to understand are the accounts of the *landnám* of Steinólfr and his neighbour and son-in-law Sléttu-Björn (S116 and S117). These *landnám* have been seen in the context of Staðarhóll's estate and of political control in Saurbær in the thirteenth century but it is hard to determine precisely how it mattered.[91] *Íslendinga saga*, which records the *Staðarhólsmál*, names Staðarhólsland and six smaller farms in Saurbær as being claimed by Órækja Snorrason in 1241.[92] The status of these other farms is unclear; they might have been part of Staðarhóll's estate but, because they are fairly well dispersed across Saurbær they do not make an obvious territorial block which might fit with the way *Landnámabók* generally represents the *landnám*. How many other properties belonged to Staðarhóll's estate in 1241 is equally unclear. It seems hard to say whether the account of *S* really related to this particular context. Certainly the division of Saurbær into the two sub-units recorded in *S* might roughly equate to something like the divide between Staðarhóll and Hvoll seen in *Sturlu saga*.[93]

If we turn to the genealogical contents of these chapters then we do at least get some sense of the status of these colonists. Little is said about Geirmundr *heljarskinn*'s descendants although he is credited with having an aristocratic Norwegian wife and a daughter (S115). Skarð's connections in the north-eastern part of Breiðafjörður are elsewhere reinforced by his daughter's marriage to Ketill *gufa* from Gufudalur. *S* says that Geirmundr had a second wife, from

---

90   Kaalund 1877–82 I: 497; ÍF I: 156, note 4.
91   I would agree with Helgi Þorláksson (2017: 206) that it 'served Sturla Þórðarson's interests' for his ancestor to be recorded as settler of all of Saurbær but the issue is how the detail furthers them.
92   SS I: 448. The farms named are Hvítadalr, Múli, Þverfell, Þverárdalr, Eysteinsstaðir (later a *hjáleiga* of Bjarnarstaðir) and Saurhóll.
93   See above p. 92.

Ísafjörður in the West Fjords, but nothing else.[94] All things considered it is rather curious that while *S* sets Geirmundr up as the leader of the settlers who took Skarðsströnd, Saurbær, the islands of Flatey and Hergilsey (S114) it has little else to say about him.[95] This might in part be explained by the fact that Skarð's occupants instead claimed descent from Steinólfr *inn lági*, as is made explicit in S116 which records a line down to lawspeaker Snorri Húnbogason from Skarð (d.1170) via his wife.[96] This link is ambiguous but perhaps it either bolstered or challenged the connection with Geirmundr. Some of Steinólfr's familial connections in S116 are relatively high-status ones with large farms in neighbouring districts (Bær in Hrútafjörður and Hvammr in Hvammssveit).[97]

---

94   A daughter of Geirmundr's by his second wife is recorded, Geirríðr, but nothing else is known about her. ÍF I: 156, note 3 records a gap in the *S* manuscript (ÁM 107) after Geirríðr's name.

95   *Geirmundar þáttr heljarskinns* and M both record a different *langfeðgatal* which stems from Geirmundr. M30 and *Geirmundar þáttr heljarskinns* both record descendants of Geirmundr. *M* traces down through Ýrr and Þorgils Oddason to Hallbera, the wife of Markús Þórðarson. *Geirmundar þáttr* traces a line from Geirmundr's daughter Arndís, through Þorgils Oddason to Skarð-Snorri (SS I: 10).

96   The genealogy of S116:

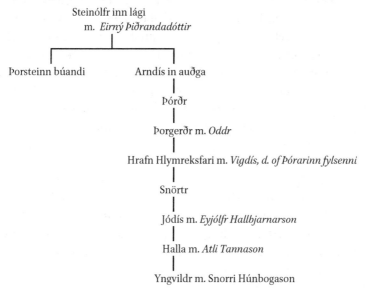

97   Helgi Þorláksson (2017: 204) suggests that *S* makes a connection between the farm at Ballará on Skarðsströnd and the farm of Geitland in Borgarfjörður to bolster Sturlungar property claims in Borgarfjörður. As with many other such links it seems so obscurely put, to me, to be a deliberate part of a tenurial claim.

S120 also gives him another *landnám* in Þorskafjörður just to the north.[98] In sum, then, the best we can probably say is that there seems to have been an effort to collect as much lore as possible about the early occupants of Skarð to create a sense of the farm's local pre-eminence. Similarly, Sléttu-Björn's descendants have a clear association with Staðarhóll, because one of them is said to have founded the farm, and they have a link to Strandir like Geirmundr did (S117, S156).

Insofar as it makes sense to summarise what *S* says about the coastal region west and north of Auðr's *landnám*, we can say that each of these chapters credits its colonists with settling districts with relatively large numbers of farms. Each of them is distinct from the other, and in the case of S111, highly unusual. The other chapters are notable for their relative lack of genealogy and therefore an absence of genealogical relationships with other areas. Sléttu-Björn is said to have had four sons but their spouses are not recorded, for instance. The *landnám* associated with each colonist make sense as *hreppar* or *hreppr*-like territories but it is more often the case here that insufficient detail is given to show genealogical charters within them.

More broadly this section has pointed out possible political ideas that lie behind the Dalir and north Snæfellsnes genealogies in *Landnámabók*. Even for Dalir, where we have other texts, these genealogies cannot always be accurately dated or firmly attributed to particular writers. Notwithstanding these problems of interpretation, I would contend that they are likely to tell us most of all about the period before 1200, because the political situations which they suggest are unlike those we have seen recounted for the thirteenth century.

To be more precise, what we have seen suggests that Hvammr, Bjarnarhöfn and probably Skarð can be seen as the major political centres highlighted by the genealogies of *S*. Of these Hvammr is clearly preeminent. Auðr *in djúpauðga* is portrayed as controller of the whole of Hvammssveit, Laxárdalur, Haukadalur and Miðdalir, and the story of Eiríkr *rauði*'s expulsion from Haukadalur makes sense as a triumph of Auðr's kin group and implies their control of inner Dalir. Auðr's donation of land to her followers or companions – the relationship is ambiguous but she is clearly seen as superior to the other settlers to whom she gives land – suggests a direct form of control over these areas, something that is reinforced by genealogical links. Þórðr *gellir*, Auðr's grandson and another key genealogical figure, is also associated with Hvammr; his

---

[98] The background of Steinólfr's wife is unknown and the rest of S116 ignores what *Þorskfirðinga saga* says about his activity in Þorskafjörður which is recorded as part of a separate narrative (not focussed on Steinólfr) in S120 (ÍF XIII: 180, 191–92, 198, 201, 209–14, 217–24).

genealogical links form a second tier of political influence for Hvammr. He himself marries into the family which is said to have controlled Helgafell; his daughters' marriages to people from Langidalr and Breiðabólstaðr suggest a weaker link but still some form of political alliance. These are, furthermore, areas with which Bjarnarhöfn and Skarð are not linked. That the *landnám* of Ingólfr *inn sterki* at Hólmslátr on Skógarströnd (S94), is not connected to Hvammr in *S* probably reflects its political separateness. It would make some sense for this sparsely populated area to be of little immediate interest to an emerging polity based around Hvammsfjörður, although admittedly we have seen Hvamm-Sturla trying to exert influence there. Skógarströnd might not be within the sphere of influence of Hvammr – or Helgafell – but could instead have been influenced by Hítardalr to the south in much the same way as we have seen hints of Þorleifr *beiskaldi* of Hítardalr being significant in Dalir.[99] More will be said on the relationship of Helgafell to Hvammssveit in Chapter 5 in connection to Snorri *goði*, who *Eyrbyggja saga* and *Laxdœla saga* say lived first at Helgafell before moving to Sælingsdalstunga.

Bjarnarhöfn and Hvammr are connected (in *S* and *Laxdœla saga*) by the sibling relationship of Björn *inn austrœni* and Auðr *in djúpauðga*. This relationship, at the notional 'top end' of a genealogy, is the only connection between their two groups of descendants.[100] Bjarnarhöfn's political influence, as implied by Björn's genealogy, is with the outer part of Hvammsfjörður: Öndverðareyrr, Drápuhlíð and, although the link is never expressed clearly, Kjallaksstaðir on Fellsströnd. Bjarnarhöfn's sphere of influence, as depicted by these relationships, is separate from those of Hvammr and Helgafell. The suggestion of a connection with Fellsströnd through 'Þorgrímr *goði*' also implies that there was at least a memory of a polity which comprised Fellsströnd and Bjarnarhöfn's sphere of influence.[101] Fellsströnd is in no way genealogically connected with anyone within Auðr's *landnám*. It is not inconceivable, however, that Fellsströnd, like Ingólfr *inn sterki's landnám*, fell between two powerful farms (Helgafell and Hvammr) and was not seen as having been strongly controlled by either.

---

99 Ingólfr *inn sterki's landnámsbær* is named as Hólmslátr which features notably in *Sturlu saga*. Its political allegiance in that text is discussed above, p. 93.
100 Note *Eyrbyggja saga's* view that Björn was settling on the *landnám* of Þórólfr Mostrarskegg (ÍF IV: 11 and p. 220 below).
101 This argument is supported by *Eyrbyggja saga's* comment that Björn's *œttmenn* were kinsmen with 'Barna-Kjallakr' from Kjallaksstaðir on Fellsströnd (ÍF IV: 15). See below p. 244 for the conflict between Kjalleklingar and Þórsnesingar;

Skarð's sphere of influence and pre-eminence is suggested by its first settler's leadership of a group of colonists who settle to the north of Skarð on the mainland and, in one case, on islands to the west. Geirmundr's dominance over his companions' *landnám* is not, however, backed up by marriages between his descendants with those of his companions. It is difficult to explain why Geirmundr is not credited with genealogical connections either more locally or with his associates. Perhaps the poor expression of Skarð's political control reflects the weakness of that control when the original *Landnámabók* was written (notwithstanding the mention in S116 of Snorri Húnbogason from Skarð shows that particular chapter had been altered after 1150). Other indicators in *S* suggest that the area around Skarðsströnd and Saurbær was not seen as a single territorial block. This contrasts with Hvammr's control over several contiguous districts (Laxárdalur, Miðdalir, Skógarströnd and Helgafell).

Different levels of territorialisation in Dalir are thus suggested by *S*. It seems extremely unlikely that *S* preserves the memory of real *landnám*, but instead it probably reflects a later political situation which shows the consolidation of groups of farms into territories, i.e. those that are represented in the text as a single *landnám*. It also needs to be borne in mind that some of the apparently large *landnám* in the north of Dalir – those of Kjallakr, Geirmundr and Steinólfr – are likely to have included relatively few farms and therefore do not represent 'large' territorial units. In this light, the large *landnám* accorded to Auðr seems yet more remarkable because most of its constituent parts are likely to have been relatively densely populated. At the same time, the form of Auðr's *landnám* shows that district-level identities mattered and could not be erased as part of any putative attempt to create a fictional territory. People still retained distinct identities within Auðr's *landnám* which were expressed in genealogical form, through the idea of their own colonists taking land within Auðr's territory.

Political ranking is also expressed in the genealogies of people within Auðr's *landnám*. Clearly Auðr, the personification of Hvammr, was pre-eminent but there is a kind of ranking below her, with Dala-Kollr (Laxárdalr) as next most significant. After him a case might be made for Hörðr of Hörðudalr being made more important through his descendants' connections with people from outside Dalir. The only comparable set of connections here are among one line of Auðr's descendants who are identified with Hvammr itself.[102] In this respect *S* gives Hörðr/Hörðudalr a special status not seen in other texts even though his *landnám* was smaller in *S* than in *Laxdæla saga*.[103]

---

102 The descendants of Óláfr *feilan* are also recorded in *Laxdæla saga* (ÍF V: 11–14).
103 This is because *Laxdæla saga* omits Ketill (S98) from its list of colonists. See above p. 167.

In some respects the description of the *landnám* around Hvammsfjörður has some distinctive-looking features. Auðr *in djúpauðga*'s *landnám* is one of a select few across the whole of *S* (other examples include Helgi *magri* in Eyjafjörður, Ingólfr in Kjalarnesþing, Skallagrímr in Borgarfjörður) in which one colonist has several other colonists settle within their large *landnám*. Auðr and Björn are relatively rare as being sibling colonists and the confused description of the *landnám* in Saurbær is unusual. The survival of *Eyrbyggja saga* and *Laxdœla saga* also demonstrate just how much material in *S* could have been derived from fuller narratives rather than the bare genealogy that it otherwise largely consists of; this area is unusual therefore for its dense coverage in surviving *Íslendingasögur*. For all this, none of these features can be seen as making it unique: all such features are found elsewhere in *S*. Where there are idiosyncracies in *S* then they most likely derive from the nature of the myths recorded rather than the interference of Sturla Þórðarson or another writer with an interest in Dalir. The fact that any coherence at all can be discerned in such a large body of genealogical material is suggestive of its having a logic or set of rules which would be difficult to invent.[104]

5 Eyjafjörður and the North-East

While for Dalir the largest *landnám* in this smaller district, that of Auðr, dominates *Sturlubók*'s account, her brother-in-law and equivalent in the north-east, Helgi *inn magri*, dominates only Eyjafjörður itself (see Map 13). To the east there are no large *landnám*, which in itself suggests that there was no belief in the kind of shared identity or political centralisation which such a *landnám* might represent. Helgi *inn magri*'s *landnám* and its internal divisions and occupants require careful consideration in themselves. However, the whole region can be considered according to the patterns suggested for Dalir too.

The account of Eyjafjörður in *S* is unusual in having an initial section about Helgi who – we find out in later chapters – colonises much of the main valley of Eyjafjörður and then grants parts of his *landnám* to two of his sons and four sons-in-law. S217 tells the story of his father's flight from Norway and his marriage with the daughter of an Irish king. Helgi was born in Ireland but came to Iceland with his wife, Þórunn *hyrna* (the daughter of Ketill *flatnefr* and sister of Auðr *in djúpauðga*), their two sons, and a group of companions. No motivation is given for Helgi's move to Iceland, despite his relatively unusual origins. S218 recounts that Helgi combined a belief in Christ with calling on the pagan

---

[104] Cf. Adolf Friðriksson & Orri Vésteinsson 2003 who emphasise just such an inventiveness.

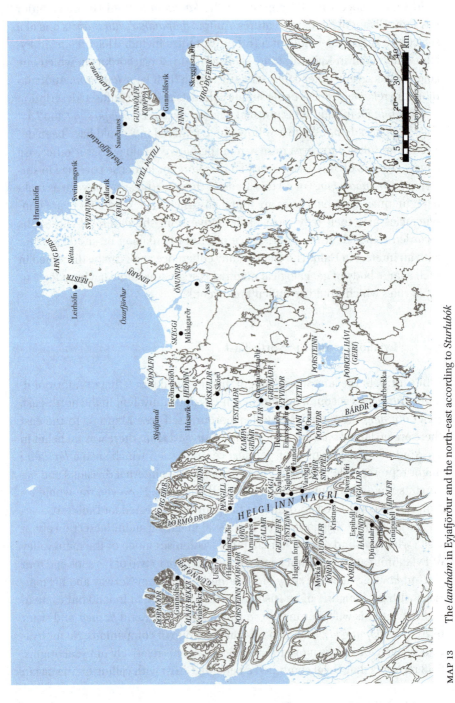

MAP 13   The *landnám* in Eyjafjörður and the north-east according to *Sturlubók*

god Þórr when going on sea voyages and in times of difficulty - a unique assertion for a colonist in S - so that in effect Þórr guides Helgi to Eyjafjörður. He is supposed to have spent his first winter at Hámundarstaðir on the coast near the mouth of Svarfaðardalur. The association of Helgi with Hámundarstaðir may be a rationalisation of the story of Helgi going up onto the mountain S calls Sólarfjöll (sun mountain(s)) to survey the region.[105] Hámundarstaðir was a large farm but otherwise unremarkable, except for the fact that Hámundr *heljarskinn*, Helgi's son-in-law, is also named in this story and makes the obvious association of Hámundr with Hámundarstaðir. One might expect Hámundr to settle at Hámundarstaðir but, as we shall see, he eventually settles at Espihóll inn syðri in Eyjafjörður. Indeed, Helgi and company are said to land in Eyjafjörður itself and settle at the farm of Kristnes, having reconnoitred the whole valley and performed some kind of hallowing ritual at every river mouth. Other elements of the story attach him to the lower part of the valley, closer to the sea.[106] Thus Helgi is associated with the whole valley in a story which seems to sit separately from the remainder of the account for the region in which individual chapters are carefully geographically arranged. The case for the separateness of this narrative is further strengthened by the fact that there is evidence that another figure was associated with Kristnes, Þorvarðr Örnólfsson from Hörgárdalur, whose family had no connection with Helgi. It looks like two stories have been recorded for one place, something the text does not reconcile, which it might typically do by explaining that the earlier settler was displaced.

Beyond this S associates Helgi and his party with most of the main valley but it leaves the outer coast of the fjord to others.[107] This suggests a distinction between the two parts of the fjord which, as we shall see, is harder to spot in other texts. If we consider the boundaries of the *landnám* accorded Helgi and his associates, then, they stretch from Kræklingahlíð (the *landnám* of Ásgrímr whose farm was Glerá in syðri, S229) in the west to where Fnjóskadalur meets Eyjafjörður on the eastern shore.[108]

---

105   Where this mountain was is unclear but it might have been the one close to Hámundarstaðir which is called Krossafjall, suggesting another Christian connection at some point (ÍF I: 250, note 2).
106   Helgi is said to have stayed temporarily at Bíldsá, a river near Kaupangr. Þórunn *hyrna* gave birth on Þórunnarey, an island, probably later Staðarey, for which see below p. 274 in connection with *Víga-Glúms saga*.
107   See below p. 193 for Þorsteinn *svarfaðr* who settled Svarfaðardalur with Helgi's permission.
108   The location and boundaries of each of Helgi's associates' *landnám* within Eyjafjörður is clear. The only possible exception actually being that eastern limit where Ásgrímr's

TABLE 2   Table showing Helgi *inn magri*'s dependent colonists in Eyjafjörður and their *landnám*[a]

Chapter	Colonist	Relationship to Helgi	Farm	*Landnám* location/boundaries
230	Hámundr	Son-in-law	Espihóll inn syðri	Merkigil to Skjalgdalsá
231	Gunnarr Úlfljótsson	Son-in-law	Djúpadalr (Stóridalr)	Skjálgdalsá to Háls
232	Auðun *rotinn*	Son-in-law	Saurbær	Háls to Villingadalr
233	Hrólfr	Son	Gnúpufell	East of Eyjafjarðará from Arnarh(v)óll southwards
234	Ingjaldr	Son	Þverá in efri (Munkaþverá)	North of Arnarh(v)óll to Þverá in ytri
235	Þorgeirr	Son-in-law	Fiskilækr	Þverá to Varðgjá
236	Skagi	Son-in-law	Sigluvík	Varðgjá to Fnjóskadalsá

a   See below p. 194 for Auðólfr, the son-in-law of Helgi outside Eyjafjörður itself (S184, S226).

Beyond the fact that Helgi's *landnám* is equated with the whole of inner Eyjafjörður, its signficance lies in the way it divides up the landscape within the valley and suggests some kind of hierarchy amongst the colonists. To deal with the latter issue first, it could be argued that a distinction should be made between those places associated with one of Helgi's sons as opposed to with one of his sons-in-law (Table 2). Thus the two *landnám* on the eastern side of the river emerge as distinct from the rest of the settlers. The fact that Munkaþverá was probably the most significant farm (and later a monastery) and that the *landnám* of Hrólfr of Gnúpufell's implicitly included Möðruvellir, the other large farm in the valley, both suggest this account is according a higher status to Helgi's sons' *landnám*. It is nonetheless remarkable that S barely mentions one of the major figures in the *Íslendingasögur*, Guðmundr *ríki* Eyjólfsson of Möðruvellir, a point which will be returned to at the end of this discussion.

The wider pattern of the information here is also suggestive of a credible idea of the past which draws on long-surviving territorial divisions and on the

landnám was probably assumed to be the river Glerá given the location of the adjacent *landnám* and its farm, Hanatún, which was probably a *hjáleiga* of the farm Glæsibær, S228). It was a *hjáleiga* of Glæsibær in 1712 (*Jarðabók* X: 182).

significance of particular farms. All the farms mentioned here are large ones, but what is interesting is that they are not necessarily the ones which feature in the narrative sources as politically active; conversely some of the more notable farms in later narratives do not appear here in connection with Helgi. Espihóll and its occupants, for example, are significant in *Víga-Glúms saga* (see Chapter 5) but the farm only appears fleetingly in the *samtíðarsögur* and never as a major player.[109] Saurbær and Gnúpufell appear as homes of fairly significant people within Eyjafjörður in both genres of saga but never as homes of *goðar* or *höfðingjar*, unlike Hrafnagil, Grund and Möðruvellir, which are all absent from the list above. The last two farms to mention from the list above, Djúpadalr and Fiskilækr as they are identified in *S*, probably represent Stóridalur and the farm of Kaupangr, referred to in *Íslendingasögur* as Fiskilækjarhverfi.[110] These barely register in other texts but probably constituted well-off farms or centres of wealth, as they did in later centuries.[111]

As regards the boundaries of these *landnám*, we can compare them with later known boundaries and see that there is a good fit between the two, just as there is for Dalir. It is perhaps a sign of the imposition of the geographically wider narrative of Helgi *inn magri* that the boundaries of his own *landnám* have to be adduced; the boundaries are not made explicit. Kristnes is a farm relatively centrally placed within the area from Glerá to Merkigil, the identifiable boundaries of Helgi's own *landnám* because of the boundaries recorded for Ásmundr's *landnám* on one side (S229) and Hámundr's to the south. Thus the placing of Helgi at Kristnes would seem more likely to be an addition to a pre-existing account of the *landnám* which derived its boundaries from real ones. This also suggests that *S*'s account here is evidence of an early version having been revised specifically to place Helgi somewhere with a Christian connection.

Just as is the case for Auðr's *landnám* in Dalir, there is something to be gleaned from the genealogical narratives for those settling within Helgi's *landnám*. Hámundr's descendants are traced in *S* almost exactly as they are in *Víga-Glúms saga*: Þórir Hámundarson lives at Espihóll inn syðri after his father, another brother lives at Grund and their half-brother was at Möðrufell. Thus a very short genealogy provides a connection from Hámundr to what were

---

109   Only S230 distinguishes between the two neighbouring farms called Espihóll, Espihóll inn nyrðri (modern Espihóll, valued at 100 hundreds in *Jarðabók* and Espihóll inn syðri (now Litlihóll, just 12 hundreds in *Jarðabók* (*Jarðabók* x: 221–23). *Hauksbók* (H187), *Víga-Glúms saga* and *Reykdæla saga* do not. *S*'s view of 'Espihóll' as being the smaller farm makes more sense in the light of the evidence for the thirteenth century.
110   ÍF IX: 54–55; ÍF X: 235.
111   *Jarðabók* X: 236–38, 305–6.

almost certainly all the largest farms within Hámundr's *landnám*. This is a model segment of a genealogical charter.[112]

The material on Helgi's sons-in-law makes them appear of high status but the genealogies associated with them are simple. Gunnarr (S231) is seen as the son of the Úlfljótr who *Íslendingabók* claims first brought law to Iceland from Norway and so is an illustrious figure; the connection is made both here and in *Íslendingabók*.[113] Beyond this, however only Gunnarr's children are mentioned and no other descendants. The next three chapters (S232–34) all provide longer genealogies but are extremely short, having just one single line of descent, followed in each case down to the late twelfth or early thirteenth century. Auðun has just one connection: a line down to Bishop Guðmundr Arason (d.1237) via Auðun's son who was the father of Eyjólfr Valgerðarson (named after his mother) through Guðmundr's grandfather Þorgeirr Hallason (d.1169).[114] In S233 and S234 the lines of Helgi's sons Hrólfr and Ingjaldr are both traced to Hvamm-Sturla from Dalir (d.1183), the former via Sturla's mother, the latter through his father. Here it looks like Sturla Þórðarson or an associate was keen to connect the Sturlungar to Helgi via the *landnám* which included the farms of Möðruvellir and Munkaþverá. Given, though, that these chapters are otherwise concise, little else is likely to have been altered from the older text. S235 is similarly brief, only mentioning the two children of Þorgeirr and his wife, while S236 has the shortest of back stories for Skagi, but says that one of his descendants was the wife of Eyjólfr Valgerðarson, the father of the more famous Guðmundr *ríki*.

Turning to the accounts of *landnám* along the outer shores of Eyjafjörður we see that they also generally respect the boundaries of *hreppar* which are recorded in the early eighteenth century, sometimes on a one-for-one basis, sometimes with more than one *landnám* within a *hreppr*. The early part of the account here does not follow a strict geographical order and is perhaps confused about the geography of the region.

To the north-east the first colonist within the early modern *sýsla* boundary is that of Úlfr *víkingr* (S214) who is said to have been a companion of Óláfr *bekkr* who settled the western half of Ólafsfjörður and lived at Kvíabekkr, one of the largest farms in the valley (Map 8). Úlfr takes Úlfsdalir, a tiny valley but has no descendants, making him look like a 'filler' colonist in a minor valley. Siglufjörður, meanwhile, is settled by a Þormóðr who seemingly had ousted Óláfr *bekkr* because they had contested Hvanndalr, a small piece of land just behind the modern town of Siglufjörður (S215). The men then resolve to share

---

112   See pp. 147–52.
113   ÍF I: 7.
114   See pp. 80–82 for Þorgeirr's descendants.

this land between them. Óláfr's line is traced down to his granddaughter who marries Karl *inn rauði* of Svarfaðardalur.[115] That Óláfr and Úlfr seemingly arrive a generation before a colonist from Svarfaðardalur probably implies some kind of superiority of Ólafsfjörður over Svarfaðardalur.

Svarfaðardalur itself has a rather unusual status because its first settler, Þorsteinn *svarfaðr*, took the valley with the agreement of Helgi (*nam Svarfaðardal at ráði Helga*). This at once subjugates Þorsteinn to Helgi but accords him a positive connection. The remainder of the chapter, however, merely gives a potted account of part of *Svarfdœla saga* and says that 'This led to the events in *Svarfdœla saga*' (*Þar af gerðist Svarfdœla saga.*). No significant genealogy is given with which to further gauge Þorsteinn's status. In a similar vein S220 gives a one-sentence account of a *landnám* for a small stretch of coast by a 'Karl' but does not mention anyone else or make any connection with *Svarfdœla saga*, which it might well have done.

Going south from Svarfaðardalur towards Helgi's *landnám* at Kristnes it seems as if S is assuming that Hámundr had retained control of the district around Árskógr because one Örn settles south of that district at Arnarnes, the name of both the farm and the small peninsula (S221). Örn is said to have been a kinsman of Hámundr, suggesting an affinity between these districts. Most of Örn's descendants are connected to three farms on Árskógsströnd (Hella, Hagi and Kálfskinn) which bolsters their connection.[116] The important exception is Örn's daughter who is said to marry Helgi's son Ingjaldr who we have seen settled at Gnúpufell (see Table 2 above). Thus Örn/Árskógsströnd is tied into the genealogy of Helgi but less directly than in central Eyjafjörður.

Hörgárdalur requires careful attention for two reasons. First, it has five colonists situated within it and second, it is regularly mentioned in saga narratives, especially *Guðmundar saga dýra*, one of the earlier texts in the *Sturlunga* compilation. The first of the five colonists takes all of the stretch of the northern side of the lower valley, up to Myrká, and is said to have lived at Fornhagi (*bjó í Haganum forna*), almost exactly central to this stretch of land (S223). His son is said to have been the ancestor of the Auðbrekkumenn, Auðbrekka being the name of one of the larger farms within the *landnám*, although no other genealogical connections are made here at all. S224 seems to show the upper part of Hörgárdalur, probably including the farm of Myrká, being taken by a Þórðr *slitandi*, who in turn is said to have given some of his *landnám* to his

---

115 See pp. 298–300 for Karl *inn rauði* in *Svarfdœla saga*.
116 It depends on where Galmansströnd is supposed to have started but either way Örn's *landnám* is virtually adjacent to Hámundr's.

kinsman, Skólmr. S224 ends by saying that Skólmr's son lived at Myrká. What might seem a fairly ordinary colonist and line of descent is seemingly aggrandised by the marriage of Þórðr *slitandi*'s son Örnólfr to Hámundr *heljarskinn*'s daughter, Yngvildr *allrasystir*, in other words a connection to the second-most important figure in local *landnám* lore (S224, S232).[117] The children of this marriage lived at Kristnes and neighbouring Kroppr. Taken all together, this does not provide a neat pattern, given that Helgi *inn magri*'s own association with Kristnes. We should probably take from it the idea that upper Hörgárdalur was being seen as more powerful and better connected than we might otherwise expect.

The next colonist in Hörgárdalur took 'all' of Öxnadalur and lived at a farm whose name is now lost but which was almost certainly at Hraun or near the lake Hraunsvatn (S225); as that next *landnám* begins at the river Þverá and goes towards the coast as far as the river Bægisá, this one actually only consists of the uppermost part of Öxnadalur. The colonist's granddaughter marries Þorvarðr of Kristnes, at once making a tie to Myrká and to Hámundr *heljarskinn*/Kristnes. Auðólfr, that next colonist, lives at Bægisá in syðri, one of two large farms of that name which sit either side of the *landnám* (and later *hreppr*) boundary (S226). More significantly, Auðólfr marries the daughter of Helgi *inn magri*, making him another of his sons-in-law. Thus Bægisá in syðri sits alongside the farms in Eyjafjörður as part of a notional top rung of a genealogical charter.

Thinking of this in terms of the map, Auðólfr's *landnám* and three others mentioned for Hörgárdalur and Öxnadalur so far, all fell within the large early modern *hreppr* of Skriðuþingsókn. Nearly all of these people have a genealogical link to Helgi *inn magri* or Hámundr, and to Kristnes, which would seem to suggest that the block of territory had some kind of shared identity and which was closely related to the reality when *S* or its *exemplar* was compiled.

To fully understand the role of Helgi *inn magri* in *S*, however, we need to consider districts further away from Eyjafjörður geographically, to other parts of the region under discussion, where *S* records there are colonists who had a genealogical connection with him. There are four such ties, one of which is to one of Helgi's sons, the other three to granddaughters. They feature places actually quite distant from Eyjafjörður, and are recorded only in chapters for these areas rather than those covering Helgi's *landnám*. Thus Helgi's son Hrólfr of Gnúpufell marries the daughter of the settler at Skörð in lower Reykjadalur (S245). From further along the northern coast of Iceland in Kelduhverfi, the

---

117   This is the least clear of the accounts in Hörgárdalur/Öxnadalur. The inland boundary of the *landnám* is unclear because the text identifies 'Drangar' as the boundary, most likely a mountain in Öxnadalur (ÍF I: 256–57, note 6).

colonist there marries the daughter of Þorgeirr at Fiskilækr. Then S254 records Arnórr settling at Reykjahlíð, at the north-east corner of lake Mývatn, and marrying the daughter of Hrólfr Helgason of Gnúpufell, the granddaughter of Helgi *inn magri*. According to S255 the son of the colonist at Grænavatn, to the south of Mývatn, i.e. the farm of Skútustaðir, married the daughter of Þórir Hámundarson of Espihóll inn syðri. From these ties it seems as if there is a notion of the decreasing importance of any tie with Helgi the further one goes east from Eyjafjörður; the tie with the son is also geographically nearest, the ties with granddaughters are further east. What is missing here is a connection between Helgi's line and districts closer to Eyjafjörður. This might imply a real disconnect between Eyjafjörður and all of the smaller neighbouring districts to the immediate east: Fnjóskadalur, Ljósavatn, Bárðardalur and Reykjadalur.

All in all, the account of Helgi *inn magri*'s *landnám* itself shows signs of having been created by an author making some revisions to a simpler, more formulaic account. The relationships have the appearance of an origin myth which people in Eyjafjörður might have created, to judge by its brevity and simplicity. What is unusual about it, perhaps, is that there is so little evidence of connections between Helgi's descendants and other local or regional figures; this distinguishes it from many of the more tangled genealogies in the Dalir chapters. The lack of ties between Helgi and colonists in areas immediately east of Eyjafjörður suggests both a lack of political relationships between the two areas and a lack of an attempt even to manipulate the text to create such an impression.

5.1   *Glæsibæjarhreppur*

Before moving on to consider regions beyond the influence of the genealogical charter associated with Helgi *inn magri*, there is one significant part of Eyjafjörður itself which warrants discussion. This is the most obviously nodal point for communications in Eyjafjörður, Glæsibæjarhreppur, which is now where the modern town of Akureyri sits. The chapters which cover almost all of what we can see later as a *hreppr*, S227, S228 and S229, stand out as having no genealogical connection to either Helgi or Hámundr. This is strange when Helgi's genealogy links him to so much of the rest of Eyjafjörður. These three *landnám* include the trading site of Gásir as well as, home to the *lögmaðr*, the leading royal official for the north and west of the country in the late thirteenth and much of the first half of the fourteenth century.[118]

---

118   Sigurðr Guðmundarson and Guðmundr Sigurðsson who was probably his son. Whether as *lögmaðr* or in his own right, Sigurðr is recorded as owning driftage rights jointly with Bishop Jörundr of Hólar (DI II: 307, 308, 309, 315–7; Sigríður Beck 2011: 153); more generally Jón Jóhannesson 1956–8, II: 226–301, esp. 255, 287, 289, 298, 300.

The first chapter of the three (S227) says that the colonist Eysteinn took land running from the river Bægisá to the edge of Kræklingahlíð, living at Lón (or Skipalón). This is close to the river Hörgá and to the trading site of Gásir, the main port for trade and communication between the north of Iceland and Norway by the thirteenth century. Eysteinn's descendants include a granddaughter who marries Víga-Glúmr, the hero of *Víga-Glúms saga*.

The first of the other two chapters, S229, describes the *landnám* of Ásmundr and Ásgrímr Öndóttssynir who, in an extended narrative, flee to Iceland before they settle. Ásmundr gets to Iceland first and is given the district of Kræklingahlíð by Helgi *inn magri*, setting up home at the farm Glerá syðri before Ásgrímr settles at Glerá nyrðri. Thus they are seen to acquire the other end of later Glæsibæjarhreppur, which had a boundary at the river Glerá. A genealogy is traced from Ásgrímr down to Hvamm-Sturla, suggesting this *landnám*'s possible importance to Sturla Þórðarson or other Sturlungar.

On the face of it the account of Eyvindr *hani*'s *landnám* in S228 is a simple one but a variety of other factors suggest that S228 relates to another important place in Eyjafjörður. Eyvindr's nickname seems to derive from Hanatún/Hanagarðr, the name of Glæsibær, a *staðr* in later centuries.[119] However, this *landnám* contains the farm Lögmannshlíð, the name that this latter farm had acquired by the late thirteenth century, and the home of the *lögmaðr*. The other thing of note, however, is that Eyvindr is said to have arrived late in the *landnám* era (*hann kom út síð landnámatíðar*) and was given his land by the Öndóttssynir of S229, themselves recipients of it from Helgi. A recorded descendant of Eyvindr's is of interest too: a line is traced to Snorri *Hlíðarmannagoði*. This Snorri features in *Ljósvetninga saga* as a mediator and thus looks locally important, even if he otherwise has a shadowy existence in the *Íslendingasögur*.[120] All the same, it is probably no coincidence that this *landnám* is also home to the only person which *S* labels *goði* in Eyjafjörður.

Put together, S227–229 give the impression that Glæsibæjarhreppur formed some kind distinctive place, most likely a politically and economically important one. Control of it seems to have been either contentious or confused; the story of the later arrival of Eyvindr *hani* might be a way to fit him into an already settled district. Further arguments cannot be pushed too far, but one possible reading of these chapters is that this area's role as a central place is being signalled in different ways by these accounts.[121] It certainly seems odd

---

119   *Jarðabók* x: 182; DI III: 519–20.
120   In *Ljósvetninga saga* Þorkell of 'Hlíð' is said to have been a friend of Guðmundr *ríki*'s son Eyjólfr, but urged restraint when Eyjólfr sought to kill someone (ÍF x: 93). See Helgi Skúli Kjartansson 1989 for Snorri *Hlíðarmannagoði*; see below p. 286, footnote 338.
121   Cf Orri Vésteinsson 2006: 315.

that the overarching genealogy of Helgi *inn magri* does not properly encompass these three *landnám* and within them we have a case of property being given and re-given. Other evidence clearly shows how important this area was as a locus for interaction with the Norwegian king. The absence of genealogical connections between its colonists and Helgi might be the product of an established tradition which set it slightly outside local socio-political networks, and possibly a centre of power despite that. This pattern self-evidently pertains to when S was compiled and the fact that this separateness is not obliterated by Sturla Þórðarson suggests it might have had the weight of tradition behind it.

5.2 Beyond Helgi inn magri's landnám *and Eyjafjörður*

While the account of Eyjafjörður is replete with *landnámsmenn*, the wider expanses and relatively sparsely populated regions to its east have fewer colonists but again mostly on the basis of one *landnáms*menn per later *hreppr*. For the sake of space, and because the physical geography is relatively simple for this region, the notional geopolitical allegiances and status of settlers will be considered in the same way as for Dalir. S gives slightly more space to the more populous districts close to Eyjafjörður than it does the end of the North Quarter where few of the settlers are credited with politically significant descendants.

Mention has already been made of the 'master' genealogy of Björn *buna*'s descendants (pp. 150–51); the most significant character on this genealogy in the north-east is Bárðr, the son of Heyjangrs-Björn (S242). Bárðr's father or grandfather was supposedly the brother of Ketill *flatnefr*, father of Björn *inn austræni* and Auðr *in djúpauðga*.[122] Bárðr took all of Bárðardalur and lived at Lundarbrekka, the valley's largest farm, before apparently moving to south-east Iceland to Gnúpar in Fljótshverfi in south-east Iceland and there being known as Gnúpa-Bárðr. His recorded descendants in S242 are Þorgeirr *goði* of Ljósavatn, then a series of other people associated with major farms in the north-east through a son who marries Fjörleif Eyvindardóttir of Grenjaðarstaðir (also S247) and a genealogy which is in agreement with *Reykdœla saga*'s account: Fellsmúli (Múli, next to Grenjaðarstaðir), 'Mývatn,' Húsavík, Helgastaðir, and, 'Fell' a relatively densely populated district a few kilometres north-east of Ljósavatn.[123] This genealogy has the effect of tying Bárðardalur to these other major farms, perhaps only on the strength of Bárðr's name, but seen on a broader geographical scale it creates a meaningful cluster of farms from around Reykjadalur.

Grenjaðarstaðir was so important in the twelfth and thirteenth centuries, as the pre-eminent *staðr* in the north-east, that it seems strange that its occupant

---

122 ÍF I *ættskrár* II and XVIII.
123 See p. 285 for Vémundr *köggurr* at 'Fell' and Öndóttsstaðir.

does not play a more prominent role in this particular genealogy.[124] In *S*, and for that matter, all other versions of *Landnámabók*, the succinct account of Grenjaðr's *landnám* is never altered. It is a rather ordinary account, which does no more than associate him with the district around Grenjaðarstaðir, probably equivalent to its tithe area, and the small valley of Laxárdalur. It does trace his genealogy down to two late twelfth-century abbots and, given that Grenjaðr is said to have been the son of a man called Hrappr, it could be that this makes him the grandson of Björn *buna* too. Unlike for Bárðr, however, a genealogical connection to Björn *buna* is not made explicit. This suggests that *S* underplays Grenjaðarstaðir's importance relative to Bárðardalur, a valley that may never have been a politically significant place given that it is remote, a long way inland, and sparsely-populated. Why this should be the case is less clear. A half-remembered story about a 'Bárðr' obviously had to involve locating him somewhere geographically with Bárðardalur being an obvious place. This could explain the valley's promotion to such a high status although at the same time recent archaeological survey suggests that it had been more populous in the tenth and eleventh centuries.[125] Neither of these options, however, seems to offer a full explanation of why Grenjaðarstaðir does not have a more explicit and illustrious *landnám* story. A political context from the twelfth or thirteenth century where Grenjaðarstaðir was somehow at odds with people who might have created *landnám* texts is also hard to find. It is more likely that this confirms that the main text of *S* was constructed before Grenjaðarstaðir was politically important.

The remaining districts to the east are best tackled geographically, beginning in Eyjafjörður itself, but only some require discussion.[126] Fnjóskadalur and Ljósavatnsskarð are districts close to Eyjafjörður and often mentioned in other narratives.[127] S243 and S244 are worth commenting on because they

---

124 See, for example, pp. 25, 53, 82, 127, 142–43 for Grenjaðarstaðir's importance.
125 Archaeological survey does seem to confirm that farms recorded in Bárðardalur in the early modern period were there in the tenth or eleventh centuries (Orri Vésteinsson 2016: 89).
126 The eastern coast of Eyjafjörður has no real signficance in *S*'s coverage (S238, 239, 240). Again, this area really is geographically remote and no genealogical connection is made with elsewhere.
127 S242 would seem to account for a significant part of early modern Ljósavatnshreppur, including as it does a single *landnám* extending from the coast at Náttfaravík, along Kaldakinn and all the way to the end of Fnjóskadalur. Þórir *snepill's* descendants are picked out as Þorgeirr *goði* of Ljósavatn – Þórir's granddaughter marries Þorgeirr *goði* – and two people from larger farms in Eyjafjörður (Stokkahlaðir, between Hrafnagil and Espihóll, and Saurbær). Þórir is placed at Lundr, in upper Fnjóskadalur, an average-sized farm in

record the *landnám* for the area around Ljósavatn, whence sprang Þorgeirr *Ljósvetningagoði*, one of the iconic figures in the story of Iceland's conversion to Christianity and, as we shall see, a key name in *Íslendingasögur* too. They seem to cover the tithe area or parish of the church at Ljósavatn as it is defined in *Jarðabók* and its earliest *máldagi*.[128] However, *S* divides what seems to have been the same piece of territory in two but for no obvious reason other than to accommodate two colonists rather than one. Given what we have seen before for Grenjaðarstaðir, it might be that *S* is actually relying on fairly scant knowledge of the *landnám* for this area. This a rather unsatisfactory explanation but S243 is quite brief and S244, where Þorgeirr *Ljósvetningagoði*'s family are placed, provides little more than Þorgeirr's line, his children, and the marriage tie to Dala-Kollr in Dalir.[129] Lacking, then, is any sense of how Ljósavatn related to Eyjafjörður or areas to the east. Equally, perhaps, this suggests the lack of control of this area from Eyjafjörður at the time of *S*'s compilation, which, as we shall see, is something notably different from the pattern visible in the thirteenth century.

The remaining accounts of *landnám* in Reykjadalur and further east provide a relatively brief account of mostly local genealogical connections with no colonists or their farms being particularly significant or insignificant. For the area around Mývatn *S* provides the kind of bipartite division of land which seems to have persisted to the present day, with *landnám* centred on Reykjahlíð and Skútustaðir (Grænavatn in *S*).[130] As we have seen, a genealogical connection with Helgi *inn magri* is identified for both these *landnám*, thus making the whole area notionally tied to Eyjafjörður but in a position which makes them the inferior party.

---

later centuries but whose name suggests a 'pagan' grove which he is said to hallow. Thus Þórir claimed all of the area around Ljósavatn, creating a single territorial block which equated to a later *hreppr* and which seems not to be identified as superior or inferior to anywhere else.

128 DI II: 438–39; *Jarðabók* XI: 124–36.
129 See above p. 169 including footnote 62; p. 186 for Kollr's status.
130 S256 records the initial settlement of a third colonist, Geiri at Geirastaðir on the western side of Mývatn but he and his son were supposedly driven out of Mývatn after they had killed the son of one Þorberg at 'Mývatn,' as also recorded in *Reykdœla saga*. They went to briefly to Geirastaðir in Húnavatnssýsla and then to Geiradalur in Króksfjörður on the northern coast of Breiðafjörður, just outside Dalir. Here we are told of Geiri's son Glúmr's marriage to Ingunn, after whom Þórðr Ingunnarson, one of Guðrún Ósvífrsdóttir's husbands was named (and of a daughter's marriage). See also pp. 284–90 for *Reykdœla saga*.

Other areas however seem completely cut off from the Eyjafjörður-centred genealogical charter of Helgi and neither do they, for that matter, form part of some alternative political structure. In S257 Öxarfjörður, the valley adjacent to Kelduhverfi, is settled by an impressive-sounding grandson of a jarl, Einarr, who arrives with two brothers with whom he hallows the land, setting up a cross at Krossá. The idea is clearly that these men took all of Öxarfjörður and, although the area covered by their *landnám* was not as populous or wealthy as Helgi *inn magri*'s Eyjafjörður, their story follows a similar pattern to that of Helgi. There is a brief genealogy of the Einarr's descendants; the most significant of these is Hrói Galtason, who in *Reykdœla saga* hired as a killer by someone from Kroppr in Eyjafjörður.[131] Hrói's role is not alluded to here but he is said to have avenged someone else and so his image is similar in both texts. S257 does not connect Öxarfjörður to other districts or personae which is no doubt a product of its sparse population and remoteness from Eyjafjörður and the idea that it was not thought to be controlled directly by anyone in Eyjafjörður.

The most important point here is that Helgi *inn magri*'s genealogy is a major structural element in the description of the *landnám* for Eyjafjörður and the north-east. Most colonists occupy a position on that genealogy somewhere. The overall genealogy seems to suggest that geographical nearness to Helgi's *landnám* within Eyjafjörður go hand-in-hand with genealogical closeness. Men who marry into Helgi's line tend to be further away from Eyjafjörður geographically. It is also important to note the limits of this genealogy as traced here – it rarely goes beyond Helgi's grandchildren and rarely suggests descendants beyond this. In geographical terms the genealogy seems to stop with Mývatn and Kelduhverfi as one travels east; Öxarfjörður and beyond would seem to be beyond the mental or political orbit for whoever has shaped S. In some parts of S there is also a slightly lesser category of colonist, one who is explicitly said to colonise an area with the consent (*at ráði*) of another settler. These do not exist within Helgi's *landnám* where in most cases he is said to have *given* land, thus showing a greater initial power differential between Helgi and those that had land within his *landnám* but then the independence of those receiving the land. The only exception to this, or the only local *landnámsmaðr* who has that slightly higher status is the one in Svarfaðardalur, giving this valley on the margin of Helgi's *landnám* a kind of affiliate status but making who owned the land more ambiguous. Either way, Svarfaðardalur is marked out as different to the main part of Eyjafjörður.

What is probably also significant is those areas which are absent from Helgi *inn magri*'s genealogy. There are two of these. First are those regions

---

131　See below p. 287.

immediately to the east of Eyjafjörður (Fnjóskadalur, Ljósavatn, Reykjadalur and Bárðardalur). The lack of any connection between Eyjafjörður and these smaller valleys must demonstrate not only a lack of influence from Eyjafjörður on those regions in the minds of the compilers of S but also a lack of its even being conceivable to assert such a claim. An alternative view, that the creators of the text were somehow sympathetic to the claims of inhabitants of the districts concerned, would seem to be ruled out by the lack of real prominence for those districts in S; they are territorially fragmented and do not have any obviously preeminent *landnámsmenn* of their own.

The second absence from Helgi's *landnám* at what was effectively the centre of Eyjafjörður, both geographically and metaphorically, are those *landnám* along Kræklingahlíð, close to the modern town of Akureyri. These must have seemed different to the text's compiler and perhaps the wider community who had knowledge of their region's past. One might speculate that because this small piece of territory was home to Gásir and the later farm of Lögmannshlíð, it made it somehow neutral or common land of some kind.

6 Conclusions

While S provides a cogent picture of past genealogical relationships, and one which probably reflects those which prevailed at the time of its writing, seeing in them any connection with twelfth- and thirteenth-century contexts is not easy. It could be argued that we should not expect to see a perfect replication of significant geopolitical patterns in a text like S with any contemporary circumstance. We could regard it as propaganda or a deliberate attempt to rewrite the past by people who felt disenfranchised, or, as Adolf Friðriksson and Orri Vésteinsson have suggested, it is a scholarly construct whose contents were essentially fiction. My contention, however, is that it is hard to imagine the politically disenfranchised or the contrary wishing to write such a text. It makes more sense for there to have been an active oral tradition about past events which was being shaped by contemporary political circumstances in some way. The term 'genealogical charter' captures the product of this tradition well, despite the caveats mentioned at the beginning of the chapter. Based on that assumption, in all probability the bulk of the text derives from before 1150.

Several more specific arguments can be put forward for the S largely retaining an early twelfth-century view of the past even if this is largely negative evidence. First, if we consider Dalir, it can be argued that a political picture in which Hvammr was the pre-eminent farm in the region need not derive from the thirteenth century when the Sturlungar were at their most powerful. In several respects S's picture of the sphere over which Auðr had control of land,

and her descendants had kinship connections, does not make sense in relation to the political set-up of the thirteenth century. *S* sees most of the valleys at the eastern end of Hvammsfjörður as part of a single territory whereas for most of the thirteenth century, it was divided between two branches of the Sturlungar. As we have also seen, Hvammr itself was hardly ever the primary home of any thirteenth-century *höfðingi* and, although it was still owned by the Sturlungar, there seems to be little interest in it in *Sturlunga saga* outside *Sturlu saga*.

If we try to look for potential earlier contexts for the writing of *S* by considering *S* alongside the narratives we have for politics post-1150 or so, then there are also problems. *S* preserves a combination of political situations which do not fit the time when Hvamm-Sturla was based at Hvammr. There are no connections between Hvammr and Staðarfell and Skarðsströnd, both of which Sturla did have. On the other hand, *S* emphasises Auðr/Hvammr's control of Miðdalir, something Sturla did not have. If we set the bar very low for seeing *S* as either a kind of passive reflection of contemporary politics, or part of an active plan to shape political discourse, then elements of *S* make sense: the ties between Auðr's Hvammr and Dala-Kollr's Hjarðarholt and Erpr's Erpsstaðir/Sauðafell look like connections between Hvammr and those same farms as occupied by Sighvatr Sturluson and Sighvatr Sturluson. If *S* were written with this in mind, however, it was done very clumsily.

Second, other contexts for *S* might also be suggested by comparison of other high-level genealogical links between Auðr/Hvammr and other places; but none match up well with descriptions of late-twelfth and thirteenth-century politics. There is, for instance, no suggestion in *Sturlunga saga* that Hvammr or the Sturlungar had close contacts with Breiðabólstaðr on Skógarströnd, something suggested by the genealogies in *S*. Similarly Helgafell, a farm of key importance in *S* through the marriage of Þórðr *gellir*'s daughter into the family there, can never be seen to have had a connection with Hvammr after 1150: after the 1180s, indeed, it also became the home of a monastery and as such plays only a small role in local thirteenth century politics. Last of all, there is no likely late-twelfth or thirteenth-century context for the portrayal of Staðarfell in *S*. Hvamm-Sturla's father had lived at Staðarfell and Sturla's brother's descendants lived there in the thirteenth century. S111, the garbled description of a story involving the family of Kjallakr, son of Björn *inn austrœni*, fighting against people from local dependent farms, can have had no visible resonance for any late-twelfth or thirteenth-century audience. Such a poorly explicated written account would have made no sense to an early audience either, but the lack of any connection between Staðarfell's history and that of Hvammr suggests that this chapter of *S* originated before the Sturlungar were powerful.

As well as the negative evidence for later contexts for *S*'s content, some slightly sketchy evidence could point to an earlier one. This would fit with Orri Vésteinsson's suggestion that the constellation of Helgafell constitutes the archetype of a pre-1000 'central area.'[132] Sverrir Jakobsson has recently emphasised the enduring connection of Ari *fróði* Þorgilsson's family with Helgafell. In effect he speculates that, although there is a more obvious connection for Ari and for his grandson Ari *sterki* with Staðarstaðr, they might have owned Helgafell and that Ari *fróði* actually lived there.[133] In these circumstances there is perhaps a reason for believing that the influence of Helgafell seen in *S* could have made sense in the first half of the twelfth century if not before. This might explain the specific form of the genealogies in Dalir but arguably has no particular bearing on what we make of the rest of the text.

For Eyjafjörður and the areas to its east, the primacy of the area on the western side of Eyjafjörður itself, in the form of the *landnám* of Helgi *inn magri* and Hámundr, fits thirteenth-century political patterns. That said, the specific configuration of the story, whereby Kristnes and Espihóll are seen as the *landnámsbæjar* in that district, rather than Hrafnagil or Grund, fits better with what we will see in *Íslendingasögur*. Indeed, given the prominence of Hrafnagil and Grund in the thirteenth century, it seems rather odd that anyone should have seen them as being entirely absent in *S*, had this part of *S* been written as late as that late. That is possible, but it would have been a very specious take on the past. For the later twelfth century, we have very little to go on but Hrafnagil also seems to have been important then, and so, so far as we can tell, the same discrepancy occurs.

Last, we might note that Möðruvellir in Eyjafjörður, the home of the pre-eminent Guðmundr *ríki* in the *Íslendingasögur*, and to sometime participants in thirteenth-century events, is absent from *S*. This could be read as a deliberate attempt to write it out of the past but it might equally fit a different, earlier political situation.

This brings us on to how and why each area's account in *S* differ. In essence, the top of the genealogy for Dalir shows a split which gives Björn *inn austrœni* and Auðr *in djúpauðga* separate territories. That we have two, albeit related groupings within a relatively small area suggests a fragmented political picture, even around Hvammsfjörður. To the north, Skarðsströnd and Saurbær have *landnámsmenn* unrelated to these two. This is probably credible for the

---

132 Orri Vésteinsson 2006: 320. His argument is that Helgafell, the nearby assembly site at Þingvellir and farm of Hofstaðir constituted an early cluster of complementary central place theophoric, assembly and social functions.
133 Sverrir Jakobsson 2015: 105; 2016: 45.

period (just) before the account of *Sturlu saga* took place in the mid-twelfth century, because as we have seen, that text shows that Saurbær and Skarðsströnd were fairly firmly in the control of people not identified with Hvamm-Sturla. The realities of political life, which always centred on individual farms, or clusters of them, was rather different, but if we accept the logic of territorial blocks in *S*, then the relationships posited for the owners of those blocks make most sense in this earlier context.

By contrast, Helgi *inn magri*'s *landnám* was vast, including what must have included well over 400 farms – one estimate suggests 593 households using nineteenth-century records[134] – making it something like three times the size of the combined size of Björn and Auðr's *landnám* combined. This therefore suggests a shared history for, or control over, far more people. That this pattern, and other elements of the story, do not easily fit local patterns observable later are suggestive of there being some kind of overlordship here even earlier than we can see it in the *Sturlunga* compilation. As we saw, there is actually no time in the *Sturlunga* account when there is not a figure with some kind of hold on the whole of Eyjafjörður. The interesting thing about Helgi's account is also how it configures relations between Eyjafjörður and districts distant from it, again, something slightly different from the pattern for Dalir. As we have seen, no connection is made between Eyjafjörður and the area immediately to its east, i.e. the most populous districts close to it, whereas there are recorded connections between Eyjafjörður and the lower, eastern side of Reykjadalur and to Mývatn, districts east of the river Laxá. One reading of this pattern might be that this was a real, mutually beneficial relationship between areas which shared a common rival, the local leaders of Ljósavatn and Reykjadalur. It would also follow that these posited relationships made sense at a time before Eyjafjörður's later dominance was quite so well established. One might even speculate that there would have been an economic logic to this connection: Some Eyjafjörður *höfðingjar* had, or sought, control of the fresh fish that Mývatn and Laxá could have provided. That such patterns are not visible in the thirteenth century certainly is due to the absence of later accounts of Mývatn; probably this in turn is the result of the differing political situation, i.e. stronger control from Eyjafjörður.[135] For the north-east, as for Dalir, the genealogy-based representations of political relations in *S* are meaningful but they are just as likely to represent earlier political realities as they are the political aspirations of *höfðingjar* in the thirteenth century.

---

134 Adolf Friðriksson & Orri Vésteinsson 2003: 148.
135 This is also different to the configuration suggested by 1250s pattern whereby Finnbjörn Helgason was appointed to control Reykjadalur and areas to its east (see above pp. 141, 143).

CHAPTER 5

The Worlds of Snorri *goði* and Guðmundr *ríki*

This chapter takes its name from two iconic figures of the *Íslendingasögur*, especially those which are set in Dalir and and Eyjafjörður respectively, although they also appear elsewhere. Snorri Þorgrímsson is the major player in *Eyrbyggja saga* and Guðmundr *ríki* is similarly pivotal in *Ljósvetninga saga*. Both appear to have been sufficiently well-known among saga writers and their audiences for both of these *goðar* to appear to a greater or lesser degree in many other *Íslendingasögur*. They provide interesting contrasts as well-known leaders because while Snorri *goði* seems generally to have been revered for his political acumen, Guðmundr is usually portrayed negatively. Some consideration will be given to this difference below.

While this chapter is certainly about these characters, its main aim is to provide readings of the local political action which is described in each of the major *Íslendingasögur* for our regions. The contention of the chapter is that these narratives generally provide an internally coherent depiction of political processes and developments. It therefore aims to interpret the sagas in terms of what they imply about the nature of political power, namely, the number and relative powers of particular *goðar*, the extent to which they suggest patterns of dispersed allegiances among *bændr*, i.e. territoriality, and how these appear to change over time. These geopolitical patterns are often significantly different to those in *Sturlunga saga* or *Landnámabók*.

Before we consider the content of the *Íslendingasögur* in detail, more needs to be said about the wider debate on their origins and nature, picking up from the discussion of genealogical charters in Chapter 4. As is well known, the anonymity of the people who had *Íslendingasögur* committed to writing, and who contributed to their construction, is the single biggest problem in our understanding them. Without knowing who wrote these narratives we have no simple way of dating the surviving or lost manuscripts of any saga. Understanding the development of the genre as a whole, both over time and from region to region or scriptorium to scriptorium is also made that much more difficult. The lack of demonstrably early manuscripts, i.e. from before about 1230,[1] also distances us from 'original' versions of these sagas. This has not stopped a

---

1 It is thought that the earliest surviving manuscript which includes any *Íslendingasaga* dates from around 1230 (Jónas Kristjánsson 1988: 217–18).

voluminous stream of analyses and interpretations of how and why sagas came into being, either as individual texts or as a group.[2]

The fundamental issue with regard to saga origins is undoubtedly that surrounding their dependency on either oral or written sources. *Íslendingasögur* were once seen as the product of a story-teller, a kind of wise man or minstrel who had memorised whole sagas.[3] This was sometimes seen as a sign of sagas' truthfulness as well.[4] The Icelandic school, with Sigurður Nordal as a major representative, was in part a reaction to this rather romantic view and stressed the opposite views: that *Íslendingasögur* were not only not written down from memory but blatantly fictional and derived, wherever possible, from other written sources.

Theodore Andersson defined the difference between these two approaches, also called, respectively, freeprose and bookprose, in this way:

> Book prosaists and freeprosaists can often be in substantial agreement on what the sources of a saga were but rarely on the form of those sources or the way in which the saga author used them. In most cases the adherent of freeprose believes in a central core of formed tradition which could (but need not) be infinitely varied by the writer, but which imparted to the saga its fundamental structure and narrative art. The believer in bookprose for the most part rejects this central core and sees the lines of a saga as the work of an author who imposed his artistic will on heterogeneous materials.[5]

The source of disagreement is the over the role of the person who had each *Íslendingasaga* committed to writing. The editors of the *Íslenzk Fornrit* series, for example, that is to say the most widely available standard editions of saga texts, have tended to seek links between texts and authors and so diminish the oral component of sagas.

The complexity of the *Íslendingasögur* as lengthy texts containing a great deal of information and, arguably, dramatic structure has been used as evidence to support the cases of both the bookprose and freeprose approach. It is because of the complexity of each individual saga that Andersson, for example,

---

2 Andersson 1964; Mundal 1977; Clover 1985; Callow 2017a.
3 Andersson 1964.
4 Bogi Th. Melsteð 1903–30.
5 Andersson 1964: 55.

thought that *Íslendingasögur* must have been composed and developed orally before being written down. His reasoning is that no narrative of this complexity could have developed completely in written form without there being some evidence of the development of what otherwise would have been a new form of literature. The absence of any preserved short or unsophisticated 'proto-saga' suggests to Andersson that sagas must have been based on a large body of orally-transmitted information in narrative form. Supporting this view it can be argued that all the *Íslendingasögur* are generally similar in style and content and none are obviously more or less sophisticated than any others, which might have been the case if authors were writing a kind of historical fiction for the first time. Thus, according to Andersson, sagas must have been fully-formed oral compositions before being written down. This is a not unproblematic assertion, as will be seen later, but less problematic than the view offered by bookprosists.

Means of analysing texts have changed since Andersson published his book nearly 60 years ago, in line with broader changes in the way history and literature are approached. Divisions still remain, however, between those who see sagas first as works of an author and those who see them as the product of an oral culture which can tell us something more broadly about society. New issues have also emerged, especially for literary critics, such as the question of the impact of foreign or ecclesiastical education on clerics.[6] Critics are more aware than ever, after more than a century's debate among professional scholars, of the difficulties of theorising about saga literature. These works need not be surveyed here. Instead arguments will be put forward which together provide a framework within which *Íslendingasögur* can be used for a historical study of medieval Iceland.

Probably the most useful proposal to come from within traditional saga scholarship on how sagas were composed has been that of the 'immanent saga' put forward by Carol Clover and borrowed from a study of oral literature in Congo.[7] In an influential article Clover points out the problems in attributing to *Íslendingasögur* an entirely oral origin as prose epics but at the same time explains how episodic oral narratives might be easily joined together when written down. Her theory is a more sophisticated version of a much older theory of saga construction, what was once called '*þáttr* theory.'[8] According to this

---

[6] Clover 1982; Bjarni Guðnason 1994.
[7] Clover 1986.
[8] Andersson (1964: 61–64). For other twentieth-century treatments of *þættir* see Ármann Jakobsson 2013.

idea *Íslendingasögur* were an assemblage of short stories or strands, *þættir*, put together by the saga author. Many strands of *þáttr* theory, however, were themselves developed, according to peoples' judgements of what a *þáttr* might have been: large or small, oral or written tales or whether *þættir* were already inserted into a larger, determining story.

Clover begins her argument by denying the possibility of *Íslendingasögur* having ever been such long, unified oral stories which might have been retold by a single person. No such prose epics exist in any recorded body of oral literature anywhere, in spite of claims to the contrary.[9] The famous case of the extensive performances by Serbian story tellers recorded and analysed by Milman Parry and Albert Lord were, crucially, metrical rather than in prose form.[10] Oral prose, of the kind which might most easily be proposed as a precursor of *Íslendingasögur*, cannot be found. What Clover proposes instead is that *Íslendingasögur* did not exist in an oral form closely resembling the written form, but that many short prose stories, whose relationship to other short stories was well-known. They existed in oral form but were not assembled as a whole until they were written down. She envisages individual members of a community telling shorter tales because of their ignorance of some of the extensive body of stories which now make up surviving written *Íslendingasögur*. She sees evidence for joint story-telling of this kind in, among other places, modern India, Mongolia and Congo.[11]

In terms of the saga origins debate this conclusion is a kind of compromise between literary approaches which would emphasise the creativity of 'authors' of *Íslendingasögur* and those that prefer to see a stronger role for oral traditions. Clover's answer, although she admits that it still presents problems, does at least get round the problem of the length of the longest *Íslendingasögur* and the limitations of individuals' memories.[12] According to this theory there was no one individual at the oral stage who had to remember the vast body of information contained in the largest sagas such as *Laxdæla saga* or *Njáls saga* and it allows for the input of an author in organising the written, surviving saga.

Andersson has made counter-arguments to Clover's ideas, citing the evidence within saga literature itself about performance.[13] The absence of oral prose forms generally may be in part because so little attention has been paid

---

9   Clover 1986: 27.
10 Lord 1960; Parry 1971.
11 Clover 1986: 16 and note 22, 24 notes 69–72.
12 Clover 1986: 38.
13 Andersson 2002, 2006: 11–12.

to the way people retell their past in prose. It may also be because recorders of oral literature are loath to write down prose, preferring to interpret what they hear as poetry. As Ruth Finnegan pointed out, prose and poetry are often only distinguishable on the written page.[14] We should also be alive to the possibility that medieval Iceland had a distinctive oral culture in which long stories were told. Finnegan's classic work reminds us of the vast array of possible forms of oral literature, if not historical oral literature. We should not underestimate the possibility that one person, particularly with the assistance of other people to help out, could retell a saga of considerable length. To us sagas may seem to have much detail which is difficult to remember, but the mere fact that everyday life must have reminded people of these stories (through places, people and genealogical relationships) must have had a considerable impact on their ability to remember a great deal. Indeed, more recent views have critiqued what an immanent saga might have constituted and moved further away from thinking in terms of there being a recognisable shape to particular oral tales.[15]

Clover's idea blurs the division between history and literature but is still concerned with it, while also allowing for some role for independent creativity in the composition of sagas. An earlier work, which incensed literary critics at the time, denied the possibility that 'authors' in a modern sense existed at all: Steblin-Kamenskij's book, *The Saga Mind*, was one of the most inflammatory works ever to be written on saga origins.[16] It put forward the idea of what he called 'syncretic truth.'[17] According to Steblin-Kamenskij there was no point in trying to analyse either the artistic merit of sagas or their straightforward historical value because, he claimed, the people who preserved them had no concept of the modern distinction between literature and history. Syncretic truth was what was simply accepted as true and passed on without question, hence the absence of claims of authorship for sagas. Steblin-Kamenskij was clearly in favour of oral saga origins rather than written ones. He defined the key features of *Íslendingasögur* which to him illustrated their oral origins and therefore the very limited role of what other critics have identified as the medieval author:

> ...the predominance of maximally simple syntactic structures connected in an elementary fashion, inconsistency in syntactic linking, irregular

---

14 Finnegan 1977: 24–28.
15 Usefully summarised and with references in Rankovic 2013.
16 Steblin-Kamenskij 1973: 49–68; see also (one of) the responses of Peter Hallberg, Hallberg 1974. See Boulhosa (2005: 34–42) for a similar discussion of Steblin-Kaminskij's impact.
17 Clover 1985: 260–62.

alternation of the past tense with the historical present and of direct speech with indirect, predominance of the simplest and most elementary words coupled with highly idiomatic expression, abundance of stereo-typed phrases, abundance of demonstrative and personal pronouns and of adverbs of place, repetition of the same word in the same sentence.[18]

There is much to be said for such a view although that is not to say that we should accept that medieval Icelanders were entirely undiscerning in receiving information nor incapable of changing it, consciously or accidentally, when writing it down.

The idea behind Steblin-Kamenskij's arguments would seem to be that we should really stop trying to read too many technicalities into these texts, things which were not seen by the people who had them written down. It seems to me that this is not unlike the way many of us receive information about our own pasts, through whatever medium. Many people are simply unwilling to believe that something they hold as true about the past is not 'the truth'. Most of us devise mental patterns of causation which we do not necessarily feel the need to question, even when asked to give a spoken narrative account of certain events. Written history provides another source on which people can choose to draw but very few of us choose to do so, or else we simply chose what to read or to interpret written sources how we like. Until the arrival of the internet it was only academic historians who had both the time and access to written material to do otherwise. Syncretic truth is not necessarily something remote or abstract, but that truth about the past which most people accept and which most people, when prompted, have to give in narrative form.[19] Saga narratives, however they were composed, are more likely to contain this kind of 'truth' because that is how most people think. As we shall see, what Steblin-Kamenskij proposed was not altogether different from the ways anthropologists have observed predominantly oral cultures understanding time, historical truthfulness and their own pasts.

Íslendingasögur, then, can be regarded as compilations of at least partially mythological information about ninth, tenth and eleventh century events.

---

18 Steblin-Kamenskij 1973: 65.
19 Carol Clover (1986: 262) notes that *The Saga Mind* had had very little influence on approaches to studies of *Íslendingasögur* by 1985. This is not altogether surprising, since to accept his ideas would have required two generations of saga scholars to utterly realign their thinking on medieval literature.

Several outline points can be made about the way these myths can be analysed. First of all, the *Íslendingasögur* have a very keen sense of place, understandable given the fact that other indicators show that *Íslendingasögur* were likely to have been first written close to where the events they relate are said to have taken place. Geography is important in these accounts, then, but so too are descriptions of people and the power they wielded. People who appear in sagas generally conform to stereotypes or roles which appear throughout *Íslendingasögur*: they can be *goðar*, *bændr*, slaves, fathers, mothers, sons or daughters who are wise, scheming, benevolent, rich, poor, or reckless with money. They can also be either Icelandic or foreign or local or from some other area of Iceland. In other words, there is a set of recognisable boxes into which most major saga characters can be fitted. It is how people who conform to these particular stereotypes are placed within the human and physical landscape that indicates how they are regarded by the text's author.

Certain information about political leadership and control is also moderately easy to extract from the *Íslendingasögur*. Some men are named as leaders (*höfðingjar* or *goðar*), and we can then trace the nature and geographical extent of their power. We can identify the rough overall number of *goðar* or leaders shown to have been active at any given time; their location and the extent of their perceived influence; the way in which *goðorð* were passed on, and other assumptions about the nature of the *goðorð*; the relationships between *goðar* and their dependants; and the relationships between *goðar*. Other people are not credited with the authority of having a *goðorð* but act in a similar way to those said to have been *goðar*. A third group are usually followers, rather than initiators of action.

It is rare for the *Íslendingasögur* give a name to a particular *goðorð*, in contrast to the sagas in the *Sturlunga* compilation which identify *goðorð* according to either the name of an *ætt* (kin group) or a place with which a *goðorð* had come to be associated. As we have seen, the first *goðorð* to be controlled by the Sturlungar was sometimes called the *Snorrungagoðorð*.[20] The *goðorð* was associated with the *ætt* of Snorri *goði*, an ancestor of the Sturlungar, and from whom the latter claimed descent. The *Íslendingasögur* practice of identifying *goðar* and *höfðingjar* but not their *goðorð* is probably the product of those sagas' lengthy oral transmission and may reflect the temporariness and fragility of each *goðorð*. *Íslendingasögur* are more concerned to highlight the power of each particular individual, i.e. by calling him *goði* (and usually where he came

---

20   *Snorrungagoðorð*: SS I: 64, 303, 304, 315, 319, 447. See pp. 57–59 above.

from), rather than to be precise about which *goðorð* he owned.[21] Thus these people are more often discussed in genealogical rather than institutional terms.

Another key aspect of sagas' ideas about the past is the chronology of events. *Íslendingasögur* do not simply retell isolated individual tales, but record several related tales in a particular chronological sequence. Relative chronology is clearly an important structuring principle in any narrative, even where absolute dating is not. Attempts are, though, sometimes made to relate particular events to the few 'known' dates, especially the *landnám* or the arrival of Christianity in 1000, but most events go undated. Underlying each narrative are, all the same, assumptions about when politics changed in certain ways.

Marriages which take place between saga characters probably have the same kind of genealogical-charter premises behind them as do those marriages recorded in *Landnámabók*. Longer narratives obviously provide the opportunity for the relationships between kin groups or places to be described, either more ambiguously or more precisely, but in essence the fuller narratives can be read in the same way as *Landnámabók* genealogies. The likelihood that fuller narratives lay behind such genealogies is strongly suggested by the presence of short narratives in *S* which read as condensed *Íslendingasögur*; the similarities between S85–86 and *Eyrbyggja saga* being a classic example of this.[22]

If a different kind of source were available for Iceland's early history, then this chapter would not only deal with the control of farms but with the ownership of land. As it is, *Íslendingasögur* are unhelpful for understanding the finer detail of how the lowland areas of Iceland were divided up and exploited, and what sort of possessory rights landholders had. What they provide is images of the past which are usually only concerned with who lived at a farm when certain events were taking place. In some cases sagas do record property transactions or changes of ownership of some farms, but usually only when ownership was a matter of dispute.[23] Nevertheless, knowing who lived where and when, in sagas' portrayals of events, suggests ideas about positive and negative political relationships.

Besides through marriages, local allegiances can be seen in acts of friendship or alliances in court cases. These relationships are sometimes between people of discernibly different social categories which may imply something

---

21 Cf. the discussion above for the twelfth and thirteenth centuries, pp. 56–70.
22 See above pp. 177–78.
23 Byock 1982: 223–28.

about power relations at the time of writing. People raised vengeance parties together and took each other to court when they were hostile to one another. When on good terms or seeking to strengthen ties they invited each other to feasts, fostered each others' children, and encouraged marriages between their children. By examining the sagas in terms of each of these kinds of social actions we can build up a more detailed picture of local power relations than through only looking at marriage or genealogical links. Most of the time, we can see that *Íslendingasögur* marriages lasted a long time and produced children, which must have been viewed by saga audiences to have had long term implications for social relations. Friendships, fostering relationships and even disputes, as elements of sagas' depiction of the past, may have been conceived of as having had shorter-term political effects.

One last point to note is that each of the texts below is dealt with in a slightly different way according to its structure and focus. The longer texts are for the west, and the main two, *Laxdæla saga* and *Eyrbyggja saga*, totalling 143 chapters between them, are discussed here in depth. The five texts on Eyjafjörður and north-east, amount to just 126 chapters between them, with *Ljósvetninga saga* being the longest at 31 chapters. These are treated more synthetically.

1 The Dalir *Íslendingasögur*

Having considered the general debates about this genre it remains to consider the more detailed text-specific issues of their dates, origins, meanings and purposes, beginning with Dalir. The arguments put forward here have a bearing on how we can understand the depictions of politics analysed below. *Laxdæla saga* and *Eyrbyggja saga* will be considered in detail first before brief comment is given to other relevant sagas.

1.1 *Laxdæla Saga*

Laxdæla saga consists of 78 chapters and 248 pages in the standard Icelandic edition. Seven pre-Reformation vellum manuscripts preserve at least part of the saga but the only vellum manuscript that preserves the whole text is *Möðruvallabók*.[24] With most of its action taking place in the Sturlungar 'heartland,' and supposedly showing an especially detailed knowledge of it,[25]

---

24   ÍF v: lxxvi, lxxx.
25   ÍF v: xxiii.

Laxdœla saga is a text which has had more than its fair share of proposed authors with Dalir connections: Snorri Sturluson (d.1241),[26] Óláfr *hvítaskáld* Þórðarson (d.1259)[27] and Sturla Þórðarson (d.1284)[28] are the most prominent among them.[29] It has also, rightly, been seen as having most features in common with chivalric romances. Notwithstanding the attributions to potential male writers, *Laxdœla saga* has also attracted the attention of critics who have seen, in its inclusion of a 'love triangle' as a major plot element (and its recording of a female *landnámsmaðr*, Unnr *in djúpúðga*, Unnr the deep-minded, as opposed to Auðr *in djúpauðga*), and an interest in saga characters' feelings, the interests of a female rather than male author. *Laxdœla saga* is also thought to have textual relationships or debts to *Landnámabók*,[30] other *Íslendingasögur* including *Eyrbyggja saga, Heiðarvíga saga, Egils saga, Fœreyinga saga* as well as Snorri Sturluson's *Óláfs saga helga*, with all of which it does share occasional similarities of content or style. It will be proposed here, however, that an earlier view on the dating of *Laxdœla saga*, suggesting an earlier origin for it, makes more sense. This rules out the attribution to the 'great men' suggested as authors by previous generations of saga scholars.

To start with then, the contents of *Laxdœla saga* suggest that a reasonably complete version of it existed by about 1200 to 1220, a date which can be

---

26   Most novel and least convincing is Margaret Arent Madelung's argument for Snorri Sturluson's authorship of *Laxdœla saga*. She takes *Laxdœla saga*'s depiction of Snorri *goði's* wiles to imply that Snorri Sturluson was playing some kind of game with his readers and in fact complimenting himself. By a tendentious line of argument based around the supposed symbolic repetition in the saga of the numbers twelve, three and two, she deduces that *Laxdœla saga* was written in 1232. Even allowing for the existence of an elite culture which took delight in the intricacies of skaldic poetry, it is hard to understand why anyone would try to communicate with their reader in such an oblique way (Madelung 1972: esp. 184, 190).

27   Hallberg argued, on the basis of comparative statistical analyses of the language of *Laxdœla saga* and other saga texts, as well as circumstantial evidence, that Óláfr *hvítaskáld* Þórðarson (the brother of Sturla, d.1259) wrote the saga (Hallberg 1963, 1965; 1968; 1978–9). See above 106, 109, 110, 113-18, 119, 122–23, 125–26 generally for their roles in thirteenth-century politics.

28   Heller 1965, 1967; Mundt 1965; 1969. See Magerøy 1971 for arguments against Mundt's idea that either Óláfr or Sturla Þórðarson were the author, an argument she based on Hallberg's ideas on language and Heller's dating of *Laxdœla saga* to the 1270s.

29   Clover 1985: 245–46, 289–90.

30   B.M. Ólsen 1908 set out the basic set of connections which have been discussed ever since (ÍF v: xxxix–xi; Jón Jóhannesson 1941: 213–16, Björn Sigfússon 1944: 66–71).

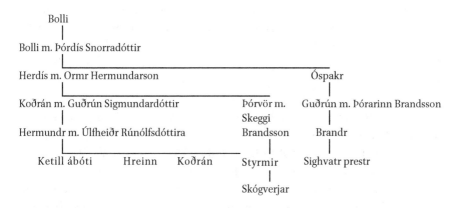

FIGURE 26   Genealogy of the descendants of Bolli Bollason in Chapter 78 of *Laxdœla saga*

inferred from the saga's genealogies. While most of the genealogies focus on the tenth century, the *höfðingi* Þorvaldr *Vatnsfirðingr* Snorrason (d.1228) and the sons of Hermundr Koðránsson (d.1197) are the last people to be mentioned in the extensive genealogies at the saga's end.[31] The basic text we have must have been written up after Þorvaldr Snorrason became worthy of note in Breiðafjörður, i.e. not before about 1209.[32] This is all the internal dating evidence there is and it leaves room for us to consider whether that genealogical material might have been added to an earlier written version of the saga which has had some cosmetic updating.

As hinted above, the genealogical information contained in *Laxdœla saga* points to a family other than the Sturlungar being responsible for writing down the saga as we have it. This was the conclusion reached by Hannes Þorsteinsson in 1912 but the idea probably never gained wider acceptance because the kin group concerned appears to have been less prominent.[33] As Hannes pointed out, the genealogy preserved in the saga's final chapter (Figure 26) has a very particular focus, being remarkable for the detailed account of descendants of Bolli Bollason and his wife Þórdís, the daughter of Snorri *goði*. It extends in

---

31   ÍF v: 83, 226.
32   SS I: 250–51 where Þorvaldr is named as a member of a group of *höfðingjar*. He is also mentioned before this date but it cannot be shown that Þorvaldr was of any real note before this reference to 1209.
33   Hannes Þorsteinsson 1912; ÍF v: xxxiv.

detail over generations otherwise not covered in the saga and would therefore appear to represent the deliberate inclusion of material by the person who commissioned the writing or copying of the saga. The genealogy of Bolli Bollason's descendants has the appearance of being what could reasonably be assumed to be one person's knowledge of their ancestry.

A look at this 'extra' piece of genealogy, above, shows how great the involvement was of this group of people in the church.[34] Within it there is a bishop, an abbot and a priest. The saga identifies Úlfheiðr, the wife of Hermundr Konráðsson, as the grand-daughter of Bishop Ketill of Hólar (1122–45) and Ketill Hermundarson as abbot of Helgafell.[35] This Ketill Hermundarson was abbot of Helgafell for four years, 1217–20.[36] Simple lines of descent are also recorded for the *goðar* Ari *inn sterki* Þorgilsson (who died in the 1190s and lived at Staðarstaðr on southern Snæfellsnes) and Þorvaldr Snorrason, though their kin groups are not recorded.[37] This all suggests the likely interests of a scribe in the first half of the thirteenth century: someone most likely connected to Abbot Ketill or living at Helgafell, the farm whose history plays such a large part in the latter parts of the saga.

It is worth setting out what we know about the political role of the people in this section of the genealogy to see whether any of their views may have influenced *Laxdœla saga*. *Sturlu saga* tells us that Hermundr Konráðsson lived at Kalmanstunga in Borgarfjörður, and possibly controlled the *Jöklamannagoðorð*.[38] In the late 1150s he was one of several local notables who sided with Einar Þorgilsson briefly against Hvamm-Sturla;[39] later Hermundr and his sons Ketill and Koðrán also probably supported Böðvarr Þórðarson (father-in-law of Hvamm-Sturla) in his dispute with Páll Sölvason.[40] In the early thirteenth century the daughter of Hreinn Hermundarson, Guðrún, became the partner/concubine of Snorri Sturluson.[41] For Ketill Hermundarson, if he inherited his father's *goðorð*, as has been suggested,[42] then his ecclesiastical role might have precluded him from taking part in secular politics in the thirteenth century: he

---

34 ÍF V: 227, notes 1 & 2.
35 ÍF V: 226–27.
36 *Skálholtsannáll* records Ketill dying twice, in 1220 and 1229, but a successor arrives in 1221 (IA 185, 187).
37 ÍF V: 83, 228.
38 Lúðvík Ingvarsson 1986–7 III: 26–33.
39 SS I: 74.
40 SS I: 74, 107, 111.
41 Their position among the elite is arguably confirmed by Guðrún's daughter by Snorri being married to Gizurr Þorvaldsson for perhaps eight years (SS I: 304, 346; above p. 74).
42 Lúðvík Ingvarsson 1986–7 III: 29.

certainly makes few appearances in *Sturlunga saga*.[43] According to *Páls saga*, Ketill Hermundarson was the servant (*þjónustumaðr*) of the Bishop of Skálholt, Páll (d.1211),[44] probably before he was made abbot of Helgafell. This would imply that Ketill spent much of his life in the church and, together with his near-absence from *Sturlunga saga*,[45] he was most likely the first member of this family not involved in secular politics.

The snippets we can glean about these people suggest that they were part of the highest echelon of western Icelandic society in the late twelfth and thirteenth century. Their relationships with other families seem ambivalent. They, like other people of *goði*-standing, helped keep peace in conflicts in the mid-twelfth century; after that they seem to have left or been ousted from secular power. This would seem to be confirmed by events recorded for 1253 when it is Þorgils *skarði* Böðvarsson – one of the Sturlungar rather than one of Ketill's descendants – who is said to have appointed someone to the *Jöklamannagoðorð*.[46]

If *Laxdæla saga* were written or copied by or for Ketill Hermundarson then we must see it as the product of an elite family with Western Quarter connections but largely absent from secular politics in the thirteenth century. Their relationship with the Sturlungar, the dominant kin group in this region, is unclear. It is difficult to say what the implications might be of Ketill's possible involvement in producing the text in its preserved form. Bolli Bollason, from whom Ketill could claim descent, is an important figure in the saga and we might suppose that he is portrayed sympathetically because Ketill was a patron of the text. In the thirteenth century, however, Bolli Bollason had a genealogical importance for more than this single family. This is proven by the existence of northern Icelandic events in *Bolla þáttr*, the text about Bolli Bollason which continues *Laxdæla saga* (in *Möðruvallabók*).[47] Bolli Þorleiksson, father of Bolli Bollason, probably therefore had more descendants still, and his image in the saga has no doubt been shaped by wider forces than simply the interests of Ketill. It is also important to stress that connecting the transmission of the text with Ketill Hermundarson gives us no guide to when the earliest version of the saga was written down.

---

43 SS I: 107, 347.
44 *Byskupa sögur* I: 140.
45 He is mentioned only once, accompanying his father at the negotiations for a settlement between Páll Sölvason and Hvamm-Sturla in 1179 (SS I: 107). His son Kári is named as a prominent supporter of Klængr Bjarnarson in 1231, a member of the Haukdælir, in events in Borgarfjörður, i.e. the traditional home of the *Jöklamannagoðorð* (SS I: 347).
46 SS II: 149; Jón Viðar Sigurðsson 1999: 174.
47 ÍF V: lxii, 230–48.

A few words ought also to be said about literary analyses of *Laxdœla saga* which often seem to me to presuppose a level of artfulness which I cannot see as being part of what a saga writer did.[48] Various arguments have been made about its structure and purpose all of which have a certain validity but, in my view, do not work as full rationales for the writing of this saga any more than they do for others. The influence of Augustine theology has been suggested, particularly in relation to the sea journeys which are a part of the text.[49] *Laxdœla* is one of those *Íslendingasögur* which has been proposed as a piece of social commentary, in this case as a critique of Iceland's violent elite, but as with all these texts the views expressed or implied in one part of the text are not the same as that in others.[50]

In recent decades Rolf Heller has been the most vigorous espouser of *Laxdœla saga*'s dependence on other written sources.[51] Such similarities are intriguing but unprovable[52] and, again, it is difficult to imagine how anyone would go about consciously influencing their text with other written information. There is no doubt a fairly close relationship in terms of content between parts of *Laxdœla saga* and *Landnámabók* but equally significant are the differences between the two. As we have seen the major female colonist is called Auðr in *Landnámabók* but Unnr in *Laxdœla saga*,[53] and the geographical order of *Landnámabók* is disrupted by the presence of the genealogy of Auðr/Unnr. It has been proposed that earlier *Íslendingasögur* based around female protagonists form major components of it (and another local saga, *Eiríks saga rauða*).[54] Female authorship has been proposed, too, but this arguably overstates the significance of female characters in the text as a whole and makes assumptions about the relationship between gender and authorship which seem untenable.[55] A better, if still circumstantial, case has been made for its sponsorship by female members of the Sturlungar in the mid-thirteenth century by Guðrún Nordal.[56]

---

48   E.g. Beck 1977.
49   Hamer 1999.
50   Clover 1985: 267–68 commenting on the ideas of Njörður Njarðvík 1972. The supposed link between the denial of access to latrines in *Laxdœla saga* to a similar (but admittedly fairly rarely recorded) instance seems unconvincing to me. The 'real' event is described in one early, annal-like section in *Íslendinga saga* for south-west Iceland in 1198.
51   Most importantly Heller 1965 and 1976a but see also Heller 1969, 1974, 1976b, 1978–9, 1998.
52   Úlfar Bragason 1986: 68.
53   Björn M. Olsen 1908.
54   Kress 1980; Conroy & Langen 1988; Conroy 1980; Cook 1998.
55   Kress 1980.
56   Guðrún Nordal 2012, 2013.

In sum it seems that for all its complexities and potentially literary qualities, most of them difficult to prove, *Laxdæla saga* must be regarded as consisting of versions of oral stories which could easily be put together without much interference from a writer, even if they were not already regarded as a single narrative. This was most likely done before c.1220 and perhaps much earlier, with the text being partly shaped by the interests of a kin group which was losing standing in the 1210s (and 1220s).

1.2 *Eyrbyggja Saga*

Eyrbyggja saga gives an account of events which supposedly took place along the north coast of Snæfellsnes between about 880 and 1030. The saga was most likely written in or close to Helgafell, in the heart of the area which the saga covers, and where there was, as we have seen, a monastery from the 1180s.[57] Questions about its authorship have been less frequently aired than for *Laxdæla saga*, probably due to critics' greater concern with the saga's structure and age. It is also generally regarded as unusual in the prominence it gives to supernatural events. At the same time it lacks an obviously dramatic hero and it has been suggested that the author was consciously trying to write a historical work.[58] Unlike *Laxdæla saga* it does not contain any obvious genealogical clues as to when it was written so proposed dates seldom differ from a general 'mid-thirteenth century.' Hallberg proposed Sturla Þórðarson as its author on the basis of its use of one particular verb, a feature it shared with works otherwise associated with Sturla.[59] Recently, analysis of the manuscripts has suggested that there was an extant 'archetype' manuscript of the surviving versions at some point in the late thirteenth century while two particular dates have been proposed for the saga's writing.[60] Torfi Tulinius has suggested a very specific context, namely, the 1250s when *höfðingjar* in western Iceland (Sturla Þórðarson and Hrafn Oddsson) were opposed to Gizurr Þorvaldsson's use of canon law to annul his first marriage, which might also support the idea of Sturla Þórðarson as author.[61] Else Mundal has proposed a date after the union with Norway because she sees the text as a critique of Iceland's elite by an author who was 'disappointed with the fall of the Icelandic Commonwealth.'[62] Most recently Elín Bára Magnúsdóttir has written a monograph to try to

---

57 DI I: 282; Orri Vésteinsson 2000: 102.
58 Andersson 2006 150–54.
59 Hallberg 1965, 1979; Torfi Tulinius 2013: 127.
60 Louis-Jensen 2013, esp. 133–39 on the manuscripts.
61 Torfi Tulinius 2013.
62 Mundal 2013: 44–45.

demonstrate Sturla Þórðarson's authorship based partly on the kinds of comparisons of wording favoured by Hallberg but, in my view, producing no stronger arguments.[63] As with other means of dating, it seems to me that the alleged concerns of the text need not be tied to very specific points in time. The role of canon law and the perceived failings of the secular elite were issues over a long period of time, well before the second half of the thirteenth century; and even if Sturla Þórðarson (1214–84) were the author, he could have written it anywhere from perhaps the 1240s to 1280s.

If we turn to the more bookprosist approaches to *Eyrbyggja saga* it is clear that they have had just as fundamental an influence as they have for *Laxdæla saga*. It has often been seen as later than the written *Laxdæla saga* because *Eyrbyggja*'s final chapter refers to a 'Laxdæla saga'[64] and multiple other borrowings are supposed by other scholars.[65] Indeed Andersson has recently suggested that *Eyrbyggja* was a response to *Laxdæla saga* and is confident that the *Eyrbyggja saga* author knew a written version of not only that text but also *Gísla saga* and *Heiðarvíga saga*.[66]

Regarding Andersson's idea that *Eyrbyggja saga* was a response to *Laxdæla saga* then the absence of *rittengsl* between the two arguably makes sense in order for the texts to offer alternative views of the same material. Certainly even their introductory genealogical material seldom overlaps. Their accounts of the *landnám* at Helgafell, as part of the story of Ketill *flatnefr* and how his children came to Iceland, disagree. *Eyrbyggja saga* suggests that the *landnámsmaðr* Þórólfr *Mostrarskegg* had power over Björn *inn austrœni*: Þórólfr shelters Björn when the latter is outlawed by the Norwegian king and it is only with Þórólfr's permission that Björn settles in Breiðafjörður. *Laxdæla saga* does not make Björn *inn austrœni* an outlaw and likewise only mentions Þórólfr in a genealogy later on. *Laxdæla* also stresses the unity of Ketill *flatnefr's* family

---

63   Elín Bára Magnúsdóttir 2015.
64   McCreesh 1993: 174–75; ÍF IV: 180.
65   See, for example, the introduction to Pálsson and Edwards' English translation (1973: 23): 'The author uses a number of written sources: several chapters derive from the *Book of Settlements* (*Landnámabók*), probably the version, now lost, of Styrmir Kárason (d.1245). The earliest extant version of the *Book of Settlements*, that of Sturla Thordarson (1214–84) in turn added material taken from *Eyrbyggja saga*, and so one text cross-fertilises another. Several sagas are referred to in *Eyrbyggja saga*: Ch. 24 gives a summary of part of *Eirik's Saga*; the killing of Snorri's father and other elements in the story refer to *Gisli's Saga*; and the author also uses *Laxdæla Saga* and *Heidarviga Saga*. Thus, while *Eyrbyggja saga* draws upon historical records, it also belongs to the great tradition of story-telling, and must be seen as fictionalised history.'
66   Andersson 2006: 150–54.

whereas *Eyrbyggja saga* says Björn remained pagan after the rest of the family became Christian. *Eyrbyggja saga* seems to be lessening the significance of Björn here. Another significant disagreement between the sagas occurs when they refer to the swapping of farms by Snorri *goði* and Guðrún Ósvífrsdóttir. Here it is clear the two rationalise the same event in different ways. The key sentence in *Laxdæla saga* says that when the swap took place: 'At that time Snorri was involved in great disputes with the *Eyrbyggjar*,'[67] whereas *Eyrbyggja saga* supposes that the move happened later and not as a direct consequence of his politicking. These are important differences but do not in themselves tell us about the relative dates of *Eyrbyggja* and *Laxdæla* and whether one was written in response to the other.

As regards *Eyrbyggja* and *Gísla saga Súrssonar*, it will suffice to note that Andersson famously used each text's version of the so-called 'Helgafell episode' to demonstrate their independence.[68] This is the episode in which Þórdís Súrsdóttir attempts to stab Eyjólfr *grái*.[69] Andersson concluded that:

> ...the author of *Eyrbyggja saga* probably knew the story of Þórdís' frustrated vengeance, but he chose to base his account on a written *Gísla saga* subject to the changes dictated by his own tradition. The variants as we have them are literary, but they ultimately reflect two oral traditions: in one of them Snorri was present at Helgafell, in the other he was not.[70]

When the actual verbal repetitions between *Eyrbyggja saga* and the two versions of *Gísla saga* are added up, however, they amount to even less than Andersson argued for. The two very different contexts for the story of the stabbing, and the way in which it fits easily into each saga, suggest instead that *Eyrbyggja saga* and *Gísla saga* record two oral accounts within which the episodes have been reshaped.

The arguments for other written antecedents for *Eyrbyggja saga* are weak. Jón Jóhannesson argued that where *Eyrbyggja saga* differed from the *Sturlubók* version of the story about Geirríðr Þórólfsdóttir's killing of Gunnlaugr, the differences reflected *Eyrbyggja*'s dependence on the lost *Styrmisbók*.[71] Direct

---

67 'Í þenna tíma átti Snorri deilur miklar við þá Eyrbyggja.' (ÍF V: 169).
68 Andersson 2006: 150.
69 ÍF IV: 22–4; ÍF VI: 116–17.
70 Andersson 1964: 172; Andersson 2006: 150.
71 S79; McCreesh 1978–79: 274; Jón Jóhannesson 1941: 41–43; ÍF IV: xvi–xvii. Geirríðr escapes punishment for killing Gunnlaugr in the S story where she is found guilty in *Eyrbyggja saga*.

connections between *Eyrbyggja saga* and *Eiríks saga* can also probably be dismissed. *Eyrbyggja saga* (Ch. 24) records the shorter version of an account of Eiríkr *rauði*'s leaving Iceland to discover Greenland (after his having killed the sons of Þorgestr Steinsson). The details about Eiríkr *rauði* are mentioned in *Eyrbyggja saga* because they form part of the author's chronological framing of his story, namely of what happened at the Þórsnessþing, and they clearly know a story about Eiríkr *rauði*. Again, we need not assume that *Eyrbyggja saga*'s writer knew our written version of *Eiríks saga rauða*.[72]

Finally the very last chapter of *Eyrbyggja saga* is of special significance with regard to this debate. The last chapter is a genealogy of Snorri *goði*'s descendants, his alleged seventeen children and a few of their descendants. For this genealogy we have another source, the very short *Ævi Snorra goða* (*The Life of Snorri goði*), which is not as lengthy as the last chapter of *Eyrbyggja saga* but, where it records the same details as the saga, it is in full agreement with it. The *Ævi* survives independently as a short list of Snorri's 21 children and his wives, and a paragraph or so of biography.[73] The agreement between them suggests that they have some close connection but is not so great as to suggest anything more than that the information about Snorri was well-known. It is hard to believe, as has been suggested from the handful of facts contained in both the saga and *Ævi Snorra goða*, that *Eyrbyggja saga* was heavily dependent on the latter.[74] A text like the surviving *Ævi* may have been the source for the last chapter of the saga but the rest of the saga most likely derived from oral traditions. The saga version of the genealogy works a bit like a genealogical charter in that it records lines of descent from several of Snorri's children.

Eyrbyggja saga is also traditionally seen as unique in its lack of apparent structure, or at least structure as defined by the influential views of Theodore Andersson.[75] *Eyrbyggja saga* is highly episodic; it does not cover just a few major disputes but several in succession, densely packed into the text. Many scholars have approached the saga as if it were put together very self-consciously with some kind of theme joining all parts of it.[76] But the lack of an obvious overall schema for the saga, the lack of clear patterns of any kind, suggests that we

---

72 Cf. ÍF IV: lxxviii.
73 ÍF IV: 185–6 for the whole text. Only *Melabók* preserves it (ÍF IV: xi–xiii, lix–lxi).
74 ÍF IV: xii.
75 Andersson 1967.
76 Clover (1986: 32) comments on *Eyrbyggja saga* in the light of '*þáttr* theory': '*Eyrbyggja saga* and *Ljósvetninga saga* in particular inspire such terms as "compilation," "patchwork," "loose assemblage of stories."' For older structural/thematic analyses see Hollander 1959; Bibre 1973; McCreesh 1978–9; McTurk 1986; Vésteinn Ólason 1991.

should not look too hard for such authorial intervention. *Eyrbyggja saga* reads essentially as a series of stories about people from a specific place,[77] organised chronologically and including skaldic verses, possibly as mnemonic devices or recalling the origins of certain parts of the saga.[78] The whole of the saga is certainly influenced by ideas on the differences between how Christians and pagans behaved but, again, not consistently so. Some stories in the saga are concerned with pagan/Christian attitudes and some clearly are not. Likewise most of the saga is concerned with Snorri *goði* but not all of it.

As with *Laxdœla saga*, the only defining element in the arrangement of the *Eyrbyggja saga* episodes is their chronology and its concern to focus on conflicts within a very small region. The full manuscript title of *Eyrbyggja saga* is *Saga Þórsnesinga, Eyrbyggja saga ok Álptfirðinga*, the saga of the people of Þórsnes, Eyrr (Öndverðareyrr or modern Hallbjarnareyri) and Álptafjörður.[79] The saga's title defines the saga as an account of three different families, associated with (effectively) three different farms (Helgafell, Öndverðareyrr and Kársstaðir (Figure 9)). The saga is thus probably a collection of family histories which have been combined. Whether they were combined at the oral or written stage is impossible to say but the shaping of the saga out of three family histories may explain the portrayals of many of the characters in the sagas. Most characters, especially the main ones, are shown in a reasonably neutral light, even someone like Snorri *goði*, who must have been revered by his descendants. Where negative portrayals come in it is when the saga deals with less important characters from outside of the three families named in the title. Vésteinn Ólason has pointed out, for example, the bias against Þorbjörn of Fróðá in the saga's so-called *Máhlíðingamál* episode.[80] In general, we can assume that the need for a version of events acceptable to all of the saga's local audience has ironed out biases in representations of many farms. But where a character like Þorbjörn was not favoured by any one of these three farms then he could come off badly. Similarly in the story in Chapters 56–62 that deals with a feud between Snorri *goði* and Óspakr Kjallaksson from Bitra, on Strandir, we have outsiders (Óspakr) who are 'othered.'

---

77   McTurk 1986: 234, 237 for the geographical extent of the saga's action. McTurk argues that the occasions when the action moves away from Snæfellsnes are designed to put local events into the context of 'Iceland's development as a nation.' The focus of the saga is nevertheless intensely local.
78   Perkins (1991: 68) includes 'scaldic verses and other poetry' as one of his types of '"kernels" for prose oral tradition concerning the söguöld [Saga Age].' Garmonsway (1940: 81) seems notable as a critic who accepted the primacy of the chronological framing.
79   ÍF IV: xxxiv; Andersson 2006: 151–52.
80   Vésteinn Ólason 1991: 188.

As suggested above for *Laxdæla saga* or any other saga, genealogies in *Eyrbyggja saga* ought to give us an idea of when the final, preserved text was written down. And, using all the genealogical information in *Eyrbyggja saga* we can trace up to seven generations from the settlement without a break; then the saga adds notes as to which powerful thirteenth century families (the Vatnsfirðingar, Sturlungar and Ásbirningar) can trace their descent from characters in the saga. This link, however, is only made in the last two chapters, Chapters 64 and 65. Just as with *Laxdæla saga*, but perhaps more clearly so here, *Eyrbyggja saga* does not integrate the genealogies at the end of the saga with the events of the saga. It could well be that the 'terminal' genealogies (and the story which accompanies the genealogy in Chapter 64) have been added to an earlier written text. This probability is increased when we take into consideration the existence of the *Ævi Snorra goða*, because it looks as if this text, too, has been copied and added to the end of *Eyrbyggja saga*.[81]

Where does this leave us, then, in trying to date the saga? Firstly, any relationship between *Eyrbyggja saga* and *Ævi Snorra goða* does not tell us that much. Equally references to clan names like the Vatnsfirðingar or Sturlungar only give a rough *terminus post quem* for, possibly, as little of the saga as its last few chapters. As with *Laxdæla saga*, these references to thirteenth century people do not help us to date the first version of the saga, only those parts which look to have been added onto that original one.

It has already been noted that *Eyrbyggja saga*'s account of Snorri *goði*'s children does not trace one particular line further than any other. This is also true of those other genealogies in the saga: most tend to end four, five or six generations after the settlement i.e. not more than about 150 years after the *landnám*. Again this suggests that the section resembling *Ævi Snorra goða* has been added onto the saga which originally did not concern itself with genealogical links to people who lived after the saga's events. This also gives us a *terminus post quem* for a lost version as early as the late eleventh century, not that anyone would argue for such an early date.[82]

It may also be significant that *Eyrbyggja saga* seems rather confused over the ancestors of Snorri *goði* in its earlier chapters, in spite of its clarity over Snorri's children and their significance in Chapter 65. In chapter seven the saga is not clear about who the wife of Þórólfr *Mostrarskegg* was; she was called

---

81 This is not incompatible with Louis-Jensen's (2013: 137) argument that it was already integral to the 'archetype' which she identifies.
82 ÍF IV: 27.

Unnr but nothing else about her is clear as 'some people say that she might have been the daughter of Þorsteinn *rauðr* but Ari Þorgilsson *inn fróði* does not include her among his children.'[83] We also have a section of the genealogy in which Þórólfr and Unnr's son, Hallsteinn, is supposed to have married Unnr's sister, Ósk. There is no reason why this might not have happened, or been remembered as happening, but it seems more likely to be the result of confusion. Thus *Eyrbyggja saga*'s muddled account of Snorri's descent from Þorstein *rauðr* – a crucial character in the Breiðafjörður settlement stories – suggests, again, that Chapter 65 has a separate origin from the rest of the saga as well as that *Eyrbyggja saga* had no connection with *Laxdæla saga* and *Sturlubók*, both of which give clear accounts of Snorri's ancestors. It may be that the comment quoted here, in which Ari *fróði* 'does not count her' (*telr hana eigi*) uses the present tense, actually does suggest its writing down in, or shortly after, Ari's lifetime.

Eyrbyggja saga's significant disagreements with *Laxdæla saga* suggest that they could not have been written by the same people. If we are looking for writers of either an initial or secondary version of *Eyrbyggja saga*, we are therefore looking for different groups of people from those named here in connection with *Laxdæla saga*. Einar Ólafur Sveinsson considered that *Eyrbyggja saga* might have been written during the abbacy of Ketill Hermundarson or his immediate predecessor, Þorfinnr Þorgeirsson, but that the saga's style suggested that the person who actually wrote it could barely be considered a learned cleric.[84] Either way, on the basis that Helgafell must have been a community small enough for the abbot to be aware of, and in control of, what his monks were doing, it seems safe to rule out the possibility that another monk at Helgafell could have written the preserved versions of *Eyrbyggja saga* and *Laxdæla saga* at about the same time.[85] Other transmitters or sponsors of the text could be posited but no particularly strong candidates emerge. Clearly there is no obvious context to be ascribed to *Eyrbyggja saga* using traditional lines of thinking.

Taking into account all the evidence put forward above it can be suggested that an early version of *Eyrbyggja saga* was written down before the beginning of the thirteenth century. The *terminus post quem* is a lot earlier; the reference

---

83   ÍF IV: 12.
84   ÍF IV: iv.
85   The early abbots of Helgafell were: Ögmundr Kálfsson, c.1184–88 (SS I: 130, 136), Þorfinnr Þorgeirsson, 1188?-1216, (SS I: 133), Hallr Gizurarson, 1221–1225/6, (SS I: 54, 60, 157, 220, 305, 307, 309), Hallkell Magnússon, 1226–44 (SS I: 339).

to Ari is suggestive of an early date; and it is hard to find a thirteenth century context for the composition of the saga. The only strong case for *rittengsl* between *Eyrbyggja saga* and another text is with the *Ævi Snorra goða*. The original written saga could have dated from any time after the births of Ketill *kappi*, Gunnlaugr and Hallsteinn who are named in Chapter 15, i.e. from the second half of the eleventh century. Given the saga's uncertainty about this trio's ancestors, we might even push this date back a further generation. The significance of *Eyrbyggja saga*'s many supernatural occurrences and the text's complex structure have often been debated; they too *may* point to an early date. While we can be almost certain that *Eyrbyggja saga* was written by a member of the community at Helgafell we cannot be certain when they wrote it down.

1.3   Other Íslendingasögur *Representing Dalir*

Of the many other *Íslendingasögur* a few others have some references to Dalir which will be noted below. These are *Heiðarvíga saga, Gísla saga Súrsonar, Eiríks saga rauða, Króka-Refs saga, Þorskfirðinga saga* (also known as *Gull-Þóris saga*) and *Brennu-Njáls saga*. Brief background comments on the content of the first three texts are made here; for the last three brief comments are made as appropriate later in this chapter.

Heiðarvíga saga is usually regarded as one of the oldest *Íslendingasögur* even though most of what survives of it is an eighteenth century attempt to retell the saga after the manuscript had been damaged by fire.[86] The reason for attributing the saga an early date, somewhere around 1200, is generally because of its complicated plot.[87] The story itself focuses on a dispute between people from Húnaþing and Borgarfjörður but can be divided into two consecutive parts, almost equal in length. The first half really centres on the actions of Víga-Styrr Þorgrímsson (the brother of Vermundr *inn mjóvi* from Bjarnarhöfn) who also appears in *Eyrbyggja saga* and, in both sagas, lived at Hraun in Helgafellssveit. After Víga-Styrr is killed Snorri *goði* exacts revenge for his kinsman's death and another killing is made by the Borgfirðingar in return. For the purposes of this study it is simply worth noting that the saga gives a very important role to Víga-Styrr; otherwise the saga does not add much to our understanding of Dalir.

---

86   ÍF III: xcviii–cxv.
87   Jónas Kristjánsson 1988: 224–25. A widely critiqued attempt was made to date the saga later but this is no more or less convincing than any other arguments put forward for dating it (Bjarni Guðnason 1994).

Gísla saga Súrssonar, like *Heiðarvíga saga*, takes place largely in districts neighbouring Dalir (the western coast of the West Fjords and Breiðafjörður). This saga is often thought to have been written early in the thirteenth century because other texts are deemed to derive information from it, rather than the other way round, although the role of oral tradition in its genesis has been emphasised more recently by Tommy Danielsson.[88] The saga is one of the small sub-group of *Íslendingasögur* known as outlaws' sagas which are almost biographies of their main character.[89] *Gísla saga* recounts how Gísli murders his brother-in-law Þorgrímr (the father of Snorri *goði*) to avenge the killing of Vésteinn and then has to live as a fugitive around Breiðafjörður.[90] Snorri *goði*'s uncle, Börkr *inn digri*, tries without success to get adequate redress for his brother's killing until Eyjólfr *inn grái*, the son of Þórðr *gellir* from Hvammr, has Gísli killed. The saga is only of interest because it confirms the image of Börkr as less powerful than his nephew Snorri and gives this arguably heroic portrayal of Eyjólfr as a member of the Hvammverjar. Þorkell, Eyjólfr's son, is far more impressively portrayed in *Laxdæla saga*, as Guðrún Ósvífrsdóttir's fourth husband and as the occupant of Helgafell.

Eiríks saga rauða is a short saga which tells the story of Eiríkr *rauði* who, having been driven out of Dalir, settles in Greenland. The saga is one of those which looks most obviously like it is actually based on other written sources – simply because it has so many similarities with several texts, including *Eyrbyggja saga* – and it can be dated to after 1264 based on internal evidence, later than many of the *Íslendingasögur* for our two regions.[91] Of *Eiríks saga*'s 14 chapters, only the first two, in which Eiríkr arrives in Dalir and is forced out, are of any concern.[92]

1.4 Laxdæla Saga

Before we analyse this lengthy text it is worth providing a brief synopsis of it (and see especially Map 7). The saga begins with the story of the family of Ketill *flatnefr* coming from Norway due to the oppression of King Haraldr *inn*

---

[88] Jónas Kristjánsson 1988: 258; ÍF VI: xii–xli; Aðalgeirr Kristjánsson 1965; Danielsson 2008: 38; Lethbridge 2013.
[89] The others being *Grettis saga Ásmundarsonar* and *Harðar saga*.
[90] The saga survives in two different versions and only in the fuller one does it say that Þorgrímr had actually killed Vésteinn, Jónas Kristjánsson 1988: 260; *Eyrbyggja saga* also says that Þorgrímr killed Vésteinn (ÍF IV: 20).
[91] ÍF IV: lxvii–lxxxv; Jónas Kristjánsson 1988: 320–22.
[92] Comments on the dispute involving Eiríkr *rauði* form a part of the discussion on pp. 254–55 in connection with *Eyrbyggja saga*.

hárfagri. Across Chapters 5 to 7 are the saga's account of the *landnám* of Unnr *in djúpúðga* Ketilsdóttir, who settles at Hvammr, and her ship's crew to whom she gives part of her *landnám* in inner Dalir (Chs. 6–9). This includes a statement of the importance of the first settler in Laxárdalur, Dala-Kollr, member of Unnr's crew, as we saw in relation to Auðr in *djúpauðga* in chapter 4. When Unnr dies her grandson Óláfr *feilan* takes over at Hvammr.

Thereafter for most of the saga the action takes place in Laxárdalur or involves its inhabitants. Höskuldr Dala-Kollsson and his half-brother Hrútr Herjólfsson at first contest their inheritance but eventually come to terms with one another (Ch. 19). Höskuldr's sons are then the focus. One son, Óláfr *pái* (peacock), moves to Hjarðarholt and his line comes to the fore but not until he has argued with his half-brother, Þorleikr. To patch up the Höskuldssynir's disagreement, Óláfr fosters Þorleikr's son, Bolli. Bolli and his foster-brother Kjartan Óláfsson emerge as great friends and promising young men. Their relationship is eventually soured, however, when Bolli takes the opportunity of Kjartan's stay in Norway to marry the woman Kjartan loves, Guðrún Ósvífrsdóttir from Laugar in Hvammssveit (Ch. 43). Bolli is Guðrún's third husband.

Kjartan marries another woman, Hrefna, but tension arises between the two couples. The theft of precious objects from Kjartan and Hrefna's home at Hjarðarholt is attributed, with good reason, to Bolli and Guðrún's household. The dispute escalates from Kjartan humiliating the Laugamenn by trapping them indoors without access to a privy, into a dispute over the ownership of the farm of Sælingsdalstunga, to Kjartan's murder, to Bolli's murder in revenge, and in turn to the killing of one of Bolli's murderers. Eventually, after Bolli's death, Guðrún moves out of the district of Hvammssveit altogether because of the intensity of the dispute (Ch. 56). To do so she exchanges farms with Snorri *goði* Þorgrímsson, her father's sometime ally at Helgafell and who emerges as her friend and ally in exacting revenge on Kjartan's brothers. Guðrún and Snorri also manage to manipulate other inviduals into carrying out the killing of Helgi Harðbeinsson (whom they had chosen as their victim, after Helgi had taken part in Bolli's killing, rather than one of the Óláfssynir, Ch. 64). The saga's last chapters see the peaceful end to the dispute, and centre on Guðrún (now living at Helgafell) and her descendants, including Bolli Bollason. Bolli Bollason marries Snorri *goði*'s daughter while Guðrún marries her fourth and final husband, the *goði* Þorkell Eyjólfsson. Þorkell dies at sea fetching timber with which to build a church, but Guðrún lives on at Helgafell, supposedly becoming Iceland's first nun and anchoress (Ch. 78).

The most obvious way to start the analysis of this saga is by considering the major political players in it. If we take the focal events of *Laxdæla saga* and we disregard its genealogical postscript which was discussed above in relation to its authorship, the saga gives labels denoting the possession of political power to 14 men. These men fall into two groups according to their roles in the saga. The first group consists of people from outside the immediate area of the saga's major events, who are called *goðar*. Descriptions of this group seem to work in a slightly different way to those for the local figures. They derive their titles from what can be considered to have been a countrywide collective memory of stories which concentrated on a relatively small number of key men. Most of these actually take very little part in *Laxdæla saga*'s events, but are still labelled as *goðar*. Thus we have Ingjaldr *Sauðeyjagoði*, Halldórr *Garpsdalsgoði*, Hallsteinn *goði* and Þórðr *Freysgoði*.[93] Figures like Þorkell *trefill* Rauða-Bjarnarson, Gestr Oddleifsson and Rúnólfr Úlfsson who are referred to as *höfðingi mikill* (great leader), but play no part at all in local politics, might also have been thought of as *goðar*.[94]

The second category of political leader contains those men who were from mid-western Iceland and, most often, are referred to as *höfðingi mikill*. Óláfr *feilan*, Höskuldr Dala-Kollsson, Óláfr *pái* and Þorkell Eyjólfsson are all described this way.[95] Other local leaders are designated in different terms but analogous terms. Þórarinn from Langidalr on Skógarströnd is the only person in the saga to be described as a *goðorðsmaðr*, a term occasionally used in the *Sturlunga* compilation to refer to *goðar*.[96] Þorgils Hölluson from Hörðudalur, by implication, must have become a *goðorðsmaðr* because he is said to have taken the *goðorð* from Þórarinn and his son.[97] Gellir Þorkelsson, the son of Þorkell Eyjólfsson, is identified as acting as a local leader but is not put into any explicit kind of political category. Gellir took over his father's leadership role after his father's death.[98] Snorri *goði*, as well as being credited with authority through his name, is said to have passed on his *mannaforráð* to Bolli Bollason on his deathbed.[99] Bolli is thereby also identified as a *goði* although his role as *goði* is not played out in the saga.

To examine *Laxdæla saga*'s approach to politics around Dalir we also need to consider the images of other local men, some of whom take important roles in events but are no ascribed any position of authority. Þórðr *gellir*

---

93   ÍF v: 28–30, 32–37, 93, 95, 98–99, 101, 126.
94   ÍF v: 20, 87, 125.
95   ÍF v: 13, 18, 66, 223.
96   SS I: 40, 162; SS II: 15, 87.
97   ÍF v: 197.
98   ÍF v: 223.
99   ÍF v: 226.

Óláfsson,[100] Ósvífr Helgason,[101] Hrútr Herjólfsson,[102] Þorleikr Höskuldsson,[103] Bárðr Höskuldsson[104] and Halldórr Óláfsson[105] all take a significant part in the saga's events and yet are never acclaimed as *höfðingjar, goðar* or *goðorðsmenn*. These men are from families active in the saga's major events and also take part in those events themselves. Two other men, Steinþórr Óláfsson (Halldórr's brother)[106] and Steinþórr Þorláksson from Öndverðareyrr (an arbitrator between the sons of Þorleikr and Óláfr *pái* and an important figure in *Eyrbyggja saga*),[107] are much less involved in the saga than those listed above but have a similar background. Indeed, two of the saga's major characters, Kjartan Óláfsson and Bolli Þorleiksson, also fall into this category because their formal political roles are hard to decipher. Bolli's single significant 'political' action, the buying of Sælingsdalstunga, is discussed below. The remainder of the local men named in the saga were most likely thought of as less influential *bændr* although they all come from farms of middling to high value, based on later sources. These include several men of some importance to the saga's narrative.[108]

Eight places were said to have been bases for *höfðingjar* in this area at one time or another. Superficially this is a large number of farms but these eight farms were not remembered as having been controlled by *höfðingjar* simultaneously. Instead, the saga effectively gives us an approximate, relative chronology indicating successive phases in which the farms were occupied by powerful men. Going through the saga, the first *höfðingi* mentioned is Óláfr *feilan* of Hvammr. His son Þórðr *gellir* is involved in politics (but never in this text called *höfðingi*) and then the farm of Hvammr disappears from the action.[109] Höskuldsstaðir is also mentioned early on in the saga, controlled by

---

100 ÍF V: 13, 21, 37–38, 47, 113.
101 ÍF V: 85–86, 91, 93, 95–98, 100–1, 111–12, 128–29, 134–35, 139–41, 145–46, 148, 150–59, 163, 169–70, 174, 176, 196.
102 ÍF V: 15–16, 44–9, 52, 70–71, 103–8, 110–11.
103 ÍF V: 18, 49, 70–73, 75, 101–8, 110–11, 129.
104 ÍF V: 18, 49, 51, 61, 70–73.
105 ÍF V: 75–76, 129, 156, 158–69, 209–11, 18–21.
106 ÍF V: 75, 129, 158, 161, 164, 168, 211.
107 ÍF V: 6, 210–11.
108 Þórðr *goddi* from Goddastaðir, Þórarinn Þórisson, Þórðr Ingunnarson, Þorsteinn Kuggason, Lambi Þorbjarnarson and Ármóðr from Þykkvaskógr and his sons Örnólfr and Halldórr.
109 *Grettis saga Ásmundarsonar* retains an image of Hvammr being powerful in a subsequent generation: Skeggi, the son of Þórarinn *fylsenni* and therefore grandson of Þórðr *gellir*, lived at Hvammr and took part in a court case together with his kinsman Þorsteinn Kuggason from Ljárskógar (ÍF VII: 90–91). It is difficult to know how to reconcile this account – from an undoubtedly late *Íslendingasaga* – with that of *Laxdæla saga*.

Höskuldr, but it is not seen as the main farm of his sons. Hjarðarholt's role as a prominent farm is similarly tied to one *höfðingi*, Óláfr *pái*. The farm is later the base of Halldórr Óláfsson until the end of the saga but, while he is involved in the dispute with the descendants of Bolli Þorleiksson, he is never called a *höfðingi*. Not long after Hjarðarholt is first mentioned, Garpsdalur is named as the home of Halldórr *Garpsdalsgoði* but this is Garpsdalur's only mention. Snorri *goði* and his farm of Helgafell are prominent from Chapter 36 of the saga until its end. Before then Helgafell is not seen as being prominent. Sælingsdalstunga in Hvammssveit is first seen as a useful political base by Kjartan Óláfsson to counter the power of the people of nearby Laugar, Ósvífr and his sons. Kjartan's death means that it falls into the hands of the people from Laugar and is then taken over by Snorri *goði* when he swaps farms with Guðrún who moves to Helgafell. Helgafell remains pre-eminent under the control of Guðrún's husband, the *höfðingi* Þorkell Eyjólfsson. Lastly Langidalr on Skógarströnd is seen as the base of the *goðorðsmaðr* Þórarinn before it is snatched away from him by Þorgils Hölluson from Hörðadalstunga.[110] Þorgils' authority is yet more fleetingly held because he is killed by agents of Snorri *goði*.[111]

What does such information about these leading men and farms tell us? If we look at where and when there were local leaders we can see that there is a discernible pattern as to who was powerful where at a given time. In the saga's first 'post-*landnám*' era there are just two people called *höfðingi*, based at Hvammr and Höskuldsstaðir respectively. In Hvammssveit, Laugar appears as the most prominent farm after Hvammr disappears from the narrative. In Laxárdalur, after Höskuldr's death, it is Óláfr *pái*, his illegitimate son, who is the valley's leading man. Óláfr lives at Hjarðarholt while his half-brothers (neither of whom is called *höfðingi*) continue to live on the south side of the valley. Returning to Hvammssveit, Sælingsdalstunga becomes the base of the leading farmer in the district when the Laugarmenn move there and Snorri *goði* lives there afterwards.

With regard to the other farms of *höfðingjar*, or the *goðorðsmaðr* Þórarinn, there is nothing in the saga's chronology to suggest that they might not have been powerful when they are said to have been. Þórarinn of Langidalr's impotence as a *goði* makes sense within the saga's general depiction of power relations.[112] He (and Skógarströnd where he lives) does not have any part to play in

---

110   ÍF V: 197–98.
111   ÍF V: 199–200.
112   Cf. Helgi Skúli Kjartansson 1989: 43–44.

the saga other than when Þorgils Hölluson displaces him. Þorgils' seizure of power suggests that he was trying to have influence over quite a large area – the area from Hörðudalur to Langidalur had tens of farms – at a time when Snorri *goði* had given up his influence on the southern side of Hvammsfjörður. This can be interpreted as Þorgils trying to take control of Skógarströnd in the absence of a neighbouring political opponent. Arguably Þorgils could not have acted in this way when Snorri lived at Helgafell. Most importantly, then, *Laxdæla saga* imagines there to have been no more than two or three *höfðingjar* who were active around the eastern end of Hvammsfjörður at any given time in the tenth and early eleventh century.

What the roles of these leaders actually encompassed can be considered further by examining their relationship with particular districts and/or farms. It is probably easiest to look first at the two districts for which the saga gives most information on individual farms and their owners. These districts, Laxárdalur and Hvammssveit, are the focus of the major disputes described. For some farms we can trace changes in ownership or the control of farms but the saga's limited view means that only for Laxárdalur can we suggest that a local leader possessed or controlled more than one farm.[113] Elsewhere around Hvammsfjörður information about ownership *per se* is not given, especially for lesser farms, as is the case in most *Íslendingasögur*. We can instead look at lesser farms' relations with more powerful ones to suggest who controlled or influenced them.

Ten farms from Laxárdalur are mentioned, more than for any other district.[114] The text presents a clear pattern in who owned or controlled which farms within Laxárdalur and the coastal trip where it meets Hvammsfjörður suggesting a territorial division between two leaders. On the north side of the river, the farm of Hjarðarholt controls the farms of Goddastaðir, Lambastaðir and Hrappsstaðir when we last hear of each of them. As a result of Þórðr *goddi*'s need for Höskuldr Dala-Kollsson's support in his divorce case Höskuldr acquires ownership of Goddastaðir.[115] Þórðr *goddi*'s fostering of Höskuldr's son

---

113   This is not evidence that *höfðingjar* could not own one or more farms, something which has often been used to show the relative poverty of *höfðingjar* before the later twelfth century. See, for example, Jón Viðar Sigurðsson 1999: 101–19.

114   Ljárskógar, Hrappsstaðir, Hjarðarholt, Goddastaðir, Lambastaðir, Dönustaðir, Leiðólfsstaðir, Höskuldsstaðir, Hrútsstaðir and Kambsnes. Those not mentioned include Vígholtsstaðir and Spágilsstaðir, two farms or *hjáleigur* belonging to the church at Hjarðarholt in the fourteenth century (DI III: 101).

115   ÍF V: 37; Byock 1988: 170–73.

Óláfr *pái* can, in this light, probably be seen as an imposition by his stronger neighbour. Óláfr *pái* is later seen running Goddastaðir, suggesting that the saga is explaining the loss of Goddastaðir's independence and how it came to belong to Hjarðarholt.[116] Óláfr *pái* is responsible for establishing Hjarðarholt on the deserted land of Hrappsstaðir (which he buys outright) and his son Halldórr later takes over the estate.

Lambastaðir may or may not have been seen by the saga as dependent in some way on Höskuldsstaðir. The farm is only mentioned by name once, when Höskuldr Dala-Kollsson arranges for Óláfr *pái*'s wedding to be held there.[117] This would seem to imply that Höskuldr, as head of Höskuldsstaðir, has some kind of control over it. Later in the saga Lambastaðir's status is more ambiguous but is probably viewed as an independent farm under Lambi Þorbjarnarson's control; Lambi lived 'at the next farm up from' Þórðr *goddi*, i.e. Lambastaðir.[118] Lambi's kinship with Óláfr *pái* is an important element later in the saga, which makes the farm's status in relation to Hjarðarholt and Höskuldsstaðir more ambiguous.[119]

South of the river Laxá, Dönustaðir is also certainly linked to Hjarðarholt. Steinþórr, the son of Óláfr *pái*, lived there when his brother Halldórr controlled Hjarðarholt.[120] Otherwise the area immediately to the south of Laxá appears to be under the influence of the legitimate sons of Höskuldr Dala-Kollsson. Þorleikr Höskuldsson, for instance, seems to own Leiðólfsstaðir.[121] Þorleikr's own abode is not entirely clear for much of the saga, but he is the last person said to have lived at Kambsnes. However, Þorleikr leaves Iceland for good and when he does so he sells his farms (*selr nú jarðir sínar*) but to whom it is not said.[122] His brother Bárðr, meanwhile, seemingly took over Höskuldsstaðir itself.[123] Therefore these brothers appear to control three adjacent farms on the southern bank of the lower half of the valley. Otherwise *Laxdæla saga* is vaguer about landownership on the southern side of Laxárdalur.

Although Kambsnes has already been seen as controlled by Þorleikr Höskuldsson, *Laxdæla saga* first mentions this farm as the base of Hrútr

---

116 Cf. Byock 1988: 173.
117 ÍF V: 51.
118 ÍF V: 21. Lambastaðir was still the next farm up the valley from Goddastaðir when *Jarðabók* was compiled (*Jarðabók* VI: 75–76).
119 See below p. 241.
120 ÍF V: 161.
121 ÍF V: 101.
122 ÍF V: 111.
123 ÍF V: 73.

Herjólfsson when he arrives in Iceland. The text never tries to reconcile the fact that both Hrútr and Þorleikr are said to have controlled Kambsnes, until a dispute is resolved whereby Þorleikr takes it over. Hrútr is said to have established himself at Kambsnes when he first arrived in Iceland but Þorleikr is said to have lived there after him.[124] The uncle and nephew fall out when Hrútr settles a tenant on land which Þorleikr deems to be his.[125] The saga simply relates that Þorleikr had this man killed and Hrútr realised that he had made a mistake over the boundary. Cementing the obvious connection between Höskuldsstaðir and Kambsnes, Þorleikr is said to have built a (new) farm there, close to the boundary of Höskuldsstaðir and Hrútsstaðir.

After Laxárdalur the only other district to be the focus of any detailed information about land is Hvammssveit. While Hvammr has a role in the *landnám* narrative for the region it is Laugar and Sælingsdalstunga that are the centre of the action; but little attention is paid to any of the other 20 or so farms we see there in *Sturlunga saga* and in later centuries.[126] Laugar is occupied by Ósvífr Helgason and his family for much of the saga and we need not doubt that the saga views them as owners of the farm. Ósvífr remains at the farm until his daughter Guðrún exchanges her home at Sælingsdalstunga for Helgafell.[127] He moves to Helgafell with Guðrún while the control of Laugar is left unexplained. Ósvífr's sons had already been outlawed by this stage of the saga and so it seems Laugar is left unoccupied or at least its role as a base of political power has ended in the view of the saga. The saga can believe that Laugar was once powerful, but that it lost that power.

Sælingsdalstunga undergoes almost the opposite transformation to Laugar. It is first mentioned as being occupied by Þórarinn, the son of Þórir *sælingr*.[128] That Þórarinn owned Sælingsdalstunga is made clear later in the saga by his being able to sell it first to Bolli Þorleiksson and then to Kjartan Óláfsson.[129] Kjartan enjoys brief possession of the farm before he is killed. His father Óláfr *pái* then offers the farm to his foster-son Bolli who lives there with Guðrún until his own untimely end.[130] This is when Guðrún swaps the farm with that of Helgafell so that Snorri *goði* and she can both escape the political pressures

---

124 ÍF v: 45, 49, 71.
125 ÍF v: 71.
126 E.g. *Jarðabók* vi: 62–81.
127 ÍF v: 170.
128 ÍF v: 86.
129 ÍF v: 146–47.
130 ÍF v: 159.

of their respective districts.[131] Snorri owns the farm until he dies. On his deathbed Snorri tells Bolli Bollason that he wishes him to take over the farm.[132] Thus at the end of the saga it is Bolli Bollason who owns Sælingsdalstunga: a descendant of Ósvífr from Laugar on his mother's side and a descendant of Höskuldr Dala-Kollsson from Höskuldsstaðir on his father's side. This seems to credit Sælingsdalstunga with connections to two locally-famous sets of people, but ultimately gives possession to someone from Laxárdalur.

Laxdæla saga's representation of Miðdalir, particularly of Sauðafell, a major farm as far as *Sturlunga saga* is concerned, is particularly noteworthy because of the way it marginalises Sauðafell and gives Hörðudalur a grander role. Sauðafell is home to a Þórólfr *rauðnefr* but it is hardly mentioned in *Laxdæla*, despite its appearance as part of the *landnám* narrative in this text as well as *S*.[133] Unnr *in djúpúðga* gives *Sauðafellslönd* to her freedman Erpr but Erpr and Þórólfr *rauðnefr* are not connected genealogically. This would seem to undermine Þórólfr and conforms to the negative view the text gives of him.[134] Indeed *Laxdæla saga* does not even give Þórólfr a patronymic. Hörðudalur features more noticeably than does Sauðafell but here too the colonisation narrative does not connect with later events. Hörðudalur is said to have been given by Unnr *in djúpúðga* to Hörðr but while Hörðr's descendants are traced to the Gilsbekkingar, as in *S*, there is no implication in the saga that this kin group still had control over Hörðabólstaðr in subsequent generations.[135] When a second narrative concerns Hörðudalur the key farm, Hörðadalstunga, is occupied by Þorgils Hölluson, a contemporary of Snorri *goði* who himself becomes a *goði*.[136] Þorgils supposedly forcibly takes the *goðorð* of Þórarinn of Langidalr but Þórarinn seeks out the help of Snorri and Snorri gives Þórarinn's son an axe, which has inevitable consequences.[137] The rather negative portrayal of both Þórólfr and Þorgils could explain why they are not attached to the genealogy of Unnr but equally significant is that the area is not seen to have anyone important living there.[138] By contrast, Þórarinn of Langidalr (one of the small

---

131   ÍF v: 169–70.
132   ÍF v: 226.
133   ÍF v: 10.
134   See above pp. 173, 202 for Erpr's association with Erpsstaðir, the farm adjacent to Sauðafell.
135   *Laxdæla saga* goes a step further than *S* in identifying the Gilsbekkingar where *S* only names the kinship of Hörðr's descendants with Illugi *inn svarti* (ÍF v: 10; S99).
136   ÍF v: 197.
137   ÍF v: 197–99.
138   *Laxdæla saga* refers to a saga of Þorgils which, had it survived might have explained things a bit better.

valleys at the eastern end of Skógarströnd) seems positively portrayed. At a push this could be connected to his geographical proximity to Helgafell. Snorri encourages the killing of Þorgil Hölluson although this is after Snorri moved to Sælingsdalstunga. The text assumes a figure of authority to have lived at the eastern end of Skógarströnd but does not give a sense of the basis of his power.[139]

Helgafell itself and Öndverðareyrr (Eyrr) are the other farms on northern Snæfellsnes whose sometime occupants are mentioned. There is a single reference to Öndverðareyrr when Steinþórr from Eyrr is chosen as an arbitrator between the Óláfssynir and Bollasynir, which, if nothing else, confirms the idea that the farm had influential occupants.[140] Helgafell comes into the narrative relatively late, as the home of Snorri *goði*, but what this tells us is intriguing given that this farm had become a monastery by the late twelfth century. In *Laxdæla saga*, Snorri *goði* lived at Helgafell but freely exchanged it with his friend Guðrún Ósvifrsdóttir in return for Sælingsdalstunga in Hvammssveit. Before this, Snorri is identified as the friend of Guðrún's father Ósvifr at Laugar. Once Guðrún is at Helgafell she marries Þorkell Eyjólfsson, something which the text shows transfers control of the property to his heirs (as Guðrún and Þorkell have no recorded children) so that Gellir Þorkelsson takes over his father's role as local politician as well as the running of the farm.[141] The subsequent position of the farm is not made clear but a genealogical line is traced from Gellir down to Ari *inn sterki* (d.1188) which at the very least confirms that the text regards Helgafell as significant.[142] Snorri, as elsewhere, is seen to keep himself out of trouble and only to support winnable legal battles; while at Helgafell he ignores Ósvifr's request for help after it is Ósvifr's household that has

---

139   In this respect, though, it may be significant that it is choosing to favour 'Langidalr' over Narfeyri as Þórarinn's base.
140   ÍF V: 210–11.
141   ÍF V: 223.
142   SS I: 229. It is tempting to think that the saga is implying that this line of men all owned Helgafell. Ari is said to have controlled half of *Þórsnesingagoðorð* although there is no explicit connection between him and Helgafell in the *samtíðarsögur*. The only information we have about Ari *inn sterki*'s estates suggests that he owned Staðarstaður. But while there is no direct evidence to suggest that Ari owned Helgafell, a charter which seemingly describes the arrangements for the establishment of the monastery at Helgafell could well have been written for him. The document is anonymous but on other grounds it has been argued that it dates from 1184x88 which fits perfectly with the date at which Ari left Iceland to go on pilgrimage. Ari may therefore have been sufficiently pious to have donated Helgafell for monastic use (SS I: 231; DI I: 281); for commentary on the document see Orri Vésteinsson 2000: 102.

had Kjartan killed. Otherwise we do not see any particular signs of Snorri's power beyond his role as a go-to figure when someone needs advice or legal help.

Turning to the northern side of Dalir itself, *Laxdœla saga* mentions just two farms but these are significant for their relationships with Hjarðarholt. Bessatunga, a relatively run-of-the-mill farm, is identified as home of Bersi, a kinsman of Óláfr *pái* who fosters Óláfr's son Halldórr.[143] Most likely the association of Bersi with this farm just derives from folk etymology and the relationship is merely a conventional fostering one which recognises Hjarðarholt's superiority to an average farm.[144] More significant is the fact that 'Hóll' is home to two brothers, Þorkell *hvelpr* and Knútr, then joined by Þórðr Ingunnarson, second of Guðrún Ósvífrsdóttir's four husbands, whose good management made the farm wealthy.[145] This farm is most likely Staðarhóll but could be Saurhóll, a part of the estate of Staðarhóll in the mid-thirteenth century.[146] On balance, perhaps, when *Laxdœla saga* says that it was the arrival of Þórðr Ingunnaron which made 'Hóll' wealthy it is crediting him with the political rise of Staðarhóll but, as with the farms in Miðdalir and Hörðudalur, it does not make an explicit connection to people in the twelfth or thirteenth century.[147] The fact that the relationship between Þórðr Ingunnarson and Guðrún failed is underpinned by an antipathy between the major farms in Saurbær and those in Hvammssveit. Certainly this antipathy is similar to that which is visible in the later twelfth century, as we saw in Chapter 3.

Before summing all of this up further, a few words need to be said about the way individuals' status is amplified or diminished by the status of their spouses. Marriage alliances, as with other kinds of social tie, can be seen as operating at two levels in *Laxdœla saga*: a local one and a regional one. At the local level there are leading men of particular valleys who dispute with each other; at the

---

143 On fostering see, for example, Miller 1990: 122–24. The places involved in the fostering (naming the home of the foster-child first, followed by their foster-home) are: Kambsnes and Hjarðarholt; Laugar and Helgafell; Hjarðarholt and Ljárskógar; Helgafell and Sælingsdalstunga; and Sælingsdalstunga and Helgafell. These ties nuance the political picture created by the pattern of marriage alliances and disputes in all *Íslendingasögur*.
144 A character called Hólmgöngu-Bersi also appears in H in connection with the settlement of Hrútafjörður. The chapter connects this Hólmgöngu-Bersi with Lundarreykjadalur in southern Borgarfjörður (ÍF I: 89). The two characters of the same name clearly had no connection.
145 ÍF V: 87.
146 SS I: 448.
147 See pp. 85–98 for Staðarhóll's twelfth-century influence.

regional level there seems to be a series of political marriages between families from different regions.

Höskuldr Dala-Kollsson is the first person from Laxárdalur to marry outside the Hvammsfjörður area. He marries Jórunn Bjarnardóttir who is said to have come from further north, from Bjarnarfjörður, just north of Steingrímsfjörður.[148] Höskuldr arranges for Óláfr *pái* to marry the daughter of Egill Skallagrímsson of Borg in Borgarfjörður, an alliance sought because with the 'best' family in Borgarfjörður.[149] That the marriage goes ahead supposes that Egill Skallagrímsson – who was well-known as a tough dealer and the subject of *Egils saga* – thought Óláfr *pái* an equally good match. In the next generation Kjartan Óláfsson and Þuríðr Óláfsdóttir also marry outside Breiðafjörður, marrying the daughter and son of Ásgeirr Auðunarson from Ásbjarnarnes in Víðidalur.[150] Again, this seems like a tie between people who were important in their respective regions.

The other category of marriages between Dalir people and outsiders are those marriages only mentioned in introductions to characters who play some part in the saga action. The marriage of Þórðr *gellir* of Hvammr, so key in many genealogies, is worth mentioning in this context: *Laxdæla saga* says he married the daughter of Miðfjarðar-Skeggi, the *landnámsmaðr* who settled Miðfjörður, just west of Dalir in the Northern Quarter (Map 1).[151] Þórðr, like the Laxdælir, is being given regional-level significance here. Two connections are also made with Gestr Oddleifsson, the *höfðingi* from Hagi (on Barðaströnd, on the southern coast of the West Fjords). Gestr's sister is said to have married Ármóðr from Þykkvaskógr, a few kilometres south of Laxárdalur,[152] while Gestr's daughter, Halla, is later identified as the mother of Þorgils Hölluson, which explains his matronymic.

The marriage alliances listed above can be said to reflect the saga's ideas about the status of local families. In all of these cases the regions from which the 'outside' partner came were relatively close to Dalir, although without being what could be considered bordering regions or valleys. Borg or the north coast of Borgarfjörður, is separated from Miðdalir/Laxárdalur by the whole of the Mýrar region; Miðfjörður and Víðidalur are separated from Dalir by Hrútafjörður (Map 1); Barðaströnd was separated from Saurbær and

---

148   ÍF V: 16.
149   ÍF V: 62.
150   ÍF V: 83, 136.
151   ÍF V: 13; for Miðfjarðar-Skeggi's *landnám* see ÍF I: 212, 213.
152   ÍF V: 87.

Skarðsströnd by sea and, by land, by several smaller inhabited fjords. Imagining alliances such as these for their ancestors probably reflected local leaders' own interests in keeping their immediate neighbours in check and a willingness to see themselves as distinct from their nearest counterparts.

Marriages within Dalir recorded in *Laxdæla saga* will be dealt with in two groups: first by looking at marriages between two powerful families and then by taking marriages involving at least one 'weaker' party i.e. people not credited with high status by the saga.

Guðrún Ósvifrsdóttir is the most remarkable figure mentioned in the saga in connection with marriage. She is important not only for being credited with four marriages but also for the political significance of these marriages in the western Icelandic political world depicted by *Laxdæla saga*. Hers are not just connections with random individuals but with men of some regional or local standing. Guðrún's first two marriages give us similar perspectives on farms and the affinities between them. Her first marriage to Þorvaldr, the son of Halldórr *Garpsdalsgoði*, is prefaced by Ósvífr's comment that the two were not of equal standing.[153] Þorvaldr lived at Garpsdalr and seems to have been a *goði* himself. That the marriage soon ended in divorce may indicate a presupposition on the part of the text that a political relationship between Laugar and Garpsdalr was bound to end in disaster, because political circumstances when the text was written made it inconceivable that such a relationship could work. Guðrún's second marriage was to Þórðr Ingunnarson. Þórðr had been married to a woman from 'Hóll' in Saurbær but his other connections indicate that he was associated with Króksfjörður, just a few kilometres from Garpsdalr.[154] Þórðr is portrayed as having important qualities for obtaining power and wealth: he improved the state of the farm at Hóll and was skilled at law. Ultimately, however, he too was unlucky. His death through the sorcery of Kotkell and family, however, means that the link between the West Fjords and Laugar never gets played out. There is a common thread here, in that the marriages between Laugar and the Króksfjörður or Gilsfjörður area were both short-lived and unsuccessful. This image suggests that it made sense to people from Dalir, but especially to people from Laxárdalur, that connections with Saurbær might end in disaster.

---

153   ÍF V: 93: 'but Ósvífr said that they might find Guðrún and he were not equals' ('en þó sagði Ósvífr, at þau myndi á kostum finna, at þau Guðrún váru eigi jafnmenni').
154   ÍF V: 87, note 1 for his father's background. His mother lived at Ingunnarstaðir in Króksfjörður (ÍF V: 94).

The third of Guðrún's marriages, to Bolli Þorleiksson, connects Laugar with Höskuldsstaðir and Hjarðarholt, both in Laxárdalur. Bolli's family controlled Höskuldsstaðir but he had been fostered at Hjarðarholt. Because of this, Laugar is in effect forming an alliance with both sides, the northern and southern sides, of Laxárdalur. The kind of 'double' loyalties which a spouse like Bolli brought to a marriage – as a *höfðingi*'s son fostered by another *höfðingi* – could have made Bolli an attractive ally. This may help to explain Ósvífr's insistence that his daughter should marry Bolli and ignore her prior attachment to Kjartan. Clearly, however, the dispute which arises between Bolli and Kjartan over Guðrún points to the inherent unsuitability of the marriage. A geopolitical metaphor could be read into this set of relationships too: it was inappropriate for a fosterling of Hjarðarholt to marry the intended marriage partner of his foster-brother. It makes sense in the light of late-twelfth or thirteenth-century (or earlier) patterns around Laxárdalur for such a relationship to be remembered as causing strife.[155] Höskuldsstaðir, Bolli's original home, was not as powerful as Hjarðarholt and so he could have been seen as upsetting the normal political order by ignoring Kjartan's prior claim to Guðrún.

Guðrún Ósvífrsdóttir's fourth marriage was to Þorkell Eyjólfsson. Þorkell, although a *goði*, is said to have been a merchant before the marriage and does not seem to be associated with any particular farm until he moves to Helgafell to live with Guðrún. This marriage therefore cannot be seen to create any new geopolitical tie but it does maintain the idea that Helgafell was run by a *goði*. The marriage of Þórdís and Bolli Bollason, however, strengthened the connection between Snorri *goði* and Guðrún, at Sælingsdalstunga and Helgafell respectively. Again, late in the saga, this is an amplification of an existing connection, that between the leading *höfðingi* in Hvammssveit and the farm of Helgafell.

Laxdæla saga also includes marriages of people lower down the social scale which are not worth setting out in detail but amplify the sense of the all-pervasive genealogical charter in the saga. Thus the Þórðr *goddi* of Goddastaðir had a failed marriage to a woman called Vigdís who was related to people from Hvammr and Sauðafell but not to anyone in Laxárdalur.[156] Another Vigdís, the wife of the troublesome Hrappr of Hrappsstaðir, has a possible Þórsnes connection but the genealogy which is accorded her in *S* seems to have been

---

155 See p. 99 for the young Sturlusynir clashing with Höskuldsstaðir.
156 Vigdís Ingjaldsdóttir, who is identified as 'the daughter of Ingjaldr; she was the daughter of the brother (*bróðurdóttir*) of Þórðr *gellir*, and the daughter of the sister of Þórólfr *rauðnefr* from Sauðafell' (ÍF v: 21).

manipulated to be more fitting for her role as the wife of someone anti-social.[157] It is also significant that the women are from relatively close by which sets the limit on the kind of range within which their husbands might marry. This differs from the way, as we have seen, the saga sees Ármóðr and his sons from Þykkvaskógr, and Þorgils Hölluson from Hörðadalstunga, as bolstered by a tie with a figure of higher standing from outside in Gestr Oddleifsson.

Laxdæla saga also shapes political relations between Hjarðarholt and other Laxárdalur farms through marriages via the union of Höskuldr Dala-Kollsson and the Irish slave Melkorka. The couple were not married but Melkorka was the mother of Óláfr *pái*; after Höskuldr's marriage, mother and son are shunted out of Höskuldsstaðir to live south of Laxá at Melkorkustaðir. Melkorka then marries and has a second son, Lambi Þorbjarnarson, by her new husband.[158] Lambi is assumed to have lived at Lambastaðir and, furthermore, supported the Óláfssynir to gain revenge for Kjartan's death.[159] Lambi's familial connection to Óláfr explains why in the saga he acts in support of Óláfr's family; his lower status is suggested by his smaller farm, and perhaps by his father's nickname (*skrjúpr*, weak).

Three further elements of the saga show its perspective in different ways. The major conflict in *Laxdæla saga* is that between Bolli and Kjartan and then their sons. This can be read as essentially a dispute between Hjarðarholt, symbolised by Kjartan and his brothers, and a series of other places: Höskuldsstaðir, where Bolli's father lived; Laugar and Sælingsdalstunga, homes to the Ósvífssons and Bolli and Guðrún; and Helgafell to which Guðrún moved and where her sons lived when they avenged their father's death. The dispute cannot be decided in favour of one side or the other, which perhaps reflects the genealogical significance of many of the characters recorded in it for a Dalir audience.

Just within Laxárdalur, disputes help define patterns of local allegiance and control. Hrútr Herjólfsson, at Hrútsstaðir, unlike in *Njáls saga*,[160] is said to have

---

157 Vigdís' only connection is a brother, Þorsteinn *surtr*, who lived at Þórsnes and fostered Vigdís' son. Comparing this account with S, it would seem that she might have been remembered as the daughter of the *landnámsmaðr* Hallsteinn Þorskfjarðargoði, father of Þorsteinn *surtr* and son of Þórólfr *Mostrarskegg*, who settled part of Króksfjörður. *Laxdæla saga* retains the names in her genealogy but no more (ÍF V: 19; ÍF I: 163–65).

158 The origins of Lambi's father, Þorbjörn *skrjúpr*, are not clear. Unlike most of the earliest recorded settlers at farms in Laxárdalur, he is not associated with a farm whose name derives from his. If it is assumed that this might have been the case then perhaps he was once associated with Þorbergsstaðir or Þorsteinsstaðir (see Map 7).

159 ÍF V: 164.

160 See below, p. 261.

been in dispute with his half-brother Höskuldr Dala-Kollsson of Höskuldsstaðir. Hrútr wins his claim to inherit half his mother's possessions, takes full possession of Hrútsstaðir, and the brothers are reconciled. A further dispute arises between Hrútr and Höskuldr's son Þorleikr over the boundary of the same two farms.[161] The second dispute, resolved in Þorleikr's favour, serves to explain Höskuldsstaðir's possession of Kambsnes, a dependent farm.

There is a final element of *Laxdæla saga* which requires comment before we attempt to summarise the text's view of local politics: the collapse of the relationship between Óláfr *pái* (Hjarðarholt) and Ósvífr (Laugar) symbolised by the cessation of their holding of feasts to which they invited one another. As leading men in their respective, neighbouring districts we could read the collapse in their relations as symptomatic of the scale of politics at which they are operating; as leading men in their respective districts they were effectively rivals. After the marriage of Bolli to Guðrún, which had the potential to cause conflict, it is Kjartan Óláfsson's attempt to buy Sælingsdalstunga, the farm adjacent to Laugar, which demonstrates real hostility because Sælingsdalstunga was next to Laugar. Equally, within Laxárdalur, Bolli and Guðrún's marriage linked Laugar to Höskuldsstaðir, the other significant farm in the valley.

To sum up, then, one reading of the wider political patterns, therefore, might be as follows. No one farm remains dominant throughout the early history of the region. In Laxárdalur Hjarðarholt supplants Höskuldsstaðir as a centre of power; in Hvammssveit, Hvammr's dominance is replaced by (or at least not as well remembered as) that of Laugar and Sælingsdalstunga. Of these farms, Laugar opposes Hjarðarholt and the contest over Sælingsdalstunga is so great that a powerful third party ends up moving there. *Laxdæla saga* does not, conversely, see the area to Laxárdalur's immediate south as a focal part of the area's past. It sees Sauðafell in quite neutral terms, but Hörðudalur (and Hundadalur) as weaker and liable to influence, not only by Hjarðarholt but from Sælingsdalstunga and Helgafell too. The people of the district of Miðdalir are not part of the genealogy of Unnr *in djúpúðga* which connects the other areas discussed. This implies that they were not remembered as being part of the same wider political community. At the end of the saga Helgafell seems to have lost some of its secular political significance, with Snorri's moving away, but gained a religious significance as the home of Guðrún who is said, in the saga's last chapter, to become a nun after building a church. Last but not least, it is worth reminding ourselves of the scale and quantity of influence of Hjarðarholt

---

161 See above p. 233 for Kambsnes.

and its occupants, as the large farm with the most clearly expressed set of relationships. Óláfr, the *höfðingi mikill* at Hjarðarholt, had a strong influence over several farms within Laxárdalur itself and social ties to other leaders across Dalir as well as marriage connections which extended to Borgarfjörður and Húnavatnssýsla.

The most striking difference between *Laxdœla saga*'s portrayal of Hvammssveit, Laxárdalur and Miðdalir with that of *Sturlunga saga* is the former's emphasis on the power of Hjarðarholt. At the same time the text's recognition of the same basic genealogy of Ketill *flatnefr*'s descendants, and, crucially, of Dala-Kollr's position within it, as in *S*, shows that the status of Laxárdalur is not really being seen as any higher than it is in *S*. If we look at how *Laxdœla saga* views particular districs in Dalir then it is immediately clear that it has no interest at all in Staðarfell or Fellsströnd, the home of the father of Hvamm-Sturla, Þórðr Gilsson, or even in Skarðsströnd, the home of the Skarðverjar who played a significant part in the transmission of *Sturlunga saga*.[162] This could be read as accidental, or as part of the lack of any real need to mention these districts due to the particular needs of the story, but more likely it shows that the creators of the text did not see these districts as being home to an important local leader. By contrast, Miðdalir is at least mentioned, perhaps because it was nearer to Laxárdalur, but more likely because it was seen as a likely home for a local leader. The fact that Sauðafell's power is so obviously ignored would probably make more sense as a product of the saga having been written at a time when Sauðafell *could* be ignored, i.e. that it was written before the thirteenth century when Sauðafell was home to a really significant local leader. More will be said about this later in this chapter.

1.5   *Eyrbyggja Saga*

Sufficient has already been said above about the structure and content of *Eyrbyggja saga* for us to go straight into a more detailed consideration of the text's depiction of politics.

The vocabulary used by *Eyrbyggja saga* to depict powerful men is noticeably different from that used in *Laxdœla saga*. Even though *Laxdœla saga* is reticent about directly identifying *goðar* or *höfðingjar*, except in epithets, *Eyrbyggja saga* is even less explicit when talking about authority.

Using the three categories outlined above for *Laxdœla saga*'s leading men, we can, however, still identify people who fit into each of them. Although

---

162   See Appendix on pp. 319–26.

Eyrbyggja saga makes very few references to politics outside of the local disputes it records, two men, Helgi *Hofgarðargoði* and Þorsteinn from Hafsfjarðarey, fit into the group of outsiders with the title of *goði*. These are, however, the kinds of vaguely defined figures whom it is hard to take seriously as fully worked out leaders in the minds of the saga's author.[163]

More local men are identified as leaders, but the words *goði* and *höfðingi* are used of hardly anyone at all. Þórðr *gellir* and Snorri *goði* are the only people referred to as *höfðingi*: Þórðr as *mestr höfðingi í Breiðafirði* (the greatest leader in Breiðafjörður)[164] and Snorri as both *höfðingi mikill* (great leader)[165] and *héraðshöfðingi* (district leader).[166] Aside from Snorri, only Arnkell Þórólfsson is explicitly called *goði*. Þorgrímr Kjallaksson is said, in effect, to have been given the role of a *goði* following the dispute between the Þórsnesingar and Kjalleklingar: he had to pay half the maintenance of the *hof* (*halda uppi hofinu at helmingi*), received a half-share of the *hof* tax (*hoftollr*) and half the *þingmenn* which formerly had belonged only to Þorsteinn *þorskabítr* (who was therefore another *goði*).[167]

The status of the leading householders at Öndverðareyrr (Eyrr), the home of the Eyrbyggjar, also requires brief comment, because the farm is of key political significance in most of *Eyrbyggja saga*'s action and figures prominently in thirteenth-century events. The leading figures from Öndverðareyrr are not identified as *goðar* in *Eyrbyggja saga*. Ásgeirr *á Eyri* and his sons, including Steinþórr who here opposes Snorri *goði* (cf *Laxdæla saga* above), are seen as locally influential men and described positively, but not given labels denoting authority.[168]

In locating centres of power belonging to *höfðingjar* or *goðar* over time, it is important to note that *Eyrbyggja saga* focuses on events covering little more than a generation. It is thus not surprising that it mentions few centres of power. It does, however, refer to the immediate post-*landnám* period when it briefly records some disputes from that era. The main bases for powerful men are Helgafell, Bólstaðr, Kársstaðir, Öndverðareyrr and Bjarnarhöfn. Of these farms Helgafell was clearly seen as the most influential farm on the north coast of Snæfellsnes. *Eyrbyggja saga* sees it as the home of Þorsteinn *þorskabítr*[169] before Snorri *goði* lived there. Bólstaðr and Kársstaðir are not seen as having had

---

163   Cf. Gunnar Karlsson 2004: 73–74.
164   ÍF IV: 16.
165   ÍF IV: 27.
166   ÍF IV: 85.
167   ÍF IV: 17.
168   ÍF IV: 12, 15, 21, 22, 33, 68 for the negative evidence.
169   ÍF IV: 14, 17–18.

any kind of influence for more than a single generation. The former was the farm of Arnkell *goði*, who is seen to be powerful until Snorri *goði* has him killed;[170] Kársstaðir's power seems to have been dependent on Snorri *goði*'s support and no one from that farm is identified as a *goði* or *höfðingi*. Öndverðareyrr and Bjarnarhöfn are both seen as *landnámsbæjar* and continue to be the homes of leading men in early disputes and in the time of Snorri *goði*. Thus Helgafell, Öndverðareyrr and Bjarnarhöfn seem to have retained influence throughout the saga while at any given time one farm in Álptafjörður had some kind of power.

More broadly in Dalir *Eyrbyggja saga* mentions the prominence of only two men, one early on, and one contemporary with Snorri *goði*. Þórðr *gellir* from Hvammr is associated with early events, as an arbitrator between the Kjalleklingar and Þórsnesingar.[171] This would suggest he was regarded as being of similar standing to Þorgrímr Kjallaksson, Ásgeirr *á Eyri* and Þorsteinn *þorskabítr*, although his label as *mestr höfðingi* otherwise sets him apart. Later on, Sturla Þjóðreksson from Staðarhóll has a similar role to Snorri *goði* in so far as he has a stake in the Bitra district on Strandir (Map 1).

A geographical tour of the districts covered by *Eyrbyggja saga* is probably the easiest way to see how it conceptualises the control and affiliations of particular farms before we go on to look at familial ties (pp. 251–52).

The small fjord of Álptafjörður (see Map 5) is the focus of many of the events in *Eyrbyggja*, and as a result the saga says a lot both directly and indirectly about land control within it. *Eyrbyggja saga* provides some detail on six farms: Álptafjörðr (Kársstaðir), Narfeyri (Geirröðareyrr), Bólstaðr, Úlfarsfell, Hvammr and Örlygsstaðir while four other Álptafjörður farms are mentioned in passing in the saga.[172] In 1702 *Jarðabók* mentions just one single additional farm in the fjord, Saurar, and records also that Bólstaðr and Hellar had been deserted.[173] This picture is denser than the coverage of the much larger valley of Laxárdalur by *Laxdæla saga*, and we can be more certain of there having been settlement continuity.

Some important chronological developments nonetheless emerge in the property disputes in Álptafjörður, which must be borne in mind during the following account of land control. At its outset the saga assumes that the whole of Álptafjörður had been controlled by one man and then by his family and

---

170   ÍF IV: 102.
171   ÍF IV: 17–18.
172   Hrísar, Hólar, Svelgsá and Hellar (ÍF IV: 57, 96, 175–76; DI VI: 39; Matthías Þórðarson 1932: 28; Guðbrandur Sigurðsson 1955–56: 45).
173   *Jarðabókð* VII : 312, 315.

dependants: Geirröðr, who is said to have settled at Narfeyri, gave out land to his freedmen and sister. This necessarily would have made issues of ownership complicated if we were to assume that later rights of inheritance had come into play in the saga's *landnám* era. That ownership issues actually do not get mentioned seems to suggest that the story of the earliest settlement was, however, not really seen in such simple terms. Secondly, the saga sees the issue of land control in Álptafjörður as a contest between two families: the descendants of Finngeirr, who had lived at Kársstaðir, and Þórólfr *bægifótr* (lamefoot) and his son Arnkell. The saga shows the success of the former group in defeating the latter. A third phase can be seen in which Snorri *goði* teams up with his associates from Kársstaðir to dominate the fjord. A short farm-by-farm account is probably the best way to explain how the saga views the pattern of landholding within the fjord.

Narfeyri is the farm at which the first settler of Álptafjörður, Geirröðr is said to have settled. In contrast with most other *landnámsbæjar* in *Eyrbyggja saga* very little is subsequently said about it. No one is recorded as living there after Geirröðr and the farm is not even mentioned in passing after the *landnám* account. This reflects the disjuncture between the *landnám* narrative and later ones rather than Narfeyri's abandonment; Narfeyri had a church by 1224, if not before, and was a notable farm in the thirteenth century.[174]

'Álptafjörðr' seems to have indicated a farm as well as a fjord and is synonymous with Kársstaðir, the largest farm in Álptafjörður. The earliest reference to the farm of Álptafjörðr comes when Finngeir, a freedman, is said to have lived here in the *landnám* period.[175] Finngeir's descendants, Þorbrandr and his sons (of whom special mention is made of Þóroddr), are subsequently all at Kársstaðir.[176] Kársstaðir can therefore be seen being handed down through the generations from father to son without interruption. The last person said to have lived there is Kárr, the son of Þóroddr after whom the farm was supposedly named.

Bólstaðr has an important part to play in *Eyrbyggja saga* as the home of Arnkell, the local leader who is eventually defeated by Snorri *goði*. Information about Bólstaðr's wealth and status for the medieval period is rather contradictory. The saga does not refer to Bólstaðr being established in the *landnám* period, and says it was abandoned after Arnkell died.[177] Effectively it suggests

---

[174] DI I: 465 and cf. Narfeyri's appearances in chapters 3 and 4 above.
[175] Cf. *M* which claims Úlfarr *kappi* as the first settler of Álptafjörður (Ólafur Lárusson 1945: 24).
[176] ÍF IV: 89, 94, 169, 170.
[177] ÍF IV: 169. The remains of a medieval farm building thought to be those of Bólstaðr were excavated in 1931 by Matthías Þórðarson who uncovered a single stone-built rectilinear

that the farm was only of prominence when Arnkell lived there.[178] It is tempting to think that the saga saw Bólstaðr as having been part of an estate which included the neighbouring farms of Úlfarsfell and Hvammr. These three adjacent farms are said to have been owned by Arnkell's father, Þórólfr *bægifótr*, but the saga's action implies that Bólstaðr was the most important, even if Úlfarsfell survived longest.[179]

Þórólfr *bægifótr* is said to have taken possession of Úlfarsfell through killing Úlfarr, a freedman who had been granted the farm by Geirröðr who settled at Narfeyri. The saga then says that Þórólfr sold the land to another freedman, another Úlfarr *kappi* (the champion), who had been the slave of Þorbrandr of Álptafjörðr. Ownership of the estate is contested by the men of Kársstaðir when Úlfarr *kappi* is killed but it appears Arnkell farms Úlfarsfell and maintains control of it until his death; after Arnkell's death, Þóroddr Þorbrandsson is said to have had both Úlfarsfell and Örlygsstaðir, with nothing said about how Þóroddr came by these properties.[180]

Örlygsstaðir not only shares the same eventual owner with Úlfarsfell but also derives its name from the person who established the farm. Örlygr was a freedman of Þorbrandr of Álptafjörðr to whom Þórólfr sold land just as Úlfarr was sold Úlfarsfell.[181] Örlygr and Úlfarr are said to have been brothers[182] and lived at their respective farms for a long time.[183] On Örlygr's death his farm became the source of a dispute between the Þorbrandssynir and Arnkell.

---

structure whose internal dimensions were approximately 22.3m x 5.8m. He thought that the house may have been built in more than one phase and was with the original structure being enlarged. Finds included a knife, pottery and 65–70 artefacts of stone or iron (Matthías Þórðarson 1932, esp. 11, 14, 16, 19–22. Byock 1989; Helgi Þorláksson 2007: 218–24).

178 The place-name element *bolstaðr* might suggest its prominence because most farms with names containing this element were usually either wealthy or had churches by the thirteenth century (Þórhallur Vilmundarson 1971: 378; Ólafur Lárusson 1939: 65–68). Svavar Sigmundsson (1979: 242, 244–45 and 1992: 133–35) sees them as having started out as specialist farming units within an early farm.

179 Byock 1988: 185; 1989: 189–90. Bólstaðr's abandonment, quite possibly in the medieval period, may have been because of the encroachment of the sea onto the farm. The ruins are under water now and it is possible that the farm was located where it was because it had waterlogged meadows, a valuable asset for cattle farming. Coastal erosion has had a serious impact on numerous wealthy farms since the middle ages, including excavated ones such as Stóraborg in the south and Siglunes in the north.

180 ÍF IV: 169.
181 ÍF IV: 14.
182 ÍF IV: 87.
183 ÍF IV: 14.

Control of the farm is not mentioned again, although the killing of Arnkell by the Þorbrandssynir at the farm suggests that Arnkell still owned it at that point. The eventual statement that Þóroddr Þorbrandsson owned both Úlfarsfell and Örlygsstaðir (*hann átti þá bæði löndin, Úlfarsfell ok Örylygsstaði*),[184] however, suggests that part of the saga's narrative should be interpreted as an explanation of the shift of ownership of farms from Bólstaðr to Kársstaðir.[185]

Before this, however, Þórólfr *bægifótr* is said to have established a new farm following his defeat of Úlfarr *kappi*, rather than continue to live at Úlfarsfell. This was Hvammr. The only later reference to Hvammr comes after Þórólfr's death. It is inherited, or at least briefly occupied, by Arnkell who spends three nights there immediately following his father's death.[186] While it seems likely that Arnkell inherited the farm, this is not made explicit; Arnkell's hasty occupation of it almost suggests that he expected the farm to fall to someone else. Hvammr, however, seems to have been a fairly marginal farm whose value would have been more strategic than economic. It was not in Álptafjörður itself but to the west of Úlfarsfell, at a higher altitude and further inland than most farms in Álptafjörður; by the end of the seventeenth century it was not even recognised as a deserted farm.[187]

In the remainder of Helgafellssveit the text names male occupants for nine farms, perhaps a third of those that might have existed in the medieval period: Helgafell itself, Þorbeinisstaðir, Spá-Gilsstaðir, Bakki (Staðarbakki), Hofstaðir, Höskuldsey, Bjarnarhöfn, Hraun (Berserkjahraun), Drápuhlíð and an unnamed farm near the former *þing* site.

Þórólfr *Mostrarskegg* is said to have been the first settler on Þórsnes, and *Eyrbyggja saga* gives the impression that he had the whole of the peninsula at his disposal. He established his home at Hofstaðir, another *landnám* farm not mentioned in the rest of the saga, but identified with Þórólfr because of the apparent connection between the place-name element *hof* and pre-Christian religion.[188] The supposition of the saga, as in S, seems to be that one person could have owned the whole of the Þórsnes peninsula.

---

184   ÍF IV: 169.
185   See generally Byock 1988: 183–202.
186   ÍF IV: 92. Arnkell 'claimed as his possession all that wealth which he and his father had owned together; Arnkell was there three nights' ('kastaði sinni eign á fé þat allt, er þar stóð saman ok faðir hans hafði átt; var Arnkell þar þrjár nætr'). This almost suggests that Arnkell's stay was of legal significance, perhaps especially as the farm was not occupied in the immediate future.
187   Hvammr is recorded in *Jarðabók* (VII: 311–12).
188   Hofstaðir was occupied in the eighteenth century (*Jarðabók* VII: 323;. Orri Vésteinsson 2007b; Lucas & McGovern 2007; Lucas 2009.

Þorsteinn *þorskabítr* is said to have been the first farmer at Helgafell, having moved his household from Hofstaðir after his father's death.[189] From then on descendants of Þórólfr and Þorsteinn continued to occupy the farm. Þorgrímr and Börkr, Þorsteinn's sons, lived there before Þorgrímr died, and the latter's son Snorri *goði* claimed a share in the property. *Eyrbyggja saga* records a dispute between Snorri and his uncle, Börkr, which results in Snorri outwitting Börkr and buying Börkr's share to take sole possession of the farm. After living at Helgafell for several years Snorri exchanged farms with Guðrún Ósvífrsdóttir of Sælingsdalstunga in Hvammssveit. *Eyrbyggja saga* differs noticeably from *Laxdæla saga* in that it does not mention what happened to Helgafell after Snorri left, although it certainly implies that none of Snorri's ancestors lived there after him, because it does not associate the farm with any of his children in Chapter 65.[190] This contrasts with the connection we saw between Þorkell Eyjólfsson's descendants and Helgafell in *Laxdæla saga*,[191] and which the author of *Eyrbyggja saga* was possibly aware of.

Eyrbyggja saga says Bjarnarhöfn was first occupied by Björn *inn austrœni*, as also recorded *S* and *Laxdæla saga*. *Eyrbyggja saga* says that one of his two sons, Kjallakr *gamli*, lived at Bjarnarhöfn after his father and it passed down the male line to Þorgrímr *goði* Kjallaksson and Vermundr inn *mjóvi* Þorgrímsson inherited the estate.[192] Vermundr, here, is still seen acting from Bjarnarhöfn until comparatively late in the saga, but in Chapter 56 he is said to have lived at Vatnsfjörðr, on the northern coast of Breiðafjörður. The idea that a character called Vermundr lived in or at Vatnsfjörðr occurs in other texts as well.[193] Vermundr *inn mjóvi* was clearly a well-known name and there must have been competing stories which have to some extent been reconciled or combined in *Eyrbyggja saga*.[194] By a circuitous route we can also see a connection to

---

189   ÍF IV: 18. *S* does not go so far as to mention Þorsteinn's move to Helgafell. *S* says that Þórólfr *Mostrarskegg* called (*kallaði*) the hill on the farm's land Helgafell (ÍF I: 125), implying that he named it, but does not make the same close association of the father and son with Helgafell as does *Eyrbyggja saga*.
190   ÍF IV: 180–84.
191   See above p. 240; Ari Þorgilsson claimed descent from Þorkell, as set out in chapter 70 of *Laxdæla* and in *Íslendingabók* (ÍF I: 28).
192   ÍF IV: 12.
193   *Grettis saga* (ÍF VII: 166), *Fóstbrœðra saga* (ÍF VI: 123). *Heiðarvíga saga* (ÍF III: 216) places him at Laugaból in Ísafjörður when he dealt with the berserks (ÍF IV: 153, note 5) but this may be a mistake by Jón Ólafsson who wrote down the saga from memory in the eighteenth century after the manuscript in his possession had been destroyed (ÍF IV: 153, note 5; ÍF III: 216, note 2, 218).
194   There are clearly implications here about constructions of the past which link Vermundr with places around Breiðafjörður but there is not space to discuss them here.

Bjarnarhöfn for Vermundr's son, Brandr: Brandr's wife Sigríðr, the daughter of Snorri *goði*, married a second time and she and her second husband (Kolli Þormóðarson) are said to have lived at Bjarnarhöfn.[195]

The upshot of these stories would therefore seem to be that Bjarnarhöfn was thought to have stayed in the possession of the male line descended from Björn *inn austrœni* through four generations to Brandr Vermundarson. With Brandr's wife's remarriage, which the saga might suppose to have happened after Brandr's death (although this is not said), the farm passed into the control of the family associated with Öndverðareyrr. The wider significance of this information is not immediately clear, especially as it comes in the saga's final genealogical chapter. If the reconstruction of the past described here reflects a reality from when the saga was written, then Bjarnarhöfn had come under the control, in some form, of Öndverðareyrr and Sælingsdalstunga (i.e. paralleling the associations of Kolli Þormóðarson and Snorri *goði*).

Eyrbyggja makes reference to a handful of other, smaller farms in Helgafellssveit whose connections or allegiances generally suggest varied relations vis-à-vis the three core farms. The ties of only three such farms are both discernible and potentially significant. The mentions of the first two, although not entirely unambiguous, hint at the increasing influence of Helgafell/Snorri *goði* at the expense of Vermundr/Bjarnarhöfn. In the south-west of the district, Drápuhlíð is home to Vigfúss, a kinsman of Vermundr of Bjarnarhöfn, whom Snorri kills; thereafter the farm plays no further part in the text. Second, Hraun was occupied at one point by Vermundr's brother, Víga-Styrr, whose daughter Snorri goði married, thus creating a significant connection to Snorri. Last, Bakki – probably modern Staðarbakki and therefore on the coast between Helgafell and Bjarnarhöfn – is identified as the home of the brother of Steinþórr from Öndverðareyrr.[196] Thus none of the more powerful figures in the text dominate this area exclusively, although the impression is given that Snorri had greatest and growing influence.

Before leaving Helgafellssveit, we should note that there are other farms which *Eyrbyggja saga* thought existed in this region's early history. Spá-Gilsstaðir in Þórsárdalur is named as the home of Spá-Gils. The exact position of this farm is not known, let alone its tenurial history. Þorbeinisstaðir is also named after its only recorded occupant, Þorbeinn or Þorbeinir. While the saga places the farm inland from Drápuhlíð and Þorbeinn is recorded as having

---

195   ÍF IV: 181.
196   ÍF IV: 33, 66–70, 75. For the more obscure Spá-Gilsstaðir and Þorbeinisstaðir see ÍF IV: 14, note 3 and 125-26, note 2.

children (one of whom married Vigfúss í Drápuhlíð) little else is known about the farm or farmer.[197]

In Eyrarsveit *Eyrbyggja saga* only makes reference to the control or occupation of Öndverðareyrr.[198] Just as S does, the saga identifies Öndverðareyrr as a *landnámsbær* and then suggests an uncomplicated transfer of the farm through the generations, from father to son. Vestarr settled and lived there first and his son, Ásgeirr, lived their afterwards.[199] Ásgeirr's son, Þorlákr *af Eyri*, is scarcely mentioned in the saga but clearly associated with Eyrr. Steinþórr *af Eyri*, Þorlákr's son, was seen as a contemporary of Snorri *goði* and is heavily involved in the saga's events. Noticeably in this generation the saga is clear that Steinþórr did not share control of Eyrr with his brothers. Þormóðr Þorláksson lived at Bakki, at least after his marriage[200] and, while the remaining Þorlákssynir (Bergþórr and Þórðr *blígr*) were probably viewed as having lived at Öndverðareyrr, neither are seen as leaders in any sense.[201] Nothing is said about who lived at Öndverðareyrr after Steinþórr. With the saga's silence we can only guess that Steinþórr's descendants, or people who saw themselves as his descendants, continued to live at Eyrr.[202] This absence of a subsequent history is remarkable considering the farm's importance to the Sturlungar in the first half of the thirteenth century and is another sign that these texts were not necessarily created by the Sturlungar.

Eyrbyggja saga has little of note to say about much of Dalir; it mostly confirms the names of local prominent leaders or colonists found in other texts. What is significant, however, is its identification of Glerárskógar in Hvammssveit as the last home of Börkr *inn digri*, uncle of Snorri *goði*. Börkr is first said to have moved from Helgafell to Fellsströnd before moving a second time to Glerárskógar, following his sale of his share of Helgafell.[203] At the same time

---

197 ÍF IV: 14 and note 3.
198 Another farm, Eið, is mentioned by name only (ÍF IV: 165).
199 ÍF IV: 12.
200 ÍF IV: 118.
201 ÍF IV: 124 for where Þórðr *blígr* is at Eyrr recovering from the wounds he received after the fighting in Álptafjörður.
202 S provides a genealogy as far as Steinþórr's son, Gunnlaugr, who married Snorri *goði*'s daughter, Þuríðr *in spaka*. *Melabók* does not include Steinþórr or his son in its account (ÍF I: 118, 119). The sagas in the *Sturlunga* compilation mention Steinþórr once, as the ancestor of the Eyrbyggjar, but only one line is traced from him (SS I: 117).
203 *Gísla saga* says that Börkr moved directly to Glerárskógar after Snorri *goði* ousted him from Helgafell (ÍF VI: 117, 137). *Laxdæla saga* seems to draw on similar traditions about Börkr. It does not show any knowledge of Börkr's political demise, perhaps because it would rather ignore such an image for someone commonly known to have lived at a large

Börkr's bones were supposedly found in the graveyard at Sælingsdalstunga, along with those of Snorri *goði*, when they were dug up by Hvamm-Sturla's wife Guðný in the late twelfth century.[204] This perhaps suggests that later traditions, or at least the later owners of Sælingsdalstunga, were willing to believe that Börkr and Snorri *goði* were not at odds, contrary to the narrative in *Eyrbyggja saga*. It is also possible that similar suppositions lay behind the separate stories about Snorri *goði* and Börkr *inn digri* moving, i.e. that a whole powerful kin group (or the centre of local power itself) moved from Helgafell to Hvammssveit.

Turning to marriages recorded in the body of *Eyrbyggja saga* (i.e. excluding the *landnám* period and the genealogy of Snorri *goði*), we see they are local, with farmers of lower status contracting marriages in the districts from Neshreppur in the west, to Álptafjörður, 20km to its east.[205] As outlined above, *Eyrbyggja saga* does not distinguish greatly between classes of people. However, it is noticeable that the saga mentions no marriages directly between the more powerful people who lived at Helgafell, Öndverðareyrr and Bjarnarhöfn. Marriages seem to be contracted between these particular farms and less wealthy ones. Thus, from Helgafell, Snorri *goði*'s sister is married to a farmer of Fróðá and Snorri marries the daughter of Víga-Styrr who was associated with Hraun. While in this second case Víga-Styrr can be assumed to have grown up at Bjarnarhöfn, he is not seen to have lived there and his descendants are not connected with that farm.[206] The only marriage involving anyone from Bjarnarhöfn itself links the farm to Mávahlíð. People from Öndverðareyrr make two marriages, one with someone from Hraunsfjörður and the other with someone from Kársstaðir. This link between Öndverðareyrr and Kársstaðir is interesting because it seems a very fragile one. The only marriage proposal which is refused in *Eyrbyggja saga* is that of Þorleifr *kimbi* Þorbrandsson to a

---

        farm in Dalir. It does identify him, along with his brother Þorgrímr, as seeking political power and forcing their own kinsman, Þorsteinn *surtr inn spaki* (from somewhere on Þórsnes), to flee his farm (ÍF V: 19, 40).

204 ÍF IV: 181.

205 The 'local' marriages in *Eyrbyggja saga* are defined here as those in which both partners are associated with farms in either Álptafjörður or to the west of this fjord, on the northern coast of Snæfellsnes. Kársstaðir (to the east) and Fróðá (to the west) mark the boundaries of the area being discussed. Þórólfr *bægifótr's* daughters, Gunnfríðr and Geirríðr, married men from Þorbeinisstaðir and Mávahlíð respectively. The daughter of Gunnfríðr and Þorbeinir from Þorbeinisstaðir was married to Vigfúss í Drápuhlíð. These marriages all involve farms which were not demonstrably centres of any kind of local power in the thirteenth century.

206 Víga-Styrr's one recorded descendant was a daughter (ÍF I: 113, 114, 115).

daughter of Þorlákr *af Eyri*. Although a marriage between the families already existed the hostilities between them were enough to prohibit further contact. The idea here is that it was difficult for a farm like Öndverðareyrr to ally itself with another powerful farm nearby; Kársstaðir was strongly connected with Snorri, the foster-brother and ally of the Þorbrandssynir. This makes the marriage mentioned above, between Kolli Þormóðarson from Öndverðareyrr and Snorri *goði*'s daughter, all the more remarkable.[207] It is only in this final chapter of the saga, its equivalent to the *Ævi Snorra goða*, that the 'rule' of no marriages between the three major farms is broken.

Other marriages, involving the family at Hvammr and, for Kársstaðir, to somewhere to the south, seem worthy of brief comment. Firstly, the Hvammr marriages stress the ties between local leaders around Breiðafjörður (Þorsteinn *þorskabítr* of Helgafell marries a daughter of Óláfr *feilan*; Þorgrímr Kjallaksson from Bjarnarhöfn marries a kinswoman of Þórðr *gellir*) but specifically it is Bjarnarhöfn and Helgafell people who marry women from the Hvammverjar rather than to people from elsewhere in Dalir.[208] The distinctive Kársstaðir tie is the marriage of Þorbrandr (Snorri *goði*'s foster-father) to a woman from the large farm of Rauðamelr in the district immediately to the south on the southern coast of Snæfellsnes (Miklaholtshreppur) of which nothing much is made in the text but reinforces the idea that Kársstaðir was a significant place and not just tied into the region immediately around Hvammsfjörður.

So far, then, a series of genealogical relationships have been set out and discussed. Some sections of *Eyrbyggja saga*, however, describe political allegiances in simpler terms. The saga includes some very short accounts of disputes which paint a simple picture of political allegiances at particular court cases. These quite bold statements about political divisions also demonstrate conceptions of regional politics.

Arguably the most important dispute in *Eyrbyggja saga*, that in which Snorri *goði* overcomes Arnkell, has already been examined at length by Jesse Byock[209] and so will not be described here. The components of this dispute, in terms of the centres of power and the farms they control in the saga, have, in any case, been set out above. In basic geopolitical terms the dispute sees the victory of Helgafell, in alliance with Kársstaðir, over Bólstaðr. It is notable that the Helgafell-Kársstaðir tie is not visible in *máldagar* or the *samtíðarsögur*.

---

207   See above p. 250.
208   ÍF IV: 14, 18.
209   Byock 1988: 181–202; Byock 1989.

The two other notable stories for geopolitics in *Eyrbyggja saga* both occur in S and are mentioned above, namely those concerning the desecration of the Þórsnessþing (chapter 9) and the outlawry of Eiríkr *rauði* (chapter 24).[210] Although we have seen a pattern whereby even in Helgafellssveit there is not a clear pattern of territorial control, when it comes to slightly larger-scale disputes, district-level mobilisation is visible in these disputes. *Kjalleklingar* is the label used to identify Þorgrímr Kjallaksson of Bjarnarhöfn and his brother-in-law Ásgeirr *af Eyri* – from the two large farms close to one another that we have seen mentioned before – when they oppose Þorsteinn *þorskabítr* of Helgafell. Þorsteinn's supporters included an earliest generation of the people from Álptafjörður and Narfeyri that have just been discussed, including Þórólfr *bægifótr*, whose son Arnkell was Snorri *goði's* rival. In a sense this conflict mostly pre-empts and deepens the text's sense of the rivalry between Helgafell with the two other most significant farms. It also suggests that the rivalry provided by Arnkell, and thus division within Álptafjörður, was a kind of aberration and that control of all of Álptafjörður from Helgafell was the normal pattern. Lastly, looking just to the west, this dispute sees two *Skógstrendingar* from the west of Skógarströnd, Þorgestr *inn gamli* (Breiðabólstaðr) and Áslákr (Langidalr) as the neutral party who ensured peace. This suggests a kind of small-scale solidarity among the leading figures of western Skógarströnd. That it was them and not figures from, say, east of Helgafellssveit gives the impression that this district was more important than the latter.

Chapter 24 of *Eyrbyggja saga* is well-known as being an account of a dispute which also appears in a shorter form in S and in its fullest form in *Eiríks saga rauða*, whereby Eiríkr *inn rauði* was forced to leave Breiðafjörður and eventually reached Greenland.[211] For our purposes it gives us a comparatively clear set of political relationships, or at least a sharp division into two sides, of several people supporting one side or other in the dispute. Þorgestr *inn gamli* is the man named as bringing the charge against Eiríkr (for killing Þorgestr's sons) and he is supported by Þórðr *gellir's* sons. *Eiríks saga rauða* and S, which give similar accounts, extend the group of men supporting Þorgestr to include Þorgeirr from Hítardalur, and Áslákr and his son from Langidalr.[212] Here and in the other texts Eiríkr *inn rauði* is supported by the same people: Þorbjörn Vífilsson,[213] Víga-Styrr, the Þorbrandssynir and Eyjólfr Æsuson from Svíney. But

---

210   See pp. 164, 177.
211   ÍF I: 130–32; ÍF IV: 197–202.
212   ÍF I: 131, ÍF IV: 198–99.
213   S records the marriage of Eiríkr's son to Þorbjörn's daughter (ÍF I: 141).

of these supposedly only Víga-Styrr attended the *þing*. Snorri *goði* was persuaded not to take the side of Þorgestr by Víga-Styrr's promise of future support.

The pattern of alliances here is unlike any described elsewhere for cases around Hvammsfjörður. Þorgestr and the Þórðarsynir (of Breiðabólstaðr on Skógarströnd) are supported by Hvammr itself (and Otradalr, far to the northwest in Arnarfjörður).[214] *Eiríks saga* also extends this support immediately to the south to Hítardalur and west to Langidalur. On the other side, while Eiríkr *inn rauði* himself is said to have lived at Eiríksstaðir in Haukadalur, he drew most of his support from the western half of the Hvammsfjörður (Hraun, Svíney, Kársstaðir) and probably from nearer to home, from Vífilsdalur.[215] The story of Eiríkr's killing of the Þorgestssynir can also be read as the expulsion of a disruptive figure in inner Dalir by Hvammr, which was opposed by a united group people in and around Helgafellssveit. The allegiances map loosely onto those seen elsewhere in *Eyrbyggja saga*, e.g. Víga-Styrr and the Þorbrandssynir acting on the same side. It also indirectly reinforces the idea of Helgafell's or Snorri's local power; Snorri does not take part in a vengeance attack in support of Þorgestr because of Víga-Styrr's intercession. It also fits a much bigger genealogical pattern as well: Snorri, as a descendant of Auðr *in djúpúðga*, is aligned with the Hvammverjar, even if he does not act in this instance.

By and large, then, *Eyrbyggja saga* presents a coherent picture of positive or antagonistic relationships between districts and major farms and presents some evidence for a growth in the influence of Helgafell. Where this fits into the wider geopolitical representation of Dalir will be discussed below.

1.6 Króka-Refs Saga

Króka-Refs saga is a short saga which primarily records the exploits of Króka-Refr, who originated from Kvennabrekka in Miðdalir, once he has left Iceland. The text is difficult to date and the earliest version of it only survives in a fifteenth-century manuscript.[216] Undoubtedly the saga is simplistic and short on detail but there is no reason to believe it is of any less use in understanding people's views of the past. It is the first five chapters of the saga, a narrative of a local dispute before Króka-Refr leaves Iceland, which is of interest for this study, even if some commentators have seen the saga as a whole as a parody.[217] The local political set up here shows some uncanny similarities with other

---

214 *Gísla saga* places Eyjólfr *grái* Þórðarson in Otradalr (ÍF VI: 69).
215 Þorbjörn Vífilsson is not associated with a particular place but in S his father is said to have been the first settler in Vífilsdalur (ÍF I: 141).
216 Rowe 1993: 369.
217 Arnold 2003: 181–208.

texts which could be dismissed as the result of enduring micro-political patterns but equally show how local political relationships were perceived in the period before c.1265, the cut-off point for this book.

The saga says, then, that Refr's father, Steinn, is was married to the sister of Gestr Oddleifsson from Barðaströnd of *Laxdæla saga* fame.[218] Steinn is said to have been rich and a good farmer but Refr was regarded as stupid but at the same time strong and good-looking.[219] Living at Sauðafell was the aggressive Þorbjörn who had bought his farm after having killed people and been forced out of many other districts of Iceland. In Miðdalir, Þorbjörn's anti-social behaviour manifests itself through his grazing his sheep on neighbouring Kvennabrekka's land.[220]

It comes as no surprise that when Steinn dies Þorbjörn becomes even less reasonable. On his deathbed Steinn warns his wife to sell Kvennabrekka and move away but she is unwilling to do so because the farm is so good. Þorbjörn is even less careful now about where his livestock graze, and his animals graze on Kvennabrekka's land night and day. His neighbours' pasture is ruined and they are without hay, preventing them from selling the farm.

Eventually Steinn's wife gets an overseer to protect her land; he stops Sauðafell's sheep from crossing the river onto their land. The dispute does not go away, however, and escalates when Þorbjörn kills Kvennabrekka's new protector. Then, finally, the problem seems to be resolved: Króka-Refr kills Þorbjörn and leaves Miðdalir. He avoids prosecution by going to see his uncle, Gestr Oddleifsson, who enables him to leave Iceland for Greenland and thence make a name for himself.

Clearly this dispute is a very simplistic one with few complexities of any kind. It could well be later than many other *Íslendingasögur* and *þættir* or else derive from a tale which has been told orally for some considerable time. Nevertheless the setting of this prefatory episode – which only really explains why Króka-Refr left Iceland – is entirely in keeping with the kind of dispute we find in *Íslendingasögur* generally. The dispute recorded is also, however, this time, one which might reflect thirteenth-century local political tensions. Sauðafell and Kvennabrekka were two of the largest farms in Miðdalir from the thirteenth century and both had churches. The tensions between Sighvatr Sturluson and his son Sturla, and Halldórr from Kvennabrekka in the first half of the

---

218 See pp. 229, 238, 241.
219 ÍF XIV: 1.
220 ÍF XIV: 3.

thirteenth century mirrors, to some extent, the tension between these adjacent farms recorded here. It may well be significant that this saga remembers a dispute between these church-farms, rather than any others, both because they were adjoining and because Sighvatr Sturluson, moving to Sauðafell, was new to Miðdalir in the same way as was Þorbjörn. Local tensions like this must have been common throughout the middle ages, but the specific rivalry *Króka-Refs saga* points up is, as we saw, visible in *Íslendinga saga*'s account of the earlier thirteenth century.[221]

A further point relates to the genealogical situations of the people from Kvennabrekka and Sauðafell. Steinn, through his unnamed wife, is connected with Gestr Oddleifsson, a positive saga character with whom many people are associated in those *Íslendingasögur* centred on the West Fjords.[222] This, however, represents another choice by the saga writer in that Refr, in this story, could conceivably have escaped Dalir through a variety of means or contacts. His link to Gestr, though, connects him with other local people who are identified in *Laxdæla saga* as related to Gestr; there Guðrún Ósvífrsdóttir and Ármóðr from Þykkvaskógr in Miðdalir are both identified as his kin.[223] There may be no great significance in the fact that at one time or another people from Laugar, Þykkvaskógr and Kvennabrekka all claimed a connection with Gestr Oddleifsson yet all these farms are relatively close to one another and of medium-high value.[224] These genealogical links might suggest an attempt on the part of *bændr* from these farms to claim a kind of identity independent of more local leaders.

---

221 See pp. 108–9 above.
222 Gestr Oddleifsson appears as a benevolent *höfðingi* and mediator. He is never really one of the leading characters in a saga although he plays his largest role in *Hávarðar saga Ísfirðings*. Clearly he was a desirable character to have in one's genealogy in the same way as was Snorri *goði*. In connection with *Króka-Refs saga* it is interesting to note that *Hávarðar saga* records the marriage and divorce of the *ójafnaðarmaðr* Þorbjörn Þjóðreksson (from Ísafjörður) and Gestr Oddleifsson's daughter (ÍF VI: 291–97, 299–314). Both sagas can therefore be seen to record a story in which Gestr Oddleifsson or his kin are at odds with an overbearing character called Þorbjörn. In both stories the Þorbjörn character is killed. Neither *Hávarðar saga* nor *Króka-Refs saga* can give Þorbjörn ancestors although S quite clearly sees the Þorbjörn Þjóðreksson from *Hávarðar saga* as the son of Þjóðrekr from Saurbær (ÍF I: 159, 182, 184–45, 190–91, 197). Perhaps both sagas retain the kernel of a much earlier story.
223 For Ármóðr, ÍF V: 87.
224 *Jarðabók* lists Laugar at 16 hundreds, Stóriskógur (Þykkvaskógr) at 60 hundreds, and Kvennabrekka as of unknown value in 1703 but having been valued at 20 hundreds 'some years before' (*fyrir nokkrum arum*) (*Jarðabók* VI: 40, 42, 89).

Another side of this story is that Sauðafell's owner, as in *Laxdœla saga*, is not given a genealogy. This is surprising given that Sauðafell was an important farm in the thirteenth century. In both *Króka-Refs saga* and *Laxdœla saga* the occupants of Sauðafell, Þorbjörn and Þórólfr *rauðnefr*, are given other positive characteristics, the one being called wealthy and the other a 'great hero'.[225] Both sagas assume that Sauðafell had an important past, but neither can or will fit the farm's previous occupants into the mainstream of genealogical knowledge. Thus *Króka-Refs saga* may or may not be an early text and it does not add anything to our picture of the major genealogical charter which the previous texts discussed are shaped around. What it does do, however, is bolster that sense of very local-level conflict and records further evidence of resistance to Sauðafell by the larger of the farms in Miðdalir.

1.7 Þorskfirðinga Saga

Þorskfirðinga saga describes disputes supposed to have taken place immediately to the north of Dalir, around Króksfjörður, in the first few generations after the *landnám*. The saga has been relatively understudied although it has recently been examined by place name expert Þórhallur Vilmundarson because it is more concerned than practically any other to connect saga characters with topographical features and farms.[226] The saga is also noted for its large number of characters whose names duplicate the names of their farms. This is one reason why the saga is thought to have been written later than many others. It is also often thought to have been written relatively late because, among other things, one of its major protagonists, Þórir Oddsson from Þórisstaðir in Þorskafjörður, has dealings with vikings who transform into dragons. Such fabulous elements are often assumed to be late, especially when, as in this case, S recounts events from a *Þorskfirðinga saga* which do not tally with the surviving independent saga.[227] Regardless of its origins, this saga provides an account of the activities of the *landnámsmenn* Steinólfr *inn lági* (who settled at Fagradalur on Skarðsströnd and at Steinólfsdalur, part of Króksfjörður to the north) and Óláfr *belgr* (who eventually settled in Ólafsdalur).[228]

The saga's early part retells Þórir's adventures outside Iceland. His father had settled in Þorskafjörður (at Uppsalir)[229] and when Þórir returns his father

---

225 ÍF IV: 21.
226 ÍF XIII: cx–cxxxiv.
227 Jónas Kristjánsson 1988: 288; Cardew 2007.
228 *Þorskfirðinga saga* gives the limits of Steinólfr *inn lági*'s *landnám* as the same as those set out in S and does not give boundaries for Óláfr *belgr*'s *landnám* (ÍF I: 159; ÍF XIII: 179).
229 ÍF XIII: 178.

is dead and a certain Hallr from Hofsstaðir (also in Þorskafjörður) is lording it over local *bændr*.[230] Þórir and Hallr fight and Þórir emerges as overall victor. Þórir then marries the daughter of Gísl from Kleifar (Gilsfjörður) who had been the intended of Óláfr *belgr*'s son, Þorgeirr. By now Þórir is beginning to build up a network of supporters and acquires more land. He therefore gets away with offending Þorgeirr Óláfsson by stealing his bride. The saga seems to see Þorskafjörður as having stronger influence over Gilsfjörður than does Ólafsdalur or Saurbær.

It is at this point that Steinólfr *inn lági* comes into the action. In order to try to secure redress for losing his bride-to-be, Þorgeirr Óláfsson pays Steinólfr to support him in the case and also enlists the help of Hallr from Þorskafjörður.[231] A protracted conflict ensues in which Þórir kills supporters of Hallr and Steinólfr.[232]

Eventually Gísl of Kleifar dies and Þórir moves swiftly to take over his farm. Óláfr *belgr* and Þorgeirr see this as a threat and turn again to Steinólfr who in turn asks for support from someone called Kjallakr, probably a Kjallakr associated with the Kjalleklingar from further south.[233] Steinólfr and Kjallakr gather together a force and go north to engage Þórir in battle. During the fight Steinólfr also gets support from Knútr from Knútsstaðir, a farm which was probably remembered as a *hjáleiga* of Tjaldanes in Saurbær.[234] Men are killed on both sides, including nine men from the Óláfsdælir, but a peace is eventually agreed.[235]

Steinólfr and Hallr maintain their hostility to Þórir and his allies. Another supporter of each group is killed before another pitched battle takes place and Steinólfr dies of his wounds.[236] After Steinólfr's death his party – his son, his son-in-law Þjóðrekr and his father, Sleitu-Björn – seek Þórir's full outlawry. The saga states bluntly that Þórir did not want to leave Iceland and instead that a large sum in compensation was paid for the killing.

One could argue about who 'won' this dispute. The saga would at least suggest a Þorskafjörður-based *höfðingi* could get away with killing his rival in

---

230   ÍF XIII: 193.
231   'Því gaf Þorgeirr Steinólfi fé til, at hann veitti Þóri umsátir, ef færi yrðr á...' (ÍF XIII: 198).
232   There is a lacuna in the MS (AM 561) of over a chapter at this point; in this it would seem that Steinólfr probably took a whale belonging to Þórir and other offences were committed against Þórir (ÍF XIII: 201–4).
233   ÍF XIII: 209.
234   ÍF XIII: 213, esp. note 1 for references.
235   ÍF XIII: 214.
236   ÍF XIII: 222–23.

Saurbær, even if he had to pay compensation. At the saga's end Þórir has defeated or gained the support of everyone at the largest farms in Króksfjörður, Gilsfjörður and managed to kill his only real opponent from anywhere as far south as Fagradalur (Map 5). Although Þórir survives politically it is not suggested that he is able to wield any power within Saurbær; there seems to be unity among the leading men in Saurbær. It could also be argued that the supposition behind Steinólfr's defeat in battle is that Saurbær could not be led effectively from a farm outside the main part of the district because Fagradalur is to its south, rather than that Saurbær is inferior to Þorskafjörður *per se*. It may be stretching the evidence but it could be significant that this saga sees the area immediately to the north as under the control of someone not from Saurbær. It imagines tension between these two districts but a certain equality between them. As we have noted for certain districts in previous texts, so this saga ignores some of the major farms within Saurbær and nearby, in this case Skarð, Staðarhóll and Hvoll. Fagradalur was certainly home to the Sturlungar at different times in the thirteenth century but it only became home to anyone significant when Sturla Þórðarson moved there in 1271, when he took it over from an otherwise unknown *bóndi*.[237]

1.8   Njáls Saga

Brennu-Njáls saga is the longest and arguably the most complex of the *Íslendingasögur* whose commitment to writing is usually dated to c.1280.[238] A key part of the first half of the saga is the events which lead up to the dispute which arises between the households of Njáll Þorgeirsson, after whom the saga is commonly known, and his friend Gunnarr. The two friends remain on good terms while their wives engineer a dispute which ultimately results in the death of Njáll, Gunnarr having died as part of another subplot. Of interest for perceptions of the west is this central dispute and the portrayals of Hallgerðr *langbrók*, Gunnarr's wife, and her father, uncle and brother: Höskuldr Dala-Kollsson, Hrútr Herjólfsson and Óláfr *pái* Höskuldsson. While most of the events of the saga take place in southern Iceland, what *Njáls saga* says about these *Laxdælir* is a different kind of political commentary to the intensely local representations as we have seen in *Laxdæla saga* and *Eyrbyggja saga*.

Njáls saga begins with the well-known scene at Höskuldsstaðir where Höskuldr asks his half-brother Hrútr for his opinion on his daughter Hallgerðr. Hrútr reluctantly admits that his niece is 'beautiful enough' but that he cannot

---

237   SS II: 235. See, for example, pp. 96, 125 above.
238   Callow 2017a: 25–26 for the debate and references.

understand how 'thief's eyes have come into our kin'.[239] This scene pre-empts what happens later in the saga. Hallgerðr marries three times and her last marriage is to Gunnarr who is helplessly drawn to her beauty and marries her in spite of her kinsmen's warnings of her troublesome past.

First it needs to be pointed out the the story about Hallgerðr *langbrók* is one which is peculiar to *Njáls saga*. Hallgerðr is mentioned in other places, but only in genealogies.[240] It would also seem that the very negative portrayal of Hallgerðr as a woman who, with the co-operation of another woman, causes conflict between men is not one which is associated strongly with where she comes from. Hallgerðr has an important role in the plot here but her negative attributes are in no way seen as having anything to do with her male kinsmen. This is perhaps surprising given that *Njáls saga* is essentially a southern Icelandic text; *Njáls saga* actually has quite a positive view of Höskuldr, Hrútr and Óláfr *pái*. All three act as law-abiding, peace-loving men. Even when Hrútr is outwitted by Gunnarr and tricked into summonsing himself (to repay his ex-wife's dowry), it is only because he himself understands the law so well.[241]

Otherwise Höskuldr and Hrútr, rather than being at odds with one another as they are in *Laxdæla saga*, here are seen co-operating. Hrútr's comment on Hallgerðr's eyes is said to have cooled their friendship but only briefly.[242] They act together on several occasions: when arranging Hallgerðr's marriages or attending them;[243] when paying compensation for the killing of Hallgerðr's first husband;[244] avoiding compensating her second husband's kin;[245] supporting their kinsman Gunnar in court.[246] The two are distinguishable, however, in that Hrútr has the more active role. Hrútr's physique and talents are described when Höskuldr's are not.[247] He is regarded as a legal expert and it is he who is most cautious about Hallgerðr's suitability as a wife. It is also Hrútr's failed marriage which first brings him and his brother into contact with Gunnarr when they dispute the repayment of her dowry.[248] Hrútr is consistently seen as

---

239   ÍF XII: 1–2.
240   She is referred to as Hallgerðr *langbrók* (long breeches) in *Laxdæla saga* and *Hauksbók* but is nicknamed *snúinbrók* (twisted breeches) in S. She is also identified in *Óláfs saga Tryggvasonar en mesta* (ÍF XII: 6, note 7).
241   ÍF XII: 64–65.
242   ÍF XII: 7.
243   ÍF XII: 30–33, 43–45, 88–90.
244   ÍF XII: 39–40.
245   ÍF XII: 51–52. Hallgerðr's second husband was Glúmr, son of Óláfr *hjalti* from Varmalækr in Borgarfjörður. He ignored the advice of his brother in marrying Hallgerðr (ÍF XII: 42).
246   ÍF XII: 130–32.
247   ÍF XII: 6.
248   ÍF XII: 20–29, 58–59, 65–68.

the more active brother in spite of the fact that Höskuldr is a *goði*. This is in contrast with *Laxdæla saga* which views him at best neutrally and certainly as a cause of conflict in Laxárdalur. In *Njáls saga* as in *Laxdæla saga* Hrútr lives at Hrútsstaðir,[249] which may only tell us that the author no doubt a widely-known fact.

Óláfr *pái* is far less important than his father and uncle are in *Njáls saga* but, like them, he supports Gunnarr. Shortly after Höskuldr's death he meets up with Gunnar at the Alþing and gives him much good advice (*réð honum mörg ráð*) and an invitation to stay at his farm.[250] Óláfr appears at court again among Gunnarr's supporters.[251] Gunnarr eventually stays at Hjarðarholt when his disputes are settled and Óláfr is credited with giving him valuable parting gifts. In the context of Gunnarr's tragic role Óláfr is even more praiseworthy for inviting him back to Hjarðarholt to escape his enemies in the south.[252] Óláfr therefore appears in a narrative which is almost separate from that involving his kinsmen, in which, as a Hjarðarholt-based leader, he acts as Gunnarr's advisor and supporter.

Events surrounding Hallgerðr shed further light on how the Laxdælir are treated by the text although several interrelated ideas emerge together here. Hallgerðr is clearly seen as causing problems, but often only when men ignore her views. Her behaviour is also explained in part as a result of her association with men who appear to have a variety of negative characteristics. Hallgerðr's Hebridean foster-father is introduced ominously, as many Hebridean characters are in *Íslendingasögur*, just before the story of her first marriage as someone who had killed many men without compensating their kin.[253] She also has a maternal uncle, Svanr, living at Svansholl in Bjarnarfjörður to the north of Steingrímsfjörður who is skilled in magic (*fjölkunnigr mjök*) and unpleasant (*ódæll ok illr viðreignar*).[254]

Hallgerðr's first marriage, arranged by her kinsmen without her consent, is to Þorvaldr Ósvífrson from Staðarfell. A series of unfortunate circumstances combine to make Hallgerðr's marriage to this local, wealthy man a disaster. Her association with her Hebridean foster-father continues through into her

---

249 ÍF XII: 6, 8, 21, 32, 39, 50, 60, 63–65.
250 ÍF XII: 151.
251 ÍF XII: 164.
252 ÍF XII: 173–74, 183.
253 ÍF XII: 29–30.
254 ÍF XII: 32. The name of Hallgerðr's kinsman Ljótr *inn svarti*, only mentioned as her travelling companion from Svansholl to Höskuldsstaðir, also has clear negative associations (ÍF XII: 36). Some MSS also identify another minion of Hallgerðr as the illegitimate son of Svanr (ÍF XII: 100, note 2).

second marriage. *Njáls saga* clearly imagines Hallgerðr as a politically and socially disruptive figure who controlled some kind of disreputable support group. At the same time, however, this can be seen to excuse her male Laxárdalur kin, especially Hrútr, who had very little influence on her. Two further points might also be read as actually distancing Höskuldr and the Laxdælir from Hallgerðr and the disruptive forces she embodies: Hallgerðr's fosterfather is never associated with a given farm in Dalir while her disreputable connections are said to have come through her (unidentified) mother.[255]

Looking in more detail at the references to Dalir in *Njáls saga*, only two significant geopolitical connections are made but they are of some interest. Þorvaldr Ósvífsson, Hallgerðr's first husband, is associated with Staðarfell while his father is said to have been at Reykjanes (and by implication lived there) when Þorvaldr died.[256] This is precious little detail in terms of a geopolitical map in comparison with what we have in *Laxdæla saga* or *Eyrbyggja saga* but it still says something about how someone imagined the past in Dalir. Plenty of other large farms might have made appropriate homes for Hallgerðr's husband and father-in-law, for instance, but Staðarfell and Reykjanes are named. It makes sense within this text for Höskuldr and Hrútr to ally with nearby Staðarfell, because it was owned by someone whose father controlled Reykhólar.

The association of Reykjanes/Reykhólar with Staðarfell is not one made anywhere else. Likewise *Njáls saga* has a unique view of 'Ósvífr.' Whereas *Laxdæla saga* associates Ósvífr Helgason with Laugar, Sælingsdalstunga and then Helgafell (for the latter two farms, in connection with his daughter Guðrún), and both *Laxdæla saga* and *Eyrbyggja saga* see Ósvífr as a descendant of Björn inn austrœni,[257] *Njáls saga* locates him and his kin in entirely different farms and does not place him genealogically. Most probably *Njáls saga* was written down by a person or persons not entirely *au fait* with the details of myths from the west of Iceland, but nevertheless it is still likely that distinct traditions about early Dalir history are preserved here. The question is really why *Njáls saga* should chose to associate Þorvaldr Ósvífrsson and his father with

---

[255] In this context it is notable how *Njáls saga* treats the relationship between Bjarnarfjörður and Laxárdalur's wealthier people. In *Njáls saga* Svanr from Bjarnarfjörður is portrayed entirely negatively. This contrasts with *Laxdæla saga* and *S*. While the latter texts are rather confused (and at odds) over the genealogical connections between the two valleys concerned, they do not mention Svanr at all but assume a positive marriage link between the two valleys.

[256] ÍF XII: 37.

[257] ÍF IV: 12; ÍF V: 85.

Reykjanes and Staðarfell and not other major mid-western farms. If such a story in any way mirrors political relationships in the period before c.1265, then a possible context for such a story might have been when, in the late twelfth century, Hvamm-Sturla married his children into the family controlling Reykhólar. Even in this case, however, it is not clear whether Sturla could still be associated with Staðarfell, given that his brother and his descendants took it over. After this period there is certainly no evidence of such a direct political connection between the two farms.

If *Njáls saga* is seen as a product of later in the thirteenth century, as it often is, then it may be trying to say that Hallgerðr, as the daughter of the owner of Hjarðarholt, was appropriately matched for the owner of Staðarfell.[258] Both farms were certainly wealthy in the thirteenth century but neither was home to any of the highest rung of local leaders. It is possible that there was a connection between the farms in the first decades of the thirteenth century when Sighvatr Sturluson took over Hjarðarholt and his closest kinsmen may have retained control of Staðarfell. That said, the conflict between Hallgerðr and Þorvaldr might be better read as a story about their respective homes being at odds. The evidence from the first half of the thirteenth century furnishes us with some occasions when this situation was apparently the case: Guðmundr *undir Felli* and the Dufgusssynir at Hjarðarholt were sometimes on opposing sides of the conflicts between the Sturlungar, as we saw.[259]

1.9 The Territories and Power of Leading Men in Dalir: Some Conclusions

The account above has outlined the basic information which these *Íslendingasögur* give about the ninth to early eleventh century. It is now time to try to synthesise this material by picking out the broader patterns of political relationships which seem to lie behind them. While the *Íslendingasögur* for Dalir and northern Snæfellsnes do not provide us with a complete account of who controlled which valleys or groups of valleys, it is remarkable that there is very little conflict between their accounts where they overlap.

Laxárdalur and Álptafjörður are the areas which are treated most fully, and which will be considered here first. The common if less detailed interest of

---

258 Andersson 2006: 2, 20.
259 The parallel is not perfect. Guðmundr seems sometimes to have been neutral in disputes involving Þórðr Sturluson and Sturla Sighvatsson but also to have more readily sided with Þórðr and his sons in more local, earlier disputes, though later been willing to support the sons of Sighvatr in larger-scale disputes. See pp. 103, 104, 106 above; Sverrir Jakobsson 2015: 134.

both sagas in Hvammssveit also allows us to comment on attitudes to power in this district's past relatively fully. The other districts are not covered in detail but some conceptions of who controlled them can still be identified.

Much has already been said about the control of farms in *Laxdæla saga*'s Laxárdalur. This saga seems to conceive of the valley being divided in two, with one local leader living on and controlling respective sides of the Laxá. Dönustaðir, the highest-valued farm in the main valley, is the only farm which we see controlled by anyone otherwise connected with the opposite side of the valley.[260] As to the territorial extent of these local leaders' control, we can see that they probably had influence over little more than one half of Laxárdalur. Immediately to the north, Ljárskógar is tied to Hjarðarholt. To the south, however, Þykkvaskógr was associated with the Bollasynir, who may have been assumed to have still controlled Höskuldsstaðir. On the other hand, Hjarðarholt's Óláfr *pái* is asked to round up the criminal tracked down in Hundadalur. In this episode the saga suggests, in effect, that Óláfr *pái* was the first person to whom a *bóndi* in Hundadalur might turn to for help. The sphere of real influence over which one of these leaders had appears to have been no more than 15 or so farms. The saga is consistent in having no place for a local leader from Sauðafell, such as there was in the thirteenth century.[261]

Snorri *goði*, who lives first at Helgafell and then at Sælingsdalstunga, is portrayed by both *Eyrbyggja saga* and *Laxdæla saga* as the most powerful man around Breiðafjörður during his lifetime. Snorri is an unusual saga *goði* in that he not only moves farm but moves from one district to another. However, it is important to remember that he is never seen acting as leader of more than one locality at a time. In this respect we can speculate that the powers attributed to him fit two moulds, one for a leader at Helgafell, the other for a leader of Hvammssveit, rather than his powers being seen as particular to him. In other words Snorri's power operates in two phases, one after the other, and his power is more limited (geographically) than it would have been if he had controlled two districts simultaneously.

While based at Helgafell, Snorri effectively takes control of the whole of Álptafjörður when he removes his only political opponent within the fjord, Arnkell. Snorri clearly then held sway over the whole of this small fjord. It would seem that a similar pattern is conceived of as persisting after Snorri moves. Þóroddr Þorbrandsson, Snorri's foster-father, owned at least three of

---

260 See p. 233.
261 Þórólfr *rauðnefr* of Sauðafell does not seem to warrant being classed as a *goði* although he does feature in events set in Laxárdalur (ÍF V: 21, 33, 35, 36).

the farms in the fjord and it seems likely that the Þorbrandssynir controlled this small fjord from Kársstaðir. The saga has no stories about the relations between Helgafell's new owners with the Þorbrandssons although it is a moot point as to whether this is significant. It seems best to conclude that the few farms in Álptafjörður are seen throughout the saga as being one political unit which was usually controlled by a locally-based leader, whether based at Helgafell or Kársstaðir. The idea that a figure like Arnkell could be imagined as living so close to Snorri *goði*, and on a seemingly poor farm, has been seen as a reason to question the credibility of *Eyrbyggja saga* as genuine tradition. But the situation can be read as two leaders locating themselves optimally within a rich district with one finally overcoming their rival.

It is conspicuous that the large farm of Narfeyri is not directly credited with a sphere of influence anywhere in the *Íslendingasögur*. Charter evidence suggests that in the thirteenth century Narfeyri was the leading farm of a territorial grouping which also included Kársstaðir. This was the case in about 1224, the likely date of the first charter for the church at Narfeyri, when the church was supposed to have taken tithes from all the farms from Örlygsstaðir in the west and Hólmslátr in the east. The only hint at Narfeyri's control of other farms is through the supposed gift of Kársstaðir by Geirröðr of Narfeyri to Finngeir (whose descendants were Þorbrandr and his sons, the allies of Snorri *goði*). Quite what this relationship might have meant is not clear; perhaps the account is imagining that although Kársstaðir was *supposed* to belong to Narfeyri, in practice it was controlled by Helgafell.

Three different farms are seen as centres of political power within Hvammssveit in both *Laxdæla saga* and *Eyrbyggja saga*. First, Hvammr itself is seen as the home of the *höfðingi* Þórðr *gellir*. *Laxdæla saga* sees Laugar as having been the home of Ósvífr when he was on equal terms with the leaders of Laxárdalur. Later Sælingsdalstunga is identified as the home of first Bolli Þorleiksson and Guðrún and then Snorri *goði*. The information relating to each of these farms helps us to build up a picture of power as it was conceived of for this region's early history.

In *Eyrbyggja saga* some idea of a local power base in Hvammssveit is suggested for Þórðr *gellir* of Hvammr. When Þórðr is said to have given his kinswoman from a neighbouring farm in marriage, it is being assumed that he had kinsmen living close to him from whom he could draw political support.[262] No saga, however, tells us any more than this about Þórðr in Hvammssveit nor

---

262 ÍF IV: 18.

does anything to explain how power came to lie with Ósvífr *inn spaki* who lived at Laugar.

The geographical extent of the power of first Ósvífr and then Snorri *goði* is also unclear. What we can say about Ósvífr's influence over Hvammssveit, though, is that it was not complete. *Laxdœla saga* says that Þórarinn Þórisson, as owner of Sælingsdalstunga, was on good terms with both Ósvífr and Óláfr *pái* at Hjarðarholt. Þórarinn's alignment towards the two parties is fairly ambivalent – it is hard to say whether he is thought to have dealt with either of them willingly or under duress – but it is significant that he has relations with both of them.[263] Ósvífr does not appear to want or be able to bully Þórarinn and so he/Laugar is not being portrayed as a dominant farm in Hvammmssveit.

Snorri *goði*'s move to Sælingsdalstunga brings out another aspect of power as it manifests itself in Hvammssveit. *Eyrbyggja saga* is explicit in saying that Snorri has a *þingmaðr* in Bitra who looks after Snorri's driftage rights on this stretch of coast. Snorri is not the only local leader seeking control of this area, however. Sturla Þjóðreksson from Saurbær also has rights in this area while two men, Þórir Gull-Harðarson and Óspakr, are seen as influential men just within Bitra.[264] Several points can be made about this image of Snorri. Snorri's control in Bitra is not exclusive and there is no sign that it expanded after the defeat of Óspakr and his fellow 'pirates.' But for clear economic reasons a *goði* from Hvammssveit had an interest in Bitra which was shared with his counterpart in Saurbær. The text also partly mirrors or pre-empts what we see in later documentary evidence. In the fourteenth century Sælingsdalstunga's church did have rights to *reki* but of the *staðir* in Saurbær it was Hvoll rather than Staðarhóll that had them.[265]

Having discussed the extent of the power of leaders from the three best-detailed districts in the region, control of the remainder of the region can be discussed more briefly due to the smaller evidence base.

In the north of the region, Saurbær is rarely mentioned and only one local leader is seen doing anything significant. This is Sturla Þjóðreksson who joined Snorri *goði* in taking action to protect their rights in Bitra. This implies that

---

263   Þórarinn is first seen selling land to Ósvífr; then acts as witness to the theft of Kjartan's sword by the Laugarmenn; sells Sælingsdalstunga to Bolli Þorleiksson; is forced to sell the farm to Kjartan; and fights with Kjartan when Kjartan is attacked by the Ósvífrssynir (ÍF IV: 86, 142, 146–48, 151, 153–54).
264   ÍF IV: 157.
265   DI II: 633; DI III: 79, 103.

Sturla was relatively powerful, arguably the most powerful man in Saurbær. Neither *Eyrbyggja saga* nor *Þorskfirðinga saga* give specific details, however.

Skarðsströnd and Fellsströnd, two areas referred to in some detail in *Sturlunga saga*, are hardly mentioned in the *Íslendingasögur*. While Barkarstaðir is linked with Börkr *inn digri*, a man possibly of some wealth and influence,[266] few other farms are mentioned at all. Not even Snorri is seen being active in these areas.

Control of the huge number of islands in Hvammsfjörður and close to Skarðsströnd is generally ignored in the *Íslendingasögur* just as they are in the *samtíðarsögur*, despite their economic importance. Helgafell also owned the group of islands known as Helgafellseyjar (and many others) in later centuries but we can say very little about their control earlier.[267] This suggests that the islands were not strategically important. Helgafell and Fellsströnd probably had economic relationships with those islands closest to them but the former, at least, drew no strong political support from *bændr* living on them.

Districts towards the western end of Snæfellsnes (Neshreppur and Eyrarsveit) are seen by *Eyrbyggja saga* as being influenced by Snorri *goði*. Fróðá is viewed as being under his complete control. After his sister's marriage to Þorbjörn of Fróðá he was called on to support his brother-in-law at court in a case involving farms in this locale. And after Þorbjörn's death the saga says that Snorri had influence over what happened to this farm: he helped arrange his sister's second marriage and the couple again lived at Fróðá.[268] Snorri is also said to have had connections with a man who lived at one of the larger farms in Neshreppur (Þrándr *stígandi* of Ingjaldshvoll).[269] The saga again supposes that Snorri had links with people who lived far to the west of Helgafell, rather than to any other district.

Eyrarsveit, or the region immediately to the west of Helgafell, is poorly described by *Eyrbyggja saga* considering its centrality to its events. However, we can see two leading families in the district, neither of which, judging by the location of their farms, are imagined as having enjoyed any significant kind of

---

266   ÍF IV: 26.
267   The earliest *máldagi* for Jónskirkja at Helgafell is from c.1274 (DI II: 116). Of the many islands only Svíney (Purkey) and Öxney are mentioned in *Eyrbyggja saga* and S with the implication that they might have been inhabited (ÍF I: 130, 131, 147; IV: 59, 198, 241). Öxney is also mentioned in *Laxdæla saga* (ÍF V: 81)
268   ÍF IV: 77.
269   ÍF IV: 165.

territorial control. The Þorgrímssynir, Vermundr *inn mjóvi* and Víga-Styrr, lived at Bjarnarhöfn and Hraun respectively. Another pair of brothers, Steinþórr *af Eyri* and Þormóðr Þorláksson, lived at farms on either side of the Þorgrímssynir, at Öndverðareyrr and Bakki respectively. Thus *Eyrbyggja saga* appears to show two powerful families living within a relatively small area. It is more likely the case that neither family is imagined as being particularly wealthy or powerful, because they owned just one wealthy farm each (Öndverðareyrr and Bjarnarhöfn).

Skógarströnd, mentioned sporadically in *Sturlunga saga*, is barely mentioned at all in either *Eyrbyggja saga* or *Laxdæla saga*. Þorgestr *inn gamli* of Breiðabólstaðr is the only likely leader identified from this area but his power is not defined.[270] Otherwise *Eyrbyggja saga* does not attribute influence over this area to any leader; and Snorri *goði* never seems to have any followers there. *Laxdæla saga*, on the other hand, does allow for the possibility that one local leader controlled the whole of Skógarströnd, but this is only implied by the presence of Þórarinn *goðorðsmaðr* from Langidalr then Þorgils Hölluson.[271] Þórarinn and Þorgils, who lived at either end of this stretch of coast, are said to have controlled the same *goðorð*. Skógarströnd would seem to be the most likely source of support on which they could both have drawn, especially when the influence of other local leaders allowed them no other realistic source of support. Whether or not this is the supposition behind *Laxdæla saga*'s references to these two men, Skógarströnd was clearly not seen as a traditional centre of political power.

In the *Íslendingasögur* the absence of any explicitly named political leader from Miðdalir, except perhaps Þorbjörn in *Króka-Refs saga*, provides a very notable contrast from the picture of politics given in *Sturlunga saga* from which we know that Sturla Sighvatsson (d.1238) and Hrafn Oddsson lived at Sauðafell for several years.[272] Neither *Laxdæla saga* nor *Eyrbyggja saga* is interested in events in this area.[273] It could be the case that *Laxdæla saga* saw control of this area shared in some way by leaders from Laxárdalur and Þorgils Hölluson in Hörðudalur.

The scale of political action in these texts and the geographical extent of the meaningful control by local leaders, requires some final comment before we

---

[270] Þorgestr is one of the characters named in the dispute involving Eiríkr *rauði* which is recorded in both *Eyrbyggja saga* and *Eiríks saga rauða*, ÍF IV: 59, 198.
[271] See p. 229 above.
[272] Probably from 1245 to 1262. See above, pp. 53, 115, 118.
[273] Helgi Þorláksson 1991a.

move to the Eyjafjörður region. It is clear that political power was every bit as localised as previous opinions have suggested. There are, however, signs of almost exclusive dominion, but only within, say, 20km radius of a leader's farm. These leaders operate a strong influence over other farms nearby often because kinsmen are supposed to have lived at those neighbouring farms. Outlying individual properties are also imagined as being held by those leaders, typically on Strandir, because of it was a source of *reki*. Leadership in almost all cases of the men identified in these texts as *höfðingjar*, but less often as *goðar*, most likely because being a *höfðingi* was thought of as synonymous with holding a *goðorð*. For Dalir and Snæfellsnes, Snorri *goði* constitutes the most powerful image of a local leader but his real power is not much different from that for other men who are pre-eminent in their district.

2   Eyjafjörður and the North-East in the *Íslendingasögur*

The five *Íslendingasögur* which take place in and around Eyjafjörður are the focus of this section: *Víga-Glúms saga, Svarfdæla saga, Valla-Ljóts saga, Reykdæla saga og Víga-Skútu* and, last, *Ljósvetninga saga*. These can be split into two sub-groups. *Víga-Glúms saga, Reykdæla saga*[274] and *Ljósvetninga saga* share a geographical focus on Eyjafjörður and the areas to its immediate east. These three sagas form the core part of what has been called an 'immanent saga' about the local leader called Guðmundr *inn ríki*.[275] Other *Íslendingasögur* mention Guðmundr (based at Möðruvellir in Eyjafjörður)[276] but he is most prominent in *Víga-Glúms saga* and *Ljósvetninga saga*; although *Reykdæla saga* has Guðmundr in a minor role, it features another prominent local leader, Víga-Glúmr, which strengthens its connection to the former pair of sagas. These three sagas also have a chronological overlap, but with *Víga-Glúms saga* seemingly beginning first and *Ljósvetninga saga* beginning last. Despite this apparent shared content, there are few overlaps of events, the exception being one

---

274   Henceforth shortened to *Reykdæla saga* although as will become readily apparent, each half of the saga's name represents a distinct narrative. See pp. 284–90.
275   Gísli Sigurðsson 2007. See above on Carol Clover's idea of the 'immanent saga', pp. 207–9.
276   TAs for previous chapters it is worth remembering that there are two farms called Möðruvellir in the wider Eyjafjörður valley system (Map 9). In what follows it will be made explicit when it is Möðruvellir in Hörgárdalur that is being referred to. 'Möðruvellir' on its own refers usually to Möðruvellir in Eyjafjörður.

story which appears in both *Víga-Glúms saga* and *Reykdœla saga*.[277] This almost suggests that these three sagas were written down in some kind of co-ordinated way or with one or more authors being aware of the content of the other sagas.

Svarfdœla saga and *Valla-Ljóts saga* work as a pair, as an almost continuous narrative of the history of the valley of Svarfaðardalur (Map 8). These sagas record disputes between two kin groups (of Þorsteinn *svörfuðr*, Ljótólfr and their respective descendants) first in *Svarfdœla saga* and then in *Valla-Ljóts saga* in a later generation.[278] Of the two, *Valla-Ljóts saga*'s action has some-thing in common with the first group of sagas mentioned above: it involves Guðmundr *ríki* and some of its action takes place partly in Eyjafjörður. *Svarfdœla saga* seems to form part of a separate and possibly later tradition because it barely mentions Guðmundr *ríki*.[279]

Given the similarities in the geographical coverage and shared personnel of *Víga-Glúms saga*, *Ljósvetninga saga* and *Reykdœla saga*, it is inevitable that they have been scrutinized intensely by literary scholars. In recent decades Theodore Andersson has provided the most significant commentary and

---

277 *Reykdœla saga* Ch. 26, *Víga-Glúms saga* Ch. 16. Opinions as to the reason for this example of supposed *rittengsl* have varied: McKinnell (1986: 9–10) along with many others thinks it is an interpolation in both sagas; Andersson (2006: 65–66) considers *Reykdœla saga* later and to have borrowed the episode from *Víga-Glúms saga*.

278 *Svarfdœla saga* is a more than usually problematic text in that the surviving manuscripts have notable lacunae although its beginning and end survive. When Iceland-based events in the saga begin they take place solely in the generation before the dominance of Valla-Ljótr of *Valla-Ljóts saga*. The nine-chapter long *Valla-Ljóts saga* is well-known for begin-ning abruptly, without the typical *Íslendingasögur* account of the *landnám* nor in fact any explicit marker as to when it takes place. By Chapter 3, however, *Valla-Ljóts saga* it is as-sumed that there had been a church at Grund in Svarfaðardalur (ÍF IX: 243) which sug-gests that it begins after Iceland's official conversion. It only covers events during the life-times of the leaders Ljótr and Guðmundr *ríki*.

279 The five *þættir* with a connection to the region, and thus included in *Íslensk fornrit* vol-ume IX, will not be discussed in this chapter because they say so little about Eyjafjörður and its neighbouring valleys. Those *þættir* are: *Ögmundar þáttr dytts* about a son of a for-mer slave of Víga-Glúmr (ÍF IX: 101); *Þorvalds þáttr tasalda* about Þorvaldr *tasaldi* Stein-grímsson from Sigluvík, the nephew of Víga-Glúmr, an identification/relationship only made explicit in *Víga-Glúms saga* and *Ögmundar þáttr dytts* (ÍF IX: 14 & note 6, 100); *Þor-leifs þáttr Jarlsskálds* about the son of Ásgeirr *rauðfeldr* from Brekka in Svarfaðardalur (ÍF IX: 215–16); Sneglu-Halli of *Sneglu-Halla þáttr* is not given a specific home and is simply of northern stock, 'norðlenzkr at ætt' (ÍF IX: 263); Þorgrímr Hallason of *Þorgríms þáttr Hallasonar* is located at Brúnastaðir in Fljót but his father's genealogical connections are not recorded.

analysis of them.²⁸⁰ His characterisations of these texts and the arguments about the causes of their interconnections and likely relative dates are more compelling than older scholarship which has generally dated the texts to later in the thirteenth century. In general Andersson sees them sharing features with the kings' sagas (about Norwegian kings) which may have been produced in northern Iceland from the mid to late twelfth century and were developing alongside *Íslendingasögur*.²⁸¹ Given their geographical focus, these three *Íslendingasögur* may well have been written in or around Eyjafjörður, perhaps in the monastery at Munkaþverá. Aside from their focus on Eyjafjörður and the districts to its east, Andersson sees the role of one notable figure in northern Icelandic politics in the later twelfth century, Þorvarðr Þorgeirsson (d.1207), as the key to understanding their origins.²⁸² In Andersson's view if Þorvarðr did not write one or more of the sagas, he commissioned or inspired their writing during his lifetime or shortly afterwards. What we know is that Þorvarðr was associated with Bishop Guðmundr *góði* of Hólar (1161–1237) and he appears to have had something to do with Guðmundr's education. He became a monk and it likely that he followed in his father's footsteps in going to Munkaþverá.²⁸³ He also appears to have been closely connected with the Sturlungar, who were certainly involved in literary production. Crucial, though, is the fact that Þorvarðr is actually mentioned in two of the texts: *Ljósvetninga saga* recalls a rather mundane saying attributed to him, while *Reykdœla saga* identifies a spear which a character in the saga had supposedly owned and then Þorvarðr had acquired.²⁸⁴ For Andersson, the recollection of such trivia in these texts means that they could not have been written very long after Þorvarðr's death, and this seems entirely likely.

Andersson also provides dates and methods for the composition of the sagas. In relative terms he thinks *Víga-Glúms saga* predates *Ljósvetninga saga* and *Reykdœla saga*. The close similarity in wording between some sections of *Víga-Glúms saga* and *Reykdœla saga* he accounts for through scribal copying rather than a coincidence in the way that they might have been delivered orally. Thus the author of *Reykdœla saga* 'knew *Víga-Glúms saga* but also knew a great deal of additional local tradition and was therefore inspired to supplement the

---

280 Andersson & Miller 1989; Andersson 1994; Andersson 2006.
281 Andersson 2012, esp. pp. 35–43.
282 Andersson 1994: 17–21.
283 Andersson 1994: 17–18.
284 ÍF x: 73, 213.

earlier text.'[285] Yet although they have characters in common, the actual narratives of *Reykdœla saga* and *Ljósvetninga saga* do not coincide, suggesting that the author of one knew the written version of the other and tried to avoid any overlap.[286] In Andersson's view *Víga-Glúms saga* dates to no later than 1210–20 but he is not precise about how much earlier, even though he points out broader similarities with *The Oldest Saga of King Olaf* which he places at about 1200.[287] As to *Reykdœla saga*, he thinks it was most likely written between 1207 and 1222[288] and that *Ljósvetninga saga* could have been produced 'around 1220'[289] or 'perhaps in the 1220s.'[290] Given the complementarity of these three texts, Andersson also wishes to group them together chronologically.

Despite all this, there are grounds for doubting such a clustering of dates. If these sagas were written down as part of the same, brief push to record local traditions it seems odd that they were not written down as a single narrative especially given that they have so much in common and would have required little reconciliation with one another. That they are not a single narrative would seem all the more peculiar if, as Andersson implies, some or all of them were written at Munkaþverá.[291] Indeed while there is a consensus that these

---

285 Andersson 2006: 65–66 (ÍF X: lx–lxix. *Víga-Glúms saga* Ch. 16 and *Reykdœla saga* Chs. 23–26 are those under discussion).
286 Andersson 2006: 82.
287 Andersson 2006: 1–2, 60–61, 64.
288 Following Hofmann 1972; Andersson & Miller 1989: 82–84; Andersson 2006: 65–66.
289 Andersson & Miller 1989: 84.
290 Andersson 2006: 119.
291 Andersson 2006: 65. There is a possible parallel between twelfth-century events and *Víga-Glúms saga* and *Ljósvetninga saga* which might support Andersson's case but he makes nothing of it. At the end of *Víga-Glúms saga* and in most of *Ljósvetninga saga*, the *goðorðsmenn* Einarr Eyjólfsson and Guðmundr *ríki* are depicted living at Munkaþverá and Möðruvellir in Eyjafjörður; Þorvarðr Þorgeirsson may have lived at Munkaþverá while his brother, the priest Ingimundr, lived at 'inner' Möðruvellir, 'á Möðruvöllu innri' for some time from in about 1172–73, renting the estate for ten hundreds, 'leigði landit tíu hundruðum' (SS I: 124). Andersson (1994: 20–21) assumes that this Möðruvellir must be the Möðruvellir in Hörgárdalur but the text is explicit in saying that it is the 'inner' Möðruvellir, in Eyjafjörður (SS I: 546–47, note 7). Andersson follows the editors of the 1946 edition of *Sturlunga saga* who suggested that this did not make sense because there were other *bændr* already living at Möðruvellir in Eyjafjörður which would have prevented Ingimundr from living there. Whether ten hundreds actually got one the whole farm is unknowable although later figures suggest he could perhaps have been renting a fraction of the farm (*Jarðabók* X: 274–8). The translators of *Sturlunga saga* trust the original's Möðruvellir innri (McGrew and Thomas 1974: 520, note 15).

three sagas were written at Munkaþverá; this too is open to question.²⁹² It is undeniable that each text shows a strong interest in Þverá itself and in some of the farms which Munkaþverá owned in later centuries. However, none of the texts are especially 'pro-Munkaþverá,' despite their interest in it as a centre of local power. We might expect a slightly more positive portrayal of Þverá than we actually get. In *Reykdœla saga*, for example, the portrayal of Þverá's most prominent occupant, Víga-Glúmr, is rather ambivalent. At one point Víga-Glúmr seems to be acknowledged as getting the better of another local leader (Skúta of Skútustaðir)²⁹³ but, at the same time, the result of the saga's key peace agreement is to transfer ownership of one particular property into the hands of farms other than Þverá. More significantly, the property concerned (Eyin mikla or Staðarey) is known to have belonged to Þverá in the fifteenth century; it might have been expected for *Reykdœla saga* to record a story explaining how it obtained the property. The transfer in *Reykdœla saga* is instead from the Reykdælir into the ownership of people from either Möðruvellir or Árskógr.²⁹⁴ This is not a story which was designed to bolster Þverá, even though it could so easily have been just by changing the outcome of the settlement.

Víga-Glúms saga is the text most obviously *about* Þverá but it is also mostly about the presence there of a disruptive and unsuccessful local leader. In the end, Víga-Glúmr gets expelled from Þverá and replaced by a more positive character, one who was the brother of the local leader at Möðruvellir. This is rather ambivalent, however, given that most of the text is about Víga-Glúmr's life at Þverá. *Ljósvetninga saga* gives a more positive role to Þverá but the farm is still not at the centre of the action: that same new occupant (Einarr Eyjólfsson) is a popular, moderate figure without being dominant.²⁹⁵

It has been suggested that *Víga-Glúms saga* was written at Þverá during the period in which the *höfðingi* Sighvatr Sturluson lived in Eyjafjörður (from 1217 until his death in 1238). This might not appear such a significant difference from Andersson's view but it does bring into consideration further issues of the text's purpose and influences. Richard North has sought further evidence for Sighvatr's sponsorship of the writing of either *Víga-Glúms saga* or the conjectured earlier version of the saga, **Þverœinga saga*, whose name appears in passing in a *þáttr*.²⁹⁶ North's view is based on the same general assumption as

---

292   See also North 2009: 270.
293   ÍF x: 236.
294   ÍF x: 203. Two documents record Munkaþverá's possession of meadows and other land there, 'Eing ok iarðar eign j myklu ey.' (DI IV: 698 (in 1446) and DI V: 303 (in 1461)).
295   See below pp. 291, 294, 297.
296   North 2009.

Andersson's, that the Sturlungar were involved in textual production but also that Sighvatr would want to connect himself to Víga-Glúmr. Sighvatr's motivation might have been to 'prove his local *óðal* (inalienable land rights) by writing a biography of Víga-Glúmr, master of Þverá' in the face of local opposition to his own arrival in Eyjafjörður as is set out in *Sturlunga saga*.[297] One sign of Sighvatr's supposed connections to the text is through the association of Víga-Glúmr's son Már with the establishment of a church (at Fornhagi in Hörgárdalur); according to the *Sturlubók* version of *Landnámabók*, but not made explicit in *Víga-Glúms saga*, Sighvatr could claim descent from Már.

North also suggests textual connections or similarities between *Sturlunga saga* and *Víga-Glúms saga* which could imply a connection with Sighvatr but they do not necessarily prove a definite connection nor which text influenced the other. North notes, for instance, that Sighvatr is remarkable for having a sharp wit like that of Víga-Glúmr. He also reiterates the similarities between the episode of the secret killing of Kálfr in *Víga-Glúms saga* (Chs. 13–15) with two other stories of killings, one in *Íslendinga saga*, that of Hafr from Hrafnagil in 1222 thought to have been carried out by Sighvatr, the other in a twelfth-century text, the *Disciplina Clericalis* by Petrus Alphonsi, a text which *may* have been available at Munkaþverá.[298] There is no denying the similarities in these stories but it is difficult to be certain whether the writer of *Víga-Glúms saga* consciously borrowed these stories and if so why they would do so. It seems no less likely to me that the author of *Íslendinga saga* might actually have cast Sighvatr in the role of Víga-Glúmr rather than that the character of Víga-Glúmr was modelled on Sighvatr.

North adduces other arguments to make the case for Sighvatr's influence but, in short, they do not go much further than others' arguments in pinning down a context for the saga's writing. One might further counter North's views by pointing out, first, that the genealogical line from Már to the Sturlungar is not made explicit in the surviving *Víga-Glúms saga*; second, that Sighvatr otherwise had no more reason (although perhaps greater means) to record local history than many other local leaders; and, third, that Grund, Sighvatr's farm, surely ought to have played a more prominent role in the saga than it does if Sighvatr were behind its writing.[299] While Sighvatr might not have wanted to record a story which showed Grund leading opposition to Munkaþverá, the

---

297 North 2009: 272; pp. 137–38 above.
298 North 2009: 272; McKinnell 1987: 11–12.
299 *Esphœlinga saga* is mentioned in the introduction to *Þórarins þáttr* (ÍF x: 143; North 2009: 258; ÍF IX: xxviii–xxxvii).

holder of Grund remains a junior opponent of Víga-Glúmr at Þverá in the surviving saga; it seems impossible to say whether the lost text shared this feature.

At the very least, then, we do not have unambiguously pro-Munkaþverá texts nor precise contexts for their writing, with the exceptions of the comments about Þorvarðr Þorgeirsson. Indeed, perhaps we should not expect a sense of corporate identity from such a small monastic house, nor from any other major farm, just as we have seen for the sagas for Dalir. Equally it is hard to see the prejudices of any other known local secular leaders or monastic establishments from later centuries in these sagas. John McKinnell's conclusion that the saga 'was most likely written at or near Thvera itself'[300] is about as certain as we can be but we have to remember that 'close to Þverá' includes many other large farms which all feature in some way in the saga and might also have had the resources and will to write sagas. Just within Eyjafjörður proper, the owners or occupants of Grund, Möðruvellir, Saurbær, Hrafnagil or one of the two farms at Espihóll might make them all potential authorship candidates. None of these farms, however, have unambiguously positive roles in any of the *Íslendingasögur* discussed in this chapter. Instead these texts show the kinds of ambiguities which might accord well with the notions discussed earlier in this book, those of an immanent saga or a 'distributed author', where a single author's prejudices do not come to the fore.[301]

Far greater ambiguity surrounds the origins of *Svarfdœla saga* and *Valla-Ljóts saga* than even the other texts analysed in this chapter. *Svarfdœla saga* will be dealt with first as it forms the first part of the Svarfaðardalur-centred narrative.

Very few scholars have ever had much to say about *Svarfdœla saga* and fewer still have had anything positive to say about it. The saga is often supposed to be a 'post-classical' saga and to have been reworked in style and content more reminiscent of fifteenth-century tastes as seen in the *fornaldarsögur* (Legendary sagas). As with the *Íslendingasögur* discussed above, an earlier date might be supposed for *Svarfdœla saga*'s origins than has often been supposed. The saga survives in just two versions: one reasonably complete one from the seventeenth century, and a single page from the fifteenth century.[302] What we do have also includes a large lacuna which follows a ten-chapter introductory section, featuring the adventures in Sweden of a Norwegian called Þorsteinn

---

300   McKinnell 1987: 13.
301   See above pp. 207–9; Rankovic 2006, 2007.
302   Boyer 1993: 626.

(from Naumadalr, i.e. Namdal, Trøndelag), a distant relative of Þorsteinn *svörfuðr*, before the remaining 18 chapters which feature descendents of Þorsteinn *svörfuðr* in and around Svarfaðardalur in Iceland. The assumption has to be that the two men called Þorsteinn are related and that, unfortunately, we are missing the account of the *landnám* of this kin group; the saga only restarts in the middle of a fight involving Þorsteinn *svörfuðr*. By contrast, the S version of *Landnámabók* does include an account of the *landnám* of Þorsteinn *svörfuðr*. This also suggests that some form of the saga existed by c.1250, if one accepts that *Sturlubók* was written in the mid-thirteenth century or, if we take the contents of *Sturlubók* to relate closely to the original *Landnámabók*, that a *Svarfdœla saga* existed a hundred years before then.

There are other grounds for not accepting the supposed evidence for a late date for *Svarfdœla saga*. The inclusion of a character with the epithet *lögmaðr* (Höskuldr *lögmaðr*) has sometimes been supposed to date the surviving *Svarfdœla saga* to no earlier than c.1300.[303] *Lögmaðr*, literally 'law man,' was the name given to a legal official in Iceland only after the introduction of the law books *Járnsíða* and *Jónsbók* in 1271–81. Yet this epithet need not be seen as indicating a post-1281 date for the saga. This nickname seems to have no significance in the text except, as is the case for the more common use of the term *goði*,[304] as a marker of high status for the character concerned. Höskuldr is briefly seen as having a role as a judge in a case in Svarfaðardalur[305] but he appears not to have had the kind of significant, regional or 'national' legal role in the way that the lawspeaker (*lögsögumaðr*) did prior to the Norwegian takeover or a *lögmaðr* did afterwards. While it is more likely that a nickname like this would have been used or remembered as Norwegian influence was beginning to be felt post-1271, there is no reason why a character might not acquire it at any point before the word had a more formal meaning. The use of this word need not undermine the notion that *Svarfdœla saga* existed much earlier.

Guðni Jónsson and Jónas Kristjánsson proposed different parts of the fourteenth century as the date for the writing down of *Svarfdœla saga* by the family associated with the farm of Urðir in Svarfaðardalur, the Urðamenn. A very brief outline genealogy of the Urðamenn appears very close to the end of the saga's final chapter.[306] In a similar way to what has been suggested above for other texts, it is easy to see that, in this case, the Urðamenn had a Svarfaðardalur

---

303   ÍF IX: lxxxviii.
304   Jón Viðar Sigurðsson 1999: 50–53 for other examples.
305   ÍF IX: 152.
306   ÍF IX: xc.

connection and that they were powerful in the fourteenth century, but if they did have the saga written down then they made few obvious efforts to glamourise their own family's past in it. None of the Urðamenn mentioned in the genealogy in *Svarfdæla saga* have any connection with any other characters in the text and the farm itself is barely mentioned at all.[307] Thus, for all its peculiarities of content, the structuring elements of *Svarfdæla saga* do not seem out of the ordinary compared to other *Íslendingasögur*. The oddities of the saga, such as its portrayal of extreme violence towards a female character, and its different epithet for Guðmundr *ríki*, calling him Guðmundr *gamli*, can be equally well explained by its having been part of an otherwise unknown tradition of storytelling as by its date.

The evidence for the date and location of the writing of *Valla-Ljóts saga* is every bit as sparse as that for *Svarfdæla saga*. Andersson and Miller put it simply: 'There is no convincing way of dating *Valla-Ljóts saga*.'[308] The saga contains no references to identifiable individuals from *samtíðarsögur* or other documentary sources. Scholars have only proposed a modest two textual connections. They have suggested that in each case those connections demonstrate that *Valla-Ljóts saga* influenced those other texts, *Bolla þáttr* and *Víga-Glúms saga* but the direction of influence is impossible to determine, even if we accept the reality of these connections. That *Valla-Ljóts saga* follows on so neatly from *Svarfdæla saga* does, however, suggest that the scribes writing down one were aware of the other's existence. The manuscript evidence does not help either, with the earliest-surviving versions of *Valla-Ljóts saga* being in seventeenth-century paper manuscripts. Indeed Andersson and Miller only supposed the text to originate in the thirteenth century; this is as good a guess as any based on the usual means by which texts are dated. Yet as with the other texts discussed in this chapter, the depictions of geopolitical action in the saga itself must be as much a guide to its likely date as other forms of evidence.

---

307 The author expresses doubt about the history of the farm of Urðir: 'Böðvarr hyggju vér, at búit hafi at Urðum, sonr Eyjólfs breiðhöfða, er Urðamenn eru frá komnir. Eyjólfr breiðhöfði var sonr Þorgils mjöksiglanda.' 'We think that Böðvarr, the son of Eyjólfr *breiðhöfði*, from whom the people of Urðir are descended, lived at Urðir Eyjólfr *breiðhöfði* was the son of Þorgils *mjöksiglandi.*' (ÍF IX: 208). Other uncertainties are raised by the author but these need not have any bearing on dating. For example, they recognise doubts over whether Karl Karlsson married Ragnhildr Ljótólfsdóttir: '...ok er þat sumra manna sögn, at hann hafi utan farit ok aukit þar ætt sína, en fleira segja, at hann hafi átt Ragnhildi Ljótólfsdóttur ok börn mörg með henni.' 'It is said by some people that he left Iceland and expanded his kin but more say that he married Ragnhildr Ljótólfsdóttir and had many children with her.' (ÍF IX: 207).

308 Andersson and Miller 1989: 85

The intertwined narratives from this region will be analysed for what they say about local politics in two groups, dealing with those longer, interrelated texts centered on Eyjafjörður first, then *Svarfdœla saga* and *Valla-Ljóts saga*.

Although it almost does not matter in which order these texts are dealt with, they will be tackled in the order in which they appear to be set, the earliest first, although of course they do overlap chronologically. *Víga-Glúms saga* takes place earliest, then *Reykdœla saga* and *Ljósvetninga saga*. *Víga-Glúms saga* comes first because the saga details the political career of Víga-Glúmr of Þverá until he is forced out of politics. *Reykdœla saga*'s events seem to be roughly simultaneous with *Víga-Glúms saga* in that it features Víga-Glúmr and Eyjólfr Valgerðarson from Möðruvellir but does not include local leaders from a later generation. Thus Einarr Eyjólfsson is at Þverá when *Ljósvetninga saga* begins but in this text it is Einarr's better-known brother, Guðmundr *ríki* from Möðruvellir in Eyjafjörður who is the focus of the action. Whereas *Víga-Glúms saga* has lots to say about the micro-politics of the main valley of Eyjafjörður, and *Reykdœla saga* deals with lower Eyjafjörður (and Reykjadalur and Mývatnssveit), *Ljósvetninga saga* is concerned more with Guðmundr *ríki*'s influence in Ljósavatn and other areas to the east of Eyjafjörður. After his death, for the final third of the text, relations with areas to the north-west of the the main valley are also the focus for his son (Eyjólfr).

2.1 Víga-Glúms Saga

Víga-Glúms saga is a fairly straightforward biography of Víga-Glúmr. Glúmr is the great grandson of Helgi *inn magri*, following the male line associated with the farm of Þverá (from Ingjaldr Helgason to Eyjólfr to Glúmr). The saga sees them as *goðar*, with Ingjaldr being the holder of an ancient *goðorð* (*forn goðorðsmaðr*).[309] His father and then Glúmr himself have adventures in Norway (Chapters 1–6) before Glúmr returns to Þverá (i.e. Munkaþverá) in Eyjafjörður (Map 9). When he returns to Þverá the farm he finds ownership of the farm is shared, with his mother owning half and the other half owned by Þorkell *hávi*, Glúmr's uncle from Mývatn, and Sigmundr, Þorkell's son. Þorkell and Sigmundr bully Glúmr's mother. In retaliation Glúmr has Þorkell expelled from the farm and kills Sigmundr (Chapters 7–10). This dispute ensures that the family from nearby Espihóll, the Esphælingar, become Glúmr's enemies for the remainder of the story. The culmination of the saga is a fight at Hrísateigr, a site midway between Þverá and Espihóll, which sees Glúmr kill Þorvaldr *krókr* Þórisson from Espihóll. Rather than Glúmr being convicted of the killing,

---

309 ÍF IX: 3.

one of his associates takes the rap (Guðbrandr Þorvarðsson of Kristnes, Chapter 23). The truth of Glúmr's guilt emerges, however, and he is convicted and forced to leave Þverá with Einarr Eyjólfsson (of Saurbær, brother of Guðmundr *ríki*) buying the farm (Chapters 25–26). Víga-Glúmr retires to neighbouring Hörgárdalur where he dies and is buried.

In geopolitical terms *Víga-Glúms saga* provides a surprisingly clear and consistent sense of how its author thought of politics in Eyjafjörður as reading this section alongside Map 9 will demonstrate. Víga-Glúmr at Þverá on the eastern side of the valley and the Esphælingar provide clear foci of support. Most characters in the text, and their associated farms, are allied to one side or the other although, as we shall see, there is a role for the brothers Einarr and Guðmundr *ríki* as a third leading party.[310] In general Víga-Glúmr and his kinsmen seem to have more friends than enemies. Their supporters cluster on the eastern side of the valley and Víga-Glúmr himself has connections to Hörgárdalur. The social network of the Esphælingar is mostly based in the inner part of the valley and to the west of Eyjafjarðará. These patterns persist all the way through the saga, and apply equally to individuals and places named in passing and those involved in disputes described at length. In this respect we have something like another genealogical charter but here, perhaps surprisingly, it is a descendant of Björn *buna*, via Helgi *inn magri*, who ultimately loses out to others.

Rather than consider the allegiances chronologically as the saga progresses, they will be set out geographically, starting in the north of Eyjafjörður and going south. In the north, then, both Hrísey and Hörgárdalur are seen as being positively associated with Víga-Glúmr. Glúmr gets his wife from Lón in Hörgárdalur while the account of the end of his life associates him with three different farms there.[311] The saga also identifies opposition between Víga-Glúmr's kinsmen at Hrísey and some of the Esphælingar's kinsmen on Árskógsströnd (at Hagi).[312] Going south into the most northerly part of inner

---

310 Öxnafell, the one-time venue for a wedding is a rare exception (ÍF IX: 67).

311 In a brief and unusual narrative Glúmr moves first to the important farm of Möðruvellir, then to Mýrká and finally he buys Þverbrekka. Glúmr's son Már is said to have lived at Fornhagi in Hörgárdalur and built a church there, where Glúmr is said to have been buried (ÍF IX: 98). There is a kind of logic to the order of the three places with which Glúmr is associated: they go from the wealthy to the middling to the poor respectively. Möðruvellir was very large, Mýrkárdalur was poorer (regardless of whether it is identified as Mýrka in Mýrkárdalur or the farm Mýrkárdalur itself). Möðruvellir had a church and was large in later centuries, the latter was very small in *Jarðabók*. The farm Glúmr dies at, Þverbrekka, old and blind, is the smallest and furthest inland. Fornhagi, identified as the place of Glúmr's burial rite at the end of the saga, was a farming of middling wealth.

312 Hrísey's occupants were Narfi and his sons Eyjólfr and Klængr, Hagi by a Þorvaldr *menni* (ÍF IX: 91–92, 94). Hagi looks like an outlier of Esphælingar support here but it is still on the western side of the fjord. There are many middle-sized farms on the outer, western

Eyjafjörður a more obvious west-east division is visible. Víga-Glúmr's supporters mainly come from a cluster of farms around Þverá itself: Laugaland and Uppsalir seem to be willingly connected to him by kinship while Hamarr is connected to him through a marriage that he enforces on the daughter of the *bóndi* there.[313] Kaupangr and Öngulsstaðir are mentioned in the text but are demonstrably neutral, something *Íslendingasögur* rarely imply about farms.[314] This we might interpret as the edge of a zone which Glúmr is seen to control. Further south, both Öxnafell and Víðines are mentioned but identifiable as neutral or slightly more favourably disposed towards the Esphælingar.[315]

On the other side of the river are the Esphælingar led by Þórir, the son of Hámundr *heljarskinn*, and his sons: the oldest son lives with him at Espihóll, another is at Grund and a third at Möðrufell.[316] Stokkahlaðir immediately to the north of Espihóll (occupied by Þórðr Hrafnsson) is also an ally. This little cluster of farms looks surprisingly similar to those mentioned in connection with Grund in the thirteenth century.[317] There is a key difference between the texts, however, because in *Víga-Glúms saga* the pre-eminent farm in the group is Espihóll, not Grund.

The southern part of Eyjafjörður, Eyjafjarðardalur, is what might be described as a contested area. Such had been the desirability of the daughter of the *bóndi* at Hamarr, for instance, that a man from Æsustaðir in Eyjafjarðardalur had been prevented by Víga-Glúmr from marrying her.[318] In other words, we see Víga-Glúmr bullying someone from this district. But there were also associates of Einarr Eyjólfsson here – Einarr's foster-father Halli at Jórunnarstaðir

---

coast which could have been portrayed as enemies of Hrísey (and by implication of Víga-Glúmr) but the point is that they are not.

313   ÍF IX: 49, 72.
314   Kaupangr, which we might expect to be an important central place is mentioned only when Glúmr arranges an 'autumn assembly' (*haustþing*) and so it might just be argued that the saga's author thinks he controlled the farm Kaupangr. Öngulsstaðir, just to the south, meanwhile, is clearly neutral because it was occupied by a farmer who acts to break up conflict between the two main groups (ÍF IX: 74, 78).
315   Öxnafell is only mentioned as a place where a wedding is held to which everyone significant in Eyjafjörður is invited ('…öllum búöndum, þeim er mestháttar váru í Eyjafirði') (ÍF IX: 67). Hlenni of Víðines offers advice to Bárðr who is a supporter of the Esphælingar and also acts as a witness for the Esphælingar (ÍF IX: 63–65, 86).
316   Þórarinn at Espihóll. Another of Þórir's sons (Þorvaldr *krókr*) lived at Grund and a third (Þorgrímr) at Möðrufell (ÍF IX: 15). When Þórir dies Þórarinn is said to set up a farm north of his father's farm. In other words, the text is providing the context for the establishment of the new farm, Espihóll nyrðri, distinguishing it from Espihóll syðri (modern Litli-Hóll). Espihóll nyrðri was the more valuable farm in later centuries, but it is unclear what hangs on this story within *Víga-Glúms saga*.
317   See above pp. 138, 139.
318   ÍF IX: 47–48.

(Figure 14) and his sons at Torfufell and Skáldsstaðir respectively – who, ultimately, are supported by the Esphælingar at court.[319] Víga-Glúmr has a former member of his household living at Tjörn but Glúmr's support for him causes friction with Halli. The very last farm in this part of the valley, Tjarnir, has connections to both sides and in some ways this rather nicely symbolises the conflict in this area.[320]

In the end, Víga-Glúmr is forced to leave his farm by the Esphælingar and the brothers Einarr and Guðmundr *ríki* Eyjólfsson.[321] Einarr took over Þverá.[322] Neither of these men appears much in the saga except towards the end when they work to defeat Víga-Glúmr. Einarr is said to have lived at Saurbær and Guðmundr at Möðruvellir. The absence of any mention of the farms closest to Saurbær and Möðruvellir might imply that this pair of farms was seen as holding sway there. It is notable that the relatively wealthy farms of Hvassafell and Hólar, the latter with a church,[323] are not mentioned. Djúpadalur and Gnúpufell are mentioned, alongside Þverá, as locations where Víga-Glúmr swears an oath of peace with the Esphælingar, which implies that they were important but we are not told who controlled them.[324] The second point is that even though Einarr replaces Víga-Glúmr at Þverá, this might not imply that the saga's author imagines the broader political situation to have changed. Other texts suggest that Einarr and Guðmundr were rivals and so it is not necessarily the case that all the western side of Eyjafjörður was now unified.[325] Thus at the end of

---

319 Both S232 and *Víga-Glúms saga* say Halli's wife was the daughter of Auðun *rotinn*, the colonist at Saurbær (ÍF IX: 57–66).

320 When Glúmr intervenes to acquire the support and the farm of his former *leysingi* at Tjörn it causes friction. This is probably because the saga author sees this district as under the control of the Esphælingar (ÍF IX: 57). At Tjarnir, further inland but on the eastern side of Eyjafjarðardalur, the genealogical connections of the owner seem to be with both the Þveræingar and the Esphælingar.

321 Guðmundr *ríki* married daughter of Atli *inn rammi* whose family had associations with Reykjaströnd, Sæmundarhlíð and Höfðaströnd in Skagafjörður (ÍF XVI: 51).

322 There is a parallel between the division of Þverá into halves in the dispute settlement in *Víga-Glúms* saga, and the farm's division into two when it was made a staðr by Bishop Björn Gilsson in 1162 (SS I: 122). The division of the farm post-1162 division is probably reflected in *Víga-Glúms* saga's account.

323 DI II: 450–51; DI III: 525–26.

324 ÍF IX: 85–86.

325 Einarr, often identified as Einarr Þveræingr, rather than by his patronymic, is seen as acting *with* his brother in narratives with a broader geographical scope. In *Njáls saga* he supports Njáll, in a role seemingly subordinate to his brother (ÍF XII: 306, 308–10). In *Óláfs saga helga* while Guðmundr *ríki* again seems to be more politically active, it is Einarr, rather than Guðmundr or any other of the leading figures named in this particular

the saga we still might have two clear leading farms, at Þverá and Espihóll, and one or two significant ones further south. After Einarr's move the saga does not say who, if anyone, might have taken control of Saurbær although the implication would seem to be that he controlled both Þverá and Saurbær.

What this all adds up to, then, is a pattern whereby Þverá is being credited with a small territory of its own around Þverá with a northern outlier in Hrísey and, at least later on, a connection with Hörgárdalur. The Esphælingar seem to control the lower, western side of the valley, and Eyjafjarðardalur seems to show them having more allies there than Víga-Glúmr. Some of the relationships between farms can be read in different ways and some farms seem to be portrayed as genuinely neutral. Given that Víga-Glúmr was, in the end, a political loser this posthumous connection might seem rather paradoxical – who would want to recall Víga-Glúmr's association with farms in Hörgárdalur after his defeat by other Eyjafjörður leaders? That said, the fact that no less than three farms were connected with him in Hörgárdalur suggests that there really was an interest in this linkage.

Beyond Eyjafjörður, the text's notable comment on other geopolitical relationships concern relations between Þverá and the Mývatn area; they are best described as failed. Relations between 'Mývatn' and Þverá are first seen when Víga-Glúmr acquires Þverá, part of which involves the expulsion of his brother-in-law Þorkell *hávi* who is sent back to Mývatn, whence he came; Þorkell had had ownership of Þverá but lost it. The second story is one that also features in *Reykdæla saga og Víga-Skútu* where Glúmr's daughter marries Víga-Skúta of Skútustaðir but the couple divorce. Together the two stories seem to suppose that Þverá and Mývatn relations could not succeed, even if attempted.

By way of brief summary here, it will have been clear that formal power relationships, in the shape of *goðar* and *þingmenn*, are no more clearly stated in *Víga-Glúms saga* than they are in the texts for Dalir. We do see farmers turning to likely *goðar* – Einarr Eyjólfsson is sought out by his foster-father – but only Víga-Glúmr's line are identified clearly as *goðar*. As far as genealogical relations go, the leading figures are all recorded as descendants of Helgi *inn magri* but via different children. The simplicity of the genealogy in the early generations after the *landnám* suggests that this too was something like a genealogical charter. The effective expulsion of Víga-Glúmr, and thus the best-established *goði* (according to the saga), suggests that the text recognises political change

---

episode, who delivers the speech which galvanises Icelandic opposition to the king (*Flateyjarbók* I: 21; II: 338–39; ÍF XXVII: 273–77).

of some kind but the shared identity of Eyjafjörður would still seem strong enough to keep Víga-Glúmr's family within Helgi *inn magri*'s genealogy.

2.2 Reykdæla saga ok Víga-Skútu

Reykdæla saga og Víga-Skútu provides two distinct foci for its events. The first focus (Chs 1–16) is Áskell *goði* Eyvindarson and his nephew Vémundr Þórisson[326] who are based in Reykjadalur and have enemies in lower and outer Eyjafjörður (Maps 8, 9 and 10). The second half of the text (Chs 17–30) centres on another of Áskell's sons, Skúta, after the deaths of Áskell and Vémundr at the hands of their Eyjafjörður enemies. Skúta, not unrealistically but also conveniently for the narrative, is absent while his kinsmen are politically active and only returns to Iceland after their deaths. He takes over Áskell's *goðorð* but rather than stay in Reykjadalur he sets up home at Skútustaðir in Mývatnssveit. The saga ends with Skúta's killing. His enemies come from different districts to aid the enemies of his father and brother. His most immediate rival was from Mývatn, from someone supported by Þorgeirr *Ljósvetningagoði*. Thus, within what was written down as a single text, we have two almost completely separate sagas which are linked only by the genealogy of the main characters. These two sets of political patterns will be set out in more detail below before the issue of the regional chronological patterning is addressed.

The first point to make about Áskell *goði* is that he is based at Grenjaðarstaðir and has control over the immediate vicinity but nowhere beyond it. As is the case for other characters, *Reykdæla saga ok Víga-Skútu* is more reticent about the homes of many of its protagonists and it identifies the home of Áskell as 'Hvammr.' This is almost certainly a former farm on the estate of Grenjaðarstaðir, identified above as the site of a major church,[327] Áskell and his kinsmen are connected in *S* to the colonist Grenjaðr by Áskell's marriage to Grenjaðr's daughter but *Reykdæla saga* makes no such link.

The saga's introductory section, when it actually identifies the homes of Áskell's kinsmen, places them on farms in Reykjadalur or nearby: his brother Helgi at Helgastaðir and nephews at Einarsstaðir and Múli (both in Reykjadalur), Tjarnir in Ljósavatnsskarð, 'Mývatn' and Húsavík (the modern port mentioned in this text), and his brother-in-law in the valley of Laxárdalur

---

[326] The text emphasises the Reykdælir ties of the Vémundr and his brothers by referring to them as Fjörleifarsynir, sons of Fjörleif, the sister of Áskell *goði* (ÍF X: 155, 159, 181, 203).

[327] ÍF X: 152, note 1 for the later place-names Presthvammur and Ásgilsstaðir; Orri Vésteinsson 2006b: 105 for the local settlement pattern and use of the label 'Hvammar' for the cluster of farms close to Grenjaðarstaðir.

to the south.³²⁸ Grenjaðarstaðir is geographically central to these other locations. Elsewhere in the text Vémundr *kögurr*, Áskell's belligerent nephew and the main protagonist in *Reykdœla saga*, is said to live at Öndóttsstaðir and then at 'Fell,' two farms in Reykjadalur.³²⁹ This chimes in with the saga's more general demonstration of Áskell's kin's influence over Reykjadalur. Áskell acts as advocate for someone at Mýlaugsstaðir when they are picked on by the occupant of Rauðaskriða, a story which might suggest the boundary of Áskell's real influence to the west of Grenjaðarstaðir. Áskell does have property elsewhere, however: he owns all or part of the islands of Flatey and Grímsey where he has driftage rights and men who protect these for him.³³⁰

As an introductory narrative this is fairly conventional stuff, in that it establishes the geopolitical links between early generations which are relevant to events later in the saga. What marks Áskell and *Reykdœla saga* out, however, is the way Áskell is consistently reasonable while some of his younger kinsmen are persistently troublesome. This is a relatively common trope in *Íslendingasögur* but Áskell has more than just the usual, lone troublesome kinsman. It is in fact Áskell's close kinsmen's relations which help define positive and negative relations in this set of stories. Both his nephews Háls (of Tjarnir near Ljósavatn, then at Helgastaðir in Reykjadalur) and Vémundr, the focal character in the early chapters, are portrayed as seeking conflict or mixing with difficult people. It is Háls who befriends a *bóndi* from Rauðaskriða in Skjálfandafljót, an

---

328 'Mývatn' is the home of Áskell's nephew Herjólfr but this is only made explicit later (ÍF X: 152, 153, 155, 172).

329 As with many negatively-portrayed characters in sagas, authors seem sometimes to have been reluctant to associate such characters with particular farms and kin groups. These place-names are not those of major farms but instead are in Reykjadalur. In a legal dispute of 1380 Öndóttsstaðir (or Öndursstaðir) was disputed by Grenjaðarstaðir and Helgastaðir, the owner of the latter having been adjudged to have given it someone else as if it were his own possession rather than being that of Grenjaðarstaðir (DI III: 352–53; ÍF X: 165, note 1; ÍF X: 177, note 5 for 'Fell'). Vémundr's wife is never named in *Reykdœla saga*, which might also be symptomatic of his anti-social behaviour and therefore people's reluctance to claim descent from him. However, in a genealogy listing all the Fjörleifarsynir, i.e. Vémundr and his brothers only Vémundr among them is given a wife, Halldóra, daughter of Þorkell *svarti* whom S also identifies as the brother of Hlenni inn gamli (S237; above, p. p. 281 footnote 315). This connection would make moderate sense, given allegiances identified elsewhere in *Ljósvetninga saga* and *Víga-Glúms saga* for Hlenni *hinn gamli*. Hlenni is said to have lived at Saurbær or Víðines (both in Eyjafjörður, the latter being a ruin near Öxnafell (ÍF IX: 36, note 2) and was not strongly allied to any other major farms apart from his acting as a foster-father to Koðrán, son of Guðmundr *ríki* from Möðruvellir. If we are looking for potential 'forgetters' of this tie between Vémundr and Hlenni then people from Eyjafjörður are obvious candidates especially, perhaps, those from Saurbær.

330 ÍF X: 170, 171.

adjacent district to Reykjadalur, a decision which ultimately leads to Háls and Vémundr being outlawed.[331] Later, again at his own initiation, Háls marries a woman from Eyjafjarðardalur (Granastaðir) only to narrowly avoid being divorced thanks to Áskell's intervention.[332] Vémundr represents a bigger problem still: he pursues the long-term conflict which, despite Áskell's repeated attempts to achieve peace, leads to their deaths.[333] Vémundr's opponents are a group of kinsmen from Eyjafjörður, a *höfðingi*, Steingrímr from Kroppr, and his brother-in-law Steinn from Árskógr.[334]

In districts inland from Grenjaðarstaðir and its small hinterland, Vémundr associates with other negatively portrayed characters/places. Thus Óþveginstunga (modern Laugasel), technically still in Reykjadalur but a long way inland and at over 300m above sea level, is home to one of Vémundr's accomplices. Vémundr also attracts support from or imposes obligations on farms in Laxárdalur, the valley linking Reykjadalur to Mývatn.[335] When he ventures into Eyjafjörður he gets support against Steinn at Árskógr from a man at Arnarnes, a few kilometres south of Árskógr.[336] There is more of a sense of the expediency of the narrative in two cases where the story needs Vémundr to be in particular places to be involved in conflict with his opponents. Thus he is said to have had a kinswoman – perhaps by marriage – at Vindheimar in Hörgárdalur just before he has a fight in that valley; he stays at a farm close to Höfði before an ill-fated attempt to steal the future wife of a man from Árskógr.[337]

The men from Kroppr and Árskógr have a different social network, one which forms a clear pattern on the map. Not surprisingly they have active supporters in lower Eyjafjörður.[338] Events connected with two markets or

---

331   Áskell refuses to support Háls at this point (ÍF x: 153–57).
332   ÍF x: 176, 194, 199.
333   For instances where Áskell and Vémundr are at odds over a course of action or a settling up of a dispute: ÍF x: 171–72, 175, 178, 184, 197.
334   Steingrímr is recalled as a *höfðingi* alongside Áskell after their deaths (ÍF x: 162–63, 202).
335   Via the farms Hraunsáss, 'Holt,' Mánahjalli and Þverá (ÍF x: 165, 166). There appears to be an especially sharp contrast in the saga between the Ljótr *hofgoði*, the supporter of Vémundr who later appears to want to have children and elderly people killed when the weather is harsh, and Áskell as opponent of Vémundr and supporter of the very young and elderly (ÍF x: 169–70).
336   ÍF x: 188, 189.
337   ÍF x: 188, 191.
338   Steingrímr's brother lived at Kristnes in Eyjafjörður and other supporters come from Öxnahóll in Hörgárdalur, Brennihóll in Kræklingahlíð (north of modern Akureyri, south of Gásir) and Höfði (ÍF x: 176, 185–90, 197). Kræklingahlíð is home to a Snorri *Hlíðarmannagoði* in *Ljósvetninga saga* who is given a speech in which he urges peace between Guðmundr *ríki* and Þorgeirr *goði* on the one side and Þorgeirr's sons on the other (ÍF x: 15). See above p. 196 for his significance in S.

trading sites – the well-known Gásir and the less well-known Knarrareyrr on the opposite side of the fjord[339] – are places the Reykdælir have to visit but which seem almost to be the 'home turf' of Steingrímr and Steinn. Outside Eyjafjörður, the farm of Lundarbrekka in Bárðardalur[340] to the east is home to a 'good *bóndi*' and the kinsman of Steingrímr at Kroppr and comes into conflict with the man at Óþveginstunga.[341] Another incident suggests Steingrímr is on reasonable terms with other lesser *bændr* in Bárðardalur but he may have been exploiting them as well, perhaps because of their association with Lundarbrekka.[342] He can also get Hrói from Öxarfjörður to try to kill

---

339 ÍF X: 172, 188.
340 DI II: 437–38 for the church at Lundarbrekka which owned 30 hundreds of the farm.
341 Hrafn is the name of the *bóndi* at Lundarbrekka in both *Reykdæla saga* and *Ljósvetninga saga*. Only in the latter, however, is he identified as the son of Þorkell *hákr* (ÍF X: 70, 74, 160–69). The relationship of the *bóndi* at Lundarbrekka to other *bændr* is a significant way in which *Reykdæla saga* and *Ljósvetninga saga* differ. In *Reykdæla saga* Hrafn is a kinsman (*frændi*) to *bændr* in lower Eyjafjörður (ÍF X: 163); in *Ljósvetninga saga* he is the son of Þorkell *hákr* whose father was Þorgeirr *Ljósvetningagoði*. Thus Lundarbrekka forms part of a different political grouping in each text. *Ljósvetninga saga* says Hrafn's wife was from Goðdalir, or related to the Goðdœlir, in a tributary valley of Skagafjörður although this has immediate significance in the saga. Hrafn does not get involved in the fight at Kakalahólar between Eyjólfr Guðmundarson (Þverá) and Hrafn's Ljósvetningar kinsmen (in this text). Eyjólfr also buys off Hrafn before the settlement following the battle. That Eyjólfr gets support from the Goðdœlir in that case is not easy to reconcile with Hrafn's connection to the Goðdœlir but his neutrality makes more sense if it is assumed that he had obligations to both sides in the dispute (ÍF X: 84, 91). Goðdalir, in the uppermost part of Skagafjörður, is a rather out-of-the-way place and it is hard to understand why *Ljósvetninga saga* seems to have a fixation with it. The Goðdœlir were associated with a *goðorð* (Gunnar Karlsson 2004: 207, 255, 256) and the 'Guðdœlir' are named as one of the significant *höfðingjar* in a list in *Landnámabók* (where all other *höfðingjar* are listed as individuals) but otherwise there is no suggestion of their importance (ÍF I: 396). No text seems to record any of members of the *ætt*.
342 ÍF X: 176–81, 194. Steingrímr agrees to buy cattle from a man from Jarlsstaðir but then was apparently slow to pay for them. There were two farms called Jarlsstaðir, one in Bárðardalur, the other in Reykjadalur and the text does not specify which of the two it is. Given that Vémundr sees it as his place to take the oxen it is possible that the Reykjadalur farm is involved. However as other farmers from Bárðardalur are mentioned in this story it seems more likely to be the Bárðardalur farm. Áskell disapproves when Vémundr tries to offer him the oxen. Part of his disapproval certainly comes from the manner in which Vémundr had obtained them and what the implications would be for him if he accepted cattle intended for Steingrímr. Part of his disapproval may also have come from their geographical origin; Áskell is not shown to have had strong connections with Bárðardalur. The cattle are returned to Steingrímr but after he has failed to pay for them and Vémundr tried to take on the legal case of the man who had sold them originally, Áskell again fails to support Vémundr.

Vémundr.³⁴³ Thus the connections that *Reykdœla saga* wishes to stress are mostly with larger farms in the northern half of Eyjafjörður and with Bárðardalur; the latter seems to be an area without a major political player so that the wealthier men of lower Eyjafjörður and Reykjadalur could vie for influence there.

As has already been noted, the second half of the text is mostly concerned with Skúta Áskelsson who buys and moves to Skútustaðir on the southern shore of Lake Mývatn (Map 10).³⁴⁴ The text sees Áskell's family retaining control of Hvammr/Grenjaðarstaðir through the continued presence there of Þorsteinn Áskelsson. Skúta is the main protagonist because, as the text says, he was not present to swear an oath of peace towards the enemies of his kinsmen.³⁴⁵ In practice, however, the story of Skúta is more about his role as the pre-eminent figure in and around Mývatn and, as a result, his relationships with leaders from Ljósavatn (Þorkell Þorgeirsson and his son Þorgeirr), Möðruvellir (Eyjólfr Valgerðarson) and Þverá (Víga-Glúmr). The leaders will be discussed below, but the relationships around Mývatn are of interest because they are the only picture of politics we have in this area from any text. In Mývatn very few farms are mentioned but Skúta is identified as being on good terms with some 'smaller' *bændr* to the south and west of the lake (Geirastaðir, 'Sandfell') and the more significant figure of Arnórr Þorgrímsson of Reykjahlíð.³⁴⁶ Arnórr appears as an ally to Skúta here whereas in the chronologically-later *Ljósvetninga saga*, he is a *þingmaðr* of Þorgeirr *goði* of Ljósavatn whom Þorgeirr and Guðmundr *ríki* have killed.³⁴⁷ He dies fighting Skúta's main enemy, 'Þorbergr at Mývatni' who is not located precisely but might also have been imagined as being from the south-west of the lake to judge from the location of the saga's action. Skúta therefore has only allies around Mývatn.

Outside of Mývatnssveit, Skúta's geopolitical relationships show some signs of continuity with what we have seen in the first half of the saga. In other words, this is not an image of a completely different leader whose role is entirely shaped by where he was based; there is a continuity of the role of this family as local leaders and therefore more of a shared origin for the two halves of the text than could have been the case. Thus in Laxárdalur, Mánahjalli is still seen as an ally, there being an absence of any other leaders in that valley.³⁴⁸

---

343   ÍF x: 164–69.
344   For recent excavations see McGovern, Harrison & Smiarowski 2014.
345   ÍF x: 203.
346   ÍF x: 204, 205–12, 226, 229.
347   ÍF x: 3, 5, 6, 7–9, 10, 12.
348   ÍF x: 221. There is an opponent of an associate of Skúta's in Laxárdalur (Þorsteinn *varastafr*) but, like other negatively-portrayed characters in *Reykdœla saga*, he is not located precisely (ÍF x: 211–13).

Bárðardalur is still a contested area in that Áskell/Skúta might gain support from weaker farmers there[349] while their rivals apparently reside at Lundarbrekka.[350] In Reykjadalur, however, Skúta seems to have support from Skörð and Ytri-Skörð in the lower part of the valley.[351] This could be seen as either a complementary view of the power of Áskell/Grenjaðarstaðir set out in the first half of the text, or else an alternative vision of it; Víga-Glúmr now has an association with nearby Breiðamýrr so either way this seems to be an area of weaker influence for the Reykdœlir.[352]

The roles of other *goðar* or *höfðingjar* have so far not been discussed yet but, of course, they are an important frame for the more detailed elements of political narrative of *Reykdœla saga*. In practice, *Reykdœla saga* leaves a lot unsaid about the main local leaders. The major figure in Eyjafjörður is Eyjólfr Valgerðarson at Möðruvellir. Without any real explanation of Eyjólfr's status or connection to other characters, he is sought by Áskell to act as his co-mediator – effectively on behalf of Steingrímr at Kroppr when Áskell acts on behalf of Vémundr.[353] Eyjólfr does then fulfill the same mediating role, an equivalent to Áskell.[354] As part of the narrative of the peace meeting after the battle at which Áskell, Vémundr and Steingrímr are killed, it also emerges that there was a connection between Áskell's kin group and Eyjólfr: Áskell's kinsman from Einarsstaðir in Reykjadalur (Einarr Konálsson) was Eyjólfr's fosterson.[355] In the second half of the text, Eyjólfr continues to work as a mediator and does so alongside his *fóstri* who supports Skúta[356] but, such is Skúta's belligerence, Eyjólfr eventually acts against him.[357]

Víga-Glúmr's relationship with Skúta is a difficult one. They act as advocates of rival *bœndr* but Víga-Glúmr supposedly brokers a peace between them by marrying his daughter to Skúta. But after Skúta disapproves of Víga-Glúmr offering a compensation payment, Glúmr orders his daughter home and marries her off to someone else, possibly a kinsman of Skúta.[358] The Skútustaðir-Þverá relationship is unsuccessful, although the existence of the story suggests the difference in standing between the two farms was not so great that such a connection was inconceivable. This tie, however, conflicts with the recorded,

---

349 Ísólfstunga (ÍF X: 225, 227).
350 ÍF X: 237.
351 ÍF X: 211–13. Ófeigr at Skörð plays a big part in *Ljósvetninga saga*. See pp. 294–95, 297.
352 ÍF X: 221–24.
353 ÍF X: 175.
354 ÍF X: 180, 184, 187, 190.
355 ÍF X: 19, 202.
356 ÍF X: 227.
357 ÍF X: 224, 226.
358 ÍF X: 230, note 2.

presumably positive, connection between Skútustaðir and Espihóll inn syðri noted in S in the previous chapter.[359] Here we have indirect evidence of a consistent portrayal of opposition between Þverá and Espihóll across texts, just with the latter story making it explicit.

The other local leader is Þorkell Þorgeirsson from Ljósavatn and his son Þorgeirr, figures well known from other sagas, including *Ljósvetninga saga*. Þorkell supports the farmer at Rauðaskriða against Háls[360] but then is absent from the saga until Chapter 18 when he is seen to support Skúta's enemy (Þorbergr 'at Mývatni'). Þorgeirr, Þorkell's son, consistently opposes Skúta and is more active in doing so than Eyjólfr Valgerðarson. Þorgeirr is seen as the more senior and politically astute partner in this alliance.[361]

To sum up, this text records the defeat of local leaders in Reykjadalur first of all and then in Mývatn. The fact that there is kinship between the two *goðar* might symbolise a sense of their shared roles in these narratives, as both Reykjadalur and Mývatn compete with, and lose to, Eyjafjörður- and Ljósavatnsskarð-based leaders who can have supporters within Reykjadalur and in Mývatnssveit. Each half of this text involves different leaders from Eyjafjörður but the result is the same in both. This sort of ignominious 'result' for Grenjaðarstaðir and Skútustaðir roughly parallels thirteenth-century relations between Eyjafjörður and districts to its east. However, it is expressed in different ways to those shown in S where certainly Skútustaðir was seen as genealogically connected to Helgi *inn magri*, but low down in the genealogy. In other words, *Reykdæla saga* lumps Reykjadalur and Mývatn together when S does not, the latter seeing Mývatn tied into Eyjafjörður's political orbit and Reykjadalur as politically separate. *Reykdæla saga* also seems to hint at the existence of local leaders who could wield power in Reykjadalur and Mývatn at the same time, however weak, territorially fragmented and, ultimately unsuccessful, their control might have been.

2.3 Ljósvetninga Saga

The action in *Ljósvetning saga* is probably most conveniently analysed in terms of action and social relationships within Eyjafjörður and Hörgárdalur, and then in relation to districts beyond these. Perhaps unsurprisingly, given that it is named after people from around Ljósavatn, it has far more to say about the latter (Maps 9 and 10).

What *Ljósvetninga saga* has to say about political relationships within Eyjafjörður and what it says can be characterised quickly. Like other sagas it

---

359 See above p. 195.
360 ÍF X: 156.
361 ÍF X: 209, 210, 217–18, 238, 239–40.

places Guðmundr *ríki* at Möðruvellir and his brother Einarr at Þverá. Guðmundr's strong influence in districts to the north-east of Eyjafjörður and the tensions that this produces are a major theme of the saga but less is said about Guðmundr's power in Eyjafjörður itself, except that we get the general sense that he was seen as overbearing. To the north, he clashes with Þorkell Geitisson from Vopnafjörður and he has difficult relations with Reykjadalur, where it seems he upsets his own *þingmenn* as well as others.

In Eyjafjörður, Möðruvellir and Þverá do sometimes work together but often Guðmundr's relationship with his brother Einarr is strained because Einarr has friendships with other leaders. The tension between the brothers is explained by a story about a conflict between them in their youth,[362] as well as Einarr marrying his daughter to one of Guðmundr's enemies (Þorkell Geitison).

The tension between Þverá and Möðruvellir is also shown by the friendly relationship between Einarr and the *goðorðsmaðr*[363] at Laugaland in Hörgárdalur, Þórir Helgason. Indeed, despite his supposedly great power, Guðmundr is said to be afraid of travelling in Þórir's territory (*sveit*).[364] At a wedding in Hörgárdalur Guðmundr's masculinity is insulted by this Þórir's wife and by a supporter of Laugaland.[365] Guðmundr also has a conflict with Þórir *Akrarskeggi*, a supporter of this man who was based somewhere near modern Akureyri.[366] Guðmundr has the latter Þórir outlawed which causes unease for his brother Einarr at Þverá, who is on good terms with Laugaland. Einarr essentially continues to side against his brother after this. It is worth noting here that, for all the many different geographical focuses of *Ljósvetninga saga* and *Víga-Glúms saga*, they both portray a connection between Laugaland in Hörgárdalur and Þverá, although they use a different family to express the connection.[367]

Also in Eyjafjörður, Víga-Glúmr's son is seen as an ally of Guðmundr *ríki*, which provides something of a contrast to *Víga-Glúms saga* where Einarr and Guðmundr enforce Víga-Glúmr's expulsion from Þverá. Víga-Glúmr's son,

---

362 ÍF x: 37–38.
363 ÍF X: 16 where Þórir is introduced explicitly as a *goðorðsmaðr* and a friend of Einarr Eyjólfsson
364 ÍF X: 17.
365 At Bægisá, one or other of the larger farms at the boundary of two *hreppar* in the centre of Hörgárdalur.
366 Guðmundr's conflict with Þórir *Akrarskeggi*, a *þingmaðr* of Þórir Helgason, associated with Akrar, somewhere in lower Hörgárdalur is mentioned in one of the two versions of *Ljósvetninga saga*. Guðmundr has Þórir *Akrarskeggi* outlawed in a case at the Vaðlaþing which puts Einarr in a difficult position because he has obligations towards both Þórir Helgason and Guðmundr. Akrar is recorded as an abandoned farm in a document of 1447 (ÍF x: 21; Andersson & Miller 1989: 68, 71).
367 In *Víga-Glúms saga* the connection is only expressed genealogically via Einarr's mother.

interestingly, is never connected to a particular farm. This perhaps reflects an awareness of the tradition about Víga-Glúmr's expulsion from Þverá or else it supposes that his son was actually living at Möðruvellir.

One other vignette shows the individuality of *Ljósvetninga saga* where it suggests the allegiances of two larger farms close to Möðruvellir: Gnúpufell appears in opposition to Guðmundr, while Saurbær appears in a neutral role but with some connection to Guðmundr. Gnúpufell was the home of two brothers, Brúni and Eilífr, who jointly owned a *goðorð* and were distantly related to the Ljósvetningar. Saurbær was home to Hlenni, a cousin of Þorgeirr *goði*. In the story, Guðmundr and the men from Gnúpufell exchange killings before a scene in which Guðmundr tracks Eilífr down to Saurbær and Hlenni prevents Guðmundr from killing Eilífr.[368] While *Víga-Glúms saga* sees many *bændr* in Eyjafjörður trying to thwart Víga-Glúmr, in *Ljósvetninga saga* it is Guðmundr who is frustrated by local farmers.[369] The association of the Gnúpfellingar and Saurbæingar with the Ljósvetningar is indicative of local opposition to Guðmundr. At the same time, the last mention of Hlenni of Saurbær identifies him as the foster-father of Guðmundr's son Koðrán. This perhaps implies some level of *modus vivendi* among the wealthier people in central Eyjafjörður, but the fact that Koðrán did not go on to inherit Möðruvellir implies that the relationship was of no real consequence.

In *Ljósvetninga saga* Eyjafjörður itself is also seen more as a single political entity than in *Víga-Glúms saga* in as much as we generally only hear about the heads of the largest farms, Möðruvellir, Þverá and, in the final third of the saga, Hrafnagil.[370] Hrafnagil is the home of Einarr Arnórsson a friend and kinsman of Eyjólfr, the son of the now deceased Guðmundr *ríki*, at Möðruvellir. Einarr at Hrafnagil supports Eyjólfr in his conflicts with the Ljósvetningar.[371] There is also some sign that this consensus works at a more localised level, through people like Hlenni at Saurbær, one of the valley's larger farms.[372]

---

[368] ÍF x: 54–57.
[369] See above pp. 281–82.
[370] Einarr Arnórsson from Hrafnagil, brother of Þóroddr *hjálmr*, is described in positive terms the first two times he is mentioned in the saga, as 'vitr maðr, göfugr ok ættstórr' and 'virðingamaðr ok vinr Eyjólfs' (Chs. 22, 23; ÍF x: 62, 71) and associated with Eyjólfr Guðmundarson but not Eyjólfr's father Guðmundr *ríki*. He is one of those saga characters that does not really say or do anything (ÍF x editor Björn Sigfússon could not tie him down to a particular *ætt* – although he has a couple of guesses – which is a good sign that he is not well-known (ÍF x: 62, note 3).
[371] ÍF x: 62, 71, 100.
[372] ÍF x: 55–7, 61–62.

One other thing to note, is that the saga suggests that Hegranessþing, in Skagafjörður, could be a regional court for a dispute involving Eyjólfr Guðmundarson of Möðruvellir and Þorvarðr Höskuldsson from Fnjóskadalur.[373] The laws would suggest that Guðmundr should have pursued this case at the Quarter Court at the annual Alþing, although provision is made for such a court to be held within a Quarter. Certainly Guðmundr *ríki* lived closer to Skagafjörður than did Þorvarðr, but not by much, and Guðmundr is not seen to have support in Skagafjörður so as to influence the case's outcome.[374] The reason this might be seen as a possibility is that we see the other famous Guðmundr, Guðmundr *dýri* Þorvaldsson manipulating the court system. This is not a parallel for Guðmundr *dýri*'s late twelfth-century disbanding of the Vaðlaþing, the spring assembly in Eyjafjörður, seemingly because he would rather have the Quarter court there or else no court at all.[375]

Outside Eyjafjörður, *Ljósvetninga saga* provides a reasonably detailed image of political relationships among some of the larger farms in Reykjadalur. Guðmundr *ríki* is said to have had supporters there, some of whom are explicitly identified as *þingmenn* and some of whom must also have been seen as *þingmenn* by the author. *Bændr* from Hagi and Reykir are identified in this implicit way.[376] Guðmundr's son Eyjólfr, has a *þingmaðr* as far away as Tjörnes.[377] Guðmundr also takes on the case of a man from Reykir, for example, against the anti-social Vöðu-Brandr. Vöðu-Brandr chooses not to live with his moderate father at Laxamýrr in lower Reykjadalur and instead lives further east, with a leading figure in Vopnafjörður (Þorkell Geitisson at Krossavík);[378] Guðmundr, in trying to pursue the case, ignores the conciliatory attitude of Vöðu-Brandr's father.[379] Gnúpar in Reykjadalur, however, was clearly home to some antisocial men one of whom is outlawed by the *bóndi* from Hagi and Arnórr from Reykjahlíð (Mývatnssveit).[380] Guðmundr and Þorgeirr *goði* are nonetheless willing to support Sölmundr from Gnúpar once Sölmundr has gained the support of the Norwegian ruler Jarl Hákon.[381]

---

373 ÍF x: 83.
374 ÍF x: 102, 215.
375 See above p. 128.
376 ÍF x: 3–5.
377 'Ísólfr *bóndi*,' no doubt at Ísólfsstaðir (ÍF x: 63).
378 Þorkell is never explicitly labelled as a *goði* so far as I can see but he is said to have had a booth at the Alþing in one text (Jón Viðar Sigurðsson 1999: 48, note 35; ÍF xi: 93).
379 The subject of *Vöðu-Brands páttr* (Chs. 8–12 of *Ljósvetninga saga*). The case is resolved peacefully in the end.
380 ÍF x: 4-5.
381 This might imply that it was only the inappropriate intervention of a Norwegian leader – and a non-royal one at that – on behalf of an outlawed man, that could lead Þorgeirr to

Yet by far the most significant figure in lower Reykjadalur (or indeed the whole of Reykjadalur) in the saga is Ófeigr at Skörð.[382] He is described as a friend of Guðmundr *ríki* and his brother Einarr but he is also identified explicitly as a *höfðingi*, something borne out by the saga's action. It is Ófeigr who leads a successful protest against Guðmundr: Guðmundr's own *þingmenn* in lower Reykjadalur turn to Ófeigr when Guðmundr fails to recognise that he is being unreasonable towards them.[383] Ófeigr also has a hand in arranging the marriage between Þorkell in Vopnafjörður and Einarr's daughter as part of a peace deal. Guðmundr regards it as an affront because this deal is done behind his back, and it certainly suggests Skörð has a stronger affiliation with Þverá than with Möðruvellir. Ófeigr also associates himself with the sons of Þorgeirr *goði* against their father and Guðmundr, but mainly does so to try to get them to settle peacefully with Guðmundr and Þorgeirr.[384]

The portrayal of the political allegiances of Þorgeirr *goði* and those of his sons from Ljósavatn seem, like those of Ófeigr in Reykjadalur, appropriate to their geographical position. They are linked to Eyjafjörður to the west, and to Reykjadalur and Mývatnssveit to the east. This is best exemplified early in the saga when Þorgeirr, allied with Guðmundr *ríki*, is pitted against his sons who

---

act inappropriately himself in opposing his sons. Unusually Þorgeirr and his sons were on opposite sides in a physical fight and in court. Þorgeirr is tricked into thinking his son Höskuldr (Vaglir, Fnjóskadalur) had been injured which made him briefly consider disassociating himself from Guðmundr (ÍF x: 6–15).

382 That Ófeigr is placed at Skörð rather than Þóroddsstaðr, also called Staðr in its *máldagi* in 1318, where Ófeigsstaðir is listed as a property of Þóroddsstaðr (DI II: 436) requires comment. Ófeigsstaðir is adjacent to Þóroddsstaðr, the *staðr* in Kaldakinn, so on other side of the valley to Skörð. Thus the story could have been manipulated or completely misremembered if, as is so often the case, the saga character owes his existence to a place-name. The story as it is here denies power to the *staðr* of Þóroddsstaðr and thus ignores what might otherwise have been seen as a conflict between Þóroddsstaðr and Möðruvellir, instead gives Skörð the role of protester against Guðmundr or Möðruvellir. There are also other place-names which include the name Ófeigr. There is an Ófeigshellir which is on the coast, close to or in the small bay of Náttfaravík, which is listed in the list of driftage rights for Munkaþverárklaustur of 1270 or earlier (DI II: 89–91). Ófeigsá is an abandoned farm in Flateyjadalur, the small valley running north-south to the west of Aðaldalur/Reykjadalur which has its mouth south of the island Flatey. There was also a tradition of using the fairly rare name Ófeigr as a personal name. An Ófeigr in the mid-thirteenth century is identified as having been involved in a dispute over farm boundaries in Reykjadalur (DI II: 1–5). In the 1318 *máldagi* for the church of Reykjahlíð an Ófeigr who lives at the farm or church is obliged to make an annual payment to the church (DI II: 429).

383 ÍF x: 117; Andersson & Miller 1989: 99–100. Guðmundr *ríki* encounters hostility when he goes to have his dream interpreted by 'Drauma-Finni' at 'Fell' in Kaldakinn, perhaps implying that this farm also sided with Ófeigr (ÍF x: 58).

384 ÍF x: 10.

support Arnórr of Reykjahlíð, Þorgeirr's *þingmaðr*.[385] Later on things are more clear cut: Guðmundr *ríki* has Þorgeirr's son, Þorkell *hákr*, killed after Þorkell had gossiped about Guðmundr's masculinity.[386] Þorgeirr and sons are also said to have claimed or reclaimed that part of their shared *goðorð* which someone else had owned. Þorgeirr had owned one third and his sons a second. Between them, Þorgeirr's sons bully a man called Arnsteinn, from Öxarfjörður, into giving up the final third of the *goðorð*.[387] This might imply some kind of influence for the Ljósvetningar in Öxarfjörður, or perhaps in other districts between Öxarfjörður and Ljósavatn but if so, then they are never seen to exercise it.

The area over which the Ljósvetningar certainly have political control is clearly demarcated by the geographical associations of members of the *ætt* across the generations; there is a sense of a centre and peripheral areas. In keeping with *Ljósvetninga saga*'s slightly later setting than *Víga-Glúms saga* and *Reykdœla saga*, Þorgeirr Ljósvetningagoði (Ljósavatn)[388] disappears from events to be replaced by his sons and eventually other descendants.[389] Of Þorgeirr's sons, Þorkell *hákr*, Höskuldr and Tjörvi are the most significant although even they appear only briefly.[390] Þorkell *hákr* is placed at Öxará and Tjörvi lived at 'Ljósavatnsskarð,'[391] both to the east of Ljósavatn, while Höskuldr was at Vaglir in Fnjóskadalur.[392] Þorvarðr, Höskuldr's son, is the *bóndi* at

---

385   ÍF x: 3, 6–15.
386   ÍF x: 46–8, 49–51, 52.
387   ÍF x: 11–15.
388   ÍF x: 3.
389   Þorgeirr's death is never mentioned. This might support the case for the saga's composition from separate *þættir*; a more coherent single narrative might have mentioned his death and the transfer of his *goðorð* to his sons as it is clear that later chapters suppose happened (see, for example, Andersson & Miller 1989: 72–74). None of Þorgeirr's sons are mentioned at all in *Víga-Glúms saga* or *Reykdœla saga*.
390   A 'Finni' is supposedly a son of Þorgeirr; the same Finni or another 'Drauma-Finni' lived at Fell in Kaldakinn (Reykjadalur) and interprets a dream for Guðmundr *ríki* but appears not to be a kinsman of the Ljósvetningar (ÍF x: 58); a 'Finni' lived somewhere in Fnjóskadalur and seems to be able to offer an opinion on the supernatural (ÍF x: 100–1). Both these locations would be on the fringes of a small territory which can be ascribed to the Ljósvetningar. The saga thus provide a loose idea of someone called Finni who may or may not have been a member of the Ljósvetningar and lived in Fnjóskadalur. *S*, which has a more extensive list of children for Þorgeirr than *Ljósvetninga saga*, names Finni/Finnr *enn draumspaki* as an illegitimate child of a 'foreign' woman (ÍF I: 275). This lower status for him makes sense in the light of the rather unclear placing of him in the saga. Finnr could also be the name of a slave of a man from Öxarfjörður in *Reykdœla saga* which a scribe or author had almost forgotten to record (ÍF x: 166, note 4).
391   ÍF x: 46, 47–48. In the C version of the text Þorkell is identified clearly with the farm of Öxará but the A version does not mention a particular farm (ÍF x: 16, 49).
392   ÍF x: 8. Sigríðr, the daughter of Þorgeirr is said to have married someone called Dagr but neither is placed geographically.

Fornastaðir while his son, another Höskuldr, was fostered at Veisa with another member of the Ljósvetningar (traced through the male line).[393] The text seems to show shades of geopolitical allegiance through this genealogy. Thus when the Veisusynir, the latest generation of the *ætt* and those living furthest west, bring about a legal action which is taken over by Eyjólfr Guðmundarson from Möðruvellir (on behalf of someone from Tjörnes), Eyjólfr is said to expect least resistance among the Ljósvetningar from Þorvarðr, who lived nearest Eyjólfr. Eyjólfr is also said to have had a *þingmaðr* at Draflastaðir in Fnjóskadalur which further suggests that the text has a notion of some kind of tailing-off of Ljósvetningar influence as one goes west from Ljósavatn. Veisa was the westerly extent of this influence; Draflastaðir the most easterly extent of Eyjólfr's influence. It is no coincidence that the fight between Eyjólfr and the Ljósvetningar occurs at Kakalahóll (modern Orustuhóll) between Veisa and Draflastaðir.[394]

If we skip back a few generations, the idea of a small-scale genealogical charter which creates a centre and periphery, makes sense of the text's confusion over the location of the possible son of Þorgeirr *Ljósvetningagoði*, Finni. Finni might have derived his origins from the place-name Finnastaðir but this is the 'wrong' side of the notional boundary between Veisa and Draflastaðir, which might explain why the saga never places him geographically. In a similar way the fringes of Ljósvetningar influences are mirrored genealogically, being to the east of Ljósavatnsskarð. In *Ljósvetninga saga*, the *bóndi* at Lundarbrekka in Bárðardalur is a son of Þorkell *hákr*, but someone who, like Þorvarðr, is arguably a fringe member of the clan, whose political allegiance is ambivalent or at least not close to his kinsmen living at the opposite end of the Ljósavatnsskarð pass.[395] The saga arguably confirms this sense of the limits of Ljósvetningar territorial influence by placing Þorvarðr's brother at Brettingsstaðir in the small valley of Flateyjardalur and then having him 'extinguished' by Eyjólfr of Möðruvellir as an act of vengeance.[396] Towards the end of the saga the 'centre' of Ljósvetningar power is only located in the person of another son of Þorkell *hákr*, who controls the *goðorð* and lives at Ljósavatn.[397]

One or two comments need to be made about the hierarchy, or relative lack of it, among the sons of Þorgeirr and their descendants. When the Þorgeirssynir are portrayed as working together against their father and Guðmundr, it is hard to distinguish their relative seniority or merits. Later in the text, however,

---

393   ÍF x: 63.
394   ÍF x: 78.
395   See p. 287.
396   ÍF x: 99–100.
397   ÍF x: 101–2.

Þorkell (Öxará) is marked out as being the person to spread rumours about Guðmundr *ríki*'s lack of masculinity; he pays the ultimate price when Guðmundr has him killed.[398] This looks like a heroic act of resistance to an Eyjafjörður-based leader but also suggests Þorkell's failure or ineptitude and yet, as just noted, his son is recorded as a *goði* and is based at Ljósavatn. Höskuldr Þorgeirsson (Vaglir) is credited with taking a leading role when he undertakes a ritual to claim the second third of their *goðorð* – in a unique instance of someone slaughtering a ram and smearing themselves in blood.[399] Quite what this might have signified about Höskuldr's desirability as an ancestor is unclear. Tjörvi, perhaps based at the farm of Ljósavatn, might be portrayed in the slightly more favourable light than the other two; he is slightly less of a warmonger than Höskuldr in one scene and it is also possible that Tjörvi's son was a *lögsögumaðr*, and by implication had controlled a *goðorð*, although this is only suggested by another text.[400] Overall there is no clear sense of hierarchy among the brothers but despite Höskuldr's role in the bloody sacrifice, his position at Vaglir, away from Ljósavatn, and his lack of significant descendants, imply that he was the least important.[401]

In sum, *Ljósvetninga saga* is the longest of all the Eyjafjörður *Íslendingasögur* and probably provides us with the most complex view of political affiliations. The scale of politics does seem to be slightly greater than we see in Dalir. This is personified by Guðmundr *ríki*'s greater geographical reach, in terms of the distribution of his *þingmenn* in Reykjadalur, and can be implied by the likely greater population density in Eyjafjörður than in Dalir. We also see the organisation of resistance to Guðmundr *ríki* by a leading figure in Reykjadalur which is symptomatic of that larger scale and greater sense of hierarchy. While Ófeigr has sometimes been identified as a *þingmaðr* of Guðmundr, the text does not say that.[402] The fact that he is identified as a *höfðingi* illustrates his role as a powerful figure within Reykjadalur; the fact that he exists and can step in as a defender of Guðmundr's *þingmenn* against Guðmundr highlights the limits of Guðmundr's control there. Greater complexity might also be shown by the role of Einarr Arnórsson at Hrafnagil in assisting Guðmundr's son against the Ljósvetningar. That said, Eyjafjörður is still not wholly dominated by Möðruvellir or any other farm, to judge by the role of Guðmundr's brother Einarr. To Eyjafjörður's east, Þórir Helgason might have

---

398 ÍF x: 46–8, 49–51, 52.
399 Andersson & Miller 1989: 134, note 29.
400 ÍF X: 12, 101 and note 2. According to *Íslendingabók* a Þorkell Tjörvason was *lögsögumaðr* for 20 years, probably 1034–53 (ÍF I: 19; IA 57,
401 Andersson & Miller (1989: 240–41, note 5) point out that the holder of Þorgeirr Hallason (d. 1169), and thus his son Þorvarðr Þorgeirsson (d. 1207), were descended from Höskuldr.
402 ÍF X: 3, note 5; Andersson & Miller 1989: 121, note 3.

dominated Hörgárdalur and/or the area equivalent to Glæsibæjarhreppur and, if so, would have constituted a more significant rival to Guðmundr/ Möðruvellir than the Ljósvetningar. Þórir is outlawed, however, with the apparent effect of removing resistance to Guðmundr in this district, so the image we have is of a leader who can influence several districts within 50km if not control them entirely. This really does mark him out as a signicant figure and make politics in Eyjafjörður appreciably different to elsewhere, albeit constructed differently here than in S.

2.4 Svarfdœla Saga

After a prefatory episode in Norway, *Svarfdœla saga* is essentially about a dispute between two factions in Svarfaðardalur (Map 8). Very little action takes place outside the valley or involves people from outside it. The key protagonists are, on the one side, Þorsteinn *svörfuðr* from Grund, his son Karl *inn rauði*, Karl *inn rauði*'s son, also called Karl, plus Klaufi, Þorsteinn's sister's son. These will be referred to collectively as the Grundarmenn for simplicity's sake. These four kinsmen come into conflict with Ljótólfr, who lived at Hof, and Ljótólfr's kinsmen and supporters. The text seems to presuppose that Þorsteinn and Ljótólfr were the leading political figures in the valley[403] but also that they lacked supporters from outside the valley. A rather dense passage in Chapter 11 sets out the idea that Þorsteinn *svörfuðr* took control of all of Svarfaðardalur, but the rest of the saga shows Ljótólfr as at least as powerful as Þorsteinn. The main part of the saga sees relatively little local political change over the course of events it relates, the few changes it does suggest implying that Þorsteinn's kin group are losing control of the valley. As part of the saga's final chapter there is a statement that Ljótólfr's son Ljótr (Valla-Ljótr) and Karl Karlsson fell out, with the result that Karl Karlsson – identifiable as a *goði* indirectly by his having had *þingmenn* – was driven out of Svarfaðardalur to Karlsstaðir in Ólafsfjörður to the north. Ljótr then had control of the whole valley (*hafði mannaforræði um allan dalinn*).[404]

Most of *Svarfdœla saga* can actually be read as an account of a conflict between the combined northern side of the valley and the coastal districts (personified by Þorsteinn/Karl and their sons) and the southern side and the inner valley (Ljótólfr). Unrest tends to occur when a supporter from one side of the river lives on the other side: two of the key sources of conflict surround the presence of allies of Ljótólfr living on the northern side of Svarfaðardalsá. First, Klaufi Snækollsson, the nephew of Þorsteinn *svörfuðr*, is brought up by Gríss, a

---

[403] '...urðu flestir at leita til vináttu, þar sem váru aðrir hvárir, Þorsteinn eða Ljótólfr.' (ÍF IX: 153).
[404] ÍF IX: 207–8.

kinsman of Ljótólfr, at Steindyrr, and he proves to be disruptive. Second, Ásgeirr *rauðfeldr* at Brekka, adjacent to Grund, was a close ally of Ljótólfr. As we shall see, it is probably a measure of the advantage that Ljótólfr's side has that it is Ásgeirr's sons who are responsible for killing Klaufi. The discussion of *Svarfdœla saga* below will look first at the supporters of the Grundarmenn, then at Ljótólfr's supporters, and last at the limited signs of support networks of both groups beyond Svarfaðardalur.

Although it is Þorsteinn *svörfuðr* whose name is associated with the name Svarfaðardalur, the saga has much less to say about him than about his son, grandson and nephew. Nonetheless, earlier parts of the saga show Þorsteinn enjoying the support of people from Þorvaldsdalur, the valley to the south of Svarfaðardalur.[405] Þorsteinn also takes the lead as the advocate for the family of the farmer at Birnunes on Árskógsströnd after the Birnunes man is killed by Þorsteinn's nephew Klaufi, Klaufi here being under the care of Gríss at Steindyrr. In the account of this latter dispute the saga says that the farmer at Hella was closely related to Klaufi, although it is unclear what that relationship was.[406] Either way, Þorsteinn and Klaufi have an interest in, and influence over, the districts at the mouth of Svarfaðardalur, which Ljótólfr does not.

Later chapters and the saga's epilogue give a clearer sense that Þorsteinn's kinsmen were remembered as being in control of the northern side of Svarfaðardalur. Klaufi is associated with the farm(s) at Klaufabrekka in the inner part of the valley, living there and dying there. He had briefly lived on the opposite side of the river close to Klaufabrekka but is forced out after he killing men at Teigsfjall, also on the southern side.[407] Karl *inn rauði* and his son Karl had a slightly more successful association with the outer part of the valley. Like Þorsteinn, Karl *inn rauði* lives at Grund but on Þorstein's advice he moves to Ufsir although seemingly retains control of Grund. It is possible that the writer of the saga is always assuming that Þorsteinn's kin controlled both of these large farms. It is while at Ufsir, however, that Karl *inn rauði* kills a man at nearby Ytra Holt (for no particularly good reason); that he is said to have lost popularity and wealth; and finally that he himself says that Ufsir had brought him bad luck.[408] His wife moves back to Grund on his advice, but his son, Karl, later moves back to Ufsir. Karl *inn rauði* is said to have been buried at Karlsá, a farm on the coast close to the northern boundary of the later *hreppr* of Svarfaðardalur.

---

405   Hávarðr and his sons (ÍF IX: 158–59, 182–83).
406   ÍF IX: 158–59.
407   At Melar before he moved (ÍF IX: 164, 173–74).
408   ÍF IX: 182–84, 187–88, 190. Holt was a notable farm (in 1318) to judge by the fact that it was the only farm other than Grund at which the priest from the church at Tjörn was obliged to perform services. Less regular services were to be performed at Holt than Grund, underlining the lesser status of Tjörn and its church relative to Grund (DI II: 457).

The saga does not mention any supporters of the Grundarmenn this far north within the valley but the linking of Karl to Karlsá probably assumes that the Grundarmenn were thought of as controlling this district. Finally, a list of the children of Karl Karlsson and the place-names which derive from their names fills out the picture of the family's connection with the northern side of Svarfaðardalur between Grund and the coast: Böggvir of Böggvisstaðir, Hrafn of Hrafnsstaðir and Yngvildr of Yngvarastaðir (Ingvarir).[409] Thus many parts of the valley to the north of Svarfaðardalsá are linked to the Grundarmenn, as well as to Árskógsströnd. The Grundarmenn have no positive or lasting connections with the area on the southern side of Svarfaðardalur.

Note should also be taken here of two significant farms which are missing from *Svarfdœla saga*. Of the wealthier farms in Svarfaðardalur which had churches, neither Urðir (with a church attested before 1200) nor Tjörn (listed in 1394) are mentioned.[410] For Urðir we *might* see Klaufabrekka as a kind of proxy for it, and for the upper part of the valley, but it is not as if the latter is even a *hjáleiga* of Urðir, or adjacent to it;[411] the farms' identities would surely have been separate in people's minds. Tjörn is simply absent although, again, neighbouring farms to its north are recorded. The implications of this will be discussed below.

It is no surprise, then, that Ljótólfr's area of dominance is to the south of Svarfaðardalsá although this is often only implied by the hostile actions of the Grundarmenn against people south of the river mentioned above. One particularly strong link is made between Ljótólfr and Ásgeirr *rauðfeldr* at Brekka on the northern side of the river. Ásgeirr and his sons are frequent supporters of Hof and Ásgeirr's daughter Yngvildr is Ljótólfr's concubine.[412] Yngvildr Ásgeirsdóttir is also married off to Ljótólfr's foreman at Hof, Skíði, and the couple set up home in Skíðadalur in upper Svarfaðarfdalur.[413] Skíði is as closely tied to Ljótólfr/Hof as Ásgeirr which is why he kills Karl *inn rauði* and is forced to leave Iceland.[414] Aside from these two men the southern side of Svarfaðardalsá is largely undescribed but this fact serves to reinforce the idea of Ljótólfr's dominance there.

When it comes to allegiances outside of Svarfaðardalur, there are equally clear and simple divisions between the sides of Þorsteinn *svörfuðr* and Ljótólfr.

---

409   ÍF IX: 207. Ingvarir was the property of the church at Tjörn (DI II: 457).
410   Orri Vésteinsson 2000: 98; SS I: 196; DI II: 456–57.
411   Such as Erpsstaðir is for Sauðafell or Hvammr for Grenjaðarstaðir, see pp. 173, 202, 284.
412   ÍF IX: especially 165–67, 174, 200–1, 202–3, 204, 205, 206. Yngvildr's unsuccessful marriage to Klaufi and subsequent mistreatment by Karl Karlsson are a significant part of the saga's later chapters (ÍF IX: 169–74, 186–88, 197–98, 200–6).
413   ÍF IX: 187.
414   ÍF IX: 192, 198.

This shows itself in two ways. First, each side has an ally to some or all of the small valleys to the west which lead into Skagafjörður: Þorsteinn's kinsmen are allied to Kolbeinn of Kolbeinsdalur – the offshoot of Hjaltadalur, the valley which was home to the cathedral of Hólar – while Ljótólfr is allied to Uni of Unadalur.[415] This pattern is not necessarily what one might expect as Unadalur, to the north, is allied to Ljótólfr, the controller of the southern side of Svarfaðardalur, but this geopolitical pattern appears consistently.[416] Second, the only other allegiances of the leaders do conform to a more obvious pattern. The Grundarmenn draw support from Héðinsfjörður and Ólafsfjörður to the north, while a case can be made for Ljótólfr drawing on support from the south if we pay any heed to the statement that he married the daughter of 'Guðmundr *gamli*' from Möðruvellir, an apparent reference to the Guðmundr *ríki* of other texts.[417]

Svarfdœla saga is quite a dense narrative and not one as obviously shaped by its own overarching genealogy as some texts discussed in this chapter, but it can be read in a fairly simple way politically. It shows a semi-isolated community with no real connection to other areas, certainly not to the south, to the likes of Guðmundr *ríki* or even a figure like Þórir Helgason in Hörgárdalur. The statement of the marriage of Ljótólfr's daughter to Guðmundr *gamli* hints at shaky knowledge of the wider genealogy for Eyjafjörður: this is probably testament to the text's separateness from other texts, as well as to Svarfaðardalur's separate identity from areas recorded as colonised by Helgi *inn magri*.

The local geopolitical logic of the text makes more sense than might first be thought. Given the importance of other farms in accounts of later politics, the choice of Hof as the home of the dominant figure in the valley looks like it might derive from the notion that early *goðar* were religious figures who had a religious function. Instead it makes more sense to see Hof as a credible early centre. It was, after all, one of the larger farms in the valley, and more centrally placed within Svarfaðardalur than the other larger farms. Nevertheless the overall pattern of politics, of the rise to dominance of the area of Hof and Vellir,

---

415   ÍF IX: 162 for Ljótólfr's support of the runaway Skíði who had fallen out with the *bóndi* at Ósland at the mouth of Kolbeinsdalur. It may also be significant that it is Karl that goes abroad from Kolbeinsárós rather than Ljótólfr (ÍF IX: 200).
416   ÍF IX: 150, 162–63, 165, 168, 170. In Chapter 11 Uni is said to have been equally related (*jafnskyldr*) to Ljótólfr and to Þorsteinn and Karl but here and later he sides with Ljótólfr. *Vatnsdœla saga* also records discord between Uni and Kolbeinn (ÍF IX: 150, note 1).
417   ÍF IX: 183.

makes sense given the other indications of Vellir's prominence by the late twelfth century.[418]

2.5 Valla-Ljóts Saga

Despite its brevity, at just eight chapters, *Valla-Ljóts saga* provides a clear sense of some aspects of local politics which often chimes in with other *Íslendingasögur*. Unlike other texts set in Eyjafjörður, it seems to give a consistent sense that the rule of *höfðingjar* is a good thing, because of diplomatic abilities of *höfðingjar*, and that it is in the best interests of 'lesser' men that they should follow the counsel of their betters.[419] It is therefore of more than usual interest to see where the troublesome *bændr* and other lesser men are located and how they relate to particular *höfðingjar*. In effect three local *höfðingjar* are mentioned – Valla-Ljótr from Vellir in Svarfaðardalur, Víga-Glúmr at Þverá and, at Möðruvellir, briefly Eyjólfr and then his son Guðmundr *ríki*. This places its action simultaneously with some of the other texts, but relatively early because it begins when both Víga-Glúmr and Eyjólfr are alive.

Three brothers form the focus of disputes which the *höfðingjar* are dragged into. The ancestry of the brothers gives them an association with Gnúpufell, next to Möðruvellir in Eyjafjörður, through one grandfather while their other grandfather was supposedly the Karl *inn rauði*, who we have just seen in *Svarfdæla saga*. Two of the brothers are portrayed as seekers of conflict, Hrólfr and Halli, while the third (Böðvarr) is seen positively, but, characteristically for a positive figure in this saga, is killed.[420] Both the troublesome brothers are connected to Guðmundr *ríki* with Halli marrying a woman who was a kinswoman of the Möðruvellingar.[421]

As the saga's title might imply it has a positive view of Valla-Ljótr, a view which is shaped mostly in relation to Guðmundr *ríki* who is generally seen in a good light, but less so than Ljótr. Guðmundr has no time for those of his supporters who seek to perpetuate disputes (Halli, Hrólfr) but he too is drawn into trying to kill Ljótr, only to fail. The whole dispute ends with a settlement which Guðmundr arranges with Skapti Þóroddsson – lawspeaker and well-known figure from other *Íslendingasögur* – so that Guðmundr maintained his honour

---

418 See above pp. 141–2 for the late twelfth century and pp. 25 for the large ministry of Vellir's church.
419 Andersson & Miller 1989: 115–18, 282–83, note 263
420 ÍF IX: 233 for introductory descriptions; ÍF IX: 252–53 for Böðvarr's death.
421 Halli's wife Signý's genealogical connection is not spelled out, however (ÍF IX: 237). A further connection between Gnúpufell and Möðruvellir, albeit of a different kind, is maintained by Eyjólfr having drowned in the river Gnúpufellsá. This is hardly a surprising connection, given that the two farms are so close, but the association need not have been made.

(*virðing*) from this point until his death. Such an outcome seems to corrolate with the idea that Guðmundr, and by extension Eyfirðingar in general, ought to recognise their inability to control Svarfaðardalur.

The first episode in which the brothers are involved is the only part of the saga which says anything about farms within inner Eyjafjörður. Here Halli kills the freedman from nearby Torfufell so as to prevent this man from marrying his widowed mother and thus making what he considers an inappropriate match. This provides a dilemma Eyjólfr at Möðruvellir because Halli is his kinsman while the man killed was his *þingmaðr*. Halli, however, goes to his grandfather at Gnúpufell who is able to get Víga-Glúmr to intercede on their behalf and to bring about a satisfactory settlement.[422] Thus there is a sense that there are two local leaders in the main part of Eyjafjörður and also that Guðmundr *ríki* is dominant close to Möðruvellir, as he is in other sagas. The text also notes that Halli had fallen out with Guðmundr's brother Einarr, implying that the saga's author thought of Einarr living at Saurbær or Möðruvellir, and being on good terms with Guðmundr.[423]

Halli's anti-social behaviour is also exemplified by his own sense that he was better than other people thought him; in broader terms this suggests that, *Valla-Ljóts saga* is more obviously opposed to Þorsteinn *svörfuðr*'s kin group than is *Svarfdœla saga*. *Valla-Ljóts saga* reminds us that Halli, as a descendant of Karl *inn rauði*, has kinsmen (still) at Grund in Svarfaðardalur and this is why he moves to that valley in a bid to exercise more power.[424] Guðmundr *ríki* expresses his doubt about Halli's ability to do this due to the power of Valla-Ljótr and his kinsmen over in Svarfaðardalur.

The difference in status between Halli and Valla-Ljótr's family – Ljótr's brother Þorgrímr and their two nephews – is exemplified in the farms associated with each. Halli is bought land at Klaufabrekka by his kinsman but his farm is said to be deficient in meadows which means meadowland has to be bought for it. Halli's unsuccessful association with Klaufabrekka replicates that of his kinsman Klaufi in *Svarfdœla saga*. Valla-Ljótr's kinsmen, by contrast, are based at larger farms in the lower part of the valley (Ufsir and Hofsá) and draw support from Tjörn.[425] Unlike in *Svarfdœla saga*, where Ljótólfr's power only seems to have extended to the southern side of the Svarfaðardalsá, *Valla-Ljóts saga* presupposes that Ljótr has support from two larger farms on the northern side of the river (Ufsir and Tjörn). Different reasons might be suggested as to

---

422 ÍF IX: 233–37.
423 ÍF IX: 239. In *Valla-Ljóts saga* it is Víga-Glúmr who still lived at Þverá (ÍF IX: 236).
424 A Þórir Vémundarson, who is most likely the son of Vémundr from Ólafsfjörður identified in *Svarfdœla saga*, is living at Grund (ÍF IX: 240, note 1). Andersson and Miller (1989: 263, note 232) identify another possible candidate.
425 ÍF IX: 239, 250, 252.

why each farm is identified here and not earlier. While Tjörn was absent altogether from *Svarfdœla saga* (and thus not seen to side with either group), Ufsir was the farm at which the Grundarmenn were unable to support themselves; such a story suggests a consistent logic across the two texts, namely that the power of Þorsteinn *svörfuðr*'s kin was thought to have reduced significantly over time.[426] There is some weak sense that the Grundarmenn were still thought of as connected to Ólafsfjörður – Valla-Ljótr certainly was not – but this tie is not seen to be even as useful as it was in *Svarfdœla saga*.[427]

One final point needs to be made about *Valla-Ljóts saga* in the context of *Svarfdœla saga* concerning the scale of political power in Svarfaðardalur. Essentially what we see is the growth of the influence of the leading figure in the valley, who is based in the lower, eastern side of it. It is probably not coincidence that the chronological setting of the texts is in the order it is; *Valla-Ljóts saga* is set later and has a leading figure from Svarfaðardalur who has sufficient control of the valley to be able to deal on a relatively even footing with Guðmundr *ríki*. At the same time, however, that control extends no further than Svarfaðardalur, which fits with the idea that such a small valley did not provide the same kind of base as Eyjafjörður did for someone seeking wider power; the saga would surely have said that about Ljótr had it been conceivable that he was more powerful.

2.6 The Territories and Power of Leading Men in Eyjafjörður and the North-East: Some Conclusions

By and large the composite picture of politics in these *Íslendingasögur* produces a coherent view rather than one where different texts contradict each another. This could reflect individual authors' knowledge of other written, but most likely oral, texts, something akin to the 'immanent saga' of Guðmundr *ríki* which Gísli Sigurðsson has proposed. It might serve repeating that for these texts, just as for those covering Dalir, this does not mean we have a narrative for actually what happened in the late tenth and eleventh centuries such as could be posited by Björn Sigfússon in the 1930s.[428]

The most obvious thing to say about these texts is simply that they are all concerned with events in a fairly restricted number of districts. First, none of them contain any action in neighbouring Skagafjörður at all, which must

---

[426] A less significant indicator of their implied reduction in influence might also be that the farm of Hella, on the coast and south of the river, was identified as home to a supporter of Klaufi in *Svarfdœla saga* but in *Valla-Ljóts saga* to a man who claimed friendship with both the Grundarmenn and Valla-Ljótr (ÍF IX 252; see above p. 299).

[427] Through Þórir Vémundarson at Grund, perhaps, see above p. 303, footnote 424. Böðvarr Sigurðarson, Halli's brother, trades with men from Kvíabekkr in Ólafsfjörður (ÍF IX: 248).

[428] Björn Sigfússon 1934.

say something about what geopolitical connections mattered to people in Eyjafjörður. It might be suggested that this reflects a kind of blind spot for saga authors, or an attempt to airbrush out the unpleasant reality of Skagafjörður's real significance or even dominance in the north. Yet this is such a significant feature of all these texts that it really does suggest that they were produced in a world where it did not make sense for Eyjafjörður to be connected to Skagafjörður. A second point is that, for *Víga-Glúms saga*, *Reykdœla saga* and *Ljósvetninga saga*, the balance of power is without doubt tipped in favour of the leading men from Eyjafjörður and Ljósavatn; we do not even have a plucky loser, or a hard-to-credit *goði* from an obscure district who somehow manages to overcome the odds. Áskell *goði* from Reykjadalur in *Reykdœla saga*, for instance, comes across as a victim, and all his other male relatives are seen as troublesome, rather than successful.

Leading men come from more or different places than we might expect based on what we saw in the contemporary sagas. Kroppr and Skörð, for example, were no doubt large farms but there is no tradition of important figures coming from these particular places which are overshadowed by other farms in other texts. As we have seen, both are identified as homes of *höfðingjar*. In the case of Kroppr, because it is close to, and midway between, Hrafnagil and Kristnes, perhaps this can be rationalised as signifying one of those two places, but I see no reason to doubt that at some point this farm could have been home to someone prominent in lower Eyjafjörður. *Reykdœla saga*'s distinctive take on lower Eyjafjörður could be dismissed as fanciful were it not for Kroppr's size and its almost identical location to other farms which served as bases for similar figures. Skörð is seen as having local significance in two texts and again makes good sense as the base of the leader of the coastal part of Reykjadalur.

In terms of territoriality, the pattern seems to be one where individual *höfðingjar* can have *þingmenn* at some remove from their own home, but also where certain of them control the equivalent of a large farm surrounded by its *hjáleigur*, such as Víga-Glúmr's Þverá or Áskell's farm and its neighbours. Perhaps the clearest signs of a concentration of landownership and/or control are in the texts covering Svarfaðardalur where Ljótólfr and Valla-Ljótr control one side of the valley and then probably the other side over the course of time, effectively becoming *goði* for the whole valley. Here, as with the narrative in *Reykdœla saga*, there might be a recognition that particular *höfðingjar* were getting more powerful with time.

Of course, the most powerful figure across the *Íslendingasögur* is Guðmundr *ríki* of Möðruvellir in Eyjafjörður, and his geographical reach is far greater than that of local leaders elsewhere in Dalir or anywhere in the north. The idea of Eyjafjörður's economic and political importance is a commonplace for the thirteenth century and more recent periods in Icelandic history, but the precise configuration of it here is what is potentially significant. Guðmundr *ríki* is clearly preeminent in Eyjafjörður, although there were other *goðar* there, and he has supporters in Reykjadalur and Tjörnes, who require managing, yet some opposition in Hörgárdalur and in Ljósavatn where there were clearly also *goðar*. *Reykdœla saga*'s connection of Grenjaðarstaðir to Mývatn, by means of a single powerful family, while unique to that text, suggests some limits to Guðmundr's influence. In some respects this picture is not dissimilar to what we see in the thirteenth century – Eyjafjörður-based leaders do seem to be superior to those in the smaller valleys to the east – but the idea of there being any leader of note in Ljósavatn, and also at Möðruvellir itself, is different. In this respect it is the equivalent of the focus of *Laxdœla saga* on Hjarðarholt, something we will come back to below. In terms of material wealth it might also suggest that Mývatn's distinctive freshwater resources were considered to be controlled by Grenjaðarstaðir rather than Möðruvellir, arguably a significant benefit to the former in countering the power of the latter.

Something also needs to be said about the text's views of the institutional underpinning of politics, i.e. the *goði-þingmaðr* relationship, in all these texts, but especially for the northern ones. The rare appearance of the word *þingmaðr* in any of these texts, or euphemisms for it, make one appreciate how much modern historiography derives its view from *Grágás* rather than these texts.[429] The relationship was undoubtedly important when invoked but perhaps was not actually as important as is sometimes suggested. In fact, what comes across is the oddity of *Ljósvetninga saga* in not only being critical of Guðmundr *ríki*, but also in frequently using the word *þingmaðr*. As we have seen here, *þingmenn* are sometimes identified when they are in distant or unexpected locations, and it might also be that a text like *Ljósvetninga saga* shows a heightened sensitivity about such issues because it was written at a time when it was contentious. In this case, specifically, it is Guðmundr *ríki*'s dealings with his *þingmenn* in Reykjadalur and Tjörnes, where this is a problem. If we assume that there was a gradual process of centralisation of power, then one possible context for this story might have been when Eyjafjörður leaders first imposed themselves on Reykjadalur. All of a sudden the nature of that relationship became important. This would most likely have been some time in the twelfth century if, as we saw, the subjugation of Reykjadalur and other parts of the east was already a given in the thirteenth century. Otherwise we

---

429 Use of the word *þingmaðr* in the major texts considered here: *Laxdœla saga*, only *Bolla þáttr*, Ch. 1, concerning Skagafjörður; *Eyrbyggja saga* Chs. 9, 12, 57; *Víga-Glúms saga*, none; *Reykdœla saga ok Víga-Skútu*, Ch. 15, in relation to an assembly, not an individual *þingmaðr*; *Ljósvetninga saga* Chs. 1, 2, 6, 7, 9, 13, 14, 21, 22, 23, 25; *Svarfdœla saga* Ch. 25; *Valla-Ljóts saga* Ch. 1.

can see *goðar* or *höfðingjar* in both regions but the ties of their supporters are mostly through kinship.

3 Conclusions

This brings us back to the question of why *Íslendingasögur* were written and how they related to the society that produced them. An easy answer is simply to say that these texts are folk stories which have no particular connection to the time in which they were written. They are undoubtedly hard to contextualise anyway; none of them work in the way that so many medieval chronicles and annals do in western Europe where the voice of the patron of a historical text is often readily visible and often relatively easy to date. What is proposed here is that these texts present stories which were close to popular views of the past current at some point in the later twelfth century. There are obviously references to thirteenth-century individuals in the surviving texts but rarely do these form an integral part of the story; they read like additions to an earlier manuscript. In terms of the scale of political activity and the relative prominence of particular farms these stories are not completely at odds with the way politics appears to have worked in each region in the period 1200–1265. However, none of the *Íslendingasögur* seem to serve to reinforce or justify the power of thirteenth-century leaders which is a further argument in favour of an earlier date for most, if not all, of the contents of the surviving texts.

The specific implications for each region are that each shows signs of varying degrees of territorial political control of the kind we see, respectively, for the twelfth century in each region. At what I would imagine as a continuous but slow concentration of power then places like Hjarðarholt and Helgafell in Dalir and on Snæfellsnes make sense as centres of influence before wealth and power had become concentrated to the extent that other farms become more strategically important, such as Sauðafell, Hvammr or Sælingsdalstunga where local leaders exercised slightly wider geographical control. For Eyjafjörður the proposed shift from Möðruvellir, 25km as the crow flies from the innermost shore of Eyjafjörður, to the likes of Hrafnagil and Grund (just over 10km and 16km respectively), makes similar sense, given that they are closer to areas of Eyjafjörður which were marginally more densely populated. Möðruvellir would have been central within Eyjafjörður but not the wider region.

Once we get beyond the top end of the political scale, *Íslendingasögur* contain a vast body of detail. As with the larger structural patterns of local politics, it is not proposed that we can pin those down to a precise point in time, but most likely that these are what are likely to have constituted a fairly commonly-accepted view of the past in the later twelfth century.

CHAPTER 6

Conclusion

This book has tried to analyse the different types of written evidence for the regions concerned up to c.1265. My suggestion is that the idiosyncrasies of these sources have led most scholars to overemphasise change in early Icelandic society at the expense of underlying structural continuity and stability. Iceland's fundamental lack of a medium of exchange or tendencies towards urbanism, and the lack of any significant economic growth underpin this. The contents of the texts concerned would seem to suggest that in about 1100 – the earliest date for which we can say much about Icelandic history from its texts – patterns of land tenure and the distribution of wealth were fairly conventional for a western European society and it stayed that way: there were larger, more stable farms in better locations and smaller or poorer farms with access to fewer resources which were more likely to be periodically abandoned. Without the economic changes of the kind seen elsewhere in medieval Europe, it seems reasonable to suggest that significant, structural political change was unlikely to have happened in Iceland: the findings of this study support this view. Most likely the motor for any changes that did occur was the influence of the increasingly powerful Norwegian king. The gradual development of Iceland's church probably added complexity to the way society worked and increased social stratification marginally. It also created a new identity for the less combative members of the elite who sought to avoid the deadly consequences of political competition in Iceland. Still, this did not in itself change the scale or workings of politics.

The premise of this book is that there is a value in examining the evidence for particular regions in greater depth than is usually done. Writing such a regional history or histories for Iceland, especially one which is intended to be comparative, has more difficulties than for other parts of medieval western Europe because of the nature of the sources. Comparing each form of narrative evidence side-by-side has, however, had the self-evident virtue of demonstrating how, in some ways, each region's history is portrayed very differently. What it has also done, particularly for the *Íslendingasögur*, is enabled geopolitical patterns for each region to be identified in those narrative texts, something which derives from looking first at each text individually rather than attempting synthesis immediately.

It is both a strength and a limitation of this book is that it has looked at Iceland's history on a genre by genre or source-by-source basis, referring to

CONCLUSION

certain, less voluminous forms of evidence (the annals and documentary evidence) only sporadically. This study still represents a significant reappraisal of the value and place of both *Landnámabók* and the *Íslendingasögur* as sources for early Icelandic history. Each, it has been argued, provide a view of Icelandic history in the twelfth century and one which sits less well with their now traditional dating to the thirteenth century. It is commonly accepted that *Landnámabók* had its origins in the early twelfth century but far less common to appraise its contents in the belief that much of that early text remains intact. For the *Íslendingasögur* it is rarely argued these days that most of the contents of most of these date to the later twelfth century as is suggested here. If we still consider the early *Sturlunga saga* texts as thirteenth-century texts – recalling the twelfth century – then it does place the *Íslendingasögur* earlier. That makes the local political patterns they depict an earlier view of the past, even if the dates of the texts and their intentions are still opaque in all sorts of ways and does not obviously help us explain how political centralisation happened in Iceland.

This book does not necessarily stand or fall, however, on whether one accepts an earlier date for *Íslendingasögur* because the analysis of the political worlds these texts create can be read as self-contained interpretations in their own right. In my view the challenge to other scholars would still be for them to pin down how and why these texts took the form they did so as to demonstrate that they really were significantly shaped by thirteenth-century or later contexts. More specifically, for the *Íslendingasögur* focussed on Eyjafjörður and the north-east, and regardless of when they were written, we might take the monastery at Þingeyrar more seriously as the place of their production: their ambivalence towards Munkaþverá might suggest this. And, for the *Sturlubók* version of *Landnámabók*, while we can undoubtedly see Sturlungar influence on some elements of the surviving text, it still reads like a text to which additions made to it, rather than one that has been significantly rewritten.

We can also now try to sum up the political histories of these two regions, although this been done to an extent in each chapter, and then suggest what this says about Iceland more broadly: a kind of political history might be written for each region based on the way the farms are represented, over time.

By about 1100 in Dalir, then, Hvammr, Bjarnarhöfn, Helgafell and Skarð were probably the pre-eminent farms because they are recorded as such in *Landnámabók*. The remaining *landnámsbæjar*, or the later estates of which they were a part, were all farms which were of above average size in later centuries and had more plentiful or varied resources than most other farms. The *Íslendingasögur*, although variable in their coverage of Dalir and northern Snæfellsnes, pick out several farms as the most important ones after the *landnám*:

Sælingsdalstunga, Laugar, Hjarðarholt, Höskuldsstaðir, Helgafell, Bjarnarhöfn, Öndverðareyrr, Bólstaðr and Kársstaðir. The last two farms in that list may not have been that significant, however, because they appear in *Eyrbyggja saga* whose highly localised coverage probably exaggerates their influence. By contrast there are also some suggestions of local leaders based in Saurbær, in Hörðudalr and in the main valley of Miðdalir, although their power is not so clearly expressed.

In the third phase of political images, portraying the mid twelfth century, Staðarhóll in Saurbær first features as a major political base for a *höfðingi*. Staðarfell joins Hjarðarholt, Helgafell and Sælingsdalstunga in what appears to have been a political rung below the pre-eminent Staðarhóll. Hvammr re-appears as a political force in the latter half of this phase, displacing Staðarhóll as the base of the pre-eminent person in Dalir. Hvoll is largely absent from the *Íslendingasögur* but is visible as a second important centre in Saurbær for this period.

In the last phase, the first half of the thirteenth century, Sauðafell rises to compete with Hvammr. Hvammr eventually ceases to be the base of a *höfðingi* as Staðarhóll re-emerges as such. The former falls back into the ranks of those large farms which are politically active but predominantly only on a regional or local scale: Skarð, Staðarfell, Hjarðarholt, Kvennabrekka, Snóksdalr (only appearing briefly), Helgafell (perhaps) and Bjarnarhöfn were other farms of this class.

Some further explanation of the development of political organisation in Dalir can also be established. The presentation of the *landnám* in *Sturlubók* is clearly a construct yet not a wholly unconvincing one in some of its basic ideas. It seems inconceivable that Iceland's colonisation was not controlled by wealthy individuals who chose the best places to live for themselves. In Dalir, Hvammr, Skarð, Helgafell and Bjarnarhöfn, the farms said to have been established by the most prominent *landnámsmenn*, would have provided some of the best places to settle. If we imagine that the first settlers brought livestock with them, and most likely a relatively large number of cattle, then areas with good meadows would have been at a premium. So too, however, would have been easily-available foods such as fish, *crustacea* and seals. Farms like Bjarnarhöfn, Helgafell and Skarð are likely to have been settled first because they were rich in good pasture and had good access to non-pastoral resources. Hvammr and the farms allegedly settled by Auðr/Unnr's companions, probably represent a genuine, slightly later phase of settlement when the population had adapted pastoral farming regimes appropriate for the landscape and so permanently settled the area further inland. It is also likely that Saurbær was settled relatively early because of its access to the sea, even if the nature of the surviving written evidence does not date the *landnám* relative to other districts to its south in Breiðafjörður.

If we hypothesise in the same way for Eyjafjörður and the north-east, which involves thinking on a larger scale, then coastal areas would seem to have been able to provide the full range of natural resources for those arriving in an empty landscape. Similarly, even if it is hard to believe in their existence of Helgi *inn magri* and Hámundr, their settling at a place like Hámundarstaðir on Árskógsströnd makes sense, as does the move to the cluster of Kristnes-Kroppr-Hrafnagil as the next political centre. The desire to maintain a pastoral economy, however, made places like central Eyjafjörður more attractive and more powerful in the longer term, because they probably had access to more (and more varied) resources in the form of coast, shielings and common land. The relative uniformity of the status of the major farms in the genealogy of Helgi most likely reflects their rough equality in the early twelfth century or before. The same suitability for pastoral farming might be credited to many farms in Reykjadalur. Mývatn, with the boon of access to a very specific resource, the lake itself, must also have been a very attractive but very small region, colonised early. Mývatn never gets into the narrative sources as a significant early centre because it must already have been seen as politically marginal by the early twelfth century; it does not even appear as a place that *höfðingjar* from other districts exploit directly for its natural resources although the genealogy connecting Helgi *inn magri* to Mývatn is strongly suggestive of one.

It warrants repeating that the *Íslendingasögur* for Eyjafjörður and the north-east have virtually no *landnám* narratives. In Eyjafjörður, local traditions may simply never have contained such stories and perhaps this left space for *Landnámabók*'s compilers to create one using more limited historical lore. That Dalir-focussed *Íslendingasögur* do have *landnám* accounts might be because political instability or competition in Dalir encouraged people to record them; the *landnám* may not have been such a contentious issue in an already-centralised Eyjafjörður region.

For Eyjafjörður and the north-east it is certainly harder to create a narrative for likely changes in the political hierarchy based on the *Íslendingasögur*. In Eyjafjörður itself the eastern half of the valley seems to be preeminent, notwithstanding Víga-Glúmr's ignominious departure from Þverá. Þverá and Möðruvellir, despite the recorded hostility to the latter, remain the key centres, with Espihóll and Kroppr having occasional importance (as opposed to Hrafnagil, Grund or Kristnes). That Ketill Þorsteinsson, the second Bishop of Hólar in Skagafjörður (d.1145), was from Möðruvellir sits well with the idea its being powerful in the twelfth century, and not uncomfortably with its being the home of a dominant figure in Guðmundr *ríki*. In general this also fits well with the pattern recently proposed by Helgi Þorláksson whereby farms which are central within a valley, rather than on the coast or else further inland, came to dominate.[1] He suggests this in relation specifically to Grund but we can perhaps see a shift from the likes of Þverá, Kristnes and even Espihóll, to Möðruvellir and then, finally, to Grund. This amounts to geographical determinism of a very refined type: we are talking about households just a few kilometres apart but ones whose leaders might be intense rivals.

It is harder still to create any chronological depth to our account for Eyjafjörður and the north-east except to say that Ljósavatn's influence emerges gradually across the texts and appears independent of Eyjafjörður. We might also posit a centralisation of power within Reykjadalur and Mývatnssveit before the recorded defeat of the Reykdœlir leaders, based at Grenjaðarstaðir, by leaders from Eyjafjörður and Ljósavatn. This makes sense as a likely regional-scale political change in the twelfth century although, as the *samtíðarsögur* make clear, the kind of overlordship portrayed there at that point (and elsewhere in Iceland) is still weak, and still was even in the 1250s, if seen from the perspective of many contemporary regions of western Europe.

This brings us to where Grund fits into this picture and why Sighvatr Sturluson moved there in the early thirteenth century. It is fair to say that Sighvatr was not the first notable figure to live at Grund, with Þorsteinn *ranglátr* Einarsson (d.1149), being associated with the farm long before him. Although Þorsteinn was posited by *Sturlunga saga* as a key figure through his inclusion in its genealogical section (*Ættartölur*), the precise influence of Grund in the twelfth century is hard to track, even if Þorsteinn's family continued to be members of Iceland's landowning elite. The best explanation for this pattern is that, while Grund was one of the top tier of farms in the twelfth century, it really owed its importance in the thirteenth century to the arrival of Sighvatr. Perhaps Sighvatr was able to move there because it was not home to, or owned by, one of the pre-existing leading families in the valley, such as we have seen at Hrafnagil and possibly still at Möðruvellir. The fairly lowly position of Grund within the *Íslendingasögur* accounts would fit with its relative lack of prominence in the twelfth century and its absence as a *landnámsbær*, with another large farm (Stóri-Dalur) being listed in its place. The fact that Grund was close to a route into Skagafjörður, and that Sighvatr owed his role in Eyjafjörður to his supporters in Skagafjörður, might have been connected. We might also speculate that Sighvatr and his successors at Grund were able to develop their financial base by buying land.

---

1 Helgi Þorláksson 2010b: esp. 77–78.

We should also consider how these detailed local pictures relate to the *landnám*. As stated above, it seems unlikely that the first generations of colonists consisted of people of equal wealth. It is likely that the journey from Norway, or anywhere else, was undertaken entirely by people who could afford to supply themselves well with sea-going vessels and sufficient livestock to survive the journey and feed their families over a winter. These people may well have taken dependents of various kinds who they eventually gave dependent farms. These farms would have been less valuable, having less and/or poorer natural resources. The model of Auðr/Unnr and her retainers is thus useful in so far as it may actually represent what happened at a micro level, rather than across districts.

It would seem, all the same, that Dalir and Eyjafjörður were distinctive. Dalir being a relatively broad, low-lying, continuous coastal strip with no extensive plains would seem to have affected the patterns of farm size. Although the information we have on this subject is mostly early modern, the stability of these patterns in that later period since the *landnám* (with the exception of a likely deforestation in some districts) argues for the early establishment of tenurial divisions. Dalir is also distinctive because it had a large number of medium-value farms (16 to 24 hundreds) in the late medieval and early modern periods. *Jarðabók*'s data would suggest that in Eyjafjörður and other areas in the northeast there is a slightly greater tendency towards a pattern of a small number of extremely large farms (60 hundreds or more) and a large number of smaller farms (12 hundreds or less) and *hjáleigur*. Although there is a risk of circularity here, the particular configuration of landscape and farm size in Dalir and Eyjafjörður may indicate that the initial settlement in Dalir was less strongly controlled than in Eyjafjörður. An alternative view might be that non-pastoral resources added to the value of many Dalir farms.

This essential geographical difference between Dalir and many other region of Iceland can be seen to influence the politics of the region into the mid-twelfth and thirteenth centuries. Political control was still weak and territorial control extremely limited. By the mid-twelfth century, however, the farms in inland areas of Dalir were sufficiently wealthy to rival those in the outer, western side of the region. While we might doubt that Hvammr was quite as important in the *landnám* process as the written evidence suggests, it was wealthy and locally significant before Hvamm-Sturla moved there: that is why he moved there.

The story of Snorri *goði*'s move from Helgafell to Sælingsdalstunga probably indicates that the latter farm had assumed as great or greater power than the former by some time before the mid-twelfth century. The absence of any myth which credits Snorri with simultaneous influence over the districts around these farms suggests that one of the most powerful figures in medieval Icelandic myth was conceived of as small-scale.

In both areas, throughout the notional period covered by the texts, *goðar* or *höfðingjar* can rarely be seen to control all of the population in any given district, even those closest to them. This is true whenever we have enough evidence to suggest the loyalties of any of the population other than the *höfðingjar* themselves. For the period before 1100, it is just about conceivable that the first *landnámsmenn*, i.e. heads of settling households, could have commanded the loyalties of the other households which settled on the territory they claimed, for a generation or two. After this period it would seem probable that personal relationships would have dictated the loyalties of heads of households and that something like the *goði-þingmaðr* relationship existed, although this early there is little we can say about the relationship of *goðar* and *bændr*.

The relationships between *þingmenn* and their legal representatives, *goðar*, were still largely personal and not institutionalised in Dalir in the twelfth and thirteenth centuries. Hvamm-Sturla and Einarr Þorgilsson could command the allegiance of individual households in different districts but not necessarily all of their wealthier neighbours; the same can be said of Guðmundr *dýri* and his rivals in the north at almost the same time. This is also true for the patterns of allegiance in disputes in Dalir the 1220s and 1230s. Farmers probably benefited from having someone other than the most immediate *goði* to act legally on their behalf when the nearest *goði* happened to be ruthless and prone to initiating violence, as the likes of Hvamm-Sturla and Einarr Þorgilsson surely were. Yet this choice was probably only open to the wealthiest tier of *bændr*, in both regions. For those *bændr* living on smaller farmsteads, no doubt with smaller households, and close to *goðar*, they can have had no choice but to follow the nearest *goði*.

Such patterns are not observable for Eyjafjörður after 1200, however. The nearest we come to this is the seemingly frantic activities of *höfðingjar* in the 1250s as they are portrayed dealing with what the sources call *stórbændr*. These men always probably interacted with poorer farmers who lived near them, either supporting them or bullying them. They, no less so than *höfðingjar*, must have been the effective rulers of small districts (a *sveit*, *byggð* or *hverfi*) across Iceland.

While there are reasons why *bændr* would not want other people to be powerful, the other side of the equation which needs to be explored is why *goðar* were not more powerful. The poverty of the natural resources available and the relative evenness of their occurrence would seem to be one explanation for the lack of political centralisation in Dalir. There were clear two broad environmental zones in the mid-west of Iceland – the coastal one where marine resources were more plentiful and the inland one where these resources were less readily available – but both zones still fed themselves predominantly on beef, mutton, and dairy products. It is probable that those on larger farms could offer those on smaller farms very little which would persuade them to support them; similarly the more powerful could only ever force the less powerful to pay dues in staples which they already had. In inner Eyjafjörður it was probably only ever the larger farms, those that eventually had churches or chapels, which were able to maintain access to coastline that provided *reki*, along the coasts of the north-east. This was a powerful motive for Eyjafjörður-based *höfðingjar* to travel through, and interfere in, Reykjadalur and other districts in the north-east. The same was true for Dalir *höfðingjar* going to Strandir, although mostly they would have had less distance to travel and fewer households to bully there. If power was still this weak in regions seemingly controlled by *höfðingjar* since the late twelfth century, it is interesting to speculate whether *höfðingjar* in the south or east of Iceland – where seemingly *ríki* had existed for longer but for which we have little narrative material – actually had greater power, however we might measure it.

The poverty of even the wealthiest people in medieval Iceland may explain partly why it was that *höfðingjar* were unable to support large retinues. There may have been some reward for young men to seek service with their local *höfðingjar* but the supply of luxury goods from Norway which arrived sporadically was not the nowhere near the lucrative reward that military service could yield in most other western European medieval societies.

There are few other signs of increasing political centralisation in either region, if we look through the range of sources and each period which they cover. It is certainly true that the lineages which ruled Dalir changed over time, as did the farms from which they operated, but there is no clear evidence that any individual in thirteenth-century Dalir actually owned much more property or controlled larger core territories than their twelfth-century predecessors. Even the Sturlusynir, who between them probably owned tens of farms, inherited only shares of their father's property. The division of inheritances probably helped to ensure that no one individual acquired increasing amounts of land, except through the occasional law suit. Our sources are occasionally quick to boast of, and possibly exaggerate, the wealth of the Sturlungar. This is especially true when they buy or acquire new property, although it is equally noticeable that the sources rarely mention their sale of property. Rented property no doubt existed in large quantity in the twelfth and thirteenth centuries, as it did in later centuries. Perhaps this is what *höfðingjar* in Dalir were gaining, little by little, over the centuries, although, again, the rents could only have come in the form of basic food stuffs and animal products. For the north there are few accounts of property purchases, the most notable of exceptions being the acquisition of Grenjaðarstaðir in 1232 by Sighvatr Sturluson.

This brings us back to the much-debated role of *goðorð*. What this book has shown is that personal relationships of all kinds mattered and that the kind of patron-client relationship of the *goði-þingmaðr* relationship was one which only mattered to certain people under certain circumstances, i.e. mostly when a well-off farmer needed support against a neighbour. *Þingmenn*, for the most part, whether willingly or unwillingly, were likely to be affiliated to a *goði*. *Goðorð* therefore tended to be in the hands of people who were *de facto* already wealthy and powerful but, perhaps like church ownership, *goðorð* were an institution that could shape a leader's status, for better or for worse. Led by *Grágás*, scholars have still tended to try to identify set numbers of *goðorð* and *goðar* but, as we have seen, individual *goðorð* are difficult to trace. No doubt *goðorð* names were changed, and their histories consciously and subconsciously altered, as it suited the political situation, in response to the balance of power between different *goðar* and between their supporters. Thus *Eyvellingagoðorð* might have become *Hafliðanautr*, both names for what was, after all, the privilege to choose judges in court, a right which required *de facto* power to make it meaningful. In this case each name probably made sense in the circumstances in which it was coined, one named after a place or regional grouping, the other after an important individual whose memory was being invoked to justify a later leader's right to the position. *Goðorð* seem to have been mostly defined geographically but with wealthier *þingmenn* more likely to able to choose a *goði* if they thought they could get away with it for a longer or shorter time. Thus the concentration of named *goðorð* in the hands of fewer *goðar* in the thirteenth century is a confirmation of the power of those men rather than the cause of it.

Finally it is worth briefly returning to consider the role of the introduction of Christianity in political developments, especially as this has often been seen as a force for increasing the wealth and power of *höfðingjar*. The usual reason for seeing the church as having an impact on politics is the development of the parish and the associated collection of tithes. Parishes and tithe collection are often regarded as forming the first territorially-defined sources of wealth extraction in medieval Iceland. Owners of farms with churches on them were entitled to keep one quarter of the tithe.

It is most likely the case that parishes, once in existence, were a territorial unit which the owners of parish churches could manipulate. But it has to be emphasised that, even though the Tithe Law was supposedly introduced in 1097, we know little about how parishes developed in most places in Iceland before the fourteenth century. Dalir has some of the better evidence for the presence of a parishes but it is not until after the period covered by this study, in the late thirteenth century, that a coherent parish system is discernible. The lack of visibility need not be an argument for the system's earlier absence, however, and it is certainly the case that many churches had been built by the end of the twelfth century. Yet the presence of churches is not the same as the collection of tithes. Some farmers would also have been exempt on the grounds of their poverty and so, all in all, this would only suggest a very gradual increase in the wealth of the leading men who had parish churches on their land, and not the sort of thing that contemporary sagas ever talk about.

In spite of the general arguments for structural political stasis, there is no denying that the representation of regional leaders is different in the thirteenth century, especially from the 1240s until saga coverage ceases. At a local level, however, it seems that they behaved in much the same way as had the people who controlled their respective farms before them. They were still required to deal with what are now identified, in the north, as *stórbændr* to maintain their political position while, at the same time, they competed with each other for the approval of the Norwegian king. *Stórbændr* is a term coined in those texts dealing with the decades leading up to the swearing of oaths to King Hákon but it seems most likely to represent a change of nomenclature rather than real change to the social hierarchy.

If the *höfðingjar* of the thirteenth century had any more wealth and power than their predecessors, it may have been due to their increasingly visible relationship with King Hákon Hákonarson. Undoubtedly the position of local leaders had always partly depended on access to luxury goods imported by merchants from Norway. In the thirteenth century, however, it would seem that the Norwegian king's interest in Iceland extended to interfering in the flow of those goods to *höfðingjar*. Not only were weapons now visibly important but also armed men, supplied by the king, to those Icelandic *höfðingjar* who commended themselves to him. If anything had altered the traditional political balance then it was most likely this input into the system, which circumvented normal political relationships. For Dalir this is as much hypothesis as it is for other regions of Iceland: the texts for before c.1200 doubtless play down the level of royal intervention in Iceland as part of a myth of local leaders' agency. For Eyjafjörður the absence of detailed narratives for this period have held us back from saying much about the region before this. It is still probably significant that Bishop Guðmundr's father Ari Þorgeirsson is recounted in an annal-like section of *Prestssaga Guðmundar góða* as bringing 30 *austmenn* (Norwegians) back with him to Iceland in 1164, in what the saga calls the 'shield summer' (*skjaldasumar*).² Thirty mercenaries made a big difference to local power in Iceland. We still see Norwegians such as Þjóstarr, Kálfr Guttormsson and Sölmundr arriving in Iceland and staying in the thirteenth century. The representation of relations between Iceland and the king in the twelfth century might warrant more careful consideration than it has been given here. In fact the early centralisation of power in Eyjafjörður, probably suggested by the genealogy of Helgi *inn magri*, coupled with the distinctive account for Glæsibæjarhreppur in *Landnámabók*, almost implies that there was something separate – Norwegian perhaps – about this district, well before we know about the royal official's farm there, Lögmannshlíð, in the very late thirteenth century. This is a big jump, but the distinctiveness of this area might suggest royal control.

One final point needs to be made, even if it is a truism. For all that 'political' activity in early Icelandic society took place at a relatively small scale and in an island-wide community of, perhaps, 50,000 people, we should not lose sight of the fact that most of its written evidence was produced by, and was about, one percent of that population. Orri Vésteinsson made the point over a decade ago that *Sturlunga saga* rarely discusses small farms but this point is almost equally true of other narrative texts. An important wider point, and one which it is still remind ourselves of, is that despite their local scale, *Íslendingasögur* are mostly about *bændr* on farms of 24–30 hundreds or more. While *Sturlunga saga* ignores these people in its account they were no doubt involved in those larger armies in thirteenth-century events and some of them are among those whose origins we cannot determine in the lists of dead at the larger battles. It is a salutary reminder of the nature of the historical record that even for a small-scale society like that of medieval Iceland, even when it is examined at this level of detail, that the lives of the poorest people are invisible to us.

---

2 SS I: 122.

Appendix: *Sturlunga Saga*

This appendix aims to provide the reader with further detail of the contents and scholarship of the source for much of Chapters 2 and 3, the contemporary sagas, especially the *Sturlunga* compilation. As is suggested in the introduction and at the beginning of Chapter 2, the source-critical issues for the narrative sources that cover the twelfth and thirteenth centuries are important, but these texts are arguably harder to interpret because they often provide a credible narrative of events. The book offers less direct critical commentary on how these texts can be treated as historical narratives and so it seemed better not to distract the reader with this material in the main text. What follows is therefore an assessment of the texts' dating and origins beginning with *Sturlunga saga*.

Sturlunga saga's perspective and origins are seemingly set out by its opening text, *Geirmundar þáttr heljarskinns*. This a short account of Geirmundr *heljarskinn*, the settler who is said to have made his home at Geirmundarstaðir, close to Skarð on Skarðsströnd. *Geirmundar þáttr* retells the story of Geirmundr's activities in Norway and at the *þáttr*'s end it traces a line down to Skarð-Snorri (d.1260). Other accounts of Geirmundr's *landnám* survive in *Landnámabók*, implying that an account of Geirmundr and his *landnám* existed well before the thirteenth century.[1] The fact that this narrative survives at all, let alone as the first narrative in the *Sturlunga* compilation is usually seen as reflecting the involvement of the Skarðverjar as the compilers. More specifically, the royally-appointed governor (*lögmaðr*) Þórðr Narfason from Skarð (d.1308) is seen as the compiler.[2] Recently, however, Helgi Þorláksson has revived and expanded on an older argument for another descendant of Geirmundr's, Þorsteinn *böllóttur* Snorrason of Melar in Melasveit, on the coast south of Borgarfjörður (d.1353?), although this makes no real difference to our assessment of the compilation.[3] Particular perspectives that appear across the compilation arguably reveal the interests of the Skarðverjar or Melamenn.

Þorgils saga ok Hafliða comes next in the surviving compilation and its contents are chronologically next as well, albeit covering the period 1117–21 rather than any earlier

---

1 ÍF I: 151–56.
2 Jón Jóhannesson 1946, xvii–xix; Tranter 1987; Hallberg 1993: 616; Úlfar Bragason 1992: 182; Úlfar Bragason 1993; Guðrún Nordal 2010.
3 Helgi Þorláksson 2012. Þorsteinn was the son of the likely compiler of the *Melabók* redaction of *Landnámabók*, as being the compiler. This view stresses the importance of Geirmundr as an ancestor figure (of Þorsteinn no less than Þórðr) rather than the farm of Skarð. Helgi also stresses that this is not incompatible with the changes the compiler makes to those sagas which survive independently (*Prestssaga Guðmundar góða* and *Hrafns saga Sveinbjarnarsonar*) and that this fits better with the date of the earliest manuscript, *Króksfjarðarbók*, of 1350–1370.

timespan. *Þorgils saga ok Hafliða* is one of the most-discussed texs.[4] It is often said to have been written comparatively early, i.e. before 1215,[5] although it has also been dated to c.1240.[6] As discussed above, the saga describes the dispute and eventual reconciliation of two chieftains from the north-west of Iceland. The dispute culminates in a confrontation at the Alþing in which Þorgils cuts off Hafliði's finger. Crucial to the saga's narrative is the role of Bishop Þorlákr and his successor, Ketill Þorsteinsson, in bringing about peace. The clerics' mediation is undoubtedly what made this saga so memorable and it has been suggested that the text was written as a parable to encourage peaceable behaviour among the secular elite.[7] It could have been, as Orri Vésteinsson suggests, that this was the first time that chieftains' power had allowed them to 'attempt to side-step accepted procedures and use force to further their objectives'.[8] The way in which this single example of chieftains' unruliness is tied to the image of Bishop Þorlákr, however, suggests that this was not necessarily a one-off event but a memorable dispute because it was bishops who were not only involved in resolving it but successful too. The genealogical content of the saga, which generally does not go back to the *landnám*, would suggest that the saga was very closely related to oral accounts or elite social memory and was limited by the knowledge contained in them.

The *Ættartölur*, an independent section of genealogies, stand after *Þorgils saga ok Hafliða* and before *Sturlu saga*. These genealogies record descendants from seven different people, from various parts of Iceland, who were probably alive in the early twelfth century: Sæmundr *fróði*, Þórðr Gilsson, Ásbjörn Arnórsson, Sigmundr Þorgilsson, Bárðr *inn svarti* Atlason, Þórðr Þorvaldsson and Þorsteinn *ranglátr* Einarsson. These were probably all *goðar* except Bárðr Atlason. The ancestors of these men are traced very briefly while their descendants are traced much more fully into the later thirteenth century. Certain sections, which come at the end of two of the seven genealogies, have been put forward as later additions to an earlier, possibly independent text. These two sections relate to the ancestors of the Narfasynir who lived at Skarð and support the idea that Þórðr (or his brother Snorri) may have had the compilation made.[9] It has also been suggested that the original version of these genealogies was written by Sturla Þórðarson (1214–84).[10] Either way, it is probable that this collection of genealogies gives us a Western Quarter perspective on the past.

---

4   Brown 1952; Jakob Benediktsson 1976a.
5   Foote 1952: 67–68.
6   Brown 1952: ix–xxix; Jakob Benediktsson 1976a.
7   Sverrir Jakobsson 1998: 7–10.
8   Orri Vésteinsson 1996: 103; Orri Vésteinsson 2000: 65–67.
9   SS II: xxv; Úlfar Bragason 1993: 33.
10   Úlfar Bragason 1993: 30.

Sturlu saga is another well-known saga from the *Sturlunga* collection because it describes the rise of Sturla Þórðarson from Hvammr. The saga shows a kind of continuity from *Þorgils saga ok Hafliða* because it describes the political defeat of the son of Þorgils Oddason, Einarr Þorgilsson, at the hands of Sturla Þórðarson. The text covers the period roughly from 1148 until Sturla's death in 1183 and was most likely first written in the early thirteenth century.[11] Its detailed account of people and places in Dalir suggests a local author. The fact that the saga seems to portray Sturla in a relatively favourable light in his dealings with Einarr Þorgilsson yet seems to show him up as out of his depth when dealing with more powerful men has troubled commentators. Although the saga is short, it has been suggested that it was originally three separate narratives, although it has been more convincingly argued that the text works as a whole, and portrays Sturla consistently throughout.[12] As Chapter 3 demonstrates, the saga reflects the harsh realities of the period it covers: Sturla comes across as ruthless but politically astute, if only effective on a local level, while Einarr Þorgilsson is seen as even more unpleasant and less competent. Again, it makes sense to see the Skarðverjar as informants to the saga's author, if not as writers of the saga itself.[13] But whoever the anonymous writer of *Sturlu saga* was, they certainly did not see Sturla Þórðarson through rose-tinted spectacles either.[14] In this connection it is also worth noting that the saga was not necessarily seen as being a biography of Sturla. A reference to what we know as *Sturlu saga* is made in *Prestssaga Guðmundar góða* where the saga is referred to as *Heiðarvígssaga*, the saga of the killing on the heath.[15] This suggests that the compiler of *Sturlunga* saw this text more as a record of a local conflict than a biography, emphasising the pivotal fight between Sturla and Einarr *Sturlu saga* was probably not seen or written purposely as propaganda for his descendants, but as a local history by someone with connections to Dalir.

By contrast *Guðmundar saga dýra* is obviously written in praise of its secular protagonist, Guðmundr *dýri* Þorvaldsson of Bakki in Öxnadalur (d.1212). The text covers the 1180s through to about 1200. Guðmundr's ultimate retirement to the monastery at

---

11 See, for example, Magnús Jónsson 2000: 35; Úlfar Bragason 2010: 25–26.
12 Foote 1984; Jakob Benediktsson 1972b.
13 Helgi Þorláksson 2009.
14 Foote 1984: 29.
15 *Prestssaga Guðmundar góða* refers to 'Heiðarvígssaga' when it records the death of Sturla Þórðarson (Hvamm-Sturla) in 1183, when *Sturlu saga* ends: 'Nú er þar komit þessi sögu, sem frá var horfit Heiðarvígssögu, ok hafa þær lengi jafnfram gengit' (Now this saga has come to where it diverged from *Heiðarvígssaga* and they have been contemporaneous for some time.) (SS I: 131; SS II: xxvi).

Þingeyrar possibly reflects him having overreached himself by killing his rival Önundr Þorkelsson in 1197. The saga's detail again suggests that it was written shortly after Guðmundr's death but as with *Sturlu saga*, it is hard to identify a particular author although an origin in Eyjafjörður seems likely.[16]

There are more complicated textual issues surrounding the origins of the biographical saga of Bishop Guðmundr Arason of Hólar (d.1237), known as *Prestsssaga Guðmundar góða* in its *Sturlunga saga* version. That said, they do not significantly affect the discussion in this book. The text survives in four longer, later variants that are usually identified as *Guðmundar saga biskups* and based on *Prestssaga* or something like it.[17] The text is annal-like in its year-by-year account of Guðmundr's life and other contemporary events, from 1161 to his consecration as bishop in 1203, but gives little detailed coverage of wider politics. All the texts demonstrate an understanding that Guðmundr was a saint-like figure even though his sanctity was never formally recognised and *Prestssaga* is not really hagiographical in style. Since the nineteenth century it has been suggested that *Prestssaga* might have been written by one of Guðmundr's acolytes, Lambkárr Þorgilsson (d.1249), who is named in *Prestssaga* and was a descendant of Þorgils Oddason of Staðarhóll in Dalir.[18] Clearly someone like Lambkárr is likely to have produced the positive, if not hagiographical, view of Guðmundr. Finally it is also notable that the compiler of *Sturlunga* was keen to avoid repetition of material and so, using the other *Guðmundar sögur*, it is possible to see how *Prestssaga* was edited with this in mind.[19]

Hrafns saga Sveinbjarnarsonar, which survives both in *Sturlunga saga* and as an independent text, records the life of Hrafn Sveinbjarnarson (d.1213), a *höfðingi* from Eyrr in Arnarfjörður in the West Fjords. Hrafn was killed at home by his local rival, Þorvaldr *Vatnsfirðingr*, in a scene which emphasises Hrafn's piety, although this quality is emphasised far less in the *Sturlunga* version. In this regard Hrafn is like Guðmundr Arason. The negative portrayal of Þorvaldr might suggest a date of composition after his death in 1228.[20]

Íslendinga saga is by far the largest individual work in the *Sturlunga saga* collection and has sometimes given its name to the whole compilation.[21] It is generally held that

---

16   Jón Jóhannesson in SS II: xxxii following Magnús Jónsson 1940.
17   Björn Sigfússon 1960b; Stefán Karlsson 1993; Úlfar Bragason 2010: 193; Haki Antonsson 2012 for wider context.
18   SS I: 150, 153, 470–72; Úlfar Bragason 2010: 193; Skórzweska 2011: 21.
19   Úlfar Bragason 2010: 202–3.
20   Björn Sigfússon 1962a; Guðrún P. Helgadóttir 1987: lxxxi–xci; Úlfar Bragason 1988; Úlfar Bragason 2010: 26, 210–26.
21   SS I: xv. See generally Björn M. Olsen 1902: esp. 385–437; Pétur Sigurðsson 1933–5; Gunnar Benediktsson 1961; Jakob Benediktsson 1972a: esp. 357–58; Guðrún Ása Grímsdóttir 1988;

Íslendinga saga was written by Sturla Þórðarson (1214–84), sometime after 1250 and possibly after *Þórðar saga kakala* and *Þorgils saga skarða* were in existence.[22] According to the author of the short introduction (*Formáli*) in *Sturlunga saga* Sturla Þórðarson wrote 'Íslendinga sögur' which recorded things Sturla himself had seen and heard as well as information from others' documents.[23] Indeed there seems far less reason to doubt that Sturla wrote *Íslendinga saga* than that he wrote many of the other works attributed to him.[24] The saga's very favourable portrayal of his father Þórðr Sturluson suggests at the very least that someone close to him wrote it.[25]

The saga itself is a political narrative which covers events across Iceland from c.1180 to 1264, with a focus on events in the north and west. The problems in interpreting this text are manifold, but stem from the fundamental difficulty that Sturla was himself involved in many of the events which are described. Detecting Sturla's point of view in the saga is sometimes difficult, but it is clear that *Íslendinga saga* was an attempt at writing political history in a different way to the typical pattern of regional or biographical sagas.

In examining the broad problem of Sturla Þórðarson's perspective on the events it is important to illustrate the variety of his political contacts and the context in which he wrote *Íslendinga saga*. Sturla was for the most part an unremarkable politician[26] and he seems to have been overshadowed by many of his more powerful kinsmen (Snorri Sturluson, Órækja Snorrason, Þorgils *skarði* Böðvarsson, Sturla Sighvatsson, Þórðr *kakali* Sighvatsson). He supported his kinsmen on a fairly pragmatic basis.[27] From the 1250s he became more prominent and was a supporter of Þórðr *kakali* and Gizurr Þorvaldsson who acted on behalf of the Norwegian king. In his later years he was expelled from his base in Borgarfjörður by Hrafn Oddsson, another agent of the king, and went to Norway in 1263. Sturla successfully ingratiated himself with King Magnús and returned from Norway in 1271 with the king's 'lawbook,' *Járnsíða*. He assumed the position of *lögmaðr*, 'lawman,' until he apparently gave up the position a year before he died. Thus Sturla lived through and took part in a volatile political scene.

In spite of the difficulties in establishing what prejudices Sturla might show in his writings and when he does show them, commentators have suggested ways of reading all or parts of *Íslendinga saga*. Sturla's account of his cousin Sturla Sighvatsson's life and death (at the battle of Örlygsstaðir in 1238) has been said to be coloured by

---

Ciklamini 1983, 1988a, 1988b; Gunnar Karlsson 1988; Úlfar Bragason 1989; Heller 1978; Helgi Þorláksson 1988.
22   Björn M. Ólsen 1902: 434–35; Jakob Benediktsson 1972; Úlfar Bragason 2010: 24–25.
23   SS I: 115.
24   Guðrún Ása Grímsdóttir 1988: 29–30.
25   Ciklamini 1983: 212–19.
26   Jón Viðar Sigurðsson & Sverrir Jakobsson 2017.
27   Guðrún Ása Grímsdóttir 1988: 24.

'Victorine and Augustinian notions'[28] whereby the latter is seen to be apologising for the brutality of his earlier deeds. The narrative certainly dwells on the cruelty of Sturla Sighvatsson's death.[29] It has also been suggested, probably correctly, that Sturla felt embarrassment at his part in the plot to remove his cousin Órækja Snorrason from the Icelandic political scene and that his account of Órækja being injured is fictional.[30] It has also been demonstrated that *Íslendinga saga*'s narrative technique is to show action from the perspective of the victims of violence rather than the aggressors.[31] Clearly Sturla generally viewed the early half of the century not as a 'golden age' but as a period most notable for its violence and the tragic consequences that this entailed for his own kinsmen and affines.

The potential for *Íslendinga saga* to mislead is clearly great: it is a large work which generally cannot be compared with any alternative account of the events it describes. The saga was written by someone whose purpose is not clear and who named himself in the account he wrote. Certainly we cannot trust his account in all respects, either because of his wilful misrepresentation of events or his incomplete memory of them.[32] Nevertheless there must be a large body of events which, because of the way they relate to one another, we can be certain Sturla could not ignore. We can also second guess how someone of Sturla's background may have viewed events and place some trust in the fact that he does not visibly paint too grand a picture of his own past. The major concerns in interpreting *Íslendinga saga* (and the two sagas still to be discussed) is about what may have been recorded at all in the first place, and how the compiler of *Sturlunga saga* altered the texts.[33]

Þórðar saga kakala is an account of the political life of Þórðr *kakali* Sighvatsson, the son of Sighvatr Sturluson and the cousin of Sturla Þórðarson who wrote *Íslendinga saga*. Þórðr is undoubtedly shown in a more positive light than some of his contemporaries might have seen him. *Þórðar saga kakala* covers the main character's political activity both in the west of Iceland and, later, in the north. Dating its composition has proved problematic on textual grounds but most commentators have preferred to see it as having been written before *Íslendinga saga*. The compiler of *Sturlunga saga* nonetheless saw this saga as a natural continuation of *Íslendinga saga* which it

---

28   Ciklamini 1988b: 239.
29   Úlfar Bragason 1986.
30   Gade 1995.
31   Gunnar Karlsson 1988: 217–20.
32   Úlfar Bragason 1986: 65.
33   Omission is something Sturla appears to have been guilty of when compiling the so-called *Resens Annal* (Rowe forthcoming).

directly follows both chronologically and in the order of the texts in the preserved manuscripts.[34]

The full text of *Þorgils saga skarða*, as mentioned above, is only found in the later *Reykjarfjarðarbók* manuscript of *Sturlunga saga* interlaced with *Íslendinga saga*. A fragment of an independent, more verbose text of the saga exists, however. From this it would seem that the compiler of the earlier version of *Sturlunga saga* has shortened the saga in order to make the text sit more neatly within the *Sturlunga* compilation as a whole and *Íslendinga saga* itself.[35] It has been suggested that the presence of the wholly independent version might reflect a greater willingness to openly challenge the Norwegian king, something which might not have been desirable when *Króksfjarðarbók* was compiled.[36] Þorgils *skarði* was another member of the Sturlungar who was politically active in the mid-thirteenth century and this account of his life is clearly partisan towards him. The saga is mostly concerned with the period 1252–8, after Þorgils had returned from a stay with the Norwegian king Hákon Hákonarson. Þorgils' political career in Iceland is characterised by two main disputes: first with the various supporters of his kinsman Þórðr *kakali* (absent in Norway), especially Hrafn Oddson and Sturla Þórðarson; and second with Þorvarðr Þórarinsson (by which time Sturla was supporting Þorgils). The first dispute ends with a reconciliation but the second only with the death of Þorgils. The saga depicts a very fluid political situation in which the most powerful men frequently change sides in disputes.

Ascribing a date and author to *Þorgils saga skarða* has not been as great a concern as it has with regard to many other sagas. Þorgils' brother-in-law, Þórðr *Hítnesingr*, was suggested as the author by B.M. Ólsen. Internal evidence suggests that the saga was written after 1275 but it has also been judged that the saga must have been written before 1284 because Sturla Þórðarson is supposed to have drawn on it to write *Íslendinga saga*.[37]

Most of these the texts describing thirteenth-century events are anonymous. Sturla Þórðarson is quite likely to have been the writer of *Íslendinga saga* and someone wishing to show individual members of the Sturlungar in a positive light was responsible for each of *Þórðar saga kakala* and *Þorgils saga skarða*. This is more than we can say for the sagas referring to twelfth-century events, *Þorgils saga ok Hafliða* and *Sturlu saga*. Their perspectives on events are less clearly one-sided. All of these sagas can be seen to have some literary shape but, nevertheless, provide a basic framework of twelfth and

---

34   Jón Jóhannesson in SS II: xli–xliii; Úlfar Bragason 1994.
35   Úlfar Bragason 1981: 161.
36   Helgi Þorláksson 2012: 82–87.
37   Jón Jóhannesson 1946: xlvii.

thirteenth century events from which we can decipher general political practices and broad geopolitical patterns. We have to be most careful in using these sources as evidence for people's motivations for undertaking political actions. Nonetheless *Sturlunga saga* provides a huge corpus of information from which the political life of the thirteenth century can be reconstructed.

Bibliography

Icelandic names are in alphabetical order by first name then patronymic or surname. The alphabetical order is: a á b c d ð e é f g h i í j k l m n o ó p q r s t u ú v w x y ý z þ æ ö ø å ä.

Primary Sources

Árna saga biskups, ed. Þorleifur Hauksson (Rit Stofnunar Árna Magnússonar á Íslandi 2, Reykjavík, 1972).
Biskupa sögur gefnar út af Hinu íslenzka bókmenntafélagi, I–II, ed. G. Vigfússon (Copenhagen, 1858–78).
Byskupa sögur I–III, ed. Guðni Jónsson (Reykjavík, 1953).
Byskupa sögur: MS Perg. fol. no 5 in the Royal Library of Stockholm, ed. Jón Helgason (Corpus Codicum Islandicorum medii aevi 19, Copenhagen, 1950).
DI = *Diplomatarium Islandicum, Íslenskt fornbréfasafn 834–1600,* I–XVI (Copenhagen & Reykjavík, 1857–1972).
Eyrbyggja saga: The Vellum Tradition, ed. F.S. Scott (Editiones Arnamagnæanæ A/18, Copenhagen, 2013).
Flateyjarbók. En samling af norske konge-sager I–III, eds. C.W. Unger, C.W. & Guðbrandur Vigfússon (Christiania, 1860–68).
Grágás 1a-1b = *Grágás. Islændernes Lovbog i Fristatens Tid*, ed. Vilhjálmur Finsen (Copenhagen, 1852–70).
Grágás II = *Grágás efter det Arnamagnæanske Haandskrift Nr. 334 fol. Staðarhólsbók*, ed. Vilhjálmur Finsen (Copenhagen, 1879).
Grágás III = *Grágás, Stykker, som findes i det Arnamagnæanske Haandskrift Nr. 351 fol., Skálholtsbók og en Række andre Haandskrifter*, ed. Vilhjálmur Finsen (Copenhagen, 1883).
IA = *Islandske Annaler indtil 1578*, ed. G. Storm (Christiania, 1888).
Íslenzk fornrit I. *Íslendingabók. Landnámabók*, ed. Jakob Benediktsson (Reykjavík, 1968).
Íslenzk fornrit III. *Borgfirðinga sǫgur*, ed. Sigurður Nordal & Guðni Jónsson (Reykjavík, 1938).
Íslenzk fornrit IV. *Eyrbyggja saga. Grœnlendinga saga sǫgur*, ed. Einar Ól. Sveinsson & Matthías Þórðarson (Reykjavík, 1935).
Íslenzk fornrit V. *Laxdœla saga*, ed. Einar Ól. Sveinsson (Reykjavík, 1934).
Íslenzk fornrit VI. *Vestfirðinga sǫgur*, ed. Björn K. Þórólfsson & Guðni Jónsson (Reykjavík, 1943).

Íslenzk fornrit VII. *Grettis saga Ásmundarsonar*, ed. Guðni Jónsson (Reykjavík, 1936).
Íslenzk fornrit VIII. *Vatnsdœla saga*, ed. Einar Ól. Sveinsson (Reykjavík, 1939).
Íslenzk fornrit IX. *Eyfirðinga sǫgur*, ed. Jónas Kristjánsson (Reykjavík, 1956).
Íslenzk fornrit X. *Ljósvetninga saga*, ed. Björn Sigfússon (Reykjavík, 1940).
Íslenzk fornrit XI. *Austfirðinga sǫgur*, ed. Jón Jóhannesson (Reykjavík, 1950).
Íslenzk fornrit XII. *Brennu-Njáls saga*, ed. Einar Ól. Sveinsson (Reykjavík, 1954).
Íslenzk fornrit XIII. *Harðar saga*, eds. Þórhallur Vilmundarsson & Bjarni Vilhjálmsson (Reykjavík, 1991).
Íslenzk fornrit XIV. *Kjalnesinga saga*, ed. Jóhannes Halldórsson (Reykjavík, 1959).
Íslenzk fornrit XV. *Biskupasögur I*, ed. Sigurgeir Steingrímsson, Ólafur Halldórsson & Peter Foote (Reykjavík, 2003).
Íslenzk fornrit XVI. *Biskupasögur II*, ed. Ásdís Egilsdóttir (Reykjavík, 2002).
Íslenzk fornrit XVII. *Biskupasögur III*, ed. Guðrún Ása Grímsdóttir (Reykjavík, 1998).
Íslenzk fornrit XXVII. *Heimskringla* II, ed. Bjarni Aðalbjarnarson (Reykjavík, 1945).
Íslenzk fornrit XXXI–XXXII. *Hákonar saga Hákonarsonar*, I–II, eds. Sverrir Jakobsson, Þorleifur Hauksson & Tor Ulset (Reykjavík, 2013).
Jarðabók Árna Magnússonar og Páls Vídalíns I–XI, eds. Bogi Th. Melsteð, Björn Karel Þórólfsson & Jakob Benediktsson (Copenhagen, 1913–43).
Hrafns saga Sveinbjarnarsonar, ed. A. Hasle (Editiones Arnamagnæanæ Series B 25, Copenhagen, 1987).
Hrafns saga Sveinbjarnarsonar, ed. Gúðrun P. Helgadóttir (Oxford, 1987).
Laxdœla saga, ed. K. Kaalund (Altnordische Saga-Bibliothek 4, Halle, 1896).
Saga Olafs konungs ens helga, eds. P.A. Munch & C.R. Unger (Christiania, 1883).
Skarðsárbók. Landnámabók Björns Jónssonar á Skarðsá, ed. Jakob Benediktsson (Reykjavík, 1958).
SS = *Sturlunga saga* I–II, ed. Jón Jóhannesson, Magnús Finnbogason & Kristján Eldjárn (Reykjavík, 1946).
Sturlunga saga. Manuscript No. 122A Fol. in the Arnamagnœan Collection, ed. Jakob Benediktsson (Early Icelandic Manuscripts in Facsimile 1, Copenhagen, 1958).
Svarfdœlasaga, Rit Handritastofnunar Íslands vol. 2, ed. Jónas Kristjánsson (Reykjavík, 1966).
Þorgils saga ok Hafliða, ed. U. Brown (Oxford, 1952).

Secondary Sources

Adolf Friðriksson 1994a. *Sagas and Popular Antiquarianism in Icelandic Archaeology*, Aldershot.
Adolf Friðriksson 1994b. 'Sturlungaminjar.' in *Samtíðarsögur* (Níunda alþjóðlega fornsagnaþingið), Akureyri: 1–15.

Adolf Friðriksson 1998. 'Ómenningararfur Íslendinga.' *Skírnir* 172: 451–55.
Adolf Fridriksson & Orri Vésteinsson 1997. 'Hofstaðir Revisited.' *Norwegian Archaeological Review* 30: 102–13.
Adolf Friðriksson & Orri Vésteinsson 2003. 'Creating a Past. A Historiography of the Settlement of Iceland.' in J. Barrett ed. *Culture, Contact, Continuity and Collapse. The Archaeology of North Atlantic Colonization, A.D. 800–1800*, Toronto: 139–61.
Aðalgeirr Kristjánsson 1965. 'Gísla saga og samtíð höfundar.' *Skírnir* 139: 148–58.
Aðils, S. 1926–7. *Den Danske Monopolhandel på Island 1602–1787*, Copenhagen.
Agnes S. Arnórsdóttir & Helgi Þorláksson 1998. 'Saga heimilis á miðöldum' in Guðmundur J. Guðmundsson & Eiríkur K. Björnsson eds. *Íslenska söguþingið 28.-31. maí 1997* I & II, Reykjavík: 31–56.
Amorosi, T. 1989. 'Contributions to the Zooarchaeology of Iceland: Some Preliminary Notes.' in E.P. Durrenberger & Gísli Pálsson eds. *The Anthropology of Iceland*, Iowa: 203–27.
Amorosi, T. 1992. 'Climate Impact and Human Response in Northeast Iceland: Archaeological Investigations at Svalbarð, 1986–1988.' in C.D. Morris & D.J. Rackham eds. *Norse and later Settlement and Subsistence in the North Atlantic*, Glasgow: 103–38.
Amorosi, T. & McGovern, T.H. 1989. 'Preliminary Report of Fieldwork in Breidafjord and Seltjarnarnes.' unpublished report.
Amorosi, T. & McGovern, T.H. 1993. 'The 1987–88 Archaeofauna from Viðey.' Unpublished report.
Amorosi, T. & McGovern, T.H. 1995. 'Appendix 4: A Preliminary Report of an Archaeofauna from Granastaðir, Eyjafjarðarsýla, Northern Iceland.' in Bjarni F. Einarsson, *The Settlement of Iceland; A Critical Approach*. Granastaðir and the Ecological Heritage, Reykjavík: 181–94.
Amorosi, T., Buckland, P. C., Edwards, K.J., Mainland, I., McGovern, T.H., Sadler, J.P., Skidmore, P. 1998. 'They did not Live by Grass Alone: the Politics and Palaeoecology of Animal Fodder in the North Atlantic Region.' *Environmental Archaeology* 1: 41–54.
Amundsen, C., Perdikaris, S., 'Fishing Booths and Fishing Strategies in Medieval Iceland: an Archaeofauna from the [site] of Akurvík, North-West Iceland.' *Environmental Archaeoology* 10: 127–42.
Andersson, T.M. 1964. *The Problem of Icelandic Saga Origins. A Historical Survey*, New Haven.
Andersson, T.M. 1967. *The Icelandic Family Saga. An Analytical Reading* (Harvard Studies in Comparative Literature 28), Cambridge.
Andersson, T.M. 1975. 'The Emergence of Vernacular Literature in Iceland.' *Mosaic* 8(4): 161–69.
Andersson, T.M. 1994. 'The Politics of Snorri Sturluson.' *Journal of English and Germanic Philology* 93: 55–78.

Andersson, T.M. 2002. 'The Long Prose Form in Medieval Iceland.' *Journal of English and Germanic Philology* 101: 380–411.
Andersson, T.M. 2005. 'Five Saga Books for a New Century.' *Journal of English and Germanic Philology* 103: 505–27
Andersson, T.M. 2006. *The Growth of the Medieval Icelandic Sagas (1180–1280)*, Ithaca.
Andersson, T.M. 2012. *The Partisan Muse in the Early Icelandic Sagas (1200–1250)*, Ithaca.
Andersson, T.M. & Miller, W.I. 1989. *Law and Literature in Medieval Iceland. Ljósvetninga Saga and Valla-Ljóts Saga*, Stanford.
Andersson, T.M. & Gåde, K.E. 1991. 'Recent Old Norse-Icelandic Studies in the German-Speaking Countries.' *Scandinavian Studies* 63: 66–102.
Andrés Arnalds 1987. 'Ecosystem disturbance in Iceland.' *Arctic and Alpine Research* 19: 508–13.
Anna Agnarsdóttir & Ragnar Árnason 1983. 'Þrælahald á þjóðveldisöld.' *Saga* 21: 5–26.
Arnold, M. 2003. *The Post-Classical Icelandic Family Saga*, Lewiston.
Ashwell, I. & Jackson, K. 1970. 'The Sagas as Evidence of Early Deforestation in Iceland.' *Canadian Geographer* 14: 158–66.
Axel Kristinsson 1986. 'Hverjir tóku þátt í hernaði Sturlungaaldar?' *Sagnir* 7: 6–15.
Axel Kristinsson 1998. 'Embættismenn konungs fyrir 1400.' *Saga* 36: 113–52.
Axel Kristinsson 2003. 'Lords and Literature: The Icelandic Sagas as Political and Social Instruments.' *Scandinavian Journal of History* 28: 1–17.
Ármann Jakobsson 1994. 'Nokkur orð um hugmyndir Íslendinga um konungsval fyrir 1262.' in *Samtíðarsögur* (Níunda alþjóðlega fornsagnaþingið), Akureyri: 31–42.
Ármann Jakobsson 1997. *Í leit að konungi: Konungsmynd íslenskra konungasagna*, Reykjavík.
Ármann Jakobsson 1998. 'Konungasagan Laxdæla.' *Skírnir* 172: 357–83.
Ármann Jakobsson 2000. 'Byskupskjör á Íslandi: Stjórnmálaviðhorf byskupasagna og Sturlungu.' *Studia theological islandica* 14: 171–82.
Ármann Jakobsson 2002. *Staður í nýjum heimi: Konungasagan Morkinskinna*, Reykjavík.
Ármann Jakobsson 2013. 'The Life and Death of the Medieval Icelandic Short Story.' *Journal of English and Germanic Philology* 112: 257–91.
Ármann Jakobsson, 2014. 'Tradition and the Individual Talent: The "Historical Figure" in the Medieval Sagas, a Case Study.' *Viator* 45: 101–24.
Árni Daníel Júlíusson 1998. 'Valkostir Sögunnar. Um Landbúnað fyrir 1700 og þjóðfélagsþróun á 14.-16. öld.' *Saga* 36: 77–111.
Árni Daníel Júlíusson 2002. 'Kvaðirnar kvaddar.' in Erla Hulda Halldórsdóttir ed. 2002. *Íslenska söguþingið 30. maí- 1. júní 2002. Ráðstefnurit* II, Reykjavík: 242–54.
Árni Daníel Júlíusson 2010. 'Signs of Power: Manorial Demesnes in Medieval Iceland.' *Viking and Medieval Scandinavia* 6: 1–29.

Árni Daníel Júlíusson 2016. *Miðaldir í skuggsjá Svarfaðardals* (Rit Þjóðminjasafns Íslands 43), Reykjavík.
Árný E. Sveinbjarnardóttir, Heinemaier, J. & Garðar Guðmundsson 2004. '14C Dating of the Settlement of Iceland.' *Radiocarbon* 46: 387–94.
Ásdis Egilsdottir 1992. 'Eru biskupsögur til?' *Skáldskaparmál* 2: 207–20.
Ásdís Egilsdóttir 2004. 'Hrafn Sveinbjarnarson, Pilgrim and Martyr.' in G. Williams & P. Bibire eds. *Saints, Sagas and Settlements*, Leiden: 29–40.
Ásgeir Blöndal Magnússon 1989. *Islensk orðsifjabók*, Reyjavík.
Bagge, S. 1986. 'The Formation of the State and Concepts of Society in 13th Century Norway.' in E. Vestergaard ed. *Continuity and Change: Political Institutions and Literature in the Middle Ages* (Proceedings of the Tenth International Symposium Organized by the Center for the Study of Vernacular Literature in the Middle Ages), Odense: 43–59.
Bagge, S. 1989. 'Theodoricus Monachus: Clerical Historiography in Twelfth Century Norway.' *Scandinavian Journal of History* 14: 113–33.
Bagge, S. 1991a. 'Propaganda, Ideology and Political Power in Old Norse and European Historiography: A Comparative View.' in J-P. Genet ed. *L'Historiographie médiévale en Europe*, Paris: 199–208.
Bagge, S. 1991b. *Society and Politics in Snorri Sturluson's Heimskringla*, Berkeley.
Bagge, S. 1996. *From Gang Leader to the Lord's Annointed. Kingship in Sverris Saga and Hákonar saga Hákonarsonar*, Viborg.
Balzaretti 2013. *Dark Age Liguria: regional identity and local power, c. 400–1020*, London.
Bandle, O. 1977. 'Die Ortsnamen der Landnámabók.' in Einar G. Pétursson & Jónas Kristjánsson eds. *Sjötíu Ritgerðir helgaðar Jakobi Benediktsson 20. júlí 1977* I, Reyjkavik: 47–68.
Barði Guðmundsson 1936. 'Goðorðaskipun og löggoðaættir.' *Skírnir* 110: 49–58.
Barði Guðmundsson 1937. 'Goðorð forn og ný.' *Skírnir* 111: 56–83.
Barði Guðmundsson 1938. 'Uppruni Landnámabókar.' *Skírnir* 112: 5–22.
Barði Guðmundsson 1953. *Ljósvetninga saga og Saurbæingar*, Reykjavík.
Barði Guðmundsson 1959. *Uppruni Íslendinga*, Reykjavík.
Barber, K. 2007. *The Anthropology of Texts, Persons and Publics: Oral and Written Culture in Africa and Beyond*, Cambridge.
Beck, H. 1977. 'Laxdæla saga – A Structural Approach.' *Saga-Book* 19: 383–402.
Bell, M. 1981. 'Seaweed as a Prehistoric Source.' in D. Brothwell & G. Dimbleby eds. *Environmental Aspects of Coasts and Islands* (British Archaeological Reports 94), Oxford: 117–26.
Benedikt Eyþórsson 2005. 'History of the Icelandic Church 1000–1300. Status of Research.' in Helgi Þorláksson ed. *Church Centres in Iceland from the 11th to the 13th Centuries and their parallels in other Countries*, Reykholt: 19–69.

Berger, A. 1978–79. 'Lawyers in the Old Icelandic Family Sagas: Heroes, Villains and Authors.' *Saga-Book* 20: 70–79.

Bibre, P. 1973. 'Verses in the Íslendingasögur.' in *Alþjóðlegt fornsagnaþing, Reykjavík 2.-8. ágúst 1973, Fyrirlestrar*, Reyjavík.

Bigg, M.A. 1981. 'Harbour Seal.' in S.H. Ridgeway & R.J. Harrison eds. *Handbook of Marine Mammals* II, London: 1–27.

Bibire, P. 2007. 'On Reading the Icelandic Sagas: Approaches to Old Icelandic Texts.' in B. Ballin Smith, S. Taylor, & G. Williams eds. *West Over Sea: Studies in Scandinavian Sea-Borne Expansion and Settlement Before 1300, A Festschrift in Honour of Barbara E. Crawford*, Leiden: 3–18.

Birna Lárusdóttir 2006. 'Settlement Organisation and Farm Abandonment: The Curious Landscape of Reykjahverfi, North-East Iceland.' in W. Davies, A. Reynolds & G. Halsall eds. *People and Space in the Middle Ages*, Turnhout: 45–63.

Birna Lárusdóttir 2007. 'Bæjanöfn brotin til mergjar.' *Árbók Hins íslenzka fornleifafélags* 98: 85–100.

Birna Lárusdóttir, Howell M. Roberts & Sigríður Þorgeirsdóttir 2012. *Siglunes. Archaeological Investigations 2011. FS480-11121*, Reykjavík.

Bisson, T.N. 2002. '*La terre et les hommes*: A Programme Fulfilled?' *French History* 14: 322–45.

Bjarni Einarsson 1961. *Skáldasögur. Um upprunu og eðli ástaskáldsagnanna fornu*, Reykjavík.

Bjarni Einarsson 1974. 'On the Status of Free Men in Society and Saga.' *Mediaeval Scandinavia* 7: 45–55.

Bjarni Einarsson 1980. 'Um Spákonuarf.' *Gripla* 4: 102–34.

Bjarni F. Einarsson 1995. *The Settlement of Iceland; A Critical Approach. Granastaðir and the Ecological Heritage*, Reykjavík.

Bjarni Guðnason 1977. 'Theodoricus og Íslenskir sagnaritarar.' *Sjötíu ritgerðir*, 107–20.

Björn Guðmundsson 1944. 'Nokkur orð um selveiði á Íslandi fyrrum og nú.' *Náttúrufræðingurinn* 14: 144–69.

Björn Lárusson 1961. 'Valuation and Distribution of Landed Property in Iceland.' *Economy and History* 4: 34–64.

Björn Lárusson 1967. *The Old Icelandic Land Registers*, Lund.

Björn Lárusson 1982. *Islands jordebok under förindustriell tid*, Lund.

Björn M. Olsen 1889. 'Ari Þorgilsson hinn fróði.' *Tímarit hins íslenzka bókmenntafélags* 10: 214–40.

Björn M. Olsen 1902. 'Um Sturlungu.' *Safn til sögu Íslands* III: 193–510.

Björn M. Olsen 1905. 'Landnáma og Eyrbyggja.' *Aarbøger for Nordisk Oldkyndighed og Historie 1905*: 81–117.

Björn M. Olsen 1908a. 'Landnáma og Laxdæla saga.' *Aarbøger for Nordisk Oldkyndighed og Historie 1908*: 151–232.

Björn M. Olsen 1908b. 'Um upphaf konungsvalds á Íslandi.' *Andvari* 33: 18–88.
Björn M. Olsen 1909. 'Enn um upphaf konungsvalds á Íslandi.' *Andvari* 34: 1–81.
Björn M. Ólsen. 1910. 'Landnáma og Gull-Þóris (Þorskfirðinga) saga.' *Aarbøger for Nordisk Oldkyndighed og Historie 1910*: 35–61.
Björn M. Olsen 1915. 'Um skattbændatal 1311 og manntal á Íslandi fram að þeim tíma.' *Safn til sögu Íslands* IV: 295–384.
Björn Sigfússon 1934. 'Veldi Guðmundar ríka.' *Skírnir* 108: 191–98.
Björn Sigfússon 1944. *Um Íslendingabók*, Reyjkavík.
Björn Sigfússon 1960a. 'Full goðorð og forn og heimildir frá 12. öld.' *Saga* 3: 48–75.
Björn Sigfússon 1960b. 'Guðmundar saga biskups Arasonar.' *KLNM* V: 542–43.
Björn Sigfússon 1960c. 'Guðmundar saga dýra.' *KLNM* VII: 543–44.
Björn Sigfússon 1962a. 'Hrafns saga Sveinbjarnarsonar.' *KLNM* VII: 16–17.
Björn Sigfússon 1962b. 'Íslendingabók.' *KLNM* VII: 493–95.
Björn Teitsson & Magnús Stefánsson 1972. 'Um rannsóknir á íslenzkri byggðarsögu tímabilsins fyrir 1700.' *Saga* 10: 134–78.
Björn Þorsteinsson 1953. *Íslenzka þjóðveldið*, Reykjavík.
Björn Þorsteinsson 1966. *Ný Íslandssaga*, Reykjavík.
Björn Þorsteinsson 1974. 'Tollr.' *KLNM* XVIII: 452–54.
Björn Þorsteinsson 1975. 'Tyende. Island.' *KLNM* XIX: 110–12.
Björn Þorsteinsson 1978. *Íslensk miðaldasaga*, Reykjavík.
Björn Þórðarson 1950. *Síðasti goðinn*, Reykjavík.
Bloch, M. 1966. *French Rural History: An Essay on its Basic Characteristics*, London.
Boden, F. 1905. *Die isländische Regierungsgewalt in der friestaatlichen Zeit*, Breslau.
Bogi Th. Melsteð 1903–30. *Íslendinga saga* I–III, Copenhagen.
Bohannan, L. 1952. 'A Genealogical Charter.' *Africa* 22: 301–15.
Bolender, Steinberg & Damiata 2011. 'Farmstead relocation at the end of the Viking Age. Results of the Skagafjörður archaeological settlement survey.' *Archaeologia Islandica* 9: 77–101.
Bonner, W.N. 1981. 'Grey Seal.' S.H. Ridgeway & R.J. Harrison eds. *Handbook of Marine Mammals* II, London: 111–44.
Bonner, W.N. 1982. *Seals and Man. A Study of Interactions*, Washington.
Boulhosa, P. 2005. *Icelanders and the King of Norway. Medieval Sagas and Legal Texts*. (The Northern World 17), Leiden.
Boulhosa, P. 2010. 'Of Fish and Ships in Medieval Iceland' in S. Imsen ed. *The Norwegian Domination and the Norse World c.1100–c.1400*, Trondheim: 175–97.
Boyer, R. 1975. 'Paganism and Literature: The So-Called 'Pagan Survivals' in the samtíðarsögur.' *Gripla* 1: 135–67.
Brady, L. 2016. *Writing the Welsh Borderlands in Anglo-Saxon England*, Manchester.
Brink, S. 1996. 'Political and Social Structures in Early Scandinavia. A Settlement-historical Pre-study of the Central Place.' *Tor* 28: 235–73.

Brooks, N.P. 1989. 'The Creation and Early Structure of the Kingdom of Kent.' in S. Bassett ed. *The Origins of Anglo-Saxon Kingdoms*, Leicester: 55–74.

Brooks, N.P. 2000. 'The English Origin Myth.' in idem. ed. *Anglo-Saxon Myths. State and Church*, London: 79–89.

Brown, J. et al. 2012. 'Shieling Areas: Historical Grazing Pressures and Landscape Responses in Northern Iceland.' *Human Ecology* 40: 81–99.

Brown, U. 1946–53. 'The Saga of Hrómund Gripsson and Þorgilssaga.' *Saga-Book* 13: 51–77.

Brown, U. 1952. 'A Note on the Manuscripts of Sturlunga saga.' *Acta Philologica Scandinavia* 22: 33–40.

Bruhn, O. 1999. *Textualisering. Bidrag til en litterær antropologi*, Aarhus.

Bryson, R.A. 1974. 'A Perspective on Climatic Change.' *Science* 184: 753–62.

Byock, J.L. 1982. *Feud in the Icelandic Saga*, Berkeley.

Byock, J.L. 1984a. 'Dispute Resolution in the Sagas.' *Gripla* 6: 86–100.

Byock, J.L. 1984b. 'Saga-Form, Oral Prehistory and the Icelandic Social Context.' *New Literary History* 16: 153–73.

Byock, J.L. 1985a. 'Cultural Continuity, the Church, and the Concept of Independent Ages in Medieval Iceland.' *Skandinavistik* 15: 1–14.

Byock, J.L. 1985b. 'The Power and Wealth of the Icelandic Church: Some Talking Points.' in J. Louis-Jensen, C. Sanders & P. Springborg eds, *The Sixth International Saga Conference, 28.7-28.8 1985: Workshop papers I–II*, Copenhagen, I: 89–101.

Byock, J.L. 1986a. 'The Age of the Sturlungs.' in E. Vestergaard ed. *Continuity and Change: Political Institutions and Literature in the Middle Ages* (Proceedings of the Tenth International Symposium Organized by the Center for the Study of Vernacular Literature in the Middle Ages), Odense: 27–42.

Byock, J.L. 1986b. 'Governmental Order in Early Medieval Iceland.' *Viator* 17: 19–34.

Byock, J.L. 1986c. 'Milliganga, Félagslegar rætur Íslendingasagna.' *Tímarit Máls og menningar* 7: 96–104.

Byock, J.L. 1988. 'Valdatafl og vinfengi.' *Skírnir* 162: 127–37.

Byock, J.L. 1989. 'Inheritance and Ambition in *Eyrbyggja saga*.' in J. Tucker ed. *Sagas of the Icelanders. A Book of Essays*, New York: 185–205.

Byock, J.L. 1990. *Medieval Iceland. Society, Sagas and Power*, Berkeley.

Byock, J.L. 1992. 'History and the Sagas. The Effect of Nationalism.' in Gísli Pálsson ed. 1992. *From Sagas to Society. Comparative Approaches to Early Iceland*, Middlesex: 43–59.

Byock, J.L. 1995. 'Choices of Honour: Telling Saga Feud, *Tháttr*, and the Fundamental Oral Progression.' *Oral Tradition* 10: 166–80.

Byock, J.L. 2001. *Viking Age Iceland*, London.

Bøe, Arne 1962. 'Jarl.' *KLNM* VII: 396–99.

Bøe, Arne 1965. 'Lendmann.' *KLNM* X: 498–505.

Callow, C. 2006a. 'Geography, Communities and Socio-Political Rrganisation in Medieval Northern Iceland.' in W. Davies, A. Reynolds & G. Halsall eds. *People and Space in the Middle Ages*, Turnhout: 65–86.

Callow, C. 2006b. 'Reconstructing the Past in Medieval Iceland.' *Early Medieval Europe* 14: 297–324.

Callow, C. 2010. 'Iceland's Medieval Coastal Market Places: Dögurðarnes in its Economic, Social and Political Context.' in J. Brendalsmo, T. Gansum and F-E. Eliassen eds. *Strandsteder, utvikinglingssteder og Småbyer i vikingtid, middelalder og tidlig nytid (ca. 800–ca.1800)*, Oslo: 213–29.

Callow, C. 2011. 'Putting Women in their Place? Gender, Landscape, and the Construction of *Landnámabók*.' *Viking and Medieval Scandinavia* 7: 7–28.

Callow 2017a. 'Dating and Origins' in Ármann Jakobsson & Sverrir Jakobsson eds. *The Routledge Research Companion to the Medieval Icelandic Saga*, London: 15–33.

Callow 2017b. 'Three recent books on Icelandic archaeology.' *Archaeologia Islandica* 12: 107–22.

Callow 2018. 'Comparing Medieval Iceland with other Regions: Problems and Possibilities.' in R. Balzaretti, J. Barrow & P. Skinner eds., *Italy and Early Medieval Europe. Papers for Chris Wickham*, Oxford: 416–29.

Callow, C. (forthcoming). 'The study of Icelandic place-names.' in S. Bassett & A. Spedding eds. *Names, Texts and Landscapes in the Early Middle Ages. A Memorial Volume for Duncan W. Probert*.

Cardew, P. 2007. 'The Question of Genre in the Late Íslendinga Sögur: A Case Study of Þorskfirðinga saga.' in B. Ballin Smith, S. Taylor, & G. Williams eds. *West Over Sea: Studies in Scandinavian Sea-Borne Expansion and Settlement Before 1300, A Festschrift in Honour of Barbara E. Crawford*, Leiden: 13–27.

Carter, Tara. 2015. *Iceland's Networked Society: Revealing How the Global Affairs of the Viking Age Created New Forms of Social Complexity*, Leiden.

Ciklamini, M. 1978. *Snorri Sturluson* (Twayne's World Authors Series 493), Boston.

Ciklamini, M. 1983. 'Biographical Reflections in *Íslendinga saga*: A Mirror of Personal Values.' *Scandinavian Studies* 55: 205–21.

Ciklamini, M. 1984. 'Veiled Meaning and Narrative Modes in *Sturlu þáttr*.' *Arkiv för nordisk filologi* 99: 139–50.

Ciklamini, M. 1988a. 'The Christian Champion in *Íslendinga saga*: Eyjólfr Kársson and Aron Hjörleifsson.' *Euphorion* 82: 226–37.

Ciklamini, M. 1988b. 'Sturla Sighvatsson's Chieftaincy. A Moral Probe.' in Guðrún Ása Grímsdóttir & Jónas Kristjánsson eds. *Sturlustefna. Ráðstefna haldin á sjö alda ártíð Sturlu Þórðarsonar sagnaritara 1984* (Rit Stofnunar Árna Magnússonar 32), Reykjavík: 222–41.

Clanchy, M.T. 1993. *From Memory to Written Record. England 1066–1307*, 2nd ed., Oxford.

Clover, C.J. 1982. *The Medieval Saga*, Ithaca.

Clover, C.J. 1985. 'Icelandic Family Sagas (*Íslendingasögur*).' in C.J. Clover. & J. Lindow eds. *Old Norse-Icelandic Literature. A Critical Guide* (Islandica 45), Ithaca: 239–315.

Clover, C.J. 1986. 'The Long Prose Form.' *Arkiv för nordisk filologi* 101: 10–39.

Clunies Ross, M. 1993. 'The Development of Old Norse Textual Worlds: Genealogical Structure as a Principle of Literary Organisation in Early Iceland.' *Journal of English and Germanic Philology* 92: 372–85.

Clunies Ross, M. 1998. *Prolonged Echoes. Old Norse myths in medieval Northern society. Volume 2: The reception of Norse myths in medieval Iceland*, Odense.

Clunies Ross, M. 2009. 'Medieval Icelandic Textual Culture.' *Gripla* 20: 163–81.

Conroy, P. 1980. '*Laxdæla saga* and *Eiríks saga rauða*: Narrative Structure.' *Arkiv för nordisk filologi* 95: 116–25.

Conroy, P. & Langen, T.C.S. 1988. '*Laxdæla saga*: Theme and Structure.' *Arkiv för nordisk filologi* 103: 118–41.

Cormack, M. 1994. *The Saints in Iceland: Their Veneration from the Conversion to 1400* (Subsidia hagiographica 78), Brussels.

Cormack, 2007. 'Fact and Fiction in the Icelandic Sagas.' *History Compass* 5/1: 201–17.

Danielsson, T. 2008. 'On the Possibility of an Oral Background for Gísla saga Súrssonar.' in E. Mundal & J. Wellendorf eds. *Oral Art Forms and their Passage into Writing*, Copenhagen: 27–41

Davies, W. 1988. *Small Worlds. The Village Community in Early Medieval Brittany*, Berkeley.

Davies, W. 2007. *Acts of Giving: Individual, Community, and Church in Tenth-Century Christian Spain*, Oxford.

Davies, W. & Fouracre, P. eds. 1992. *The Settlement of Disputes in Early Medieval Europe*, Cambridge.

Davies, W. & Fouracre, P. eds. 1995. *Property and Power in the Early Middle Ages*, Cambridge.

Davies, W. & Fouracre, P. eds. 2010. *The Languages of Gift in the Early Middle Ages*, Cambridge.

Dennis, A., Foote, P. & Perkins, R., trans. 1980. *Laws of Early Iceland: Grágás I. The Codex Regius of Grágás with Material from Other Manuscripts* (University of Manitoba Icelandic Studies 3), Winnipeg.

Donner, W.W. 1992. 'Lineages and land disputes on a Polynesian outlier.' *Man* 27: 319–39.

Duby, G. 1953. *La société aux xie et xiie siècles dans la region mâconnaise*, Paris.

Dumville, D. 1977a. 'Sub-Roman Britain: History and Legend.' *History* 62: 173–92.

Dumville, D. 1977b. 'Kingship, Genealogies and Regnal Lists.' in P. Sawyer & I.N. Woods eds. 1977. *Early Medieval Kingship*, Leeds: 72–104.

Durrenberger, E.P. 1988. 'Stratification without a State: the Collapse of the Icelandic Commonwealth.' *Ethnos* 53: 239–65.

Durrenberger, E.P. 1989. 'Anthropological Perspectives on the Commonwealth Period.' in E.P. Durrenberger & Gísli Pálsson eds. *The Anthropology of Iceland*, Iowa: 228–46.

Durrenberger, E.P. 1991. 'The Icelandic Family Sagas as Totemic Artefacts.' in R. Samson ed. *Social Approaches to Viking Studies*, Glasgow: 11–17.

Durrenberger, E.P. 1992. *The Dynamics of Medieval Iceland. Political Economy and Literature*, Iowa.

Einar Arnórsson 1930a. 'Alþingi árið 930.' *Skírnir* 104: 6–48.

Einar Arnórsson 1930b. 'Alþingi árið 1000.' *Skírnir* 104: 68–106.

Einar Arnórsson 1930c. 'Alþingi árið 1262.' *Skírnir* 104: 116–34.

Einar Arnórsson 1941. 'Kristinitökusagan árið 1000.' *Skírnir* 115: 79–118.

Einar G. Pétursson 1977. 'Geirmundar þáttur heljarskinns og Sturlubók.' in Bjarni R. Einarsson ed. *Bjarnígull sendur Bjarna Einarssyni sextugum*, Reykjavík: 10–12.

Einar G. Pétursson 1986. 'Efling kirkjuvaldsins og ritun Landnámu.' *Skírnir* 160: 193–222.

Einar Ólafur Sveinsson 1937a. 'The Icelandic Family Saga and the Period in which their Authors Lived.' *Acta Philologica Scandinavia* 12: 71–90.

Einar Ólafur Sveinsson 1937b. *Sagnaritun Oddaverja. Nokkrar athuganir.* (Studia Islandica 1), Reykjavík.

Einar Ólafur Sveinsson 1940. *Sturlungaöld*, Reykjavík.

Einar Ólafur Sveinsson 1953. *Age of the Sturlungs*, trans. Jóhann S. Hannesson, Ithaca.

Einar Ólafur Sveinsson 1958. *Dating the Icelandic Sagas. An Essay in Method.* (Viking Society for Northern Research. Text Series 3), trans. G. Turville-Petre, London.

Elín Bára Magnúsdóttir 2015. *Eyrbyggja saga. Efni og höfundareinkenni.* (Studia Islandica 65), Reykjavík.

Ellison, R. 1986–89. 'The Alleged Famine in Iceland.' *Saga-Book* 22: 165–79.

Erlingur Hauksson 1993a. 'Íslenskir selir.' in Páll Hersteinsson & Guttormur Sigbjarnarson eds. 1993. *Villt íslensk spendýr*, Reykjavík: 188–201.

Erlingur Hauksson 1993b. 'Farselir við Ísland.' in Páll Hersteinsson & Guttormur Sigbjarnarson eds. *Villt íslensk spendýr*, Reykjavík: 202–13.

Erlingur Sigtryggsson 1986. 'Einn óþarfasti maður í sögu vorri? Deilur Guðmundar Arasonar og veraldarhöfðingja.' *Sagnir* 7: 12–15.

Evans-Pritchard, E.E. 1940. *The Nuer*, Oxford.

Faulkes, A. 1978–79. 'Descent from the Gods.' *Mediaeval Scandinavia* 11: 92–125.

Featherstone, S. 'Jack Hill's Horse: Narrative Form and Oral History.' *Oral History* 19: 59–62.

Fenton, A. 1986. 'Seaweed Manure.' in idem ed. *The Shape of the Past*, II, Edinburgh: 48–82.

Fentress, J. & Wickham, C. 1992. *Social Memory: New Perspectives on the Past*, Oxford.

Finnegan, R. 1970. 'A Note on Oral Tradition and Historical Evidence.' *History and Theory* 9: 195–201.

Finnegan, R. 1977. *Oral Poetry*, Oxford.

Finnegan, R. 1985. 'What is Orality – If Anything?' *Byzantine and Modern Greek Studies* 14: 130–49.

Finnur Jónsson. 1920–24. *Den oldnorske og oldislandske litteraturshistorie* I–III, 2nd ed., Copenhagen.

Foote, P. 1952. *Notes on the Prepositions OF and UM(B) in Old Icelandic and Old Norwegian Prose* (Studia Islandica 14), Reykjavík.

Foote, P. 1965. 'An Essay on the Saga of Gisli and its Icelandic Background.' in G. Johnston, trans. 1965. *The Saga of Gisli*. London: 93–134.

Foote, P. 1975. 'Træl, Alment, Norge og Island.' *KLNM* XIX: 13–19.

Foote, P. 1984. *Aurvandilstá. Norse Studies*, ed. M. Barnes, H. Bekker-Nielsen & G.W. Weber, Odense.

Frank, R. 1973. 'Marriage in Twelfth- and Thirteenth Century Iceland.' *Viator. Medieval and Renaissance Studies* 4: 473–84.

Friðrik G. Olgeirsson 2000. 'Ritun byggðarsögu á 20. öld.' *Saga* 38: 249–66.

Fritzner, J. 1886–96. *Ordbog over det gamle norske sprog* I–III, Christiania.

Gade, K.E. 1995. '1236: Órækja meiddr ok heill görr.' *Gripla* 9: 115–32.

Garðar Guðmundsson 1996. 'Gathering and Processing of Lyme-grass (Elymus arenarius L.) in Iceland: an Ethnohistorical Account.' *Vegetation History and Archaeobotany* 5: 13–23.

Garmonsway, G.N. 1940. 'Eyrbyggja saga.' *Saga-Book* 12: 81–92.

Gilsenan, M. *Recognizing Islam. Religion and Society in the modern Middle East*. London and New York, 1982.

Gísli Sigurðsson 1994a. 'Bók í stað lögsögumanns – Valdabarátta kirkju og veraldlegra höfðingja?' in Gísli Sigurðsson, Guðrún Kvaran & Sigurgeir Steingrímsson eds. *Sagnaþing helgað Jónasi Kristjánssyni sjötugum 10. apríl 1994*, Reykjavík: 207–32.

Gísli Sigurðsson 1994b. 'Aðrir áheyrendur – önnur saga? Um ólíkar frásagnir Vatnsdælu og Finnboga sögu af sömu atburðum.' *Skáldskaparmál* 3: 30–41.

Gísli Sigurðsson 2002. *Túlkun íslendingasagna í ljósi munnlegrar hefðar: tilgáta um aðferð* (Stofnun Árna Magnússonar á Íslandi 56), Reykavik.

Gísli Sigurðsson 2007. 'The Immanent Saga of Guðmundr ríki.' in J. Quinn, K. Heslop & T. Wills eds. *Learning and Understanding in the Old Norse World*, Turnhout: 201–18.

Glauser, J., Hermann, P. & Mitchell, S.A. eds. 2018. *Handbook of Pre-Modern Nordic Memory Studies: Interdisciplinary Approaches*, Turnhout.

Glendinning, Robert J. 1969. 'Arons saga and Íslendinga saga: A Problem in Parallel Transmission.' *Scandinavian Studies* 41: 41–51.

Gluckman, M. 1965. *Politics, Law and Ritual in Tribal Society*, Oxford.

Goody, J. ed. 1968. *Literacy in Traditional Societies*, Cambridge.

Goody, J. 1977. *The Domestication of the Savage Mind*, Cambridge.

Grønlie, S. 2006. *Íslendingabók. Kristni saga. The Book of Icelanders. The Story of the Conversion* (Viking Society for Northern Research Text Series 18), London.
Grönvald, K., Niels Óskarsson, Sigfús J. Johnsen, Clausen, H.B., Hammer, C.U., Bond, G. & Bard, E. 1995. 'Ash layers from Iceland in the Greenland GRIP ice core correlated with oceanic and land sediments.' *Earth and Planetary Science Letters* 135: 149–55.
Guðbrandur Sigurðsson 1955–56. 'Eyðibýli í Helgafellssveit.' *Árbók hins íslenzka fornleifafélags* 54: 44–65.
Guðmundur Finnbogason 1930. 'Alþingi árið 1117.' *Skírnir* 104: 107–15.
Guðmundur Ólafsson, Smith, K.P. & McGovern, T.H. 2010. 'Surtshellir: A Fortified Outlaw Cave in West Iceland." in J. Sheehan & D. O'Corráin eds. *The Viking Age: Ireland and the West. Proceedings of the Fifteenth Viking Congress, Cork, 2005*, Dublin: 283–297.
Guðni Jónsson 1960. 'Genealogier.' *KLNM* V: 247–49.
Guðrún Ása Grímsdóttir 1982. 'Um afskipti erkibiskupa af íslenzkum málefnum á 12. og 13. öld.' *Saga* 20: 28–62.
Guðrún Ása Grímsdóttir 1988. 'Sturla Þórðarson.' in Guðrún Ása Grímsdóttir & Jónas Kristjánsson eds. *Sturlustefna. Ráðstefna haldin á sjö alda ártíð Sturlu Þórðarsonar sagnaritara 1984* (Rit Stofnunar Árna Magnússonar á Íslandi 32), Reykjavík: 9–36.
Guðrún Nordal 1989. 'Eitt sinn skal hverr deyja.' *Skírnir* 163: 72–94.
Gúðrun Nordal 1992. '*Sturlunga saga* and the Context of Saga Writing.' in J. Hines & D. Slay eds. *Introductory Essays on Egils saga and Njáls saga*, London.
Guðrún Nordal 1998. *Ethics and Action in Thirteenth Century Iceland*, Odense.
Guðrún Nordal 2012. 'Text in Time. The Making of Laxdæla.' Paper given at the 15th International Saga Conference, Aarhus, 5th–11th August 2012.
Guðrún Nordal 2013. 'Skaldic citations and settlement stories as parameters for saga dating' in E. Mundal ed. *Dating the Sagas. Reviews and Revisions*, Copenhagen: 195–212.
Gúðrun Sveinbjarnardóttir 1992. *Farm Abandonment in Medieval and Post-Medieval Iceland: an Interdisciplinary Study*. (Oxbow Monograph 17), Oxford.
Guðrún Sveinbjarnardóttir 2012. *Reykholt. Archaeological Investigations at a High Status Farm in Western Iceland*, Publications of the National Museum of Iceland 29, Reykjavík.
Gunnar Benediktsson 1961. *Sagnameistarinn Sturla*, Reykjavík.
Gunnar Harðarson 1987. 'Enn um Íslendingabók.' *Tímarit Máls og menningar* 48: 374–77.
Gunnar Karlsson 1972. 'Goðar og bændur.' *Saga* 10: 5–57.
Gunnar Karlsson 1975. 'Frá þjóðveldi til konungsríkis.' *Saga Íslands* II: 1–54.
Gunnar Karlsson 1977. 'Goðar and Höfðingjar in Medieval Iceland.' *Saga-Book* 19: 358–70.

Gunnar Karlsson 1979. 'Stjórnmálamaðurinn Snorri.' in Gunnar Karlsson ed. *Snorri, átta alda minning*, Reykjavík: 23–51.
Gunnar Karlsson 1980a. 'Völd og auður á 13. öld.' *Saga* 18: 5–30.
Gunnar Karlsson 1980b. 'Icelandic Nationalism and the Inspiration of History.' in R. Mitchinson ed. *The Roots of Nationalism*, Edinburgh: 77–89.
Gunnar Karlsson 1983. 'Um valdakerfi 13. aldar og aðferðir sagnfræðinga.' *Saga* 21: 270–75.
Gunnar Karlsson 1984. 'Saga í þágu samtíðar eða Síðbúinn ritdómur um Íslenska menningu Sigurðar Nordals.' *Tímarit Máls og menningar* 45: 19–27.
Gunnar Karlsson 1985a. 'Dyggðir og lestir í þjóðfélagi Íslendingasagna.' *Tímarit Máls og menningar* 46: 9–19.
Gunnar Karlsson 1985b. 'The Ethics of the Icelandic Saga Authors and their Contemporaries: A Comment on Hermann Pálsson's Theories on the Subject.' in J. Louis-Jensen, C. Sanders & P. Springborg eds, *The Sixth International Saga Conference, 28.7-28.8 1985: Workshop papers I-II*, Copenhagen, I: 381–99.
Gunnar Karlsson 1988. 'Siðamat Íslendingasögu.' in Guðrún Ása Grímsdóttir & Jónas Kristjánsson eds. *Sturlustefna. Ráðstefna haldin á sjö alda ártíð Sturlu Þórðarsonar sagnaritara 1984* (Rit Stofnunar Árna Magnússonar á Íslandi 32), Reykjavík: 204–21.
Gunnar Karlsson 1992. 'Ritunartími Staðarhólsbókar.' in Gísli Sigurðsson & Þorleifur Hauksson eds. *Sólhvarfasumbl samanborið handa Þorleifi Haukssyni fimmtugum 21. desember 1991*, Reykjavík: 40–42.
Gunnar Karlsson 1992. 'A century of research on early Icelandic society.' in A. Faulkes & R. Perkins eds. *Viking Revaluations. Viking Society Centenary Symposium 14–15 May 1992*, London: 15–25.
Gunnar Karlsson 1994. 'Nafngreindar höfðingjaættir í Sturlungu.' in Gísli Sigurðsson, Guðrún Kvaran & Sigurgeir Steingrímsson eds. *Sagnaþing helgað Jónasi Kristjánssyni sjötugum 10. apríl 1994*, Reykjavík: 307–16.
Gunnar Karlsson 1996. 'Viðhorf Íslendinga til landnámsins.' in Guðrún Ása Grímsdóttir ed. *Um Landnám á Íslandi. Fjórtán Erindi*, Reykjavík: 49–56.
Gunnar Karlsson 2000. *A History of Iceland*, Minnesota.
Gunnar Karlsson 2004. *Goðamenning. Staða og áhrif goðorðsmanna í þjóðveldi Íslendinga*. Reykjavík.
Gunnar Karlsson 2007. 'Valdasamþjöppun þjóðveldisaldar í túlkun fræðimanna.' in Benedikt Eyþórsson & Hrafnkell Lárusson eds. *Þriðja íslenska söguþingið 18.-21. maí 2006: Ráðstefnurit*, Reykjavík: 205–13.
Gunnar Karlsson 2008. 'Stofnár Þingeyraklausturs.' *Saga* 46: 159–67.
Gunnar Karlsson 2009. *Lífsbjörg Íslendinga frá 10. öld til 16. aldar. Handbók í íslenskri miðaldasögu* III, Reykjavík.
Gunnar Karlsson 2011. 'Íslendinga saga Jóns Jóhannessonar.' *Saga* 49: 196–202.

Gurevich, A.J. 1968. 'Wealth and Gift-Bestowal among the Ancient Scandinavians.' *Scandinavica* 7: 126–38.

Gurevich, A.J. 1971. 'Saga and History: The 'Historical Conception of Snorri Sturluson.' *Mediaeval Scandinavia* 4: 42–53.

Gurevich, A.J. 1990. 'Free Norwegian Peasantry Revisited.' *Historisk Tidskrift* 69: 275–84.

Haki Antonsson 2012. 'Salvation and Early Saga Writing in Iceland: Aspects of the Works of the Þingeyrar Monks and Their Associates.' *Viking and Medieval Scandinavia* 8: 71–140.

Haki Antonsson 2017. 'Árna saga biskups as Literature and History.' *Journal of English and Germanic Philology* 116: 261–85.

Hallberg, P. 1963. *Óláfr Þórðarson hvítaskáld, Knýtlinga saga och Laxdæla saga. Ett forsök till språklig författarbestämning* (Studia Islandica 22), Reykjavík.

Hallberg, P. 1965. 'Óláfr hvítaskáld, Knýtlinga saga och Laxdæla saga, En motkritik.' *Arkiv för nordisk filologi* 80: 123–56.

Hallberg, P. 1969. 'Jóns saga helga.' *Afmælisrit Jóns Helgasonar*, 59–79.

Hallberg, P. 1978–79. 'Ja, Knýtlinga saga und Laxdæla sind Schöpfungen eines Mannes.' *Mediaeval Scandinavia* 11: 179–92.

Hallberg, P. 1979. 'Eyrbyggja sagas ålder – än en gång.' *Acta Philologica Scandinavica* 32: 196–219.

Hallberg, P. 1983. 'Sturlunga saga – en isländsk tidsspegel,' *Scripta Islandica* 34: 3–28.

Hallberg, P. 1993. 'Sturlunga saga.' in P. Pulsiano & K. Wolf eds. *Medieval Scandinavia: An Encyclopedia*, New York: 616–18.

Halldór Hermannsson 1930. *The Book of Icelanders (Íslendingabók)* (Islandica 20), Ithaca.

Halldór Hermannsson 1943. 'Goðorð í Rangárþingi.' *Skírnir* 117: 21–31.

Halldór Hermannsson 1948. 'Ari Þorgilsson fróði.' *Skírnir* 122: 5–29.

Hallfreður Örn Eiríksson 1970. 'Þjóðsagnir og sagnfræði.' *Saga*: 268–296.

Halsall, G. 1995. *Settlement and Social Organisation: The Merovingian Region of Metz*, Cambridge.

Halvorsen, E.H. 1965. 'Langfeðgatal.' *KLNM* X: 311–13.

Hamer, A. 2008. *Njáls saga and its Christian Background. A Study of Narrative Method*. Unpublished PhD thesis, Rijksuniversiteit Groningen.

Hamre, Lars 1974. 'Tiend, Noreg.' *KLNM* XVIII: 280–87.

Hanna, E., Jónsson, T. & Box, J.E. 2004. 'An analysis of Icelandic climate since the nineteenth century.' *International Journal of Climatology* 24: 1193–1210.

Hannes Þorsteinsson 1912. 'Nokkrar athuganir um íslenzkar bókmenntir á 12. og 13. öld.' *Skírnir* 86: 126–48.

Haraldur Matthíasson 1950. 'Landnám milli Þjórsár og Hvítár.' *Skírnir* 124: 113–51.

Harrison, R. & Maher, R.A. eds. 2014. *Human Ecodynamics in the North Atlantic. A Collaborative Model of Humans and Nature through Space and Time*, Lanham.

Hastrup, K. 1979. 'Classification and Demography in Medieval Iceland.' *Ethnos* 44: 182–91.

Hastrup, K. 1985. *Culture and History in Medieval Iceland: an anthropological analysis of structure and change*, Oxford.

Hastrup, K. 1990. *Island of Anthroplogy: studies in past and present Iceland*, Viborg.

Haugen, E. ed. 1972. *First Grammatical Treatise*, 2nd ed., London.

Helgi Skúli Kjartansson 1986. 'Hverju jók Ari við Íslendingabók?' *Tímarit Máls og menningar* 47: 385–86.

Helgi Skúli Kjartansson 1989. *Fjöldi goðorða samkvæmt Grágás. Erindi flutt á málstefnu Stofnunar Sigurðar Nordals 24.-26. júlí 1988* (Félag áhugamanna um réttarsögu. Erindi og greinar 23), Reykjavík.

Helgi Skúli Kjartansson 1994. 'De te fibula... Samtíð Sturlunga í spegli Laxdælu.' in Gísli Sigurðsson, Guðrún Kvaran & Sigurgeir Steingrímsson eds. *Sagnaþing helgað Jónasi Kristjánssyni sjötugum 10. apríl 1994*, Reykjavík: 377–88.

Helgi Skúli Kjartansson 2005. 'Thin on the Ground. Legal Evidence of the Availability of Priests in 12th Century Iceland.' in Helgi Þorláksson ed. *Church Centres in Iceland from the 11th to the 13th Centuries and their parallels in other Countries*, Reykholt: 95–102.

Helgi Þorláksson 1979a. 'Snorri Sturluson og Oddaverjar.' in Gunnar Karlsson ed. *Snorri, átta alda minning*, Reykjavík: 53–88.

Helgi Þorláksson 1979b. 'Stórbændur gegn goðum. Hugleiðingar um goðavald, konungsvald og sjálfræðishug bænda um miðbik 13. aldar.' in Bergsteinn Jónsson, Einar Laxness & Heimir Þorleifsson eds. *Söguslóðir. Afmælisrit helgað Ólafi Hanssyni sjötugum 18. september 1979*, Reykjavík: 227–50.

Helgi Þorláksson 1982a. 'Rómarvald og kirkjugoðar.' *Skírnir* 156: 51–67.

Helgi Þorláksson 1982b. 'Stéttir, auður og völd á 12. og 13. öld.' *Saga* 20: 63–113.

Helgi Þorláksson 1983. 'Helgi Þorláksson svarar.' *Saga* 21: 275–79.

Helgi Þorláksson 1988a. 'Var Sturla Þórðarson þjóðfrelsishetja?' in Guðrún Ása Grímsdóttir & Jónas Kristjánsson eds. *Sturlustefna. Ráðstefna haldin á sjö alda ártíð Sturlu Þórðarsonar sagnaritara 1984* (Rit Stofnunar Árna Magnússonar 32), Reykjavík: 127–46.

Helgi Þorláksson 1988b. 'Gráfeldir á gullöld og voðaverk kvenna.' *Ný Saga* 89: 40–53.

Helgi Þorláksson 1989a. *Gamlar götur og goðavald. Um fornar leiðir ok völd Oddaverja í Rangárþingi* (Ritsafn Sagnfræðistofnunar 25), Reykjavík.

Helgi Þorláksson 1989b. 'Mannfræði og saga.' *Skírnir* 163: 231–48.

Helgi Þorláksson 1991a. 'Sauðafell. Um leiðir of völd í Dölum við lok þjóðveldis.' in Magnús Stefánsson, Gunnar Karlsson & Helgi Þorláksson eds. *Yfir Íslandsála. Afmælisrit til heiðurs Magnúsi Stefánssyni sextugum 25. desember 1991*, Reykjavík: 95–109.

Helgi Þorláksson 1991b. *Vaðmal og verðlag. Vaðmál í utanlandsviðskiptum og búskap Íslendinga á 13. og 14. öld*, Reykjavík.

Helgi Þorláksson 1992a. 'Snorri goði og Snorri Sturluson.' *Skírnir* 166: 295-320.

Helgi Þorláksson 1992b. 'Social Ideas and the Concept of Profit in Thirteenth Century Iceland.' in Gísli Pálsson ed. *From Sagas to Society. Comparative Approaches to Early Iceland*, Enfield Lock: 231-45.

Helgi Þorláksson 1994. 'Þjóðleið hjá Brekku og Bakka. Um Leiðir og völd í Öxnadal við lok þjóðveldis.' in *Samtíðarsögur* (Níunda alþjóðlega fornsagnaþingið), Akureyri: 335-49.

Helgi Þorláksson 2001. 'Fé og virðing.,' in idem ed. *Sæmdarmenn. Um heiður á þjóðveldisöld*, Reykjavík: 96-134.

Helgi Þorláksson 2002. 'Sturla Þórðarson. Minni og vald.' in Erla Hulda Halldórsdóttir ed.: 319-41.

Helgi Þorláksson 2003. 'Fiskur og höfðingjar á Vestfjörðum.' *Ársrit Sögufélags Ísfirðinga*, 43: 67-82.

Helgi Þorláksson 2005. 'Why were the 12th century staðir established?' in idem ed. *Church Centres in Iceland from the 11th to the 13th Centuries and their parallels in other Countries*, Reykholt: 31-59.

Helgi Þorláksson 2006. 'Walruses at Reykjavík' in Bryndís Sverrisdóttir ed. *Reykjavík 871±2. Landnámssýningin. The Settlement Exhibition*, Reykjavík: 34-35.

Helgi Þorlákson 2007. 'Veraldlegar valdamiðstöðvar, hvernig urðu þær til? Samanburður Reykholts og Bólstaðar' in Benedikt Eyþórsson & Hrafnkell Lárusson eds. *Þriðja íslenska söguþingið 18.-21. maí 2006: Ráðstefnurit*, Reykjavík: 214-24.

Helgi Þorláksson 2009. 'Sturlusaga og Einar Þorgilsson' in Guðmundur Jónsson, Helgi Skúli Kjartansson, Vésteinn Ólason eds. *Heimtur. Ritgerðir til heiðurs Gunnari Karlssyni sjötugum*, Reykjavík: 215-29.

Helgi Þorláksson 2010a. 'Kings and Commerce: The foreign trade of Iceland in medieval times and the impact of royal authority.' in S. Imsen ed. *The Norwegian Domination and the Norse World c.1100-c.1400*, Trondheim: 149-73.

Helgi Þorláksson 2010b. 'Milli Skarðs og Feykis. Um valdasamþjöppun í Hegranesþingi í tíð Ásbirninga og um valdamiðstöðvar þeirra.' *Saga* 48:2, 51-93.

Helgi Þorláksson 2011. 'Jón Jóhannesson og íslensk sagnfræði.' *Saga* 49: 203-10.

Helgi Þorláksson 2012. 'Sturlunga - tilurð og markmið.' *Gripla* 23: 53-92.

Helgi Þorláksson 2013. 'Ódrjúgshálsar og sæbrautir. Um samgöngur og völd við Breiðafjörð á fyrri tíð.' *Saga* 49: 94-128.

Helgi Þorláksson 2017. 'The Bias and Alleged Impartiality of Sturla Þórðarson.' in Jón Viðar Sigurðsson & Sverrir Jakobsson eds. *Sturla Þórðarson: Skald, Chieftain and Lawman*, Leiden: 200-11.

Helle, K. 1981. 'Norway in the High Middle Ages: Recent Views on the Structure of Society.' *Scandinavian Journal of History* 6: 161-89.

Helle, K. 2011. 'Hvor står den historiske sagakritikken i dag?' *Collegium Medievale* 24: 50-86.

Heller, R. 1961. 'Laxdæla saga und Sturlunga saga.' *Arkiv för nordisk filologi* 76: 112-33.

Heller, R. 1965. 'Laxdæla saga und Knýtlinga saga. Studien über die Beziehungen zwischen den beiden Sagas.' *Arkiv för nordisk filologi* 80: 95–122.

Heller, R. 1966. 'Þóra frilla Þórðar Sturlusonar.' *Arkiv för nordisk filologi* 81: 39–56.

Heller, R. 1967. 'Knýtlings saga. Bemerkungen zur Enstehungsgeschichte des Werkes.' *Arkiv för nordisk filologi* 82: 155–74.

Heller, R. 1969. 'Der Verfasser der Laxdæla saga und sein Verhältnis zur Sturlubók.' in Jakob Benediktsson ed. *Afmælisrit Jóns Helgasonar 30. júní 1969*, Reykjavík: 80–91.

Heller, R. 1974. 'Laxdæla saga und Landnámabók.' *Arkiv för nordisk filologi* 89: 84–145.

Heller, R. 1976a. *Die Laxdæla saga: Die literarische Schöpfung eines Isländers des 13. Jahrhunderts*, Berlin.

Heller, R. 1976b. 'Fóstbræðra saga und Laxdæla saga.' *Arkiv för nordisk filologi* 91: 102–22.

Heller, R. 1977. 'Hrafns saga Sveinbjarnarsonar und Isländersagas.' *Arkiv för nordisk filologi* 92: 98–105.

Heller, R. 1978. 'Sturla Þórðarson und die Isländersagas. Überlegungen zu einer wichtigen frage in der Sagaforschung.' *Arkiv för nordisk filologi* 93: 138–44.

Heller, R. 1978–79. '*Knýtlinga saga* und *Laxdæla saga*: Schöpfung *eines* Mannes?' *Mediaeval Scandinavia* 11: 163–78.

Heller, R. 1986. 'Anmerkungen zur Arbeit des Verfassers der Laxdæla saga.' in R. Simek, Jónas Kristjánsson & H. Bekker-Nielsen eds. *Sagnaskemmtun: Studies in Honour of Hermann Pálsson on his 65th Birthday, 26th May 1986* (Philologica Germanica 8), Vienna: 111–20.

Heller, R. 1998. '*Laxdæla saga* und *Færeyinga saga*.' *Alvíssmál* 11: 85–92

Henige, D. 1974. *The Chronology of Oral Tradition: Quest for a Chimera*, Oxford.

Henige, D. 1982. *Oral Historiography*, New York.

Hermann, P. 2007. 'Íslendingabók and History.' in P. Hermann, J.P. Schødt & R. Tranum Kristensen eds. *Reflections on Old Norse Myths* (Studies in Viking and Medieval Scandinavia vol.1), Turnhout: 17–32.

Hermann Pálsson 1960–63. 'Athugasemd um Arons sögu.' *Saga* 3: 299–303.

Hermann Pálsson 1962. *Sagnaskemmtun Íslendinga*, Reykjavík.

Hermann Pálsson 1965a. 'Fyrsta málfræðiritgerðin og upphaf íslenskrar sagnaritunar.' *Skírnir* 139: 159–77.

Hermann Pálsson 1965b. 'Upphaf Íslandsbyggðar.' *Skírnir* 139: 52–64.

Hermann Pálsson 1967. *Helgafell. Saga höfuðbóls og klausturs* (Snæfellsnes II), Reykjavík.

Hermann Pálsson 1986. *Leyndarmál Laxdælu*, Reykjavík.

Hermann Pálsson & Edwards, P., trans. 1972. *The Book of Settlements. Landnámabók*, Winnipeg.

Hermann Pálsson & Edwards, P., trans. 1973. *Eyrbyggja saga*, Edinburgh.

Herschend, F. 1994. 'Models of Petty Rulership: Two Early Settlements in Iceland.' *Tor* 26: 163–91.
Heusler, A. 1911. *Das Strafrecht der Isländersagas*, Leipzig.
Hollander, L.M. 1959. 'The Structure of Eyrbyggja Saga.' *Journal of English and Germanic Philology* 58: 222–27.
Hreinn Benediktsson ed. 1972. *The First Grammatical Treatise* (University of Iceland Publications in Linguistics 1), Reykjavík.
Hörður Ágústsson 1987. 'Íslenski torfbærinn' in Frosti F. Jóhannsson ed., *Íslensk þjóðmenning I. Uppruni og umhverfi*, Reykjavík: 229–344.
Iceland. 1942. (Great Britain, Naval Intelligence Division: Geographical Handbook Series B.R. 504), Cambridge.
Innes, M. 2000. *State and Society in the Early Middle Ages*, Cambridge.
Jackson, K. 1961. *The International Popular Tale and Early Welsh Tradition*, Cardiff.
Jakob Benediktsson 1961. 'Hauksbók.' *KLNM* VI: 250–51.
Jakob Benediktsson 1969. '*Landnámabók*: Some Remarks on Its Value as a Historical Source.' *Saga-Book* 17: 275–92.
Jakob Benediktsson 1971. 'Sogn. Island.' *KLNM* XVI: 380–81.
Jakob Benediktsson 1972a. 'Sturlunga saga.' *KLNM* XVII: 355–59.
Jakob Benediktsson 1972b. 'Sturlu saga.' *KLNM* XVII: 359–60.
Jakob Benediktsson 1974a. 'Landnám og upphaf allsherjarríkis.' *Saga Íslands* I: 155–96.
Jakob Benediktsson 1974b. 'Markmið Landnámabókar: Nýjar rannsóknir.' *Skírnir* 148: 207–15.
Jakob Benediktsson 1974c. 'Ting. Island.' *KLNM* XVIII: 359–60.
Jakob Benediktsson 1976a. 'Þorgils saga ok Hafliða.' *KLNM* XX: 384–85.
Jakob Benediktsson 1976b. 'Þorgils saga skarða.' *KLNM* XX: 385.
Jakob Benediktsson 1976c. 'Þorlákr helgi Þórhallsson.' *KLNM* XX: 385–88.
Jakob Benediktsson 1976d. 'Årböcker. Island.' *KLNM* XX: 435–37.
Jakobsen, A. 1986. 'Om forfatteren av Sturlu saga.' *Scripta Islandica* 37: 3–11.
Janus Jónsson 1914. 'Sturla Þórðarsonar. Sjö alda afmæli.' *Almanak hins íslenszka Þjóðvinafélags* 40: 69–79.
Jesch, J. 1985a. 'Some Early Christians in Landnámabók.' in J. Louis-Jensen, C. Sanders & P. Springborg eds, *The Sixth International Saga Conference, 28.7-28.8 1985: Workshop papers I-II*, Copenhagen, I: 513–29.
Jesch, J.1985b. 'Two Lost Sagas.' *Saga-Book* 21: 1–14.
Jesch, J. 2008. 'Myth and cultural memory in the Viking diaspora.' *Viking and Medieval Scandinavia* 4: 221–26
Jones, G. 1952. 'History and Fiction in the Sagas of the Icelanders.' *Saga-Book* 13: 285–306.
Jón Hnefill Aðalsteinsson 1984. 'Önnungar.' *Saga* 22: 31–40.

Jón Hnefill Aðalsteinsson 1985. 'Blót og þing. Trúarlegt og félagslegt hlutverk goða tíundu öld.' *Skírnir* 159: 123–42.

Jón Böðvarsson 1968. 'Munur eldri og yngri gerðar Þorláks sögu.' *Saga* 6: 81–94.

Jón Guðmundsson 1896–1902. 'Um ættir og slekti.' *Safn til sögu Íslands* III: 701–28.

Jón Thor Haraldsson 1988. *Ósigur Oddaverja* (Ritsafn Sagnfræðistofnunar 22), Reykjavík.

Jón Helgason 1976. 'Þorláks saga helga.' *KLNM* XX: 388–91.

Jón Jóhannesson 1941. *Gerðir Landnámabókar*, Reykjavík.

Jón Jóhannesson 1954. 'Sannfræði og uppruni Landnámu.' *Saga* 2: 217–29.

Jón Jóhannesson 1956–58. *Íslendinga saga* I–II, Reykjavík.

Jón M. Samsonarson 1954–58. 'Var Gissur Þorvaldsson jarl yfir öllu Íslandi?' *Saga* 2: 326–65.

Jón Viðar Sigurðsson 1989. *Frá goðorðum til ríkja. Þróun goðavalds á 12. og 13. öld* (Sagnfræðirannsóknir. Studia historica 10), Reykjavík.

Jón Viðar Sigurðsson 1998. 'Heimili, þingmennska, frændur og vernd á þjóðveldisöld.' in Guðmundur J. Guðmundsson & Eiríkur K. Björnsson eds. *Íslenska söguþingið 28.-31. mai 1997* I & II, Reykjavík: 107–16.

Jón Viðar Sigurðsson 1999. *Chieftains and Power in the Icelandic Commonwealth*, trans. Jean Lundskær-Nielsen, Viborg.

Jón Viðar Sigurðsson 2000. 'Allir sem sjá líta þó ekki jafnt á: sagnaritun um íslenskar miðaldir fram um 1300.' *Saga* 38: 33–57.

Jón Viðar Sigurðsson 2007. 'Stórkirkjur, sagnaritun og valdamiðstöðvar 1100–1400.' in Benedikt Eyþórsson & Hrafnkell Lárusson eds. *Þriðja íslenska söguþingið 18.-21. maí 2006: Ráðstefnurit*, Reykjavík: 225–33.

Jón Viðar Sigurðsson 2006. 'Noen hovedtrekk i diskusjonen om det islandske middelaldersamfunnet etter 1970.' *Collegium Medievale* 18: 106–43.

Jón Viðar Sigurðsson 2009. 'Hugleiðingar um hreppa, bændagildi og goðorð.' in Guðmundur Jónsson, Helgi Skúli Kjartansson, Vésteinn Ólason eds. *Heimtur. Ritgerðir til heiðurs Gunnari Karlssyni sjötugum*, Reykjavík: 243–55.

Jón Viðar Sigurðsson 2013. Review of Úlfar Bragason, *Ætt og saga: Um frásagnarfræði Sturlungu eða Íslendinga sögu hinnar miklu. Speculum* 88: 863–64.

Jón Viðar Sigurðsson 2014. 'The making of a 'skattland': Iceland 1247–1450.' in Steinar Imsen ed. *Rex Insularum. The King of Norway and his 'skattlands' as a political system c.1260–c.1450*, Bergen: 181–225.

Jón Viðar Sigurðsson & Sverrir Jakobsson 2017. 'Sturla Þórðarson, the Politician.' in Jón Viðar Sigurðsson & Sverrir Jakobsson eds. *Sturla Þórðarson: Skald, Chieftain and Lawman*, Leiden: 1–7.

Jón Steffensen 1968. 'Population, Island.' *KLNM* XIII: 390–92.

Jónas Kristjánsson 1975. 'Bókmenntasaga.' *Saga Íslands* II: 147–258.

Jónas Kristjánsson 1980. 'Annálar og Íslendingasögur.' *Gripla* 4: 295–319.

Jónas Kristjánsson 1981. 'Learned Style or Saga Style?' in U. Dronke, Guðrún P. Helgadóttir, G.W. Weber & H. Bekker-Nielsen eds. *Specvlvm norroenvm. Norse Studies in memory of Gabriel Turville-Petre*, Odense: 260–92.

Jónas Kristjánsson 1988. *Eddas and Sagas. Iceland's Medieval Literature*, trans. P. Foote, Reykjavík.

Kaalund, K. 1877–82. *Bidrag til en Historisk-Topografisk Beskrivelse af Island*, I–II, Copenhagen.

Kári Gíslason 2009. 'Within and Without Family in the Icelandic Sagas.' *Parergon* 26: 13–33.

Kellogg, R. 1994. 'What is a Saga?' in Gísli Sigurðsson, Guðrún Kvaran & Sigurgeir Steingrímsson eds. *Sagnaþing helgað Jónasi Kristjánssyni sjötugum 10. apríl 1994*, 2 vols., Reykjavík: 497–503.

KLNM = Kulturhistorisk leksikon for nordisk middelalder, I–XXII (Copenhagen, 1956–78).

Kress, H. 1980. 'Meget samstavet må det tykkes deg: Om kvinneopprör og genretvang i Sagaen om Laksdölene.' *Historiskt Tidskrift* 3: 266–80.

Kristján Eldjárn 1956. *Kuml og haugfé úr heiðnum sið á Íslandi*, Akureyri.

Kristján Eldjárn 1960. 'Gård, Island.' *KLNM* V: 445–47.

Kristján Eldjárn 2000. *Kuml og haugfé úr heiðnum sið á Íslandi*. 2nd edition, Reykjavík.

Kristján Eldjárn 2016. *Kuml og haugfé úr heiðnum sið á Íslandi*. 3rd edition, Reykjavík.

Kuper, A. 1982. 'Lineage Theory: a Critical Retrospect.' *Annual Review of Anthropology* 11: 71–95.

Lancaster, W.W. 1981. *The Rwala Bedouin Today*, Cambridge.

Lethbridge, E. 2013. 'Dating the Sagas and *Gísla saga Súrssonar*.' in E. Mundal ed. *Dating the Sagas. Reviews and Revisions*, Copenhagen: 77–113.

Lethbridge, E.D. 2007. *Narrative Variation in the Versions of Gísla saga Súrssonar*, unpublished PhD thesis, Department of Anglo-Saxon, Norse and Celtic, University of Cambridge.

Lethbridge, E. & Quinn, J. eds. 2007. *Creating the Medieval Saga: Versions, Variability, and Editorial Interpretations of Old Norse Saga Literature*, Odense.

Lincoln, B. 2014. *Between History and Myth: Stories of Harald Fairhair and the Founding of the State*, Chicago.

Lindow, J. 1997. '*Íslendingabók* and Myth.' *Scandinavian Studies* 69: 454–64.

Long, A-M. 2017. '*Sturlubók* and Cultural Memory.' in Jón Viðar Sigurðsson & Sverrir Jakobsson eds. *Sturla Þórðarson: Skald, Chieftain and Lawman*, Leiden: 56–69.

Lord, A.B. 1960. *The Singer of Tales*, Cambridge, Mass.

Louis-Jensen, J. 2013. 'Dating the Archetype. *Eyrbyggja saga* and *Egils saga Skallagrímssonar*.' in E. Mundal ed. *Dating the Sagas. Reviews and Revisions*, Copenhagen: 133–47.

Lucas, G. ed. 2009. *Hofstaðir. Excavations of a Viking Age Feasting Hall in North-Eastern Iceland* (Institute of Archaeology Monograph Series 1), Reykjavík.

Lucas, G. & McGovern, T.H. 2007. 'Bloody Slaughter: Ritual Decapitation and Display at the Viking Settlement of Hofstaðir, Iceland.' *European Journal of Archaeology* 10: 7–30.
Lúðvík Ingvarsson 1986–87. *Goðorð og goðorðsmenn* I–III, Egilsstaðir.
Lúðvík Kristjánsson 1980–86. *Íslenzkir sjávarhættir* I–V, Reykjavík.
Lüning, K. 1990. *Seaweeds. Their Environment, Biogeography, and Ecophysiology*, New York and Chichester.
Lýður B. Björnsson 1978. 'Eigi skal höggva.' *Skírnir* 152: 162–65.
Lönnroth, L. 1968. 'Styrmir's Hand in the Obituary of Viðey.' *Mediaeval Scandinavia* 1: 85–100.
Lönnroth, L. 1975. 'The Concept of Genre in Saga Literature.' *Scandinavian Studies* 47: 419–26.
Lönnroth, L. 1976. *Njáls saga: A Critical Introduction*, Berkeley.
Madelung, A.M.A. 1972. *The Laxdæla saga: Its Structural Patterns*, Chapel Hill.
Magerøy, H. 1959. 'Guðmundr goði og Guðmundr ríki. Eit motivsamband.' *Maal og Minne 1959*: 22–34.
Magerøy, H. 1971. 'Har Sturla Þórðarson skrivi Laxdæla saga?' *Maal og Minne 1971*: 4–33.
Magnús Jónsson 1940. *Guðmundar saga dýra. Nokkrar athuganir um uppruna hennar og samsetning* (Studia Islandica 8), Reykjavík.
Magnús Jónsson. 2000. 'Sturlungar ryðja sér til rúms.' *Sagnir* 21: 34-
Magnús Már Lárusson 1956a. 'Árna saga biskups.' *KLNM* I: 251.
Magnús Már Lárusson 1956b. 'Arons saga.' *KLNM* I: 251.
Magnús Már Lárusson 1956c. 'Biskupa sögur.' *KLNM* I: 630–31.
Magnús Már Lárusson 1957. 'Bonde. Island.' *KLNM* II: 95–97.
Magnús Már Lárusson 1959a. 'Fostring.' *KLNM* IV: 544–45.
Magnús Már Lárusson 1959b. 'Framfœrsla.' *KLNM* IV: 556–58.
Magnús Már Lárusson 1960. 'Fylgð.' *KLNM* V: 37–38.
Magnús Már Lárusson 1961. 'Hovedgård. Island.' *KLNM* VI: 707–10.
Magnús Már Lárusson 1962a. 'Hreppr.' *KLNM* VII: 17–22.
Magnús Már Lárusson 1962b. 'Hundrað.' *KLNM* VII: 83–87.
Magnús Már Lárusson 1962c. 'Hungrvaka.' *KLNM* VII: 88–89.
Magnús Már Lárusson 1962d. 'Jóns saga helga.' *KLNM* VII: 617–18.
Magnús Már Lárusson 1962e. 'Jordejendom. Island.' *KLNM* VII: 671–77.
Magnús Már Lárusson 1963a. 'Kirkegård, Island.' *KLNM* VIII: 399–402.
Magnús Már Lárusson 1963b. 'Kloster. Island.' *KLNM* VIII: 544–46.
Magnús Már Lárusson 1964a. 'Kristni saga.' *KLNM* IX: 356.
Magnús Már Lárusson 1964b. 'Kyrka. Island.' *KLNM* IX: 636–39.
Magnús Már Lárusson 1965a. 'Landskyld. Island.' *KLNM* X: 282.
Magnús Már Lárusson 1965b. 'Laurentius saga.' *KLNM* X: 354–55.

Magnús Már Lárusson 1966. 'Máldagi.' *KLNM* XI: 264–66.
Magnús Már Lárusson 1967a. *Froðleiksþættir og sögubrot*, Reykjavík.
Magnús Már Lárusson 1967b. 'Odelsrett.' *KLNM* XII: 492.
Magnús Már Lárusson 1968a. 'Páls saga biskups.' *KLNM* XIII: 90–91.
Magnús Már Lárusson 1968b. 'Privatkirke.' *KLNM* XIII: 462–67.
Magnús Már Lárusson 1970. 'Á höfuðbólum landsins.' *Saga* 9: 40–90.
Magnús Stefánsson 1974. 'Tiend. Island.' *KLNM* XVIII: 287–91.
Magnús Stefánsson 1975. 'Kirkjuvald eflist.' *Saga Íslands* II: 57–144.
Magnús Stefánsson 1978. 'Frá goðakirkju til biskupakirkju.' *Saga Íslands* III: 111–257.
Magnús Stefánsson 1988. 'Drottinsvik Sturlu Þorðarsonar.' in Guðrún Ása Grímsdóttir & Jónas Kristjánsson eds. *Sturlustefna. Ráðstefna haldin á sjö alda ártíð Sturlu Þórðarsonar sagnaritara 1984* (Rit Stofnunar Árna Magnússonar á Íslandi 32), Reykjavík: 147–83.
Magnús Stefánsson 2000. *Staðir og staðamál: studier i islandske egenkirkelige og beneficialrettslige forhold i middelalderen*, Bergen.
Magnús Stefánsson 2005. 'De islandske stadenes egenart og eldste historie.' in Helgi Þorláksson ed. *Church Centres in Iceland from the 11th to the 13th Centuries and their parallels in other Countries*, Reykholt: 117–25.
Mahoney, D. 2016. 'The Political Construction of a Tribal Genealogy from Early Medieval South Arabia.' in E. Hovden, C. Lutter & W. Pohl eds. *Meanings of Community across Medieval Eurasia. Comparative Approaches* (Brill's Series on the Early Middle Ages, 25), Leiden: 163–82.
Matthías Þórðarson 1932. 'Bólstaður við Álftafjörð. Skýrsla um rannsókn 1931.' *Árbók hins íslenzka fornleifafélags 1932*: 1–28.
Maurer, K. 1852. *Die Enstehung des isländischen Staats und seiner Verfassung*, München.
Maurer, K. 1907–38. *Vorelesungen über altnordische Rechtsgeschichte* I–V, Leipzig.
McCreesh, B. 1978–79. 'Structural Patterns in the Eyrbyggja saga and Other sagas of the Conversion.' *Mediaeval Scandinavia* 11: 271–80.
McCreesh, B. 1993. 'Eyrbyggja saga.' in P. Pulsiano & K. Wolf eds. *Medieval Scandinavia: An Encyclopedia*, New York: 174–75.
McGaffey, W. 1970. *Custom and Government in the Lower Congo*, Los Angeles.
McGovern, T.H. 1989. 'A Comparison of the Greenlandic Eastern and Western Settlements.' *Hikuin* 15: 27–36.
McGovern, T.H., Harrison, R. & Smiarowski, K. 2014. 'Sorting Sheep and Goats in Medieval Iceland and Greenland: Local Subsistence, Climate Change, or World System Impacts?' in Harrison, R. & Maher, R.A. eds. *Human Ecodynamics in the North Atlantic. A Collaborative Model of Humans and Nature through Space and Time*, Lanham: 153–76.
McGovern, T.H., Orri Vésteinsson, Adolf Friðriksson, Church, M., Lawson, I. Simpson, I.A., Árni Einarsson, Dugmore, A., Cook, G., Perdikaris, S., Edwards, K.J., Thomson,

A.M., Adderley, P., Newton, A., Lucas, G., Ragnar Edvarðsson, Aldred, O., Dunbar, E. 2007. 'Landscapes of Settlement in Northern Iceland: Historical Ecology of Human Impact and Climate Fluctuation on the Millennial Scale.' *American Anthropologist* 109: 27–51.

McTurk, R. 1986. 'Approaches to the Structure of Eyrbyggja saga.' in R. Simek, Jónas Kristjánsson & H. Bekker-Nielsen eds. *Sagnaskemmtun: Studies in Honour of Hermann Pálsson on his 65th Birthday, 26th May 1986* (Philologica Germanica 8), Vienna: 223–37.

Mehler, N. & Gardiner, M. 2007. 'English and Hanseatic Trading and Fishing Sites in Medieval Iceland: Report on Initial Fieldwork.' *Germania* 85: 385–427.

Mehler, N. 2015. 'The Sulphur Trade of Iceland from the Viking Age to the End of the Hanseatic Period.' in I. Baug, J. Larsen, S. Samset Mygland eds. *Nordic Middle Ages – Artefacts, Landscapes and Society* (University of Bergen Archaeological Series 8), Bergen: 193–212.

Meulengracht Sørensen, P. 1974. 'Saga um Ingólf og Hörleif: Athugasemdir um söguskoðun Íslendinga á seinni hluta þjóðveldisaldar.' *Skírnir* 148: 20–40.

Meulengracht Sørensen, P. 1977. *Saga og samfund. En indføring i oldislandsk litteratur,* Copenhagen.

Meulengracht Sørensen, P. 1988. 'Historiefortælleren Sturla Þorðarson.' in Guðrún Ása Grímsdóttir & Jónas Kristjánsson eds. *Sturlustefna. Ráðstefna haldin á sjö alda ártíð Sturlu Þórðarsonar sagnaritara 1984* (Rit Stofnunar Árna Magnússonar á Íslandi 32), Reykjavík: 122–26.

Meulengracht Sørensen, P. 1992. 'Some Methodological Considerations in Connection with the Study of the Sagas.' in Gísli Pálsson ed. *From Sagas to Society. Comparative Approaches to Early Iceland,* Enfield Lock: 27–41.

Meulengracht Sørensen, P. 1993. *Saga and Society. An Introduction to Old Norse Literature* (Studia Borealia, Nordic Studies Monograph Series 1), trans. J. Tucker, Odense.

Miller, W.I. 1983a. 'Justifying Skarpheðinn: Of Pretext and Politics in the Icelandic Bloodfeud.' *Scandinavian Studies* 55: 316–44.

Miller, W.I. 1983b. 'Choosing the Avenger: Some Aspects of the Bloodfeud in Medieval Iceland and England.' *Law and History Review* 1: 159–204.

Miller, W.I. 1986. 'Dreams, Prophecy and Sorcery: blaming the Secret Offender in Medieval Iceland.' *Scandinavian Studies* 58: 101–23.

Miller. W.I. 1988a. 'Some Aspects of Householding in the Medieval Icelandic Commonwealth.' *Continuity and Change* 3: 321–55.

Miller, W.I. 1988b. 'Ordeal in Iceland.' *Scandinavian Studies* 60: 189–212.

Miller, W.I. 1990. *Bloodtaking and Peacemaking. Feud, Law and Society in Saga Iceland,* Chicago.

Miller, W.I. 1993. *Humiliation: And Other Essays on Honor, Social Discomfort, and Violence*, Ithaca, NY.
Miller, W.I. 1997. *The Anatomy of Disgust*, Cambridge, MA.
Miller, W.I. 2000. *The Mystery of Courage*, Cambridge, MA.
Miller, W.I. 2003. *Faking It*, Cambridge.
Miller, W.I. 2006. *Eye for an Eye*, Cambridge.
Miller, W.I. 2008. *Audun and the Polar Bear. Luck, Law, and Largesse in a Medieval Tale of Risky Business*, Leiden.
Miller, W.I. 2014. *Why is your axe bloody? A Reading of Njáls Saga*, Oxford.
Moisl, H. 1981. 'Anglo-Saxon Royal Genealogies and Germanic Oral Tradition.' *Journal of Medieval History* 7: 215-48.
Mundal, E. 1977. *Sagadebatt*, Oslo.
Mundal, E. 1984. 'Íslendingabók, ættar tala og konunga ævi.' in *Festskrift til Ludvig Holm-Olsen på hans 70- årsdag den 9. juni 1984*, Øvre Ervik: 255-71.
Mundal, E. 2013. 'The Dating of the Oldest Sagas about Early Icelanders.' in E. Mundal ed. *Dating the Sagas. Reviews and Revisions*, Copenhagen: 31-54.
Mundt, M. 1969. *Sturla Þórðarson und die Laxdæla saga*, Bergen.
Njörður P. Njarðvík 1972. 'Laxdæla saga - en tidskritik?' *Arkiv för nordisk filologi* 86: 72-81.
North, R. 2009. 'Sighvatr Sturluson and the authorship of *Víga-Glúms saga*.' in W. Heizmann, K. Böldl & H. Beck eds. *Analecta Septentrionalia: Beiträge Zur Nordgermanischen Kultur- Und Literaturgeschichte*, Berlin: 256-80.
O'Connor, R. 2002. *Icelandic Histories and Romances*, Stroud.
Ogilvie, A.E.J. 1981. *Climate and Society in Iceland from the medieval period to the late eighteenth century*, unpublished PhD thesis, School of Environmental Sciences, University of East Anglia, Norwich.
Ogilvie, A.E.J. & Jónsdóttir, I. 2000. 'Sea Ice, Climate and Icelandic Fisheries in the Eighteenth and Nineteenth Centuries.' *Arctic* 53(4): 383-94.
Ogilvie, A.E.J. & Trausti Jónsson 2001. '"Little Ice Age" Research: A Perspective from Iceland.' *Climate Change* 48: 9-52.
Ogilvie, A.E.J., Woollett, J.M., Smiarowski, K., Arneborg, J., Troelstra, S., Pálsdóttir, A. & McGovern, T.H. 2009. 'Seals and sea ice in medieval Greenland.' *Journal of the North Atlantic* 2: 60-80.
Olsen, O. 1966. *Hørg, hov og kirke: Historiske og arkæologiske vikingetidsstudier*, Copenhagen.
Orning, H. 2008. *Unpredictability and Presence. Norwegian Kingship in the High Middle Ages*, trans. A. Crozier, Leidene.
Orri Vésteinsson 1994. 'Skjalagerð og sagnaritun.' in Sverrir Tómasson ed. *Samtíðarsögur* (Níunda alþjóðlega fornsagnaþingið), Akureyri: 626-37.

Orri Vésteinsson 1996. *The Christianisation of Iceland: Priests, Power and Social Change 1000–1300*, unpublished PhD thesis, University College London.
Orri Vésteinsson 1998a. 'Íslenska sóknaskipulagið og samband heimila á miðöldum' in Guðmundur J. Guðmundsson & Eiríkur K. Björnsson eds. *Íslenska söguþingið 28.-31. mai 1997*, 2 vols, Reykjavík: 147–66.
Orri Vésteinsson 1998b. 'Patterns of Settlement in Iceland. A Study in Pre-History.' *Saga-Book* 25: 1–29.
Orri Vésteinsson 2000. *The Christianization of Iceland: Priests, Power and Social Change*, Oxford.
Orri Vésteinsson 2006a. 'Central areas in J. Arneborg & B. Grønnow eds. *Dynamics of Northern Societies. Proceedings of the SILA/NABO Conference on Arctic and North Atlantic Archaeology, Copenhagen, May 10th–14th, 2004* (Publications of the National Museum Studies in Archaeology & History 10), Copenhagen: 307–22.
Orri Vésteinsson 2006b. 'Communities of Dispersed Settlements: Social Organisation at the Ground Level in Tenth- to Thirteenth-Century Iceland' in W. Davies, A. Reynolds & G. Halsall eds. *People and Space in the Middle Ages*, Turnhout: 87–113.
Orri Vésteinsson 2007a. 'A Divided Society: Peasants and the Aristocracy in Medieval Iceland.' *Viking and Medieval Scandinavia* 3: 117–39.
Orri Vésteinsson 2007b. '"Hann reisti hof mikið hundrað fóta langt": um uppruna hoförnefna og stjórnmál á Íslandi á 10. öld.' *Saga* 45: 53–91.
Orri Vésteinsson, 2009. 'Upphaf goðaveldis á Íslandi.' in Guðmundur Jónsson, Helgi Skúli Kjartansson & Vésteinn Ólason eds. *Heimtur. Ritgerðir til heiðurs Gunnari Karlssyni sjötugum*, Reykjavík: 298–311.
Orri Vésteinsson, 2014. 'Shopping for identities. Norse and Christian in the Viking Age North Atlantic.' in I. Garipzanov & R. Bonté eds. *Conversion and Identity in the Viking Age*, Turnhout: 75–91.
Orri Vésteinsson 2016. *Fornleifar fremst á Bárðardal vestanmegin. Mýri, Mjóidalur, Íshóll og Litlatunga* (Fornleifastofnun Íslands FS630-04193), Reykjavík.
Orri Vésteinsson 2017. 'Local church organisation and state formation in medieval Iceland.' in Guðrún Sveinbjarnardóttir & Bergur Þorgeirsson eds. *The Buildings of Medieval Reykholt. The Wider Context*, Reykjavík: 53–72.
Orri Vésteinsson, Árni Einarsson & Magnús Á Sigurgeirsson 2004. 'A New Assembly Site in Skuldaþingsey, NE-Iceland.' in Garðar Guðmundsson ed. *Current Issues in Nordic Archaeology. Proceedings of the 21st Conference of Nordic Archaeologists, 6–9 September 2001, Akureyri, Iceland*, Reykjavík: 171–79.
Orri Vésteinsson, Árný Björnsdóttir, Hildur Gestsdóttir & Heinemaier, J. 2019. 'Dating religious change: Pagan and Christian in Viking Age Iceland.' in *Viking Settlers of the North Atlantic: An Isotopic Approach. Journal of Social Archaeology* 19: 162–80.

Orri Vésteinsson, Church, M.J., Dugmore, A.J., McGovern, T.H. & Newton, A.J. 2014. 'Expensive errors or rational choices: the pioneer fringe in Late Viking Age Iceland.' *European Journal of Post-Classical Archaeologies* 4: 39-68.

Orri Vésteinsson & Hildur Gestsdóttir 2014-18. 'The colonization of Iceland in the light of isotope analysis.' in *Viking Settlers of the North Atlantic: An Isotopic Approach* (*Journal of the North Atlantic* Special Volume 7): 137-45.

Orri Vésteinsson & McGovern, T.H. 2012. 'The Peopling of Iceland.' *Norwegian Archaeological Review* 45: 206-18.

Orri Vésteinsson & McGovern, T.H. & Keller, C. 2002. 'Enduring Impacts: Social and Environmental Aspects of Viking Age Settlement in Iceland and Greenland.' *Archaeologia Islandica* 2: 98-136.

Ólafía Einarsdóttir 1964. *Studier i kronologisk metode i tidlig islandsk historieskrivning* (Bibliotheca historica Lundensis 13), Stockholm.

Ólafía Einarsdóttir 1968. 'Om de to håndskrifter af Sturlunga saga. 1. Króksfjarðarbók og Reykjarfjarðarbók.' *Arkiv för nordisk filologi* 83: 44-80.

Ólafur Arnalds, Hallmark, C.T. & Widding, L.P. 1995. 'Andisols from Four Different Regions of Iceland.' *Soil Society of America Journal* 59: 161-69.

Ólafur Halldórsson 1966. *Helgafellsbækur fornar* (Studia Islandica 24), Reykjavík.

Ólafur Halldórsson 1979. 'Sagnaritun Snorra Sturlusonar.' in Gunnar Karlsson ed. *Snorri, átta alda minning*, Reykjavík: 113-38.

Ólafur Hansson 1966. *Gissur jarl*, Reykjavík.

Ólafur Lárusson 1939. 'Ortnamn. Island.' *Nordisk kultur* 5: 60-75.

Ólafur Lárusson 1944. *Byggð og saga*, Reykjavík.

Ólafur Lárusson 1945. *Landnám á Snæfellsnesi*, Reykjavík.

Ólafur Lárusson 1958a. *Lög og saga*, Reykjavík.

Ólafur Lárusson 1958b. 'On Grágás – the oldest Icelandic code of law.' in Kristján Eldjárn ed. *Þriðji Víkingsfundur. Third Viking Congress, Reykjavík 1956* (Fylgirit, *Árbók hins íslenzka fornleifafélags* 1958), Reykjavík.: 77-89.

Ólafur Lárusson 1960a. 'Goði og goðorð.' *KLNM* v: 363-66.

Ólafur Lárusson 1960b. 'Grágás.' *KLNM* v: 410-12.

Ólafur Lárusson 1960c. 'Gårdsnavne, Island.' *KLNM* v: 642-45.

Parry, A. ed. 1971. *The Making of Homeric Verse. The Collected Papers of Milman Parry*, Oxford.

Patzuk Russell, R. 2017. *The development of education and Grammatica in Medieval Iceland*. Unpublished PhD thesis, University of Birmingham.

Páll Bergþórsson 1985. 'Sensitivity of Icelandic Agriculture to Climatic Variations.' *Climatic Change* 7: 109-37.

Páll Bergþórsson 1998. 'The Effect of Climatic Variations on Farming in Iceland.' *International Congress on the History of the Arctic and Sub-Arctic Region, Reykjavík*, June 1998.

Páll Sigurðsson 1886. 'Um forn örnefni, goðorðaskipan og fornmenjar í Rangárþingi.' *Safn til sögu Íslands* II: 498–557.

Perkins, R. 1978. *Flóamanna saga, Gaulverjabær and Haukr Erlendsson* (Studia Islandica 36), Reykjavík.

Perkins, R. 1991. 'Objects and oral tradition in medieval Iceland.' in R. McTurk & A. Wawn eds. *Úr Dölum til Dala*, Leeds: 239–66.

Pétur Sigurðsson 1933–35. 'Um Íslendinga sögu Sturlu Þórðarsonar.' *Safn til sögu Íslands* VI (2), Reykjavík.

Pétur Urbancic 1963. 'Landnám og hreppar í Austur-Húnavatnssýslu.' *Mímir* 2: 26–43.

Peters, E. 1960. 'The Proliferation of Segments in the Lineage of the Bedouin in Cyrenaica.' *Journal of the Royal Anthropological Institute* 90: 29–53.

Peters, E. 1990. *The Bedouin of Cyrenaica: Studies in Personal and Corporate Power*, Cambridge.

Pittock, A.B. et al. eds. 1978. *Climatic Change and Variability: a Southern Perspective*, Cambridge.

Pohl, W. 2016. 'Genealogy: A Comparative Perspective from the Early Medieval West.' in E. Hovden, C. Lutter & W. Pohl eds. *Meanings of Community across Medieval Eurasia. Comparative Approaches* (Brill's Series on the Early Middle Ages, 25), Turnhout: 232–69.

Porter, J. 1970–71. 'Some Aspects of Arons saga Hjörleifssonar.' *Saga-Book* 18: 136–66.

Price, T.D. & Hildur Gestsdóttir 2014–18. 'The peopling of the North Atlantic: isotopic results from Iceland.' in *Viking Settlers of the North Atlantic: An Isotopic Approach* (*Journal of the North Atlantic* Special Volume 7, 2014–2018): 146–63.

Rankovic, S. 2006. *The Distributed Author and the Poetics of Complexity: a Comparative Study of the Sagas of Icelanders and Serbian Epic Poetry*, unpublished PhD dissertation, University of Nottingham, Nottingham.

Rankovic, 2007. 'Who Is Speaking in Traditional Texts? On the Distributed Author of the Sagas of the Icelanders and Serbian Epic Poetry.' *New Literary History* 38: 293–307.

Rankovic, S. 2013. 'The Temporality of the (Immanent) Saga: Tinkering with Formulas.' in E. Mundal ed. *Dating the Sagas. Reviews and Revisions*, Copenhagen: 119–54.

Riddell, S. 2015. 'Harp Seals in the Icelandic Archaeofauna: Sea Ice and Hard Times?' *Archaeologia Icelandica* 11: 57–72.

Riddell, S., Egill Erlendsson, Guðrún Gísladóttir, Edwards, K.J., Byock, J. & Zori, D. 2018. 'Cereal cultivation as a correlate of high social status in medieval Iceland.' *Vegetation History and Archaeology* 27: 679–96.

Roberts, H.M. & Elín Ósk Hreiðarsdóttir 2013. 'The Litlu-Núpar burials.' *Archaeologia Islandica* 10: 104–30.

Ronald, K. & Healey, P.J. 1981. 'Harp Seal.' in S.H. Ridgeway & R.J. Harrison eds. *Handbook of Marine Mammals* II, London: 55–87.

Rowe, E. 1993. 'Króka-Refs saga.' in P. Pulsiano & K. Wolf eds. *Medieval Scandinavia: An Encyclopedia*, New York: 369-70.

Rowe, E. forthcoming. *The Medieval Annals of Iceland: A First English Translation*, 2 vols.

Ryder, M.L. 1983. *Sheep and Man*, London.

Samson, R. 1992. 'Goðar: Democrats or Despots?' in Gísli Pálsson ed. *From Sagas to Society. Comparative Approaches to Early Iceland*, Enfield Lock: 167-88.

Sawyer, P.H. 1987. 'The Process of Scandinavian Christianization in the tenth and eleventh centuries.' in B. Sawyer, B., P. Sawyer, P. & I.N. Wood eds. *The Christianization of Scandinavia. Report of a Symposium held at Kungälv, Sweden 4-9 August 1985*, Alingsås: 68-87.

Schledermann, H. 1975. 'Tyende.' *KLNM* XIX: 98-107.

Schmid, M.M.E., Dugmore, A.J., Orri Vésteinsson & Newton, A.J. 2017. 'Tephra isochrons and chronologies of colonisation.' *Quaternary Geochronology* 40: 56-66.

Scholes, R., Phelan, J. & Kellogg, R. 2006. *The Nature of Narrative. Fortieth Anniversary Edition, Revised and Expanded*, Oxford.

Shryock, A. 1997. *Nationalism and the Genealogical Imagination: Oral History and Textual Authority in Tribal Jordan* (Comparative Studies on Muslim Societies 23), Berkeley.

Sigríður Beck 2011. *I kungens frånvaro. Formeringen av en isländsk aristokrati 1271-1387*, Gothenburg.

Sigurdson, E. 2016. *The Church in Fourteenth-Century Iceland. The Formation of an Elite Clerical Identity*, Leiden.

Sigurður Líndal 1969. 'Sendiför Úlfljóts. Ásamt nokkrum athugasemdum um landnám Ingólfs Arnarsonar.' *Skírnir* 143: 5-26.

Sigurður Líndal 1974a. 'Ísland og umheimurinn,' *Saga Íslands* I: 199-223.

Sigurður Líndal 1974b. 'Upphaf kristni og kirkju.' *Saga Íslands* I: 227-88.

Sigurður Líndal 1976. 'Ætt. Island.' *KLNM* XX: 591-94.

Sigurður Líndal 1984. 'Lögfesting Jónsbókar.' *Tímarit lögfræðinga* 32: 182-95.

Sigurður Líndal 1992. 'Löggjafarvald og dómsvald í íslenzka þjóðveldinu.' *Skírnir* 166: 171-78.

Sigurður Nordal 1940. *Hrafnkatla* (Studia Islandica 7), Reykjavík.

Sigurður Nordal 1942. *Íslenzk menning* I. *Arfur Íslendinga*, Reykjavík.

Sigurður Nordal 1957. *The Historical Element in the Icelandic Family Sagas* (The Fifteenth W.P. Ker Memorial Lecture), Glasgow.

Sigurður Nordal 1958. *Hrafnkels saga Freysgoða. A study*, trans. R.G. Thomas, Cardiff.

Sigurður Vigfússon 1882. 'Rannsókn í Breiðafjarðardölum og í Þornesþingi og um hina nyrðri strönd.' *Árbók hins íslenzka fornleifafélags* 1882: 60-105.

Sigurður Þórarinsson 1944. *Tefrokronologiska studier på Island* (Geografiska Annaler 26), Copenhagen.

Sigurður Þórarinsson 1956. 'Ísland þjóðveldistímans og menning í ljósi landfræðilegra staðreynda.' *Skírnir* 130: 236-48.
Sigurður Þórarinsson 1958. 'Iceland in the Saga Period. Some Geographical Aspects.' in Kristján Eldjárn ed. *Þriðji Víkingsfundur. Third Viking Congress, Reykjavík 1956* (Fylgirit, *Árbók hins íslenzka fornleifafélags* 1958), Reykjavík: 13-24.
Sigurður Þórarinsson 1961. 'Population Changes in Iceland.' *Geographical Review* 51: 519-33.
Sigurður Þórarinsson 1974. 'Sambúð lands og lýðs í ellefu aldir.' *Saga Íslands* I: 29-97.
Sigurður Þórarinsson 1976. 'Gjóskulög og gamlar rústir. Brot úr íslenskri byggðasögu.' *Árbók hins íslenzka fornleifafélags*: 5-38.
Sigurður Þórarinsson. 'Jarðvísindi og Landnáma.' *Sjötíu Ritgerðir helgaðar Jakobi Benediktsson 20. júli 1977* II: 645-76.
Simon, J. 1976. 'Snorri Sturluson. His Life and Times.' *Parergon* 15: 3-15.
Simpson, I., Dugmore, A.J., Thomson, A. & Orri Vésteinsson 2001. 'Crossing the Thresholds: Human Ecology and Historical Patterns of Landscape Degradation.' *Catena* 42: 175-92.
Simpson, J. 1957-61. 'Advocacy and Art in Guðmundarsaga dýra.' *Saga-Book* 15: 327-45.
Simpson, J. 1973. 'Guðmundr Arason: A Clerical Challenge to Icelandic Society.' in *Alþjóðlegt fornsagnaþing Reykjavík 2.-8 ágúst 1973. Fyrirlestrar*, 2 vols, Reykjavík. [http://www.sagaconference.org/SC02/SC02_Simpson.pdf]
Skovgaard-Petersen, I. 1960. 'Islandsk egenkirkevæsen.' *Scandia* 26: 230-96.
Skórzewska, J. 2011. *Constructing a Cult: The Life and Veneration of Guðmundr Arason (1161-1237) in the Icelandic Written Sources* (The Northern World, 51), Leiden.
Sólveig Hauksdóttir 1974. 'Snorri Sturluson og konungsvaldið.' *Mímir* 21: 5-11.
Smith, K.P. 1995. 'Landnám: the Settlement of Iceland in Archaeological and Historical Perspective.' *World Archaeology* 26: 319-47.
Smith, K.P. & Parsons, J.P. 1989. 'Regional Archaeological Research in Iceland: Potential and Possibilities.' in E.P. Durrenberger & Gísli Pálsson eds. *The Anthropology of Iceland*, Iowa: 170-202.
Spiegel. G.M. 1983. 'Genealogy: Form and Function in Medieval Historical Narrative.' *History and Theory* 22: 43-53.
Spiegel, G.M. 2016. 'Structures of Time in Medieval Historiography.' *The Journal of Medieval History* 19: 21-33.
Steblin-Kamenskij, M.I. 1973. *The Saga Mind*, trans. K.H. Ober, Odense.
Stefán Aðalsteinsson 1981. *Sauðkindin, landið og þjóðin*, Reykjavík.
Stefán Aðalsteinsson 1991. 'Importance of Sheep in Early Icelandic Agriculture.' *Acta Archaeologica* 61: 285-91.
Stefán Aðalsteinsson 1996. 'Uppruni íslenskra húsdýra' in Guðrún Ása Grímsdóttir ed. *Um Landnám á Íslandi. Fjórtán Erindi*, Reykjavík: 73-80.
Stefán Karlsson 1964. 'Aldur Hauksbókar.' *Fróðskaparit* 13: 114-21.

Stefán Karlsson 1985. 'Guðmundar sögur biskups: Authorial Viewpoints and Methods.' in J. Louis-Jensen, C. Sanders & P. Springborg eds, *The Sixth International Saga Conference, 28.7-28.8 1985: Workshop papers I–II*, Copenhagen, II: 983–1005.

Stefán Karlsson 1988. 'Alfræði Sturlu Þorðarsonar.' in Guðrún Ása Grímsdóttir & Jónas Kristjánsson eds. *Sturlustefna. Ráðstefna haldin á sjö alda ártíð Sturlu Þórðarsonar sagnaritara 1984* (Rit Stofnunar Árna Magnússonar 32), Reykjavík: 37–60.

Stefán Karlsson 1993. 'Guðmundar sögur biskups.' in P. Pulsiano & K. Wolf eds. *Medieval Scandinavia: An Encyclopedia*, New York: 245–46.

Stefán Karlsson 1999. 'The Localisation and Dating of Medieval Icelandic Manuscripts.' *Saga-Book* 25: 138–58.

Stein-Wilkeshuis, M. 1982. 'The Rights to Social Welfare in Early Medieval Iceland.' *Journal of Medieval History* 8: 343–52.

Stein-Wilkeshuis, M. 1986. 'Laws in Medieval Iceland.' *Journal of Medieval History* 12: 37–53.

Stein-Wilkeshuis, M. 1987. 'Common Land Tenure in Medieval Iceland.' *Recueils de la société Jean Bodin* 44: 575–85.

Stenberger, M. 1943. *Forntida gårdar i Island*, Copenhagen.

Strömbäck, D. 1975. *The Conversion of Iceland. A Survey*, trans. P. Foote (Viking Society for Northern Research, Text Series, vol. 6), London.

Sturla Friðriksson 1972. 'Grass and Grass Utilization in Iceland.' *Ecology* 53: 785–96.

Sturla Friðriksson 1973. 'Crop Production in Iceland.' *International Journal of Biometeorology* 17: 359–62.

Svanhildur Óskarsdóttir 1992. 'Að kenna of rita tíða á millum: Um trúarviðhorf Guðmundar Arasonar.' *Skáldskaparmál* 2: 229–38.

Svavar Sigmundsson 2009. *Nefningar*, Reykjavík.

Sveinbjörn Rafnsson 1974. *Studier i Landnámabók. Kritiska bidrag till den isländska fristatstidens historia* (Bibliotheca Historica Lundensis 31), Lund.

Sveinbjörn Rafnsson 1975. 'Saga Íslands I–II.' (Review) *Skírnir* 149: 210–22.

Sveinbjörn Rafnsson 1979. 'Um kristnitökufrásögn Ara prests Þorgilssonar.' *Skírnir* 153: 167–74.

Sveinbjörn Rafnsson 1982. 'Skriftaboð Þorláks biskups.' *Gripla* 5: 77–114.

Sveinbjörn Rafnsson 1985. 'Um Staðarhólsmál Sturlu Þórðarsonar.' *Skírnir* 159: 143–59.

Sveinbjörn Rafnsson 2001. *Sögugerð Landnámabókar. Um íslenska sagnaritun á 12. og 13. öld*, Reykjavík.

Sveinbjörn Rafnsson 2017. '*Landnámabók* and Its *Sturlubók* version' in Jón Viðar Sigurðsson & Sverrir Jakobsson eds. *Sturla Þórðarson. Skáld, Chieftain and Lawman*, Leiden.

Sveinn Skúlason 1856. 'Æfi Sturlu lögmanns Þorðarsonar og stutt yfirlit þess er gjörðist um hans daga.' *Safn til sögu Íslands* I: 503–639.

Sveinn Víkingur 1970. *Getið í eyður sögunnar*, Reykjavík.

Sverrir Jakobsson 1998a. 'Griðamál á ófriðaröld.' in Guðmundur J. Guðmundsson & Eiríkur K. Björnsson eds. *Íslenska söguþingið 28.-31. mai 1997*, 2 vols, Reykjavík: 117-34.

Sverrir Jakobsson 1998b. 'Friðarviðleitni kirkjunnar á 13. öld.' *Saga* 36: 7-46

Sverrir Jakobsson, 2002. 'Braudel í Breiðafirði? Breiðafjörðurinn og hinn breiðfirski heimur á öld Sturlunga.' *Saga* 40: 150-79.

Sverrir Jakobsson 2005. *Við og Veröldin. Heimsmynd Íslendinga 1100-1400*, Reykjavík.

Sverrir Jakobsson 2007a. 'Strangers in Icelandic Society.' *Viking and Medieval Scandinavia* 3: 141-57.

Sverrir Jakobsson. 2007b. 'Hauksbók and the Construction of an Icelandic World View.' *Saga-Book* 31: 22-38.

Sverrir Jakobsson 2008. 'The Peace of God in Iceland in the 12th and 13th centuries' in P. Krafl ed. *Sacri canones servandi sunt. Ius canonicum et status ecclesiae saeculis XIII-XV*, Prague: 205-13.

Sverrir Jakobsson 2009. 'The Process of State Formation in Medieval Iceland.' *Viator* 40: 151-70.

Sverrir Jakobsson 2010. 'Heaven is a Place on Earth: Church and Sacred Space in Thirteenth-Century Iceland.' *Scandinavian Studies* 82: 1-20.

Sverrir Jakobsson 2013. 'Konur og völd í Breiðafirði á miðöldum.' *Skírnir* 187: 161-75.

Sverrir Jakobsson 2015. *Saga Breiðfirðinga I. Fólk og rými frá landnámi til plágurnar miklu*, Reykjavík.

Sverrir Jakobsson 2016. *Auðnaróðal. Baráttan um Ísland 1096-1281*, Reykjavík.

Thornton, D.E. 1992. 'A neglected genealogy of Llewellyn-Ap-Gruffudd.' *Cambridge Medieval Celtic Studies* 23: 9-23.

Thornton, D.E. 2002. 'Identifying Celts in the Past: A Methodology.' *Historical Methods* 35.2: 84-91.

Torfi H. Tulinius 2013. 'Dating Eyrbyggja saga. The Value of "Circumstantial" Evidence for Determining the Time of Composition of Sagas about Early Icelanders.' in E. Mundal ed. *Dating the Sagas. Reviews and Revisions*, Copenhagen: 115-32.

Torfi H. Tulinius 2016. '*Hvers Manns Gagn*. Hrafn Sveinbjarnarson and the Social Role of Icelandic Chieftains Around 1200.' *Saga-Book* 40: 91-104.

Tranter, S.N. 1987. *Sturlunga saga. The Rôle of the Creative Compiler* (European University Studies I. German Language and Literature 941), Frankfurt am Main.

Turville-Petre, G. 1953. *Origins of Icelandic Literature*, Oxford.

Turville-Petre, J. 1978-81. 'The Genealogist and History: Ari to Snorri.' *Saga-Book* 20: 7-23.

Úlfar Bragason 1981. 'Frásagnarmynstur í Þorgils sögu skarða.' *Skírnir* 155: 161-70.

Úlfar Bragason 1986. 'Hetjudauði Sturlu Sighvatssonar.' *Skírnir* 160: 64-78.

Úlfar Bragason 1988. 'The Structure and Meaning of *Hrafns saga Sveinbjarnarsonar*.' *Scandinavian Studies* 60: 267-92.

Úlfar Bragason 1989. '"Hart er í heimi, hórdómur mikill" Lesið í Sturlungu.' *Skírnir* 163: 54-71.
Úlfar Bragason 1991. 'The Art of Dying.' *Scandinavian Studies* 63: 453-63.
Úlfar Bragason 1992. 'Sturlunga saga: Textar og rannsóknir.' *Skáldskaparmál* 2: 177-206.
Úlfar Bragason 1993. 'Um ættartölur í *Sturlungu*.' *Tímarit Máls og menningar* 54: 27-35.
Úlfar Bragason 1994. 'Um samsetningu Þórðar sögu kakala.' in Gísli Sigurðsson, Guðrún Kvaran & Sigurgeir Steingrímsson eds. *Sagnaþing helgað Jónasi Kristjánssyni sjötugum 10. apríl 1994*, 2 vols., Reykjavík: 815-22.
Úlfar Bragason 2004. 'The Politics of Genealogy in *Sturlunga saga*.' in J. Adams & K. Holman eds. *Scandinavia and Europe 800-1350*, Turnhout: 309-21.
Úlfar Bragason 2010. *Ætt og saga: um frásagnarfræði Sturlungu eða Íslendinga sögu hinnar miklu*, Reykjavik.
Úlfar Bragason 2013. 'Arons saga: Minningar, mýtur og sagnaminni.' Ritið: *Tímarit Hugvísindastofnunar Háskóla Íslands*, 13(3): 125-45.
Vansina, J. 1985. *Oral Tradition as History*, Madison.
Vestergaard, T.A. 1988. 'The System of Kinship in Early Norwegian Law.' *Mediaeval Scandinavia* 12: 160-93.
Vésteinn Ólason 1998. *Dialogues with the Viking Age*, Reykjavík 1998.
Vésteinn Ólason 1971. 'Nokkrar athugasemdir um Eyrbyggja sögu.' *Skírnir* 145: 5-25.
Vésteinn Ólason 1973. 'Concentration of Power in 13th Century Iceland and its Reflection in Some Íslendingasögur.' in *Alþjóðlegt fornsagnaþing. Reykjavík 2.-8 ágúst 1973. Fyrirlestrar* II. hefti, Reykjavík.
Vésteinn Ólason 1991. '"Máhlíðingamál": authorship and tradition in a part of *Eyrbyggja saga*.' in R. McTurk & A. Wawn eds. *Úr Dölum til Dala. Guðbrandur Vigfússon Centenary essays* (Leeds Texts and Monographs, New Series 11), Leeds: 187-203.
Vilhjámur Árnason 1991. 'Morality and Social Structure in the Icelandic Sagas.' *Journal of English and Germanic Philology* 90: 157-74.
Viðar Pálsson 2003. '"Var engi höfðingi slíkr sem Snorri?": Auður og virðing í valdabaráttu Snorra Sturlusonar.' *Saga* 41: 55-96.
Viðar Pálsson 2017. *Language of Power. Feasting and Gift-Giving in Medieval Iceland and Its Sagas*, Ithaca: 2017.
Vries, J. de 1964-67. *Altnordische Literaturgeschichte* I-II, 2nd ed., Berlin.
Wastl, M., Stötter, J. & Caseldine, C.J. 2001. 'Sea-Ice-Climate-Glacier Relationships in Northern Iceland Since the Nineteenth Century: Possible Analogues for the Holocene.' in P.D. Jones, A.E.J. Ogilvie, T.D. Davies & K.R. Briffa eds. *History and Climate. Memories of the Future?*, New York: 187-200.
West, C. 2012. 'Dynastic Historical Writing.' in S. Foot & C. Robinson eds. *The Oxford History of Historical Writing, Volume II: 600-1400*, Oxford: 496-516.

Whaley, D. 2000. 'A useful past: historical writing in medieval Iceland.' in M. Clunies Ross ed. *Old Icelandic Literature and Society*, Cambridge: 161–202.
Wickham, C.J. 1988. *The Mountains and the City. The Tuscan Appenines in the Early Middle Ages*, Oxford.
Wickham, C.J. 1995. 'Gossip and Resistance among the Medieval Peasantry.' *Past and Present* 160: 3–24.
Wickham, C.J. 2005. *Framing the Early Middle Ages*, Oxford.
Wood, I. 1987. 'Christians and Pagans in Ninth-century Scandinavia.' in B. Sawyer, P. Sawyer, & I.N. Wood eds. 1987. *The Christianization of Scandinavia. Report of a Symposium held at Kungälv, Sweden 4–9 August 1985*, Alingsås: 36–67.
Zori, D., Byock, J., Erlendsson, E., Martin, S., Wake, T., & Edwards, K.J. 2013. 'Feasting in Viking Age Iceland: sustaining a chiefly political economy in a marginal environment.' *Antiquity* 87: 150–65.
Zori, D. & J.L. Byock 2014. *Viking Archaeology in Iceland. Mosfell Archaeological Project*, Turnhout.
Zori, D. 2016. 'The Norse in Iceland.' *Oxford Handbooks Online*. DOI: 10.1093/oxfordhb/9780199935413.013.7
Þorkell Bjarnason 1883. 'Um fiskveiðar Íslendinga og útlendinga við Ísland að fornu og nýju.' *Tímarit Hins íslenzka bókmenntafélags* IV: 166–242.
Þorsteinn Þórarinsson 1974. 'Þjóðin lifði en skógurinn dó.' *Ársrit Skógræktarfélags Íslands*: 16–29.
Þorvaldur Thoroddsen 1892–1904. *Landfræðisaga Íslands. Hugmyndir manna um Ísland, náttúruskoðun þess og rannsóknir, fyrr og síðar* I–II, Reykjavík.
Þorvaldur Thoroddsen 1908–22. *Lýsing Íslands* I–IV, Copenhagen.
Þorvaldur Thoroddsen 1913–15. *Ferðabók. Skýrslur um rannsóknir á Íslandi 1882–1898* I–IV, Reykjavík.
Þóra Ellen Þórhallsdóttir 1996. 'Áhrif búsetu á landið.' in Guðrún Ása Grímsdóttir ed. *Um Landnám á Íslandi. Fjórtán Erindi*, Reykjavík: 149–70.
Þórhallur Vilmundarson 1971. '-stad. Island.' *KLNM* XVI: 378–84.
Þórhallur Vilmundarson 1977. 'Ólafur chaim.' *Skírnir* 151: 133–62.
Ævar Petersen 1979. 'Varpfuglar Flateyjar á Breiðafirði og nokkurn nærliggjandi eyja.' *Náttúrufræðingurinn* 49/2–3: 229–56.
Ævar Petersen 1993. 'Rostungar við Ísland að fornu og nýju.' in Páll Hersteinsson & Guttormur Sigbjarnarson eds. 1993. *Villt íslensk spendýr*, Reykjavík: 214–16.
Ævar Petersen 2008. 'Seabird harvest in the Arctic.' in Merkel, F. and Barry, T. eds. *CAFF International Secretariat, Circumpolar Seabird Group* (CAFF Technical Report No. 16), 50–58. [https://www.caff.is/expert-groups-series/circumpolar-seabird-expert-group-cbird]
Ævar Petersen 2010. *Fuglalíf í Flatey á Skjálfanda* (Náttúrufræðistofnun Íslands NÍ-10001), Reykjavík.

Ævar Petersen, Árni Björnsson & Eysteinn G. Gíslason 1989. 'Breiðafjarðareyjar.' *Árbók Ferðafélag Íslands* 1989: 17–218.

Ævar Petersen & Gaukur Hjartarson 1993. *Vetrarfuglatalningar: Áragangur 1989* (Fjölrit Náttúrufræðistofnunar 23), Reykjavík.

Index

Icelandic names are in alphabetical order by first name then patronymic or surname. The alphabetical order is: a á b c d ð e é f g h i í j k l m n o ó p q r s t u ú v w x y ý z þ æ ö ø å ä.

Certain freqently mentioned places, concepts and terms are omitted, e.g. Dalir, Breiðafjörður, Eyjafjörður, *goði, goðorð, þing*, discussion of which can usually be found via the list of contents or under specific proper nouns, e.g. *Eyvellingagoðorð*. Individuals without patronymics or matronymics are listed before those with them. References to notes indicate the page on which the item can be found. Most clergy have been identified as such, e.g *prestr, djákn*.

Adolf Friðriksson 187n, 201
aðalból 5, 157
Aðaldalur 4n, 294n
   see also Reykjadalur
Akranes 35n
Akrar 291n
Akureyjar 39n
Akureyri 4, 29–30, 195, 201, 286n, 291
Alþing 10, 12, 18, 32n, 48n, 65, 86, 88n, 110, 127, 129, 262, 293
Andersson, Theodore M. 206–7, 208–9, 220, 221, 222, 270n, 271–73, 274–75, 278, 297n
Andreas Brandsson (d. 1254) 139n
annal 2, 47n, 61, 65, 79, 109, 216, 218, 307, 309
Annales School 1
archaeology 5, 6–9, 10, 29, 31, 36, 38, 39n, 41n, 147, 198, 310
archbishop, of Niðarós 21, 48, 49
   see also Eiríkr
Ari Ingimundarson 139n
Ari Þorgeirsson (d. 1166) 67, 127, 317
Ari *fróði* Þorgilsson, priest, scholar (d. 1148) 9–10, 11, 59, 86, 150, 154, 155–56, 157, 161n, 169, 203, 225, 226, 248, 249n
Ari *inn sterki* Þorgilsson (d. 1188) 59, 61, 72, 216, 236
Arnarbæli 106
Arnarfjörður 74, 75, 255, 322
Arnkatla Þórðardóttir 170
Arnkell Þórólfsson 244, 245, 246–48, 253, 265, 266
Arnleif Þórðardóttir 177n
Arnóra Gunnbjarnardóttir 173
Arnóra Þórðardóttir 177n
Arnórr Hrútsson 171

Arnórr Þorgrímsson 195, 288, 293, 295
Arnórr Tumason (d. 1221) 49, 142
Arnþrúðarsynir 79n, 127, 128, 132n, 140
Arnþrúðr Fornadóttir 79n, 127
Aron *kjúkabassi* 136
Aron Hjörleifsson (d. 1255) 17, 62, 102–3, 119n, 120n, 136n
Arons saga Hjörleifssonar 17, 62n, 111
Atli *inn rammi* Eilífsson 282n
Atli Hrútsson 171
Atli Tannason 183
Auðbrekka 131, 193
Auðbrekkumenn 193
Auðólfr 190, 194
Auðr *in djúpauðga* Ketilsdóttir 150n, 155, 159, 161–62, 163, 164–67, 168n, 169–70, 171, 172, 173–74, 176–78, 179, 184, 185, 186–87, 191, 197, 201, 202, 203, 204, 214, 218, 255, 310, 313
   Unnr *in djúpúðga* 164n, 214, 218, 224–25, 228, 235, 242, 310, 313
Auðun *stoti* Válason 175, 179n
Auðun *rotinn* Þórólfsson 190, 192, 282
austmaðr (Norwegian), byname and generic term 71, 73, 104, 162, 317
autumn 37n, 132
autumn assembly 10n (*leið*), 281n (*haustþing*)
Álfr í Dölum 172, 173
Álfr Snorrason 96
Álftanes, Mýrar 123
Álof Þorgeirsdóttir 70, 72n
Álptafjörðr, Álptafjörður 22, 33n, 163n, 175, 177–79, 223, 245–48, 250n, 251n, 252, 254, 264, 265, 266
Álptfirðingar 223
Ármann Jakobsson 207

INDEX 363

Ármóðr Þorgrímsson of Þykkvaskógr 230n, 238, 241, 257
Ármóðssynir 172, 241
Árna saga biskups 15n, 17, 48n
Árnessýsla 104
Árnesþing 12, 45
Árni Auðunarson (d. 1238) 104, 106
Árni Hjaltason, Abbot of Þverá (d. 1252) 139n, 141
Árni *óreiða* Magnússon (d. 1250) 73
Árni Pálsson (d. 1952) 19
Árni Þorláksson, Bishop of Skálholt (d. 1298) 15n, 17, 73n
Árskógr 23, 132, 144, 193, 274, 286
Árskógsströnd 131, 193, 280, 299, 300, 311
Ásbirningar 46, 48, 69, 73, 74, 76, 77, 81, 82, 83, 135, 224
Ásbjarnarnes, Víðidalur 238
Ásbjörn Arnórsson 320
Ásbjörn Hallsson 83
Ásgarðr 77, 92, 94, 95, 97, 104, 111
Ásgeirr, who killed Sámr 178
Ásgeirr *rauðfeldr* 270, 298, 299, 300
Ásgeirr *æðikollr* 169n, 170n
Ásgeirr Auðunarson 238
Ásgeirr Erpsson 173
Ásgeirr Kjartansson 170n
Ásgeirr *af/á Eyri* Vestarsson 177, 244, 245, 251, 254
Ásgeirsá, Víðidalur 87
Ásgilsstaðir 284n
Ásgrímr of (Munka)þverá 140n
Ásgrímr Þorsteinsson (d. 1285) 122, 143
Ásgrímr *auðgi* Þorvaldsson (d. 1178) 64, 78, 80
Ásgrímr Öndóttsson 163, 189, 196
Áskell *goði* Eyvindarson 66, 284–86, 287n, 288, 289, 305
Áslákr Þorbergsson 177n, 253, 254
Ásmundr Öndóttsson 163, 191, 196
Áss, Skagafjörður 72
Ástríðr Hrólfsdóttir 176n
Ávík, Strandir 91

Bakki (Staðarbakki) in Helgafellssveit 248, 250, 251, 269
Bakki, Öxnadalur 47, 64, 78, 83, 129, 130, 131, 134, 139n, 321
Ballará 58n, 116, 183n

Barð 25
Barðaströnd 59n, 91, 238, 256
Barði Guðmundsson (d. 1957) 63, 64, 157
Barkarstaðir 181n, 268
barley 30n
Baugsstaðir, Árnessýsla 104n
Bárðardalur 30, 195, 197, 198, 201, 287–88, 289, 296
Bárðr *inn svarti* Atlason 320
Bárðr Hallason 281n
Bárðr Heyjangrs-Bjarnarson (Gnúpa-Bárðr) 197, 198
Bárðr Höskuldsson 170, 230, 232
Bárðr *prestr* Snorrason 71, 117
Bárðr Þorkelsson 116
Bedouin 149, 150, 151
Beinir Hjaltason 173
Bergþórr Jónsson (d. 1232) 111n
Bergþórr Þorláksson 251
berserks 249n
Berserkseyrr 102
Bersi *inn auðgi* Vermundarson (d. 1202) 72–73
Bersi Véleifsson (Hólmgöngu-Bersi) 237, 237n
Bessatunga 237
Birnunes 299
bishop 6, 9, 15, 19, 20, 24, 25, 45, 144, 155, 156–57, 159, 216, 320
Bishops' sagas (*biskupasögur*) 9, 15n, 45
Bitra, Strandir 107, 114, 223, 245, 267
Bíldsá 189n
Bjarnareyjar 36, 37n, 103n
Bjarnarfjörður 238, 262, 263n
Bjarnarhöfn 22, 98, 102, 111, 119, 121n, 158, 162, 165, 174, 175, 176n, 177, 178, 179, 180–81, 184, 185, 226, 244, 245, 248, 249–50, 252, 253, 254, 269, 310
Bjarnarstaðir 182n
Bjarni Árnason (d. 1227) 103n
Bjarni Snorrason 124
Björn *drumbr* Dufgusson 71, 121, 122
see also Dufgusssynir
Björn *kægill* Dufgusson 71
see also Dufgusssynir
Björn Gilsson, Abbot of Þverá (d. 1181) 46n
Björn Gilsson, Bishop of Hólar (d. 1162) 46, 282n
Björn Helgason (Heyjangrs-Björn) 197

Björn *inn austrœni* Ketilsson   150n, 160n, 162, 163, 164, 165, 174–76, 176n, 177n, 179, 180, 185, 187, 197, 202, 203, 204, 220–21, 248, 249, 250, 263
Björn *inn sterki* Kjallaksson   160n, 176n, 180
Björn Sigfússon (d. 1991)   19, 291n, 304
Björn *buna* Veðrar-Grímsson   150–51, 159, 161, 162, 197, 198, 280
Björn Þorsteinsson   77–78
Blund-Ketill Geirsson   169
Blönduhlíð, Skagafjörður   139n
boat   38n
Bohannan, Laura (d. 2002)   148–49
Bolla þáttr   217, 278, 306n
Bolli Bollason   170, 215–16, 217, 229, 240
Bolli Þorleiksson   170, 170n, 171, 172, 215, 228, 230, 231, 234–35, 240, 241, 242, 266, 267n
Book of Icelanders, see *Íslendingabók*
Book of Settlements, see *Landnámabók*
Borg, Borgarfjörður   46, 72, 98, 169, 238
Borgardalr   175
Borgfirðingar   226
Borgarfjörður   8, 27n, 33n, 46, 50, 51, 53, 55, 72, 76, 83, 86, 98, 122, 123, 138, 141n, 168–69, 183n, 187, 216, 217n, 226, 237n, 238, 243, 261n, 323
boundary
   farm   27, 28n, 234, 242, 294
   hreppr   4, 19n, 159, 180–81, 291, 299
   landnám   157, 158, 159, 180–81, 182, 189–90, 191, 194, 196
   ministery   21
   sýsla   4, 192
bólstaðr, place-name element   247n
Bólstaðr   244–45, 246–47, 248, 253, 310
bóndi (pl. *bændr*)   12, 36, 42, 48, 54, 56, 60n, 74n, 84, 91, 92, 95, 97, 100–4, 106, 107, 108, 110, 111, 112, 113, 114, 117, 119, 125, 129, 130, 132, 133, 134, 136, 138, 139n, 141, 142, 144, 145–46, 205, 211, 230, 257, 258, 259, 265, 268, 273n, 280, 281, 285, 287, 287n, 288–89, 292, 293, 295–96, 301n, 302, 314, 318
   see also *stórbóndi*
Brady, Lindy   2n
Brandr Daðason   79n
Brandr Eyjólfsson (Arnþrúðarson)   79n
   see also Arnþrúðarsynir

Brandr Gellison   87
Brandr Jónsson, Abbot of Þykkvibær, Bishop of Hólar (d. 1264)   118, 120
Brandr Knakansson   82
Brandr Kolbeinsson (d. 1246)   52, 75, 80, 143
Brandr Sæmundarson, Bishop of Hólar (d. 1201)   81, 127
Brandr Tjörvason   81n
Brandr Vermundarson   250
Brandr Þorkelsson (Vöðu-Brandr)   293
Brandr Þórarinsson   215
Brandr Þórhallsson   100–1
Brattavöllr   132
Breiðabólstaðr, Borgarfjörður   169, 169n
Breiðabólstaðr, Skógarströnd   175, 177, 181n, 185, 202, 254, 255, 269
Breiðabólstaðr, Vestrhóp, Húnavatnssýsla   82, 85–86, 128
Brekka see Ósbrekka; Skeggjabrekka
Brekka, Svarfaðardalur   271n, 299, 300
Brennihóll   286n
Bretalækr   116n
Brettingsstaðir   296
Brimilsvellir   175
Brunná   60, 89, 112
Brúnastaðir   271n
Brúni Hrólfsson (?)   92
búð   37n
Búðardalr, Laxárdalur   37n
Búðardalr/-ur, Skarðsströnd   22n, 40n, 96, 109, 181
Búlandshöfði   175
byggð   6, 145, 314
Byock, Jesse L.   13, 17, 18
Bægisá farms, river   130, 194, 196, 291n
Bær, Hrútafjörður   183
Böðvarr Barkarson   89, 94, 94n
Böðvarr Eyjólfsson   278n
Böðvarr Sigurðarson   302, 304n
Böðvarr Þórðarson   58, 59, 60, 71, 74, 75, 77, 99, 110, 113, 114, 116, 118, 119, 120, 124–25, 216
Böggvir Karlsson   300
Böggvisstaðir   300
Börkr Guðmundarson (Öxna-Börkr)   136n
Börkr Kálfsson   92, 93
Börkr *inn digri* Þorsteinsson   168, 178, 181, 227, 249, 251–52, 268

INDEX

canon law 219, 220
cattle 2, 7, 23n, 27, 30, 31, 32, 107, 118, 247n, 287n, 310
cemetery 8, 252
charcoal making 32, 33
charter, *see máldagi*
church, building, property, and individual churches 19–26, 28n, 30, 31, 34, 35, 36, 38n, 39–40, 41, 42n, 48, 72n, 76–77, 78, 94, 96, 108, 109n, 130n, 143, 144, 199, 228, 232n, 242, 246, 247n, 256–57, 267, 271n, 275, 280n, 282, 284, 287, 294n, 299n, 300, 302n, 315, 316, 317
see also church owner, *staðr*
private church 20, 48
see also *staðamál*
church-farm, *see staðr*
church owner 19, 76–77, 111, 316
church, the 13, 19–26, 30, 31–32, 35, 40, 46, 80, 82–83, 217, 308, 316
climate 29–30
Clover, Carol 154, 207–9, 218, 222, 270
colonisation *see landnám*
Commonwealth (*Þjóðveldið*) 10, 13, 134, 219
concubine (*frilla*) 70, 75, 102, 105, 119, 300
contemporary sagas see *samtíðarsögur*
crustacea 35–36, 37, 162, 310
Cyrenaica 149

Dagr, husband of Sigríðr Þorgeirsdóttir 295n
Dala-Kollr *see* Kollr
Dalamaðr 100n
Dalasýsla 3, 5, 35, 166
Davies, Wendy 2
deacon (*djákn*) 21, 73n (*subdjákn*) 82, 100, 108, 118
demography, see population
diocese, *see* see
Disciplina Clericalis 275
Djúpadalr/-ur 23n, 25, 190, 191, 282
Draflastaðir 23, 296
Drangar 194n
Drangareka 51n
Drauma-Finni see Finni Þorgeirsson
Drápuhlíð 185, 248, 250–51, 252n
driftage, see *reki*
Dritvík, Snæfellsnes 37n
Duby, Georges (d. 1996) 1

Dufgus Þorleifsson 71, 72, 100, 101, 103, 104, 106, 112, 117n, 122, 125
Dufgusssynir, the sons of Dufgus Þorleifsson 107, 112, 114, 115, 117n, 121, 122, 264
see also Björn *drumbr*, Björn *kægill*, Kolbeinn *grön*, Svarthöfði
Dufnall Erpsson 173
Durrenberger, Paul 14
Dynhagi 131
Dýrfirðingagoðorð 58
Dögurðará, river 165, 180
Dögurðarnes (Dagverðarnes) 116, 181
Dönustaðir 232n, 233, 265

Eastern Quarter 4, 12, 25, 45, 82
East Fjords 75
Edwards, Paul 220n
eggs, see wildfowl
Egill Skallagrímsson 170, 238
Egill Sölmundarson (d. 1297) 73
Egils saga Skallagrímssonar 214, 238
eider ducks see wildfowl
Eið 251n
Eilífr *skyti* Hrólfsson (?) 292
Eilífr Ketilsson 168
Einar Ólafur Sveinsson (d. 1984) 225
Einarr Arnórsson 292, 297
Einarr Eyjólfsson 46n, 273n, 274, 279, 280, 281–82, 283, 291, 292, 294, 297, 303
Einarr Grímsson(?) of Gaddsvík (d. 1254?) 139n
Einarr Hallsson of Möðruvellir 64n, 65–66, 134
Einarr Helgason (Ingibjargarson) 89n, 95
Einarr Ketilsson 174
Einarr Konálsson 289
Einarr Þorgeirsson 200
Einarr Þorgilsson (d. 1185) 60, 61, 76n, 88–89, 90, 92, 94–96, 97, 99, 112, 216, 314, 321
Einarr Þorgrímsson (d. 1254) 139n
Einarsstaðir 88, 142
Eindriði Hrútsson 171
Eiríkr Ívarsson, Archbishop of Niðarós (d. 1205) 21, 48
Eiríkr *rauði* Þorvaldsson 163, 165, 174–75n, 181n, 222, 227, 254, 269n
Eiríks saga rauða 181n, 218, 222, 226, 227, 254, 255, 269n

Eiríksstaðir 255
Eirný Þiðrandadóttir 183n
Eldey, island off the south-west coast of Iceland 37
Eldjárn of Fljótsdalshérað 82
Eldjárn *prestr* Steingrímsson 82n
Elín Bára Magnúsdóttir 219–20
ell 23n
England 153n
Erlendr *prestr* Hallason 92, 94–95
Erpr 165, 166, 167, 172–73, 235
Erpsstaðir 167, 173, 202, 235, 300n
Esjuvellir, see Hesjuvellir
Esphælingagoðorð 57
Esphælingar 279, 280–81, 282, 283
Esphælinga saga 275n
Espihóll 34, 65, 82, 133, 137, 191, 198n, 203, 276, 278, 279, 281, 283, 290, 311, 312
    Espihóll inn nyrðri 191n, 276, 281n
    Espihóll inn syðri (Litli-Hóll) 189, 190, 191, 195, 276, 278, 279, 281, 282, 290, 311, 312
exports 27n, 36
Eyfirðingar 54, 141, 144, 303
Eyjafjarðardalur 5, 281, 282n, 283
Eyjafjarðarsýsla 4, 5
Eyjardalsá 23
Eyjólfr Brandsson (d. 1293) 79n
Eyjólfr Guðmundarson 196n, 287n, 292–93, 296
Eyjólfr Hallbjarnarson 183n
Eyjólfr *prestr* Hallsson (d. 1210) 40n, 78, 83n
Eyjólfr Ingjaldsson 278
Eyjólfr Kársson (d. 1222) 100, 101n, 102
Eyjólfr Narfason 280n
Eyjólfr Valgerðarson 46n, 192, 279, 288, 289, 290, 302, 302n 303
Eyjólfr Valla-Brandsson, priest, then Abbot of Munkaþverá (d. 1293) 78n, 141
Eyjólfr *breiðhöfði* Þorgilsson 278n
Eyjólfr *ofsi* Þorsteinsson (d. 1255) 53, 54, 75, 140–41, 143
Eyjólfr *grái* Þórðarson 221, 227, 254
Eyjólfr Æsuson 163n, 181n, 254
Eyrarbakki 35n
Eyrarland 175
Eyrarsveit 28n, 31n, 37n, 40n, 251, 268
Eyrbyggjar 221, 244, 251n

Eyrbyggja saga 18, 33n, 57n, 61, 152n, 161, 163n, 166, 175, 176n, 177, 178–79, 181n, 185, 187, 205, 212, 213, 214, 219–26, 227, 230, 243–55, 249n, 252n, 260, 263, 265–69, 306n, 310
Eyrar-Snorri see Snorri Pálsson
Eyrr, Arnarfjörður 75
Eyrr, *see* Narfeyri; Öndverðareyrr
Eysteinn Rauðólfsson 196
Eysteinsstaðir 182n
Eyvellingagoðorð 90, 91, 316
Eyvindr *eldr* 171
Eyvindr *hani* 196
Eyvindr *austmaðr* Bjarnarson 162

Fagradalr/-ur/Fagradalur 39n, 89, 96, 97, 97n, 106n, 125, 182, 258, 260
Fagraskógr 132n
Family sagas, see *Íslendingasögur*
farm abandonment 7–8, 181n, 245, 246, 247n, 291, 294n, 308
farmstead *see lögbýli*
Fell see Staðarfell
Fell, district near Ljósavatn 197, 197n, 285, 294n, 295n
Fell, Kollafjörður 35n
Fellsendi 77, 100–1, 108, 111
Fellsmúli *see* Múli
Fell-Snorri *see* Snorri Þórðarson
Fellsstrendingar 181
Fellsströnd 33, 103, 104, 109, 110, 111, 112, 125, 159, 160, 165, 166, 176, 179–81, 185, 243, 251, 252, 268
feudalism 54
Fifth Court (*Fimmtadómr*) 12
Finnastaðir, Eyjafjörður 23n
Finnastaðir, Fnjóskadalur 296
Finnbjörn Helgason (d. 1255) 52n, 53, 54, 82n, 141, 143, 204n
Finnegan, Ruth 209
Finngeirr 163n, 175, 246, 266
Finni Þorgeirsson (Drauma-Finni, Finnr *enn draumspaki*) 294n, 295n, 296
Finnr Hallsson 86
First Grammatical Treatise (*Fyrsta málfræðiritgerðin*) 9
fish and fishing 2, 5, 27, 29, 35–38, 113, 162, 204, 310
    beinahákarl 37

INDEX

cod 35, 37, 37n
haddock 35
hákarl (shark) 38n
herring 37
lumpfish 37, 37n, 38n
salmon 27, 35, 36, 38
skreið (stockfish) 36, 37
trout 35, 36, 38
fishing nets 36
fishing seasons 37
fishing stations (*verbúð*) 29, 36, 37
Fiskilækjarhverfi 191
Fiskilækr 190, 191, 195
Fjörleif Eyvindardóttir 197, 284n
Fjörleifarsynir 284n, 285n
Flatey, Breiðafjörður 31n, 41, 42, 46, 50–51, 53, 73, 74n, 101n, 102, 113, 114, 116, 183
  see also monastery
Flatey, off Flateyjardalur, north-east 36, 41n, 285, 294n
Flateyjarbók 283n
Flateyjardalur 296
Fljót 63–64, 129, 132, 271n
Fljótadalsherað 82, 88
Fljótamannagoðorð 57, 57n, 63–64, 66, 132
Fljótshverfi 197
Flóabardargi, battle 115, 136n, 141
Flóamenn 74
Flugumýrarbrenna 47, 140n
Flugumýrr 53, 121, 122, 139, 140
Fnjóskadalsá 190
Fnjóskadalur 4, 23, 33, 42, 81, 82, 127, 129, 130, 133, 135, 141, 189, 195, 198, 199n, 201, 293, 294n, 295, 296
Fnjóskdælir 143
Formáli, part of the Sturlunga saga compilation 17, 323
Fornhagi 193, 275, 280n
Forni Söxólfsson 79, 140
Fornungar 69, 79, 132n, 140
fosterage, fostering relationships 17, 48, 49, 73, 74, 127, 228, 237, 240, 253, 263, 265, 281, 283, 285n, 289, 292
Frakkanes 35n
freedman (*leysingi*) 165, 172, 235, 246, 247, 303
Fróðá 22n, 86, 90, 175, 178, 179, 223, 252, 252n, 268

Færeyinga saga 214
föstumatr 36

Gaddsvík 139n
Galmansströnd 193n
Galtardalsá 180
Galtardalstunga 92, 93, 97, 181n
Gamlavík 175
Garðar, Akranes 105
Garða-Snorri see Snorri Illugason
Garmonsway, George 222n
Garpsdalr/-ur 22, 35n, 60, 75, 123, 231, 239
Garpsdalsgoði see Halldórr *Garpsdalsgoði*
Gásir 142, 195, 196, 201, 286n, 287
Geiri 199n
Geirastaðir in Húnavatnssýsla 199n, 288
Geirmundarstaðir 22, 22n, 181, 319
Geirmundar þáttr heljarskinns 17, 76n, 183n, 319
Geirmundr heljarskinn 163–64, 181, 182–83, 184, 186, 319, 319n
Geirr *auðgi* Þorvaldsson (alive in 1288) 80, 80n
Geirríðr Geirmundardóttir 183n
Geirríðr Þórólfsdóttir 175, 221, 252n
Geirröðareyrr – see Narfeyri
Geirröðr/Geirrøðr 175, 246, 247, 266
Geitland, Borgarfjörður 183n
Geldingaholt, Skagafjörður 83n, 118n, 130
Gellir Þorkelsson 170, 236
Gellir Þorsteinsson 71, 73, 73n
genealogical charter 147, 150, 152, 158–61, 164, 167, 168, 169, 172, 176, 179, 180, 184, 192, 194, 195, 200, 201, 205, 212, 222, 240, 258, 280, 283, 296
Geodætisk Institut 30n
Gestr Oddleifsson 172n, 229, 238, 241, 256, 257
Gilsbakki, Borgarfjörður 83, 86
Gilsbekkingar 235
Gilsfjörður 96, 114, 158, 239, 259, 260
Gizurr Hallsson (d. 1206) 76n, 78
Gizurr Þorvaldsson (d. 1268) 47n, 50, 51–56, 52n, 55n, 62, 73–74, 75, 79, 84n, 99, 107, 113, 115, 121, 138, 139–40, 141, 143, 216, 219, 323
Gísl (Gils) of Kleifar in Gilsfjörður 259
Gísla saga Súrssonar 152n, 220, 221, 226–27, 251n, 255n

Gísli Markússon (d. 1258)   73n
Gísli Sigurðsson   304
Gísli Súrsson   227
Gísli Þórðarson   173n
Gjaflaug Kjallaksdóttir   160n, 176n, 180
Glerá, farms and river   163, 189, 191, 196
Glerárdalur   107
Glerárskógar   105, 105n, 107, 251
Glúmr Eyjólfsson (Víga-Glúmr)   196, 270, 271n, 274–75, 276, 279–84, 288, 289–90, 291–92, 302, 303, 305, 311
Glúmr Geirason   199n
Glúmr Óláfsson   261n
Glæsibæjarhreppur   33, 195–201, 298, 318
Glæsibær   23, 190n, 196
Gnúpar, Fljótshverfi   197
Gnúpar, Reykjardalur   293
Gnúpfellingar   292
Gnúpufell   23, 137–38, 139n, 190, 191, 193, 194, 195, 282, 292, 302, 303
Gnúpufellsá   302n
goats   27, 31
Goðdalir   287n
Goðdœlir   287n
Goddastaðir   230n, 232–33, 240
Gottskálksannáll   109
Grani Óláfsson   168
Granastaðir   286
grave goods   8
grazing rights   35n, 256
   see also pasture
Grágás   10–11, 10n, 18, 62, 91, 306, 316
Greenland   65n, 163, 222, 227, 254, 256
Grenjaðarstaðir   25, 36, 40n, 52n, 53, 66, 78, 78n, 82, 83, 127, 142–43, 197, 198n, 199, 284, 285, 286, 288, 289, 290, 300n, 306, 312, 316
Grenjaðr   198, 284
Grettis saga Ásmundarsonar   230n, 249n
Grímr Hrútsson   171
Grímr Mág-Snorrason   87
Grímr *þingaprestr* Snorrason   81
Grímsey   29, 36, 102, 285
Grímseyjarför   137n
grís-, place-name element   32n
Gríss   298–99
Grjótá = Grjótgarðr   127
Grjótgarðr   23n, 127

Grjótvallarmúli   182
Gróa Dala-Kollsdóttir   170n
Gróa Geirleifsdóttir   176n
Grund, Eyjafjörður   23, 25, 34, 46, 61n, 65, 74n, 77–78, 83, 134, 135–40, 143, 144, 191, 203, 275–76, 281, 307, 311–13
Grund, Svarfaðardalur   271n, 297–300, 302, 303
Grundarmenn   69, 298–301, 304
Grýtubakki   25
Grænavatn   195, 199
Grænlendinga saga   181
Guðbrandr Þorvarðsson   280
Guðlaugr Þorfinnsson   171
Guðmundar saga biskups   15n, 322
Guðmundar saga dýra   17, 40n, 63, 65–66, 67, 79, 80, 82n, 83n, 126, 127, 128, 129, 134, 193, 321–22
Guðmundr of Sakka (Sökku-Guðmundr)   141
Guðmundr *góði* Arason, Bishop of Hólar (d. 1237)   15n, 48, 49, 67, 79, 81, 82, 83, 110, 127–28, 135, 136n, 141, 142–44, 192, 272, 317–18, 322
Guðmundr Árnason   106
Guðmundr Brandsson (d. 1151)   90, 90n, 107
Guðmundr Böðvarsson (d. 1275)   124
Guðmundr *ríki* Eyjólfsson (Guðmundr *gamli*)   19n, 68, 190, 192, 196n, 203, 205, 270–71, 272, 273n, 278, 279, 280, 282, 285n, 286n, 288, 291–95, 296–98, 301–4, 305–6, 311
Guðmundr Gíslsson (d. 1246)   141
Guðmundr Hallsson(?) at Hrafnagil   84n139, 140
Guðmundr *umboðsmaðr* Óláfsson(?)   118, 120n, 121, 123
Guðmundr Sigurðsson   195n
Guðmundr *undir Felli* Þórðarson   76n, 103, 104, 106, 109, 110–11, 112, 264
Guðmundr Þorgeirsson, lawspeaker (1123–34)   86
Guðmundr *dýri* Þorvaldsson (d. 1212)   46–47, 48, 63, 64, 66, 68, 78–80, 83, 127–30, 131–35, 145, 292, 314, 321–22
Guðni Jónsson (d. 1974)   277
Guðný Böðvarsdóttir (d. 1221)   70, 71, 72, 73, 99n, 252
Guðrún Bjarnadóttir   71, 74

INDEX 369

Guðrún Hreinsdóttir 216
Guðrún Nordal 14, 218
Guðrún Óspaksdóttir 215
Guðrún Ósvífrsdóttir 171, 199n, 221, 227, 228, 231, 234–35, 236, 237, 239, 240, 241, 242, 249, 257, 263, 266
Guðrún Sigmundardóttir 215
Guðrún Þorgilsdóttir 89n
Gufudalur, Barðaströnd 106, 182
Gunnar Karlsson (d. 2019) 12, 13, 16, 18, 44, 57, 59, 62, 63n, 65, 67, 142, 143
Gunnarr Hámundarson 260–62
Gunnarr Hlífarson 168
Gunnarr Úlfljótsson 192
Gunnarr Þorgrímsson, lawspeaker 82
Gunnarsstaðir 92, 93, 97–98
Gunnbjörn Erpsson 173
Gunnfríðr Þórólfsdóttir 252n
Gunnlaugr Steinþórsson 179n, 221, 251n
Gunnlaugr Þorbjarnarson 224n, 226
Gunnsteinn Hallsson 60n, 112n
Gunnsteinn Þórisson 88
Guttormr Kálfsson (d. 1234) 80, 139n

Haffjarðarey (Hafsfjarðarey) 61n
Hafliðanautr, goðorð 90, 316
Hafliði Másson (d. 1130) 19n, 32n, 78, 85–88, 90, 91, 320
Hafr of Hrafnagil 275
Hagi, Árskógsströnd 193, 280, 293
Hagi, Barðaströnd 59n, 238
Hagi, Reykjadalur 293
Halla Eyjólfsdóttir 183n
Halla Gestsdóttir 238
Halla Þórðardóttir 74
Hallbera Hrafnsdóttir 83
Hallbera Snorradóttir, wife of Mág-Snorri 87, 88n
Hallbera Snorradóttir (d. 1231) 71
Hallbera Snorradóttir, wife of Markús Þórðarson 183n
Hallberg, Peter 214n, 219, 220
Hallbjarnareyri, *see* Öndverðareyrr
Hallbjörg Bárðardóttir 170
Halldís Erpsdóttir 173
Halldóra Eyjólfsdóttir, Abbess of Kirkjubær (d. 1210) 79n
Halldóra Steinmóðardóttir 168
Halldóra Tumadóttir 71, 136

Halldóra Þorkelsdóttir 285
Halldóra Þórhallsdóttir 171
Halldórr *Garpsdalsgoði* 229, 231, 239
Halldórr Ármóðarson 230
Halldórr Bergsson (d. c.1151) 89n
Halldórr Helgason 143n
Halldórr Jónsson 108, 256
Halldórr Óláfsson 170n, 230, 231, 233, 237
Halldórr *djákn* Vilmundarson 118–20, 123n
Halldórr *slakkafótr* Þórarinsson 89n
Hallfríðr Þorbjarnardóttir 170
Hallgerðr *langbrók/snúinbrók* Höskuldsdóttir 170, 170n, 260–61, 262, 263, 264
Halli Sigurðarson 302–3, 304n
Halli *inn hvíti* Þorbjarnarson 281–82
Hallkell Magnússon, Abbot of Helgafell (d. 1244) 225n
Hallr of Hofstaðir in Þorskafjörður 259
Hallr Arason of Höskuldsstaðir 108
Hallr Arason of Jörvi 99
Hallr Gizurarson (d. 1253) 76n
Hallr Gizurarson, Abbot of Helgafell then of Þykkvabær (d. 1230) 76n, 102–3, 225n
Hallr *prestr* Gunnarsson 83n
Hallr *prestr* Gunnsteinsson 61, 76
Hallr Hrafnsson, Abbot of Þverá (d. 1190) 82–83
Hallr Jónsson 138
Hallr Kleppjárnsson (d. 1212) 63, 65, 67n, 79, 80, 82n, 84n, 135, 139n
Hallr Styrmisson 87n
Hallr Styrsson 170
Hallr *prestr* Teitsson 86
Hallsteinn Þorbjarnarson 224n
Hallsteinn Þórólfsson *Þorskfjarðargoði* 178, 225, 226, 229, 241n
Hallvarðr *gullskór* 55
Hallveig Ormsdóttir 48, 51
Hallveig Þorgrímsdóttir 171
Hamarr 281
Hanatún 190n
handgenginn maðr 54n
Haraldr *hárfagri*, king of Norway 154, 162, 163, 227–28
Haraldur Matthíasson (d. 1999) 157n
Harðbakur 39n
harpoon 36
Haugsnes, Skagafjörður 80

Haukadalur, Árnessýsla 9
Haukadalur, Dalir 77, 106, 107, 108, 111, 163, 164, 165, 170, 171, 184, 255
Haukdæla þáttr 17, 79
Haukdælir 15n, 24, 45, 50, 72, 73, 79, 86, 99, 108, 217n
Haukr Erlendsson (d. 1334) 152, 156
Haukr Ormsson, Víga-Haukr 65n
Haukr Þorgilsson 59n
Hauksbók *see* Landnámabók
hay 29, 30, 37n, 42, 256
Hákon, jarl 293
Hákonar saga Hákonarson 15–16, 53
Hákon *galinn* Fólkviðarson 113
Hákon Hákonarson, king of Norway 1n, 48, 49, 52n, 53, 317, 325
Hákon Þórðarson (d. 1198) 132–33
Hálfdan Sæmundarson (d. 1265) 71
Hálfdanartunga, Skagafjörður 131n
hálfkirkja 19–20, 97n
Háls, Eyjafjörður 190
Háls, Fnjóskadalur 67, 80, 129, 135, 285–86
Hámundarstaðir 189, 311
Hámundr *heljarskinn* 65n, 189, 190, 191–92, 193, 194, 195, 203, 281, 311
Hámundr Gilsson 72n
Hávarðar saga Ísfirðings 257n
Hávarðr of Þorvaldsdalur 299n
Hebrides 165, 262
Hegranessþing, Skagafjörður 12, 293
Heiðarvíga saga 174, 214, 220, 226, 227, 249n
Heiðarvígssaga *see* Sturlu saga
heimaland 23
Heinaberg 97
Heinrekr, Bishop of Hólar (d. 1261) 52n, 141
Helga Aradóttir 72
Helgafell, farm and monastery 17n, 22, 29, 35n, 40, 46, 77, 87, 102, 103n, 113, 118, 119, 120, 162, 164, 168, 175, 176, 177–79, 181n, 185, 186, 202, 203, 216, 217, 219, 220, 221, 223, 225, 226, 227, 228, 231, 232, 234, 236, 237n, 240, 241, 242, 244, 245, 248, 249, 250, 251, 252, 253, 254, 255, 263, 265–66, 268, 307, 309, 310, 313
Helgafellseyjar 268
Helgafellssveit, district 31n, 111, 112, 177, 178, 226, 248, 250, 254, 255
Helga Óláfsdóttir 168
Helgastaðamál 82n

Helgastaðir, Reykjadalur 82n, 83, 133, 139, 142, 197, 284, 285
Helga Sturludóttir the younger 71, 73
Helga Sturludóttir the older 71
Helga Þórðardóttir 74
Helgi *Hofgarðargoði* 244
Helgi Áskelsson 284
Helgi *inn magri* Eyvindarson 159, 161, 162, 167, 187, 189n, 190, 191–92, 193–95, 196, 197, 199–201, 203, 204, 279, 280, 283, 284, 290, 301, 311, 318
Helgi *prestr* Halldórsson (d. 1191) 132
Helgi Harðbeinsson 228
Helgi Höskuldsson 170n
Helgi *bjóla* Ketilsson 162
Helgi Skúli Kjartansson 17–18
Helgi Þorláksson 13, 13n, 312, 319
Hella, Árskógsströnd 193, 299, 304
Hellar, Helgafellssveit 245n
Heller, Rolf 214n, 218
Helluhólmr 40n
Henry III, king of England 36n
heraðsþing 175
hersir 151
Héðinsfjörður 301
héraðshöfðingi 244
Herdís Bersadóttir (d. 1233) 71
Herdís Bolladóttir 170, 215
Herdís Sighvatsdóttir 81
Hergilsey, island 39n, 183
Herjólfr Eyvindarson 171
Herjólfr Þórisson 285n
Hermann Pálsson (d. 2002) 220n
Hersteinn Blund-Ketilsson 168, 169n
Hesjuvellir (Esjuvellir) 23n
Hítardalr/-ur, farm, monastery & valley 46, 61, 62, 77, 93, 123, 125, 185, 254, 255
see also monastery
Hítarnes, Mýrar 75, 118
Hítdælagoðorð 56, 61
Hjallasandur 37
Hjaltadalur 46
Hjalti Helgason (d. 1244) 143n
Hjalti Magnússon (d. 1248) 51
Hjalti Þorkelsson 173
Hjarðarholt 72, 89, 90, 93, 101, 104, 106, 107, 122, 125, 168, 171, 173, 202, 228, 231, 232–33, 237, 240, 241, 242–43, 262, 264, 265, 267, 306, 307, 310

INDEX

hjáleiga 5, 27, 32, 127, 132n, 164n, 182n, 190n, 232n, 300, 305, 313
Hjálmr Ásbjarnarson (d. 1227) 82n
Hjörleifr Gilsson (d. 1227) 102, 111, 119n, 120n
Hlaðir 131
Hlenni *inn gamli* Ormsson 281n, 285n, 292
Hlíð *see* Lögmannshlíð
Hneitir of Ávík 91
hof (hall/temple) 175, 244, 248
Hof, Skagafjörður 81
Hof, Svarfaðardalur 298, 300, 301
Hofsá 303
Hofstaðir, Helgafellssveit 175, 203n, 248–49
Hofstaðir, Mývatnssveit 31, 38, 41n
Hofteigr, Jökuldalur, eastern Iceland 86
hoftollr (*hof* payment) 244
holt place-name element 33n
Holt, Fljót 63–64
Holt, Laxárdalur, north-east 286n
Holt (Stóraholt) 97n
Holt (Ytra Holt) Svarfaðardalur 299
Holtahyrna 182
Hornbrekka 132n
Hornstaðir 104, 106
horse 8, 27, 35n, 50n, 96, 106, 116, 117, 119
horse fight 96
Hólar, Álptafjörður 245n
Hólar, episcopal see in Hjaltadalur in Skagafjörður 6, 9, 12, 15n, 19, 21, 22, 46, 48, 52n, 79, 83, 127, 134, 138, 141, 143, 152, 196n, 216, 272, 301, 311, 322
Hólar, Eyjafjörður 23n, 80, 139, 282
Hóll (Saurhóll or Staðarhóll) 237, 239
Hólmslátr 92, 93, 97, 116, 175, 177n, 185, 266
Hrafn Karlsson 300
Hrafn Oddsson (d. 1289) 53, 54, 55, 75, 110, 112, 114, 115, 117, 118, 119n, 120–21, 122–25, 219, 269, 323, 325
Hrafn *Hlymreksfari* Oddsson 183n
Hrafn Sveinbjarnarson (d. 1213) 65n, 101, 102, 322
Hrafn Úlfhéðinsson, lawspeaker 82, 83n
Hrafn Þorkelsson(?) of Lundarbrekka 287n
Hrafnagil 23, 25, 65, 79, 80, 82, 84, 134, 135, 136, 137–38, 139, 140, 144, 191, 198n, 203, 275, 276, 292, 297, 305, 307, 311, 312
Hrafns saga Sveinbjarnarsonar 17, 101, 319, 322
Hrafnsstaðir 300

Hrafnssynir, sons of Hrafn Sveinbjarnarson 102
Hrafsi Ljótólfsson 160
Hrani Koðránsson (d. 1254) 53, 54
Hrappr, father of Grenjaðr 198
Hrappr Sumaliðason 173
Hrappsstaðir 173, 232, 233, 244
Hraun, Helgafellssveit 226, 248, 250, 252, 255, 269
Hraun, Öxnadalur 194
Hraunsáss 286n
Hraunsfjörður 175, 179n, 252
Hraunskarð 35n
Hraunsvatn 194
Hrefna Ásgeirsdóttir 170n, 228
Hreinn *prestr* Hermundarson (d. c.1183) 83, 215, 216
hreppr 18–19, 19n, 20, 62n, 111, 133, 145, 157n, 159, 165, 180–81, 184, 192, 194, 195, 197, 199n, 291n, 299
hreppsmaðr 62n
Hrísar 245n
Hrísateigr 279
Hrísey 280, 283
Hrói Galtason 200, 287
Hrólfr Helgason 190, 192, 194, 195
Hrólfr Sigurðarson 302
Hrútafjörður 22, 32n, 183, 237n, 238
Hrútr Herjólfsson 171, 172, 228, 230, 233–34, 241–42, 260, 261, 262, 263
Hrútsstaðir 232n, 234, 241, 262
Hundadalr/-ur 108, 167, 242, 265
Hundi 167, 179
hundrað (hundred) 23, 27–28, 119, 273n
Hungrvaka 15n
Húnaflói, bay 115
Húnavatnssýsla, region 33n, 34n, 46, 127, 157n, 243
Húnaþing 11, 226
Húsavík 25, 197, 284
Hvammr 284n
Hvammr, part of Grenjaðarstaðir 284, 288, 300n
Hvammr, Helgafellssveit 245, 246, 247, 248, 253
Hvammr, Hvammssveit 4, 24n, 25, 46, 49, 60, 89, 90, 94, 95, 98, 99n, 104, 105, 106, 110, 116, 125, 127, 159, 160, 162, 164, 165, 166, 167, 168, 169, 177, 178, 179, 181, 183, 184–85, 186, 201, 202, 227, 228, 230, 231,

234, 238, 240, 242, 245, 255, 266, 307,
   309, 310, 313, 321
Hvammsfjörður   4, 33, 37n, 41n, 76n, 77, 98,
   108, 115, 117, 123, 124, 150, 162, 164, 180,
   181n, 185, 187, 202, 203, 232, 238, 253,
   255, 268
Hvammsför   104, 105, 106
Hvamm-Sturla *see* Sturla Þórðarson
   (d. 1183)
Hvanndalr   192–93
Hvassafell   66–67, 127, 133, 139, 139n, 282
hverfi   6, 314
Hvítadalr   182n
Hvítá, Borgarfjörður   51
Hvítárbrúarfundr   51
Hvoll   22, 77, 89, 92, 182, 260, 267, 310
Hænsa-Þóris saga   168, 169
Höfðahverfi   142, 143
Höfðaströnd   282n
Höfði   23, 142, 143, 144, 286, 286n
Höfn   103, 104, 110
höfuðból   5
Hörðabólstaðr   235
Hörðadalstunga   231, 232, 235, 241
Hörðdælir   108
Hörðr   167, 186, 235
Hörðudalur   107, 111, 167, 174, 232, 235, 237,
   242, 269
Hörgá   196
Hörgárdalur   25, 47, 66, 67, 78, 79, 80n, 81, 82,
   127, 129, 130, 131, 132, 133, 135, 139–40,
   144, 189, 193, 194, 270n, 273n, 275, 280,
   283, 286, 290, 291, 298, 301, 306
Höskuldr *lögmaðr*   277
Höskuldr Bollason   170
Höskuldr Dala-Kollsson   170, 228, 229, 231,
   232, 233, 235, 238, 241, 242, 260, 261, 262,
   263, 277
Höskuldr Þorgeirsson   294n, 295, 297
Höskuldr Þorvarðsson   296
Höskuldsstaðir, Laxárdalur   77, 99, 105, 108,
   230, 231, 232n, 233, 234, 235, 240, 241,
   242, 260, 262n, 265, 310

Illugi *inn rammi* Ásláksson   177n
Illugi *inn svarti* Hallkelsson   235n
Illugi Jósepsson   131
imports   32, 36n, 317

Ingibjörg Guðmundardóttir   79–80
Ingibjörg Snorradóttir   71, 74
Ingibjörg Þorgeirsdóttir (d. c.1160)   70, 71
Ingibjörg Þorgilsdóttir   94
Ingimundr *prestr* Einarsson (d. 1169)   60, 90
Ingimundr Jónsson (d. 1231)   111n
Ingimundr *prestr* Þorgeirsson
   (d. 1189)   8181, 127, 273
Ingimundr Þorkelsson(?)   106
Ingjaldr *Sauðeyjagoði*   229
Ingjaldr Helgason   190, 192, 193, 279
Ingjaldr Óláfsson   168, 268
Ingjaldshvoll/-hóll   268
Ingólfr Arnarson   187
Ingólfr *inn sterki* Ánason   175, 177n, 185, 185n
Ingvarar *see* Yngvarastaðir
iodine   35
Ireland, Irish people   187, 241, 262
Ísafjörður   87, 88, 183, 249n, 257n
Ísleifr Hallsson (d. 1227)   83, 83n
Íslendingabók   9, 10, 86, 155, 155n, 156, 156n,
   161n, 168, 169, 192, 249, 297n
Íslendinga saga   15, 16, 17, 44, 49, 50, 53, 54n,
   58, 59, 63, 72, 91, 98, 99, 100, 101, 103n,
   107, 110, 112, 121, 122, 126, 134, 136, 138,
   142, 182, 218n, 257, 275, 322–25
Íslendingasögur   3, 6, 9, 10, 11, 12, 13–15, 17,
   19n, 26, 32, 36, 39, 40n, 56, 57, 59, 64, 65,
   66, 69, 76, 84, 92, 102, 111, 135, 137, 144,
   147, 148, 152, 153, 154, 155, 155n, 157, 159,
   160n, 161, 166, 181n, 187, 190–91, 196, 199,
   203, 205–307
Ísólfsstaðir   293n
Ísólfstunga   289n
Ívarr Hrútsson   171
Ívarr Sigurðarson(?) of Múli   142n

Jakob Benediktsson   156n
Jarðabók Árna Magnússonar   23n, 28–29,
   31n, 33, 35, 36, 37n, 39, 39n, 41, 42, 97,
   181n, 190n, 191n, 199, 233n, 245, 247n,
   257n, 280n
Jarteinasaga Guðmundar biskups   17
Járnsíða   277, 323
Jordan   150
Jódís Eyjólfsdóttir   183n
Jón of Bakki   139n
Jónas Kristjánsson (d. 2014)   277

INDEX

Jón Brandsson (d. 1211)   71, 111
Jón Eyjólfsson   78, 78n, 139n
Jón Jóhannesson (d. 1957)   10n, 155, 156, 221
Jón Ketilsson (d. 1192)   63
Jón Loptsson (d. 1197)   45, 47–48, 49, 78, 102n, 129
Jón Ólafsson (d. 1779)
Jónsbók   277
Jónskirkja at Helgafell   268
Jóns saga helga   15n
Jón Viðar Sigurðsson   11, 12, 13n, 16, 17, 18, 19, 68
Jón *murti* Snorrason (d. 1231)   49, 58, 71
Jón Sturluson (d. 1254)   51–52, 59, 123
Jón Tóstason   136n
Jón Þorgeirsson   105–6, 109
Jón Þorgilsson (d. c.1152)   89n
Jón *krókr* Þorleifsson (d. 1229)   71, 106
Jón Ögmundarson, saint, Bishop of Hólar (d. 1121)   9, 15n
Jórunnarstaðir   281
Jórunn Bjarnardóttir   238
Jórunn Hafliðadóttir   87
Jórunn Kálfsdóttir   80
judges   11–12, 101, 316
Jöklamannagoðorð   216, 217
Jökulsá   53, 143
Jörfi   106
Jörundr Hrútsson   171
Jörundr Þorsteinsson, Bishop of Hólar (d. 1313)   196n

Kakalahóll   287n, 296
Kaldakinn (Köldukinn)   127, 198n, 294n, 295n
Kalmanstunga, Borgarfjörður   216
Kambsnes   232n, 233–34, 237, 242
Karl Karlsson   278n, 298, 299, 300, 300n
Karl *inn rauði* Þorsteinsson   193, 193n, 298, 299, 300, 301n, 302, 303
Karlsá   299, 300
Karlsstaðir   298
Kaupangr   23n, 189n, 191, 281
Kálfr of Stokkahlaðir   275
Kálfr Brandsson (born c.1240)
Kálfr Guttormsson (d. 1234)   65, 78, 80, 82n, 131, 134, 135, 139, 318
Kári Ketilsson   217n

Kárr *munkr* Geirmundarson   101n
Kárr Hrútsson   171
Kárr Þóroddsson   246
Kársstaðir   175, 223, 244, 245, 246, 247, 248, 252, 253, 255, 266, 310
Kelduhverfi   194, 200
Keldur   78
Ketill, *þingmaðr* of Einarr Þorgilsson   92, 94n
Ketill of Ketilsstaðir   167, 174, 186
Ketill *inn einhendi* Auðunarson   168
Ketill *flatnefr* Bjarnarson   150, 162, 187, 197, 220–1, 227, 243
Ketill Hermundarson, Abbot of Helgafell (d. 1220)   215, 216, 217, 225
Ketill *kappi* Þorbjarnarson   224n, 226
Ketill *prestr* Þorláksson, lawspeaker (d. 1273)   62, 110, 118
Ketill Þorleifsson   92
Ketill Þorsteinsson, Grundar-Ketill (d. 1173)   77–78, 135
Ketill Þorsteinsson, Bishop of Hólar (d. 1145)   83, 216, 311, 320
Ketill Þorvaldsson   65n
Ketill *gufa* Örlygsson   182
Ketilsstaðir, Hvammssveit   180
Ketilsstaðir, Hörðudalshreppur   167, 174
king, kingship   1, 15, 50, 51, 52–53, 54, 55–56, 58, 60, 62, 80, 82n, 99, 114, 120, 125, 163, 187, 197, 220, 227–28, 262, 271, 276, 283n, 308, 317–18, 323, 325
Kirkjubær, convent   79
Kirkjufjörður   175
Kjallakr Bjarnarson 160, 163, 165, 176, 176n, 179, 180, 185n (Barna-Kjallakr), 186, 202, 249 (Kjallakr *gamli*)   259
Kjallakr, jarl in Jämtland   176n
Kjalleklingar   176n, 185n, 244, 245, 254, 259
Kjarlarnes   73, 162
Kjalarnesþing   187
Kjartan Ólafsson   170n, 171, 228, 230, 231, 234, 237, 238, 240, 241, 242, 267n
Kjartan Þorvaldsson   82, 96
Klaufabrekka   299, 300, 303
Klaufi Snækollsson   298, 299, 300n, 303, 304
Kleifar   259
Kleppjárn Einarsson   174
Kleppjárn Klængsson (d. 1194)   65, 80, 84n

Klofasteinar 181, 182
Klofningur 42, 180
Klængr Bjarnarson (d. 1241) 217n
Klængr Eyjólfsson (Arnþrúðarson) 79n
Klængr Kleppjárnsson (d. 1219) 82
Klængr Narfason 280n
Knarrareyrr 287
Knútr of Hóll 237
Koðrán Guðmundarson 285n, 292
Koðrán Hermundarson (d. 1189) 215, 216
Koðrán Ormsson 215
Kolbeinn of Kolbeinsdalur 301
Kolbeinn *ungi* Arnórsson (d. 1245) 48–49, 50, 51–52, 54n, 73, 80, 82, 107n, 112, 113–15, 116, 117, 136, 137, 138, 139n, 141, 143, 145
Kolbeinn *grön* Dufgusson 71, 121, 122, 139n see also Dufgusssynir
Kolbeinn Sighvatsson (d. 1238) 71, 142, 144
Kolbeinn Sigmundarson of Kolbeinsdalur 301
Kolbeinn Tumason (d. 1208) 47, 48, 63, 72, 81–82, 91, 129, 130, 131, 134–35
Kolbeinn Þórðarson 173
Kolbeinsdalur 300
Kolbeinsstaðahreppur 75
Kolbeinsstaðir 62, 107, 118, 119n
Kolbrandr Skíðason 106
Kolfinna Hallsdóttir 87
Kolgrafarfjörður 179n
Kolgrafir 175
Kolgrímr of Bjarnarhöfn 119, 120, 121n
Kollafjörður 35n, south-west Iceland
Kolli Þormóðarson 250, 253
Kollr, Dala-Kollr 166, 167, 169–70, 172, 186, 199, 202, 228, 243
Kolr 175
Kotkell 239
Kónall Steinmóðarson 168
Krákunesskógr 33n
Kristján Eldjárn (d. 1982) 8
Kristnes 162n, 189, 191, 193, 194, 203, 280, 286n, 305, 311, 312
Kroppr 194, 200, 286, 287, 289, 305, 311
Krossafjall 189n
Krossanes 66, 70
Krossavík 293
Krossá 200
Króksfjarðarbók 16, 60n, 105n, 319, 325

Króksfjörður 199, 239, 241n, 258, 260
Kræklingahlíð 66, 189, 196, 201, 286n
Kúgaldi Hrútsson 171
kúgildi see hundrað
Kvennabrekka 93, 108, 255, 256, 257, 310
Kvennahóll 105, 106
Kvíabrekkr 192, 304n

Lambastaðir, Laxárdalur 232, 232n, 233, 241
Lambastaðir, Mýrar 58n
Lambi Þorbjarnarson 230n, 233, 241
Lambkárr Þorgilsson (d. 1249) 322
Langadalsá 175
Langahlíð (Skriða) 80n, 81, 129, 131
Langdælir 177
langfeðgatal 155, 183n
Langidalr/-ur 60, 87n, 121, 123, 175, 177, 185, 229, 231, 232, 235–36, 254, 255, 269
landnám 1, 3, 7, 8–9, 26, 27, 32, 147–204, 212, 220, 224, 228, 234, 235, 238n, 244, 246, 248, 252, 258, 271n, 277, 283, 309, 310–11, 313, 319, 320
Landnámabók 3, 9, 26, 56, 135, 142n, 147, 148, 150, 152, 154–58, 160, 161, 163n, 171, 176, 181, 182, 184, 186, 198, 205, 212, 214, 218, 220n, 275, 277, 287n, 309, 311, 318, 319
  Hauksbók (H) 152, 154, 156, 181, 191n, 236n, 261n
  Melabók (M) 154, 155n, 156n, 158n, 181, 222n, 261n, 319
  Skarðsárbók (Sk) 154
  Sturlubók (S) 32n, 87n, 147, 150, 152, 153, 154, 156, 158–204, 221, 225, 275, 277, 309, 310
  Þórðarbók (Þ) 154, 156
landownership 5, 27, 28n, 30, 34, 49, 50–51, 60, 78, 83, 88, 89, 93, 94n, 103n, 117, 127, 131, 137, 146, 157, 159, 160–61, 164n, 169n, 200, 202, 203, 212, 228, 232, 233, 234, 236, 242, 245–48, 256, 263, 266–67, 268, 274, 279, 283, 303, 305, 312, 315–16
  ecclesiastical 13, 19–25, 23n, 31, 34, 35, 39n, 40, 48, 274, 287n
land registers *see Jarðabók Árna Magnússonar*
Langadalsá 175
Langdælir 177
Laufás 23, 64, 133, 143
Laufæsingagoðorð 64, 66
laug (hot spring) 99

Laugaból, Ísafjörður 249n
Laugaland 23, 32n, 65, 127, 129, 130, 131, 281, 291
Laugar 92, 94, 95, 97, 105, 228, 231, 234, 235, 236, 237n, 239, 240, 241, 242, 257, 257n, 263, 266, 267, 310
Laugarbrekka, Snæfellsnes 58n
Laurentius saga biskups 15n
laws 9, 10–11, 17, 18, 20, 86, 192, 293
  see also canon law; *Grágás*; *Járnsíða*; *Jónsbók*
lawman (*lögmaðr*) 195, 196, 277, 319, 323
lawspeaker (*lögsögumaðr*) 10, 48, 59, 62, 79, 82, 83, 86, 183, 277, 302
Laxá, place-name 38
Laxá, Laxárdalur, Dalir 233, 241, 265
Laxá, Skógarströnd 175
Laxá, near Mývatn 204
Laxárdalur, valley in Dalir 32, 37n, 41n, 42, 77, 93, 99, 106, 107n, 111, 114, 116, 165, 167, 169–72, 173, 169n, 173n, 184, 186, 228, 231, 232, 233, 234, 235, 238, 239, 240, 241–42, 241n, 243, 245, 261, 262, 263, 264, 265, 265n, 266, 269, 288n
Laxárdalur, north-west of Mývatn 83, 142, 143, 198, 284, 285, 288
Laxdæla saga 18, 32, 36, 40, 97, 161, 164n, 165n, 166, 167, 169, 171, 172, 173, 174, 178, 185, 186, 187, 208, 213–19, 220–21, 223, 224, 225, 227–43, 244, 245, 249, 251n, 256, 257, 258, 260, 261, 262, 263, 265, 266, 267, 268n, 269, 306
Laxdælir 171, 238, 260, 262, 263
Lárentius Kálfsson, Bishop of Hólar (d. 1331) 15n
leið see autumn assembly
Leiðólfsstaðir 232, 233
Leirhöfn 143
lendr maðr 48, 54n, 127
livestock 28, 29, 30, 31, 35, 41n, 42, 118, 119, 120, 256, 310, 313
Ljárskógar 106, 230n, 232n, 237n, 265
Ljósavatn 23, 195, 197, 198n, 199, 201, 204, 279, 285, 288, 290, 294, 295, 296, 297, 305, 306, 312
Ljósavatnshreppur 198n
Ljósavatnsskarð 67, 198, 284, 290, 295, 296
Ljosvetningagoðorð 57, 66–67, 297n

Ljósvetninga saga 18, 40, 142n, 196, 205, 213, 222n, 270, 271, 272, 273, 274, 279, 285n, 286, 287n, 288, 289n, 290–98, 305, 306
Ljósvetningar 66, 287n, 292, 295, 296, 297, 298
Ljótólfr of Ljótólfsstaðir 160n
Ljótólfr *goði* Alreksson 271, 298, 299, 300, 301, 303, 305
Ljótólfsstaðir (Ljótsstaðir), Fellsströnd 160n
Ljótr *hofgoði* 286n
Ljótr *inn svarti* 262n
Ljótr Jónsson of Bakki 139n
Ljótr Ljótólfsson (Valla-Ljótr) 141, 271n, 298, 302, 303, 304, 305
Loftr Hálfdanarson (d. 1312) 137
Loftr Markússon 65n
longhouse 7, 8
Lón (Skipalón) 196
Lundr, Fnjóskadalur 199n
Lundr, Lundarreykjadalur, Borgarfjörður 72n
Lundarbrekka 23, 24n, 197, 287, 289, 296
Lundarreykjardalur 71, 72
Lúðvík Ingvarsson (d. 2011) 44, 57, 62, 63, 64
lögbýli 5, 27
lögmaðr see lawman
Lögmannshlíð 23n, 32n, 196n (Hlíð)
lögrétta 10
lögsögumaðr see lawspeaker

Madelung, Margaret 214n
Magerøy, Hallvard 214n
Magnús Gizurarson, Bishop of Skálholt (d. 1237) 51, 76
Magnús *lagabætir* Hákonarson, king of Norway (d. 1280) 15, 323
mannaforráð 12, 67, 68, 142, 169, 229, 298
Matthías Þórðarson (d. 1961) 246n
Maurer, Konrad (d. 1902) 10
Mág-Snorri of Múli 87–88
máldagi 2, 21, 22, 23, 24, 25, 28, 35, 40n, 41, 144, 199, 236n, 253, 266, 268n, 281n, 294n
Mánahjalli 286n, 288
Mána-Ljótr 57
Máni Snorrason 57
Már Glúmsson 275, 280n
Már Hallvarðsson 168
Már Hrútsson 171

Mávahlíð 22n, 178, 252
McKinnell, John 271n
meadow (*engi*) 22, 30, 247n, 274, 303, 310
Melabók see Landnámabók
Mela-Snorri see Snorri Markússon
Melamenn 155n, 319
Melkorka 170n, 241
Melkorkustaðir 241
Melar, Melasveit 319
Melar, Svarfaðardalur 299n
Melr, Miðfjörður 35n, 88, 105n, 319
Melrakkaslétta 4, 34, 39n, 41, 143
mercenaries 120, 318
merchant 240, 317
Miðdalir 4, 25, 46, 77, 93, 98, 100, 101, 103, 106, 107, 108, 111, 123, 165, 167, 171, 172, 173, 177n, 184, 186, 202, 235, 237, 238, 242, 243, 255, 256, 257, 258, 269, 310
Miðfirðingar 100
Miðfjarðar-Skeggi 238
Miðfjörður, Húnavatnssýsla 35, 88, 116, 117, 238
Miklabær, Skagafjörður 80, 127, 139
Miklagarðr 23, 24n, 25, 138, 140n
Miklaholt, Miklaholtshreppur 102, 120n, 123
Miklaholtshreppur 253
Miller, William I. 13, 14, 17, 102n, 237n, 278, 297n
ministry (*þing*), parish, tithe area 21, 22n, 24, 25, 109, 198, 199, 302n, 316–17
monastery 22, 34, 39n, 46, 83, 144, 152, 270n, 309
   Flatey 46, 73
   Helgafell 22, 46, 113, 202, 219, 236
   Hítardalr 46, 61
   Keldur 78
   Munkaþverá 22, 39n, 46, 66, 127, 144, 190, 272, 276
   Möðruvellir, Hörgárdalur 270n
   Saurbær, Eyjafjörður 78
   Þingeyrar 34, 46, 48, 83, 127, 134, 309, 322
Mundal, Else 219
Mundt, Marina 214n
Munkaþverá, *see* Þverá
Múli (Fellsmúli), Reykjadalur 142, 197, 284
Múli, Saurbær, Dalir 88, 182
Myrká 131, 193–94, 280n
Mýlaugsstaðir 285
Mýrar, district 58n, 61n, 72, 98, 118, 123, 238

Mýrkárdalur 79, 131
Mýrkjartan, Irish king 170n
Mývatn, lake 4, 5, 38, 41, 42, 195, 197, 199, 200, 204, 279, 283, 284, 285n, 286, 288, 290, 306, 311
Mývatnssveit, district 4, 7, 30, 31, 141, 279, 284, 288, 290, 293, 294, 312
Möðrufell 78, 83n, 139, 191, 281
Möðruvallabók 213, 217
Möðruvellingagoðorð 57, 63, 66
Möðruvellingar 69, 302
Möðruvellir, Hörgárdalur 66, 67, 82, 129, 131, 133, 135, 139, 273n, 280n, 292
Möðruvellir, Eyjafjörður 23, 63, 64, 65, 66, 83n(?), 127, 134(?), 138, 190, 191, 192, 203, 270, 273n, 274, 276, 279, 282, 285, 288, 289, 291, 292, 293, 294, 296, 297, 298, 301, 302, 303, 305, 306, 307, 311, 312

Narfeyri (Geirröðareyrr) 22, 60, 75, 110, 111, 112, 121, 175, 177, 236n, 245, 246, 247, 254, 266
Narfi Snorrason (d. 1202) 59n, 76n, 118
Naumadalr (Namdal), Trøndelag 277
Náttfaravík 198n, 294n
Neshreppur, district 4, 28n, 31n, 252, 267, 268
Niðarós, archepiscopal see, Norway 20, 48, 49
Nigeria 148
Nikulás Bergsson, Abbot of Þverá (d. 1159) 46n
Nikulás Oddsson 114, 118, 136n
Njáll Þorgeirsson (Brennu-Njáll) 260, 282n
Njáls saga (Brennu-Njáls saga) 64, 103n, 150, 208, 226, 241, 260–64, 282n
Njörður Njarðvík 218n
North Atlantic Biocultural Organisation (NABO) 7
North, Richard 274–75
Northern Quarter 4, 10, 11, 25, 30n, 46, 47, 52, 53, 55, 74, 85, 90, 91, 116, 158, 238
Norway 1, 2, 7, 8, 14, 20, 48, 49, 50, 51, 52, 53, 54, 56, 62, 72, 73, 80, 85, 104, 113, 114, 115, 117, 118, 126, 127, 129, 135, 136, 151, 162, 163n, 165, 182, 187, 192, 196, 197, 219, 227, 228, 277, 279, 298, 313, 315, 317, 319, 323, 325
   see also king, kingship

INDEX

Oddaverjar 45, 47, 48, 55, 70, 73, 74, 76, 78, 89
Oddi, Rángárvallasýsla 9, 45, 52, 73, 74, 76
Oddi Þorgilsson (d. 1151) 89, 96
Oddr, father of Hrafn Hlymreksfari 183n
Oddr Þórarinsson (d. 1255) 53–54
Oddr Önundarson see Tungu-Oddr
Ogilvie, Astrid 39n
ordination 20–21, 46, 59
Ormr *inn mjóvi* 175
Ormr Erpsson 173
Ormr *prestr* Fornason 65n, 79n, 132
Ormr Hermundarson 215
Orrahóll 181n
Orri Vésteinsson 18, 19, 22n, 24, 27n, 148n, 187n, 201, 203, 284n, 318, 320
Orustuhóll see Kakalahóll
Otradalr, farm in Arnafjörður 255
overgrazing 32
óðal rights 157, 275
Ófeigr Eiríksson (d. 1254) 139n
Ófeigr Önundarson 142n, 289n, 294, 297
Ófeigshellir 294n
Ófeigsá 294n
Óláfr *belgr* 175, 176, 182, 258, 259
Óláfr *hjalti* 261n
Óláfr Hjörleifsson, Abbot of Helgafell (d. 1302) 17n, 120n
Óláfr *pái* Höskuldsson 168, 169n, 170n, 228, 229, 230, 231, 233, 234, 237, 238, 241, 242, 260, 261, 262, 265, 267
Óláfr Jónsson 139
Óláfr *bekkr* Karlsson 192–93
Óláfr *hvítaskáld* Þórðarson, *subdjákn* (d. 1259) 71, 106, 109, 214
Óláfr Þorsteinsson, canon at Saurbær (d. 1204?) 65, 78, 127
Óláfr *feilan* Þorsteinsson 167, 168, 169, 178, 186n, 228, 229, 230, 253
Óláfsdalur 7, 176, 258, 259
Óláfsdælir 259
Óláfsfjörður 129, 132, 133, 192, 193, 298, 301, 303n, 304
Óláfs saga helga 214, 282n
Óláfs saga Tryggvasonar en mesta 261n
Óláfsvík 175, 176
Óláfsvíkurenni 175
ómagi (dependent) 19

Órækja Snorrason (d. 1245) 49–51, 71, 73, 80, 98, 109, 110, 139n, 181, 182, 323, 324
Ósbrekka 132
Ósk Þorsteinsdóttir 178, 225
Ósland, Kolbeinsdalur, Skagafjörður 301n
Óspakr Bollason 215
Óspakr Kjallaksson 223, 267
Ósvífr Helgason 230, 231, 234, 235, 236, 239n, 242, 263, 266, 267
Óttar Bjarnarson 176n
Óþveginstunga 286

parish see ministry
pasture 8, 27, 28, 30, 31, 32, 34, 42, 256, 310
Páll *prestr* Hallsson 60–61, 110, 112, 121, 122, 123
Páll Jónsson, Bishop of Skálholt (d. 1211) 15n, 21n, 61, 217
Páls saga biskups 15n, 61, 217
Páll *prestr* Sölvason (d. 1185) 47, 216
peat 27, 33
Perkins, Richard 223n
pig 27, 31, 32
poetry 209, 214n, 223
political centralisation 6, 12, 13, 47, 63, 64, 67–68, 112, 128, 145–46, 187, 306, 309, 312, 314, 315, 316, 318
population 5, 11, 42, 43, 142, 200, 297, 318
precipitation 29–30, 31
Presthólar 25
Presthvammur 284n
Prestssaga Guðmundar góða 15n, 17, 67, 81, 126, 127, 128, 317, 319n, 321, 322
priest 19, 20, 21, 59, 60, 62, 65, 95, 107, 117, 127, 131, 132, 140, 216, 273, 299n
Purkey see Svíney

Quarter 4, 10, 49
see also Eastern Quarter, Northern Quarter, Southern Quarter, Western Quarter
Quarter courts 12, 293

Ragnhildr Ljótólfsdóttir 278n
Rangárvellir, region in southern Iceland 12, 55, 78
Rauðalækr 131
Rauðamelr, Kolbeinsstaðahreppur 61, 118, 119, 168, 253

Rauðasandr, district on Barðaströnd 73n
Rauðaskriða 285, 290
Rauðmelingagoðorð 56, 61
Rauðseyjar 39n
Refr (Króka-Refr) 255–57
reki 22, 32, 34, 36, 40, 50, 91, 267, 270, 285, 294n, 315
Reykdælagoðorð 57, 66
Reykdæla saga 191n, 197, 199n, 200, 270, 271, 272, 273, 274, 279, 283, 284–90, 295, 305, 306
Reykdœlir 143, 144, 274, 284n, 287, 289, 312
Reykholt, Borgarfjörður 8, 46, 51, 98, 169
Reykhólamenn 80
Reykhólar 42, 60n, 74n, 80, 90, 111n, 114, 117, 263, 264
Reykholt 8, 46, 51, 98, 169
Reykhyltingar 90n
Reykir 293
Reykjadalur 4, 25, 30, 33, 38, 40, 53, 66, 78, 82, 83, 88, 133, 141, 142, 143, 144, 194–95, 197, 199, 201, 204, 279, 284–85, 286, 287n, 288, 289, 290, 291, 293, 294, 295n, 297, 305, 306, 311, 312, 315
Reykjahlíð 195, 199, 288, 293, 294, 295
Reykjahverfi 4n
Reykjanes 35n, 38n, 75, 89, 173, 264
Reykjarfjarðarbók 16, 325
Reykjaströnd, Skagafjörður 282n
Reykjavík 4, 161
Reyknesingagoðorð 56, 60, 90
rittengsl 226, 271n
ríki 12–13, 52, 67, 114, 135, 136, 145, 315
Rjúpa Þorkelsdóttir 170
Rúfeyjar 39n
Rúnólfr Nikulásson 132
Rúnólfr Úlfsson 229

Sa'ada 149
Sagas of Icelanders see *Íslendingasögur*
Sakka 79n, 127, 132n, 141
salt 35n
samtíðarsögur (contemporary sagas) 3, 9, 12, 13, 14, 15, 44, 56, 58, 69, 84, 85, 92, 97, 126, 148n, 151, 191, 236n, 253, 278, 304, 312, 317, 319–26
 biskupasögur 9
 Sturlunga saga 3, 6, 9, 14, 15–17, 28, 32n, 33n, 35, 36n, 38n, 40n, 41, 45, 46n, 55n, 57, 59, 60n, 61, 62, 64, 65, 68, 69, 73, 75n,
76, 77, 79n, 80n, 82, 83, 86, 90, 97n, 100, 103, 105n, 121n, 123, 126, 136n, 137, 138, 141, 143, 144, 173n, 174n, 193, 202, 204, 205, 211, 217, 229, 234, 235, 243, 251n, 268, 269, 273n, 275, 309, 312, 318, 319–26
Sandfell 288
Sandkirkja 132n
Sandr 132n
Sauðanes 142
Sauðafell 1n, 25, 46, 49, 50, 53, 55, 57, 93, 94, 98, 100, 101, 104n, 106, 107, 108, 110, 114, 115, 118, 122, 123, 124, 125, 165, 167, 172, 173, 202, 235, 240, 242, 243, 256, 257, 258, 265, 268, 300, 307, 310
Sauðafellsför 49n
Sauðafellslönd 167, 235
Sauðafellsmenn 173
Saurar 245
Saurbæingar 110, 292
Saurbæjarhreppur 4
Saurbær, district in Dalir 4, 22, 25, 33, 35, 53, 61, 77, 85, 88, 89, 90, 92, 95, 96, 99, 109, 112, 114, 122, 125, 166, 173, 176, 179–80, 181, 182, 183, 186, 187, 203, 204, 237, 238, 239, 257n, 259, 260, 267, 268, 310
Saurbær, farm in Eyjafjörður 23, 25, 65, 78, 83, 127, 134, 139, 140, 190, 191, 199n, 276, 280, 282, 283, 285n, 292, 303
Saurhóll 182n, 237
Saxahvoll 35n
Sámr Barkarson 178
sea-ice 39n
seals, seal hunting 38–40
seaweed (dulse/*söl*, *fjörugrös*, wrack) 31, 34–35
 see, episcopal 6, 12, 19
 see also Hólar; Skálholt
Seldælir 74
Selsker, skerry 40n
Setberg 22
settlement, the – *see* archaeology; *landnám*
settlement patterns 11, 27, 29, 33–34, 43, 55, 105n, 157, 167, 180, 185, 186, 197, 284n, 307
sheep 2, 23n, 27, 30, 31, 32, 118, 256
ship 32n, 143, 313
Sighvatr *prestr* Brandsson 215
Sighvatr Böðvarsson (d. 1266) 54, 60
Sighvatr Sturluson (d. 1238) 46, 48, 49, 50, 51, 57, 58, 60, 62, 63, 65, 67, 70, 71, 72, 73n, 74, 76, 77, 78, 80, 85, 98, 99, 100–2, 105,

INDEX

108, 109, 110, 117n, 122, 124, 125, 135, 136,
    137, 139, 142–43, 145, 202, 256, 263, 273,
    274, 312, 316, 324
    see also Sturlusynir
Siglufjörður   192
Siglunes   36, 247n
Sigluvík   190, 271
Sigmundr Snorrason   117
Sigmundr Þorgilsson (d. 1118)   320
Sigmundr Þorkelsson   279
Signý Guðmundardóttir   79n
Sigríðr Arnórsdóttir   74
Sigríðr Eldjárnsdóttir   82
Sigríðr Hafliðadóttir   87
Sigríðr Sighvatsdóttir   74, 136
Sigríðr Snorradóttir   250
Sigríðr Tumadóttir   81
Sigríðr Þorgeirsdóttir   295n
Sigurðr *kerlingarnef*   92, 94–95
Sigurðr *svínhöfði*   175, 178
Sigurðr Guðmundsson   195n
Sigurðr Ormsson (d. 1235)   63, 63n, 64, 65,
    67n, 72, 134–35
Silfrastaðir, Skagafjörður   80
Skagafjörður   6, 9n, 11, 12, 13, 25, 46, 47, 48,
    50, 52, 53, 54, 55, 63, 72, 73, 75, 77, 78, 79,
    80, 81, 82, 83, 91, 114, 115, 118n, 127, 128,
    130, 134, 135, 136, 137, 139n, 145, 146,
    282n, 287n, 293, 301, 304, 305, 311, 312
Skagfirðingar   54, 80
Skagi Skoptason   190, 192
Skallabúðir   37n
Skallagrímr Kveldúlfsson   187
Skapti Þóroddsson, lawspeaker   302
Skarð   22   35, 39n, 42, 59, 61, 74, 76n, 96, 105n,
    109n, 117, 118, 122, 163, 181, 182, 183, 184,
    185, 186, 260, 309, 310, 319, 320
Skarðsárbók see Landnámabók
Skarð-Snorri *see* Snorri Narfason
Skarðsströnd, district   35n, 37n, 39, 40, 58n,
    59, 89, 96, 109, 110, 112, 116, 165, 166, 179,
    180, 181, 183, 186, 202, 203, 204, 239, 243,
    258, 268, 319
Skáldsstaðir   282
Skálholt, episcopal see in Árnessýsla   6, 9, 12,
    15n, 17, 19, 20n, 21, 24, 45, 46, 51, 73n, 79,
    118, 152, 159n, 217
Skálholtsannáll   216n
skáli (hall)   32n
Skálmarnesmúli   91

Skeggi Brandsson   215
Skeggi Gamlason (d. 1148)   92
Skeggi Skinna-Bjarnarson *see*
    Miðfjarðar-Skeggi
Skeggi Þórarinsson   230n
Skeggjabrekka   132n
Skinnastaðir   143n
Skíðadalur   300
Skíði of Skíðadalur   300, 301n
Skíði Þorkelsson (d. 1235)   105–6
Skjaldarvík   131
skjaldasumar (shield summer)   317–18
Skjalgdalsá   190
Skjálfandafljót   285
Skorravík   104, 109
Skógarströnd, district   33, 35n, 77, 93, 103,
    165, 167, 174, 176, 177, 179, 181n, 185, 186,
    202, 229, 231, 232, 236, 254, 255, 269
skógartollur   33
skógr place-name element   33n
Skógstrendingar   254
Skólmr   194
Skraumuhlaupsá (Skrauma)   165, 174, 175
skreið see stockfish
Skriðukot   164n
Skriðuþingsókn   194
Skúmr Kjartansson   170n
Skúta Áskelsson (Víga-Skúta)   274, 283, 284,
    288, 289, 290
Skútustaðir   195, 199, 274, 283, 284, 288, 290
Skörð   194, 294, 305
slave   159, 241, 247, 271n, 295n
Sléttu-Björn (Sleitu-Björn)   182, 184, 259
Sneglu-Halli   271n
Sneglu-Halla þáttr   271n
Snorri *Hlíðmannagoði/Hlíðarmannagoði*
    Eyvindarson   196, 286n
Snorri í Múla *see* Mág-Snorri
Snorri Húnbogason (d. 1170)   183, 186
Snorri Illugason (Garða-Snorri)   105n
Snorri Kálfsson of Melr in Miðfjörður
    (d. 1175)   88, 105n
Snorri Markússon (Mela-Snorri)
    (d. 1313)   155n
Snorri *prestr* Narfason (Skarð-Snorri, d.
    1260)   75n, 105n, 106, 107, 109–10, 111,
    112, 117, 121, 123, 124, 183n, 319
Snorri Narfason (d. 1332)   320
Snorri Pálsson (Eyrar-Snorri of
    Narfeyri)   105n, 121, 124

Snorri Sturluson (d. 1241)   8, 13n, 46, 48–51,
    52, 56, 58, 70, 71, 72–74, 76, 90–91, 98,
    103n, 104, 107, 110, 124, 168, 169, 214, 216,
    323
    see also Sturlusynir
Snorri Sturluson the younger (d. 1306)   123,
    124
Snorri *goði* Þorgrímsson   57, 87, 88n, 148,
    168, 178–79, 181n, 185, 205, 211, 214, 215,
    220, 221, 222, 223, 224, 226, 227, 228, 229,
    231, 232, 234–36, 240, 243, 244–45, 246,
    249–50, 251–52, 253, 254, 255, 257n, 265,
    266, 267–68, 269, 270, 313–14
Snorri *prestr* Þórálfsson (d. 1244)   136n
Snorri Þórðarson (Lauga-Snorri)
    (d. 1238)   105, 108, 125
Snorri *prestr* Þórðarson (Fell-Snorri)   105n,
    111, 121, 123, 123n
Snorri Þórðarson, father-in-law of Snorri í
    Múla   87
Snorrungagoðorð   49, 56, 57, 58, 59, 104, 211
Snóksdalr   22, 77, 100–1, 108, 310
Snæfellsnesjökull   4
Snörtr Hrafnsson   183n
Sogn, Norway   151
Solveig Sæmundardóttir (d. 1254)   50, 73
Southern Quarter   11, 25, 45, 53, 55
Sólarfjöll   189
Spain   2
Spá-Gilsstaðir   248, 250
Spákonuarfr   34n
spring   37, 38n   132
spring assembly (*vorþing*)   10, 293
staðamál   20, 48
Staðarey (Eyin mikla), Eyjafjörður   189n, 274
Staðarfell (Fell)   22n, 76n, 90, 94, 103, 105n,
    109, 110, 111, 159–61, 181n, 202, 243, 262,
    263, 264, 310
Staðarhóll   22n, 25, 53, 60, 76n, 85, 87, 89n,
    96, 99, 110, 112, 117n, 121, 122, 125, 181, 182,
    184, 237, 237
    (Hóll)   239, 245, 260, 267, 310, 322
Staðarhólsmál   181
Staðarhólsmenn   69
staðr, church farm   13, 19–20, 23n, 25, 34, 36,
    48n, 72n, 77, 82–83, 99, 101, 111, 127, 142,
    157, 196, 198, 294n
Staðr (Þóroddsstaður), Kaldakinn   127, 142,
    294n

Staðr, Reykjanes   75
Staðr (Staðarstaðr), Snæfellsnes   98, 99n,
    116, 117, 118, 119, 120, 125
Stafaholt, Borgarfjörður   122, 123
Stafá   175
Steblin-Kamenskij, Mikhail (d. 1981)   209–10
Steindyrr   299
Steingrímr Hrútsson   171
Steingrímr Örnólfsson   286, 287, 289
Steingrímsfjörður, Strandir   22, 40, 127, 238,
    262
Steinn of Kvennabrekka   256, 257
Steinn Hrútsson   171
Steinn *mjöksiglandi* Vígbjóðsson   164n, 175
Steinn Þorbjarnarson   286, 287
Steinn Þorfinnsson   168
Steinólfr *inn lagi* Hrólfsson   182, 183, 184n,
    186, 258, 259
Steinunn Sturludóttir   71, 111n, 139n
Steinvör Sighvatsdóttir (d. 1271)   71, 137
Steinþórr Óláfsson   170n, 230, 233
Steinþórr Þorláksson   179n, 230, 236, 244,
    250, 251, 269
stockfish (*skreið*)   36
Stokkahlaðir   137, 198n, 281
Stóraborg   247n
stórbóndi (pl. *stórbændr*)   13, 137, 145–46, 314,
    317
Stóridalr   190, 191
Stóriskógur   257
Strandir, region   22, 40, 50n, 91, 93, 163, 181,
    184, 223, 245, 270, 315
Strendir   110
Sturla Sighvatsson (d. 1238)   17, 49, 50, 51, 58,
    59, 61, 62, 71, 73, 75, 85, 93, 98, 100,
    102–11, 114, 122, 123, 124, 256, 264n, 269,
    323–24
Sturla Þjóðreksson   87, 88, 245, 267–68
Sturla Þórðarson (Hvamm-Sturla)
    (d. 1183)   14, 46, 47, 57, 66, 70, 71, 72,
    73, 75, 76n, 81, 89, 90, 92, 93–99, 107, 112,
    127, 130, 131, 139n, 158, 159, 160, 171, 185,
    192, 196, 202, 204, 216, 217n, 243, 264,
    313, 314, 321, 321n
Sturla Þórðarson, lawspeaker, writer
    (d. 1284)   15, 16, 50–51, 53, 54, 55, 57,
    58, 59, 60, 71, 74, 75, 77, 80, 84, 99, 100,
    103n, 109, 110, 112, 113, 114, 115, 116, 117, 118,
    120–21, 122–24, 125, 138n, 150, 155, 156,

160–61, 181, 182n, 187, 192, 196, 197, 214,
    219–20, 260, 320, 323–24, 325
Sturlubók see Landnámabók
Sturlu saga   14, 17, 57, 61, 70, 87, 88, 92–98,
    111, 112, 129, 131, 182, 185n, 202, 203, 216,
    320, 321
    (Heiðarvígssaga)   322, 325
Sturlu þáttr   16, 17, 123, 124
Sturlunga, Sturlunga saga see samtíðarsögur
Sturlusynir, sons of Hvamm-Sturla
    Þórðarson   46, 72, 73, 74, 76, 98, 99,
    124, 315
    see also Þórðr Sturluson (d. 1237)
    Sighvatr Sturluson (d. 1238); Snorri
    Sturluson (d. 1241)
Styrmir Hermundarson   215
Styrmir Hreinsson   86
Styrmir Kárason (d. 1245)   150, 156, 220n
Styrmir Þórisson   74n, 136–37
Styrmisbók see Landnámabók
Styrr Gilsson   95n
Styrr Þorgrímsson (Víga-Styrr)   163n, 170, 174,
    226, 250, 252, 254, 255, 269
sulphur   27n
Sumarliði Hrappsson   173
Sunnlendingar   52
Surtr Bollason   170
Svalbarð, Svalbarðsströnd   23n
Svalbarð, Þistilfjörður   39n
Svalbarðsströnd, district in Eyjafjörður   139n
Svanr Bjarnarson   262, 263n
Svanshóll, Bjarnarfjörður   262
Svarfaðardalsá   298, 300, 303
Svarfaðardalur   1, 5, 8n, 25, 30n, 65n, 79, 127,
    128, 129, 130n, 131, 132, 133, 140, 141, 142,
    144, 145, 189n, 193, 200, 271n, 276, 277,
    298–305
Svarfdæla saga   193, 270, 271, 276, 277, 278,
    279, 298–304, 306n
Svarthöfði Dufgusson   71, 75, 113, 121, 122
    see also Dufgusssynir
Sveinn Sturluson (d. c.1203)   71
sveit   6, 145, 291, 314
Svelgsá   245n
Sverrir Jakobsson   1n, 4, 203
Svertingr Þorleifsson   71, 106, 107n, 109, 110,
    116, 117n
Sviðnur   39n
Svignaskarð, Borgarfjörður   125

svín-, place-name element   32n
Svínadalur   32n
Svínafell   72
Svíney   180, 181, 254, 255, 268n
Svínfellinga saga   17
Svínfellingar   53, 72, 75, 134
Sweden   276
sýsla   4, 192
Sælingsdalur   32, 99
Sælingsdalstunga   22n, 25, 89, 95, 96, 97n,
    113, 185, 228, 230, 231, 234, 235, 236,
    237n, 240, 241, 242, 249, 250, 252, 263,
    265, 266, 267, 307, 310, 313
Sæmundarhlíð, Skagafjörður   282n
Sæmundarsynir, sons of Sæmundr Jónsson of
    Oddi (d. 1222)   52
Sæmundr Ormsson (d. 1252)   75
Sæmundr fróði Sigfússon (d. 1133)   45, 320
Sökkólfr   167, 179
Sökkólfsdalur   167
Sölmundr austmaðr   71, 73, 318
Sölmundr of Gnúpar   293
Söxólfr Fornason   79n, 130, 131

Tanni of Galtardalstunga   92, 93
Teigsfjall   299
Teitr Guðmundarsson (d. 1186)   139n
Teitr Styrmisson   112, 113, 114, 115
tephra layers   7
territoriality   12, 18, 93, 102, 106, 124, 126, 131,
    186, 201, 205, 254, 267, 269, 270, 290,
    305, 313, 316
timber (viðr)   32, 34, 228
tithe   18, 19, 20, 21, 22n, 109n, 316
    see also ministry
Tithe Law (Tíundalög)   20, 316
Tiv   148–49, 151
Tjaldanes   22, 97, 109, 259
Tjarnir, Eyjafjarðardalur   282
Tjarnir, Ljósavatnsskarð   284, 285
Tjörn, Eyjafjörður   282
Tjörn, Svarfaðadalur   132, 299, 300, 303, 304
Tjörnes   4, 34, 39, 40, 41, 293, 296, 306
Torfi prestr Guðmundarson   104, 107, 108
Torfi Tulinius   219
Torfufell   282, 303
Tómas Þórarinsson (d. 1253)   74
trade   36, 106, 195, 196, 287
Trøndelag   277

Tumi Kolbeinsson (d. 1184)   72, 81
Tumi Sighvatsson the older (d. 1222)   49, 63, 65, 71, 102, 137n, 142
Tumi Sighvatsson the younger (d. 1244)   71, 112, 114, 116, 117, 136
Tungu-Oddr (Oddr Önundarson)   168, 169
turf   8

Ufsir   128, 299, 303, 304
Unadalur   301
Uni   301
Unnr in djúpúðga see Auðr in djúpauðga
Uppsalir, Eyjafjörður   281
Uppsalir, Skagafjörður   131n
Uppsalir, Þorskafjörður   258
Urðamenn   277, 278
Urða-Steinn   132n
Urðir   65, 79n, 132, 277, 278n, 300
Úlfheiðr Rúnólfsdóttir   215
Úlfheðinn Gunnarsson   82
Úlfar Bragason   16
Úlfarr kappi   175, 246n, 247, 248
Úlfarsfell   175, 245, 247, 248
Úlfr víkingr   192, 193
Úlfsdalir   192

vaðmál   23n
Vaglir   294n, 295, 297
Valgerðr Sighvatsdóttir   116
Valla-Ljótr see Ljótr Ljótólfsson
Valla-Ljóts saga   141, 270, 271, 276, 278, 279, 302–4, 306n
Valshamarr   103, 105
Varðgjá   190
Varmalækr, Borgarfjörður   261n
Vatn   164, 171
Vatnabúðir   37n
Vatnsdalur   75
Vatnsdæla saga   301n
Vatnsfirðingar   49, 87, 98, 107, 224
Vatnsfjörðr, Ísafjörður   216, 249
Vatnshorn   77, 164
Veisa   296
Veisusynir   296
Vellir   25, 79n, 127, 128, 132n, 140, 141, 301–2
Vermundr inn mjóvi Þorgrímsson   178, 226, 249, 250, 269
Vestliðaeyrr   174n

Vestliði Ketilsson   174
Véleifr inn gamli   170n
Vémundr   303n
Vémundr kögurr Þórisson   197n, 284, 285, 286, 287n, 288, 289
Viðar Pálsson   13n
Vigdís Hallsteinsdóttir (?)   240–41
Vigdís Ingjaldsdóttir   240
Vigdís Óláfsdóttir   168
Vigdís Sturludóttir   71, 73
Vigdís Þórarinsdóttir   168
Vigdís, daughter of Þórarinn fylsenni   183n
Vigfúss of Valshamarr   103, 105
Vigfúss Björnsson   250, 251, 252n
Vigfúss Gunnsteinsson   60–61, 75, 76n, 112, 114, 123–24, 125
Villingadalr   190
vinátta (formal friendship)   119
Vindheimar   286
Víðdælir   100
Víðidalur, Húnavatnssýsla   87, 238
Víðines, Skagafjörður   48, 281, 285n
Víðivellir   67, 81
Vífill Ketilsson   163n, 167
Vífilsdalr/-ur   97n, 167
Víga-Glúmr see Glúmr Eyjólfsson
Víga-Styrr see Styrr Þorgrímsson
Vígholtsstaðir   232n
Vopnafjörður   30n, 82, 291, 293, 294
Vöðu-Brandr see Brandr Þorkelsson
Vöðu-Brands þáttr   293n

weapons   56, 95, 106, 130, 138, 235, 267n, 272, 317–18
Western Quarter   11, 24, 52, 60, 75, 77, 87, 217, 320
West Fjords   27n, 29, 38n, 39, 45, 49, 50, 51, 58, 65n, 73, 74, 75, 88, 101, 102, 111n, 113, 115, 117, 124, 163, 181, 183, 227, 238, 239, 257, 322
whale, whale meat   34, 35, 40, 259n
wildfowl   34, 40–41
wood, woodland (skógr)   22, 27, 32–33, 34, 42 see also timber

Yngvarastaðir (Ingvarir)   300
Yngvildr Atladóttir   183n
Yngvildr Ásgeirsdóttir   300

INDEX

Yngvildr *allrasystir* Hámundardóttir   194
Yngvildr Karlsdóttir   300
Yngvildr Þorgilsdóttir   89n
Ytra-Fell   104n, 106
Ytra Holt see Holt, Svarfaðardalur
Ytri-Skörð   289
Ýrr Geirmundardóttir   183n

þáttr (pl. *þættir*)   207, 256, 271, 274, 295
þáttr theory   207–8, 222
Þingeyjarsýsla   4, 5, 11, 25, 49, 126
Þingeyrar see monastery
þingmaðr   12, 14, 18, 49, 59, 62n, 64, 67, 68, 72, 89, 90, 91, 92–97, 100, 106, 126, 128, 129, 132, 133, 134, 244, 267, 283, 288, 291, 293, 294, 295, 296, 297, 298, 303, 305, 306, 314, 316
Þingvellir, site of the Alþing   10
Þingvellir, Helgafellssveit   203n
Þjóðrekr Sleitu-Bjarnarson   257n, 259
þjónustumaðr   217
Þjóstarr, *austmaðr*   103n, 104n, 318
Þorbeinir   250, 252n
Þorbeinisstaðir   248, 250, 252n
Þorbergr of Langidalr   175, 177n
Þorbergr *höggvinkinni* of Mývatn   288, 290
Þorbergr Hrútsson   171
Þorbergr Óláfsson   170n
Þorbergsstaðir   105n, 241
Þorbjörg *digra* Óláfsdóttir   170n
Þorbjörn of Sauðafell   256, 257, 269
Þorbjörn *inn Haukdælski* of Vatn   163–64, 170, 171
Þorbjörn *skrjúpr*   241n
Þorbjörn Einarsson   174
Þorbjörn *inn digri* Ormsson   175, 178, 223, 268
Þorbjörn Vífilsson   163n, 254, 255n
Þorbjörn Þjóðreksson   257n
Þorbrandr Þorfinnsson   163n, 246, 247, 253, 266
Þorbrandssynir   247, 248, 253, 254, 255, 266
  see also Þorleifr *kimbi* Þorbrandsson; Þóroddr Þorbrandsson
Þorfinnr Önundarson (d. 1197)   79
Þorfinnr Þorgerisson, Abbot of Helgafell (d. 1216)   225
Þorgeirr *kornasylgja*   136n

Þorgeirr Brandsson (d. 1186)   81
Þorgeirr Hallason (d. 1169)   66, 70, 80, 81, 83, 127, 129, 192
Þorgeirr Óláfsson   259
Þorgeirr *Ljósvetingagoði* Þorkelsson   170n, 197, 198n, 199, 284, 286n, 287, 288, 290, 292, 293, 294, 295, 296
Þorgeirr Þorvarðsson
Þorgeirr Þórðarson   190, 195
Þorgeirr Þórhaddsson of Hítardalur   163n, 254
Þorgerðr Bolladóttir   170
Þorgerðr Egilsdóttir   168
Þorgerðr Gísladóttir   173
Þorgerðr Höskuldsdóttir   170n
Þorgerðr Þorsteinsdóttir   170n
Þorgerðr Þórðardóttir   183n
Þorgestr *inn gamli* Steinsson   163n, 177n, 181, 254, 255, 269
Þorgestr Þórhallsson(?)   174
Þorgils Hólasveinn   139n
Þorgils *mjöksiglandi*   278n
Þorgils *skarði* Böðvarsson (d. 1258)   52–53, 54, 59, 71, 99, 117, 118, 119, 120, 121, 122, 123, 124, 126, 136, 138n, 141, 143, 217, 323, 325
Þorgils Gunnsteinsson   75, 99n
Þorgils Hölluson   229, 231, 232, 235, 238, 241, 269
Þorgils Oddason (d. 1151)   32n, 60, 61, 85, 86, 87–90, 91, 96, 173n, 181n, 183n, 321, 322
Þorgils Oddsson   103n, 104
Þorgils saga ok Hafliða   14, 17, 60, 70, 85, 86, 87, 88, 90, 91, 92, 93, 97, 105n, 126, 319–20, 321
Þorgils saga skarða   16, 17, 54, 117, 120, 134, 136, 140, 323, 325
Þorgils Snorrason (d. 1201)   59, 60, 112
Þorgils Snorrason of Skorravík   109
Þorgils Sveinsson (d. 1254)   139n
Þorgrímr of Þykkvaskógr   171
Þorgrímr Hallason   271n
Þorgrímr Kjallaksson (= Þorgrímr *þöngull*?)   160n, 177, 181, 185, 244, 245, 249, 252n, 253, 254
Þorgrímr Ljótólfsson   303
Þorgrímr *alikarl* Vigfússon   82, 129, 130, 131, 133, 134, 135, 136
Þorgrímr Þorsteinsson   168, 178, 227

Þorgrímr Þórisson 281n
Þorgríms þáttr Hallasonar 271n
Þorkell *hávi* of Mývatn 279, 283
Þorkell of Hlíð 196n
Þorkell *hvelpr* of Hóll 237
Þorkell *prestr* of Hvammr 94n
Þorkell *prestr* of Sauðafell(?) 123
Þorkell Dufnalsson 173
Þorkell Eyjólfsson 170, 227, 228, 229, 231, 236, 240, 249
Þorkell Geitisson 291, 293, 294
Þorkell Hrútsson 171
Þorkell *trefill* Rauða-Bjarnarson 229
Þorkell Tjörvason, lawspeaker 297
Þorkell Þorgeirsson, father of Þorgeirr Ljósvetningagoði 288, 290
Þorkell *hákr* Þorgeirsson, son of Þorgeirr Ljósvetningagoði 287n, 295, 296, 297
Þorkell *inn svarti* Þórisson 285n
Þorlákr *af Eyri* Ásgeirsson 251, 253
Þorlákr Ketilsson (d. 1240) 61–62, 107, 134, 135
Þorlákr Þórhallsson, saint, Bishop of Skálholt (d. 1193) 15n, 20n, 61, 159, 320
Þorláks saga helga 15n
Þorlákssynir 251
  see also Bergþórr Þorláksson; Steinþórr Þorláksson; Þórðr blígr Þorláksson; Þormóðr Þorláksson
Þorleifr *kimbi* Þorbrandsson 252
Þorleifr *skeifa* 71, 72n
Þorleifr Ketilsson 82
Þorleifr *beiskaldi* Þorleiksson 46, 61, 77, 92, 93, 95, 98, 185
Þorleifs þáttr Jarlsskálds 271n
Þorleikr Höskuldsson 170, 228, 230, 233, 234, 242
Þorljótr Hrútsson 171
Þormóðr *inn rammi* Haraldsson 192
Þormóðr Þorláksson 251, 269
Þorsteinn *svarfaðr/svörfuðr* 189n, 193, 271, 277, 298, 299, 300, 301n, 303, 304
Þorsteinn *varastafr* 288n
Þorsteinn Áskelsson 288
Þorsteinn Egilsson 168
Þorsteinn *ranglátr* Einarsson (d. 1149) 61n, 65n, 77, 78, 86, 135, 312
Þorsteinn Eyjólfsson see Urða-Steinn
Þorsteinn Gellisson 90

Þorsteinn Ívarsson 90
Þorsteinn Kuggason 230n
Þorsteinn *þorskabítr* Þórólfsson 253
Þorsteinn Gellisson 90
Þorsteinn *surtr inn spaki* Hallssteinsson 178, 241n, 252
Þorsteinn Kuggason 230n
Þorsteinn *rauðr* Óláfsson 168, 171, 178, 225
Þorsteinn *böllóttur* Snorrason (d. 1353?) 319
Þorsteinn *búandi* Steinólfsson 183
Þorsteinn Þorgilsson of Hafsfjarðarey 61, 244
Þorsteinn Þorgnýsson 276–77
Þorsteinn *þorskabítr* Þórólfsson 177, 178, 244, 245, 249, 253, 254
Þorsteinsstaðir 241n
Þorvaldr of Bægisá, kinsman of Guðmundr *dýri* 130
Þorvaldr *menni* 280n
Þorvaldr, *þingmaðr* of Einarr Þorgilsson 92
Þorvaldr Gizurarson, priest then canon at Viðey (d. 1235) 76n
Þorvaldr *auðgi* Guðmundarson (d. 1161) 78–79
Þorvaldr Guðmundarson, son of Guðmundr *dýri* 63, 64, 65, 80
Þorvaldr Halldórsson 239
Þorvaldr Ósvífrsson 262, 263, 264
Þorvaldr *Vatnsfirðingr* Snorrason (d. 1228) 49, 73, 101, 107, 109, 214, 215, 322
Þorvaldr *krókr* Þórisson 65n, 279, 281n
Þorvalds þáttr tasalda 271n
Þorvaldur Thoroddsen (d. 1921), geographer 31n, 39
Þorvarðr *auðgi* Ásgrímsson (d. 1186) 64, 80
Þorvarðr Höskuldsson 293, 295, 296
Þorvarðr Ormsson (d. 1194) 65n
Þorvarðr Þorgeirsson (d. 1207) 66, 67, 80, 81, 82, 83, 129, 132, 133, 272, 273n, 276
Þorvarðr Þórarinsson (d. 1296) 54, 55, 136, 137, 138, 140, 141, 143, 325
Þorvarðr Þórðarson 139, 140
Þorvarðr Örnólfsson of Kristnes 194
Þorvarðr Örnólfsson of Miklagarðr 140n, 189
Þórarinn *balti* 116
Þórarinn of Langidalr 229, 231–32, 235–36, 269
Þórarinn Brandsson 215
Þórarinn Grímsson (d. c.1217) 100–1

INDEX

Þórarinn Ragabróðir Óleifsson 168
Þórarinn Sveinsson 123
Þórarinn Tómasson (d. 1246) 74n
Þórarinn *fylsenni* Þórðarson 183n, 230n
Þórarinn Þórisson of Espihóll nyrðri 281n
Þórarinn Þórisson of Sælingsdalstunga 230n, 234, 267
Þórarinn Þórólfsson 178
Þórarins þáttr 275n
Þórarna Ásgeirsdóttir 173
Þórdís Daðadóttir 79n
Þórdís Einarsdóttir 174
Þórdís Guðlaugsdóttir 171
Þórdís Óláfsdóttir 168
Þórdís Snorradóttir, daughter of Snorri *goði* 215–16, 240
Þórdís Snorradóttir, daughter of Snorri Sturluson 71
Þórdís Súrsdóttir 221
Þórðarbók see Landnámabók
Þórðar saga kakala 17, 115, 116, 134, 136, 323, 324, 325
Þórðr *goddi* 230n, 232–33, 240
Þórðr *slítandi* 193, 194
Þórðr Andréasson (d. 1264) 55
Þórðr Arndísarson 183n
Þórðr Gilsson, father of Hvamm-Sturla 57, 90, 92, 94, 159, 171, 243, 320
Þórðr *Hítnesingr* 118, 325
Þórðr Hrafnsson 281
Þórðr Kollason 100
Þórðr Ingunnarson 170, 199n, 230n, 237, 239
Þórðr Narfason (d. 1308) 319, 320
Þórðr *gellir* Óláfsson 164n, 168, 169, 178, 181n, 184, 202, 227, 229, 230, 238, 240n, 244, 245, 253, 254, 266
Þórðr *kakali* Sighvatsson (d. 1256) 51–53, 54, 59, 71, 73n, 75n, 99, 103n, 112–17, 118, 119n, 122, 124, 125, 136, 138, 139, 140, 141, 143, 145, 323, 324, 325
Þórðr Skatason 173
Þórðr Sturluson, grandson of Sturla Þjóðreksson 87
Þórðr Sturluson (d. 1237) 46, 49, 50, 58, 59, 60n, 62n, 70, 71, 72–73, 74, 75, 76, 77, 80, 98, 99, 100, 101, 102, 103, 104, 105, 106, 108, 109, 110, 111, 112, 124, 125, 126, 264n, 323
see also Sturlusynir

Þórðr *munkr* Þorgeirsson 81, 117
Þórðr *blígr* Þorláksson 251
Þórðr Þórarinsson 64, 133
Þórðr *köttr* Þórðarson 170
Þórðr *tiggi* Þórðarson, son of Þórðr Sturluson (fl. 1234–1241) 51
Þórðr Þorvaldsson 320
Þórðr *prestr* Önundarson 82
Þórðr *Freysgoði* Özurarson 229
Þórhallr Finnsson 88
Þórhallr Hrútsson 171
Þórhallr Svartsson 92, 93
Þórir Akrarskeggi 291
Þórir *sælingr* 234
Þórir Gull-Harðarson 267
Þórir Hámundarson 65, 191, 195, 281
Þórir Helgason 291, 297–98, 301
Þórir Oddsson 258–59, 260
Þórir *snepill* Ketilsson 198n
Þórir Vémundarson 303n, 304n
Þórisstaðir, Þorskafjörður, West Fjords 258
Þóroddr *hjálmr* Arnórsson 292n
Þóroddr Tungu-Oddsson 168
Þóroddr Þorbrandsson 246, 247, 248, 265
Þóroddsstaðir *see* Staðr
Þórólfr of Hundadalur 108
Þórólfr *rauðnefr* 235, 240, 252n, 254, 258, 265n
Þórólfr *bægifótr* Björnsson 246, 247, 248, 253
Þórólfr *Mostrarskegg* Örnólfsson 162, 163n, 164, 174, 175, 176, 177, 178, 185n, 220, 224, 225, 241n, 248, 249
Þórólfr Sigmundarson 139n
Þórsnes, peninsula 22, 175, 177, 223, 240, 241n, 248, 252n
Þórsnesingagoðorð 56, 58, 59, 112, 236
Þórsnessþing 11, 58, 104, 222, 254
Þórunn Gunnarsdóttir 168
Þórunn *hyrna* Ketilsdóttir 187, 189n
Þórunnarey 189n
Þórvör Ormsdóttir 215
Þrándr *stígandi* Ingjaldsson 268
Þuríðr Arnbjarnardóttir 170n
Þuríðr Eyvindardóttir 167–68
Þuríðr Gizurardóttir 72
Þuríðr Höskuldsdóttir 170
Þuríðr Kolgrímsdóttir 119
Þuríðr Ormsdóttir 114

Þuríðr Óláfsdóttir   170n, 238
Þuríðr *in spaka* Snorradóttir   251n
Þuríðr Sturludóttir, d. of Hvamm-Sturla   70, 71, 72
Þuríðr Sturludóttir (d. 1288), d. of Sturla Sighvatsson   115
Þuríðr Þórðardóttir   87–88
Þverá, river in Öxnadalur   194
Þverá (Munkaþverá, Þverá in efri), farm and monastery in Eyjafjörður   22, 34, 39n, 46, 66, 67n, 79n, 81, 83, 127, 135, 138, 140n, 141, 144, 190, 192, 198, 272, 272–74, 275, 276, 279, 280, 281, 282, 283, 287n, 288, 289, 290, 291–92, 294, 302, 303n, 305, 309, 311, 312
Þverá, Laxárdalur, north-east   83, 142, 143, 286n
Þverá in litla (Þverá in ytri)   54, 122n, 141, 143, 190
Þverárdalr, Saurbær   182n
Þverbrekka   280n
Þverfell   182n
Þveræingagoðorð   57, 64
Þveræingar   282n
Þykkvaskógr (Stóriskógur)   172, 230n, 238, 241, 257, 265

Æsa Þorgrímsdóttir   181n
Æsustaðir   281
ætt   76, 211, 271n, 295, 296
ættfaðir   172, 177
Ættartölur, part of the *Sturlunga saga* compilation   17, 65, 73, 77, 89n, 312
Ævi Snorra goða   57, 148, 222, 224, 226, 253
Ævarr Ketilsson   87n

Ögmundar þáttr dýtts   271n
Ögmundr Kálfsson, Abbot of Flatey then Helgafell (d. 1188)   225n
Ögmundr *sneis* Þorvarðsson (d. 1237)   63, 66, 67, 81, 82, 129, 130, 133, 135
Ölkofra þáttr   32n
Öndóttsstaðir   197n, 285
Öndverðareyrr (Hallbjarnareyri)   40n, 111, 119, 125, 175, 177, 179, 185, 223, 230, 236, 244–45, 250, 251, 252–53, 269, 310
Öngulsstaðir   140, 281
Önundarbrenna   47, 79, 129, 131
Önundr Þorkelsson (d. 1197)   47, 64n, 65, 66, 79, 129, 130, 131, 132, 133, 134, 322
Örlyggr   175
Örlygsstaðir, Álptafjörður   245, 247, 248, 266
Örlygsstaðir, Skagafjörður, Battle of, (1238)   50, 74, 85, 105, 109, 110, 137, 142, 323
Örn of Arnarnes   193
Örnólfr Ármóðarson   230n
Örnólfr Kollason   88
Örnólfr Þorvarðsson   140n
Örnólfr Þórðarson   194
Öxará   295, 297
Öxarfjörður   4, 141, 142, 143, 200, 287, 295
Öxfirðingagoðorð   57
Öxna-Börkr *see* Börkr Guðmundarson
Öxnadalsheiði   63, 91
Öxnadalur   25, 47, 63, 64, 78, 129, 131, 139n, 194, 321
Öxnafell   280n, 281, 281, 285n
Öxnahóll   131, 139n, 286
Öxney   103, 268n